THE HANDBOOK OF
AUSTRALIAN
LANGUAGES

—————— VOLUME 5 ——————

THE HANDBOOK OF
AUSTRALIAN
LANGUAGES

—————— VOLUME 5 ——————

Grammatical sketches of Bunuba, Ndjébbana and Kugu Nganhcara

Edited by R.M.W. Dixon and Barry J. Blake

OXFORD
UNIVERSITY PRESS

OXFORD

UNIVERSITY PRESS

253 Normanby Road, South Melbourne, Australia

Oxford University Press is a department of the
University of Oxford. It furthers the University's
objective of excellence in research, scholarship, and
education by publishing worldwide in

Oxford New York

Athens Auckland Bangkok Bogotá Buenos Aires
Calcutta Cape Town Chennai Dar es Salaam Delhi
Florence Hong Kong Istanbul Karachi Kuala
Lumpur Madrid Melbourne Mexico City Mumbai
Nairobi Paris Port Moresby São Paulo Singapore
Taipei Tokyo Toronto Warsaw

with associated companies in Berlin Ibadan

OXFORD is a trade mark of Oxford University Press
in the UK and in certain other countries

National Library of Australia
Cataloguing-in-Publication data:

Dixon, Robert M. W.
A handbook of Australian languages. v. 5.

Bibliography
Includes index.
ISBN 0 19 554998 8.

1. Australian languages. I. Blake, Barry J. II. Title.

499.15

Printed by the Bookmaker Pty Ltd, Australia

Contents

**AUSTRALIAN ABORIGINAL LANGUAGES: THEIR
CONTEMPORARY STATUS AND FUNCTIONS
by Mary Laughren**

NDJÉBBANA by Graham McKay

KUGU NGANHCARA by Ian Smith and Steve Johnson

List of Maps

Preface

In editing the *Handbook of Australian Languages* we have published good quality grammatical sketches as they became available. It was just the luck of the draw that all of the 16 grammars in the first four volumes were of non-prefixing languages (see Map 1). However, we are now pleased to present Volume 5, including two languages of the prefixing type – Bunuba, from the south Kimberley region of Western Australia; and Ndjébbana, from central Arnhem Land. Indeed, the third language represented in this volume – Kugu Nganchara, from western Cape York Peninsula in North Queensland – has pronominal enclitics which normally attach to the word immediately preceding the verb; this may be the stage immediately before the development of prefixing (the enclitics to the word preceding the verb become proclitics – and then prefixes – to the verb).

There is generally little argument as to whether or not a language has prefixes. The other parameter that is often invoked in Australian studies is Pama-Nyungan versus non-Pama-Nyungan. We included a grammar of Yukulta in Volume 3 (published in 1983). At that time Yukulta was considered Pama-Nyungan, defined in terms of lexicostatistic counting. But then the goalposts were moved and Pama-Nyungan/non-Pama-Nyungan was defined in quite different terms, one major criterion being pronominal forms. According to this, Yukulta is now considered non-Pama-Nyungan (as also are Bunuba and Ndjébbana). Dixon is firmly of the opinion that the Pama-Nyungan idea has no significant basis, and that it has in fact held back Australian studies. His ideas are set out briefly in *The rise and fall of languages* (Cambridge University Press, 1997) and in considerable detail in a two volume work *Australian languages: their nature and development* (Cambridge University Press, forthcoming).

Volumes 1–3 of the *Handbook* were published within Australia by ANU Press and these editions have sold out. They were also published, in hardback format, by John Benjamins in Amsterdam and copies are still available from them.

The contributors to the *Handbook* supplied copy on disc. We are greatly indebted to Barbara Upton and Barbara Kelly for preliminary editing and especially to Vicki Webb and Julie Reid who completed the editing and combined the various contributions into a harmonious whole.

R.M.W. Dixon
B.J. Blake

September 1998

Contributors' Addresses

Mary Laughren, Department of English, University of Queensland, St. Lucia,
  Queensland, 4072.
  <mary@cltr.uq.edu.au>

Alan Rumsey, Department of Anthropology, RSPAS, Australian National
  University, Canberra, ACT, 2600.
  <alan.rumsey@anu.edu.au>

Graham McKay, Department of Linguistics Edith Cowan University, Mount
  Lawley Campus, Perth, W.A., 6050.

Ian Smith, Department of Languages, Literatures and Linguistics, York
  University, North York, Ontario, Canada, M3J 1P3.
  <iansmith@yorku.ca>

Abbreviations

A	transitive subject function	EMPH	emphatic
ABL	ablative case	ENT	entire group/entity
AFFIRM	affirmation particle	ERG	ergative case
ABS	absolutive case	EXC	exclusive
ALL	allative case	EXCL	exclamation clitic
AUG	augmented	EXT	extent
AV	aversative	FEM	feminine
CARD	cardinal Pronoun	FUT	future tense
CAU	causal case	HIST	historic
CAUS	causative	HORT	hortative
CF	counterfactual	HUNTOBJ	object of hunt
CHAR	characterised by	IMP	imperative
CLAN	member of clan X	INF	infinitive
CNC	indeterminate concord suffix	INFIN	infinitive
		INCHO	inchoative case
COM	comitative suffix	INST	instrumental case
COM1	comitative 1	INT	interrogative/ indefinite
COM2	comitative 2		
CONTMP	contemporary	INTRANS	intransitiviser
CTP	contemporary	IRG	irregular
CTV	continuative	IRR	irrealis
DAT	dative case	ITR	iterative
DAT	dative pronoun	JUST	'pointless' clitic
DATA	dative pronoun (DAT) as Agent marker	LINK	linking clitic
		LOC	locative case/location
(A)			
DEF	definite	MAY	'probably' clitic
DEM	demonstrative	MIN	minimal
DESID	desiderative	N	nominal
DITR	ditransitive	NEGPOSS	negative possibility
DUR	durative	NONFACT	nonfactual clitic
DU	dual	NP	noun phrase
DYAD	dyadic	NRN	non-remote negative
		nsg	non-singular

O	transitive object
OBL	oblique pronominal cross-reference
ON	only
PAIR	pair
PAST	past tense
PER	perlative
PL	plural
POSS	possessive pronoun
PRES	present tnese
PROX	proximad
PURP	purposive inflection
R	restricted person
RE	realis
RECIP	reciprocal
REDUP	reduplicated
REFL	reflexive/reciprocal/ intransitiviser
REM	remote
REP	repetition
S	intransitive subject function
SEM	semblative
SG	singular
SUB	subordinate clause
SUBORD	subordinator
particle	
THEN	'then' clitic
TR	transitiviser
U	unrestricted
UA	unit augmented
V	verb
VOC	vocative case
YK	'you know' clitic

*	idiomatic (non-literal) phrase
+	boundary between elements in a compound,
-	boundary between stem and (inflectional or derivational) affix or clitic
#	pause (when gloss is given), sudden break (when no gloss is given)
!	RESPECT form
^	precedes

Glosses for kin terms

B	brother
D	daughter
F	father
H	husband
M	mother
S	son
W	wife
Z	sister
X+	elder X, X = B or Z
X-	younger X, X = B or Z

1	first person
2	second person
3	third person
2PP	second person propositus
3PP	third person propositus

Symbols

'	boundary between preverb and inflected root
↑	rising pitch
↓	falling pitch
$	'mother-in-law' word

Institutions, Programs, etc.

AACLAME Australian Advisory Council on Languages and Multicultural Education.
ABC Australian Broadcasting Corporation.
AEP Aboriginal and Torres Strait Islander Education Policy.
AIATSIS Australian Institute of Aboriginal and Torres Strait Islander Studies.
AILF Australian Indigenous Languages Framework.
ALIP Aboriginal Languages Initiatives Program.
AnTEP Anangu Teacher Education Program.
ASEDA Aboriginal Studies Electronic Data Archives (AIATSIS).
ATSIC Aboriginal and Torres Strait Islander Commission.
ATSILIP Aboriginal and Torres Strait Islander Languages Program.
BRACS Broadcasting for Remote Aboriginal Communities Scheme.
CAAMA Central Australian Aboriginal Media Association.
CALL Centre for Australian Languages and Linguistics (Batchelor College).
DEET Department of Education, Employment and Training.
KRALC Katherine Regional Aboriginal Languages Centre.
LOTE Languages Other than English.
NAATI National Accreditation Authority for Translators and Interpreters.
NALP National Aboriginal Languages Program.
RATE Remote Area Teacher Education (Batchelor College).
SAL School of Australian Linguistics.
SIL Summer Institute of Linguistics.
SSABSA Senior Secondary Assessment Board of South Australia.
TSIMA Torres Strait Media Assocation.
WMA Warlpiri Media Association.

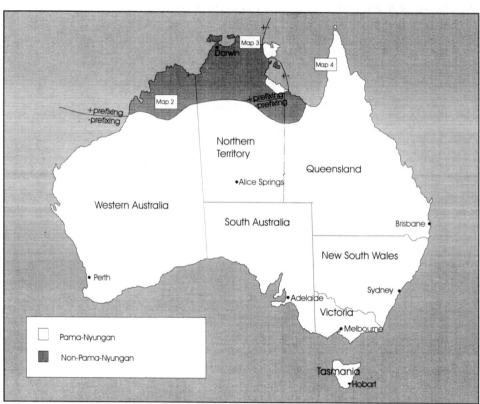

Map 1: Australia (with key to maps 2, 3 and 4)

Australian Aboriginal languages: their contemporary status and functions
by Mary Laughren

1. INTRODUCTION

Paradoxically, over the past 25 years or so as the number of Australian Aboriginal and Torres Strait Islander languages being used as people's primary language of communication decreases in Australia (McGregor 1988a and 1994:xi–xiv, Schmidt 1990, Walsh 1993), the range of uses to which they are put and the media in which they are expressed have diversified in quite remarkable ways (Black 1993, McKay 1996), as has the quantity and quality of language documentation and linguistic research relating to these languages. An excellent overview of linguistic research into Australian Aboriginal languages carried out in the same period is provided by Austin (1991b).

The purpose of this chapter is twofold: firstly, to briefly describe some of these developments and to indicate where further information about them can be found; secondly, to point to linguistic research and documentation in the field of Aboriginal and Torres Strait Islander languages which relates to the contemporary use and expression of these languages.

Most of the developments in language use and documentation reported on in this chapter have come about as a result of actions taken by Aboriginal people, both those who speak a traditional Aboriginal language and those who don't. In some cases these have been collective actions as those taken by national organisations such as the Aboriginal Languages Association, or by people working in educational institutions and community groups. The impetus for some language recording and language instruction programs has come from individuals. The most productive and successful projects usually result from cooperative partnerships between Aboriginal language speakers and people with a diversity of other skills – linguistic, organisational, artistic, pedagogic and political.

Section 2 deals with the place of Aboriginal languages in relation to national language policies adopted by the Commonwealth Government. Section 3 provides a brief description of some of the many and varied language education programs which involve Australian Aboriginal languages and their speakers. Section 4 reports on some of the innovative ways in which Aboriginal languages are being used and expressed. Section 5 gives an overview of some of the linguistic research and documentation of Aboriginal languages relating to the topics covered in the preceding sections.

2. ABORIGINAL LANGUAGES WITHIN AN AUSTRALIAN NATIONAL LANGUAGE POLICY

Since the late 1980s very significant financial support for many of the initiatives relating to Aboriginal language programs derives from the place given to Aboriginal languages within the official national policies on language which have been developed and implemented by the Commonwealth Government. These initiatives typically include measures to document languages in a way that makes knowledge about the language accessible to Aboriginal people and to the general public in addition to linguistic scholars. The National Policy on Languages (Lo Bianco 1987), while recognizing English to be the national language, recommended support for Aboriginal and Torres Strait Islander languages as well as for the teaching of languages other than English. The adoption of this policy by the Federal Government in 1987 led to the setting up of the Australian Advisory Council on Languages and Multicultural Education (AACLAME) to oversee the implementation of the policy which included the inauguration of the National Aboriginal Languages Program (NALP), the smallest of AACLAME's six programs in financial terms.[1]

2.1 NATIONAL ABORIGINAL LANGUAGES PROGRAM

The National Aboriginal Languages Program (NALP) was a submission-based program administered by the Department of Education, Employment and Training (DEET) with a budget of three million dollars over four years, 1987 to 1991. Riley-Mundine and Roberts (1990:9–10) estimated that in the 1988–89 financial year alone, the 53 projects funded by NALP involved some 91 languages which they conservatively estimated to have assisted some 5,600 people. The sector whose submission received the greatest percentage (34%) of funding in that financial year was Aboriginal communities or corporations, followed by schools (27%) and Aboriginal language/education centres (22%).

2.2 ABORIGINAL AND TORRES STRAIT ISLANDER LANGUAGES PROGRAM

Under the Australian Language and Literacy Policy adopted by the Commonwealth Government in 1991, NALP gave way to the Aboriginal Languages Initiatives Program (ALIP) initially administered by DEET but which, as the Aboriginal And Torres Strait Islander Languages Program (ATSILIP), came under the Aboriginal and Torres Strait Islander Commission (ATSIC) in 1992–93. Through ATSILIP, a wide range of grass-roots initiatives involving Aboriginal languages have continued to receive considerable financial support. Some of these programs will be described in §3.

2.3   REGIONAL ABORIGINAL LANGUAGE RESOURCE CENTRES

One of the most productive outcomes of these successors to NALP has been the establishment and function of Regional Aboriginal Language Resource Centres around Australia funded under these programs, although some of these centres, such as the Language and Culture Centre of the Institute for Aboriginal Development (IAD) in Alice Springs, predate these Commonwealth programs. These centres are represented at the national level by the Aboriginal and Torres Strait Islander Corporation of Languages (formerly called the Federation of Aboriginal and Torres Strait Islander Languages or FATSIL).[2] McKay (1996:94) observes that language centres which are under the control of local Aboriginal people generally 'provide a relatively stable focus for language activities (because most of them receive some recurrent funding) ... and provide coordination and access to expertise and equipment'. The Regional Aboriginal Language Resource Centres operating in 1996 are listed in the appendix.

These Centres channel money from a variety of government sponsored programs relating to Aboriginal languages. They are involved in language documentation (speaker surveys, language needs surveys, language recording and analysis, production of grammars and dictionaries), in language in education programs, and in training local people to work in language-related jobs (Marmion 1994). These Centres facilitate productive cooperation between Aboriginal people with an interest in language matters, linguists, educationalists and others.

2.4   ABORIGINAL AND TORRES STRAIT ISLANDER EDUCATION POLICY

The Aboriginal And Torres Strait Islander Education Policy (AEP) was developed in conjunction with the national language policy implementation with the aim of improving general education outcomes for Aboriginal people. Since 1989 it has provided some financial backing for education programs which promote Aboriginal languages although the bulk of funding has been directed at English language programs and other aspects of education. For example, in the Northern Territory in 1993, $365,000 was distributed as grants for AEP Initiative #2 'Support for Aboriginal Languages in Schools' (reports on some of the programs funded by these grants are given in *Aboriginal Education News*, No. 5 (1994)), while in 1995, $385,000 was allocated to AEP Initiative #2 'Support for Aboriginal Languages in Schools' out of total AEP (NT) allocations for all 24 initiatives of \$13,341,762 as reported in *Aboriginal Education News*, No. 6 (1995). Over the nine years of its operation the AEP will have channelled large amounts of Commonwealth funding (\$214 million in the first triennium (Baldauf et al. 1996:33)), via state and territory education systems, into Aboriginal education.

2.5   LANGUAGES OTHER THAN ENGLISH

In terms of its contribution to educational programs involving Aboriginal language instruction, it is the strong support for the teaching of languages other than English in the 1981 and 1991 national language policies, reversing previous educational policies, that has had positive tangible consequences with the incorporation of Aboriginal languages into state education Languages Other Than English (LOTE) programs (§3.2). In states which had previously sought to exclude the use or study of Aboriginal languages from classrooms, the adoption of LOTE policies provided a window of opportunity for those seeking a place for the inclusion of Aboriginal language study in school programs. The development of both the Australian Indigenous Languages Framework (§3.2.7) and the Western Australian Ministry of Education's Framework for the Teaching of Aboriginal Languages in Primary Schools (§3.2.5.4) results from the LOTE-Aboriginal Language nexus.

3.   ABORIGINAL LANGUAGES IN EDUCATION

Around Australia there are many types of informal and formal education programs which involve the use of an Aboriginal language (see Hartman & Henderson (eds) (1994) for descriptions of a wide range of such programs). Most are situated within the framework of formal educational institutions, some supported by regional language resource centres (§2.3), while others are solely run by language resource centres. Some target children, while others target adults. Some target Aboriginal people while others target non-Aboriginal people.

Bilingual education programs involve the use of an Aboriginal language, in addition to English, as the language of instruction in formal school programs as well as the Aboriginal language constituting a subject of study in some form. They are aimed at students for whom the Aboriginal language is the dominant language. Other programs are concerned with the teaching of and/or about an Aboriginal language to people for whom it is not the first or dominant language. These language instruction programs take a number of forms as shown by the brief descriptions given in §3.2.

3.1   BILINGUAL EDUCATION PROGRAMS

Although, since colonial times, the educational practice in some church-run schools in Aboriginal communities has included the use of the pupils' home language as a language of instruction, overall this practice has been exceptional in the Australian Aboriginal context in which English has been the favoured language of instruction, while mastery of the English language – both spoken and written – has been one of the main goals of formal schooling (Gale 1990, 1994a and Nicholls 1994).[3]

3.1.1   BILINGUAL EDUCATION PROGRAMS IN THE NORTHERN TERRITORY.

The best known and documented bilingual education programs in Aboriginal Australia are those which have operated in schools in the Northern Territory, which of all the Australian states and territories has the highest number of people who speak an Aboriginal language and whose population has the highest percentage of Aboriginal people, 22 per cent of the total population (Gardner 1991:8–9). Bilingual education programs were initiated by the Whitlam Labor Government in 1973 when formal schooling in the Northern Territory was the responsibility of the Northern Territory Division[4] of the Commonwealth Department of Education.[5] These programs were typically set up in communities in which the first language of children entering school was an Aboriginal language -- either a traditional language, or, in the Roper River area, Kriol.[6]

The motivation for setting up and maintaining these programs stemmed from a belief that schooling in their own language would enhance the academic achievements of Aboriginal children. It was argued that children would more readily learn to read and write their own language, than they would standard Australian English, a language of which most children had little, if any, knowledge on coming to school. Having acquired literacy skills in their own language, it was thought that the transition to mastery of basic English literacy would be relatively simple and quick. It was also expected that official sanctioning of the local Aboriginal language as a language of instruction and also as a legitimate school 'subject' would mitigate against the negative self-image that seemed to be often associated with poor academic achievement in Aboriginal school children. It was also seen as a way of breaking down the barrier between the school and the Aboriginal community in which it was situated, making school less 'foreign' by integrating the community language and culture within the traditional school setting.

These ideas are explicit in a number of reports which were very influential in the setting up of bilingual education programs such as that of Watts, McGrath and Tandy (1973), and also in the 1975 film *Not to lose you my language* commissioned by the Australian Department of Education to promote its bilingual education policy and publicize some of the newly established programs. They have also informed the criteria by which the NT Department of Education has formally evaluated individual programs. Very few rigorous studies comparing academic achievement levels of Aboriginal children in bilingual programs and those in English-only programs have been carried out. A notable exception is the research reported by Gale, McClay, Christie and Harris (1981) in which they measured significantly higher achievement scores for Milingimbi children in bilingual education as opposed to those of children not receiving any classroom instruction in their own language.

Northern Territory Bilingual Education programs were set up at the request of and in consultation with members of the relevant Aboriginal communities, although programs have not been set up in all communities requesting them. Linguists have been employed to work with local Aboriginal people and school personnel in setting up and developing these programs which have required them to carry out a wide variety of tasks including:

- recording and documenting the language;
- establishing practical orthographies;
- producing dictionaries and grammars;
- making earlier linguistic research and documentation accessible to non-linguists engaged in the conduct of bilingual education programs;
- providing adult literacy classes for language speakers (especially the teaching assistants employed by the Department of Education to teach the school-children to read and write their own language and to provide instruction on a range of subjects in the local language);
- instructing non-Aboriginal school personnel in local Aboriginal language;
- constructing 'primers' to aid teachers and teaching-assistants to teach children to read and write their language;
- assisting local people, particularly the Aboriginal Literacy Workers employed by the Department of Education, to produce written materials in their language;
- undertaking sociolinguistic research relevant to school programs and needs in their communities; and
- working with community members and school staff to develop appropriate local curricula, lesson content and teaching materials.

In 1974 five positions for field linguists and one senior supervising linguist position in the Darwin office were created. By the late-1970s there was a Commonwealth Department of Education linguist at Maningrida, Yirrkala, Umbakumba, Yuendumu and Papunya. In 1997 four field linguists with regional responsibilities are employed by NTED to assist Aboriginal language in education programs in the Yolngu-speaking area of Eastern Arnhem Land, in central and western Arnhem Land, in the Tennant Creek and Barkly Region, and in the Central Australian region.

In the late-1970s teacher-linguists were appointed to some schools to support those teaching in bilingual education programs. Teacher-linguists are accredited teachers with some knowledge of and/or interest in Aboriginal languages, who are charged with the coordination and implementation of bilingual programs through cooperation and consultation with linguists, classroom teachers and teaching assistants, school principals, literacy workers and others.

Although at the outset, additional supervisory positions were created in the Darwin and some regional offices of the Department of Education to assist and coordinate the Northern Territory bilingual education programs (both the Aboriginal language and English language components of those programs), these positions have been eliminated and the field linguists, previously based in remote Aboriginal communities, have been relocated to offices in urban centres, their roles becoming more administrative than in the early days of the programs. In addition to the specialist staff employed by the Department of Education in Aboriginal communities – linguists, assistant teachers, literacy workers, teacher-linguists, literature production supervisors – the setting up and implementation of many bilingual education programs was enabled by the work of linguists attached to non-government organizations such as the churches and missions and the Summer Institute of Linguistics (SIL), working in cooperation with the Department of Education. Conversely, bilingual education programs in non-government schools in the Northern Territory have benefited from knowledge, experience and resources gained in the government sector.

The Northern Territory Bilingual Education programs have been extremely influential in providing models for the use of Aboriginal languages in education, in fostering research and in documentation of Aboriginal languages and language situations in cooperative partnerships between speakers of Aboriginal languages, linguists, educationalists and others. The recent development of many of the 'new' forms of expression of Aboriginal languages – written language in print, in film and video, in electronic format – as well as the new linguistic genres, can be traced back to these programs (§4).[7] Likewise, much of the documentation and analysis of Aboriginal languages spoken in the Northern Territory in the past 25 years has been carried out in the context of these bilingual education programs.

Since 1973 bilingual education programs in the Northern Territory have operated in the following languages: Anindilyakwa, Arrernte, Burarra, Kuninjku, Kriol, Kunibidji/Ndjebbana, Luritja, Maung, Murinhpatha, Nunggubuyu, Pintupi, Pitjantjatjara, Tiwi, Warlpiri, and Yolngu Matha languages including Dhuwaya, Djambarrpuyngu, Gälpu, Gumatj and Gupapuyngu. Research has been carried out into these and other languages such as Nakkara (Central Arnhem Land), Mudburra (Elliot area), Warumungu (Tennant Creek) and languages spoken in the Barkly Tablelands area to the east of Tennant Creek and also those spoken in the Gulf area of the Northern Territory (Hoogenraad 1993) in the context of planning and supporting educational programs.

Not all bilingual programs have been equally successful. Many have waxed and waned. Serious long-term and detailed evaluation of NT bilingual education programs has yet to be done. Much could be gained to inform on-going government policy and policy implementation if the data from good evaluative studies were available.

3.1.2   BILINGUAL EDUCATION PROGRAMS BEYOND THE NORTHERN TERRITORY. While in the Northern Territory and also in South Australia bilingual education programs have been conducted in both government and non-government schools, in states such as Western Australia and Queensland, with sizable communities in which the first language of the majority of community members is an Aboriginal language, programs similar to the Northern Territory Bilingual Education Programs have mainly been undertaken in non-Government schools, whether run by Church organizations or by independent Aboriginal community groups such as the Nomads group (or 'Strelly mob') in Western Australia. In many of the schools in the Yankunytjatjara and Pitjantjatjara-speaking region of South Australia, originally under mission control, there has been a long history of bilingual education promoting Pitjantjatjara literacy, although in recent years there has been less emphasis placed on these approaches.

Outside the Northern Territory, one of the most extensive network of bilingual education programs operates within the Catholic Education system in the Kimberley region of Western Australia (Lee 1993). These programs typically operate in primary schools based in small remote communities such as Ringers Soak (Yaruman) whose Jaru-English bilingual program is described in some detail by McKay (1996:55–67). In addition to having local community support, the Catholic Education system provides specialist support through visits from a teacher-linguist and supports ongoing formal training for the Aboriginal teaching personnel. Another program based in Western Australia briefly described by McKay (1996:128) is the one operating at the Parnngurr Independent Community School near Newman, where children are taught to read and write their first language which is a Western Desert language.

At Aurukun in north west Queensland, bilingual school programs in the Wik-Munkan language which emerged as the mission lingua franca have operated at various times since the mid 1970s. No support for such programs was given by the Queensland Department of Education until the adoption of its LOTE policy which includes Aboriginal language study (§3.2.4).

3.2   LANGUAGE INSTRUCTION PROGRAMS

Language instruction programs involving Aboriginal languages are often classified as being either language learning or language awareness (or learning about language) programs (Amery 1994:141), although logically language learning programs would have to involve an increase in awareness about the language being learned. Close inspection of Aboriginal language learning programs – their operation, the motivations behind them, the expected outcomes – suggests that few provide students with the basis for learning to speak or write the language, but that they do make students aware of the existence and nature of these languages and their speakers. Where a language is no longer the primary language of communication, it is most unlikely that it will ever regain this position, so that the aim of teaching about such a language is not to provide the student with an alternative language of primary communication, but has more to do with other roles that knowledge of a language fulfil (Harper 1996).

Aboriginal language programs operate in private and state-run schools at the present time. Most have been set up on the initiative of particular teachers, largely depending on them for their successful operation. With the renewal of interest in second-language learning in Australian schools resulting from the 1987 National Language Policy (§2), most states and territories have included Aboriginal languages within the scope of their Languages Other Than English (LOTE) programs. In some cases this has meant system-wide support for school-based instruction in Aboriginal languages for both Aboriginal and non-Aboriginal children and an attempt to develop coherent system-wide policies such as the Western Australian Ministry of Education's Framework for the Teaching of Aboriginal Languages in Primary Schools (§3.2.5.3).

The aim of language instruction programs is to teach an Aboriginal language, requiring students to learn to understand, speak, read and write the language, or to acquire some subset of these linguistic skills. They differ from the Aboriginal bilingual education programs described above which were typically set up for the benefit of children who come to school already knowing an Aboriginal language which they may use as their primary language.

Programs which seek to enable Aboriginal people, both adults and children, to understand and speak the language of their forebears are sometimes referred to as Language Revival Programs or Language Restoration Programs.[8] In some cases, these languages are still known to some speakers in the community who provide a resource and stimulus for those wanting to acquire knowledge of the language. In other cases, the languages are no longer spoken by any living soul, the only knowledge of them being contained in the form of written records, and in some cases, voice recordings. The Kaurna programs described below are of this sort, as is the Yorta-Yorta program in Victoria. Other programs, commonly known as Language Maintenance Programs, aim to encourage Aboriginal people, especially children, to maintain and strengthen their knowledge of their community language(s), although it is not necessarily their primary or dominant language. A number of these programs are described in McKay (1996) and in Hartman and Henderson (eds) (1994). Some Aboriginal people have elected to learn about Aboriginal languages spoken not by their immediate forebears, but by people from distant communities where the language is still the dominant language.

Other Aboriginal language programs in schools are targeted mainly at non-Aboriginal students, such as the Warlpiri program at the Mt. Evelyn School in Victoria, the Victor Harbour Pitjantjatjara Program in South Australia and some of the Arrernte programs taught in Alice Springs schools. Formal Aboriginal language courses are also delivered by a number of institutions to adults (mainly non-Aboriginal, but not exclusively so) seeking to learn the language often for professional purposes. In many Aboriginal communities in northern Australia, Aboriginal language courses are provided for non-Aboriginal personnel such as teachers, nurses and police stationed in Aboriginal communities through the local school or through Aboriginal language resource centres (§2.3).

A brief description of some of the formal Aboriginal language courses offered around Australia is given below.

3.2.1   NORTHERN TERRITORY. In addition to the bilingual education programs described in §3.1.1, a variety of Aboriginal language and culture programs have operated in schools and other institutions throughout the Northern Territory since the 1970s, a sample of which are mentioned here. (See Coleman and Strauss (1996) for a brief up-to-date account of Aboriginal language programs currently operating in the northern region of the Northern Territory.)

[a] *Arrernte.* Students at the Alice Springs High School have been offered courses in Arrernte, the language of Alice Springs and the surrounding area, at various times since the 1970s. Arrernte has also been

taught at the Catholic High School (Bowden 1994) and at some primary schools in Alice Springs. The instruction has usually been given by Arrernte instructors working in partnership with classroom teachers, linguists and others. The Institute for Aboriginal Development has played an important role in providing instructors, appropriate language materials, and language-teaching expertise.

A very ambitious Arrernte language education project was launched in 1993. This is the *Intelyape-lyape Akaltye* or *Arrernte Early Childhood Development Project* funded by the Bernard van Leer Foundation, involving cooperation between the Yipirinya School,[9] the Our Lady of the Sacred Heart Primary School in Alice Springs, and the Ltyentye Apurte School at Santa Teresa to the east of Alice Springs (Hartman et al. 1995).[10] This project aims to establish a model process for the implementation of education programs in communities where Aboriginal language and culture are dominant.

The Institute for Aboriginal Development based in Alice Springs has been running language-learning courses in Arrernte as well as in other central Australian languages such as Warlpiri, Pitjantjatjara and Pintupi since the early 1970s, and has been publishing ancillary materials: dictionaries, pedagogical grammars, and language-learning courses consisting of printed materials, audio and video tapes. Teaching resources in Arrernte produced as a result of the *Intelyape-lyape Akaltye* project are available through IAD Press.

[b] *Yolngu.* Yolngu languages constitute a complex network of closely related language varieties which belong to the Pama-Nyungan language family. Yolngu language speakers occupy the north-east section of Arnhem Land including the off-shore islands. Their neighbours to the south and west speak languages much more distantly related to those of the Pama-Nyungan family. The Northern Territory University offers courses in the Yolngu languages of north-east Arnhem Land as part of its degree programs (McKay 1996:152–3).

Because of dramatic changes in demographic patterns brought about with the establishment of mission settlements in the Yolngu-speaking area prior to World War 2, some language varieties – once the markers of particular kin group membership – have flourished, becoming virtual lingua francas while others have waned. In an attempt to reinforce among young speakers the use of linguistic difference as a marker of kin group affiliation, what is essentially a dialect revitalisation project has been organized on Galiwin'ku (Elcho Island) (McKay 1996:124–5). This is mainly an oral language program but does involve some written language as well. (See also Christie (1994) for further information about language programs in north-east Arnhem Land.)

[c] *Nunggubuyu.* Kriol is the primary language of most Aboriginal people living at Numbulwar on the eastern coast of Arnhem Land although the traditional Nunggubuyu language is still spoken by older people, some of whom have initiated a Nunggubuyu language revitalization program in collaboration with the school and the NTED linguist responsible for that area, Melanie Wilkinson (McKay 1996:134, Nicholls 1994). Although an attempt

was made to establish a bilingual Nunggubuyu–English bilingual education program at Numbulwar in the 1970s, it was not successful, partly through lack of institutional and professional support, and partly because of the decline in the use of the traditional language by the then school-aged children.

[d] *Maningrida languages.* At Maningrida, a multi-lingual community on the north coast of Arnhem Land, a variety of language in education programs have operated over the years, including formal bilingual programs in several languages. A program which links language education with learning about the local environment, known as the 'Land and Language Project' (McKay 1996:126), involves school children in data collection and observation alongside teachers and community members and also draws on research on local flora, fauna and land forms by outside scientists. Part of the project is the creation of an encyclopaedic picture reference through the collaboration of the NTED regional linguist, Carolyn Coleman, with natural scientists and knowledgeable local people (Coleman 1991).

[e] *Katherine, Roper River Area.* McKay (1996:139–41) reports on a number of language revival programs supported by the Katherine Regional Aboriginal Languages Centre (KRALC) in the Roper River area of the Northern Territory, which is a predominantly Kriol-speaking area.

One is the Mangarrayi language program at the Jilkminggan School near Katherine, where adult Mangarrayi speakers support the efforts of Aboriginal teaching assistants who understand the language well. The program aims to develop the children's Mangarrayi language competence since the primary language of the children in this community is no longer Mangarrayi, but Kriol. The availability of linguistic documentation in the form of a grammar and wordlist has been one the factors in the program's success, according to McKay.

Other programs which involve elderly speakers of traditional Aboriginal languages teaching children something of those languages operate in schools at Ngukurr (Alawa, Marra, Ngalakgan, Ngandi, Ritharrngu, Rembarrnga and Nunggubuyu), Barunga (Jawoyn, Dalabon, Mayali, Rembarrnga) and Hodgson Downs (Alawa). (For a fuller account of language programs in the Katherine area see Angelo (1996)).

While these programs, along with those conducted at Numbulwar, are unlikely to 'revive' languages in terms of causing young people to abandon Kriol and adopt their people's traditional language as their primary language, they do serve a meaningful social function in fostering greater awareness of linguistic and cultural diversity and in maintaining cultural and social solidarity between generations of close kin.

[f] *Barkly and Sandover Regions.* Hoogenraad (1994) discusses some 13 Aboriginal studies programs involving an Aboriginal language which have operated in some 32 schools (including outstation schools) in the Barkly and Sandover regions of the Northern Territory since 1990. These programs are typically initiated and run by Aboriginal language speakers who are also teachers or student teachers, mainly Batchelor College graduates (§3.4). The languages in which these programs have operated are Alyawarr, Garrwa, Kaytetye, Jingili, Wampaya, Warlpiri, Warumungu, Yanyuwa.

While noting the interest in the Aboriginal community and especially among Aboriginal teachers for Aboriginal language to be formally integrated into school programs, Hoogenraad observes that these grassroots language programs tend to be of rather short duration, quickly losing direction and failing to develop (Hoogenraad 1994:184). In order to prevent this from occurring, he concludes that Aboriginal people presenting local Aboriginal studies programs in a formal education context require help with curriculum development, lesson plans, development of teaching materials and accessing and adapting existing materials, training in appropriate teaching techniques and with liaison between school staff and the local community to establish appropriate roles for all involved.

These same requirements have been judged necessary by others involved in similar education initiatives and were reflected in the infrastructure put in place for those bilingual education programs which did function well, and which are reflected in the Western Australian Framework for the Teaching of Aboriginal Languages in Primary Schools (§3.2.5.3).

3.2.2   VICTORIA. A variety of courses in languages traditionally spoken in Victoria, such as Yorta Yorta, Wemba Wemba and Ganai, as well as languages still spoken in the Northern Territory (Yolngu Matha and Warlpiri) operate throughout Victoria.

[a] *Yorta Yorta.*   Yorta Yorta was spoken in the Murray River–Barmah Forest area between Deniliquin, N.S.W. and Shepparton, Victoria. The Worawa Aboriginal College at Healesville, Victoria, has set up a Yorta Yorta language course which has been accredited as a Victorian Certificate of Education subject. This program has been built around the language materials produced by the Yorta Yorta language revival program initiated by Mrs. Geraldine Briggs who learnt the language from her mother. She has been helped to develop this program by Dr. Heather Bowe, a linguist from Monash University (McKay 1996:145–6).

[b] *Wemba Wemba.*   Wemba Wemba was spoken in the southern New South Wales-northern Victoria area. People of Wemba Wemba ancestry in the Echuca area of Victoria have established language awareness programs and are working towards the creation of a Wemba Wemba language learning program with help from Luise Hercus, a linguist at the Australian National University, who has produced a grammar and dictionary of Wemba Wemba (McKay 1996:146–7).

[c] *Ganai.*   Ganai (or Gaanai) was spoken by people living in Victoria's Gippsland district whose way of life was described in considerable detail by nineteenth century ethnologists, particularly Howitt (1904), who referred to both the people and their language as Kurnai. Aspects of the language pieced together from historical sources is now taught at the Koorie Open Door on Education school at Morwell by Lynette Dent, who formerly taught the Bundjalung course at Monash University's Gippsland campus.

[d] *Yolngu Matha.*   Using the excellent teaching materials compiled by Don Williams (1981), Yolngu Matha speakers from north-east Arnhem

Land have given lessons about their language and culture to students in Years 11 and 12 at Worawa College (Amery 1994:144).

[e] *Warlpiri.* At the Mount Evelyn Christian School in Victoria, courses in the Warlpiri language of the Tanami Desert area of the Northern Territory are provided for Year 9 and 10 non-Aboriginal children (McKay 1996:153–4). Warlpiri speakers visit the school to teach part of the course which encompasses both language and culture, and pupils visit Yuendumu in southern Warlpiri country as part of a week-long school excursion once a year.

3.2.3   SOUTH AUSTRALIA. The South Australian Department for Education and Children's Services has developed a draft state-wide policy for the use of Aboriginal languages within the state, which remains to be officially adopted. An up-to-date survey of Aboriginal language programs in South Australian schools is provided by Wilson (1996).

[a] *Pitjantjatjara.* Amery (1994:144) reports that a language-learning program has operated for over ten years at Victor Harbour Primary school in South Australia, where non-Aboriginal students are taught Pitjantjatjara. This program is linked to a student-exchange program with the school at Fregon situated in the Pitjantjatjara-speaking area of northern South Australia. A similar exchange program between the Goolwa school in the south of South Australia and another Pitjantjatjara-speaking community in the state's north, Indulkana, has also been put in place (Amery 1994:144).
    Pitjantjatjara language courses for adults have been conducted for many years by Bill Edwards, Mona Tur and others at the University of South Australia, which has published an outstanding Pitjantjatjara learner's course (Eckert and Hudson 1991).
    Pitjantjatjara/Yankunytjatjara programs have been offered in Adelaide schools to students many of whom are from the Nunga communities of the coastal and southern part of South Australia. (*Nunga* is the term for Aboriginal person used in the southern part of South Australia, borrowed from Aboriginal languages traditionally spoken in that area.) Amery (1994:143) observes that although these Western Desert languages are spoken by people traditionally resident in the northern part of South Australia and the southern Northern Territory, they have generally been well received by Nunga children and their families. In fact, Amery claims that these programs helped 'in paving the way for Nunga language reclamation programs by setting the pedagogical and political precedent of an Aboriginal language being taught officially in the urban classroom' (Amery 1994:143).

[b] *Kaurna.* Other language heritage programs taught in the context of formal education programs involve the teaching of Kaurna, the language once spoken in the Adelaide area. These programs are possible because this language was well documented in the first half of the nineteenth century by the German missionary scholars, Teichelmann and Schürmann (Amery 1993, 1996; Simpson 1993). Both Kaurna and Ngarrindjeri language programs have been documented by the South Australian Aboriginal Education Unit in a video entitled *Living languages.*

Kaurna is taught to all Aboriginal students at the Kaurna Plains School in South Australia as the school LOTE (Varcoe 1994). It is also taught by Cherie Watkins, a Nunga woman, and linguist Rob Amery at the Para West Adult Campus of Inbarendi College to Year 11 level Aboriginal and non-Aboriginal adult students and at Tauondi Inc. (formerly Aboriginal Community College) Port Adelaide within a nationally accredited TAFE Aboriginal Cultural Instructors and Tourism course. All the students in the latter program are Aboriginal, some of them Kaurna. Kaurna has also been taught to members of the Kaurna community by Rob Amery at Warriparinga (Sturt River) at the invitation of the Kaurna Heritage Committee (Amery 1996).

Some ex-students from the Inbarendi program have been incorporating some elements of the Kaurna language into Aboriginal Studies offerings at a number of schools. There are early signs that some bits of Kaurna language such as greetings, leave-takings and kin terms are beginning to spread within the Kaurna community amongst people who have had no direct contact with the formal Kaurna language programs. Many speeches of introduction and welcome are now delivered using Kaurna at public events, openings of organisations, exhibitions etc. Some Kaurna children are being officially named with Kaurna names. Some Kaurna signage is going up within some institutions (Amery, personal communication). (See also Amery (1993 and 1996).)

[c] *Adnyamathanha.* Adnyamathanha is the traditional language of the Flinders Ranges area of South Australia. McKay (1996:147) reports on initiatives taken by people of Adnyamathanha background, including speakers of the language, to have week long literacy workshops run by linguist Dorothy Tunbridge who has extensively researched and documented Adnyamathanha language and culture.

3.2.4   QUEENSLAND. Since 1991 a number of language programs have been introduced into Queensland schools under the LOTE umbrella. Most of these have been introduced for the benefit of Aboriginal children in rural Queensland where Aboriginal languages are still spoken or where some knowledge of them has been maintained. Some of these school based programs have been documented by the Department of Education on a video called *Which Language.* These include a Djabugay program at Kuranda, a Kala Lagaw Ya program on Thursday Island, a Gugu Yimidhirr program at Hopevale, a Gugu Yalanji program at Mossman, Dyirbal language programs at Tully and Mt Garnet, and a Wik-Munkun program at Aurukun.

[a] *Djabugay.* Djabugay is the language traditionally spoken in the Kuranda area of north Queensland, however, only a few Djabugay speakers are still alive. At the Kuranda State (Primary) School in north Queensland where about one third of the pupils are Aboriginal, all classes are given an introduction to the Djabugay language and culture for one period a week in a five or six week block each year (Johnson 1994, McKay 1996: 136-148). This program can be seen as a 'language heritage' program for those pupils who are Djabugay, while it constitutes a 'language awareness' and 'language learning' program for all students. Among the educational resources used in

this program is the Djabugay dictionary, produced with assistance from the Australian Institute of Aboriginal and Torres Strait Islander Studies (AIATSIS) Dictionaries Project (§5), and pedagogical grammar books. There is also a Djabugay language program at Smithfield High School in Cairns.

[b] *Kalaw Kawaw Ya.*   A LOTE accredited language learning program in the Kalaw Kawaw Ya language of the Western Torres Strait operates at Thursday Island State High School (McKay 1996:77, Walton and Babia 1996:7–26).

[c] *Guugu-Yalanji and Guugu-Yimidhirr.*   Other LOTE accredited Aboriginal language courses are offered in two other languages of eastern Cape York Peninsula: Guugu-Yalanji taught at Mossman High, Guugu-Yimidhirr at Peace Lutheran College (Walton and Babia 1996:9).

[d] *Other languages.*   Yugambeh programs have been run in traditional Yugambeh country in the Gold Coast area of south east Queensland.
  While most programs involve the language traditionally spoken in the school area, at Urandangie in north western Queensland there have been attempts to teach Alyawarr in the local school rather than the traditional Warluwarra language. Although Alyawarr is an Arandic language traditionally spoken within the Northern Territory, speakers of this language now live in communities on the Queensland side of the Northern Territory-Queensland border, in country where the traditional languages are no longer spoken.

3.2.5   WESTERN AUSTRALIA. The last few years has seen a resurgence of locally initiated language research and teaching activity in this state. In addition to the language programs described below, the Nyungar language has been taught in the south west for many years, while a number of language programs are operating in both the Pilbara and Kimberley regions.

[a] *Western Desert Languages.*   Courses in Aboriginal languages spoken in the south west of the Western Desert language area were offered for many years to students at the former Mt. Lawley College of Advanced Education and at the West Australian Institute of Technology by both Wilf Douglas and Eric Vászolyi (see Vászolyi 1982). An intensive Wangkatja course is also held each year for adult students at Kalgoorlie College (Smith 1989). Both Eric Vászolyi who wrote an excellent teaching grammar of Wangkatja (Vászolyi 1979) and Wilf Douglas who, since the 1950s, has documented Aboriginal languages of Western Australia, including Western Desert languages of the Warburton Ranges area, the Nyungar languages of the south west of the state and the Wajarri language of the Murchison area, have long been involved in Aboriginal language teaching in Western Australia.

[b] *Walmajarri.*   Although Walmajarri is still spoken by many middle-aged and elderly people in communities in the southern part of the Kimberleys, most Walmajarri children speak Kriol as their primary language,

although many have a good passive knowledge of the language. (For documentation of Fitzroy Valley creole see Fraser 1977, Hudson 1981, Thies 1987.) Walmajarri is a language which has been extensively documented mainly by linguists formerly with SIL, Joyce Hudson and Eirlys Richards, with a published grammar and dictionary. A substantial portion of the Bible has also been published in an diglot Walmajarri-English version, and there are other Walmajarri written materials (McGregor 1988b:172–8).

The Walmajarri language has been taught to children of Walmajarri background at a number of schools in Walmajarri communities including the Yakanarra Community School near Fitzroy Crossing in Western Australia (McKay 1996:139), Gogo School also near Fitzroy Crossing (Wrigley 1994).[11]

[c] *Nulungu Catholic College.* While programs which aim to teach people to understand and speak (and/or read and write) an Aboriginal language typically also involve teaching about the language, its speakers, their history and culture, some language heritage programs are less ambitious, in the sense that their explicit aim is to impart some knowledge about a language and its speakers, not primarily (or at all) to teach people to actually use the language. An example of such a program is the one run at the Nulungu Catholic College in Broome, Western Australia (McKay 1996:152).

[d] *Framework For The Teaching Of Aboriginal Languages In Primary Schools.* The Western Australian Ministry of Education's Framework for the Teaching of Aboriginal Languages in Primary Schools (Hudson 1994; McKay 1996:142–5; Wrigley 1994) makes provision for a variety of language programs including language awareness programs which can be taught under the LOTE umbrella in the many and varied Aboriginal language situations which are found in that state. One of the main planks of this framework is the requirement for a school-based language team – teacher, community language specialist, Aboriginal Education Worker, Linguist – very much like the successful Northern Territory Bilingual Education Programs. This framework was developed by Joyce Hudson and has been piloted in a number of schools since 1992. This program foreshadows the national Australian Indigenous Languages Framework (AILF) described below §3.2.7.

3.2.6   NEW SOUTH WALES. The New South Wales Board of Studies has identified ten languages for use in schools and the development of a Years 7–10 Framework for Aboriginal language programs is in progress. In the western part of the state, both Paakantyi and Ngiyampaa programs are operating. Brief descriptions of some of the other New South Wales language courses follow.

[a] *Bundjalung.* Sharpe (1993) describes a number of Bundjalung language courses that have been run in Bundjalung country in southern Queensland and in north eastern New South Wales and also in Victoria as a unit in the Associate Diploma level course in Koorie Studies at Monash University College, Gippsland. (*Koorie* is a word from languages of the north coast of New South Wales meaning 'person' or 'Aboriginal person'

which is commonly used in New South Wales and Victoria with the latter meaning.) Some of these courses have been initiated by Bundjalung people (such as those organised by the Kumbumerri Aboriginal Corporation in southern Queensland) and have been taught by native speakers of Bundjalung, only very few of whom are still alive.

[b] *Gumbaynggir.* The initiatives taken by the Muurrbay Aboriginal Language and Culture Cooperative based in Kempsey to foster a revival of knowledge of the Gumbaynngir language once spoken to the south of the Bundjalung area are described by McKay (1996:45–54 and 105). The few remaining speakers of the language work with other Gumbaynngir people and others using both speaker expertise and available linguistic documentation. Their efforts have been directed towards both adults and children, including direct teaching within the context of the local school attended mainly by local Aboriginal children.

[c] *Awabakal.* The Awabakal language revival program (which operated from 1979 to 1984) described by Heath (1982) is similar in a number of ways to the Kaurna (§3.2.3.2) program in that the language ceased to be a primary language of communication at the end of the nineteenth century, but had been extensively documented with a dictionary and grammar in the early part of that century by the missionary Threlkeld working in close collaboration with an Awabakal man, Birabahn (Simpson 1993). It is this material which Aboriginal people living in traditional Awabakal country in the Newcastle-Lake Macquarie area have been able to draw on for knowledge about the language.

3.2.7   AUSTRALIAN INDIGENOUS LANGUAGES FRAMEWORK. An important initiative of the 1990s to extend knowledge about Aboriginal languages to Australian school children in all states and territories is the Commonwealth Government funded development of the *Australian Indigenous Languages Framework* (AILF) which was co-hosted by the Northern Territory, the New South Wales Boards of Studies and the Senior Secondary Assessment Board of South Australia (SSABSA) which managed the project. It drew on linguistic and educational expertise from all around Australia aiming 'to provide a national framework for the introduction of Aboriginal and Torres Strait Islander languages into the upper secondary school' (McKay 1996:100). AILF is a national curriculum project funded under the Innovative Languages Other than English (ILOTES) Program administered by the Commonwealth Department of Employment, Education, Training and Youth Affairs.

The Framework has been deliberately designed to be flexible enough to deal with the wide range of different situations which may be found in schools across Australia, from schools with no Aboriginal or Torres Strait Islander pupils to those with a majority of Aboriginal or Torres Strait Islander pupils for whom a local Aboriginal language may be the first or dominant language. The AILF process has involved research and consultation leading to the production of pedagogical support materials in various forms: printed matter, videos, CD-ROM.

Material resources that have been developed to support AILF programs include a textbook *Australia's Indigenous Languages* together with a CD-ROM compiled by David Nathan of AIATSIS, exemplar material *Australian Indigenous Languages in Practice* and the *Australian Indigenous Languages Framework*.

AILF has been fully accredited for Years 11 and 12 in South Australia, though the universities differ in the status they accord it as far as university entrance is concerned. AILF is also fully accredited in Victoria, Western Australia and the Northern Territory.

AILF has also fostered the trialing of proposed curricula guidelines and resources and the setting up of pilot programs in schools in the following states and territories (Rob Amery, personal communication).

[a] *South Australia.* In South Australia an AILF program in Pitjantjatjara/Yankunytjatjara is currently being taught at the Port Augusta Secondary School, while since 1994 the Kaurna Language Reclamation Program has been operating at Inbarendi College in Elizabeth (§3.2.3.2). In Semesters one and two of 1994, the Oodnadatta Aboriginal School ran an Antikirinya Year 11 language revitalisation program. (Antikirinya is a Western Desert language spoken at the most south-eastern part of the Western Desert language region.)

[b] *Victoria.* The Worawa College Yorta-Yorta and Yolngu Matha (Gupapuyngu) programs described in §3.2.2.1 and §3.2.2.3 are AILF pilot programs.

[c] *Western Australia.* In 1996 AILF pilot programs giving instruction about two languages of the Pilbara area, Yinjibarndi and Nyangumarta, were operating at the Hedland High School, Port Hedland.

[d] *Northern Territory.* At Kormilda College, Darwin, a Year 11 program, 'Indigenous Languages of the School', based on the Framework has been established, and was accredited by the NT Board of Studies for 1997. This is basically a Language Awareness Program which involves students in a survey of languages spoken by students at the school and languages of the local area as well as giving general background about Australian languages.

In 1994 the Catholic High School in Alice Springs ran an Eastern Arrernte First Language Maintenance program, as an AILF pilot program (§3.2.1).

3.3   ABORIGINAL LANGUAGES AND ABORIGINAL TEACHER EDUCATION

A very significant consequence of the bilingual education programs in Northern Territory schools in which the key teaching role is played by local Aboriginal people has been the development of appropriate teacher training courses at institutions such as Batchelor College (Crowe 1994). Since the late 1970s an increasing number of Aboriginal people who speak an Aboriginal language as their primary language have moved from the role of 'teaching assistant' to that of registered 'classroom teacher' obtaining formal qualification through a course of study usually well integrated into both Aboriginal community life and the routine of the community school. An awareness of the importance of the local Aboriginal languages in the education process has led to innovative teaching programs such as the Batchelor College Aboriginal Languages Fortnight run in local communities with the collaboration of linguists, College staff, community members and the students (McKay 1996:96–100).

Responding to the need to train Aboriginal teachers to teach in the schools in their communities, specialized teacher education courses have also been established in other states. In South Australia the Anangu Teacher Education Program (AnTEP) operates out of the University of South Australia, providing on-site training for Aboriginal Education Workers and prospective teachers in the Pitjantjatjara-speaking communities of the state's north (Gale, M.-A. 1996). (*Anangu* is the Pitjantjatjara word for 'person' and more particularly for 'Aboriginal person'.) In Western Australia, similar courses are offered by institutions such as Pundulmurra College (Sharp and Injie 1994). In Queensland, specialist TAFE courses in Aboriginal languages and linguistics for Aboriginal students have been developed by TAFE Queensland (1995).

The Northern Territory University offers an Australian Indigenous Languages Strand within the Graduate Diploma in Applied Linguistics which includes the subject 'Teaching Australian Indigenous Languages' which attempts to cover the wide range of language-teaching contexts and programs described above (see Walton and Babia 1996). (See also Tindale (1994) for discussion of the type of professional training required by Aboriginal people teaching their languages in the Central Australian context.)

The Institute for Aboriginal Development (Alice Springs) produces printed materials and videos such as *Teaching Our Way* which provide instruction about setting up and running language programs. It also provides on-the-job training for Aboriginal language instructors.

3.4   ABORIGINAL LANGUAGES AND ABORIGINAL LINGUISTS

In conjunction with the setting up of bilingual education programs in the Northern Territory (§3.1.1), a School of Australian Linguistics (SAL) was established in 1974 as part of Darwin Community College to provide courses in linguistics and Aboriginal language literacy to speakers of Aboriginal languages. These courses were especially directed at Aboriginal Literacy Workers employed in schools with bilingual education programs to produce written materials in the local language to support the classroom based programs. As noted by McKay (1996:99), over the years SAL 'developed a much broader view of its role in helping indigenous people to work towards maintaining their languages'. SAL was very successful in developing the literacy skills of its students and also in raising their level of linguistic awareness. Many SAL graduates supported various bilingual education programs and provided language teaching courses. They have also collaborated with linguists in researching and documenting their languages and in making the results of their work available to other speakers of their language (McKay 1991). Hoogenraad (1994) notes the dominant role of Batchelor College graduates in initiating and conducting Aboriginal language programs in their community schools.

SAL was one of the first education establishments to take its courses to the students in their communities, a model later followed by Batchelor College's Remote Area Teacher Education (RATE) program and the University of South Australia's AnTEP program (§3.3). As part of the reorganization of the tertiary education sector in the late 1980's, SAL was incorporated into Batchelor College and renamed the Centre for Australian Languages and Linguistics (CALL).

The TAFE Queensland course referred to in §3.3 above is also designed to provide appropriate education for Aboriginal and Torres Strait Islander people who wish to research, record, maintain and teach their own languages.

The Australian Linguistic Institutes[12] held at the University of Sydney in 1992, at La Trobe University in 1994, and at the University of Queensland in 1998 offered special courses of relevance to Aboriginal language speakers and others working in language education and documentation programs.

AIATSIS has also played a useful role in providing expert instruction in specific language documentation techniques, especially in the area of Aboriginal language lexicography (AIATSIS Annual Report 1992–3: 13–14; Thieberger 1993).

4.　NON-TRADITIONAL MODES OF LINGUISTIC EXPRESSION

4.1　WRITTEN LANGUAGE IN PRINT

Because of the emphasis most of the bilingual education programs put on the teaching of literacy in Aboriginal languages as well as on the use of the written language in various forms as a teaching tool, a considerable quantity of local written material in a wide variety of genres has been produced (Black 1993, Eckert 1982, Gale 1992 and 1994b, Goddard 1990 and 1994, Marett 1987).

Over the past 25 years most written forms of Aboriginal language authored by speakers of the language have emerged as printed matter – often locally produced books incorporating illustrations by local Aboriginal artists, charts, maps, photographs. Most of these have been published by school-based literature production centres or more recently by community-based language resource centres.[13]

The Aboriginal language education programs, especially the bilingual education programs in the Northern Territory and elsewhere, have been the catalyst for a large quantity of linguistic research and documentation which will be discussed in §5. The byproducts of much of this research have been locally printed curriculum materials, teaching aids, wordlists, documentation of local physical and social environment, story books, local history.

4.1.1 ABORIGINAL LITERATURE FOR THE GENERAL PUBLIC. The 1980s and 1990s have seen the production of a number of publications of high standard in which the original text in a Aboriginal language is printed side by side with an English translation. Most of these texts are basically transcribed and edited versions of oral literature texts, while others were produced as written texts by their authors, writing in an Aboriginal language.

Some examples of the former are Strelhow's *Songs of Central Australia*, Warlukurlangu Artists' *Yuendumu Doors*, Hercus & Sutton's *This is what Happened*, Rockman and Cataldi's *Warlpiri Dreamings and Histories: Yimikirli*, Dixon and Duwell's *The honey-ant men's love song and other Aboriginal song poems*, Dixon and Koch's *Dyirrbal Song Poetry*, Koch's *Kaytetye Country*, the Reads' *Long Time-Olden Time*, Bradley's *Yanyuwa Country: The Yanyuwa people of Borroloola tell the history of their land* and Vaarzon-Morel's *Warlpiri Women's Voices*.[14] These works were produced through partnerships between speakers of Aboriginal languages and professional linguists, anthropologists or historians and have been published by both specialist publishers in the case of Aboriginal Studies Press and IAD Press, and general publishing houses such as Harper Collins Publishers and University of Queensland Press. In the Introduction to *Yanyuwa County*, Bradley describes the complex collaborative process that he engaged in with Yanyuwa speakers and others to produce the collection of Yanyuwa language texts with their English translations, explications and illustrations.

Similar partnerships have also led to the successful publication of the works of Aboriginal writers, writing in their own languages. These texts have typically been published by publishers specialising in Aboriginal subjects. The foremost publisher of books for the general public written in Aboriginal languages with an English translation is IAD Press, attached to the Institute for Aboriginal Development (Alice Springs), which publishes a wide range of books and videos relating to Aboriginal languages (dictionaries, grammars, language-learning course materials, story books) as well as books on Aboriginal history, education, social issues, environment and culture. Magabala Books based in Broome, Western Australia, is another publisher which specializes in works produced by Aboriginal authors, some of which have been presented in the original Aboriginal language with an English version.

Spoken texts in a number of Aboriginal languages were incorporated into the sound component of *The Red Earth*, a major ballet commissioned by the Australian Ballet Company which had its debut in 1996. These Aboriginal language texts were subtitled in the way that the lyrics of operas sung in languages other than English are subtitled for the audience. While products of Aboriginal technology and culture such as tools, weapons, shelters, body ornamentation, paintings and engravings have been used by non-Aboriginal Australian artists, film-makers and others as props in their portrayals of Australian subjects, as have traditional Aboriginal music and songs which have been incorporated into 'mainstream' musical compositions, it is probably the first time that spoken language has been used to create such artistic effects. As the decline of these Aboriginal languages as primary means of linguistic communication continues, they are partially acquired by another ethnic group to assume a sort of decorative function.

4.1.2   MAJOR   TEXTS   TRANSLATED   INTO   ABORIGINAL LANGUAGES.

[a] *Aboriginal Language Bibles.* By far the most challenging exercises in translation from English into an Aboriginal language are the many bible translations that have been accomplished by teams of translators trained in both linguistics and translation techniques who work in close consultation and partnership with speakers of Aboriginal languages. Where there is written literature in an Aboriginal language, the Bible typically constitutes the largest single text written in that language. Significant sections of the Bible have been translated into the following Australian languages: Alyawarr, Anindilyakwa, Burarra, Djambarrpuyngu, Eastern Arrernte, Gumatj, Gurindji, Kalaw Kawaw Yaa, Kuku-Yalanji, Kunwinyku, Martu Wangka, Maung, Murrinhpata, Ngaanyatjarra, Nunggubuyu, Pintupi, Pitjantjatjara, Tiwi, Walmajarri, Warlpiri, Western Arrernte, Wik-Munken, Yanyuwa as well as into Kriol (Steve Swartz, personal communication). Bible translations into other Aboriginal languages which are no longer spoken also exist, some dating from the nineteenth century.

Bible translators associated with the Summer Institute of Linguistics-Australian Aborigine and Islander Branch (SIL-AAIB), and with a variety of Christian Church organizations, have also been active in promoting Aboriginal language literacy and in providing training to Aboriginal people in linguistics and translation. They have also carried out extensive linguistic research and documentation. One of the areas of linguistic investigation pioneered by Bible translators in the context of Australian Aboriginal languages is that of discourse structure analysis (Eckert 1982, Godfrey 1979 and 1985, Kilham 1977, McGregor 1987, Reynolds 1988, Sayers 1976, Swartz 1988).

[b] *Translations of English Literary Works.* The translation of *Alice in Wonderland* into Pitjantjatjara is perhaps the most significant work of English literature to have been translated into an Aboriginal language (Sheppard 1992). Many shorter children's stories have been translated into Aboriginal languages in the context of bilingual education programs.

4.2   ABORIGINAL PLACE NAMES

All over Australia are place names derived from the original local Aboriginal language names. These place names are in some cases the only remaining linguistic trace of the pre-European population. In the past three decades, with the recognition of Aboriginal Land Rights in some parts of Australia, and more recently of Native Title, and also as part of a general renaissance of acknowledgement of Australia's Aboriginal heritage, Aboriginal place names have, in response to Aboriginal requests, replaced English language place names as the official place name for many of the townships and outstations with a majority Aboriginal population. This has been especially marked in the Northern Territory. With the establishment of many new Aboriginal community locations as part of the 'outstation movement' in the Northern Territory and Western Australia in particular, the Aboriginal place name has been officially adopted and marked on relevant maps.[15]

4.3   WRITTEN LANGUAGE ON VIDEO

An outstanding example of the use of video technology for language and literacy instruction is the nine part series of video programs targeted at Warlpiri children entitled *Manyu-wana*, produced by the Warlpiri Media Association, based at Yuendumu, Northern Territory. The finance for the original three programs in the series was provided by a NALP grant (§2.1). This series, with English subtitles, was screened on national television by SBS in 1995. The Yiyili Community School in the Kimberley area of Western Australia has produced a similar set of two videos called *Jiyabinggiddi Gooniyandi* which 'presents the (Gooniyandi) language in written and spoken form in a lively and relevant way' (McKay 1996:148).

4.4   WRITTEN LANGUAGE IN ELECTRONIC MEDIA

As new technologies came into Aboriginal communities, written language also appeared in electronic form to be read and interacted with via a computer screen, as well as being used in film and video media. McKay (1996:104–5) describes some of the educational uses to which computer technology has been put in Aboriginal language teaching.

Both video and computer technology in education have proven very popular with many Aboriginal people. As video technology is more readily acquired than computer expertise, Aboriginal people tend to be more active and creative in their uses of video, using video cameras to produce teaching materials. With computer technology, the main use is a more passive one in the school setting, as adults and children manipulate ready-made materials such as HyperCard Stacks.

The Aboriginal Studies Electronic Data Archives (ASEDA) set up and maintained by AIATSIS has exploited the new computer technology to create an ever expanding archive of written Aboriginal language data from electronic files deposited by linguists and others. This archive makes Aboriginal language data readily available to a wide range of users from Aboriginal language communities to academic research linguists (Nash and Simpson 1989, Simpson and Nash 1987, Thieberger 1993).

The AIATSIS HyperCard interactive education kit *Aboriginal Languages* produced by Nick Thieberger as part of the AIATSIS Dictionaries Project (Thieberger 1992 and 1993) allows users to find out a large amount of information about Aboriginal languages and their speakers. It addresses a general audience and is a very useful resource for language awareness programs.

4.5   STANDARDISED ORTHOGRAPHIES

The nature of most Aboriginal bilingual education programs and language teaching programs require the standardisation of the writing system for each language used, as do the requirements of bible translations into Aboriginal languages.[16] Standardised practical orthographies, usually created by linguists and language speakers involved with Aboriginal language literacy programs, have exerted considerable influence beyond their original uses. Today, many people seeking to publish material containing Aboriginal language, be they linguists, journalists, scientists, or historians, are aware that standard orthographies exist and seek to use them. This practice makes their work more readily accessible to people with a knowledge of the relevant language and its writing conventions, as well as facilitating cross-linguistic comparisons.[17]

4.6 ABORIGINAL LANGUAGES AND THE MASS MEDIA: RADIO, TELEVISION, FILM, SOUND RECORDINGS

4.6.1 CENTRAL AUSTRALIAN ABORIGINAL MEDIA ASSOCIA-TION.

The 1980s saw the birth of Aboriginal radio and television (Michaels 1986, Willmot 1984).[18] Central Australian Aboriginal Media Association (CAAMA) Radio based in Alice Springs has been broadcasting in languages such as Arrernte, Kaytetye, Luritja, Pitjantjatjara and Warlpiri as well as in English to central Australian communities since the early 1980s, following the success of a weekly thirty minute program in Arrernte, Pitjantjatjara, and English on Alice Springs commercial radio station 8HA in the late 1970s. Aboriginal language-speaking broadcasters have anchored programs as diverse as the 'news' and popular music request shows.[19]

CAAMA also supports the professional recording, broadcast and sales of music by central Australian bands and choirs performing songs in Aboriginal languages. Cassette tapes of musical performances by local Aboriginal bands are extremely popular among the Aboriginal people (§4.5). Some of these are sold with the song lyrics written on the cover sheet.

Imparja Television, another arm of CAAMA, which operates the commercial television licence in Alice Springs, broadcasts some programs, such as those in its *Nganampa Anwernekenhe* series about Aboriginal subjects with speech in Aboriginal languages subtitled in English for the wider audience.

4.6.2 TORRES STRAIT MEDIA ASSOCIATION.

The Torres Strait Media Association (TSIMA), based in Thursday Island, has been broadcasting since 1985, mainly in Torres Strait Creole[20] with occasional broadcasts in the traditional languages such as Kalaw Kawaw Ya, Kala Lagaw Ya and Miriam Mir (McKay 1996:79–80).

4.6.3 WARLPIRI MEDIA ASSOCIATION.

Since 1983 the Warlpiri Media Association (WMA) at Yuendumu, Northern Territory, has broadcast television programs in Warlpiri to the local community. Its employees have videoed a wide range of subjects ranging from local meetings, ceremonial performance, sporting events, documentaries of significant local historical events, traditional crafts to children's programs. The highly successful video series *Manyu-wana* (§4.2) was produced by WMA in cooperation with film-maker David Batty, Yuendumu School teacher-linguist, Wendy Baarda, school children and adults from the Yuendumu and Willowra communities.

4.6.4 PURANYANU RANGKA KERREM ABORIGINAL RADIO. Puranyanu Rangka Kerrem Aboriginal Radio, based in Halls Creek, Western Australia, broadcasts programs in the local Kija and Jaru languages, some other Aboriginal languages and English (McKay 1996:103).

4.6.5 ERNABELLA TV. Over the past ten years, Ernabella, a Pitjantjatjara and Yankunytjatjara-speaking community in the far north of South Australia, has produced a very impressive quantity of high quality video programs with local people speaking their language. Many of these videos have as their subject the documentation of traditional life-styles in Pitjantjatjara country. A number of educational videos featuring local actors speaking Pitjantjatjara have been made for the adult community.

4.6.6 BROADCASTING FOR REMOTE ABORIGINAL COMMUNITIES SCHEME. The Broadcasting for Remote Aboriginal Communities Scheme (BRACS) is a Commonwealth Government sponsored scheme which provides Aboriginal and Torres Strait Islander communities with broadcasting equipment and expertise for local broadcasting which they can use to produce and broadcast locally made programs with local content and language (House of Representatives Standing Committee on Aboriginal and Torres Strait Islander Affairs (1992:55–6)). TSIMA, WMA, Ernabella TV, and Puranyanu Rangka Kerrem Aboriginal Radio have made use of BRACS as have other Aboriginal communities around Australia.

4.6.7 NATIONAL BROADCASTERS AND ABORIGINAL LANGUAGES. Since the late 1980s, there has been a resurgence of interest in Aboriginal Australia which has been reflected in a marked increase in the nationwide broadcasting of programs relating to Aboriginal people. The Australian Broadcasting Corporation (ABC) radio and television have broadcast several series of programs with Aboriginal content including documentaries with extensive passages of spoken Aboriginal languages. A smaller quantity of like material has also been programmed by the commercial channels.

4.6.8 ABORIGINAL LANGUAGES IN FILM. Very few mass release films feature any Aboriginal language. A notable exception was the very popular 'Women of the Sun' series 'Alinta the Flame' made for television and screened nationally by the Australian Broadcasting Corporation in which the actors from north east Arnhem Land spoke in their Yolngu Matha throughout. Most films with large quantities of Aboriginal language spoken on them have been made by specialist ethnographic film-makers, often in collaboration with AIATSIS which distributes them through its Aboriginal Studies Press.

4.7 NON-TRADITIONAL ORAL FORMS OF ABORIGINAL LANGUAGE USE

The changes in social, occupational and cultural practices that have occurred in Aboriginal Australia since the colonial period have given rise to many new speech genres (Black 1993) as well as to changes in Aboriginal languages including the birth of new creole languages. Singing in Aboriginal languages – traditional songs, popular songs translated into Aboriginal languages from English or other Aboriginal languages, new compositions in Aboriginal languages – is used as an effective teaching device in the educational programs described in §2, including language reclamation programs such as the Kaurna language programs (Amery 1996).[21]

With the adoption of Christian religious practices where use of an Aboriginal language has been encouraged have come genres such as prayers and hymns in Aboriginal languages. In the face of language death, hymn singing in the traditional language may be one of the last uses of the language to survive -- even after people may no longer know what each word in the hymns means. McKay (1996:109–10) reports:

> At Borroloola (in the Northern Territory's Gulf country) Christian songs in language are the only form in which children spontaneously use traditional languages in the school playground (...). Similarly, at Ngukurr on the southern edge of Arnhem Land, hymns are reported to be the 'most common form of language usage'.

Harper (1996) reports similar findings in Northern Cape York.

In the 1970s Warlpiri people in the Northern Territory created a series of religious rituals enacting major Bible stories using traditional musical, dance and body decoration forms. People of high ritual status crafted verses in carefully chosen words to fit the chosen musical frames and poetic conventions. These 'Christian Purlapa' (*purlapa* is a Warlpiri word for an open corroboree) were very popular with Warlpiri people of all ages and are still performed at major Christian Festivals such as Christmas and Easter. In the Jaru speaking country of the east Kimberley region of Western Australia, the Catholic Mass is celebrated in Jaru, along with Jaru hymns. Recordings of the Ernabella Church Choir singing hymns in Pitjantjatjara and of the Hermansburg Choir singing hymns in Western Arrernte are extremely popular with Aboriginal people in central Australia, where they are played alongside popular Western and Country music as well as non-religious songs performed by local Aboriginal bands in Aboriginal languages and English.

There is a long tradition of non-religious song-making by Aboriginal people in Australia which continues today in communities where Aboriginal languages are still spoken. Some Aboriginal bands such as the *Warumpi* band from Papunya in central Australia and the *Yothu Yindi* group from eastern Arnhem Land which perform songs in English and in local Aboriginal languages have gained national and even international popularity.

Reading aloud in an Aboriginal language is another new oral form which has been fostered by Aboriginal language programs in schools and which is used by Aboriginal language broadcasters. Some Aboriginal language speakers have become very adept in this rather specialized language genre.

4.8   INTERPRETING AND TRANSLATION SERVICES IN
       ABORIGINAL LANGUAGES

The need for competent interpreting and translation services to
facilitate communication between speakers of Aboriginal languages and
English speakers has been well documented (Bell 1995, Brennan 1979,
Carroll 1995, House of Representatives Standing Committee on Aboriginal
and Torres Strait Islander Affairs 1992). It is particularly acute in the area of
the administration of justice in which the greatest efforts have been made to
provide interpreting services for court proceedings and judicial hearings.
Other government departments which provide essential services to Aboriginal
people such as the Department of Social Security have also made provision
for the employment of Aboriginal language interpreters on a regular basis in
areas of Australia where a significant proportion of their clientele are speakers
of Aboriginal languages who lack a good command of standard Australian
English. The Alice Springs Hospital has done likewise, responding to the
urgent need for accurate communication in the delivery of health services.
The Northern Territory government has also employed the services of
Aboriginal interpreters and translators in its efforts to engage Aboriginal
language speakers in its consultations about a projected Constitution.
       The only long term provider of commercial Aboriginal language
interpreting and translation services in Australia is the Alice Springs based
IAD which also provides interpreter training (see Elwell 1982b). Successful
IAD graduates have been accredited by the National Accreditation Authority
for Translators and Interpreters (NAATI).
       Because of their special involvement in translation, SIL has provided
training, both on an informal and formal basis, for many Aboriginal people
on their translation teams. Some of their training strategies have been codified
in a translators' training manual (Kilham 1996) which supports the accredited
SIL Certificate in Translation course. In more recent years, Batchelor College
in the Northern Territory has also offered accredited courses in interpreting
and translation for Aboriginal students.
       While the need for good translation and interpreting services is still
acutely felt in many parts of Australia, such are the difficulties involved in
training people to be highly competent in these fields, which presuppose a
native-speaker-like mastery of at least two languages, that it seems unlikely
that this need will ever be more than very poorly met.

5.   ABORIGINAL LANGUAGE RESEARCH AND
       DOCUMENTATION

Since the 1960s there has been a resurgence of research into
Australian Aboriginal languages, with the results of that research being
published in a variety of forms (Austin 1991b). Aboriginal language
programs of the types described in the preceding sections have drawn heavily
on language documentation presented in the form of descriptive grammars,
dictionaries and wordlists (Austin 1983 (ed.), 1991a, Goddard and
Thieberger 1997, Simpson 1993). Language in education programs

have also initiated much of this research and documentation, recognising it as a prerequisite for the success of their programs.

AIATSIS has played an important role in lexicographic documentation by funding linguistic research grants and by assisting publication costs through their 1992 Aboriginal Dictionaries Project (AIATSIS Annual Report 1992–3: 12–13; Thieberger 1992, 1993)[22], of wordlists or dictionaries of over forty languages. It complemented the earlier AIATSIS National Lexicography Project (Nash and Simpson 1989) which assisted people all over Australia to apply modern computer technology to their lexicographic enterprises. This project also funded the computer keyboarding of words from manuscript and typescript sources. These dictionary projects have also been part of the on-going ASEDA project (§4.3).

The Tasmanian Aboriginal Centre has undertaken research into the interpretation of written records of Tasmanian languages and has developed a dictionary and computer database (ATSIC Annual Report 1994–5: 4.5.3).

As well as making the fruits of linguistic research into Aboriginal languages readily accessible to Aboriginal people and others engaged in a variety of language related enterprises, the 1990s has seen the publication of a number of works about Australian languages aimed at the general public and the wider educational market. This popularisation of language documentation is seen in works such as Blake (1991), Dixon (1991), Dixon, Ramson and Thomas (1990), *Macquarie Aboriginal Words* published in 1994, and Walsh and Yallop (eds) (1993). As Aboriginal language studies becomes a more significant component of Aboriginal studies in school curricula as anticipated by the AILF project, it is likely that more of these popular works of high quality will appear.

Language in education projects have inspired research into a number of psycholinguistic and sociolinguistic areas relating to Aboriginal languages: language speaker surveys (Hoogenraad 1993, Hudson and McConvell 1984, McGregor 1988a, Sandefur and Sandefur 1979, Thies 1987), child language and language acquisition (Bavin and Shopen 1985a, Lee 1987, Leeding 1979), language change (Black 1982, Lee 1987, McConvell 1991, Sayers 1982), Aboriginal English (Eades 1984 and 1988, Harkins 1994, Kaldor and Malcolm 1991, Thies 1987), language maintenance (Ash 1994, Bavin and Shopen 1985b, Devlin 1990, McConvell 1994, McConvell and McKay 1994), bilingualism and code-switching (McConvell 1985), language registers (Alpher 1993, Buyuminy and Sommer 1978, Laughren 1984), literacy (Gale, K. 1983, Gale, M.-A. 1992, Goddard 1990, McKay 1982a), systems of classification of natural species and environmental features (Coleman 1991, Waddy 1982), and language and mathematical conceptualisation (Harris, P. 1991) to name just some.[23]

In coming years as Aboriginal language speakers literate in their own languages play more significant teaching and administrative roles in formal education institutions, it is not unreasonable to expect that they will contribute in many ways to the further dissemination of knowledge about their languages and will participate in the critical evaluation of language education programs that needs to be done to inform better language policy with regard to Aboriginal languages.

ACKNOWLEDGMENTS

I want to acknowledge the very generous assistance of Rob Amery who supplied information about many of the language in education programs reported on in this chapter and who provided very useful critical comment on an earlier draft, and also to Diana Eades. I am also indebted to Robert Hoogenraad and Jeanie Bell for reading early drafts and for the improvements they proposed.

APPENDIX A: REGIONAL ABORIGINAL LANGUAGE RESOURCE
CENTRES (1996)

Queensland
    Djabugay Tribal Aboriginal Co-operative, Kuranda
    Guugu Yimidhirr Language Centre, Hopevale
    Kombumerri Aboriginal Corporation for Culture, Rochedale
    Thoorgine Education Centre, Pialba
    Torres Strait Islander Art and Craft Corporation, Townsville

New South Wales
    Muurrbay Aboriginal Language and Culture Co-operative, Sherwood via
        Kempsey
    Niigarr Lingo Gumbi NSW, Trangie

Northern Territory
    East Arnhem Language Centre, Yirrkala
    Language and Culture Centre, Institute for Aboriginal Development, Alice
        Springs
    Kardu Numida Incorporated, Port Keats
    Katherine Regional Aboriginal Language Centre
    Nauiyu Nanbiya Language Centre, Daly River
    Papulu Apparr-Kari Language Centre, Tennant Creek (also known as the
        Barkly Region Aboriginal Languages Centre)
    West Arnhem Minjilang, Croker Island

South Australia
    Yaitya Warra Wodli Language Centre, Port Adelaide

Tasmania
    Tasmanian Aboriginal Language Program, Hobart
    North and North-West Region, Launceston

Victoria
    Lordjba Victoria, Mebourne

Western Australia
    Wangkanyi Ngurra Tjurta Aboriginal Corporation, Kalgoorlie
    Noongar Languages and Culture Centre, Bunbury
    Yamaji Language Centre, Geraldon
    Wangka Maya Pilbara Aboriginal Language Centre, Port Hedland
    Kimberley Language Resource Centre, Halls Creek (with annexe in
        Fitzroy Crossing)
    Mirima Dawang Woorlab-gerring, Kununurra

---

[1] See Riley-Mundine and Roberts (1990: chapter one) for a succinct account of national
language policy developments as they related to Aboriginal languages from the release of

the report by the Senate Standing Committee on Education and the Arts in 1984 up to 1990. For additional information and discussion see House of Representatives Standing Committee on Aboriginal and Torres Strait Islander Affairs (1992). See Baldauf et al. (1996) for more recent information.

[2] See House of Representatives Standing Committee on Aboriginal and Torres Strait Islander Affairs (1992:43–4 & 83–7) for recommendations relating to Regional Language Centres followed in subsequent policy development and implementation.

[3] See also McKay (1996:113) for a brief summary of Bilingual Education programs involving Australian Aboriginal languages and also Harris, S. (1995) for an historical evaluation of Northern Territory bilingual education programs.

[4] This Division became the Northern Territory Department of Education (NTED), a Northern Territory Government Department formally independent of the Commonwealth Government, in 1979 as part of the 'self-government' process.

[5] For a brief account of these, see McKay (1996:113–17). For a fuller account, see Gale (1990) and references therein, Harris et al. (1984), Harris and Jones (1991), articles by Baarda, Christie, Gale, Harris, Lanham et al., and Nicholls in Hartman and Henderson eds. (1994), articles by Devlin and Cataldi in Walton and Eggington eds. (1990). Also see Northern Territory Department of Education (1986), annual reports from N.T. schools with Bilingual Programs and NT Bilingual Education Newsletters. Informative articles dealing with NT bilingual education programs since their inauguration have been published in *The Aboriginal Child at School* (renamed *Australian Journal of Indigenous Education* from 1996) published by The Department of Education, The University of Queensland, St. Lucia.

[6] For information about Kriol-English bilingual education programs see Allen (1985), Gale (1983), and Murtagh (1979). For documentation of Roper River Kriol see Graber, (1987), Harris, (1986), Rhydwen (1992a, 1992b and 1996), and Sandefur (1985).

[7] There are very few examples of written Aboriginal languages being incorporated into Australian English literary texts. Katherine Susanah Prichard's *Coonardoo* in which some of the Aboriginal characters' dialogue and songs are in written in Western Australian languages is rather exceptional.

[8] Amery (1994:140–58) makes finer-grained distinctions between language programs and provides a useful set of terms to refer to them. See also the terminology used by other scholars and that adopted by the Australian Indigenous Languages Framework (see §3.2.7) summarised in McKay (1996:21).

[9] The Yipirinya school in Alice Springs is an independent school for Aboriginal children run by a local Aboriginal board of management in which schooling has been offered in three Aboriginal languages in addition to English: Arrernte, Warlpiri and Luritja (Cook and Buzzacott 1994).

[10] Santa Teresa is an Eastern Arrernte-speaking community. Classes in Eastern Arrernte language and literacy have been part of the school program in various forms since the mid-1970s (Reynolds 1994).

[11] Wrigley (1994) also describes the Kija language program at Gogo School.

[12] These two-week long institutes, jointly sponsored by the Australian Linguistic Society and the Applied Linguistic Association of Australia, are held biennially.

[13] In most cases Aboriginal language literature production has been funded directly or indirectly by government bodies: Education Departments, Aboriginal Arts Board of the

Australia Council, NALP, ALIP and ATSILIP, AIATSIS etc.

[14] Cassette tapes of the original oral versions from which the written texts were derived, are also commercially available for both Dixon & Koch's *Dyirrbal Song Poetry* and the Reads' *Long Time, Olden Time*. The latter has also been distributed on CD-ROM with integrated graphic and sound contents.

[15] See Amery (1996) for the role of the study of place names in the Nunga country of South Australia in the context of Kaurna language reclamation and language in education programs. See also Tunbridge (1988) for an excellent study of Adnhamathanha place names and their significance in the Flinders Ranges area of South Australia.

[16] See also McKay (1996:107–9). Earlier researchers into Aboriginal language and culture such as the Berndts, Capell, Elkin and Tindale used, as much as possible in their published work, standarised Aboriginal language writing systems agreed upon by the scholarly community.

[17] Some examples of recent published work reporting scientific research which incorporates information gained from Aboriginal language speakers using the Aboriginal language written in standardized orthographies are Burbidge et al. (1988), Latz (1995), *Punu: Yankunytjatjara Plant Use* (1988), and a series of publications on traditional Aboriginal plant uses in the Northern Territory of Australia as well as various reports by the Conservation Commision of the Northern Territory (CCNT).

[18] For further information about the development of Aboriginal radio broadcasting services see articles in *Aboriginal Newsletters* Nos 35 (1979), 72 (1980), 100 (1982), 113 (1982) and *Aboriginal Newsletter, Central Australia* Vol. 4, No. 1 (1986).

[19] Radio stations run by Aboriginal people broadcasting programs targeted at Aboriginal audiences operate in many parts of Australia, but CAAMA has been the longest and most consistent broadcaster of programs in Aboriginal languages.

[20] See Shnukal (1988).

[21] Aboriginal Studies Press (AIATSIS, Canberra) sells high quality recordings of traditional and new forms of Aboriginal music from around Australia. Excellent examples of the latter are to be found on *Modern Music of Torres Strait* recorded by Beckett and *Songs from the Kimberleys* recorded by Alice Moyle. AIATSIS also maintains the most extensive archive of Aboriginal language audio recordings (speech and song). This collection is currently being 'digitised' to enhance its longevity. CAAMA (Alice Springs) also markets contemporary Aboriginal language music (see §4.6.1). A set of three audio-tapes with booklets of lyrics featuring both traditional and contemporary Aboriginal music from the Kimberleys, Western Australia, has been produced by the Garnduwa Amboorny Wirnan Aboriginal Corporation (Broome) and is marketed by A Jovial Crew (Fremantle).

[22] This was funded via the Aboriginal Languages Initiatives Program (ALIP) (§2.2).

[23] The references to work in their areas given in this section are by no means exhaustive, but merely indicative of the range of research referred to.

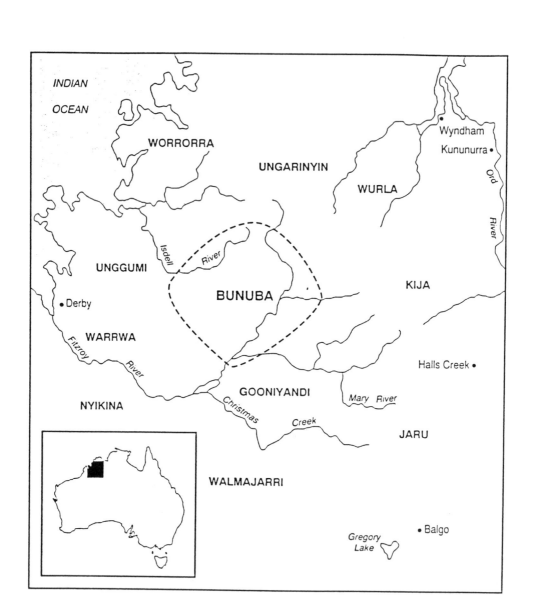

Map 2: Bunuba and neighbouring language areas (boundary approximate)

Bunuba
by Alan Rumsey

1. INTRODUCTION

Bunuba is a non-Pama-Nyungan language, spoken mainly in and around Fitzroy Crossing, in the far north of Western Australia. It is closely related to only one other language, Gooniyandi (McGregor 1990), the two together comprising what O'Grady, Voegelin and Voegelin (1966) called the Bunaban family.

1.1 LINGUISTIC TYPE

Like most other non-Pama-Nyungan languages, Bunuba has complicated verb inflection, including pronominal prefixes which cross-reference one or two participants in the clause (S, or A and O), pronominal suffixes which cross-reference an extra participant (usually a beneficiary), and two series of tense-mode markers (one prefixal, the other suffixal) which in various combinations signal six distinct tense-mode categories. Unlike the neighbouring northern Kimberley languages, Bunuba has no noun classes.

The person/number system is unusual in that, instead of an inclusive-exclusive distinction in the first person, there is a distinction between Unrestricted (corresponding to the traditional category of first person plural inclusive, but not dual inclusive), and Restricted (first person dual inclusive and exclusive, and first person plural exclusive).

Case relations are indicated by phrase-level clitic elements, which usually are added only to the first word of the noun phrase. These include an ergative marker, which can occur on all kinds of lexical noun phrases and personal pronouns. Its use always indicates that there is a semantically patient- or goal-like participant involved in the process described by the verb, but it need not be a prefixally cross-referenced O, nor do the subjects of all bivalent verbs take the ergative marker. Instead, verbal cross-reference and nominal case marking operate according to two distinct, cross-cutting systems, one syntactic and the other more directly semantic.

Phonologically, Bunuba has the usual three vowels and six consonant positions, but is unusual in making extensive use of a contrast between /i/ and /iy/ in unstressed syllables, and in having a lamino-dental glide /yh/.

1.2   LANGUAGE NAME AND DIALECT VARIATION

The name Bunuba has also been spelled 'Bunapa', 'Punaba', 'Buniba' and 'Bunaba'. 'Bunaba' was by far the most common spelling up until the mid-1980s, and I deferred to it in my own writings until then (for example, in Rumsey 1982a). But, although the phonetic difference is slight, Bunuba is undoubtedly the correct phonemic form of the word, so when a new generation of literate speakers began to take up that spelling in about 1984, I gladly switched to it.

Bunuba speakers recognise two regional dialects of the language, which, as in many areas of Australia, are distinguished as 'heavy' versus 'light'. 'Light' Bunuba is identified with the southern and eastern portions of Bunuba country, and 'heavy' Bunuba with the northern and eastern regions. The latter is also referred to as 'Unggumi Bunuba', because it is (rightly) thought to share some of its distinctive features with Unggumi, a Northern Kimberley language which bordered it to the north-west.

In strictly linguistic terms, the differences between the two regional dialects are slight. I have not systematically compared their vocabularies, but I would be surprised if they differed by more than ten percent. Phonologically, the 'heavy' dialect is characterised by a much more frequent occurence of /yh/, a phoneme which it shares with Unggumi (uniquely in the Kimberleys as far as I know; see §2.1.2d for a partial parallel from elsewhere in Western Australia). In many words where 'heavy' Bunuba speakers have /yh/ (including for example, the frequently occurring auxiliary verb root /YHA/), 'light' speakers instead have /y/. Grammatically, the main differences between the two dialects concern some aspects of verb morphology, including some of the pronominal prefixes, and some of the tense/mode forms. These will be pointed out below.

1.3   TERRITORY AND NEIGHBOURS

Among the Bunuba as elsewhere in Australia (Merlan 1981, Rumsey 1993), languages are directly associated with tracts of country, in which they are said to have been installed during the Dreamtime. The Bunuba language belongs to a large region in the southern Kimberley bounded (very roughly) by the Fitzroy River to the south-east, the Leopold Range to the north-east, the Oscar Range to the south-west, and the Napier Range to the north-west. The traditional languages of neighbouring regions are all non-Pama-Nyungan ones, and include: Ungarinyin, Unggumi, Warrwa, Nyikina, Gooniyandi, and Kija. Grammatically, Ungarinyin and Unggumi are typical Northern Kimberley languages, each with extensive verbal cross reference, four noun classes, and no syntactic case marking (i.e., ergative or accusative) on the noun. Warrwa and Nyikina are Nyulnyulan languages, with S and A cross-referenced by verb prefixes and O by suffixes. Gooniyandi is the most closely related to Bunuba, and typologically similar to it in most respects (with some exceptions, noted below). Kija is a Jarragan language, with two noun classes, no syntactic case marking, and extensive verbal cross-reference (for further details on all these languages, see McGregor 1988c and works cited therein). The rates of lexical resemblance between Bunuba and nearby languages, based on 100 to 200-word lists, are as follows:

Ungarinyin	24%	Gooniyandi	45%
Unggumi	20%	Kija	20%
Warrwa	11%	Walmajarri	24%
Nyikina	15%		

All fluent speakers of Bunuba also speak at least one other Aboriginal language. The other languages they most commonly speak are Gooniyandi, Kija and Walmajarri, a Pama-Nyungan language (cf. §1.4 below). All also speak Kriol and/or other varieties of English.

1.4   SPEECH STYLES

Most older speakers of Bunuba (above approximately sixty years old) retain a good speaking knowledge of the so called Gun.gunma style, which was formerly used between a man and his mother-in-law, whether potential or actual. Many, perhaps most Aboriginal languages have such a 'mother-in-law style', but usually it differs from the everyday language only in vocabulary. Gun.gunma also differs from everyday (jadajada or 'straight') Bunuba in grammar: any everyday auxiliary verb, whether monovalent or bivalent, can be replaced by a single, distinctively Gun.gunma auxiliary, which is formally monovalent and cross-references O with an optional oblique pronominal suffix. This is described in §5.

1.5   PRESENT SITUATION

There are currently about one hundred speakers of Bunuba, most of whom live in Fitzroy Crossing, either at Junjuwa, a housing block on the grounds of the former United Aborigines Mission, or in the new Fitzroy Crossing town site about two kilometres to the south. Most of Bunuba territory is in prime cattle country, and as elsewhere in northern Australia where this is the case, Bunuba people up until the 1960s lived mainly on cattle stations, where they provided a permanent labour pool that could be drawn on as demanded by the seasonal pastoral regime. The Aboriginal employees' pay consisted mainly or entirely of rations for themselves and their families. This situation changed drastically in the late sixties, when federal legislation required Aboriginal pastoral workers to be paid the same award wages as others. As elsewhere, the reaction of Kimberley pastoralists was to evict most or all of their Aboriginal residents, claiming that they could no longer afford to maintain them on a live-in basis. This coincided with an increasing influx of Aborigines from desert areas to the south into the Fitzroy

Valley (including more Walmajarri people, who had begun moving there at least a generation earlier, and then Wangkajunga and others from further south). The result of these two developments was that the Aboriginal population of the town grew from a small number in 1950, most of whom were Bunuba, to between seven hundred and one thousand by the early seventies (Kolig 1981:14–20). At the time of my first visit to Fitzroy Crossing in 1975, most of those people were living on the ground in camps spread over a large area around its periphery. By then the Bunuba and Gooniyandi were far outnumbered in the Fitzroy area by people whose traditional affiliations were to country far to the south in the northern reaches of the Western Desert (cf. Kolig 1981).

Having suffered less disruption from European settlement, the desert people brought with them languages (Walmajarri and Wangkajunga) which were still being learned by children as their first language. This had probably ceased to be the case among the Bunuba by the 1950s, since there were not many fully fluent speakers under thirty years of age when I first began studying the language in 1978. When linguists from the Summer Institute of Linguistics began working in Fitzroy Crossing in 1967, they accordingly chose Walmajarri as their target language for Bible translation and literacy training, and for this and other reasons it had by 1978 become easily the most conspicuous of the ten or so Aboriginal languages in the area. Fortunately, this had a kind of 'spin off' effect on the others, especially Gooniyandi and Bunuba, whose speakers were keen to see them become better known as the indigenous languages of the Upper Fitzroy Basin. For example, having become involved in production of a feature film about Jandamarra, a famous Bunuba 'outlaw' of the 1890s, Bunuba people have insisted that all the dialogue be spoken in Bunuba (with English subtitles), and have put in many hours of work to help translate the script.

Under the auspices of the Kimberley Language Resource Centre, 15 to 20 Bunuba speakers convened a three-day workshop in 1989 to decide on a practical orthography for their language (see Wrigley 1990 and §2.1 below). Since then, several of the senior generation have attended literacy classes, and the orthography has been used to produce an illustrated wordbook (Kimberley Language Resource Centre 1991) and book of stories (Marr, Oscar and Wirrunmarra 1990). More recently, KLRC workers have assisted in the production of an excellent illustrated volume of 28 stories by eleven Bunuba speakers (Kimberley Language Resource Centre, forthcoming). The effect of all this on the long-term survival of the language remains to be seen, but as for the current trend, I can report that more young adult speakers and semi-speakers of the language have been showing an active interest in it in the 1990s than in 1978.

1.6   PAST INVESTIGATIONS

As far as I know, the first linguist to record any Bunuba was Arthur Capell in the 1930s. His notes on the language run to about 250 pages, much of it in typescript. His phonological and grammatical analysis of the language did not get very far, but much of the lexical information, elicited sentences and running text are useful if approached with a critical eye in light of the present description. All of his material has been deposited with the Australian Institute of Aboriginal and Torres Strait Islander Studies in Canberra (after surviving with me on the roof of a swamped Holden somewhere near the Western Australian border in 1979). To my knowledge, the only published results of his study were brief comparative notes in Capell (1940).

'Bunaba' is mentioned and a few supposedly Bunuba words cited in Worms (1949) and Nekes and Worms (1953), but they are unreliable.

Further work was done on Bunuba in the 1950s and '60s by Howard Coate. He recorded some useful text material and probably the first sound recordings of the language. This material too is deposited with the Australian Institute of Aboriginal and Torres Strait Islander Studies in Canberra.

My own work on Bunuba began in a small way in 1976, during the time I was studying Ungarinyin at Mowanjum, near Derby. At that time, Howard Coate told me about his work on Bunuba and urged me to take it up. As there were no Bunuba speakers living permanently at Mowanjum, the best I could do was to work on it very briefly with a Bunuba visitor (who was stranded there for a week or so during the wet). After finishing my PhD thesis on Ungarinyin in 1978, I began working on Bunuba with the main body of speakers at Fitzroy Crossing. But although I have since made seven return visits there (in 1979, 1980, 1984, 1987, 1990, 1993 and 1995), my understanding of the language has developed slowly, because, owing to other commitments, I have always had to keep these visits short, and so the total amount of time I have spent in fieldwork on Bunuba is still only about seven months. Eventually, after at least another six months' fieldwork, I hope to publish a fuller description of the language than the present one.

My early writings on Bunuba include a brief unpublished (though widely circulated) tentative description of the phonology and some of the morphology (Rumsey n.d., written in 1980) and a published account of the mother-in-law style (Rumsey 1982a). I still consider the first to have been essentially correct as far as it went, except that, mainly on morphophonemic grounds, I now interpret the lamino-palatal continuant as a glide /yh/ rather than a lateral /lh/ (see §2.1). I still stand by most of what I said in Rumsey (1982a) also, except that I failed to note contrasts in some forms between / i / and /iy/, and between /j/ and /dj/. Thus I now spell the word for 'mother-in-law' madjali rather than majali (see §2.1, §5).

My more recent publications on Bunuba include studies of the grammar of reported speech (Rumsey 1994) and of the person/number system (Rumsey 1996).

Bunuba and Gooniyandi culture and society have received little anthropological attention in comparison to the northern Kimberley area, but valuable studies have been done by Erich Kolig of European-Aboriginal interaction in the Fitzroy Crossing area (Kolig 1972, 1977) and of ritual life in the area, especially among the Walmajarri and Wangkajunga (Kolig 1981). There has also been a PhD thesis done at Australian National University by Bernard Moizo concerning community politics at Junjuwa (Moizo 1991).

TABLE 2.1 *Bunuba phonemes*

CONSONANTS

	Bilabial	Lamino-dental	Apico-alveolar	Apico-post-alveolar	Lamino-palatal	Dorso-velar
Stops	b	th	d	d̲	j	g
Nasals	m	nh	n	n̲	ny	ng
Laterals			l	l̲	ly	
Rhotics			r r	r̲		
Glides	w	yh			y	

VOWELS

	FRONT		BACK
HIGH	i		u
LOW		a (short) aa (long)	

2.   PHONOLOGY

2.1   PHONEMES AND THEIR REALISATION

The phonemes I recognise for Bunuba are as in Table 2.1 above.

2.1.1   A NOTE ON SPELLING. The spelling system used here is in most respects the same as the one which was decided upon at the Bunuba Spelling Workshop (see §1.5) and used in the *Bunuba Wordbook* (Kimberley Language Resource Centre 1991; cf. Wrigley 1990) and in my transcriptions in *Bunuba Stories* (Marr, Oscar and Wirrunmarra 1990). The ways in which it differs are: 1) in the use of aa to distinguish the long low vowel phoneme from the short one; 2) in the use of yh instead of lh to spell the lamino-dental continuant; 3) in the use of ng instead of n̲g for the velar nasal. For present purposes 1) is important because it allows us to register a phonemic distinction that would otherwise be missed, 2) because it more accurately reflects the phonological structure of the language, and 3) because it saves underlining to be used for consonants of one kind only — the apico-post-alveolars, as decided upon at the workshop. In those few words which contain a sequence of n followed by g, the two are separated by a dot (n.g) so as to distinguish this sequence from the velar nasal.

Readers who are used to other orthographies should note that, presumably because of its greater familiarity to Bunuba speakers who are literate in English, th has been chosen for the lamino-dental stop rather than dh, but this should not be taken to mean that it differs in voicing from the other stops: th spells a *voiced* sound (just as it often does in English).

2.1.2   PRONUNCIATION.

[a] *Stops and nasals.* The stops are nearly always fully voiced when not occurring at the beginning of words, and voiced, or voiceless and non-aspirated at the beginning of words. Occasionally they are aspirated, usually for definite expressive purposes, for example, a woman calling out emphatically to her son as ['cʰukʰu] 'son'. As in most Australian languages, oral articulation is identical for every pair of stop and corresponding nasal. Lamino-dentals are produced with contact between the blade of the tongue and the upper teeth. The tongue is laterally spread (rather than bunched); the tip sometimes rests between the teeth, but does not always reach that far. For the lamino-palatals, the tongue is also spread, and there is a considerable area of contact between the blade and the mid-palate, with the tip resting somewhere around the alveolar ridge. For the apico-post-alveolars, the tip of the tongue either extends straight up and contacts a small part of the mid-palate, or is pointed backwards so that there is a small area of contact between the bottom of the tongue and the mid-palate. The other three articulatory labels on the top line of the consonant chart should be self explanatory. The apical series contrast only within words. Pairs illustrating this contrast are:

nada 'short'	jada 'straight'
bidi 'thigh'	widigi 'stick insect'
gananganja 'emu'	gananyi 'digging stick'
gungunu 'black'	Gun.gunma 'mother-in-law talk'

Pairs illustrating the contrasting laminal series are:

tharra 'dog'	jarraa 'far away'
thinga 'foot'	jingirri 'lower arm'
yatha 'sit'	ngaja 'younger brother'
nhungu 'husband'	nyungga 'be asleep'
nganhing 'lick'	lanyi 'freshwater eel'

The contrast between /j/   and /d/-/j/   is made by holding the tongue against the roof of the mouth longer for dj than for j. It is illustrated by the following pairs:

majali 'cicatricising stone'	madjali 'mother-in-law'
lajalaja 'pocket country'	malwadja 'mud'

[b] *Laterals.* All the laterals are produced with the blade or tip of the tongue contacting the roof of the mouth at the same place as for their corresponding stops and nasals. The back part of the tongue is raised for /ly/, low for / l/ and of intermediate height for /l/. The palatal lateral, and the contrast between the two apical laterals, occur only word internally. Examples showing the l/l contrast are:

galu 'penis'	galu 'road'
dulu 'heart'	duluga 'die'
malngarri 'red'	malngirri 'lightning', 'thunder'

The full three-way contrast is shown by:

> walarri 'ghost gum, snappy gum'
> balarra 'outside'
> walyarra 'sand'

[c] *Rhotics.* /rr/ is an apico-alveolar trill or tap. /r/ is a retroflex continuant: it is produced without any contact between the tip of the tongue and the roof of the mouth, but with the tip pointed up or back, and air allowed to pass over it. All word-initial rhotics are of the latter variety. Examples of the contrast within words are:

> jirigi 'bird' (generic) jirrin.gin 'owlet nightjar'
>   (Aegotheles cristata)
> garuwa 'water' garra 'throw'

[d] *Glides.* The bilabial and lamino-palatal glides are pronounced much as in English and in other Australian languages. The lamino-dental glide is unlike any sound I have ever heard anywhere except in the neighbouring language Unggumi (but cf. Wordick 1982:10–12 regarding a lamino-interdental glide phoneme in the Pilbara language Yindjibarndi, and Dench (1995:26) regarding one of the pronunciations of Maduthunira /th/). Bunuba /yh/ is generally produced without any contact between any part of the tongue and either the roof of the mouth or teeth. Except for the fact that it cannot comprise a syllable nucleus, it is phonetically more vocalic than consonantal, since it is produced with even less constriction of the oral aperture than there is for the high vowels. The tongue is laterally spread, just as for /th/ and /nh/, and there is a very slight movement of the tongue towards the same articulatory target as is reached in the production of those two consonants. The other main reason for placing this segment with the lamino-dentals is that it has the same effect on preceding high vowels (see below). My reasons for placing it with the glides rather than the laterals, and therefore for spelling it yh rather than lh (as I formerly did, and as the workshop orthography does) are: 1) the absence of apical tongue contact, which it has in common with the other glides, but with none of the laterals; 2) the fact that the 'light' dialect, and the speech of many of the younger people, has /y/ (rather than /l/ or /ly/) in place of /yh/; and 3) the fact that in certain morphological environments (§3.4.12a, §3.4.3b, rule 6) it alternates with a stop — a kind of alternation which the other Bunuba glides w and y (and Unggumi /yh/) also undergo, but which none of the laterals undergoes.

Some speakers have the /yh/ phoneme in only two or three words, and some have it perhaps in only one word, which is, however, a frequently used one: miyha 'meat'. I have only ever heard this word pronounced as miya by a Walmajarri man who professed only a 'hearing' knowledge of Bunuba. In the speech of fully-fledged Bunuba speakers, it is always pronounced as miyha, and contrasts as a minimal pair with -miya, a suffix meaning 'merely, only, alone'. Other pairs illustrating the contrast in most Bunuba people's speech are:

> mirriyhini 'rainbow' jiyirri 'kingfisher'
> ligayhina 'west' jamayina 'axe'

[e] *Low vowel*. The pronunciation of /a/ is determined both by stress and by the nature of the preceding and/or following consonants. In unstressed syllables, it is realised as [ʌ]. Examples are:

/bina/	'ear'	→	[ˈbɪnʌ]
/galamuda/	'turkey bustard'	→	[ˈgalʌmʊdʌ]
/ngindaji/	'this (one)'	→	[ˈŋɪn̪dʌd͡ʒi]

In stressed syllables, when followed by /w/, /a/ is fronted (though not as far as cardinal **æ**). Examples are:

| /jawiy/ | 'forehead' | → | [ˈd͡ʒaˤwi] |
| /gawarra/ | 'sun' | → | [ˈgaˤwʌrʌ] |

Elsewhere in stressed syllables, /a/ is realised as [a]. Examples are:

| /tharra/ | 'dog' | → | [ˈd̪arʌ] |
| /gambinyi/ | 'egg' | → | [ˈgambiɲi] |

The long vowel /aa/ is pronounced [aː]. Examples of its contrast with / a / are:

| baali | 'trail, track' | | balinja | 'flat stone' |
| jarraa | 'far away' | | tharra | 'dog' |

[f] *High front vowel*. The phoneme /i/ is realised as:

[i] directly before /y/ or /i/ (cf. §3.2.1a), word-finally after palatal segments, and before /ny/ or /j/ except when following /w/. Examples are:

/-miya/	'only'	→	[miyʌ]
/giḻiy/	'blood'	→	[ˈgɨḻi]
Compare /gili/	'bindi-eye'	→	[ˈgɨlɪ]
/darrali-ingga/	'whip snake-ERG'	→	[ˈdarʌliˈŋgʌ]
/ngirrginya/	'hunger'	→	[ˈŋɨrgiɲʌ]
/gijalu/	'raw, unripe'	→	[ˈgid͡ʒʌlu]
/ngawiji/	'father's mother, son's children'	→	[ˈŋaˤwɪd͡ʒi]
/balanyja/	'flat' (spelled balanja, see §2.2)	→	[ˈbalʌɲd͡ʒʌ]

[ɨ] (a high central vowel) before velar and apico-post-alveolar consonants. Examples are:

/biliga/	'middle'	→	['bɩlɨgʌ]
/mingali/	'hand'	→	['mɨŋʌlɩ]
/bidi/	'upper leg, thigh'	→	['bɨɖɩ]
/gilili/	'shoulder blade'	→	['gɨlɨlɩ]
/jirali/	'before, long ago'	→	[ʤɨ'ɽʌlɩ]

When followed by /r/, all the vowels, but especially /i/, take on an r coloration (acoustically characterisable by a lowered third formant). Under those conditions, syllables which would otherwise have primary stress tend to lose it, as in the last example above. In some words with g or b followed by /ir/, the /i/ merges completely with the following /r/, resulting in what sounds more like a consonant cluster than a distinct syllable. Examples are:

/giriywa/	'wind'	→	['gɽiwʌ]
/biriyali/	'conkerberry bush'	→	['bɽiyʌlɩ]
/biray/	'come out'	→	[bɽe]

[ɨ̌] (a mid-to-high central vowel) before or after lamino-dental consonants. Examples are:

/thinga/	'foot'	→	['d̪ɨ̌ŋʌ]
/nhi/	'his, her'	→	[n̪ɨ̌]
/miyha/	'meat'	→	['mɨ̌ɣʌ]

(Note in the first example, thinga→ ['d̪ɨ̌ŋʌ], the effect of a preceding laminal consonant overides that of a following velar, which would otherwise result in the first vowel being pronounced as [ɨ].)

In all other environments besides the ones mentioned above, /i/ is pronounced [ɩ]. Examples are:

/jilya/	'green branch'	→	['ʤɩλʌ]
/gimani/	'knee'	→	['gɩmʌnɩ]
/ngirri/	'spinifex'	→	['ŋɩrɩ]
/winyin.ga/	'escape'	→	['wɩɲɩngʌ]
/jinali/	'spear'	→	['ʤɩnʌlɩ]

The difference between word final /i/ (→[ɩ]) and /iy/ (→[i]) is difficult for speakers of English (and indeed, of other Aboriginal languages) to hear, as we are used to [ɩ] occurring only in closed syllables (i.e., where it is followed by a consonant). But it is a very important difference, as it is the sole mark of present versus past tense for some verbs (§3.4.4). Given that consonants do not generally occur word-finally in Bunuba, one might be tempted to regard word-final [i] as /i/   and assign [ɪ] to a distinct phoneme (perhaps a central vowel, as the neighbouring language Kija has been claimed to have). But such a solution would be uneconomical for Bunuba, as the i-ɪ distinction is limited almost entirely to word-final position, where [ɪ] is considerably more frequent than [i] (cf. Stokes 1982 regarding the neighbouring language Nyikina, where word-final /iy/ is also distinct from /i/, but where this distinction is apparently realised by length rather than vowel quality). Furthermore, the recognition of word-final /y/   allows us also to account for the occurrence of phonetic mid-vowels, which are also limited to word-final position (as discussed under [h] below).

[g] *High back vowel.* The phoneme /u/ is realised as:

[u] word-finally; when followed by /m/, /ng/, /wi/   or /wu/; and in stressed syllables except when followed by /r/, /rr/, or /wa/. Examples are:

/dumurru/ 'chest'	→	['dumɷru]
/jalungurru/ 'good'	→	['ɟalu‚ŋɷru]
/yuwid/ 'copulate with'	→	['yuwɪd]
/muḻu/ 'eye'	→	['muḻu]
/dubarra/ 'dry out'	→	['dubʌrʌ]
/gulwula/ 'waterhole'	→	['gulwɷlʌ]

[ɔ^] when followed by /wa/. Examples are:

/duwa/ (+WU2) 'hit'	→	['dɔ^wʌ]
/yuwana/ 'one'	→	['yɔ^wʌɳʌ]

[ɷ] elsewhere. For examples see dumurru, jalungurru, and gulwula above. Other examples are:

/bururru/ 'pubic hair'	→	['bɷɽɷru]
/wanggura/ 'crow'	→	['waŋgɷɽʌ]

[h] *Some phonetic mid vowels and their phonemic status.* Bunuba has phonetic mid vowels, [e], [ɔ] and [o]. In previous, tentative analyses by Capell and Coate, these were recognized as distinct phonemes /e/ and /o/, as in Northern Kimberley languages such as Ungarinyin and Worrorra. But this is uneconomical for Bunuba, because the phonetic mid vowels are limited almost entirely to word-final position. The mid front vowel can be accounted for in the same way as I discussed for word final [i] above, that is as a sequence of vowel followed by /y/. Examples are biray as in [f] above, and the following:

/ganday/ 'bad, old'	→	['gaɳḓe]

/manggay/ 'wife'   →   ['maŋge]

/ngay/ 'I am'   →   [ŋe]

This sequence contrasts with /ayi/ which in word-final position is pronounced as a diphthong [ai] or [ʌi]. Thus, compare the above examples with:

/ngayi/ 'no, not'   →   [ŋai]

/mayi/ 'vegetable food'   →   [mai]

[ɔ] occurs in a handful of words, such as ['yɔraɡɪ] 'dingo', where it is, for some speakers, in free variation with [æɷ], suggesting that it is a realisation of /awu/. It seems to occur only in the first two syllables of words having at least four syllables (and therefore a secondary stress on the third, as discussed in §2.3). Otherwise /awu/ is pronounced [æu], as in, for example, gawu 'lungs', or [æwɷ], as in thawuru 'beard' and jawawurru 'kookaburra'.

[o] occurs only as a realisation of word-final /a/ followed by the dative/genitive postposition /-u/ (~/-gu/). That is, /a+u/ is realised as [o] (as distinct from the various realisations of /awu/ discussed immediately above). For examples see § 3.2.1b.

[i] *Phonetic long vowels.* [iː] occurs in a few words, where for most speakers it freely alternates with [iɪ]. Since [iyi] does not occur, I take [iː] and [iɪ] to be realisations of /iyi/. The maximally high front quality of the first phase of the [iɪ] realisation is accounted for among the conditioning factors for /i/ discussed above. Examples are:

/ngiyirri/ 'we R' (see §3.3.1) →   ['ŋiɪrɪ] ~ ['ŋiːrɪ]

Compare /ngirri/ 'spinifex'   →   ['ŋɪrɪ]

/wiyi/ 'woman'   →   [wiː] ~ [wiɪ]

[uː] occurs in some words, where I take it to be a realisation of /uwu/. Examples are:

/muwurru/ 'club'   →   ['muːru]

/juwurru/ (male subsection term)→   ['ʤuːru]

It is instructive to compare the female counterpart of juwurru, which is pronounced ['ɲaʼwɷru], strongly suggesting the analysis /ju-wurru/ ~ /nya-wurru/. (See §3.2.3h regarding -wurru.)

There is a long mid-to-high central vowel [ɨ̂ː], which occurs in only one word that I know of - ['bɨ̂ːrɨɡʌ] 'north' (compare /birrinyi/ 'sky' →['bɪriɲi]; /biyirri/ 'they'→ [biyɪrɪ] ~ [biːrɪ]). As this vowel is of a quality which otherwise occurs only as an allophone of /i/ in the environment of lamino-dental consonants (as described above), I take this particular phonetic long vowel to be a realisation of /iyhi/. [aː] occurs as a realisation of /a/-/a/ at certain morpheme boundaries (see §3.4 below). It might therefore seem justified to regard all instances of [aː] as sequences of two vowels /aa/ instead of recognising a distinct long vowel phoneme. The reason I have not done so is that, in my analysis, sequences of two vowels do not otherwise occur within morphemes. (For practical purposes, it makes little difference, given that the long vowel is in any case spelled aa.)

2.2 PHONOTACTICS

In order to specify which Bunuba phonemes can occur at what positions within words, we must distinguish among words of various classes, and among different kinds of morpheme boundaries within them. As discussed in §3, almost all Bunuba finite verbal constructions consist of two words, a preverb followed by an inflected auxiliary. Apart from the interjection a'ga and some of the inflected auxiliaries, no Bunuba word begins with a vowel. Phonetic high vowels do sometimes occur at the beginning of other words, but, except in inflected auxiliaries (where the difference is distinctive), these vowels alternate freely with yi and wu, as in most Australian languages.

The difference between apico-alveolar and apico-post-alveolar consonants is not distinctive word-initially. Phonetically, segments of both kinds occur, but unlike in many other Australian languages, where all initial apicals are phonetically retroflex, in Bunuba they are generally apico-alveolar unless there is a d̲, n̲, or l̲ in a subsequent syllable (interestingly r does not have the same effect). Compare, for example /dumurru/ 'chest' → ['dumɔru] with /dul̲u/ 'heart' → [ɖul̲u].

/ly/ and /rr/ do not occur word-initially, nor does /yh/, except in ø-prefixed forms of the auxiliary YHA (see §3.4.3b, after rule 9). Otherwise, all consonants may occur word-initially.

All consonants may occur between two vowels within a word. The only consonants that occur word finally are n, ny, ng and l, all of which do so very infrequently, and /y/ which does so rather more frequently. All vowels (including aa) may occur word-finally.

The frequencies of these segments in initial and final position within Bunuba words other than preverbs or auxiliaries are shown in Table 2.2. This table is based on a lexical sample of 1177 items. It is worth noting that the sole recorded instance of a word-final ny is in a reduplicative, onomatopoetic bird name (gil̲inygil̲iny 'galah'), as are two of the three instances of final ng. Also note that, since I have not yet been able to recheck my entire lexical file since becoming aware of the distinctive difference between word-final /i/ and /iy/, it is likely that the incidence of word final y is somewhat higher than shown by this table, and the instance of word-final i somewhat lower.

A wide range of two-consonant clusters occur within morphemes, and an even wider range at morpheme boundaries. The latter are discussed in §3. The intramorphemic clusters I have found are shown in Table 2.3. The clusters d̲b, nhg, lyw, yd, and yw have so far been found in only one word

TABLE 2.2 Occurrence of Bunuba phonemes in initial and final positions

	Initial	Final		Initial	Final
b	12.1%	0%	m	14.6%	0%
th	3.1%	0%	nh		0%
				0.6%	
d	3.1%	0%	n	1.1%	0.4%
j	10.6%	0%	ny	3.6%	0.1%
g	17.5%	0%	ng	10.6%	0.3%
Stops in total	46.4%	0%	Nasals in total	30.5%	0.8%
l	5.7%	0.3%			
r	1.3%	0%	i	0%	37.6%
w	11.8%	0%	u	0%	20.4%
y	4.6%	3.2%	a	0%	37.7%
Glides in total	16.4%	3.2%	Vowels in total	0%	95.7%

each. The cluster nng has not yet been found, but would be expected to occur from the above patterning.

Some generalisations that can be drawn from Table 2.3 are as follows:

1. As in most Australian languages, the most highly favoured cluster is nasal followed by stop. In clusters of this kind, all possible homorganic sequences occur.

2. The other permitted manner sequences are: stop-stop (rare); nasal-nasal; and lateral, rhotic (rr only) or glide followed by stop, nasal or glide. We can make sense of these restrictions by grouping laterals, rhotics and glides together as continuants and positing a scale of consonant strength: stop>nasal>continuant. In these terms, the second member of a cluster may not be of lower strength than the first.

3. Peripheral consonants (labials and velars) do not appear as the first member of a cluster except in the sequences mb, ngb and ngg (where the second member is also peripheral).

4. Except in homorganic clusters and some with a lamino-palatal and apical (dj, nj and yd), the second consonant in the cluster is always a peripheral one.

5. All clusters with two apical or two laminal consonants are homorganic.

TABLE 2.3 *Bunuba intramorphemic two-consonant clusters*

	b	th	d	d̲	j	g	m	nh	ng	w
d					dj					
d̲	d̲b									
m	mb									
nh		nhth				nhg				
n	nb		nd			n.g	nm		nng	
n̲				n̲d	n̲j	n̲g	n̲m			
ny	nyb				nyj	nyg				
ng	ngb					ngg̲				
l						lg	lm		lng	
l̲						l̲g	l̲m		l̲ng	l̲w
ly	lyb				lyj					lyw
rr	rrb					r rg̲	rrm		rrng	rrw
yh								yhnh		
y	yb		yd			yg			yng	yw

Note: because of 5, it was decided at the Bunuba Spelling Workshop (see §1.5) that the number of letters used to spell homorganic laminal clusters should be kept down by showing their palatal or dental quality on only one of the consonants. Accordingly, I spell /nhth/, /nyj/, /lyj/ and /yhnh/ as nth, nj, lj, and ynh respectively.

The only intra-morphemic three-consonant clusters I have found so far are lmb, l̲ngg, and lngg. In terms of the patterning summarised in 1–5 above, these clusters are of the most highly expected sort, since: the consonants are in the order weak-stronger-strongest; the last two consonants in each case comprise a homorganic cluster of the favoured kind; and the places of articulation of the tri-consonant cluster as a whole are non-periheral followed by peripheral.

2.3 STRESS

Monomorphemic words of one, two, or three syllables have primary stress on the first syllable. Those with four or five syllables have primary stress on the first syllable and secondary on the third. Examples of stress-marked two-to-four syllable words can be found among the forms cited in §2.1 above. A five-syllable example is:

> miljidawurru 'storm from the south' → ['mɪλ ʤi̪da'wɔ ru]

Words with vowel-reduced /ir/ sequences (as discussed in §2.1) are treated as if the rule for stress placement follows that of vowel reduction, as evident from the examples given there.

Polymorphemic words show other, more complicated stress patterns which are best discussed as the morphology is introduced.

3.   MORPHOLOGY

As an introduction to both the morphology and syntax of Bunuba, it will be useful to begin with a bird's eye view of the grammar of the most common kinds of simple sentence, so that the reader can see the system as a whole.

The heart of almost any Bunuba sentence is the verb complex. I call it a complex because in almost every instance it consists of two elements: a preverb followed by an auxiliary. The preverb is the part that carries most of the lexical meaning of the complex — the relatively concrete and specific aspects of its meaning which can be glossed by English verb roots such as 'go', 'die', 'see' etc. The auxiliary carries most of the more abstract, grammatical aspects of meaning: tense (time of the narrated event relative to that of the speech event), aspect (absolute temporal contour of the event), mode (the speaker's judgement of its likelihood or desirability), etc.

The auxiliary (separated from the preverb by an apostrophe in my transcriptions) also carries information about the identity of the participants in the event being described. Consider the following example:

(1)   (ngayini) jira'luwaniy
          (I)   fall 1sg-WU-PAST
          I fell down.

The prefix I- (→lu) on the auxiliary root WU specifies who underwent the falling, that is, the speaker 'I'. The prefix is obligatory in this context: there is no way to say 'I fell down' without including such a prefix. This means that, although it is possible to add to the sentence the word ngayini 'I', the actor in the clause will always already be fully specified without it. In fact, as you might expect, the use of independent pronouns is rather rare in such sentences. Now consider another example:

(2)   thatharra'waniy
          stand 3sg-WU-PAST
          He/she stood up.

Here the obligatory prefix ø- specifies that the actor is third person singular, that is, a single actor who is someone other than the speaker of this sentence or its addressee. In this instance, the information about the actor is not nearly as specific as in (1). Thus a fuller version of (2) might be:

(3)   gurama thatharra'waniy
          man   stand 3sg-WU-PAST
          The man stood up.

But in the actual use of a sentence such as (2), the specification 3sg would usually be enough to allow the actor's identity to be inferred from the context, for example, from a more explicit referring expression in the preceding text, as was the case in the narrative from which (2) was actually taken. Unlike in English, sentences such as (2), with no independent pronouns or noun phrases referring to the participants, are always fully grammatical in Bunuba:

any verb complex is always a potential sentence by itself. This is true not only of intransitive sentences such as (1) to (3), but of transitive ones such as I am about to discuss.

In Bunuba as in every language, some of the verbs construe the processes they describe in such a way as to implicate two participants, which are of the kind commonly referred to by Australianists as 'agent' and 'object'. The verb complexes which are of this kind, the bivalent ones, have auxiliaries which obligatorily refer to both these kinds of participant. An example is:

(4)   ngayini-ingga   dalja'lunbunugu
        I-ERG   rear 1sg>3nsg-WU2-PAST-pl
        I reared them.

Here the prefix combination on the verbal auxiliary specifies that the agent of the action was the speaker and that the object was a plurality of beings not including the speaker or addressee. (Here as elsewhere, > (or <) in my interlinear glosses points from the agent or subject specification to the object one.) Notice that when the (optional) personal pronoun for 'I' is included in such a sentence (as it actually was in this one), it usually does not take the same bare form it did in (1), but instead takes the ergative marker -ingga. Unlike in many Australian languages, in Bunuba this is true of nouns and pronouns of all kinds, not just some of them. There is in Bunuba no distinct accusative case marker for the objects of bivalent verbs. These occur in the same bare form as do the sole participants in (1) and (3).

There are, however, a number of oblique cases for specifying relations such as possession, location, source, destination, cause, purpose, instrument (shown by the same marker as ergative), accompaniment, etc. And any verb complex may take an optional oblique pronominal suffix which refers to someone who is affected by or implicated in the action or state of affairs predicated by the verb ('His dog died *on him*', 'He killed a kangaroo *for me*', etc.).

3.1   PARTS OF SPEECH

[a] *Nominals*. These may be distinguished as free lexemes which are able to occur with the case markers discussed in §3.2.1. They include the following subclasses:

Pronouns, which show distinctions of number within the root and special suppletive stem forms for oblique cases, and refer to participants in the speech situation;

Deictics/Demonstratives, which locate a referent in relation to the particulars of the speech situation;

Kin terms, which have distinct vocative forms, a partially distinct system of number and possessive inflection, and can take a dyadic suffix.
As far as I know, there is no formal basis for a distinction between adjectives and other nominals.

[b] *Verbal words*, which include the *preverb* and *auxiliary*. These are distinguished from each other and from all others on the basis of what affixes they take.' The preverb and auxiliary together behave in some ways like a single word and in other ways like separate words. To show the kind of intermediate status of the boundary between preverb and auxiliary I indicate it with an apostrophe rather than a full space between the two.

[c] *Adverbs*. These are distinguished from verbal words by not being able to take any of the same affixes, and from nouns by being able to occur in bare form in construction with an inflected verb complex on which they are not cross-referenced.

[d] *Mode particles* comprise a small, closed set of words which have the same formal characteristics as adverbs except that they show a stronger tendency to occur clause-initially, and to be restricted in what tense-mode forms of the verb they can occur with. They are functionally distinct in that they always modify the entire clause rather than just its predicate.

[e] *Interjections*. These are distinct from all the above in not being syntactically integral to the clause, and in therefore frequently occurring as single-word utterances. Some of them are phonologically aberrant.

3.2   NOUN MORPHOLOGY

As will already be evident from the overview above, number and case relations in Bunuba are marked partly on the verb and partly on the noun. The devices by which they are marked on the noun must be described both at the level of single words and at the level of the noun phrase. In terms of their distribution, they belong to the phrase level. That is, in multi-word noun phrases, they usually occur only once in the phrase, at a specifiable position within it (its first word). But they must also be discussed at the level of the word, because most of them vary in form depending on the final phoneme of the word they occur on. (Compare the possessive marker -s in English, which goes on the last word of the possessor NP, e.g., 'the queen of England's crown', and varies in realisation, [z], [ʒ], or [əz], depending on what phoneme that word ends with.) The distribution of these markers within the phrase will be discussed in §4.2.2 below. For now, I will limit the discussion to the case and number marking of single-word noun phrases only.

3.2.1   CASE MARKERS

[a] *Ergative/instrumental* -ingga. When this marker is added to words with final -a the resulting /a-i/ sequence is pronounced [e] (just as /ay/ is when word-final or before consonants).   For example:

gurama-ingga   →   [gʊɾʌmeŋgʌ]
man-ERG

When -ingga is added to words ending in u, it displaces the u. For example:

gayangurru-ingga   →   [ɡayʌŋɶrʊŋɡʌ]
echidna-ERG

When -ingga follows final /i/ or /iy/, the resulting single vowel is always fully high-front (unlike word final i) and usually somewhat over-long. For example:

rarrgi-ingga   →   [ɾarɡiˑŋɡʌ]
stone-ERG/INST

When following other word-final consonants (which occur mainly on English borrowings), -ingga is pronounced [ʊŋɡʌ]. (Note that its / i / vowel therefore behaves somewhat differently from what is specified in §2.1.2f for /i/ before velar consonants within words, where it is pronounced as [ɨ].)

NPs on which this marker occurs are usually ones which are cross referenced on the verb as its subject, as in (4) above. In such instances, we can say as a first approximation that the function of this marker is to indicate that the NP on which it occurs is an AGENT within the event, situation or process described by the verb – that it refers to an actor that *acts upon* someone or something. (For further details see §4.1.1.) Where the NP is not a cross-referenced one, it is usually in instrumental function rather than ergative. Examples are:

(5)   jinali-ingga malmurru-ingga   jabirri-ingga
        spear-INST   little.wooden.tipped.spear-INST   shovel.spear-INST
            baljarringi-ingga gula'wida
            boomerang-INST   try/test 3sg<3nsg-YHA-PAST
        They tried it with spears, with little wooden-tipped spears, with shovel spears, and with boomerangs.

(6)   mingali-ingga   gaygaytha'yirrangarri
        hand-INST   cut 3sg<1R-RA2-PAST-CTV
        We (R) used to cut [fence posts] by hand.

(7)   waliwali-ingga niy-ya   wadba'wirrma
        sides-INST   him-REP   get/catch 3sg<3nsg-MA2-PAST
        They grabbed hold of him by the sides.

Instrumental phrases (but not ergative ones) are often formed with a combination of the COMITATIVE1 marker followed by the ERGATIVE/ INSTRUMENTAL. Where both ergative and instrumental NPs are present in the same clause and the instrument is not a part of the agent (e.g. a body part), there is a strong preference for this compound case marker (COM1+INST) over INSTrumental alone as the means of expressing the instrumental function. Thus (8), for example, was said by Bunuba speakers to be ungrammatical without the inclusion of COMITATIVE1 -ngarri.

(8)   gurama-ingga   muwurru-ngarri-ingga
       man-ERG   club-COM1-INST
       dangayga'nganbuni
       hit 1sg<3sg-WU2-PAST
       The man hit me with a club.

Alerted by informants' judgements on this matter, I have searched through many texts and been unable to find a single exception to the above generalisation.

Note that in (7) above, and in other examples such as the Bunuba glosses for 'He's lying *on his belly*' (see [c] below), the INSTrumental marker is used for functions which in many other languages would be covered by the locative case. In such examples, where the NP in question refers to a body part, the sense can usually be construed as instrumental as well. But the same marker, -ingga (or one of the same form at least), also occurs on expressions of time and place, where the sense seems purely locative. Examples are:

nginda-ngarri-ingga   ngurru-ngarri-ingga
this-COM1-ERG/INST?   that-COM1-ERG/INST?
this side   that side

jarra-ngarri-ingga   baburru-ingga
?(cf. jarraa 'distant')-COM1-ERG/INST?   down-ERG/INST?
other side   underneath

ngarranggani-ingga
long ago-ERG/INST?
in the [mythic] past

Citing Gooniyandi cognates of the first two of these forms, and the resemblance between the Gooniyandi ergative marker (-ngga) and a locative form found in many Pama-Nyungan languages, McGregor (1990:179) suggests this might provide evidence that the Gooniyandi ergative form has arisen from an ancient locative. The Bunuba evidence suggests this even more strongly (perhaps for a common ancestral language of Bunuba and Gooniyandi), for in Gooniyandi the present-day locative usage is apparently limited to just those two forms (ibid.), whereas in Bunuba it is freely productive for expressions of time and place.

[b] *Dative* -gu/-u. The -gu variant of this marker occurs only after word-final nasals and stops (which means that it is very infrequent and found mainly on borrowed words). Examples are gan.gan-gu 'for clapping' (i.e., clapsticks), warrgam-gu 'for work', job-gu 'for soap' and wug-gu 'for cooking. When the -u variant follows word-final a, the resulting form is sometimes pronounced with a diphthong [au], but more often with a phonetic mid vowel [o]. For example:

garuwa-u   →   ['gaɽʌwo] or ['gaɽʌwau] 'for water'
water-DAT

Note that the sequence a-u behaves differently in this respect from awu, which is realised as [au] (§2.1.2h). That is my main reason for taking the form of this dative allomorph to be -u rather than -wu.

When -u follows word final -i that vowel is sometimes elided and sometimes not. For example:

> rarrgi-u   →   ['ɽarɡɪu] or ['ɽarɡu] 'for money'
> money-DAT

When -u follows word final u, the result is a phonetic half-overlong vowel [uː]. Elsewhere -u is pronounced as [u]. (Note that the 'elsewhere' environment here includes word final /y/ in such words as /muway/ 'camp' and /gandiy/ 'spinifex resin', even though they end in phonetic vowels, [e] and [i]. In this respect these words behave differently from words ending in phonemic vowels, which supports the analysis of them as ending in /y/.)

The functions of the dative case include the following:

Possession. Examples are:

> ngaala-u   manggay   gananganja-u thangani
> another-DAT   wife   emu-DAT   mouth/language
> another man's wife   emu's language

> ngawiy nginda-u   gurama-u mingali
> aunt   this-DAT   man-DAT   hand
> this one's aunt/auntie for this one   the man's hand

> dirrag   janjuwa-u
> truck   Junjuwa (Community)
> the Junjuwu truck

As can be seen from these examples, the dative marker can be used both for alienable possession and for inalienable. But though it is grammatical in the latter function, it is not very frequently used for it. Especially for body-part possession the preferred means of expression are possessive pronouns (§3.3).

Purpose. In this function, -gu/-u occurs both with syntactically productive purposive constructions, and with others where it behaves more like a derivational device, for creating nouns from preverbs. Examples of the latter are:

> yathayatha-u   gangan-gu
> sit-sit-DAT   clap-clap-DAT
> saddle   clapsticks

A more complex example, with -u occurring in construction with a preverb and accompanying root is:

> (9)   lundu-ngarri   wanday-ma-u
>   stick-COM1   pick up and carry-MA2-DAT
>   'with a stick for picking up and carrying' (i.e., a swag)

Examples of sentences with true purposive NPs are:

(10)   jirali   bininybalu   gandiy-u   thudga'wirrmangarri
       before   spinifex   resin-DAT pull.up 3sg<3nsg-MA2-PAST-CTV
       In the olden days they used to pull up spinifex for [making] resin.

(11)   nawanu manja'wirrmangarri   rayl-u
       hole   make 3sg<3nsg-MA2-PAST-CTV   rail-DAT
       They used to make holes [in fence posts] for the rails.

Similar purposive constructions are made by combining -gu/-u with a
preverb, as discussed in §4.4.2, where I treat them as non-finite clauses.
       Other functions of the dative marker overlap considerably with those
of OBLique cross-reference on the verb (for which see §3.4.9). These include
the indication of the addressee of verbs of speaking, the beneficiary, and the
'about' relation ('They felt ashamed about him', etc.). For all of these functions,
OBLique cross reference is far more frequently used than are dative-marked
NPs, and when an NP in one of these functions is cross referenced by an
OBLique pronominal, the dative marker can be omitted from the NP.

       [c] *Locative* -yuwa/-juwa. The -juwa form occurs after stops and
nasals (and after I in English borrowings), -yuwa elsewhere.
       The range of senses conveyed by this marker includes most of those
of English 'on', 'at,' and 'in'. It is used both for spatial location (muway-
yuwa 'at the camp', nawanu-yuwa 'in/on the hole') and for temporal
(jirali(-yuwa) 'yesterday', garrwaru-yuwa 'in a day', nginji walyay-
yuwa 'you small-loc', i.e., 'when you were small'). Although in some
contexts its meaning is similar to the locative sense of -ingga (as in [a]
above), there are subtle differences between the two. Compare, for example
(12) and (13) .

(12)   thanybana-yuwa   baga'ray
       back-LOC   lie 3sg-RA-PAST
       He was lying on his back [i.e. on someone else's back].

(13)   guda-ingga   baga'ray
       belly-ERG/INST   lie 3sg-RA-PAST
       He was lying on his (i.e. his own) belly.

       Although primarily a local case, the locative has at least one kind of
secondary, syntactic function in clauses of reduced transitivity. Consider, for
example:

(14)   ngayini-ingga   gilandirri-ya   lundag
       I-ERG   big-REP   1sg>3nsg-YHA-PAST-pl
       I bin grow'm up [i.e. I raised them].

(15)   gilandirri-ya   wudiyg   ngarragi-yuwa
       big-REP   3nsg-NI-PAST-pl me-LOC
       They bin git big longa me [i.e. They grew up on me/under my tutelage].

These two sentences occurred in the same text, about ten pages apart. They both refer to the same biographical 'facts', but present them in a rather different light. In (14), with a bivalent verb and ergative-marked agent pronoun, the speaker is highlighting her own active role in fostering the growth of the children in question (who are not hers, but the white station owner's) whereas in (15), with a monovalent verb and locative marking on the erstwhile 'agent', she is placing that role more in the background and focussing on the children's growth as such (cf. §4.1.1 regarding clause types, valence and transitivity).

[d] *Allative* -yawu/-jawu. The -jawu form occurs after stops and nasals, -yawu elswhere. (I have as yet recorded no examples of this marker after English-derived l, so its realisation there remains to be determined.)

The allative is used to specify motion 'to', 'as far as', or 'into'. Examples are:

(16) wadjay   yanarri-yawu
      go 3sg-RA-PAST   town-ALL
      He went to town.

(17) thada'wirrantha   garanya-yawu
      scoop with hands Past- 3sg<3nsg-RA2-du   earth.oven-ALL
      The two scooped it into the earth oven.

As with the dative, the functions of the allative overlap with those of OBLique cross-reference on the verb, which can also be used to indicate the goal of monovalent verbs of motion (see §4.1 below). An example of a sentence using both of these means at once is:

(18) niy-ingga wadayngarrinhingi   mamu-yawu
      he-ERG   go/come 3sg-RA-PAST-CTV-3sgOBL   corpse-ALL
      He was coming to the corpse.

This is an unusual example in that it is rare to find both an allative-marked NP and OBLique cross reference to it within the same clause. The same is true of dative NPs, as discussed in [b] above. But whereas the overlapping functions discussed there are most often realised by verbal cross-reference alone, here the preferred means is ALLative marking alone. Thus a more usual variant of (18) would be a clause without the OBLique marker -nhingi on the verb. This difference may be related to the fact that the preferred candidates for verbal cross-reference of all kinds (including OBLique) are human or other animate actors, whereas allative-case marked NPs usually refer to inanimate ones.

In some of its uses the meaning of the allative seems similar to some purposive uses of the dative case. Examples are:

(19) wadburrangarri   wanggu-yawu
      go/come 3nsg-RA-CTV   bush.potatoes-ALL
      They go for bush potatoes.

(20)   ngindaji   gurama   wadjay   mayi-yawu
        This   man   go/come 3sg-RA-PAST   [vegetable] food-ALL
        This man went for food.

Bunuba speakers consistently translate these and other such sentences with 'for' rather than 'to the' or the like. But if the allative marker takes on a purposive meaning in such contexts (which in my texts are limited to clauses with wad+RA 'come'/'go'), it does not entirely overlap with the dative in this function, because it is only used when there is also a local component to the meaning: directed motion towards the referent of the allative-marked NP as the means by which the actor tries to accomplish the 'purpose' in question. Thus, while the dative could be used in place of the allative in (19) and (20) (with a slight change of meaning), the allative is not a permissible replacement for the dative in (10) and (11).

[e] *Ablative* -nhingi/nhi. The form -nhi is limited to rapid or casual speech and is usually replaced by -nhingi when transcribing tapes or in elicited speech.
In its local uses, this marker is the inverse of the allative, indicating the place or direction *from which* an action or process originates. Examples are:

(21)   jarraa-nhingi   wadjay
        far away-ABL   go/come 3sg-RA-PAST
        She came from far away.

(22)   nyirra-nhingi   burrum-jawu   wadngay
        there-ABL   Broome-ALL   go 1sg-RA-PAST
        From there I went to Broome.

(23)   wurrga'yanhi   thanybana-nhingi   ngurru   dulu-yuwa
        put YHA-PAST-3sgOBL   back-ABL   there   heart-LOC
            jabirri   birayga'raynhi
            shovel.spear arrive 3sg-RA-PAST-3sgOBL
        He put the shovel spear in from his back and it came through to his heart.

The ablative is also used in reference to time. When used in relation to some reference point in the past, it has the sense of 'after' or 'since'. Examples are:

(24)   nyirraji-nhingi   wariyga'yiyirrwaniy   yalurru
        that-ABL   start out 1R-WU-PAST   [place name]
        After that we (R) left for Yalurru.
(25)   jirali-yuwa   warrgam'gila   walyay-nhingi   yaranggi
        before-LOC   work 3sg<1sg-RA2   small-ABL   Leopold Downs
        I worked at Yaranggi in the past, from when I was small.

Note the contrast in (25) between the temporal use of the locative, which (redundantly) locates the predicated action entirely in the past without specifying a beginning or ending point, and the use of the ablative (in the phrase walyay-nhingi) which specifies a beginning point, but does not by itself specify any endpoint.

The ablative is also used to specify the (more or less immediate) source or origin of something. Examples are:

(26)   wadba'wuluma   nangala-nhingi
         get FUT-3sg<1sg-MA2   [subsection term]-ABL
         I have to get [a wife] from the Nangala subsection.

(27)   nga(g)'gila   banda-nhingi
         eat PRES-3sg<1sg-RA2   ground-ABL
         I eat [it] from the ground [i.e., cooked in an earth oven].

(28)   banggarri   daliy-ba'wurrangarri   gurama-nhingi
         [place name]   call-ITR 3sg<3nsg-RA2-CTV   Aboriginal-ABL
         'Banggarri' is what they call it in the Aboriginal language.

The notion of 'source' here is one which shades over into what we might think of as 'cause'. Examples are:

(29)   tharra-nhingi   milwa'niy
         dog-ABL   mad 3sg-NI-PAST
         He got mad because of the dog.

(30)   yunggu-mili-nhingi   yatha'raynyangarri   yunggu-yuwa
         scrub-CHAR-ABL   sit 3sg-RA-PAST-SUB-CTV   scrub-LOC
         Because [he was a] scrub man he always used to sit down in the scrub.

Especially when used to specify an origin or source, the ablative frequently functions as a kind of adnominal case, that is, to construct a noun phrase which modifies another noun rather than the verb or clause as a whole. Examples are:

         ngilamungga-nhingi   bilanyi
         east-ABL   snake
         a snake from the east

         gunjilan-nhingi   malngarri
         Queensland-ABL   red [i.e., European]
         a European from Queensland

         jalnggangurru-nhingi   lundu
         doctor-ABL   stick
         stethoscope

[f] *Perlative* -binyi/-bilinyi. This case indicates general orientation 'towards', movement 'through' or 'along', or location 'in the midst of'. I have been unable to discover any difference in meaning between the two variant forms, -binyi being characterised as 'light' Bunuba and -bilinyi as 'heavy'. Examples are:

(31)   nga(g)'birrantha   gurrgarinja   nungganba-binyi
        eat 3sg<3nsg-RA2-PAST-du   [place name]   Noonkenbah-PER
        The two [dogs] ate him [dingo] at Gurrgarinja, over in the Noonkenbah area.

(32)   thinga-bilinyi   ganba'ranhi
        foot/track-PER   follow PAST-3sg<3sg-RA2-3sgOBL
        He [flying fox] followed him along [kangaroo] by his tracks.

(33)   banga'ray   ngurru   walyarra-binyi
        return 3sg-RA-PAST   over there   sand-PER
        He went back over there right through the sand.

(34)   galu-binyi   wad'jay
        road-PER   go 3sg-RA-PAST
        He went along the road.

The perlative is regularly used on NPs referring to bush foods, where it is usually glossed by Bunuba speakers as 'for'. Examples are:

(35)   ngayini gawiy-binyi   wad'bungay
        I   fish-PER   go FUT-1sg-RA-exc
        I will go for fish.

(36)   nginji miyha-binyi   gamanba'wura
        you   meat-PER   hunt FUT-2sg-RA
        You hunt for meat.

These sentences were given as part of a connected text in which a Bunuba woman (Casey Ross) was explaining traditional male and female roles by means of an imaginary conversation between a husband and wife. The use of the perlative in them is typical in that the bush produce referred to is entirely hypothetical, rather than actual (as McGregor 1990:186 also points out for Gooniyandi). In this sense it contrasts both with the dative and the allative, which, if they replaced it in (35) for example, would change the sense to, respectively, 'I will go for the fish' and (less likely) 'I will go to the fish'.

Curiously, in some of its local uses, the perlative is glossed by Bunuba speakers as 'from' rather than in a way which would indicate movement 'toward'. Examples are:

(37)   wad'jay   baljuwa-binyi   diyga'wunarriyngarriy
        go 3sg-RA-PAST   behind-PER   find 3nsg<3sg-NGARRI-PAST
        He came from behind and found them.

(38)   girrgara'miy   ngiyangiyamungga   ngilamungga-binyi
        run 3sg-MA-PAST   south   east-PER
        He [kangaroo, trying to evade flying fox] ran from east to south.

See also (232). It is perhaps significant that such examples are, as far as I know, limited to phrases in which the perlative is used with an expression which is itself inherently 'orientational' or 'directional' (by far the most frequent being baljuwa, as in (37); cf. McGregor 1990:187). They also seem to be limited to contexts in which there are at least two participants involved, one generally in pursuit of the other. Perhaps the perlative phrase in such contexts is to be understood as oriented from the point of view of the second actor, so that, for example, a movement 'from behind' is also a movement 'toward'. Alternatively, as pointed out by Barry Blake (personal communication), it may be that the basic sense of -binyi here is 'through', the sense of 'from' being conditioned by its context of use: 'He came through the behind' being interpreted as 'He came from behind'.

[g] *Comitative1* -ngarri. This marker can usually be glossed as 'with' or 'accompanied by'. As in Gooniyandi (McGregor 1990:187; 346-7), it is used when there is an unequal relationship between the thing accompanied and the thing accompanying it — either a whole-part relationship or one in which the two are being treated as of unequal salience. Examples are:

(39)   wiyi-ngarri waḏjay↑
         woman-COM1   go 3sg-RA-PAST
         Did he have the woman with him when he went?

(40)   birayga'wurraynthangarri   miyha-ngarri
         arrive 3nsg-RA-PAST-du-CTV   meat-COM1
         The two arrived with the meat.

Comitative1 phrases frequently function adnominally. Examples are:

mulurru   guluma-ngarri
catfish   bristle-COM1
catfish with bristles

rarrgi yingiy-ngarri
stone   name-COM1
stones that have names [i.e. inquest stones]

gurama   muḻu-ngarri
[Aboriginal] man   eye-COM1
magician, 'clever fellow'

In examples such as the last of these, -ngarri is really functioning as a derivational device, that is, to coin new expressions whose meanings are not necessarily predictable from the sum of their parts. Comitative -ngarri is sometimes also used in one-word 'headless' or 'exocentric' phrases in which this is even more patently so. Examples are:

garriy-ngarri
edible.water.lily.root-COM1
species of water lily which has an edible root

gambinyi-ngarri
'egg' [jocular expression for 'testicle']-COM1
male dog [a word for them which is used to 'swear' at them]

As mentioned under [a] above, and exemplified by (8) -ngarri phases are frequently further marked with instrumental -ingga. Another example is:

(41)   garuwa-ngarri-ingga   ngulyba'yangarri
        water-COM1-ERG/INST   soft PAST 3sg<3sg-YHA-CTV
        She used to soften it with water.

In light of the above discussion of the uses of -ngarri, it could be argued that -ingga in sentences such as (8) and (41) is being used in its agentive sense rather than its instrumental one. That is, -ingga - marked expressions such as muwurru-ngarri and garuwa-ngarri could be taken to refer to the agents of the actions in question — i.e. the 'one with a club' and the 'one with water' respectively. But this is untenable, at least for these particular sentences, because it would not accurately represent their meanings: 'The man with the stick hit me' and 'The one with water used to soften it' do not have the same meanings as 'The man hit me with a stick' and 'She used to soften it with water', and (8) and (41) are appropriately glossed only by the latter. (Examples such as these also show that -ngarri truly functions as a clause-level case marker in Bunuba, rather than just as phrase- or word- level 'stem forming affix' as the 'having' suffix has been claimed to be in many Australian languages, for example in Dixon 1976:203–310; cf. Rumsey 1980b.)

[h] *Comitative2* -guda. This marker is also used for relationships of 'accompaniment', and may in some contexts be in free variation with comitative1. But in at least some of its uses, the meaning is subtly different (as I pointed out in Rumsey 1980b, where, however, I failed to characterise the differences adequately). One clue as to the difference may be drawn from the fact that most nouns marked with -guda refer to human or other animate actors, whereas the great preponderance of those marked with -ngarri refer to inanimate ones. In contexts where either can be used to refer to an animate actor, another clue as to their semantic difference is provided by the different treatment given to the two kinds of comitative phrases in pronominal cross-reference on the verb. Johnny Marr aptly demonstrated the difference for me with an imaginary question-and-answer sequence which began with (39), to which the reply was:

(42)   ngay wiyi-guda   wad'burrayntha
        yes woman-COM2   go 3nsg-RA-PAST-du
        Yes, he went with the woman.

A better gloss for (42) might actually be 'He and the woman went'. For note that the verb in (42) cross-references its subject as dual, whereas the subject of (39) is treated as singular. Looking through the texts I have recorded, I have found several instances where -guda - marked nominals referring to animate actors are similarly taken into account in cross-reference, and none where -ngarri-marked nominals are. Another -guda example is:

(43) nginji-guda   wad̲'biyirra   maangi
      you-COM2   go FUT-1R-RA   mate
      Let's you and I go, mate.

When the speaker, George Nayindu, and I we were going over this sentence and I asked for a gloss of nginji-guda by itself, he said 'you too', which is consistent with the way others have glossed -guda when used on pronouns. There are, on the other hand, no instances in my texts of Comitative1 -ngarri on personal pronouns, nor has it ever been glossed for me as 'too'.

All the above evidence suggests that comitative2 is in at least some contexts used to indicate a relationship of accompaniment in which the accompanying entity plays a more nearly equal role in the action than he/she/it does in the case of a Comitative1 phrase. Sentences (41) and (42) exemplify a kind of limiting case in that the 'accomplice' plays the *same* role as the accompanied party (with regard to the propositional content of the sentences anyway: the *textual* or 'pragmatic' status of the two participants is no doubt different). This is not always so, as shown by the following:

(44) bulumana-guda   nga(g)'jiyirrangarri   dina
      bullock-COM2   eat PAST-3sg<1R-RA2-CTV   dinner
          nyirra-yuwa   yawad̲a-guda
          that-LOC   horse-COM2
      We'd eat our dinner there with the bullocks and horses.

(45) gurraga'yiyidiyngarri   linygurra-guda
      cross.over 1R-NI-PAST-CTV   saltwater.crocodile-COM2
      We (R) used to cross over [the Fitzroy River at Lanji] right amongst the
      saltwater crocodiles.

From the context it was clear that the bullocks and horses were not also eating their dinner, and that the crocodiles did not also cross the river. But they were involved in these episodes as salient actors in their right, which is seldom if ever the case with -ngarri-marked NPs.

Like -ngarri phrases, -guda ones are quite often used adnominally. An example is the phrase walyay-guda bulumana in the following:

(46) yungga'yiyirrudangarri   bulumana↓
      let go PAST-3nsg<1R-YHA-CTV   cow
          walyay-guda   bulumana↓
          small-COM2   cow
      We (R) would let the cows go with their calves.

As indicated by the downward arrows, the phrase walyay-guda bulumana was spoken on a separate intonation contour, as a kind of afterthought. When focussing on that phrase by itself, the speaker, Billy Oscar, glossed it as 'cow and calf'. Clearly (46) entailed not only that those cows that had calves were sent, but that the calves were sent with them. Here again, there is a contrast with -ngarri, which in this context could be used to mean the former.

In other adnominal uses, especially on inanimate nouns, and in exocentric uses, it is not so clear that the meaning of -guda differs from that of -ngarri. Examples are:

thingi-guda	rarrgi	dirrili-guda
cooking stone -COM2	stone	heavy-COM2
cooking stone		heavy one

[i] *Causal* -winja. This is very rarely used. I have recorded only three examples in jadajada ('straight', everyday) Bunuba, which are as follows:

(47) jirali   gurama   wudijga'rayningarri
      before   blackfella   spear 3sg-RA2-REFL-PAST-CTV
         wiyi-winja
         woman-CAU
      The olden-days blackfella[s] use to spear one another over women.

(48) malngarri-winja   garuwa nyaga'wirriyningarri
      European-CAU   water   spear 3nsg-WU2-REFL-PAST-CTV
      They used to fight each other because of [the effect] of 'whitefella water' [i.e., grog].

(49) rarrgi-winja   milwa'ani
      stone/money-CAU   angry 3sg-NI-PRES
      He's feeling angry because of the money.

As mentioned under [e] above, the ablative marker -nhingi is sometimes also used to indicate the cause of something. The marker -winja is more specialised in that function in that it is only used when the consequences are bad. So for example in order to say 'He's feeling good because of the money', one cannot use rarrgi-winja, but must use rarrgi-nhingi instead (cf. McGregor 1990:188 regarding an identical form with similar but not identical functions in Gooniyandi).

3.2.2   NOMINAL NUMBER MARKING. Number marking in Bunuba is complex in that there are four distinct sets of number categories which operate somewhat differently on words of different classes. Number marking on the verb is described in §3.4.6. Number marking on oblique pronouns is discussed in §3.3.1. Number markers used on lexical nouns, proper names and absolutive pronouns are as follows:

[a] *Dual and plural markers.* The number markers that occur on common nouns and demonstrative, endophoric and interrogative pronouns (§3.3.2) are: DUAL -arri and PLURAL -yani. Word-final vowels are usually omitted before -arri. Examples are:

/buga-arri/ → ['bugʌrɩ] 'two children'
child-DU

/rarrgi-arri/ → ['ɽargʌrɩ] 'two rocks'
rock-DU

/lu<u>nd</u>u-arri/ → ['luɳ̩dʌrɩ] 'two trees'
tree-DU

An exception is:

/ngurru-arri/ →['ŋɷru,ʌrɩ] 'those two'
that-DU

Words ending in /iy/ ([i]) preserve their high front vowel, as in, for example:

/larrgariy-arri/ → ['largʌɽi,yʌrɩ] 'two boab trees'
boab.tree-DU

Examples of the use of -yani are:

/ngaa-yani/ → ['ŋaːyʌnɩ] 'which ones'
which-PL

/larrgariy-yani/ → ['largʌɽi,yʌnɩ] 'boab trees'
boab.tree-DU

/yinggirri-yani/ → ['ɩŋgɩriyʌnɩ] 'you (PL)'
you (nsg)-PL

Note that these two nominal number categories are given interlinear morpheme labels which are distinct from those for the dual and plural number categories in the pronominal cross-reference system on verbs: upper case DU and PL for the former and lower case pl and du for the latter (as per McGregor 1990). This is because the two systems do not always agree with each other. Thus while one would normally expect dual or plural cross-reference for phrases referring to animate beings, such as buga-arri and ngaa-yani above, phrases referring to inanimate beings, such as rarrgi-arri and lu<u>nd</u>u-arri, more often take singular cross-reference on the verb. And among third person NPs, those (mostly animate) ones which are cross referenced as dual or plural are usually not marked for number on the noun or noun phrase.

[b] *Pair marker* -way. This marker occurs on personal names, where it indicates that the person named is one of a pair, the other member of which is not named, but is usually specified by the cross-referencing pronominals on the verb and/or by another word in the phrase. Examples are:

(50)   jimarri   bindayminyi-way   yatha'yiyirrayntha
        mate   [man's name]-PAIR   sit 1R-RA-PAST-du
        yilngarri-wiya
        altogether-DEF
        My mate Bindayminyi and I have been sitting down [together] for a long time.

(51)   nyirra-miya wad'jiyirraynthangiyirri   wulamada-way
        there-ON   go 1R-RA-PAST-du we (R)   [a name]-PAIR
        We two, Wulumada and I, went to that very place.

The same marker also occurs in a closely related function on some pronouns
(§3.3.1) and a homophonous one with a very different function on human
relationship terms (§3.2.3b).

3.2.3   OTHER NOMINAL MARKERS.

[a] *Dyadic* -langu. This suffix occurs on human relationship terms
to refer to a set of people who stand to each other in the relationship specified
by the term. Examples are:

madjali-langu   gunda-langu
mother.in.law-DYAD   male.cross.cousin-DYAD
mother-in-law and son-in-law   two male cross-cousins [of each other]

jimarri-langu   mana-langu
mate-DYAD   elder.brother-DYAD
two mates [or each other]   two brothers [of each other]

                          also: ngaja-langu
                                    younger.brother-DYAD
                                    two brothers [of each other]

As evident from the last two examples, in the case of non-self-
reciprocal terms (i.e., where those in the relationship call each other by
different terms), either term can be taken as the basis for the dyadic
expression (unlike in some other Aboriginal languages, where there is a
regular preference for one or the other, as described by Merlan and Heath
1982).
       This suffix also occurs with reduplicated forms (§3.2.4) of the
relationship terms to refer to a set of more than two people, all of whom are
related to each other in the specified way. Examples are:

jimajimarri-langu   manamana-langu
mate-REDUP-DYAD   elder.brother-REDUP-DYAD
[three or more] mates [of each other]   [three or more] brothers [of each other]

[b] *Third person propositus* -way. This marker occurs on human
relationship terms, where it relates them to some textually given participant
(whether singular or non-singular) from whom the relationship is reckoned,

which in the anthropological literature is known as the *propositus* — a label I
have adopted here in order to acknowledge the difference between this kind
of relationship and that of 'possession' in Bunuba grammar (as opposed to
English where the two are conflated). Examples are:

madjali-way
mother.in.law-3PP
his mother-in-law

nhunhungu-way(-yani)
husband-REDUP-3PP(-PL)
their husbands

Note that this sufix has the same form as the PAIR marker discussed in
§3.2.2b. As far as I can tell, the resemblance is fortuitous.

[c] *Second person propositus* -wulu/bulu. Second person
counterpart of the above, this marker occurs only on human relationship
terms, where it glosses as 'your' (where the 'you' in question can be singular
or plural). The form -wulu occurs after vowels, -bulu after consonants.
Where the final syllable of the term consists of a nasal consonant followed by
a vowel, the vowel is omitted and the -bulu variant is used. Examples are:

gunda-wulu   →   gundawulu 'your cousin'
male.cross.cousin-2PP

ngarranyi-wulu   →   ngarranybulu 'your mother'
mother-2PP

nyaanyi-wulu   →   nyaanybulu   'your mother's brother'
mother's.brother-2PP

The form for 'your father' is irregular in that it not only loses its final vowel
but also changes its final consonant, assimilating it to the following labial:

ngawungu-wulu   →   ngawumbulu 'your father'
father-2PP

Note that there is no distinct marker for first person propositus. That is
indicated either by a possessive pronoun (see §3.3) or by zero, that is, by the
absence of a possessive phrase or propositus marker. The lack of a positive
formal marker of this function can be related to the fact that, in most contexts
among the Bunuba as elsewhere (cf. Merlan 1982) the speaker or first person
is the most expected (functionally 'unmarked') point for relationships to be
reckoned from.

[d] -mili '*characterised by*'. This marker is used to form nominal
expressions which characterise a person (or other being) by association with
the thing or process referred to. Examples are:

garuwa-mili
water/alcohol-CHAR
drunkard

milwa-mili
trouble/bad.temper-CHAR
trouble maker, bad tempered person

wula-mili	bu-mili
speak -CHAR	'moo' [sound made by cow]-CHAR
lawyer	cow

As the last two examples show, this marker can be used with preverbs as well as nominals (the derived form itself being a nominal).

[e] -wanggu *'countryman'*, used with place names to refer to a person associated with the place: warrgali-wanggu 'person from Warrgali country'; ngalarra-wanggu 'person of Ngalarra country', etc.

[f] -warrawarra *'countrymen'*, used to refer to the group of people associated with the place: danggu-warrawarra 'Danggu (Geikie Gorge); yilimbirri-warrawarra 'Yilimbirri people', etc.

[g] -ngurru. This marker is hard to gloss because it occurs only infrequently, in analysable expressions. They are all nominal and generally refer to kinds of agent, instrument or quality. Examples I know of are: jalngga-ngurru 'bush doctor, clever fellow', where jalngga occurs as a preverb, which in combination with the root MA2 means 'to heal or magically manipulate someone's body'; jandama-ngurru 'needle (traditionally made from bone)', where janda is a preverb which in combination with MA2 means 'to pierce'; jada-ngurru 'straight (one)', where jada is a nominal root also meaning 'straight (one)'. There are other words of the same sort which end in ngurru, but are not analysable; for example jalungurru 'quiet, good, gentle (one)', where jalu does not occur by itself or in other analysable combinations.

[h] -wurru. Like -ngurru above, this element is only semi-productive. Many nominals end with it, but most of them are unanalysable. Exceptions include: walyaywurru 'little one' (walyay 'little'); jalungurruwurru 'good one', 'that's good' (jalungurru 'good'); balanggarrawurru 'big mob' (balanggarra 'many'); and yaninjawurru, an often used expression related to yaninja 'Alright', but meaning something like 'Yes indeed' or 'So be it!'.

[i] -alu/-nalu *'from — to(ward)the speaker'* . Closely related to the (far more productive) PROXimad verb suffix (§3.4.8), this marker occurs on nominal or pronominal expressions of place or direction, to which it adds the meaning 'from — to/toward here'. Examples are:

rawurranalu	ngurrubilinyalu
above-nalu	there-PER-alu
from above to(wards) here	from over there to(wards) here

Compare also the word minaluga 'to here, in this direction', which is unanalysable in present-day Bunuba, but includes the element -alu. The initial element mi has no meaning in present Bunuba (the word for 'here' being nginda, the same word as for 'this' — §3.3.2a). But it is suggestively similar to the M-class 'place' prefix of Ungarinyin and other Northern

Kimberley languages which have noun classes. Compare for example Ungarinyin munowalu, which has a similar meaning to Bunuba minaluga 'from over there to here', but which in Ungarinyin contrasts with jinowalu 'from him over there to here', nyinowalu 'from her over there to here', etc. (Rumsey 1982b:32–3,132). If not a result of borrowing, this may provide evidence for the existence of noun classes in the proto-language from which Bunuba has evolved.

3.2.4   NOMINAL REDUPLICATION. Bunuba nominal words are reduplicated to indicate plurality or other amplification. Formally, it is done in at least five distinct ways:

[a] the first syllable is repeated, for example:

mabilyi 'little (one)'   →   ma'mabilyi 'little ones'
ranggumana 'light (one)' →   ra'ranggumana 'light ones'

[b] the second syllable is repeated, for example:

ganday 'bad, old'   →   ga'ndaynday 'old ones'

ngarranyi 'mother'   →   nga'rrarranyi 'mothers'

[c] the first two syllables are repeated, for example:

ngarranyi 'mother'   →   ngarra'ngarranyi 'mothers'

jalungurru 'good (one)'   →   jalu'jalungurru 'good ones'

minthini 'heavy (ones)'   →   minthi'minthini 'heavy ones'

ranggumana 'light (one)' →   ranggu'ranggumana 'light (ones)'

[d] the first vowel and all consonants before the second vowel are repeated, for example:

gilandirri 'big'   →   gi'lilandirri 'very big'

langgula 'firewood'   →   la'ngganggula 'lots of firewood'
(Gun.gunma word)

nada 'short'   →   na'dada 'short ones'

jalungurru 'good (one)'   →   ja'lalungurru 'good ones'

minthini 'heavy (ones)'   →   mi'nthinthini   'heavy ones'

[e] the entire word or root is repeated. Most examples of this involve words of two syllables, but the resulting forms differ from those of type [c]

above (and all the others as well) in that they retain primary stress on the first syllable. Examples are:

nhungu-way 'her husband'	→	'nhungunhungu-way 'their husbands'
mamu 'devil'	→	'mamumamu 'devil-devil'

As can be seen from the above examples, some words reduplicate in more than one way. Others reduplicate in only one way. I have been unable to discover any phonological factors conditioning the preferred form of reduplication, or any differences in meaning associated with each. What has been pointed out to me is that, for forms such as ranggumana and minthini which reduplicate in both ways, pattern [c] is typical of the 'heavy' Bunuba and pattern [d] of 'light'.

3.3   PRONOUN MORPHOLOGY

3.3.1   CARDINAL PRONOUNS. The patterning of Bunuba pronominals (both free-standing and bound ones) differs from that in other Australian languages (except for Gooniyandi) with respect to how they treat the distinction between the inclusion versus exclusion of the addresee in the non-singular series. To show how, I first display the free-standing personal pronouns, arranged in terms of the usual distinction between inclusive and exclusive. This is done in Table 3.1a, which shows the absolutive forms only. (The other, oblique forms pattern somewhat differently with respect to this distinction; they are described further on in this section.)

Note that the PLURAL marker used with these pronouns is of the same form as the one used with nouns (§3.2.2a) and the dual marker the same as the PAIR marker used for proper names (§3.2.2b). The dual marker -arri that occurs on nouns (§3.2.2a) does not occur on pronouns.

The non-singular stem forms can obviously be analysed as including a non-singular marker -rri, which is similar in form to -arri (§3.2.2a), and to non-singular markers used with the pronominal prefixes in the verb complex (§3.4.3).

Note that the inclusive/exclusive distinction is made only when the number of people being referred to is three or more, and that the 'exclusive' form, ngiyirri, also serves as the base of the first person dual form. Since the PAIR marker -way is optional in this context, ngiyirri is potentially ambiguous between first person dual and first person plural exclusive. Given this lack of full fit between the Bunuba first person forms and inclusive/exclusive functions, it seems preferable not to try to draw the distinction in those terms, but to introduce others which will allow us to draw it in a unitary way. McGregor (1989, 1990) has done this for Gooniyandi, using the terms 'restricted' *vs* 'unrestricted'. In terms of this distinction, the Bunuba pronominal categories may be reanalysed as in Table 3.1b (cf. McGregor 1990:169 regarding Gooniyandi, and Rumsey 1996, where a distinctive feature analysis of this system is proposed; cf. also Roberts 1996 and McGregor 1996).

TABLE 3.1a *Absolute Pronouns: Inclusive vs Exclusive*

PERSON	SINGULAR	DUAL	PLURAL
1ST	ngayini	ngiyirri(-way)	inclusive: yaarri(-yani) exclusive: ngiyirri(-yani)
2ND	nginji	yinggirri(-way)	yinggirri(-yani)
3RD	niy	biyirri(-way)	biyirri(-yani)

TABLE 3.1b *Absolute Pronouns: Restricted vs Unrestricted*

PERSON	SINGULAR	NON-SINGULAR
1ST	ngayini	unrestricted: yaarri restricted: ngiyirri
2ND	nginji	yinggirri
3RD	niy	biyirri

Table 3.2 *Oblique Pronouns*

first person singular	ngarragi
first person restricted	ngiyirrangi, ngiyirrangu, ngiyirranggu
first person dual exclusive	ngiyirrantha
first person unrestricted	yarrangi, yarrangu, yarranggu
second person singular	nganggi
second person plural	yinggirranggi, yinggirrangi
second person dual	yinggirrantha
third person singular	nhi, nhu
third person plural	biyirrangi, biyirrangu, biyirranggu
third person dual	biyirrantha

Note that in the interest of terminological consistency I am here using the term 'restricted' in the special sense established by McGregor with respect to Gooniyandi, namely that the referent set of ngiyirri is restricted either by the exclusion of the addressee or by the exclusion of all others besides the addressee.

When the PAIR marker -way is used on the first person restricted form ngiyirri it can only refer to the speaker and some other person besides the addressee, not to the pair of speaker and addressee (see §3.4.6 for the same restriction on dual number on the verb).

The pronouns shown in the Tables 3.1a and 3.1b are used: with comitative2 (as in (43)); with the ergative marker in agent role (as in (4)); and in bare form for other major syntactic functions (see §4). There is another set of oblique pronoun stems which are used: 1) in bare form as possessive pronouns; 2) with other case markers besides comitative2 or ergative; and possibly also 3) in bare form as the subject of a reflexive-reciprocal verb (see §4.3). This set of pronouns is shown in Table 3.2.

As far as I can tell, there are no differences of meaning associated with any of the variant forms. The sets of variants are phonologically regular in that each of them includes one ending in a nasal followed by i. If we take that variant as the basic form in each category, the other variants could be explained as resulting from the (semantically redundant) addition of the dative case marker, either in its -u variant (which displaces final /i/ as per §3.2.1[b]) or in its -gu variant, which is the one that we would expect if the final vowel of the base form were omitted, leaving a final nasal consonant (§3.2.1[b]), compare §3.2.3[c] regarding vowel deletion).

The 3sg form nhu has been said to be 'heavy' and nhi 'light'.

The restricted/unrestricted distinction applies to these pronouns in the same way as to the absolutive ones (and to all the pronominal series on the verb as well: §3.4.3, §3.4.9), but the number marking works somewhat differently. In place of -way and -yani, the non-singular number markers here are -ntha and -ng- (which are similar or identical to those used on verbs; see §3.4.6). And unlike the dual (or PAIR) *vs* plural number marking on absolutive pronouns and verbs, -ntha and -ng- here are obligatory in that each of the non-singular oblique pronouns includes one of them or the other. There are no unsuffixed general non-singular forms like those in the right column of Table 3.1b. Accordingly, the first person restricted forms on the second line of Table 3.2 are not limited to 'plural' functions like the -yani forms in Table 3.1a, but are also used to refer to the pair of speaker and addressee. The dual form ngiyirrantha, like ngiyirriway, *cannot* be used for that pair, and so can be considered a 'dual exclusive' form.

In their possessive function, any of these forms may combine with a number marker (§3.2.2a) indicating the number of the 'possessed'. An example is:

ngarrag(i)-arri	nyaanyi	nganggi-yani	buga
my-DU	maternal uncle	your-PL	child
my two maternal uncles		your children [three or more]	

ngiyirrantha-yani   jugu
belonging.to.us.two (exc)-PL   son
the three or more sons of us two

Appearances notwithstanding, it is only the number of the possessor which is really marked at the level of the word here. As discussed and exemplified in §4.2.2 below, the number markers -arri and -yani operate at the phrase level.

3.3.2   OTHER FREE-STANDING PRONOUNS. In the previous section (§3.3.1) I have placed niy/nhi and biyirri/biyirrangi together with the free-standing personal pronouns mainly because they are similar in having two distinct roots which are used with different sets of case markers. By contrast, all the third person pronouns discussed in this section have a single form which is used with all case markers. All of them can also occur in phrases marked for dual or plural number with the markers discussed in §3.2.2.

[a] *Demonstrative and endophoric pronouns*. Bunuba has two pairs of deictic pronouns, one of which is used primarily for pointing to something in the context of situation ('demonstrative' or 'exophoric' reference) and the other of which is used primarily for pointing to something in the linguistic context ('endophoric' reference).
   One of the demonstratives refers to things relatively close to the speaker ('proximal') and the other to things relatively distant ('distal'). The forms are:

Proximal: nginda, ngindaji this (one)
Distal: ngurru   that (one)

As far as I know, the two proximal forms have exactly the same deictic value, that is, are used in reference to things within the same spatial range relative to the speaker. The only difference I know of is that, while either may be used as an independent pronoun, only ngindaji is ever used attributively, that is, in expressions such as ngindaji gurama 'this man' (see, e.g., (20) as opposed to just ngindaji 'this' or 'this one').
   The endophoric deictics are:

nyirra, nyirraji   this, that (one)

Nyirraji differs from nyirra in the same way as ngindaji does from nginda, that is, not in its deictic value but in its being used attributively (although, unlike with nginda, I have one or two examples of nyirra being used attributively).
   These words are used *only* endophorically, to refer to something or someone nearby in the linguistic context, i.e. to mean something like 'the one that has just been referred to'. To repeat a reference to something that has been referred to further back in the text – 'the former', 'the one mentioned a while ago' – the third person pronouns from Table 3.1 are used (see for

example §6.1, lines 5, 15 and 21). In other words, the difference in deictic value between nyirra(ji) and niy/biyirri within the linguistic context is similar to that between nginda(ji) and ngurru within the space of the speech situation.

Besides being used to refer to participants in the narrated event, nyirra(ji) (but not niy) is also used to refer to more-or-less extensive sections of the text itself (just as are 'this' and 'that' in English). See for example (131), which comes from a text in which the nyirraji in (131) refers to an immediately preceding episode.

[b] *Interrogative/Indefinite Pronouns.* As in most Australian languages, Bunuba has words which are used both for questioning the identity of something and treating it as indefinite. These are:

ngunda	'who?', 'someone'
ngaa	'where?', 'somewhere'
nginjaga	'what?', 'something'
nginjayha/nginjaya	'when?', 'sometime'

From the English speaker's viewpoint, an unexpected use of ngaa is to ask the name of someone or the word for something: not 'What do they call him/it/her?', but, literally 'Where do they call him/her/it?'.

There are two words which are functionally related and formally similar to the above (both of them perhaps based on ngaa), but which do not combine interrogative and indefinite functions in the same way. One is ngaanyi 'what', which is used only for questions, either to mean 'where to' (for example ngaanyi wadjay 'Where did (s)he go') or 'what', in questions about linguistic or other action (ngaanyi gima 'What did (s)he say/do?').

The other related form is ngaala, which seems never to be used for questions, but rather as a kind of indefinite quantifier meaning 'some', 'any' or 'different (one)'.

All of the above words may combine in phrases with the full range of semantically appropriate case and number markers. There is at least one such phrase whose meaning is not necessarily predictable from the English viewpoint: ngaa-nhingi 'where-ABL', which can be used to mean 'how much', 'how many'. More predictably, 'what for' is nginjaga-u ('what'-DAT).

3.4   VERB MORPHOLOGY

As in most non-Pama-Nyungan languages, the verb in Bunuba is quite complex in form, including affixes which convey kinds of grammatical information which in many languages (including English as well as the Pama-Nyungan languages of Australia) are conveyed by separate words. The sequence of order classes which comprise the two-word Bunuba Verb Phrase is represented on the following vertical axis.

1	PREVERB
2	ASPECT
3	QUALIFIER
4	TENSE/MODE PREFIX
5	OBJECT PRONOMINAL
6	SUBJECT PRONOMINAL
7	ROOT
8	REFLEXIVE/RECIPROCAL MARKER
9	TENSE/MODE SUFFIX
10	NUMBER
11	SUBORDINATE MARKER
12	PROXIMAD
13	OBLIQUE PRONOMINAL
14	CONTINUATIVE
15	QUALIFIER

This is of course a composite picture, which shows all the order classes together even though all of them are seldom if ever filled at once. The number which usually are filled ranges from about four to seven, as can be seen from the interlinear gloss lines in example sentences throughout this chapter and in the appended texts. It is also a somewhat over-simplified picture with respect to the order in which the affixes occur. While the order of elements in 1–11 is, as far as I know, invariant, I have recorded occasional examples where affixes normally in positions 12 and 13 have occurred in the reverse order.

The same goes for classes 13 and 14. In addition to their somewhat looser ordering relative to each other, order classes 12–15 also differ from 4–10 in that the elements which occur in them are nearly all identical in form to ones which occur on, or as, words of other classes — mostly with related functions (see §3.4.8-12). Given that all of the oblique pronominals of class 13 (§3.4.9) are similar or identical to corresponding free-form oblique pronouns (§3.3.1), they could be regarded as clitics rather than suffixes. But that would pose an ordering paradox in that the continuative aspect marker, which generally comes after the oblique pronominals (class 14), is more suffix-like in not occurring with a related function on words of any other class.

Not all the order classes are equally likely to be filled. Classes 11 and 12 are seldom filled, while classes 4, 6, 7 and 9 are always filled if the verb is finite, and 1 is always filled if the verb is non-finite. The order of presentation in this section will be to start with classes 7 and 1; then work through the other obligatory classes 4, 6 and 9 and, for bivalent verbs, 5; and finally the non-obligatory classes 2, 3, 8 and 10–15.

3.4.1   THE ROOTS AND THEIR CONJUGATION CLASSES. As far as I know, there are only ten verb roots in Bunuba. The form of each of them varies considerably depending on what comes before and after it (as described in §3.4.3). The roots in what I take to be their underlying forms are shown in Table 3.3. Five of the roots are formally bivalent, taking obligatory prefixes which index two participants (usually corresponding to the traditional notions of 'Object' and 'Agent'). Five are formally monovalent, in that their obligatory pronominal prefixes cross-reference or index only one participant in the clause. Bivalent verbs can be converted to monovalent ones through the addition of a reflexive marker, indicating self-directed action, whereby the agent of an action is also its undergoer. One of the five monovalent verbs, NA, is reflexive in both form and meaning ('talk to oneself/each other'), but has no corresponding non-reflexive form.

Six of the ten roots only ever occur with an accompanying preverb, which carries most of the lexical meaning of the resulting verbal expression. The major exception is the root MA, which often occurs by itself as a 'framing verb' where it can be glossed 'say' or 'do' (see §4.3.3).

NI and YHA sometimes occur with nominals or derived preverbs, where NI can be glossed as 'become' and YHA as 'make into' or 'treat as (a) —'. Nominals do not seem to be able to be used in bare form in such constructions unless they end in a, which is also the only vowel that preverbs end in. Otherwise the nominal in this construction adds a or ga (cf. §3.4.2 regarding ga on the end of preverbs). Examples: are gandaya+NI, 'become bad' (cf. ganday, 'bad'), lanyga+NI 'become daytime' (cf. lanygu 'daytime') and jalungurra+YHA 'make good/well' (cf. jalungurru 'good', 'well'). The other roots are hard to gloss in isolation because they never occur that way. They are not meaningless, but their meanings are abstract, classificatory ones, of the kind McGregor (1990:557–72) has analysed in Gooniyandi. The most basic opposition in that analysis is between what McGregor calls 'accomplishments' *vs* 'extendibles', that is, processes which have an inherent point of completion versus those which do not (McGregor 1990:201–2). This distinction is clearly fundamental to the Bunuba system as well, and indeed, to many other languages around the world, where it is more commonly known by the terms *telic* (having an end) versus *atelic* (lacking an end), which I will use here, with the following stipulation. As McGregor has pointed out to me, it is often unclear in the literature whether these terms are being used in reference to the meaning of the verb itself, or to that of the clause as a whole. The clause can clearly be telic even when the verb itself is not inherently so – as for example in the sentence 'He went to the shop' (William McGregor, personal communication). In Bunuba as in Gooniyandi, the classification which is made by the choice among alternative verb roots (McGregor's 'classifiers') pertains to the verb only. So even in a Bunuba sentence corresponding to the above (*job*-gu wadjay 'He went to the shop'), the verb root (RA) is of the atelic set, since the process predicated by the verb itself is not inherently telic but only becomes so by the specification of a goal in the rest of the clause.

It is perhaps somewhat pointless to assign such a small, closed set of verb roots to conjugation 'classes', but they do vary with respect to the affixes they take for indicating tense/mode. Bunuba has up to six tense/mode

TABLE 3.3 *Bunuba Verb roots*

Root	Valence	Semantic Characteristics	Present Irrealis	Past/ exclusive
MA	1	telic: active	-iy(a)	-iy
RA	1	atelic: active or stative	-ngiy(a)	-y
NI	1	telic: action or change of state	-ø	-y
WU	1	telic: active	-iy(a)	-aniy
MA2	2	telic: active	-iy(a)	-ø
WU2	2	telic: impact upon	-iy(a)	-nu/ni/n
YHA/YA	2	telic: transfer	-iy(a)	-ø
RA2	2	atelic: active	-y	-ø/yi
NGARRI	2	telic: move or change	-ø	-y
reflexive	(2→)1	telic or atelic	-ø	-ni
NA	1 (REFL)	telic	-ø	-ni

categories (fewer for some verbs), each of which is signalled by a particular combination of prefix and suffix. There are only three suffixes which enter into these combinations: zero, PRESent IRRealis and PAST/exclusive (see §3.4.4 for details). A zero suffix occurs with the same value in two of the tense/mode categories for roots of all classes. The two suffixes which are involved in signalling the other four categories vary in form depending on the root. The roots, and associated present irrealis and past/exclusive suffixes, are shown in Table 3.3. When bivalent verbs are reflexivised (§3.4.5) they take a distinctive set of tense/mode suffixes, which do not vary by root, but are the same for all reflexivised verbs. These are also shown on the table. The last root on the list, which means 'say/speak to each other', could be taken to be either nay or na with reflexive marker y. I prefer the latter.

The variation between the root forms yha and ya is partly regional (see §1.2) and partly age-related (§2.1.2). The form of most of the these roots undergoes phonological changes when they combine with some of the pronominal prefixes. These are best discussed after the prefixes have been introduced in §3.4.3.

The semantic features I have specified for these roots appropriately characterise *most* of their uses, but there are many apparent exceptions, especially regarding distinctions more delicate than the basic one between telic and atelic. I have not yet been able to push the analysis of those distinctions as far as McGregor has done for Gooniyandi, but it is clear that the data are similar in many respects. (For readers who might be interested in comparing the two systems, the first nine Bunuba roots in Table 3.3 from top to bottom correspond most closely in function to Gooniyandi MI, I, BINDI, ANI, MI, BINI, DI, A and ARRI respectively.)

3.4.2   THE PREVERB. Almost every Bunuba verb phrase includes a preverb, which carries most of its lexically specific content. Preverbs end in a wider range of phonemes than do other parts of speech – including stop consonants – and the morphemes which follow them in the verb complex differ in their phonological realisation depending on the shape of the preverb. This is discussed in §3.4.3 and §3.4.4 below, where I describe how, in general, preverb-final stops and nasals condition 'hardening' of following elements (-j instead -y, b instead -w, etc.). When the preverb ends in g, it is usually deleted. Expressed in terms of ordered phonological rules, this deletion follows the consonant strengthening. Examples are:

/wug'bila/   → wu'bila 'I'll cook it.'
cook FUT-3sg<1sg-RA2

    Compare: mila'wila
                see FUT-3sg<1sg-RA2
                I'll see him/her/it.

/ngag'yarrag/   → nga'jarrag 'We (U) ate it.'
  eat PAST-3sg<1U-RA2-pl
    Compare: ngag'urrag   mila'yarrag
               eat PAST-3sg<2nsg-RA2-pl   see PAST-3sg<1U-RA2-pl
               You (pl) ate it.   We (U) saw him/her/it.

When the preverb in such a sequence ends in a nasal consonant, it tends to assimilate in place of articulation of the following stop. Examples are:

/nganhing'bayi/   → nganhim'bayi
  lick FUT-3sg<3sg-RA2-exc   He'll lick it. / Let him lick it.

/ngalany'ganbirrag/   → ngalang'ganbirrag
  sing (ensorcel) PRES-1U<3nsg-RA2-pl   They're singing [to ensorcel] us.

Many, perhaps most, preverbs can combine with more than one root, usually with obvious continuities of meaning. The sets of alternative combinations for each preverb are small: usually only two or three. The most common kind of alternative set is a pair, one monovalent and the other bivalent. Examples are:

wula+MA speak   mila+RA look around
wula+RA2 speak to   mila+RA2 see

gunaga+WU rotate   banga+RA come back
gunaga+NGARRI (cause to) rotate   banga+NGARRI bring back

tharrga+NI get down   duwadga+RA break, be broken
tharrga+RA2 lower   duwadga+YHA (cause to) break

As these examples show, the subject of the monovalent verb can correspond to either of the two roles cross-referenced on the bivalent verb: in the wula, mila and banga examples it corresponds to the actor and in the other three to the undergoer of the action.

The contrast between telic and atelic action types which distinguishes RA and RA2 from the other verb roots (§3.4.1) is also to some extent expressed in the form of the preverbs. It is only in combination with one of those two (atelic) roots that we find preverbs ending in stop consonants. For those (otherwise) stop-final preverbs which also occur with telic roots (i.e., those other than RA and RA2), the preverb when in such a combination adds -ga. Examples are:

wulug+RA2 swallow, drink   dangaj(ba)+RA2 assault, belt up
wulugga+MA have a drink   dangajga+WU2 hit, kill

gurrad(ga)+RA hop along (generally used of marsupials, frogs, etc. for their
          way of getting around)
gurradga+WU jump (generally used of people, for a single jump)

Indeed, it is rare to find preverbs ending in consonants at all except in combination with RA or RA2 (see §7.1). Nasal-final preverbs which combine with those roots also tend to add -ga when paired with other roots. Examples are:

judiny+RA crouch
judinyga+WU bend over

ngalany+RA sing
ngalanyga+MA2 sing someone (to seduce them or make them sick)

The ending -ga in the previous six examples could be analysed as a punctual aspect marker. I have not done so, because it is in part phonologically conditioned (no such marker being available to preverbs ending in vowels) and because so many Bunuba preverbs end in invariant ga. As a look at the list in §7.1p-w will show, most of them could be seen as inherently punctual, but this is only a general tendency, perhaps reflecting an earlier stage at which aspect marking on the preverb was more systematic and productive (cf. McGregor 1990:241–2 regarding Gooniyandi, where an analogous ending -gi- functions as an inceptive aspect marker).
    Some preverbs, especially those ending in vowels, enter into telic / atelic contrasts without any associated difference in form. An example is wula, which occurs not only with MA and RA2 (as above), but also with RA, usually in the reduplicated form wulala, to mean 'talk at length' ('talk-talk'). As suggested by this example, verb complexes with roots from the atelic set are often reduplicated. Also they are often marked for continuative and/or iterative aspect, and pairs of verbs which I have elicited for differences of aspect have often differed in the verb root as well. Examples are:

(52) giyga'niy
      get.up 3sg-NI-PAST
      He got up.

(53) giygiyg'jayngarri
      get.up-REDUP 3sg-RA-PAST-CTV
      He kept getting up all the time.

(54) waya'limiy
      call.out 1sg-MA-PAST
      I called out.

(55) waya-wa'ngay
      call.out-ITR 1sg-RA-PAST
      I was calling out.

3.4.3   PRONOMINAL PREFIXES.

[a] *Monovalent Verbs.* Monovalent verbs take one pronominal prefix, in order class 6. The prefixes which are readily segmentable are shown in Table 3.4 on the following page (see Table 3.5 and the following discussion for (2sg and 3sg) forms of NI and RA for which a prefix is not readily segmentable; see §3.4.3b and §3.4.4 for some modifications to the form of these prefixes in future and irrealis verbs).

As is evident from Table 3.4, except within the future tense/mode, only the 3sg and/or non-singular prefixes are the same for all roots. The non-singular prefixes have variants which may be specified on phonological and morphological grounds as follows:

The 1nsg variants with initial consonants occur in the past indicative only — yiyirr and yarr when the preceding element within the verb complex ends in a vowel or continuant, and jiyirr and jarr elsewhere. For example, compare (56) with (57), and (58) with (59).

(56)	girrgara'yarrmiy	(57)	ngaanyi jarrmiy
	run 1U-MA-PAST		what 1U-MA-PAST
	We (U) ran.		What did we (U) say?
(58)	yatha'yiyirray	(59)	wad̲jiyirray
	sit 1R-RA-PAST		go 1R-RA-PAST
	We (R) sat.		We (R) went.

The same phonological conditioning applies to third person non-singular forms. Compare, for example, (60) with (61). For further examples, see (15), (19), (48), (108), and (112).

(60)	yatha'wurray	(61)	wad̲burray
	sit 3nsg-RA-PAST		go 3nsg-RA-PAST
	They sat.		They went.

Among the 2nsg allomorphs, gurr and urr occur in the past indicative only: urr when a preceding element in the verb complex ends in a vowel or continuant; gurr elsewhere. In all other tense/modes (where it is always preceded by a vowel, as per §3.4.4), the form of the 2nsg prefix is -nggurr. Examples are:

(62)	wad̲gurray	(63)	yatha'urray
	go 2nsg-RA-PAST		sit 2nsg-RA-PAST
	You (nsg) went.		You (nsg) sat.

Table 3.4 *Pronominal prefixes for monovalent verbs*

	Singular	Non-singular
1	ng (for RA and NI) l (for MA and WU)	Restricted: jiyirr/yiyirr/iyirr Unrestricted: jarr/yarr/arr
2	ngg/gingg (for RA) y/j/nj (for MA and WU) ø (for all future verbs)	nggurr/gurr/urr
3	ø	burr/wurr

Table 3.5 *Singular-prefixed forms of monovalent verbs, indicative mode*

	RA	NI	MA	WU
PAST				
1	ngay	nginiy	limiy	luwaniy
2	ginggay/nggay	ngindiy	jimiy/yimiy	yuwaniy
3	jay/ray/yay/ay	niy	miy	waniy
PRES				
1	ngira	ngini	lima	lu
2	nggira	nthi	njima	nju
3	ra	ni	ma	wu

(64) wad'ginggurra
go PRES-2nsg-RA
You (nsg) are going.

(65) ngaanyi gurrmiy
what   2nsg-MA-PAST
What did you (nsg) say?

(66) wad'bunggurra
go FUT-2nsg-RA
You (nsg) will /should go./Go!

(67) yatha'wunggurrantha
sit Fut-2nsg-RA-du
You two will/should sit. / You two sit!

(68) nginjaga   girrgara'anggurrmiya
why   run away IRR-2nsg-MA-PRES.IRR
Why do you all want to run away?

Before the intial m of MA (which is the only nasal consonant that ever follows them), the final -rr- of all the non singular prefixes optionally changes to n, for example,

yarrmiy (→yanmiy)
1U-MA-PAST

wurrmiy (→wunmiy)
3nsg-MA-PAST

By contrast with the non-singular prefixes, most of the irregularities among the singular ones are specific to certain roots. Since the total set of roots involved is small, and the number of allomorphs relatively large, it seems best to display the full set of singular-prefixed monovalent roots. These are shown in Table 3.5, in the (present and past tense) indicative mode only, as the pronominal prefixes for all the other tense/mode forms are transparently related to those of the present indicative.

The ginggay variant of the RA 2sg (PAST) is found after stop and nasal consonants, nggay after vowels and continuants (cf. §3.4.4a regarding the regular insertion of -gi- in a similar environment in bivalent verbs; and McGregor 1990:122–3 for a more general process of this kind in Gooniyandi). Examples are:

(69)   wad̲ginggay
       go 2sg-RA-PAST
       You went.

(70)   ngalany'ginggay
       sing 2sg-RA-PAST
       You sang.

but

(71)   yatha'nggay
       sit 2sg-RA-PAST
       You sat.

(72)   bayala'nggay
       swim 2sg-RA-PAST
       You swam.

The 3sg past form jay is found after stops and nasals, ray after vowels and ay mainly after continuants. Examples are:

(73)   wad̲jay
       go 3sg-RA-PAST
       He/she went.

(74)   ngalany'jay
       sing 3sg-RA-PAST
       He/she sang.

(75)   yatha'ray
       sit 3sg-RA-PAST
       He/she sat.

(76)   warirr'ay
       itch 3sg-RA-PAST
       He/she itched.

The ay variant is sometimes also used after stops in place of jay, e.g. wad̲ay instead of wad̲jay for 'He/she went'. I have recorded this in the speech of only two people, both of them elderly at the time and now deceased. Living speakers do not identify this usage with any particular dialect, but say it is simply incorrect.

The -yay variant occurs occasionally after vowels and continuants instead of -ray. Examples are:

(77)   wala'yay
       cry 3sg-RA-PAST
       He/she cried.

(78)   bayala'yay
       swim 3sg-RA-PAST
       He/she swam.

Unlike the variation between jay and ay, this one seems to be specific to certain preverbs, some usually or always taking ray and others yay. The yay form can be understood as an analogical development based on jay, since jay occurs in the same environments where other forms beginning in j (such as 1nsg jiyirr and jarr above) have corresponding y-initial forms after vowels and continuants. The jay form itself is so irregular that it is probably best regarded as a unique, fused form of prefix and root.

The same is true of the 2sg forms of NI, which show unexplained intrusive homorganic and lamino-dental stops.

In the MA column, the 2sg variant jimiy occurs when the verb is free-standing or follows a root-final stop or nasal, yimiy elsewhere.

The form of the roots (or combinations of prefix plus root) vary among the non-singulars in similar ways to what is shown in Table 3.5 for the singular forms. Except for the irregular fused forms noted above, these variations can be accounted for by taking the (ø-prefixed) 3sg present indicative forms as the basic forms, and positing the following morpho-phonological processes:

1) The r of RA is lost in the following environments: after ng (1sg) and ngg (final consonants of 2sg) in the past indicative (as shown in Table 3.5); after the irrealis marker -giy- (see §3.4.4c and (113)) and the future marker (see e.g. (141)); and after r r (the final consonant of all nsg prefixes) in all tense/modes. Examples of the latter occur in (58) to (64) and (66).

2) The w of WU is lost after l and nj (as shown in Table 3.5), and after r r except when the root vowel u has been displaced by a suffix (see §3.4.4). Examples are (129) and:

'yiyirru   'ginggurru   'arru
PRES-1R-WU   PRES-2nsg-WU   1U-WU-PRES

3) When the n of NI follows r r, the (impermissible) sequence r r n is replaced by d. Examples are:

wudiy   wadi
3nsg-NI-PAST   FUT-1U-NI

4) With the exception of the forms generated by 1) and 2) above, sequences of stop or lateral plus root-initial consonant are broken up by inserting a vowel: u before w and in guw(u)-marked irrealis forms (§3.4.4c), i elsewhere (see Table 3.5 for examples: -njima, luwaniy, etc.)

[b] *Bivalent Verbs*. Bivalent verbs take two pronominal prefixes, or what may in some instances be better regarded as a single, complex one, in order classes 5 and 6. These prefixes specify the person and number (singular versus non-singular) of the verb's subject (see §4.1) and object. Like the pronominal prefixes for monovalent verbs, the ones for bivalent verbs vary according to what root they occur with. But the amount of variation is less, so the whole set of them can be presented in a single list of basic forms, showing root-specific alternatives where they occur. There is again considerable variation in the form of the prefixes as between past and present indicative, the form of the other tense/modes being the same as for the present indicative, except for some 2sg subject forms as noted in §3.4.4. The pronominal prefixes used in the present and past indicative are shown in Tables 3.6 a-c.

TABLE 3.6a *Bivalent Pronominal prefixes with first person subject*

Object /Tense	1sg Subject	1R Subject	1U Subject
2sg PRES	iny	irriny	
2sg PAST	nginy	yirriny	
2nsg PRES	anggirriny	irriny(birr)	
2nsg PAST	irriny	yirriny(birr)	
3sg PRES	l	i(yi)rr	arr
3sg PAST	l	yi(yi)rr	yarr
3nsg PRES	lun	irrir	adir
3nsg PAST	lun	yirrir	yarrir

Table 3.6b *Bivalent pronominal prefixes with second person subject*

Object /Tense	2sg Subject	2nsg Subject
1 sg PRES	in	nbirr (RA2, NGARRI, YHA) nd (MA2, WU2)
1sg PAST	yin	nginbirr (RA2, NGARRI, YHA) yind (MA2, WU2)
1R PRES	in	inbirr (RA2, NGARRI, YHA) ind(MA2, WU2)
1R PAST	yin	yinbirr (RA2, NGARRI, YHA) yind (MA2, WU2)
3sg PRES	inj	nggurr
3sg PAST	iy (MA2, YHA, WU2) y (RA2,NGARRI)	urr
3nsg PRES	(i)njun	nggurrir (NGARRI)
3nsg PAST	yun	urrir (RA2, YHA) urr (NGARRI, WU2) irru(ru)n (MA)

As far as I know, the choice among the alternative forms shown on these tables by parentheses is largely a matter of free variation. Certain speakers consistently use the fuller forms, but it seems to be more a matter of personal differences than regional ones (cf. §3.4.4).

For all of the prefixes in Tables 3.6a-c which begin with y or w, it is strengthened to j or b respectively when the preceding element ends in a stop or nasal, just as for the monovalent prefixes as discussed in §3.4.4a. Examples may be found in §6.1, 1.2, and in §3.4.2.

Notice that almost all of the prefix combinations in Tables 3.6a-c end in consonants, or pairs of them, and that all the bivalent verb roots (like all the monovalent ones) begin with consonants. This means that the prefixed verbs in their underlying forms contain sequences of two or three

consonants. Actually-occurring Bunuba verb forms can be specified by the
rules listed after the tables, which operate to simplify those clusters.

1. Before the root MA2, prefixes ending in d, g, j or l add u (cf.
§3.4.3a, rule 4) and prefix-final r optionally changes to n (cf. §3.4.3a). For
an example of the latter see (162). Examples of the addition of u occur in (79)
to (82).

(79)   ngayaga'ngindumag
         ask PAST-1sg<3nsg-MA2-pl
         They asked me.

(80)   nganja-ma'angguma
         bite-INT PAST-2sg<3sg-MA2
         Did he/she/it bite you?

(81)   m idga'injuma
         tie on PRES-3sg<2sg-MA2
         You tie it up.

(82)   manja'iluma
         make PRES-3sg<1sg-MA2
         I make it.

2. Following d, g, r, or l, the root WU2 loses its initial w. Examples
are (83) to (86).

(83)   walanggala'wundu
         forget.about 3nsg<3nsg-WU2-PRES
         They forget about them.

(84)   wula'inggu
         talk/tell PRES-2sg<3sg-WU2
         He tells you.

(85)   wurrala'yirrirunu
         punch 3nsg<1R-WU2-PAST
         We punched them.

(86)   garrga'lun
         leave 3sg<1sg-WU2-PAST
         I left him/her/it.

Following rr, the deletion of w is optional. For example, one hears
expressions such as the following both with and without the w:

(87)   dalja 'yarr(w)un
         rear 3sg<1U-WU2-PAST
         We reared him/her.

3. Following n or ny, the w of WU2 strengthens to b (cf. § 2.2).
Examples are (88) and (89).

(88)   wula'ilunbu
         talk 1sg>3nsg-WU2-PRES
         I talk to them.

(89)   wula'irrinybu
         talk 1R>2-WU2-PRES
         We talk to you.

4. Sequences of rr followed by YHA are pronounced da. For
example:

(90)   ngangga'yada
         give PAST-3sg<1U-YHA
         We[U] gave to him/her.

5. Sequences of n followed by YHA are pronounced nda. An
example is (91).

(91)   wurrga'wunda
         put 3nsg<3sg-YHA
         He/she put them.

6. Sequences of ny followed by YHA are pronounced nja. For example:

(92)   ngangga'nginja
         give to PAST-1sg>2sg-YHA
         I gave to you.

7. Following y, the initial consonant of YHA is omitted. An example is (93).

(93)   ngangga-ma'iya
         give-INT PAST-3sg<2sg-YHA
         Did you give to him/her?

8. The sequence of r followed by YHA is pronounced sometimes as ra and sometimes as da. For example, the following phrase (94) has been recorded in both the alternate forms shown:

(94)   yungga'yirrira/yirrida
         let go PAST-3nsg<1R-YHA
         We let them go.

9. Before the root YHA, prefixes ending in l or g add i. For example,

(95)   ngangga'liyha   (96) biyga-ma'anggiyha
         give PAST-3sg<1sg-YHA   burn-INT PAST-2sg<3sg-YHA
         I gave to him/her.   Did it burn you?

It is only in examples such as the above (i.e., where YHA is preceded by a vowel), or where it occurs with the ø- prefix (i.e., 3sg<3sg) that YHA is ever pronounced with the lamino-dental glide. In these environments, some speakers instead pronounce it with a lamino-palatal glide, as ya. In the other environments, specified in 4 to 8 above, all speakers pronounce it in the same way.

10. The initial consonants of RA2 and NGARRI are omitted following (prefix-final) consonants. This means that the only prefix combination after which they are *not* omitted (since it is the only one without a final consonant) is 3sg<3sg, as exemplified by the following:

Table 3.6c *Bivalent pronominal prefixes with third person subject*

	3sg Subject	3nsg Subject
Object /Tense		
1 sg PRES	n an (WU2 only)	nbirr (RA2, NGARRI, YHA; also attested with WU2) nd (MA2, WU2)
1 sg PAST	ngin ngan (WU2 only)	nginbirr (RA2, NGARRI, YHA) ngind (MA2, WU2)
1R PRES	i(yi)n	inbirr (RA2, NGARRI, YHA) ind (MA2, WU2)
IR PAST	(y)i(yi)n	yinbirr (RA2, YHA, NGARRI) yind (MA2, WU2)
1U PRES	an	anbirr (RA2, YHA, NGARRI) and (MA2, WU2)
1U PAST	yan	yanbirr (RA2, YHA, NGARRI) yand (MA2, WU2)
2sg PRES	ngg	mbirr
2sg PAST	angg	ngimbirr anggimbirr(+WU) ('Heavy' Bunuba)
2nsg PRES	nggun	nggunbirr (RA2, NGARRI, YHA; also attested with WU2 and MA2) nggund (WU2, MA2)
2nsg PAST	in	anbirr (YHA, RA2, NGARRI) and (MA2, WU2)
3sg PRES	ø	(w)urr
3sg PAST	ø	wirr
3nsg PRES	wun	unbirr, wunbirr (RA2, NGARRI, YHA; also attested with WU2) (w)und (MA2, WU2)
3nsg PAST	wun/win	wunbirr (RA2, NGARRI, YHA; also attested with WU2) wund(MA2, WU2)

(97) mila'ra
      see PAST-3sg<3sg-RA2
      She/he saw him/her/it.

(98) diyga'ngarriy
      find PAST-3sg<3sg-NGARRI-PAST
      He/she found her/him/it.

Even with 3sg<3sg, the initial consonants of these two roots are pronounced only in the past tense. For example, the corresponding present indicative forms of the above are mila'a 'He/she sees him/her/it' and diyga'arri 'He/she finds him/her/it'. Given the extremely limited distribution of the ra and ngarri forms in comparison to the a and arri ones it is tempting to regard the latter as the basic forms of these roots, and to account for the others by assuming that consonants are inserted before vowel-initial roots in the past indicative (as McGregor (1990:208) does in the face of similar facts from Gooniyandi). I prefer to regard the consonant-initial forms as basic, for two reasons. First, under the alternative analysis there is no way to account for why *these particular* consonants (r and ng) should be the ones that get inserted where they do. Secondly, assuming the consonant-initial forms as basic allows us to specify the difference between past and present indicative bivalent verbs in a consistent way. For, as a look at Tables 3.6a-c will reveal, the great majority of present indicative verb prefixes differ from the corresponding past indicative ones only by absence of the initial consonant (the same is true of the 2nsg and 3nsg monovalent verb prefixes, as discussed in §3.4.3a). It is consistent with this pattern to say that, for those pairs of -ø prefixed forms (i.e. 3sg<3sg ones) which differ only by the presence or absence of an initial consonant, the consonant is a part of the root, which gets deleted according to the same rule which deletes prefix-initial consonants (i.e., a rule which applies to prefixed verb forms, rather than to the prefixes as such).

3.4.4   TENSE AND MODE. As shown in the order-class schema at the beginning of §3.4, tense and mode are signalled both by prefixes in position 4 and by suffixes in position 9. (Now that the forms of the bivalent verb prefixes have been described, we may also add that, within the indicative mode, the difference between past and present tense is also signalled partly within position 5 or 7.) Each of the six tense/mode categories is realised by a particular combination of prefix and suffix. The prefixes vary in form depending on the pronominal element they precede and the suffixes according to what root or verb stem they follow. Before describing that variation, and the functions of each of the six categories, I will begin with an overview of the tense/mode system, showing the combinations of prefix and suffix for each category. This is done in Table 3.7

[a] *Present Indicative and Past Indicative.* Almost all of the verb examples shown so far (in §3.4.3) have been in the indicative mode, which is used to make assertions without any qualification as to the likelihood, necessity or desirablity of the states of affairs they are describing: 'She saw him', 'I make it', etc. The present indicative is used to make such assertions about a time more or less coinciding with the time of speaking, sometimes extending into the definite future. For example, just as one can say in English 'Tomorrow we go' (instead of 'will go') when we have made definite plans to go, so Banjo Wirrunmarra once said to me, as we rehearsed our plans the night before a bush trip: Yarrangi-yawu muway maaningarri wadjiyirra 'Tomorrow we go to our country'. By contrast, the past indicative is always used about matters prior to the time of speaking.

The formal realisation of the present/past distinction within the indicative mode is very complex, in that it occurs in three different places, but may be present or absent in any or all of them depending on the root and/or pronominal prefix. Turning first to the PAST suffixes, as shown in Table 3.3, two of the roots – MA2 and YHA – have none, and a third – RA2 – has one which is not always used. As far as I can tell that suffix is always available to disambiguate between present and past forms of RA2 where the

TABLE 3.7 *Tense/mode marking on theVerb*

Category	Order class 4 (prefix)	Order class 9 (suffix)
past indicative	ø	PAST (see Table 3.3 for forms)
present indicative	ø / gi/i	ø
future	wu(/bu)	ø / exclusive (see Table 3.3)
past irrealis	(g)a/(g)iy/guw	PAST (see Table 3.3)
present irrealis	(g)a/(g)iy/guw	PRESent IRRealis (see Table 3.3)
future irrealis	(g)a/(g)iy/guw(u)	ø

prefixes do not, but it is not used always or only under those conditions. For example, mila wunag can mean either 'He saw them' or 'He sees them', and 'I saw him' can be either mila la or mila layi (as opposed to mila ila 'I see him').

The pronunciation of verbs with the suffixes -yi and -y is as described in §2.1.2. Note how the analysis of word-final [i] as /iy/ is supported by the fact that it allows us to posit a single past tense suffix /y/, 'which yields [i] when added to verb roots ending in /i/ (NI and NGARRI) and [e] when it comes after the /a/ of RA.

As elsewhere in Bunuba morphology, past suffixes beginning in a vowel displace preceding vowels. Thus the root wu followed by -aniy is pronounced [wani] and ma followed by -iy is pronounced [mi] .

I am unable to specify exactly where each of the three past/exclusive allomorphs for WU2 occurs, but the general tendency is for -nu to occur when the previous syllable has an u in it, -n when there would otherwise be an odd number of syllables, and -ni elsewhere (cf. McGregor 1990:212–15).

The present indicative allomorph i occurs before bivalent pronominal prefixes which begin with l, m or ng, and immediately before the roots MA2 and YHA (i.e., in 3sg<3sg forms where the pronominal prefix is

As for the class 4 prefixes, present indicative gi occurs when there is no preverb or when the preverb ends with a consonant. Examples are /ngalany'ganburrag/ > ngalang'ganburrag in §3.4.2, (263), and (99) and (100) below.

(99) ngaanyi gi-ø-ma > gima
      what   PRES-3sg-MA
      What's (s)he saying?

(100) wad'gi-ng-ra >...gingira
      go PRES-1sg-RA
      I'm going.

(For ng-ra > ngira in (100) see §3.4.3a, rule 4)

The i of gi- is dropped when followed by a vowel. Examples are:

(101) ngag'gi-urr-ra >...gurra
      eat PRES-3sg<3nsg-RA2
      They're eating it.

(102) wirrij'gi-arr-ra-y >...garray
      scratch PRES-1U-RA2-REFL
      We're scratching ourselves.

(For ra > a see §3.4.3b, rule 10).

ø-). It sometimes also occurs before nthi (2sg present indicative form of the root NI, see Table 3.5), and before the ø-prefixed 3sg form of the root MA (see Table 3.5).

Elsewhere the present indicative prefix is the same as the past indicative, ø. For all monovalent verbs and for most bivalent ones the difference between present and past indicative is still signalled in the form of the pronominal prefixes (and for most by suffixes as well), but for bivalent verbs in some of the person–number combinations, such as 3nsg<3sg, there is, for many speakers, no difference. For other combinations, especially where the relevant morphological difference is between i and yi, the phonetic difference is extremely small, indeed for some speakers not recognised at all, neither in their pronunciation nor in their comments on it. Others persist in making the distinction almost every-where, but even the most assiduous Aboriginal grammarian I have ever worked with, Johnny Marr, has sometimes treated the difference between 1sg<2sg yin (past) and in (present) as optional, saying that the latter was 'all right' but short way'.

When the root RA2 occurs in the past indicative in combination with a preverb which ends in a stop or nasal consonant, and the following pronominal prefix is ø- or begins with a consonant other than y or w, an element gi (homophonous with one variant of the present indicative marker but morphologically distinct from it), is added to break up the sequence of consonants (cf. §3.4.3). Examples are:

/ngag'-ø-ra/   →   nga(g)'gira 'He/she ate it'.
eat 3sg<3sg-RA2

/wug'-l-ra/   →   wu(g)'gila 'I ate it'.
eat 3sg<1sg-RA2

/warrgam'-l-ra/   →   warrgam'gila 'I worked (it)'.
work 3sg<1sg-RA2

The complex, sometimes redundant, sometimes non-existent tense marking within the indicative mood makes it hard to decide exactly what and what not to show in interlinear glosses. For those roots which always take tense suffixes (WU2, NGARRI, and all of the monovalent roots), this can be regarded as their *primary* means of the present *vs* past indicative marking, since it is the only one of the three means (tense suffix, tense prefix or suppletive pronominal prefix) which is used with all preverbs and in all person–number combinations. Accordingly, for those roots, my interlinear glosses show tense only once, in order class 9. For the other roots YHA, MA2 and RA2 I show PRESent versus PAST, where they are distinguished, in class 4 or 5. For RA2 I always include a gloss for the PAST suffix when it is used, but do not treat its absence as a positive indication of PRESent tense in class 9. In those verb complexes where there is no positive mark of this distinction at all I do not include PRES or PAST in the interlinear glosses, but usually presuppose one or the other in my free translations, depending on how the sentences were translated in the context in which they occurred.

[b] *Future.* As shown in (103) to (110), FUTure marking conveys a wide range of meanings, their least common denominator being that they all project into the future (cf. McGregor 1990:520). There is no formally distinct category of imperative verbs in Bunuba, and FUTure forms with second

person subjects are the standard way of making commands. Speakers also use FUTure forms to: 1) express a wish to do something, or that someone or something else do something ('I wanna...', 'He should...', 'Let it...'); 2) impute obligation ('They/I/you gotta...'); 3) express future conditionality ('If you..., then I will...', cf. (257)); and 4) simply to talk about future events ('He will...', 'I will'). Unlike in English, 'if' and 'when' clauses in Bunuba which refer to future events ('Next month when /if I...', etc.) are regularly in the FUTure tense/mode rather than present (or non-past).

As with the present indicative, the future prefix variants with initial stop consonant (in this case b) occur when there is no preverb, or when the preverb ends in a consonant. The vowel of wu/bu is lost before following vowels. Examples of both these kinds of conditioning are in (103) to (107).

(103)   ngaanyi wu-ø-ma > ...buma
         what   FUT-2sg-MA
         What will you say?

(104)   wulug'wu-iyirr-ra > ...biyirra
         drink FUT-1R-RA
         We (you and I) will drink. / Let's drink.

(105)   ngangga'wu-in-yha > ...winda
         give FUT-1sg<2sg-YHA
         Give to me. / You will/must give to me.

(106)   yatha'wu-arr-ra > ...warra
         sit FUT-1U-RA2
         Let's sit. / We'll sit.

(107)   ba'wu-nggurr-ni-gi > ...wunggudigi
         paint up FUT-2nsg-NI-pl
         You (pl) paint up. / You have to/will/should paint up.

As shown on Table 3.4 and exemplified by (36), (103) and (264), future monovalent verbs with 2sg subjects take a ø- pronominal prefix. The same is true of bivalent verbs when they have a 2sg subject and 3sg object. For an example see (260). For all other person/number categories, the form of the pronominal prefixes for future verbs is the same as for present indicative.

In all of examples (103) to (107) the subject of the FUTure verb is or includes the addressee (person spoken to). Where this is not the case, FUTure verbs take a suffix of exactly the same form as the PAST (indicative and irrealis) suffix for that particular root (as specified by Table 3.3). Because its function is so different in this context (when it occurs on verbs with FUTure prefix), I have labelled this suffix 'exc' for exclusive, i.e., excluding the addressee. Examples are (108), (109), and (110).

(108)   ngaanyi wu-wurr-ma-iy > ...buwurrmiy
         what   FUT-3nsg-MA-exc
         What will they say?

(109)   yatha'wu-ng-ra-y > ...wungay
         sit FUT-1sg-RA-exc
         I will sit.

(110)   wuḻug'wu-iyirr-ra-y >   ...biyirray
         drink FUT-1R-RA-exc
         We (not including you) will drink.

It might seem as though the exclusive marker adds nothing to the meaning of
future verbs, as their prefixes already specify whether the subject does or
does not include the addressee. This is true of examples such as (108) and
(109), but not of (104) and (110), where the subject is first person restricted.
For, as shown in §3.3.1, the Restricted category can be used either for 'You
(sg) and I' or for 'I and other(s) not including you'. Thus the presence or
absence of the exclusive suffix in pairs such as (104) and (110) serves to
implement a semantic distinction which cuts across the Restricted-
Unrestricted one, and is of the Inclusive-Exclusive sort which is much more
commonly found in Australian languages (for details, see Rumsey 1996).
    The exclusive marker is also significant on third person singular
verbs, since without it they would be identical to second person singular
ones, both taking a ø- pronominal prefix in the future tense/mood. For
example, compare (103) with ngaanyi bumiy 'What will (s)he say'.

    [c] *Irrealis (Past, Present and Future).* IRRealis marking is used to
convey uncertainty or non-factuality, the nature and degree of which are
usually further specifed in the same clause by modal adverbs or
postpositions. Perhaps the most frequent of these, for all three tenses in the
irrealis mode, is ngayi 'not'. Irrealis verbs cannot by themselves be used to
negate a proposition ('He doesn't...', 'They didn't...'), or to tell someone
not to do something. In these functions, the irrealis verb must be
accompanied by ngayi.
    Past Irrealis is also used for imputing: past unmet obligation ('ought
to have...', 'should have...'; past intention or incipience ('wanted to...',
'was going to...'); and past counterfactual conditionality ('If you had...,
then I would have'; cf. §6.1, line 23).
    Present Irrealis is used for all the above in the present tense, and
(with ngayi 'not' and second person subject) for telling someone not to do
something.
    Future Irrealis is used for expressing future possibility ('might...',
'can [in future] ...', etc.). With ngayi it is variously glossed as 'will not...',
'not gonna...', 'don't/doesn't wanna...', and, with second person subjects,
as 'Don't...'. I have so far been unable to find any difference in meaning
between these negative commands with future irrealis and those with present
irrealis.
    The irrealis prefix variants with initial g occur in the same
environments as the stop-initial present and future prefixes: when there is no
preverb or when the preverb ends in a consonant. In these environments giy
is found before w- and ø- pronominal prefix (i.e., immediately preceding the
root); ga is found before a (yielding [gaː]; guw before i, and guwu elsewhere.
Where the preverb ends in a vowel or consonant other than a stop, iy is
found before -w and -ø (as for giy above) and a elsewhere. The following

forms illustrate all these kinds of conditioning, and the various functions of the irrrealis mode discussed above. (Most of the phrases shown could serve more than one of those functions in various contexts; the glosses are those given by informants for each example in its original context of use or elicitation.)

(111)   ngayi   ga-arr-ma-iy-g > ...gaarrmiyg
        not   IRR-1U-MA-PAST-pl
        We [U] didn't say.

(112)   ngayi wad'giy-wurr-ra-ngiy > ...giywurrangiy
        not   go IRR-3nsg-RA2-PRES.IRR (i.e., present irrealis)
        They don't want to go.

(113)   wad'giy-ø-ra-ngiy > ...giyangiy
        go IRR-3sg-RA-PRES.IRR
        Can't he go? / He ought to go.

(114)   ngayi guw-iyirr-ma-ø-nhingi > ...guwiyirrmanhingi
        not   IRR-1R-MA-FUT.IRR-3sgOBL
        You and I are not going to say to him.

(115)   ngayi ngag'guwu-nj-ra-ø > ...guwunja
        not   eat IRR-3sg<2sg-RA2-FUT.IRR
        Don't eat it.

(116)   ngayi-ma guwu-nj-ma-iy-nhingi > ...guwunjumiynhingi
        not-INT   IRR-2sg-MA-PAST-3sgOBL
        Why didn't you say to him? [For nj(ø>u)-ma, see §3.4.3a, rule 4]

(117)   ngayi girrgara'iy-ø-ma-iy > ...iymiy
        not   run away IRR-3sg-MA-PRES.IRR
        He's not running away.

(118)   diyga'iy-wunbirr-ngarri-y-g > ...'iywunbirrarriyg
        find IRR-3nsg<3nsg-NGARRI-PAST-pl
        They were going to find them.

(119)   wad'giy-ø-ra-y> ...giyay
        go IRR-3sg-RA-PAST
        He was going to go.

(120)   ngayi nyaga'a-njun-wu-ø-gV> anjunbugu
        not   spear IRR-3nsg<2sg-WU2-FUT.IRR-pl
        Don't spear them. [For n(w>)b see §3.4.3b, rule 3; for gV>gu, see §3.4.6b.]

3.4.5 REFLEXIVE-RECIPROCAL MARKING. Like many other Australian languages, Bunuba has a single grammatical category for indicating both the reflexive relation ('did to themselves') and the reciprocal one ('did to each other'). (The two are of course logically distinct only where the subject is non-singular.) Reflexive-Reciprocal is indicated by a suffix immediately after any of the five bivalent roots, which transforms them to monovalent stems. The pronominal prefixes and tense/mode prefixation for reflexive verbs are the same as for the corresponding bivalent forms with third person singular objects (see Tables 3.6a-c, §3.4.3b, and §3.4.4). The form of the reflexive suffix varies somewhat according to the root, as do the tense mode suffixes for reflexive stems. The variants are shown in Table 3.8. The suffix forms -iy and -ay displace preceding vowels, yielding wiy ([wi]) and ngarray ([ŋʌre]) respectively. Examples of reflexivised verbs are (121) to (125).

TABLE 3.8 *Reflexive-reciprocal verb suffixes*

Root(s)	Reflexive-reciprocal suffix	Past suffix when reflexivised	Present Irrealis suffix when reflexivised
MA2, RA2, YHA, NA	- y	- n i	- ø
WU2	- i y	- n i	- ø
NGARRI	- a y	-(r a y) n i	- ø

(121) ninthila'l-ma-y-ni > ...limayni
       pinch 1sg-MA2-REFL-PAST
       I pinched myself.

(122) mila'wu-nggurr-ra-y-g > ...wunggurrayg
       look at FUT-2nsg-RA2-REFL-pl
       Look at yourselves/each other.

(123) ngangga'wirr-yha-y-ni > ...widayni
       give 3nsg-YHA-REFL-PAST
       They gave to one another.

(124) wula'yirr-wu-iy-ni > ...yirrwiyni
       talk 1R-WU2-REFL-PAST
       We talked to one another.

(125) diyga'il-ngarri-ay > ...ilarray
       find 1sg-NGARRI-REFL
       I'm finding myself [my own tracks, etc.].

For further examples of Reflexive-Reciprocal verbs, see (47), (48), (102), and (243) to (247).

3.4.6   NUMBER SUFFIXES. In order class 10, (after the tense-mode suffix if there is one), any verb whose subject and/or object is non-singular or first person Restricted or Unrestricted may take a plural suffix -g(V). In the same position, any of those verbs except the first person Unrestricted ones may alternatively take a dual number suffix -ntha. Note that only one order class is available for indicating number even for bivalent verbs. For those verbs, dual or plural specification is available for Agent or Object but not both. Where neither of those is singular (or 1U when the number suffix is dual), nothing in the verb itself indicates whether the number marking applies to A or to O. This can usually be determined from the context, as in (127).

[a] *Dual*. The dual verb suffix -ntha, like the DUAL nominal marker -arri (§3.2.2), indicates that the referent consists of exactly two entities (but see §3.2.2 regarding the somewhat different conditions under which these two markers are used). Examples are:

(126) baburruga   tharrga'wudiy**ntha**
      downward   get.down 3nsg-NI-PAST-du
      The two got down.

(127) gurama wad̲gira nyirali-ngarri...   mila'wunggurra**ntha**
      man   is coming stolen wife-COM1   look FUT-3nsg<2nsg-RA-du
      A man is coming with a wife he has stolen; look at the two of them [said by
      Brolga to the other birds around him].

For further examples of dual number marking, see (17), (31), (40), (42), (50) and (51).

    There is one kind of pair which can*not* be referred to with -ntha: the pair of speaker and addressee. Although first person Restricted pronominals may be used for that pair, when they do so they cannot co-occur with dual number marking (cf. §3.3.1 for the same restriction regarding Dual number marking on free-standing pronouns). Dual number marking may occur with 1R, as shown by (51), but when it does so, the referent can only be a pair consisting of the speaker and one more person other than the addressee. Thus, for example the phrase wad̲ jiyirrayntha in (51) cannot be used to mean 'You and I went', whereas the same phrase without the suffix -ntha can be (although it then becomes potentially ambiguous between first person dual and exclusive, as discussed in §3.3.1).

[b] *Plural*. The plural suffix -g(V) indicates that its referent (S, A or O as above) consists of three or more entities. The optional vowel (V) is sometimes a phonemically indeterminate central vowel [ə] (in which case I don't include it in my phonemic transcriptions), and is sometimes within the allophonic range of /a/, /i/ or /u/ (§2.1.2), depending on the vowel in the previous syllable, to which it assimilates. Examples are:

(128) ngangga'widag(a)
      give to PAST-3sg<3nsg-YHA-pl
      They gave to him/her.

(129) jira'wunggurrugu
      fall FUT-2nsg-WU-pl
      You (pl) will fall.

(130) ngiyirrimuway-yawu   ban̲ga'iyirrayg
      We (R)   camp-ALL   go back 1R-RA-PAST-pl
      We went back to the camp.

For other examples see (4), (14), (15), (79), (107), (111), (118), (120), (122); §6.1 lines 1, 10, 11, 13, 14, 20, 23; and §6.2 lines 2 and 14.

    Note that when the plural suffix is used with 1R as in (130) it in effect distinguishes between first person dual and first person plural exclusive, as there must be more than two referents (cf. §3.3.1 regarding the independent pronouns, and §3.4.4b above for a cross-cutting inclusive-exclusive distinction within the dual number).

3.4.7   SUBORDINATE CLAUSE MARKER. In order class 11, any verb which is in a textually appropriate position may take a suffix -nya, which marks the clause in which it occurs as a subordinate one. For examples, see (30) and §4.4.1. Though the position of this suffix is relatively central within the verb complex, its function lies at the level of sentence syntax. See §4.4.1 for discussion.

3.4.8   PROXIMAD SUFFIX. In order class 12 (or sometimes 13 or 14), any verb of motion may take a suffix -ali which specifies that the motion is toward the speaker. The suffix is similar in form to the postposition described in §3.2.1i, but with a somewhat different function. For examples of this suffix, see (21), (189), (236), and §6.2, line 21. Other examples are:

(131)   nyirraji-nhingi   banga'ray-ali
        that-ABL   return 3sg-RA-PAST-PROX
        After that he came back this way.

(132)   yuwurra'wurrmiynhali   muwurru-ngarri
        rush in 3nsg-MA-PAST-3sgOBL-PROX   club-COM1
        They rushed in this way towards him with clubs.

As illustrated by (132), the a of ali displaces any preceding vowel (in this case the i of 3sg OBL nhi).

Sometimes the relevant orientation toward the speaker is not in the spatial context of the actual speech situation, but in that of some narrated event into which the speaker is projecting himself as though he were there. This is true, for example of (132) above, which came as the climax of a story about a wife stealer. The culprit has been chased and chased by a mob of offended husbands, who have finally caught up with him and rush in for the kill with clubs after he has managed to dodge all their spears. The narrator tells the story from the viewpoint of the wife stealer, enlivening it by talking as though he were right there next to the protagonist — a practice commonly used by good story tellers around the world (compare, for example, Hanks 1990 regarding Mayan Indians).

3.4.9   OBLIQUE PRONOMINAL SUFFIXES. In order class 13 (or sometimes 12 or 14), any verb may take an optional pronominal suffix referring to another participant besides the one(s) referred to by the pronominal prefixes: a person or thing which is involved in the action, state or relation predicated by the verb, but in a less central role than the one(s) referred to by the prefixes. The wide range of functions served by these suffixes is discussed and exemplified in §4.1.1. In form, they are identical to the independent oblique pronouns shown in Table 3.2, with one partial exception: the 3sg form -nhi/-nhu has an alternative form -nhingi, which has no free standing counterpart (but which makes it identical to the Ablative case postposition, in both of *its* variants; see §3.2.1e). The choice between these two allomorphs seems to be largely a matter of free variation except that -nhingi is seldom if ever used when the verb is also marked with a following continuative aspect suffix. For examples of the use of oblique pronominal suffixes, see (18), (23), (32), (114), (116) and (132).

3.4.10 CONTINUATIVE ASPECT. In order class 14 (or sometimes 13 or 12), any verb (as far as I know) can take a suffix -ngarri, which indicates that the action, state or relation predicated by the verb is one which is spread out in time: one which takes place continuously or as a matter of course. For examples, see (6), (10), (11), (18), (19), (28), (30), (40), (41), (44) - (48) and (52). This suffix is identical in form to the Comitative1 suffix (§3.2.1g). There is perhaps some commonality of meaning between these two morphemes, insofar as both have as one of their uses a kind of *characterising* function. Compare for example the adnominal and derivational uses of COM1 discussed in §3.2.1g ('eyed one' for 'magician', 'egged (i.e., big-balled) one' for dog, etc.) with continuative verb examples such as (19), (30), (41) and (47) which describe characteristic activities of, respectively, Aboriginal women, Aboriginal men, 'scrub men', and 'olden days blackfellas'.

3.4.11 ITERATIVE ASPECT. In order class 2 (immediately following the preverb), semantically appropriate verb complexes may take a suffix -wa/-ba, which indicates that the event or process described is one which takes place as a series of repetitions of the same action. This suffix occurs far less frequently than the continuative aspect suffix, and almost always in combination with one of the two atelic roots RA or RA2 (§3.4.1). It is perhaps at the borderline between being an inflectional suffix and a derivational one, in that the meaning of iterative-marked expressions is sometimes not fully predictable from the sum of their parts, as for example in (137). An interesting intermediate case is the contrast between daliya+MA2, 'to name' and daliyba+RA2 'to call, refer to as —', where the former refers to a unique event which establishes the name, and the latter to the repeated uses of it (see (28)).

There are also some preverbs ending in -ba or -wa which occur *only* in that form, e.g., warrba (+WU2) 'flog', rirrwa (+RA2) 'pull', nyunba (+YHA/RA2) 'rub on', 'paint', where the final syllable perhaps originated from an iterative suffix but can no longer be analysed as one.

The -ba variant of the iterative suffix occurs after stops, nasals and y, and the -wa variant elsewhere. Examples are:

(133) nangguraj-ba'ngay
       limp-ITR 1sg-RA-PAST
       I limped along.

(134) waya-wa'ngay
       sing out-ITR 1sg-RA-PAST
       I kept singing out.

(135) dangaj-ba'a
       hit/kill-ITR PRES-3sg<3sg-RA2
       He's bashing him.

(136) burij-ba'yirrayngarri
       play-ITR 1R-PAST-1R-CTV
       We'd play about.

(137) mila-wa'ranhi
       look-ITR PRES-3sg-RA-3sgOBL
       He's looking around for him.

Compare: (138) mila'a
                 look 3sg<3sg-RA2
                 He's looking at him.

In (136) the iterative marker on the preverb occurs along with the continuative marker in the same verb complex, the combination meaning something like 'do repeatedly for a long time or on a regular basis' (this particular example comes from a story by Nancy Rogers about what she used do on bush trips with her grandmothers; in Kimberley Language Resource Centre forthcoming).

The iterative suffix sometimes occurs on preverbs not accompanied by an auxiliary, when they are being used with the dative postposition in a purposive construction (§3.2.1b; see also §4.4.2). An example is:

(139)   ganba'wurra   dangaj-ba-u
         follow/chase 3sg<3nsg-RA2   hit/kill-ITR-DAT
         They chased him in order to bash him up

3.4.12 VERBAL QUALIFICATION. In final position on the preverb (order class 3) or the inflected auxiliary (class 15) any verb complex may take one of a set of adverb-like modifying suffixes which I call 'qualifiers'. Most of these are not used very often, and I don't have a big enough sample to allow many firm generalisations, but it is clear that at least some of them can occur alternatively on either the preverb or the auxiliary, while some are used mainly (and some perhaps exclusively) on the preverb. All of the verbal qualifying suffixes I know of can also occur on words of other classes in similar or identical form with related or identical meanings. The suffixes with identical forms on words of other classes are described in §3.5.2. Here I will describe two qualifying suffixes which have somewhat different forms when they occur on verbs.

[a] *REPetition suffix* -yha(y)/tha(y)/ya(y)/ja(y).   This suffix has a wide range of meanings on words of all classes (see §3.5.2a below and compare McGregor's (1990:459–74) much fuller treatment of a functionally very similar morpheme in Gooniyandi; cf. also Rumsey (1982b:130-1) for the Ungarinyin cognate). On verbs, it is usually glossed as 'again'.

In most environments, the first two variants of this suffix, with lamino-dental consonants, are in free or dialectal variation with the other two (with lamino-palatals) as described in §1.2 and §2.1.2 (compare the yh/y variation in the root YHA, §3.4.1). Among speakers who use the yh variant elsewhere, there seems to be a tendency to avoid it when the previous syllable has a lamino-dental consonant, as illustrated by some of the gaps in the examples below. Within both the lamino-dental pair and the lamino-palatal one, the variant with a stop consonant occurs in the usual hardening environments, and the one with y or yh elsewhere. For all four variants, the presence or absence of the final y is, as far as I know, a matter of free variation. Even single speakers use both alternatively in some of the same environments. Some of the examples of this suffix which I have recorded (mostly from elicitation) are:

(140) yatha-ya'ra   (141) wad-thay(/jay)'way
       sit-REP 3sg-RA-PRES   go-REP FUT-3sg-RA-exc
       He's sitting down again.   He must go again.

(142) nginjaga giyga-yha(/ya)'inthi
       why   get up-REP 2sg-NI-PRES
       Why are you getting up again?

(143) ngag'ayi-yay
       eat 3sg<3sg-RA2-PAST-REP
       He ate [it] again.

Sometimes this suffix when used on the auxiliary is glossed as 'still' rather than 'again'. For example, compare the following with (140) (both with glosses as provided by Johnny Marr):

(144) yatha'ra-yhay
       sit 3sg-RA-REP
       He's still sitting down.

For other examples of the the REPetition suffix, see (7), (14), (15) and (112).

[b] *LINKing suffix* -nga. I have recorded this suffix in this form only on preverbs, where it seems to be a reduced version of a suffix -ngana, which occurs with the same value on preverbs, and on words of other classes as well (§3.5.2b). Its function is to link the meaning of the verb to something that has come before it in the text. Examples are:

(145) ngangga'yanbida   gula-nga'wada
       give to PAST-1U<3nsg-YHA try-LINK FUT-1U-YHA
       They gave it to us, so we'll try [to make something of it].

(146) ngayag'gina   wula-nga'wulunu
       ask PRES-1sg<3sg-RA2   talk-LINK FUT-3sg<1sg-WU2-exc
       He's asking me, so I'll answer him.

When I repeated (146) without the -nga suffix and asked Johnny Marr how the meaning would differ, he said the second part would then just mean 'I'll talk to him'.

3.5   OTHER PARTS OF SPEECH. The other parts of speech besides nouns, pronouns and verbs are morphologically simple, and in general are distinguished more by how they do or don't combine with other elements in the clause than by their own internal form (see §3.1 for details). Here I will provide just a few examples of each, referring the reader to §4 for further details regarding their uses within the clause.

3.5.1   ADVERBS. These are independent words which modify or further specify the meaning of the verb or clause. As far as I know, they may occur at any position within the clause. The relevant dimensions of meaning include at least the following:

[a] *Time*. Examples are:

(147) **garrwaru**   wa(d̲>)n̲'ngay   janjuwa-yawu
afternoon/yesterday   go 1sg-RA-PAST   Junjuwa-ALL
Yesterday I went to Junjuwa.

(148) wirray   nawanu-yuwa   baga'irayngarri   **jirali**
hill.kangaroo   cave-LOC   stay 3sg-RA-PAST-CTV   before
Before [a long time ago] a hill kangaroo was stopping in a cave.

(149) **warra**   mila'winya
by.and.by   see FUT-2sg<1sg-RA2
I'll see you by and by.

For further examples, see (10) and (199).

[b] *Spatial Orientation*. Examples are:

(150) rirrwa'yirrantha   **baburru**   wal̲ibirri-yawu
pull/drag PAST-3sg<1R-RA2-du   down   [Fitzroy] river-ALL
We dragged it [a big hill kangaroo they had killed] down to the river.

(151) yawad̲a-yuwa   garra'larriy   **rawurra**
Horse-LOC   throw 3sg<1sg-NGARRI-PAST   up
I threw him up on to the horse.

For further examples, see (38) and §6.1, line 16.

[c] *Manner*. Examples are:

(152) **walinggan̲i** nyaga'lunu
half way   spear 3sg<1sg-WU2-PAST
I speared him halfway [i.e, wounded him with out killing him].

(153) **yilngarri**   girrgira'miy
altogether   run away 3sg-MA-PAST
She ran away altogether.

Other examples are baliya 'going quickly', barrba 'going on foot', yungu 'sort of, a little bit' and madijay 'truly'. For more, see §7.1.w.

3.5.2   MODE PARTICLES. The line between adverbs and particles is difficult to draw for Bunuba according to the usual criterion of open versus closed class membership, as there are not many adverbs, and it is not clear that they are an open-ended class. But a class of *mode* particles can be clearly distinguished from adverbs and other word classes on syntactic grounds, in that they are strictly ordered with respect to the verb complex, and do not occur with verbs of all six of the tense/mode categories, but only with certain ones of them. Bunuba does not seem to have as many such words as the neighbouring language Ungarinyin (Rumsey 1982b:166–76), no doubt at least in part because it has a richer system of tense/mode marking within the verb complex (§3.3.4). But there are at least two words which would seem to qualify as mode particles under this definition.

[a] ngayi 'not'. The uses of ngayi as a negative particle have already been extensively illustrated in §3.4.4c. When it occurs in construction with verbs they are always of irrealis mode (in any of its three tenses), and it always precedes the verb. (It is also used as a negating element in combination with words of other classes at the phrase level, for which see §4.2.2; and as an interjection, as in §7.1z).

[b] mayhay 'maybe'. This particle is rare in comparison to the functionally similar suffix -yarra (§3.5.3f). In all my examples it occurs before the verb, which is in indicative mode or future tense/mode. Examples are:

(154)   mayhay   winya'yina
         maybe   hear PAST-1sg<2sg-RA2
         Maybe you listened to me.

(155)   mayhay wad'buwurrayg
         maybe   go FUT-3nsg-RA-exc-pl
         Maybe they will go.

3.5.3   QUALIFYING CLITICS. These have already been introduced in §3.4.12, where I described two of them which occur in variant forms which are specific to the verb. Here I will describe the variants of those two morphemes that occur on words of other classes, and some other qualifying clitics that occur in the same form on verbs as elsewhere. When occurring on words of other classes, as on preverbs and auxiliaries, the qualifying clitics always come last, following all suffixes or postpositions if there are any. With words of all classes, the meaning of most or all of these clitics often applies to a larger chunk of text than just the word they are attached to, as will be evident from the examples below.

[a] *REPetition* (compare §3.4.12a). The allomorphs of this suffix on words other than verbs are iya/ya/iyha/yha. Appropriate English glosses for it vary widely according to context, as evident from the examples below (see Rumsey 1982b:130–1 and McConvell 1983 for close parallels from Ungarinyin and Gurindji, and McGregor 1990:459–74 for a very thorough and revealing analysis of a functionally similar morpheme in Gooniyandi.)

(156)   ngindaji   julungurru-**yha**   gurama
         this   good-REP   man
         This is the man who's good.

(157)   diyga'wunarriyngarri   ngaala-**ya**   gurama
         find 3nsg<3sg-NGARRI-PAST-CTV other/different-REP   man
         He keeps finding yet another mob of men. [Compare the common Aboriginal English expression 'different again'.]

(158)   nyunba'wurrangarri   nyirraji-ingga-**ya**
rub 3sg<3nsg-RA2-CTV   that-INST-REP
They would rub it with that stuff too.

(159)   nginji-**ya** yingiy   baga'nggira   jurrguna
you-REP   name   stay/be 2sg-RA-PRES   [country name]
You yourself have the name Jurrguna.

(160)   nyanangarri-**ya** balbala'wurrmiy
many-REP   flee 3nsg-MA-PAST
All of them fled. [cf nyanangarri balbala wurrmiy, 'Many fled']

(161)   nhu-**iya**   janda'mayni
3sgOBL-REP   pierce 3sg-MA2-REFL-PAST
He stabbed himself on purpose.

[b] *LINKing* (compare §3.4.12b). The form this clitic takes on
words other than preverbs (and sometimes there as well) is -ngana. It is
usually glossed as 'and', 'so' or 'or' [in the inclusive sense: 'maybe this,
maybe that, maybe both']. Examples are:

(162)   jabil-**ngana** wadba'yi(rr>)nmangarri   banda-**ngana**
shovel-LINK   get PAST-3sg<1R-MA2-CTV   dirt-LINK
thuruga'yidangarri
cover/bury PAST-3sg<1R-YHA-CTV
So we'd get a shovel and pack dirt in around it [the fence post].

(163)   mingali-ingga   gaygaytha'yirrangarri   nginjaga-ma-**ngana**
hand-INST   cut PAST-3sg<1R-RA2-CTV   what-INT-LINK
We used to cut [fenceposts], or do whatever, by hand.

(164)   rayl nyana-nyana bawij-**ngana**   jamurrga'yhangarri
rail   big-REDUP   post-LINK   pile.up PAST-3sg<3sg-YHA-CTV
He'd stack up a big pile of rails and fence posts.

For another example, see §6.2, line 16.

[c] *INTerrogative/indefinite* -ma. The most frequent use of this clitic
is to form yes/no questions. Examples are:

(165)   ngurru-**ma**   yatha'ra   bang-juwa
that one[distal, see §3.3.2a]-INT   sit PRES-3sg-RA   bunk-LOC
Is that him sitting over there on the bunk?

(166)   ngayaga-ma'iyma   (167)   ngayini-**ma**
ask-INT PAST-3sg<2sg-MA2   I/me-INT
Have you asked him?   [Who] me?

A related, and perhaps more basic function of this clitic is to mark something as indefinite or unknown (cf. §3.3.2b regarding the interrogative/indefinite pronouns). An example is:

(168) nya<u>na</u> bulumana wad'burrangarri   ngaa-**ma**
       big   bullock   take 3sg<3nsg-RA2-CTV   where-INT
       They would take those big bullocks somewhere.

[d] *SEMblative* -jangi. This clitic is used to form expressions which liken something to something else. Examples are:

(169) baljarrangi-**jangi** ba<u>ndi</u>y   (170) nya<u>na</u>wulu-**jangi**
       boomerang-SEM   arm(s)   big   paperbark-SEM
       arms like a returning boomerang [i.e., crooked]   big as a paperbark tree

(171) ma<u>l</u>ngarri-u-**jangi** thanga<u>ni</u> wirriwirriy'wurrmag-wiya
       white people-DAT-SEM language scratch/write 3sg<3nsg-MA2-pl-DEF
       Now they write it [Bunuba] just like white people's languages.

(172) warara'yay   yaninga-**jangi**
       walk around 3sg-RA-PAST   now-SEM
       He walked around just like [they do] now.

(173) ga<u>lga</u>l_a-**jangi**'miy
       laugh-SEM 3sg-MA-PAST
       He smiled.

[e] *DEFinite* -wiya. This clitic usually can be glossed as 'definitely' or 'completely' (cf. McGregor 1990:487, 339–43). Examples are:

(174) baga'ra-**wiya**   winthali
       stay 3sg-RA-PRES-DEF   fire
       Fire remains for all time [for context see §6.1; line 19].

(175) niy-**wiya** yatha'rangarri
       he-DEF   sit 3sg-RA-PRES-CTV
       He's sitting by himself.

Just as the uses of -yarra ([f] below) overlap considerably with those of the mode particle mayhay (§3.5.2b), so those of -wiya overlap with those of the adverb yilngarri (§3.5.1c). The two sometimes occur in combination, as in the following, which also exemplifies the use of -wiya on a preverb, and twice in the same clause.

(176) yilngarri-**wiya**   yatha-**wiya**'ngira   ngi<u>nda</u>-yuwa
       completely-DEF   sit-DEF 1sg-RA-PRES   here-LOC
       I stay here for good.

Six clauses later in the same text, the same speaker (Johnny Marr) said ngi<u>nda</u>-yuwa yatha'wurrayg-wiya 'They stay here for good'. Here and elsewhere (see also (174)), I have not been able to discover any difference in meaning according to whether -wiya is put on the preverb or on the auxiliary.

[f] -yarra/-jarra 'perhaps'. Examples are:

(177)   lu<u>nd</u>u-**yarra**   wara'ra   yiyirrmiynhingi
         tree-perhaps   stand.up 3sg-RA-PRES   1R-MA-PAST-3sgOBL
         We thought maybe he was a tree standing up there.

(178)   garrga-**yarra**'wanbini
         leave-perhaps FUT-1U<3sg-WU2-exc
         He might leave us.

(179)   thurranda muway-**yarra** nyirra-yuwa   baga'yiyirray
         two   camp/day-perhaps   that.one-LOC   camp 1R-RA-PAST
         We camped there for perhaps two days.

[g] -miya 'only', 'just', 'exactly'. Examples are:

(180)   wiyi-**miya**   lamajga'yhangarri
         woman-ON   pick.up 3sg<3sg-YHA-PAST-CTV
         He picked up only the woman.

(181)   warra-**miya**   diyga'larriyngarri   mu<u>l</u>u-ingga
         later.on-ON   find 3sg<1sg-NGARRI-PAST-CTV   eye-INST
         Only later did I discover them [mythic turkey eggs] with my own eyes.

(182)   ngurru-**miya**   brayga'yiyirrayngarri   *dob* lumunggan
         that/there-ON   arrive 1R-RA-PAST-CTV   [place name]
         Then we'd come out right there at Top Limungan.

[h] -ala / -gala 'first', 'before'. Both variants are found, apparently in free variation, after vowels and y. After other consonants only the -ala variant occurs. Examples are:

(183)   nginji   yatha'wura   ngi<u>nd</u>aji-**ala**
         you   sit FUT-2sg-RA   this.one-first
         You stay there; [let] this one [go] first.

(184)   niy-**ala** (also attested as niy-**gala**) wad'jay
         he-first   go 3sg RA-PAST
         He went first.

(185)   *miydwag*   nyirraji-**ala**   yatha'iray
         meatwork   that.one-first   sit/be 3sg-RA-PAST
         There used to be a meatworks there before.

3.5.4 INTERJECTIONS. Phonologically aberrant interjections include: gaj 'Come on!' (no other independent words end in stops); ag'a 'not so' (no other independent words begin with a vowel or are stressed on the last syllable if they have more than one); āy 'Aha! ', 'I see' (aberrant initial vowel and nasalisation) and ngāy 'yes, that's right' (nasalisation). For some other common interjections, see §7.1z.

4.   SYNTAX

4.1   SENTENCE TYPES.

4.1.1   SIMPLE SENTENCES WHICH INCLUDE A VERB. The most common types of simple sentence in Bunuba - those which include a verb - have already been briefly introduced at the beginning of §3. As will be clear from that description and from the many examples in §3.4, any well-formed verb complex can stand by itself as a grammatically complete clause or sentence in Bunuba (as in other prefixing languages of northern Australia). But all such verb complexes may also be accompanied in the same clause by one or two NPs referring to the same participants which are also referred to ('cross-referenced') by the pronominal prefixes on the verb. When they are present, those NPs function partly to provide further information about the identity of the participants. For example in (3), the presence of the noun gurama tells us that the one who stood up was not just someone other than the speaker, but that it was a man.

But through their case marking (§3.2.1), cross-referenced NPs also tell us something about the nature of the role played by their referents in the event or state of affairs described by the verb. This information may seem entirely redundant, merely duplicating information which is already encoded in the verb by the pronominal prefixes, with their distinct forms for each of the roles S, A and O. But this is not so. For ergative case marking is not limited to NPs in construction with bivalent verbs, but is sometimes also used on NPs which are functioning as the subject of *mono*valent verbs (especially when these include an OBLique suffix). Moreover the apparent 'agent' of a double-prefixed, bivalent verb sometimes appears in absolutive rather than ergative case. In short, there are two systems of case roles implemented by NP marking versus verb marking, with partial, but not full overlap between them.

In order to see how they differ, it is useful first to look at the verb-marking system on its own, to see what kind of roles are associated with each kind of pronominal prefix. As a preliminary to this, consider the forms of the prefixes. For simplicity's sake, in my morpheme by morpheme glosses of bivalent verbs, I have treated the double pronominal prefixes as single units, with labels such as 3sg<1sg, 1R>2sg, etc., where the arrow points from what I have called 'subject' to 'object'. But it can be readily seen from Tables 3.6a-c that most of the bivalent prefixes can be broken down into two elements, one for each of the two cross-referenced participants. Where this is the case, comparison with Tables 3.4 and 3.5 shows that the monovalent prefixes generally resemble the bit of the bivalent prefix which cross-references the performer of the action rather than its undergoer (e.g. 1sg -I-, 2nsg -y-/-j-, 1U yarr).   Furthermore the bit corresponding to the under-goer of the action often differs from the other one by the addition of -n (perhaps a surviving trace of an old accusative marker). This evidence is partial but as far as it goes it supports the positing of a common category of 'subject' for monovalent and bivalent verbs which identifies S with A rather than with O.

This is also supported by the distribution of the 'exclusive' suffix (§3.4.4b), which when occurring with a bivalent verb is conditioned solely by the nature of its subject (as for monovalent verbs), not its object. This evidence is stronger than that provided by the form of the pronominal prefixes, as it applies across the full range of person/number combinations for subject and object, whereas the forms of the prefixes identify S with A for most but not all such combinations (some failing to provide clear evidence for the pairing of *any* two of the three terms S, A and O).

Now that I have clarified what I mean by 'subject' as opposed to 'object', let us consider the range of ways in which participants of those kinds figure in the events, relations, or states of affairs predicated by the verb complexes in which they figure (still limiting the discussion for now to participant role-marking by pronominal prefixes only).

Examples of monovalent verb complexes in grammatically complete clauses without any accompanying subject NP include (1), (2), (12), (13), (16), (19), (21), (22), (24), (29), (33), (37), (38), (39), (40), (42), (45), (49), (52)–(78), (99), (100), (103), (25), (104), (107)–(114), (117), (119), (126), (129), (131)–(134), (136), (137), (140)–(142), (144), (147), (153), (155), (172), (173), (176), (179) and (182). A look at these examples (which are typical of the semantic range of monovalent verbs; cf. §7.1p-v) shows that what the great majority predicate of the subject is some kind of movement through space ('go', 'come', 'leave', 'stand up', 'run', 'limp along', arrive', etc.), state of being, ('lie', 'sit' 'stay', 'itch', etc.) or change of state ('grow up', 'get mad', 'die', etc.). A smaller, but still sizeable number predicate actions which may be performed without an overall movement through space ('call out', 'sing', 'cry', 'paint up', 'smile', etc.). What all of them have in common is that the states or actions they describe need not involve more than one participant.

Bivalent verb complexes in clauses without accompanying subject or object NPs include (5), (6), (17), (25), (26), (27), (28), (31), (41), (79)–(98), (101), (105), (115), (118), (120), (128), (135), (138), (139), (146), (149), (150), (151), (152), (154), (178) and (181). A look at these examples again reveals a wide variety of predicates ('raise', 'try/test', 'cut', 'take', 'hit', 'pull up', chop', 'scoop', 'work', 'eat', 'spear' 'see', etc.; cf. §7.1r-v). All of them have in common that they can and *almost* always do explicitly involve two participants in distinct roles, one corresponding to the subject pronominal prefix and one to the object prefix. The exceptions to this are of two kinds. First, there are examples such as (25) and (41), where the object is not explicit, and the 3sg object prefix is arguably being used as a 'dummy' element in an order class which must be filled because of the choice of a bivalent root (class 15); rather like the 'it' in English 'It's raining' (cf. §3.4.5 regarding the prefixes used for reflexive/reciprocal verbs). The second kind of exception, the inverse of the first, are verbs such as jirrbala+WU2 'be in pain', which cross-reference the experiencer of the pain in object position, and take dummy 3sg subject prefixes which never cross-reference an explicit subject NP.

The grammatical subject of the bivalent verb (as specified by the formal criteria discussed above) is almost always the initiator and controller of the predicated action or process, and the grammatical object an undergoer of it without control over it (exceptions include walanggala+RA2 'lose, forget about'; yajili+RA2 'dream (about)'; dawungga+MA2 'like').

In short, with no more fudging than is usual on the part of linguists, Bunuba monovalent and bivalent verbs may be described as 'intransitive' and 'transitive' respectively. So why haven't I done so, insisting instead on the less usual terms 'monovalent' and 'bivalent'? To see why, we must first turn to a consideration of the other system of participant role marking, which is realised mainly by ergative versus absolutive case marking on the NP.

So far (since we have been concerned mainly with morphology) there have been only three examples of clauses with bivalent verbs and explicit NP subjects: (4), (8) and (14). Some more examples are:

(186) ngindaji-ingga   gurama gayga'wuma   winthali
       this-ERG   man   chop FUT-3sg<3sg-MA2 firewood
       This man has to cut the firewood.

(187) winthali-ingga   biyga'nginda   thinga
       fire-ERG   burn 1sg<3sg-YHA-PAST foot
       The fire burned my foot.

(188) nyirra-ingga   bananggarra'wunu
       that one-ERG   steal 3sg<3sg-WU2-PAST
       That one stole her [another man's wife].

In each of these examples, the NP which is cross-referenced by the subject pronominal is marked with the ergative postposition. This is almost always the case in clauses of this kind (i.e., with bivalent verb and overt NP subject). In a sample of 135 such clauses, that occurred over approximately five hundred pages of Bunuba text, the NP subject of the bivalent verb was ergatively marked in 124, or 92 per cent of them. In all of the other eleven examples, the subject NP was in unmarked, absolutive form, just as for the subjects of monovalent verbs. Examples are:

(189) *jidniy gidman*   yungga'windagali
       Sidney Kidman   send.ahead/let go PAST-3nsg<3sg-YHA-pl-PROX
       Sidney Kidman sent them ahead in this direction.

(190) jirali gurama gudaya'wunbunungarri   wiyi
       before man   try/keep after 3nsg<3sg-WU2-PAST-CTV women
       The olden-days man used to keep after women [i.e. wouldn't take no for an answer].

What are we to make of examples such as these? Infrequent as they are, the absence of the ergative marker in them cannot be dismissed as a mistake, for Bunuba speakers when presented with them regard them as fully grammatical. Rather, the difference between the absence of the ergative marker here and its presence in the examples such as (186) to (188) is a meaningful one, which can be related to the *degree* of transitivity of the clause as a whole, as per Hopper and Thompson (1980). For Hopper and Thompson, transitivity is not a matter of a simple two-way distinction between transitive and intransitive verbal categories, but a scale along which a number of different aspects of the clause's meaning tend to vary together. These include: 1) punctuality (whether the action takes place at a point in time or over an extended duration); 2) telicity (whether the action reaches a distinct endpoint or goal); 3) the degree of individuation of the object (definite versus indefinite, referential versus non-referential); and 4) the degree to which the object is affected by the action.

In my sample, all eleven of the exceptional clauses such as (189) and (190) are, for clauses with bivalent verbs, relatively low in transitivity according to at least one of Hopper and Thompson's criteria, and unusually high in none. Sentences (189) and (190), for example, are low in punctuality and telicity, and of indetermimate object-affectedness. Their objects are also fairly low in individuation, the 3nsg prefix in (189) referring to a participant that has been introduced in the previous clause only as biyirri   nyanangarri 'They, a big mob', and the referent of wiyi in (190) being generic rather than specific. None of the other nine examples involves a verb of violent impact, or predicates an action which consumes or extinguishes the object.

Now let us consider the other, converse kind of 'exceptional' clause, in which the ergative marker is conspicuous by its presence rather than by its absence, that is, when it appears on the subject of a monovalent verb. An example is:

(191)   niy-ingga   waḏʼjay
         the.former-ERG   come 3sg-RA-PAST
         He [previously mentioned] came up.

This comes from a story in which Emu is deprived of food while all the other birds are allowed to eat. Finally he is permitted to come and get some on condition that he eat only a little and leave the rest for Peaceful Dove. The clause in (191) comes at the point in the story when Emu has eaten a little and been told to leave the rest. The presence of the ergative marker on niy which refers to Emu, can perhaps be related to the established presence by this point within the text of a highly salient *goal* (the food) towards which Emu's movement is directed. It is also relevant to consider what comes immediately after (191) in the story, which is:

(192)   dagurra'waniy   waḻibirri-yawu   ngag'gira
         go.down 3sg-WU-PAST   river-ALL   eat PAST-3sg<3sg-RA2
         He went down to the river.   He ate it.

Somewhat unexpectedly, there is no explicit mention between (191) and (192) of Emu actually taking the food. But given what happens in the second clause of (192), it is obvious that he has done so. Within the sequence of (191) and (192) as a whole, the ergative marker in (191) may perhaps be understood both as the marker of agency in an implicit act of taking, and as an 'anticipatory' ergative marker for the Agent of ngag'gira especially given that there is no other intervening NP after (191) referring to the same participant (cf. Haviland 1979:154ff. on 'ergative hopping'). In any case, the food which is the object ngag'gira, as a key 'participant' in the story, remains given as a definite referent without any overt NP referring to it in that clause, just as our understanding of (191) can presuppose it as Emu's implicit goal.

Indeed ergative marking in Bunuba always presupposes another participant in the clause besides the one referred to by the ergative-marked NP, regardless of whether its verb is monovalent or bivalent. To see the evidence for this, we need to consider some other, more typical examples.

Although it is not at all unusual in Bunuba for ergative marking to occur with monovalent verbs, (191) is very unusual in one respect. Usually in such clauses, the verb occurs with an oblique pronominal suffix (§3.4.9). An example is (18). Others are (193) to (195).

(193) wariyga'waniynhingi   gayangurru-ingga
       start out 3sg-WU-PAST-3sgOBL   echidna-ERG
       The echidna started out towards him.

(194) nyirraji-ingga   baga'ranganggi
       this one-ERG   sleep 3sg-RA-PRES-2sgOBL
       This one is sleeping with your wife [lit., sleeping, affecting you].

(195) nyaga'wuninya-ingga   gurama
       spear 3sg<3sg-WU2-PAST-SUB-ERG   man
         gamanba'raynhi
         hunt.around [for] 3sg-RA-PAST-3sgOBL
       The man who speared him was looking around for him.

In terms of Hopper and Thompson's criterion of 'affectedness' of the object, these clauses are clearly lower in transitivity than examples such as (186) to (188) where the ergative-marked NP occurs with a bivalent verb. Both sets of examples are typical in this respect: as will be apparent from the discussion of pronominal prefixes above, clauses with bivalent verbs do tend to be higher in Hopper and Thompson-style transitivity than those with monovalent verbs; and this is true even when the monovalent verb is accompanied by an OBLique suffix and/or an ergative marked subject NP. But within the range of transitivity displayed by clauses with monovalent verbs and overt NP subjects, there is a further division between those with ergative marking and those without it. These are of higher and lower transitivity respectively, insofar as those with ergative marking implicate a second object-like participant that ranks relatively highly in terms of Hopper and Thompson's other object property: individuation (definiteness and referentiality). For example, compare (18) 'He came to the corpse' with (20) 'The man went for food'. These two clauses are very similar in that both use the same verb, wad+RA 'come'/'go', with an allative-marked NP referring to a goal of the action. But the goal NPs differ in both definiteness and referentiality, which is associated with the difference between Ergative subject marking in (18) and Absolutive in (20) (cf. also (130)).

Returning now to the question of why I have avoided using the terms 'transitive' and 'intransitive' in reference to verbs, it should be clear that there is only a very loose fit between the kind of agent-object relations that are marked on the NP and those that are marked on the verb. The difference is not just one of differential mapping of A, S and O onto Ergative (A) and Absolutive (S, O) case for the former versus subject (S, A) and object (O) for the latter. Rather, there is not a single, common set of S, A and O categories which underlies the different pairings. Instead there are two sets of more or less overlapping basic categories which operate at distinct levels: the verb-marking system at the level of the verb complex and the NP-marking system (with the help of the pronominal clitics) at the level of the clause and beyond. The former is true in that the choice of pronominal prefixes, which realise the verb's version of S, A and O roles, is entirely determined by the choice of verb root. When the root is one of the five bivalent ones (even if reflexivised), the prefixed pronominals *must* be from the bivalent set, with distinct form classes for A and O (§3.4.3b), and when it is monovalent, they must be from the monovalent set, with a single form class for S (§3.4.3a). Given these formal constraints, there is no room for variable treatment of A and O according to the *degree* of semantic or pragmatic transitivity of the clause in which the verb occurs. Rather, the prefixes operate in conjunction with the specific meanings of preverbs and their paired roots, in terms of which Bunuba speakers know, for example, that the experiencer of pain is the grammatical *object* of the verb jirrbala+WU2 'be in pain', and an experiencer of pleasure the grammatical *subject* of dawungga+MA2 'like'. By comparison to the choice between monovalent and bivalent prefixes, the choice between ergative and absolutive marking for subject NPs is far less highly constrained by the choice of verb root or preverb. Grammatically, the only absolute requirement for ergative marking is that there *be* a subject NP, that is, one cross-referenced by a subject pronominal prefix (which in practice is usually, but by no means always, from the bivalent set). There must also be an object (though it needn't be present as an NP in the clause), and if the verb is bivalent, that object can only be the participant which is cross-referenced in object position. If the verb is monovalent, the object is almost always cross-referenced by an (otherwise optional) OBLique pronominal clitic. Where the object of such a clause (with monovalent verb) is also present as an NP, it is usually marked with an oblique case postposition, the most common one being allative, as in (18) and (193), and the second most common one being dative.

The discussion so far may be summarised by saying that the grammar of basic participant roles in Bunuba is characterised by two cross-cutting distinctions, one a simple two-way division between monovalent versus bivalent verb prefixation and the other a sliding scale of multiple co-varying properties of the clause which together comprise its 'transitivity'. The four types of clause which result in these two distinctions are shown in Table 4.1 on the following page. (To simplify the presentation, the verb prefixes have been omitted, but it is to be understood that verbs in the first column have monovalent prefixes cross-referencing the ergative or absolutive NP,

TABLE 4.1 *Major Bunuba Clause Types*

Verb: Clause:	Monovalent	Bivalent
High transitivity	NP-ERG V$_1$-OBL NP(-obl) e.g.,(18),(192),(193)	NP-ERG V$_2$ NP-ABS e.g., (186)–(188)
Low Transitivity	NP-ABS V$_1$ (NP-obl) e.g., (1),(20),(130)	NP-ABS V$_2$ NP-ABS e.g., (189),(190)

V$_1$ monovalent verb (i.e. with obligatory subject prefix)
V$_2$ bivalent verb (i.e. with obligatory subject and object prefixes)
OBL   oblique pronominal suffix to verb
obl   oblique case nominal postposition (dative, allative, etc.)

and those in the second column have bivalent prefixes cross-referencing the ergative or one absolutive NP as subject and an absolutive NP as object. The word order shown is not to be taken as a significant indicator of participant role relations.)

4.1.2   SIMPLE SENTENCES WITHOUT VERBS. Most Bunuba sentences have a verb, but unlike in English, not every sentence in Bunuba requires one. Those which do not have one generally consist of two juxtaposed NPs, the referents of which are being equated with each other, or where the referent of the first is being characterised by the second (see McGregor 1990:292–317 for a very full treatment of similar sentences in Gooniyandi). Examples are (196) to (198). For another example, see (156).

(196)   nginda ligi jinjinarra   muway
        that   west [place name]   place
        There to the west is the place [called] Jinjinarra.

(197)   *linrawi*   bunuba-ngarri-miya
        Linroy [Station]   Bunuba-COM1-ON
        Linroy Station is/has only Bunuba.

(198)   ngindaji ngarragi jimarri
        this   my   friend
        This is my friend.

Some verbless sentences include additional elements besides just the two NPs. This is illustrated by (199), where, in the absence of a verb to carry the tense marking, the speaker (Billy Oscar) uses a temporal adverb.

(199)   ngi<u>nd</u>aji   janjuwa   jirali
         this   Junjuwa   before
         This used to be Junjuwa.

4.2   PHRASES

4.2.1   VERB PHRASES. The traditional notion of 'verb phrase', a verb plus its object, is not very useful for describing or understanding Bunuba syntax, for there is, as far as I know, no evidence that the object NP is any more immediately related to the verb than is its subject. Bunuba is better described as having a *phrasal verb,* in that almost all its verbs consist of two words: preverb and auxiliary, as described in §3.4.

4.2.2   NOUN PHRASES. My discussion of Bunuba simple sentences above (§4.1) assumed the noun phrase (NP) as a possible constituent of sentences with verbs, and as a necessary constituent of those without verbs. A noun phrase in Bunuba can be defined as a word or group of words which may: 1) enter into a relationship of cross-reference with a single pronominal prefix on the verb; and 2) combine with a single nominal case-marking clitic in one of the functions discussed in §3.2.1.

In all the Bunuba texts I have recorded, the majority of noun 'phrases' consist of a single word. Two-word NPs are fairly common (I counted 56 of them in a sample of five hundred lines of text), three-word NPs rare (ten in my sample), and NPs of four or more words very rare (none in my sample, but occasionally attested elsewhere). NPs always include at least one word of the nominal class (and usually consist entirely of them). Other than that, I know of no formal restrictions on the kinds of words that they may consist of. In particular, there is nothing like the distinction one finds in many languages between nouns and adjectives, according to which every noun phrase must contain a noun or pronoun as its 'head', with adjectives optionally present as 'modifying' or 'attributive' elements. Thus, for example, each of the words yuwa<u>n</u>a 'one', <u>ga</u>n<u>d</u>ay 'bad', 'old', and ngarragi 'my' may be used by itself as a complete NP.

For most multi-word Bunuba NPs it is possible to distinguish between modifying words and modified ones. This is a relative distinction in that a given word may modify another word in the phrase and itself be modified by a third (like the *big* in English 'very big bulls'). And for Bunuba it is a purely functional distinction rather than a formal one, in that modifier and modified are not classes of words (as are adjective and noun), but uses to which words are put.

Within the Bunuba NP there is a strong preference for the order modifier^modified (in striking contrast to Ungarinyin on one side (Rumsey 1982b:138) and Gooniyandi on the other (McGregor 1990:251), where the preferred order is modified^modifier). Where this relation was evident in my textual sample of multi-word NPs, the modifying word preceded the modified in 64 out of 70 instances, or 91 per cent of the time. (McGregor (personal communication) reports the same for the nearby Nyulnyulan language Warrwa.) Examples are:

(200) ganday gurama
       bad/old   [male] Aboriginal
       old Aboriginal man

(201) malngarri   yingiy
       red/European name
       European name

(202) mayaru-u winthali
       house-DAT firewood
       firewood for the house

(203) mabilyi bulumana
       small   ox
       calf

(204) gurrgarinja muway
       [place name]   camp/place
       Gurrgarinja camp

(205) ngurru muway
       that   camp/place
       that place

(206) mamulgu-yuwa muway
       sacred.object-LOC camp/place
       ceremony ground

(207) ngayi   walyay bulumana
       not   little cattle
       not few [i.e., many] cattle

See also the last three examples in §3.2.1e.

Examples showing the exceptional order modified^modifier are (208) and (209).

(208) gawarra   yuwana
       sun/hour   one
       one hour / one o'clock

(209) gilandirri yarrangi
       big/great   our (U)
       our lord [God]

Both of these expressions also occur with the reverse word order. Likewise, (202) was repeated a few lines later in the same text as winthali mayaru-u, and (203) paralleled by:

(210) *olgolguman*   bulumana gandaynday
       old female-REDUP   cattle   bad/old-REDUP
       old old cows

For most such expressions I am unable to say what difference there is, if any, between the meaning of 'normal' word order versus the inverted one. (More intensive study might well turn up differences of the general kind discussed in McGregor (1990:249–76), albeit with considerable differences of detail, given the big difference in NP word order norms between Bunuba and Gooniyandi.) For some NPs, word order *is* clearly significant, in distinguishing between pairs of the following sort:

(211) mulu   ngadi
       eye   blind
       blind person

(212) ngadi   mulu
       blind   eye
       blind eye

(213) bina ganday
       ear   bad
       stupid person

(214) ganday bina
       bad   ear
       bad ear

Expressions such as (211) and (213) are perhaps best treated as derived ones, in which the word order modified^modifier signals their special status as constructions which do not contain their own 'head' or ultimate 'modified', which remains only implicit ('exocentric constructions'; compare English 'bootblack', 'birdbrain'). If so, this derivational device in Bunuba is only possible because the order, modifier^modified is otherwise so prevalent that deviations from it stand out as special.

Note from examples such as (208) and ngarragi jimarri in (198) that one instance of the modifier-modified relation is that between possessor and possessed. Those can be constructed either with possessive pronouns, as in these examples (see also §3.3.1), or with a noun or other NP referring to the possessor, marked with the dative case, as exemplified in §3.2.1b. As suggested by the examples there and here, the order modifier^modified is somewhat less prevalant for both kinds of possessive phrase than for other NPs, but still clearly the predominant one. There is perhaps a subtle difference in emphasis associated with the different orders, as suggested by the tendency for Bunuba speakers to translate the possessive phrases with the order possessed^possessor with 'for': 'auntie for this one', etc.

As distinct from possessive phrases, those expressing a part-whole relation do not use the dative case, but simply juxtapose the words for whole and part. Examples are (215) and (216).

(215)   thangani   jamayina   (216)   manba   thinga
        mouth   axe   rump   foot
        axe blade [i.e., the part that 'eats']   heel [cf. also madari]

Note that the word for the part precedes the one for the whole. This is regularly the case for such phrases. It seems to be an exception to the normal order modifier^modified, though it is perhaps less clear which is which in these phrases than in the others discussed above, or if the relationship is even one of 'modification' at all.

The NPs in which the order modifier^modified is most strictly ad-hered to (invariably, as far as I know) are those where the modifier is a de-monstrative pronoun (§3.3.2a), such as (205) and ngindaji gurama in (20).

I have already mentioned that most NPs consist entirely of words of the nominal class. As far as I know, the only other words that may occur in them are adverbs and the particle ngayi 'not' (§3.5.2a), both always as modifying words. Examples are (217), (218) and (207).

(217)   jirali   gurama   (218)   ngayi   yalurru
        before   Aborigine(s)   not   [place name]
        early-days Aborigine(s)   not Yalurrru

In addition to NPs which are structured in terms of modifier and modified, there are also sequences of nominal words which can be interpreted as coordinate noun phrases. Sometimes the second and succeeding nominals are marked with the LINKing clitic (§3.5.2b), and sometimes not. Examples are:

(219) nalija   miyha-ngana
     tea   meat-LINK
     tea and meat

(220) wiyi   gurama
     woman   man
     a woman and a man

See also (5), where there is a sequence of four nouns all in instrumental role in the clause, each marked with an ERGative/ INSTrumental case marker. It seems to me debatable whether collocations of this kind are best regarded as a single coordinate NP or as four separate ones, but if the former, it would mean that case-marked coordinate NPs are distinguished from other complex NPs by having their case marking distributed over the whole NP as opposed to the more usual pattern which I will now describe.

As mentioned at the beginning of §3.2, all of the number and case markers described in that section operate at the level of the phrase, usually occurring only once in an NP even where it consists of more than one word. This fact about them was sidestepped in that section (concerned as it was with morphology) by using only one-word NPs as examples. I will now turn to the syntax of case and number marking within NPs of more than one word. In most such NPs, the case or number marker goes on the first word of the phrase. Sentences including one or more examples of this within case-marked NPs are (221) to (224). For other examples, see (48), (186) and §6.1, line 10.

(221) bilthiba'ngina   ganday-ingga malngarri
     assault PAST-RA2-1sg<3sg   bad-ERG   red/whiteman
     A bad whiteman beat me up.

(222) ngindaji-ingga gurama   ngurru-u gurama gima
     this-ERG   man   that-DAT man   3sg-MA-PRES
     This man tells that man.

(223) wariyga'waniy   ngaala-yawu   muway
     shift 3sg-WU-PAST   different-ALL   camp/country
     He shifted to a different camp.

(224) yarrangi-yawu   muway   maaningarri wad'jiyirra
     our (U)-ALL   camp/country   tomorrow   go 1R-RA
     Tomorrow we go to our country.

An example of a possessive phrase showing the same pattern is:

(225) ngindaji-u   gurama miyha
     this-DAT   man   meat
     this man's meat

The dual and plural number markers that are used with NPs (§3.2.2) also occur most often on the first word of the phrase. Examples are:

(226) ngarragi-arri   nyaanyi
     my-DU   maternal uncle
     my two maternal uncles

(227) nyirra-yani gurama
     this-PL   man
     these men

See also the examples at the end of §3.3.1.

When an NP is marked for case and number, the two markers almost always occur on the same word, the number marker before the case marker. Examples occur in the following sentences:

(228)   nhu-yani-ingga garrawu   wadba'wurrma
         his-PL-ERG   relations take 3sg<3nsg-MA2
         His relations take him.

(229)   gurama-arri-ingga   nganggaʻnginbidantha
         man-DU-ERG   give to PAST1sg<3nsg-YHA-du
         Two men gave it to me.

(230)   wiyi-arri-u   rarrgi
         woman-DU-DAT   stone/money
         The two women's money.

Though it doesn't happen very often, more than one case marker can occur in the same noun phrase. By far the most frequently occurring combination is Comitative1 followed by Instrumental, as discussed in §3.2.1a and exemplifed by (8) and (41). Instrumental also combines with Perlative in a similar function, as exemplified by the following.

(231)   miynhingarri   bunuba-binyi-ingga
         3sg-MA-PAST-3sgObl-CTV   Bunuba-PER-INST
         he said to him in Bunuba [preceded by a quote]

Without the preceding perlative marker, -ingga here could be interpreted as an ergative marker, and the clause glossed as 'The Bunuba [person] said to him', whereas with it it can only mean 'in the Bunuba language'. In other contexts perlative does seem to be able to combine with ergative. A possible example is:

(232)   nginda-yani-ingga   ganba'wirrayi
         this-PL-ERG   follow/chase 3sg<3nsg-RA2-PAST
         baljuwa-binyi-ingga
         behind-PER-ERG
         This mob chased him from behind.

I say this is only a *possible* example because what I have labelled the ergative marker may actually be serving the locative function discussed in §3.2.1a. This is true of all attested examples of the combination binyi-ingga.

When NPs with more than one word occur with more than one case marker, all of the case markers still tend to occur on the first word of the phrase, in the order which is logical for the phrase as a whole. Examples with two case markers are:

(232a)   bindayiminyi-u-ingga   jamayina   duwa'wunu
         Bindayiminy-DAT-INST   axe   hit 3sg<3sg-WU2-PAST
         He hit it with [the blunt end of] Bindayiminyi's axe.

(233) manyanji-u-ngarri   jamayina   wad'jayali
       Manyanji-DAT-COM1   axe   come 3sg-RA-PAST-PROX
       He came with Manyanji's axe.

(234) wiyi-ngarri-ingga gurama miyngarragi
       woman-COM1-ERG   man   3sg-MA-PAST-1sgOBL
       The man with a wife told me.

Compare also the complex NP in (171).

      Examples with three case markers are:

(235) wiyi-ngarri-u-ingga   jamayina   duwa'wunu
       woman-COM1-DAT-INST   axe   hit 3sg<3sg-WU2-PAST
       He hit it with the axe belonging to a man with a wife.

(236) mayaru-u-ngarri-ingga lundu   wad'jayalu
       house-DAT-COM1-INST   wood   come 3sg-RA-PAST-PROX
       He came with the wood for the house.

In NPs with a number marker and more than one case marker, the number marker precedes all case markers. An example is (237).

(237) wiyi-arri-u-ingga   rarrgi wadba'ma   balyamarada
       woman-DU-DAT-INST   money get 3sg<3sg-MA2 car
       He bought the car with the two women's money.

      While complex NPs such as those in (231) to (237) are apparently fully grammatical in Bunuba, and of undoubted interest to linguists, they are very rarely produced unless elicited (as all these examples were). In the approximately five hundred pages of Bunuba texts that I have checked for this, there are no more than a handful of double case marked phrases with combinations other than Comitative1 plus Instrumental, and I have been unable to find any at all with three case markers or a number marker and two case markers. Even in elicited speech, there is a tendency to offer less densely packed expressions as preferable alternatives to the above. For example, in the sentence which was first offered by Johnny Marr to gloss my English in (237), he did not use the expression wiyi-arri-u-ingga, but instead said thurranda wiyi-u-ingga, using the separate word thurranda 'two' instead of the DUAL suffix -arri (which in other, less complex NPs is used more often than thurranda). When I proposed the alternative Bunuba version in (237) he accepted it, but not in preference to his own version.
      Case markers occur more often in combination with the 'other' nominal markers discussed in §3.2.3 (which could be described as 'stem forming affixes'). Any of the latter always precedes any or all of the former. Examples are:

(238)   ngawungu-way-nhingi   wadba'ma
        father-3PP-ABL   get PAST-3sg<3sg-MA2
        He got it from his father.

(239)   ban.ga'wura   ngawumbulu-yawu
        return-FUT-2sg-RA   father-2PP-ALL
        Go back to your father.

(240)   warrgali-wangg(u>ø)-ingga   miyngarragi
        Warrgali-countryman-ERG   3sg-MA-PAST-1sgOBL
        The person from Warrgali country said to me [followed by quote].

Compare also the order of morphemes in (171) malngarri-u-jangi   thangani
'like white people's language'.
      Discontinuous noun phrases are rare in Bunuba, but exactly how
rare they are depends upon what you choose to interpret as a single NP
versus two or more NPs with the same referent. Examples of collocations
which could be taken to include discontinuous NPs are (241), (242) and
(253).

(241)   ngarragi-ingga   matha'nginbirrag   jirali   gandaynday
        my-ERG   tell PAST-1sg<3nsg-RA2-pl before   old-REDUP
        My old before-ones [i.e., relations from long ago] told me.

(242)   walyay niy   dumurru-yuwa jirigi
        little   that.one chest-LOC   bird
        on that little bird's breast (from §6.1, line 21)

      The fact that case markers generally only occur one-per-phrase in
Bunuba can be taken as evidence for the discontinous-phrase analysis of
examples such as (241) as opposed to the (also grammatical) alternative
version of (241) with ergative markers on both ngarragi and gandaynday.

4.3   REFLEXIVE-RECIPROCAL CLAUSES

      The morphology of reflexive-reciprocal verb marking has been
described in §3.4.5, along with some examples of its use in clauses without
subject NPs. In terms of the discussion in §4.1, these verbs are neither
monovalent nor bivalent, but intermediate between the two, their prefixes
having some of the features of each (as described in §3.4.5). When they
occur in clauses with NP subjects, these are also intermediate or variable on
the scale of transitivity, since the subject NP is sometimes ergative-marked
and sometimes not. Examples are:

(243)   jirali   gurama ganba'wurrayningarri
        before   man   chase 3nsg-RA2-REFL-PAST-CTV
        Olden-days people used to chase each other.

(244) biyirri-ingga nyaga'wurriyni
       they-ERG   spear 3nsg-WU2-REFL-PAST
       They speared each other.

(245) nhu wurrbinya jalungurru(>a)'yhayni
       he   alone   good/well 3sg-YHA-REFL-PAST
       He cured himself all by himself. (For u>a, see §3.4.1.)

(246) nyirraji gurama nhithila'mayni
       that   man   pinch 3sg-MA2-REFL-PAST
       That man pinched himself.

(247) nginda-yani-ingga mila'wurraynigi
       that-PL-ERG   look/see 3nsg-RA2-REFL-PAST-pl
       These ones looked at one another.

(248) binaynintha   biyirrantha wurrbinya
       3nsg-NA-REFL-PAST-du they two   alone
       They two alone said to each other.

For another example, see (47). As indicated by these examples, the presence versus absence of ergative marking on the subject of reflexive/reciprocal clauses is less clearly correlated with differences in their overall semantic transitivity than for active clauses of the kind discussed in §4.1. When the subject is non-singular, there is some tendency for ergative marking to be associated with reciprocal meanings (action upon one another) rather than reflexive (action by each upon him/herself), but the correlation is not perfect.

Another unusual feature of these clauses is that, when the subject is an independent pronoun, it is sometimes the oblique-stem form rather than Absolutive one (for the sets of forms see §3.3.1). Examples are (245) and (248). When this happens, ergative marking is not available as a further option on the same pronoun, since the ergative marker can be used only on an absolutive base form (§3.3.1). I am unable to say exactly how the clauses with oblique-stem pronouns differ in meaning from those with Absolutive or Ergative ones, but when I asked Banjo Wirrunmarra how to say 'They speared themselves' (after he had just given me (244) for 'They speared each other'), he used a different preverb janda 'pierce', 'stab' and for the subject the oblique 3pl pronoun biyirrangu. In commenting later on this, Johnny Marr translated biyirrangu in this context as 'for themselves'.

As Bill McGregor has pointed out to me, another possible interpretation of sentences such as (245) would be to see the oblique pronoun as not filling the subject role, but instead meaning something like 'by oneself', specifying that the actor did it alone. To test this out I asked Johnny Marr if niy-ingga 'he-ERG' could be used in the sentence along with nhu wurrbinya and he volunteered: niy-ingga wurrbinya jalungurru ayhaynu, nhu wurrbinya. He and two other senior Bunuba speakers all found it ungrammatical to have both biyirrantha and biyirri-way (the corresponding absolutive form) both present in sequence in (247) but found either acceptable by itself in the sentence. All this weighs against McGregor's suggested interpretation, but the matter requires further, text-based exploration.

4.4   COMPLEX SENTENCES.

4.4.1   FINITE SUBORDINATE CLAUSES. As described in §3.4.7,
subordinate clauses with full verbs are marked in the verb complex by a
suffix -nya. The range of functions served by these clauses is quite wide,
including at least the following.

[a] *Relative.* These are -nya clauses which function as 'modifiers'
in complex NPs (cf. §4.2.2). Accordingly, they almost always come before
the noun they modify rather than after it. An example is:

(249)   diyga'larrinya   gurama wad'jay
          find PAST-3sg<1sg-NGARRI-SUB   man   go 3sg-RA-PAST
          The man I found has gone.

The relative clause together with the noun it modifies (diyga'larrinya
gurama) form a single noun phase within the main clause. Where
appropriate, this NP can itself occur with an ergative case marker specifying
its role within the main clause. Being the first word of the NP, the verb
complex usually takes the case marker for the NP as a whole (cf. §4.2.2).
See for example (195). Another example is:

(250)   ginyirriga'wuninya-ingga   gurama   mila'a
          cuckold 3sg<3sg-WU2-PAST-SUB-ERG   man   see PRES-3sg<3sg-RA2
          The man whom he has cuckolded sees him.

As in most Australian languages which have subordinate clauses
with pronominal prefixes on the verb, it can be seen from the above examples
that the form of the Bunuba subordinate marker is the same regardless of the
syntactic functions of the relevant coreferential noun in the main and
subordinate clauses (A-A, O-A, O-S, etc.). As far as I know this noun may
be in any function in the main clause, though S, A, and O are the most
common, and relative clauses with any other case marking but ergative (or
zero) are very rare. S, A and O are also the most usual functions of the
common NP in the relative clause.

[b] *Temporal.* Examples are:

(251)   birayga'iraynya   ngag'ira
          emerge 3sg-RA-PAST-SUB   eat/burn PAST-3sg<3sg-RA2
          When he came out he had got burned. (§7, Text A, line 17)

(252)   warrba'wirruninyangarri   buja'niynya
          pound 3sg<3nsg-WU2-PAST-SUB-CTV   finish 3sg-NI-PAST-SUB
                   bininybalu   garra'wirrarriyngarri
                   spinifex grass   throw [away] 3sg<3nsg-NGARRI-PAST-CTV
          When they had pounded it [to extract the resin], when it was finished, they
          threw away the spinifex grass.

[c] *Locative*. These clauses are similar to type [a] in that they are used to form noun-like expressions, which in this case refer to places. Unlike the examples in [a], these are generally 'headless' expressions — without an accompanying noun that they modify. Most of them are proper names which identify particular places in the landscape with reference to events that took place there during the time of creation (ngarranggani). Examples are:

(253) mila'wayi   galu wara'raynya
       see FUT-3sg<3sg-RA2-exc   penis stand 3sg-RA-PAST-SUB
       jularrga
       euro
       He will look at [the place] 'Where Euro's Penis Stood Up'.

(254) ngindaji   muway   wulugga'winarriynthanya
       this   place   swallow 3nsg>3sg-NGARRI-PAST-du-SUB
       This place is 'Where he [Long Neck Turtle] Swallowed the Two'.

[d] *Causal* (See also (30))

(255) wanjali   burrmiynhingarri
       leaf   3nsg-MA-PAST-3sgOBL-CTV
       yaninga   nalija   giwurrma-nhi
       now   tea   PRES-3nsg-MA-3sgOBL
       gurama   duluga'waniynya
       man   die 3sg-WU-PAST-SUB
       They used to call it [tea] wanjali but now they call it nalija because a man died [who had a name sounding like wanjali].

[e] *Conditional*

(256) buju   bina'iywurrayginyanganggi
       if   show IRR-3sg<3nsg-RA2-PRES IRR-pl-SUB-2sgOBL
       mila'anjay
       see IRR-3sg<2sg-RA2-PRES IRR
       If they want to show it to you, you can see it.

(257) buju ngag'gunjanya   warraynga   duluga'anju
       if   eat IRR-3sg<2sg-RA2-SUB after.a.while die IRR-2sg-WU
       If you eat it you might die after a while.

For a counterfactual example, see §6, Text A, line 23.

4.4.2 PURPOSIVE CLAUSES. As discussed and exemplified in §3.2.1, one of the uses of the dative marker -gu/-u with NPs is to indicate a purposive role within the clause. The same marker is used on preverbs in a similar function. Examples are in (139) and (258).

(258)   winthali   gaygaytha'yirrangarri   mayaru-u winthali
         fire/firewood cut up PAST-3sg<1R-RA2-CTV   house-DAT   fire/firewood
         mayi   wug-gu
         food   cook-DAT
         We'd cut firewood for the house, for cooking the food.

In (258) the expression mayi wug-gu 'for cooking food' could be taken as
most immediately linked either to winthali (comprising a complex NP 'wood
for cooking food'), or with winthali gaygaytha'yirrangarri ('We'd cut
wood...for cooking food'). In either case, the purposive relation marked by
-gu must be seen as applying to both of the preceding words, not just to the
preverb. So it is clear that, at least when formed from preverbs, dative-
marked purposive constructions are true clauses, albeit non-finite ones.

4.3.3   MA FRAMING CONSTRUCTIONS. As in the neighbouring
language Ungarinyin (Rumsey 1982b:157–66, 1990), much use is made in
Bunuba of a kind of framing construction which from the English viewpoint
looks like a form of quotation. As in Ungarinyin, there is only one Bunuba
verb which may be used for this purpose: monovalent MA. Like the other
roots listed in Table 3.3, MA occurs in combination with various preverbs,
where it carries most of the grammatical information for the clause, including
abstract distinctions of action-type which are associated with the choice of
one verb root or another (see §3.4.1-2). But unlike any of the other roots,
MA also occurs frequently without an accompanying preverb, always as a
framing verb, in which function it can be glossed more concretely as 'say' or
'do'.

(259)   garrga-yarra'wanbini   miy
         leave-perhaps FUT-1U<3sg-WU2-exc   3sg-MA-PAST
         He_i said he_j might leave us.

(260)   mila'wa   jiyirrmiyg   nginda-yani   mayi
         look FUT-3sg<2sg-RA2   1R-MA-PAST-pl   this-PL   [bush] food
         'Look at this' we said, 'these are bush tucker'.

Sometimes the material which is framed by MA is to be understood
not as actual speech, but as 'inner speech', i.e. thought or intention. Thus,
for example (259) could in some contexts be used to mean 'He thought he
might be leaving us'.
    Usually when MA is used as a framing verb, it is suffixed with an
oblique pronominal, which refers either to the addressee, or, less frequently,
to the person or object which the reported speech or thought is about.
Examples are:

(261)   yaninga   ngayaga'warrma   limiybiyirrangi
         now   ask FUT-3sg<1U-MA2   1sg-MA-PAST-3plOBL
         'Now we'll have to ask him' I said to them.

(262) nginji-guda   wurrba'wuni   gimananggi
       you-COM2   sit.down FUT-3sg-NI   PRES-3sg-MA-2sgOBL

He wants him to sit down with you. [Lit. He$_i$ is doing/saying with regard to you: he$_j$ should sit down with you.]

When the MA framing verb is accompanied by an NP referring to its subject, that NP is sometimes ergatively marked and sometimes not (about 64 per cent of the time versus 36 per cent respectively in a textual sample containing 45 MA clauses with subject NPs). In that respect, MA framing clauses behave much like other clauses with monovalent verbs with an explicit 'goal' as discussed in §4.0 (e.g., (193), (194) and (195)). But they differ from other such clauses in that quite often (in 8 out of 29 instances in my sample) they include an ergative-marked subject NP even in the absence of an OBLique pronominal suffix on the verb. Elsewhere (Rumsey 1994) I have argued that this is because the Hopper and Thompson style 'object properties' that are associated with Ergative case marking on the subject NP in Bunuba framing clauses include not only those of the addressee (as cross-referenced by the optional pronominal suffix), but also those of the framed locution (i.e., its degree of 'individuation' as a discrete speech event).

5.   GUN.GUNMA 'MOTHER-IN-LAW TALK'

As elsewhere in Aboriginal Australia the social relationship between a Bunuba man and his mother-in-law has traditionally been one of great circumspection and decorum, which used to be marked linguistically by the use of a special speech style known as Gun.gunma (as opposed to the everyday, unmarked variety known as jadajada 'straight' Bunuba). In another publication, written at a much earlier stage in my study of everyday Bunuba (Rumsey 1982a), I gave a brief description of the grammar of Gun.gunma and a rather fuller account of its use in social interaction, exemplified with reference to a transcript of a staged Gun.gunma conversation between a Bunuba man and woman playing the part of son-in-law and mother-in-law. Here, after a few remarks about the contexts in which Gun.gunma was used, I will focus mainly on its formal features as compared with those of everyday Bunuba.

5.1   CONTEXTS OF USE

Nowadays, Gun.gunma is little used in actual conversations, but it is well remembered by everyone over the age of about sixty, and still used by them when telling traditional stories in which they take the parts of characters related to each other in the appropriate way.

Given the available evidence, it is not entirely clear in what sorts of situations Gun.gunma was formerly used. In my earlier account (ibid.) I reported that Bunuba people related to each other as mother-in-law and son-in-law (hereafter referred to as madjali-langu) had been permitted to speak to each other, provided they averted their gaze and spoke slowly and softly to each other in Gun.gunma. This is what I had been told by the four senior Bunuba people who provided the information on which that account was based. Indeed, the Bunuba woman from whom I first learned about Gun.gunma in 1979 (now deceased) explicitly contrasted Bunuba practice to the neighbouring Ngarinyin in this respect: among the Ngarinyin, in-laws could not talk to each other because there was no special form of the language so as to allow it. More recently I have been told by one Bunuba man (her junior by about fifteen years and unavailable to me at the time because he was away on work as a stockman) that actual madjali-langu could not speak to each other, and that Gun.gunma was used when they were merely within earshot of each other. In any case when telling stories in which characters are related as mother-in-law to son-in-law, Bunuba narrators portray them as speaking Gun.gunma to each other, and not merely within earshot (for an example, see Rumsey 1982a:179).

It is also relevant to note that the relationships which were marked by the use of Gun.gunma include not only ones between a man and his actual wife's mother, but also between people who stand in the right relationship for such a marriage to take place. In my earlier account I tried to show that it is not always clear who does and does not stand in such a relationship, and I concluded from several different sorts of evidence that the Gun.gunma register provided 'a rather flexible set of speech forms and strategies', by means of which the madjali relationship among actual or *prospective* affines was 'selectively invoked or partially effaced' (ibid.). It could well be that the use of Gun.gunma in *direct* interaction between madjali-langu was confined mainly or entirely to potential in-laws rather than actual ones (i.e, those linked through an actual marriage or, perhaps, betrothal). In any case, though some of the details of my earlier description were incorrect (see below for amendments), I think the available evidence still supports my conclusions about the social uses of Gun.gunma — in some ways even more strongly than before.

5.2   THE STRUCTURE OF GUN.GUNMA

5.2.1   PERSON REFERENCE. As in many speech situations around the world which are characterised by relatively high social 'distance' between or among those who are speaking to each other (Brown and Levinson 1987, Brown and Gilman 1960; Rumsey 1982a:174–5), madjali-langu avoided addressing each other in the second person singular, instead substituting non-singular forms, even when addressing a single person (for examples see Rumsey 1982a:169–71). Contra Rumsey (1982a), this was not a restriction on what could be said in Gun.gunma, but more specifically on how madjali-langu could address (and thereby refer to) each other. Thus, although the conversation transcript in Rumsey (1982a) shows the conversants addressing each other with 2nsg forms only, in another text — a traditional myth told in Gun.gunma — I have come across several instances of 2sg forms used when the narrator is speaking in the voice of characters who are not related to each other as madjali-langu. (Another respect in which my earlier account was somewhat inaccurate is in referring to the forms used between madjali-langu as 'plural'; most of them are actually 'non-singular' forms, not positively marked for plurality with a number suffix (cf. §3.2.2, §3.4.6).)

5.2.2 PATTERNS OF WORD REPLACEMENT. So far, I have come across about two hundred distinctively Gun.gunma vocabulary items, many of which are included in the lists in §7 (each identified by a preceding $ sign). Many of these items show the sorts of many-to-one relations to the everyday vocabulary which have been widely reported for similar registers in other Australian languages. So for example the Gun.gunma word jayirriminyi is said to have been used in place of thangani, 'mouth', 'language', 'speech', 'story', and also yingi 'name'; jalimanggurru for the three otherwise distinct boomerang types listed in §7.1j; jimara for at least six otherwise distinct spear types, including three listed in §7.1j, etc. (see §5.2.3 below for verb examples). But unlike in the well-known case of Dyirbal (Dixon 1971), Bunuba people do not say that all or even most words of the everyday language had to be replaced in the appropriate speech situations by an equivalent expression made up entirely of Gun.gunma words. When I was eliciting vocabulary from them in both Gun.gunma and everyday Bunuba, for most of the items on my list they said that when speaking Gun.gunma they would simply use the same word as the everyday one. This included most of the five hundred or so everyday items listed in §7. And in all of the Gun.gunma texts I have recorded, that is what the speakers do. Moreover they sometimes use everyday words even in places where there is an available alternative Gun.gunma expression. What they seem to strive for is not total avoidance of everyday vocabulary, but a fairly even distribution of Gun.gunma items throughout the utterance, usually including at least one per clause. The average number of words in each clause is about the same as between Gun.gunma and everyday speech: although many Gun.gunma words when considered in the abstract may seem 'vague' in comparison to their everyday counterparts, when using Gun.gunma words, speakers make little attempt to compensate for this by paraphrasing (see Rumsey 1982a for further discussion and exemplification of all the above points).

The Gun.gunma words themselves do tend to be longer than everyday ones. Several that I can recognise (and probably a lot more that I cannot) are similar to those in other Kimberley languages, from which they have apparently been borrowed, often with obscure end bits apparently added to them. Examples are debarra+$AUX, 'die', cf. Ungarinyin debarr, 'die'; dambalngu, 'place', 'camp', cf. Ungarinyin dambun, Wurla dambu, 'place', 'camp'; mangarrinyi, 'vegetable food', cf. Ungarinyin mangarri, 'vegetable food'; ngumbana, 'husband', cf. Walmajarri ngumbana, 'husband'; and jayirriminyi, 'mouth', 'language', 'speech', 'story', 'name', cf. Kija jarrak, 'speak'.

In a few cases, I have been given two different Gun.gunma translations of the same everyday word. Examples may be found in §7.1 under: muway 'place, camp' (sec. h); wurrga+YHA 'put, put in place' (sec. r); ngangga+YHA 'give' (sec. r) and duluga+WU 'die' (sec. v). I have been unable to discover any difference in meaning or appropriate use among any of these alternative forms. They have usually been given by different people and may reflect differing familiarity with nearby languages from which Gun.gunma forms have been borrowed.

Some of the Gun.gunma expressions are everyday words used in a figurative way, or resemble everyday words with related meanings. Examples are langgula 'firewood', cf. the everyday word langgurra 'hollow log'; and the euphemism thingga+$AUX for 'defecate', thingga+WU2 being the everyday expression for 'lay an egg'. In view of examples such as these, it is inapproprite to regard Gun.gunma as simply an alternative 'code' by means of which Bunuba speakers mechanically translated everyday utterances into 'equivalent' Gun.gunma ones. Rather, it was part of a more general mode of deportment in which people also drew creatively upon the figurative and other euphemistic possibilities of the everyday language. This aspect of Gun.gunma becomes more apparent when one looks at how it is used in connected texts as opposed to formal elicitation (see Rumsey 1982a, and, for another example, (269) below, which comes from a myth told in Gun.gunma).

5.2.3   THE GUN.GUNMA VERB COMPLEX. As described in §3.4, almost every Bunuba 'verb' consists of a combination of a preverb and following inflected root functioning as an auxiliary verb. In Gun.gunma speech, any of the ten everyday Bunuba verb roots, whether monovalent or bivalent, may be replaced by a single distinctive mother-in-law auxiliary (as in the neighbouring language Jaru; see Tsunoda 1981:182, 215–17). This Gun.gunma auxiliary is itself complex, consisting of an unanalysable element mal followed by an inflected root which behaves in almost all respects like the everyday root NI. The final consonant of mal in such combinations is omitted in the only place where it would otherwise be immediately followed by the n of NI, in the third person singular past (where the subject pronominal prefix is ø-).

The Gun.gunma auxiliary (i.e., mal+NI) occurs mainly in combination with everyday preverbs, this apparently sufficing to mark the verb complex as a whole as Gun.gunma speech. Indeed, where people use everyday preverbs while speaking in Gun.gunma, they almost invariably use the Gun.gunma auxiliary, and in elicitation sessions when supplying Gun.gunma versions of everyday verb complexes for which they know of no distinct Gun.gunma preverb, they *always* use it. Examples are:

	Everyday Expression	Gun.gunma Expression
(263)	galgala'miy laugh 3sg-MA-PAST He laughed.	galgala'ma'niy laugh MAL 3sg-NI-PAST He laughed.
(264)	girarra'way crawl FUT-3sg-RA-exc Let him crawl around.	girarra'mal'buniy crawl MAL FUT-3sg-NI-exc Let him crawl around.
(265)	ngayi mindija'aluma not believe IRR-3sg<1sg-MA2 I couldn't believe it.	ngayi mindija'mal'guwunguniy not believe MAL-IRR-1sg-NI-PAST I couldn't believe [it].

The only way in which the NI of the Gun.gunma auxiliary MAL+NI behaves differently from the everyday verb NI is in the third person singular present indicative, where the present marker is ga rather than the expected gi (§3.4.4a). For the other Gun.gunma present indicative forms besides 3sg (i.e., where there is a non-ø person-number prefix coming in between mal and ni), the form of the present indicative prefix is as described in §3.4.4a. Examples of both these kinds are:

	Everyday Expression	Gun.gunma Expression

(266) gawarra giyga'ni
sun   get up 3sg-NI-PRES
The sun is coming up.

giyga'mal'gani
get up MAL PRES-3sg-NI-PRES
[The sun] is coming up.

(267) giyga'nthi
get up 2sg-NI-PRES (see §3.4.4a)
You are getting up.

giyga'mal'ginthi
get up MAL PRES-2sg-NI-PRES
You are getting up.

Note from the above examples (263-7) that the Gun.gunma auxiliary consistently marks the distinction between present and past by both a prefix (ga-/gi- versus ø-) and suffix (-ø versus -y). It differs in this respect from all the everyday verb roots in that none of them consistently uses both of these methods at once: MA2 and YHA have no tense suffixes in the indicative mode, and none of the roots takes present indicative prefixes consistently across all person-number categories except when there is no preverb or when the preverb ends in a consonant (which means that in some verb complexes the present-past indicative distinction is not marked at all; see §3.4.4). The more consistent semantic specificity of the Gun.gunma auxiliary in this respect (to the point of redundancy) could be seen as a fortuitous consequence of the fact that it pairs the everyday root NI with a preceeding element which ends in a consonant (mal), which otherwise happens only rarely for any verb root. In any case it is an exception to the tendency for Gun.gunma forms to have less specific meanings than their everyday counterparts.

One way in which the Gun.gunma auxiliary behaves more normally in this respect is in its simplified marking of valency relations. Note that in (265), the Gun.gunma auxiliary replaces a bivalent root even though it is itself monovalent. This happens quite often in Gun.gunma (there being no other way to turn a verb complex with an everyday preverb into Gun.gunma). In this particular example it means that the object is simply not cross-referenced in the Gun.gunma utterance. Often in such Gun.gunma verb complexes the object does get cross-referenced, using an optional OBLique pronominal suffix (the everyday uses of which are described in §3.4.9, 4.1). Examples are:

	Everyday Expression	Gun.gunma Expression

(268) lamajga'winja
get (someone) FUT-1sg>2sg-YHA
I'll pick you up [to take on a trip].

lamajga'mal'bunginiyinggirrangi
get MAL FUT-1sg-NI-2plOBL
I'll pick you up. (Rumsey 1982a:171)

(269) ngayi nyaga'iywirrunu
notspear IRR-3sg<3nsg-WU2-PAST
They did not spear him.

ngayi gan.gurra'mal
not touch MAL
'giywudiynhi
IRR-3nsg-NI-PAST-3sgOBL
They did not 'touch' [i.e.spear] him.

For a few such pairs, the subject of the Gun.gunma auxiliary corresponds not to the subject of the everyday bivalent root, but to its object. This is shown in (270).

(270) jirrbala'anbu   jirrbala'mal'gingini
       hurt 1sg<3sg-WU2-PRES   hurt MAL PRES-1sg-NI-PRES
       I'm in pain.   I'm in pain.

For all such pairs that I know of, the object of the everyday verb is in an 'experiencer' role of the sort which is more commonly associated with the subject of other everyday verbs of feeling and knowing. In that respect, the form of pronominal cross-reference on the Gun.gunma auxiliary, if simpler than that on everyday roots (or perhaps *because* it is simpler) is more directly sensitive to considerations of (Hopper and Thompson-style) transitivity (cf. §4.1).

6.   TEXTS

6.1   CROCODILE AND PARROT (JOHNNY MARR)

This is a traditional story which tells of how humankind almost lost the use of fire, and how it was rescued for us by Crimson-winged Parrot (accounting also for why he now has a red mark under his wings). Similar versions of the story are told over much of the Kimberley region, and variants of it are told at least as far away as the southern reaches of the Western Desert (David Rose, personal communication). Like many such 'just-so' stories from around the world, it ends in a counterfactual conditional statement, which in this case provides a good illustration of one of the uses of the Bunuba -nya clause (cf. §4.4.1e).

1.   lalanggarra   ngarranggani   muja'yha
       crocodile   Dreamtime   burrow in PAST-(3sg<)3sg-YHA
       In the Dreamtime Crocodile burrowed in[to the sand].

2.   rawurra   winjuwiy   jajalingga   jirigi
       above   [place name]   crimson.winged parrot   bird
       gaman'birrag
       search PAST-3sg<3nsg-RA2-pl
       Up at Winjuwiy Gorge the Crimson-winged Parrot mob looked for him.

3.   jajalingga   jirigi   wurrba'niynhi
       crimson winged parrot   bird   sit.down 3sg-NI-PAST-3sgOBL
       The crimson-winged parrot sat down on top of him.

4.   rawurranali   jajal   jajal   miynhi
       from above   3sg-MA-PAST-3sgOBL
       From on top he called to him 'jajal jajal'.

5. niy   lalanggarra-ingga   winya'ra
    that.one crocodile-ERG   hear PAST-3sg<3sg-RA2
    He, Crocodile heard him.

6. dumbula'waniy   ngurrubilinyalu
    come around 3sg-WU-PAST   from that side
    He came around from that side.

7. girrgara'miy   baburruga
    run 3sg-MA-PAST down
    He ran down.

8. garuwa nyanungga'waniy
    water   dive 3sg-WU-PAST
    He dived into the water

9. winthali-ngarri   jirigi-ingga
    fire-COM1   bird-ERG/INST
    with the fire and with that bird

10. nyanangarri-ingga gurama mila'wirrag
    many-ERG   man   see PAST-3sg<3nsg-RA2-pl
    Many men saw him.

11. winthali   baburru   bada'iywirrunugu
    fire   below   seize IRR-3sg<3nsg-WU2-PAST-pl
    They wanted to get the fire back.

12. nyanungga'wurraniygi-nhi
    dive.in PAST-3sg<3nsg-WU-PAST-3sgOBL
    They dived in after him.

13. ngayi winthali-ingga birrirra   nga(g)'bunag
    no   fire-ERG   flame   eat/burn PAST-3nsg<3sg-RA2-pl
    But no, they were burned by the hot flame.

14. yura'wirrunugi
    fear PAST-3sg<3nsg-WU2-PAST-pl
    They were frightened of it.

15. niy-ingga   jajalingga   nyanungga'waniynhi
    that.one-ERG crimson-winged parrot   dive.in 3sg-WU-PAST-3sgOBL
    The parrot dived for it.

16. bada'wunu   girrgara'ra   rawurruga
    seize 3sg<3sg-WU2-PAST run PAST-3sg<3sg-RA2   upward
    He got it and quickly ran [with] it back up to the surface.

17.   birayga'raynya   ngag'ira
        emerge 3sg-RA-PAST-SUB   eat/burn PAST-3sg<3sg-RA2
        When he came out he had got burned.

18.   garra'ngarriy   winthali   birrirra
        throw 3sg<3sg-NGARRI-PAST   fire   flame
        He threw the fire down.

19.   baga'rawiya   winthali
        sit/be 3sg-RA-PRES-DEF fire
        The fire is there for all time

20.   gunggala   wurama'wirrag   balara
        firestick   gather PRES-3sg<3nsg-RA2-pl   outside/everywhere
        and people find firesticks everywhere.

21.   walyay niy   dumurru-yuwa jirigi
        little   that.one chest-LOC   bird
            baga'ranhi   manmali
            sit/be 3sg-RA-PRES-3sgOBL red
        And on that little bird's breast he's got a red mark

22.   nyirraji-ingga   bada'wunu   winthali
        this-ERG   seize 3sg<3sg-WU2-PAST   fire
        this one [that] stole the fire.

23.   jajalingga   ngayi-ya   bada'iywuni-nya
        crimson.winged parrot   not-REP   seize IRR-3sg<3sg-WU2-PAST-SUB
            winthali   lalanggarra-nhingi   baburruga
            fire   crocodile-ABL   below
            wuruga'ranya   babuburruga garuwa-yawu
            take.away PAST-3sg<3sg-RA2-SUB below   water-ALL
            nyanungga'ra   gunggala   ngayi-nga
            dive [for] PAST-3sg<3sg-RA2   firestick   not-LINK
            yatha'arrayg
            sit IRR-1U-RA-PAST-pl
        And if Crimson-winged Parrot hadn't stolen fire from Crocodile down there by
        diving down under the water and taking away the fire we wouldn't have any
        firesticks.

6.2   HOW AND HOW NOT TO TREAT CATTLE (BILLY OSCAR)

Most Bunuba men have worked as stockmen on cattle stations —
the older ones for much of their lives (cf. §1.5). In recent years they have
been partly displaced in this work by new forms of mechanisation, including
helicopter mustering. This has its disadvantages in comparison to the older
ways of managing cattle, as described here by Billy Oscar. (Note that here as
elsewhere, English loan words are italicised.)

1.   mayuru   yatha'ngaynya   *majirrima* 'yiyidangarri
           house   sit 1sg-RA-PAST-SUB   muster PAST-3sg<1R-YHA-CTV
           When I was at the station we used to do mustering.

2.   bulumana-yawu   wariyga'yiyirruningarri
           cattle-ALL   start.out 3sg<1R-WU2-PAST-CTV
           We used to start out towards the cattle.

3.   wadjiyirrayngarri   *majarrima* 'yiyidag
           go 1R-RA-PAST-CTV   muster PAST-3sg<1R-YHA-pl
           We'd go and muster them.

4.   luwa'yiyidangarri   *dinagem*-jawu
           drive PAST-3sg<1R-YHA-CTV   dinner.camp-ALL
             wurrga'yidangarri
             put PAST-3sg<1R-YHA-CTV
           We drove them along 'till dinner camp and put them there.

5.   ngaala   gurama *dina*-yawu wadburrayngarri   mayi-yawu
           whatever man   dinner-ALL   go 3nsg-RA-PAST-CTV   food-ALL
           Some of the men would go for their dinner.

6.   nga(g)'birrangarri
           eat PAST-(3sg<)3nsg-RA2-CTV
           They would eat.

7.   mayi buja'wirrununyangarri   nga(g)'birranya
           food   finish 3sg<3nsg-WU2-PAST-SUB-CTV   eat PAST-3sg<3nsg-RA2-SUB
             banga'wurrayngarringiyirrangi
             return 3nsg-RA-PAST-CTV-1R.OBL
           When they had finished their meal they would come back for us.

8.   ngiyirri*na*   yungga'yinbidangarri   mayi-yawu   *dina*
           we (R)   now   send PAST1R<3nsg-YHA2-CTV   dinner-ALL   dinner
           They would send us in for our food then, our dinner.

9.   ngirrginyi nga(g)'jiyirrangarri
           hunger   eat PAST-3sg<1R-RA2-CTV
           Hungrily we ate it.

10.   yawada wadba'yiyirrmangarri   banga'yiyirrayngarri
           horse   get PAST-3sg<1R-MA2-CTV   return 1R-RA-PAST-CTV
           Then we would get our horses and go back again.

11.   garrwaru bulumana-yawu   wadjiyirrayngarri
           afternoon   cattle-ALL   go 1R-RA-PAST-CTV
           In the afternoon we'd go back to the cattle.

12.   bayiyga'yiyirrunmangarri

meet PAST-3sg<1R-MA2-CTV
We'd meet up with them.

13.   luwa'yiyidangarri   balarra
       drive PAST-3sg<1R-YHA-CTV   open country
       We'd drive them over the open range.

   [section of text omitted]

14.   jalungurru-ya   mabilyi bulumana   ngarranyi-ngarri-ya
       quiet/good-REP little   cattle   mother-COM1-REP
          wad'burraygngarri
          go 3nsg-RA-PAST-pl-CTV
       The calves were able to go around quietly with their mothers.

15.   yungu   dalja'miyngarri   *bulug*
       little bit   grow up 3sg-MA-PAST-CTV   bullock
          bulumana   nyananingga
          cattle   big-REDUP-ERG
       Until they would grow up to be bullocks, really big bullocks.

16.   *epa*-ngana nyanana   nyana-ya   wudiygngarri
       heifer-LINK big-REDUP big-REP   3nsg-NI-PAST-pl-CTV
       The heifers would grow up.

17.   buga-ngarri   wudiygngarri
       offspring-COM1 3nsg-NI-PAST-pl-CTV
       They would come to have calves of their own.

18.   bulumana   dalja'wurrmiyngarri
       cattle   grow 3nsg-MA-PAST-CTV
       The cattle would grow.

19.   nyanangarri nyanangarri bulumana dalja'miyngarri
       big.mob   big.mob   cattle   grow 3sg-MA-PAST-CTV
       It would grow into a really big herd.

20.   yaninga birrinyi-ngarri-ingga   ganbanba'a
       now   sky-COM1 (helicopter)-ERG chase-REDUP PRES-3sg<3sg-RA2
       Nowadays the helicopter chases after them.

21.   ganba'a   jarraa-nhingi
       chase PRES-3sg<3sg-RA2   far.away-ABL
          ganba'ali
          chase PRES-3sg<3sg-RA2-PROX
       It chases them from a long way off, chases them this way.

22.   biliga   buga   nhi *gab* burrga'ma
       in between   offspring its calf get.tired 3sg-MA-PRES
       The calves get tired along the way.

23.   yawurragi-ingga   maaningga didiya'ma

dingo-ERG	at.night	chase 3sg<3sg-MA2

The dingo chases them at night

24. nganja'ma
    bite PRES-3sg<3sg-MA2
    and bites them.

25. ngag'a   dangayiga'wu   ngag'a
    eat PRES-3sg<3sg-RA2   kill 3sg<3sg-WU2-PRES   eat PRES-3sg<3sg-RA2
    He eats them, kills them and eats them.

7. VOCABULARY

The same set of Bunuba vocabulary items is presented below: in
§7.1 organized by semantic field and in §7.2 in alphabetical order. The words
listed include all those used in examples and text in §1-6 except for proper
names and grammatical items discussed in §3, and several hundred of the
other most commonly used or especially interesting Bunuba words. In both
lists Gun.gunma words are identified by $ before the word (cf. §5), words
said to be specific to the 'heavy' dialect are identified by (H) after the English
gloss and those specific to the 'light' dialect by (L) (cf. §1.2).

7.1 VOCABULARY IN SEMANTIC FIELDS

NOMINALS

A - Body Parts
gungulu; $winjala; head
gunygunyu, $bungbungu; brain
wirrili, $yambarra; hair on head
    or body
marruli, marrul-ngarri; grey
    hair
jawiy; forehead
mirrngi, $nganthi gun.gunu; face
mulu, $miyamburru; eye
wirrimalmal, $wanbinyi;
    eyebrow
wura; nose
bina, $man.ga; ear
nganybalgu, $wunbali; cheek,
    earlobe, temple (i.e., side of
    head)
langulu; chin, jaw
guji; chin
limimiy; jaw
thangani, $jayirriminyi; mouth

malawu; lip
thawuru; beard
minju, $liji; tooth
thalanyi; tongue
langari, $thalirrgi; saliva
winyi; neck, throat
birrmindi, $bandari; shoulder
    (also, figuratively, 'son')
gilili; shoulder blade
garri; armpit
bandiy; arm
juwumbu; elbow
jingirri; lower arm
mingali; hand, finger
miljani, $lirra; fingernail, toenail
ngamu; breast, milk
dumurru, $mantha dumurru;
    chest
lamani; rib
wumbarra; hip
waliwali; sides, flanks
gulgu; waist
guda, $mala; belly, stomach, guts

dinjili, $yalu; navel, umbilical
  cord
dulu; heart
gundawunda; kidney
gawu; lungs
miliy; liver
lirriy; large intestine
thanybana; back, spine
nyiyidi, $balma; lower back
manba; buttocks, rump
gawaru; anus, faeces
bidi; thigh
gimani; knee
jawulu; calf
garrawu; shin
luwu; ankle
thinga, $jarrgambirri; foot,
  footprint, track
madari; heel
galu; penis
ngaljarri, ngaljarri ganji;
  testicles
mariy; semen
bururru; pubic hair
jindili; vagina
gumbu, $gumbulu; urine
nganthi; body, trunk
bilina; skin
guju; bone
giliy; blood
min.ga; fat, marrow
nguyulu; sweat
bilwili; sore

B - Human Classification
gurama, $baliya; man, person,
  Aborigine
wiyi, $nyumbayngga; woman
buga, $banjani; child, baby,
  offspring
gunduwa buga; boy
wangarri; adolescent boy
bunungguli; bachelor
miyanggu; fully initiated man
ganaynggu buga; girl
yumburra wiyi; young,
  marriageable-aged woman
bunda; promised wife
gurama-ngarri wiyi, $baliya-
  ngarri nyumbayngga; married

(literally 'man-with') woman
wiyi-ngarri gurama,
  $nyumbayngga-ngarri baliya;
  married (literally 'woman-
  with') man
juwurru; (male) subsection term
nangala; (female) subsection term
nyawurru; (female) subsection
  term
nyirali; stolen wife
galarra; widow, widower
jalnggangurru; Aboriginal
  'doctor'
jandangurru; boss, owner
malanyi; bad hunter
malmali, manmali, malngarri;
  white (literally 'red') person
mamu; corpse, devil, ghost
midmidmili; policeman (literally
  'one who's always tying up
  [people]')
limba; policeman

C - Human Relationship
nyaanyi; mother's brother
ngarranyi; mother, mother's sister
ngawungu; father, father's brother
ngawiy; father's sister
miymiy; mother's mother
jabiy, jaminyi; mother's father
ngawiji; father's mother, son's
  child
gilagi; father's father
mana; older brother
ngaja; younger brother
manay; older sister
ngajanyi; younger sister
jugu; son (man speaking), son or
  daughter (woman speaking)
ngabiy; daughter (man speaking)
gunda; male cross-cousin
nhungu, $ngumbana; husband
manggay; wife
madjali; mother-in-law
jimarri; mate
maangi; mate
D - Mammals
gayangurru; echidna ('porcupine')
jawula; marsupial mouse
walamba, $jalangana; big white

kangaroo species
wanjirri; river kangaroo species
wirray; big red hill kangaroo,
  male
barawu; big red hill kangaroo,
  female
wangay; wallaby species (black at
  the tip of his tail)
wiriyirri; rock wallaby
jularrga; euro
nyawa; tail
yawurragi; dingo
tharra, $jurrumbulu; dog
jarringgi; flying fox
bangali; bat
yawada; horse
bulumana; bullock, cow
gugunja; sheep

E - Reptiles
linygurra; saltwater crocodile
lalanggarra; fresh water crocodile
janggurru; short-necked turtle
waywurru; long-necked turtle
lunggura; bluetongue lizard
wawili; frilled lizard
ganbararra; sand goanna
baaniy; big goanna
wawanyi; small goanna
wabada; water goanna
bilanyi; snake (generic)
buwunyungu; black nosed python
darrali; whip snake
ngalana; death adder
ngunybulu; black snake
nilamarra; brown snake
lunburru; king brown snake

F - Birds
jirigi; bird (generic)
gambinyi; egg
burunu; nest (in tree)
jalmarra; wing feather
gananganja; emu
gurranda; brolga
mayada; pelican
jiyirri; kingfisher
galamuda; turkey bustard
thindijali; bush fowl
julayi; black swan

juwijbani, jurrguna; bower bird
milwirri; dove (red eyed)
balarara; pigeon
thiyila; tawney frogmouth
diyadiya; peewee
gurriranggul; butcher bird
jiyani; night bird
duwumbu; owl
wadawiy; spotted nightjar (L)
banangga; spotted nightjar (H)
jirrin.gin; owlet nightjar
wanggura; crow
jawawurru; kookaburra
jindiwirrinyi; willy wagtail
gulara; cuckoo
gurarri; sulpher-crested cockatoo
dirrari; black cockatoo
gilinygiliny; gallah
jajalingga; crimson winged parrot
ganjali; kite hawk
warrana; wedge-tailed eagle
bulungbulung, bulumbulung;
  spoonbill
jibilyugu; duck
lawala; black duck
garranggarrang; diver duck
thuthulu; pheasant coucal

G - Fishes
gawiy; fish (generic)
mulurru; catfish
balga; barramundi
lanyi; freshwater eel
guluma; bristle, spike (on catfish,
  etc.)

H - Insects, etc.
milnggi; antbed
thawunu; ant
jimani; sugarbag (generic)
wida; bee (generic)
naa, nayha; a type of sugarbag
  found in trees, the bee that
  makes it (also used for English
  honey)
ngarrwali; sugarbag found in the
  ground, the bee that makes it
milalani; scorpion
ganbarri; centipede
widigi; stick-insect

bininyi; maggot, cockroach
wurrirali; brown blowfly
ngirrinyi; common fly
gulinyi; mosquito
jungunyi; mosquito, fruit fly
walimarrgu; butterfly, moth
nurangarri; caterpillar
lajini; grub
baanu; spider
bambarri; mussel
ngalja; brown frog
balngawuna; green frog
jirragi; white frog
burrmuru; dragon fly
gindili; grasshopper
lamburra; termite
lun.ga; head louse

I - Language, Ceremony, etc.
yingiy, $jayirriminyi; n a m e
thangani, $jayirriminyi;
    language, story, speech,
    (literally 'mouth')
Gun.gunma; mother-in-law talk
    (see §5)
jadajada; (straight-REDUP)
    everyday Bunuba (as opposed
    to Gun.gunma 'mother-in-law
    talk')
jajal jajal; call of the crimson
    winged parrot
barawurru; fighting ground,
    dancing ground, clearing
bilji; red ochre
gumbarri; yellow ochre
mawurra; white ochre
ngarranggani; Dreamtime
lalani; dreaming

J - Artefacts, etc.
baljarrangi, $jalimanggurru;
    returning boomerang type
gali, $jalimanggurru; returning
    boomerang type
mandi, $jalimanggurru; non-
    returning boomerang type,
    used for hunting
gangan-gu; clapsticks (literally:
    'for clapping')
gananyi; digging stick

muwurru; club (nulla nulla)
jinali, $jimara; spear (generic)
jabirri, $jimara; shovel spear,
    fighting spear
jimbila, $jimara; bottle spear
warrba, $jimara binjari-jangi;
    barbed spear (the Gun.gunma
    expression literally means
    'spear like a hook')
madu; single-piece spear
malmurru; little wooden-tipped
    spear
ngawalu; spear thrower, woomera
garruna, garrwuna; shield
majali; cicatricising stone
mamulgu; sacred object
jamayina, $mayinday; axe
gurra; stone axe
gunggala; fire drill, firestick
jandamangurru; needle
ramburra; fishing net
galwaya; double-log raft
wiyidiy; dilly bag
yamadi; coolamon
baadi; pannikin
garanya; earth oven
thingi; cooking stone
jagula, $danji; shell pubic cover
rarrgi, $ngarramili; stone,
    money
wandu; bough shade
mayaru; house
balyamarada; motorcar
yathayatha-u; saddle (literally:
    'for sit-sitting')
birrinyi-ngarri; (sky-COM)
    helicopter

K - Fire, Food, Water
miyha, $nyajinda; meat
mayi, $mangarrinyi; vegetable
    food
winthali, $langgula; fire,
    firewood ($langgula is attested
    in the latter sense only)
wanggu; bush potato
wajarri; boab nut
windi; charcoal
birrgi; charcoal
wumbularri, $wumulu; hot coals

gambunu; ashes
binja; smoke
birrirra; flame
garuwa, $ngawagi; water, grog
nalija; tea
maali; creek
walibirri; river
winjarugu; soak
gulwula; waterhole
winjiy; rain

L - Celestial, Weather
gawarra; sun
lanygu; daytime
mangulu; shade
gilinymana; moon
wadanyi; star
maaningga; night-time
mirriyhini; rainbow
birrinyi; sky
ngumurru; cloud
manybu; fog
giriywa; wind
malngirri; thunder, lightning
miljidawurru; storm from the
    south

M - Geography
muway, $mangana, $dambalngu;
    place, camp
waandu, $waandu mangana; hut,
    humpy
baali; road, path, track
yanarri; town
banda; ground, dirt, earth
walyarra; sand
rarriwalu; river gravel
malwadja; mud
galadi; white clay
thuninyi; dust
nawanu; hole in ground, cave
galanganja; blacksoil plain
lajalaja; pocket country, i.e.,
    terrain with lots of pockets
balili; hill
rarrgi, $ngarramili; rock (also
    money)
rirrwili; pebble

N - Arboreal, etc.
lundu, $girili; tree, stick, wood
jilya; green (branch, nut, etc.)
wanjali; leaf
yunggu; scrub
wanamindi; root
wirruwu; flower
bilgi; grass
malagalay; prickle
gadjari; waterlily species (leaves
    arrow-shaped, flowers about
    5-7 cm across)
guyhu; waterlily species (flowers
    about 15 cm across)
garriy-ngarri; waterlily species
    with edible root
garriy; root of the garriy-ngarri
    water lily
jangga mayi; waterlily seedpod
ganji; seed
garringga; river red gum tree
muraga; bloodwood tree
warrulu, warrwulu; coolibah tree
walarri; ghost gum, snappy gum
marrira; leichhardt tree
ngiyali; bohemia tree
larrgari; boab tree
gunanggi; fig tree
warrgali; wattle tree
wulu; paper bark tree
jiyinjili; tea tree species
gandiwali; tea tree species
yinngani; yam
gili; bindi-eye
biriyali; conger berry bush
ngirri; spinifex with small, sharp
    blades
bininybalu; spinifex with large,
    relatively soft blades, used for
    making wax
gandiy; spinifex resin
yarrara, ngalthirri-guda;
    pandanus tree
ngalthirri; pandanus nut cluster

*O - Expressions of Quality or
    Quantity*
yuwana, $yimanjarri; one
thurranda, $yimiyandi; two
ngalgurru; three, a few

thurranda, $yimiyandi; two

ngalgurru; three, a few

nyanangarri; many

balanggarra; many, big mob

wulungarri, N: big mob, pack (of people, dogs, etc.)

ngaala; another, some, any, different (cf §3.3.2b)

wina; any?; (as in 'Is there any food for me?)

baljuwa; behind, last

baljuwa-ngarri, $burinya-ngarri; behind, last one

wurrbinya; alone, by oneself

gungunu; black

ngirigangara; white

malmali, manmali; red

nyana; big

balarra; open, full

gilandirri; big (used mainly of humans and animals)

wal(y)ay, wanyay, $yimangali; small, few

mabilyi; little, little one

girrabu, girrabungarri; long, tall

guba; roundish, stocky, 'nuggetty'

minybali, munybali; thin, skinny

jada, jadangurru; straight, right, proper

yiningga; just like that

digulngara; crooked (road, etc.)

jarinybara; crooked (boomerang, etc.)

balinja; flat, flat stone

jambala; hot

ngirrilya; cold, cool

jirri; wet

jumbulu; dry

danji; hard, strong

ngulyba; soft

minthini; heavy

dirrili; heavy

ranggumana; light (weight)

dagula; deep

lada; shallow

nayirri; sharp

thamani; blunt

laari; sweet

yaninggaya; new

jiraliga; old

jalungurru, $yirrimbali; good, gentle, quiet

ganday, $yiyuwurru; bad, old

nuna; smart

bina ganday, $bina yiyuwurru; stupid, insane (literally 'ear bad')

yirabanggu; frightened, cowardly

galangarri; wrong

wangini; dead

gijalu; raw, unripe

mula; ripe, cooked

muthura; rotten

bilwili; sick

ngirrginyi; hungry, hunger

thamada; deaf

ngadi; blind

milwa; angry, bad temper, trouble

bulirrgirri; bald

VERBS

P - Motion

wad+RA, $biriy+$AUX; go, come

wad+RA+ali(PROX), $briy+RA +ali(PROX); come

warara+RA; walk around

mulurrug+RA; wander around

gaman(ba)+RA; go hunting/foraging

wathayga+WU; go in, enter

dagurra+WU; go down

gurraga+NI; cross over, ford

giyga+NI; wake up, get up, come out, emerge

yuwurra; rush in, swarm

giygiyg+RA; keep waking up, getting up, coming out, emerging

birayga+RA; arrive, emerge

bayiyga+MA2; meet

banga+RA; go back

banga+RA+PROX; come back

gunaga+WU; turn around, turn over

gunaga+NGARRI; (cause to) rotate

dumbul+WU; go around, come around, avert

ganba+RA2, $duduba+$AUX;

follow
lamajga+YHA; get (someone), take
(someone) away
yungga+YHA; let go, send ahead
didiya+MA, $banjama+RA2;
chase
luwa+YHA; drive (cattle, etc.)
yurgula+WU2; pass by
girarra+RA/MA; crawl
gurrad(ga)+RA; hop
gurrad(ga)+RA2; make jump,
make hop
gurradga+WU; jump
nangguraj+RA; limp
malga+RA, $jarrnguri+RA;
dance
balbal+MA, $girrajga+$AUX; flee
balbala+RA, $girrajga+$AUX; fly
(balya+)girrgara+MA/RA,
$gurrayga+$AUX; run, run
away
winyin.ga+NI, $daraga+NI, V:
escape
burij(ga)+RA; play
burij(ga)+RA2; play with, dance
(a corroboree)
jira+WU, $warrwala+WU; fall
thatharra+WU; stand up
bara+NI, $ngambaj+$AUX; climb
up
tharrga+NI; climb down, get off
bayala+RA; swim
jurug+RA; bathe, swim
jurug+RA2; dive for (e.g.
waterlily roots)
juruga+NI; go down into the
water, drown
muba+WU; drown
nyanungga+NI; dive

Q - Rest, State
yatha+RA, $thany+RA; sit, stay
wurrba+NI, $darraman.ga+WU;
sit down
thandawa+RA, sit cross-legged
judiny+RA; crouch
judinyga+WU, bend over
giyga(/gijga)+NI,$ngambaj+NI;
get up, wake up
wara+RA; stand

baga+RA, $murrag+RA,
$murraba+RA; lie down,
stay, sleep
lirrba+WU2; be angered by
jirrmala+YHA; be shamed by
garwayla+RA; be dead
milu+RA, $thanya+$AUX; be alive
burrga+MA; get tired
nyungga+MA2; be asleep
ngirrginyga+NI; be hungry
ngalmana+NI; be thirsty
lumbirayj+RA; float around
ngilba+MA; spread around (fire,
etc.)
dubarra+NI; dry out
dumbul+WU; go around, come
around, avert

R - Induced position
wurrga+YHA, $wanyala+RA2,
$gulmun.ga+$AUX; put, put in
place
tharrga+RA2; put down, lower
bara+RA2; take upward
jamurrga+YHA; heap up
dadga+NGARRI; hang up
gurrij(ga)+RA2,
$mirringga+$AUX; hold on
to, look after, tend
wandayga+MA2; pick up on to
shoulder(s) and carry
wandayga+RA2; carry on
shoulder(s)
jilaj+RA2; carry underarm
wad(ga/ba)+RA2, $biriy+RA2;
take
wadba+MA2, $wanyala+WU2;
get, catch
banga+NGARRI; take back
banga+NGARRI+PROX; bring back
garrga+WU2, $wanyala+$AUX;
leave
rirrwa+RA2, $rirra+$AUX; pull
widjal+RA2; jerk
thubajga+RA2; push
garra+NGARRI, $wanyala+
NGARRI; throw
garra+RA/RA2; go throwing
(e.g., fishing line)
winyin.ga+NGARRI; hide

muja+YHA; burrow into the
   ground
wal̲anggala+WU2; lose, forget
diyga+NGARRI, $birayla
   +RA+OBL, $birayla+$AUX;
   find
diyga+WU; find (a camping place)
ngangga+YHA, $wanyala+$AUX,
   $yirrgi+YHA; give

S - Affect
dangayga+WU2,
   $yinbarra+$AUX; hit, kill
warij+RA2/MA2; kill
dangayba+RA2; assault (L)
bilthiba+RA2; assault (H)
duwa+WU2; hit (H)
warrba+WU2; flog, pound
dug+RA2; pound, grind
wurrala+WU2; punch
thuwan+MA; kick
ninthila+MA2; pinch
julya+MA; squeeze
nyaga+WU2; spear, stab
wud̲ijga+RA2; throw spear at
janda+MA2; pierce
dungga+MA2; pierce
thada+RA2; scoop with hands
wirriyga+MA2; dig
rawuga+YHA/RA2; bury
wirriyga+RA2; scratch
wirriywirriyga+MA2/RA2; write
yiriyirij(ga)+RA2/RA, V:
   straighten (spears) by heating
gayga+MA2; cut (e.g., sugar bag)
gaygay(tha/ga)+RA2,
   $mal̲amal̲a(ga)+$AUX; cut
wirrin.ga+RA2; scrape
duwarrga+RA; be broken, break
duwarrga+YHA, $nguwanygula+
   YHA/$AUX; break (i.e., cause
   to break)
thalma+RA2; divide in half
thanggaltha+RA2; quarter (meat,
   etc.)
wa(wa)+YHA/WU2; singe (the
   hair off a carcass)
bad̲a+WU2; seize, take away
banan̲ggarra+WU2; steal (meat,
   swag, wife etc.)

wuruga+RA2; take away, steal
ban̲ga+NGARRI; bring back
lirrba+WU2; tear up
dungga+RA; burst
biyga+YHA; burn (tr), set fire to
biyga+MA2; brand (cattle)
nga(g)+RA2; burn (of sun), eat
nga(g)+RA, $duwiya+$AUX; be
   burning (wood, etc.), eat
wu(g)+RA2, $wuga+$AUX; cook
wuba+YHA; cook
barrga+YHA; stoke (a fire)
m id̲ga+MA2; tie on, tie up
m in̲a+YHA; roll up (swag, etc.)
thud̲ga+MA2; pull up
burra+RA2; rub
nyunba+YHA; paint
ba+NI; paint up for corroboree
manjimanji+RA; draw
thuruga+YHA/NGARRI; cover,
   bury
manja+MA2/RA2,
   $ngarangaraga+GG Aux; make,
   build
wirama+RA2; forage, gather
thirridga+WU2; winnow, peel,
   strain
ginyirriga+WU2; betray, double-
   cross, cuckold
j al̲ngga+MA2; heal or magically
   manipulate someone's body

T - Attention
lingga+NI, $lirri+RA/$AUX; wait
lingga+RA2; wait for
mila+RA2, $yilga+MA2; see,
   look at
mila+RA2+CTV; stare at
mila+RA; look around
gaman(ga/ba)+RA2,
   $girribinyga+RA2; look for
gaman.ga+MA+OBL; look for
winyi+RA2; hear, listen to
dawungga+MA2; like
m ind̲ija+MA2; believe
yura+WU2; fear
bina+RA2; show
binarriya+MA2; show (H)
yuniya+MA2; show (L)

U - Talking, etc.
MA; say
wuḻa+MA, $gamalg+RA; speak
wuḻa+RA2, $gamalg+RA2; talk to
wuḻa (ḻa)+RA; talk at length
matha+RA2,
    $gamalg+RA(+OBL); tell, tell
    about, indicate
jawiy+RA2 V: tell, inform
ngayaga+MA2, $gamalg; ask (for)
ngayag+RA2; ask
burrganyga+RA2; ask about
waya+MA, $gurraya+$AUX/MA;
    call out
waya+RA; be calling out, keep
    calling out
wayi+RA, $gurraya+$AUX/RA;
    be calling out
bu+MA; moo
daliya+MA2; name
daliyba+RA2; call (refer to as...)
ngalany+RA; sing
ngalany(ga)+MA2/RA2; sing
    someone (to seduce or make
    ill)
guḏaya+WU2; keep after, try in
    vain to persuade

V - Corporeal
nga(g)+RA2,
    $jangani+$AUX/RA2; eat
nganja+MA2; bite
thaya+RA2; feed
wulug+RA; drink
wulug+RA2, $janganiya+$AUX;
    drink, swallow
wuluga+MA, $janganiya+$AUX;
    have a drink
wuluga+NGARRI; swallow
gulmurr+RA2; vomit
ngajirr+RA/MA; sneeze
yajili+RA2; dream (about)
gambay+RA; yawn
wab+RA; smell (intr: 'it smells to
    me', etc.)
bu+YHA; blow
nganhingga+MA; lick
nganhing+RA2; lick
bungbung+RA2; kiss
julurr+WU; marry

yuwid+RA2; copulate with
thingga+WU2; lay an egg
$thingga+$AUX; defecate
dalja+MA; grow up
dalja+NI; get big
dalja+WU2; rear
wulwul+MA (with OBL cross
    reference for experiencer); be
    in pain
jirrbal+WU2 (with Obj. cross
    reference for experiencer); be
    in pain
warirr+RA; itch
warirra+MA; scratch oneself
duluga+WU, $garrwayla+$AUX,
    $debarra+$AUX; die
wala+RA, $yarrinyin; cry
galgaḻa+MA; laugh

W - Other Verbs and Adverbials
gula+RA; try, test (see §3.4.12b)
wariyga+WU, $girrbi+RA,
    $banja+NI; start out, start
    going, shift oneself
ngada+RA2; make camp
barrba; going on foot, going on a
    journey
baliya; going quickly
gurrugurru; quickly, suddenly
wambaḻa; slowly, gradually
buja+WU2; finish
buja+NI; be finished
yungu; sort of, a little bit
yilngarri; altogether, for good,
    completely
madija; really, truly
walinggaṉi; half way, partially
mal; Gun.gunma verbal auxiliary
    root (see §5.2.3)

X - LOCATION
biyhirriga; north
ngiyamungga; south
ngilamungga; east
ligi(wurra); west (L)
ligayhina; west (H)
jibirri; downstream
wathila, $malambarra; nearby
jarraa; far away
rawurra; up, on top

biliga; halfway, middle, in
    between
rawurruga; upward
baburru; down
baburruga; downward
baburruingga; underneath
ngindangarringga; this side
ngurrungarriingga; other side
jarrangarringga; other side
ngurrubilinyalu; from that side
minaluga; to here, in this direction
balara; outside, everywhere

Y - TIME

nyirramiya $jamuniwa,
    $gumbuniingga; yesterday
yaninga; now
yaningiya, $ngajarri; now, today
maaningarri, $gumbuningarri;

morning, tomorrow
garrwaru; afternoon
jirali; before, for a long time,
    forever
warra; later, by-and-by
warraynga; after a while

Z - INTERJECTION

yuway, $yawu; yes
ngayi, $wumilay; no, not
a'ga; not so
āy; ha!
gaj, $gay; Come on!
yaninja(wurru),
    $ngajarri(wurru); O.K., all
    right
wilagurru, 'Alright', 'finished'
ngāy; yes, that's right

7.2   ALPHABETICAL VOCABULARY

a'ga, INT: not so
āy, INT: ha!
ba+NI, V: paint up for
    corroboree
baadi, N pannikin
baali, N: road, path, track
baaniy, N: big goanna
baanu, N: spider
baburru, N: down
baburruga, N: downward
baburruingga, N: underneath
bada+WU2, V: seize, take away
baga+RA, V: lie down, stay,
    sleep
balanggarra, N: many, big mob
balara, N: outside, everywhere
balarara, N: pigeon
balarra, N: open, full
balbal+RA, V: fly
balbala+MA, V: flee
balga, N: barramundi
balili, N: hill
balinja, N: flat, flat stone
baliya, ADV: going quickly
$baliya, N: man, person,
    Aborigine
$baliya-ngarri nyumbayngga,

N: married (literally 'man-
    with') woman
baljarrangi, N: returning
    boomerang type
baljuwa, N: behind, last
baljuwa-ngarri, N: behind, last
    one
$balma, N: lower back
balngawuna, N: green frog
balyamarada, N: motorcar
bambarri, N: mussel
banangga, N: spotted nightjar
    (H)
bananggarra+WU2, V: steal
    (meat, swag, wife etc.)
banda, N: ground, dirt, earth
$bandari, N: shoulder (also,
    figuratively, 'son')
bandiy, N: arm
banga+NGARRI+PROX, V: bring
    back
banga+NGARRI, V: take back
banga+RA+PROX, V: come back
banga+RA, V: go back
bangali, N: bat
$banja+NI, V: start out
$banjama+RA2, V: chase

$banjani, N: child, baby
bara+NI, V: climb up
bara+RA2, V: take upward
barawu, N: big red hill
   kangaroo, female
barawurru, N: fighting ground,
   dancing ground, clearing
barrba, ADV: going on foot,
   going on a journey
barrga+YHA, V: stoke (a fire)
bayala+RA, V: swim
bayiyga+MA2, V: meet
b idi, N: thigh
b ilanyi, N: snake (generic)
b ilgi, N: grass
biliga, N: halfway, middle, in
   between
b ilina, N: skin
bilji, N: red ochre
bilthiba+RA2, V: assault (H)
b ilw ili, N: sick
b ilw ili, N: sore
bina ganday, N: stupid, insane
   (literally 'ear bad')
$bina yiyuwurru, N: stupid,
   insane (literally 'ear bad')
bina+RA2, V: show
bina, N: ear
binarriya+MA2, V: show (H)
b ininybalu, N: spinifex with
   large, relatively soft blades,
   used for making wax (cf.
   ngirri).
bininyi, N: maggot, cockroach
binja, N: smoke
birayga+RA, V: arrive, emerge
$birayla+RA+OBL, V: find
$birayla+RA, V: arrive, emerge
$biriy+$AUX, V: go
$biriy+A+ali(PROX), V: come
$biriy+RA2, V: take
birrgi, N: charcoal
birrinyi, N: sky
birrinyi-ngarri, N: (sky-
   COM) helicopter
birrirra, N: flame
birrmindi, N: shoulder (also,
   figuratively, 'son')
biyga+MA2, V: brand (cattle)
biyga+YHA, V: burn (tr), set

fire to
biyhirriga, N: north
bu+MA, V: moo
bu+YHA, V: blow
buga, N: child, baby, offspring
buja+NI, V: be finished
buja+WU2, V: finish
bulirrgirri, N: bald
bulumana, N: bullock, cow
bulungbulung, bulumbulung, N:
   spoonbill
bunda, N: promised wife
bungbung+RA2, V: kiss
$bungbungu, N: brain
bunungguli, N: bachelor
burij(ga)+RA, V: play
burij(ga)+RA2, V: play with,
   dance (a corroboree)
$burinya-ngarri, N: behind,
   last one
burra+RA2, V: rub
burrga+MA, V: get tired
burrganyga+RA2, V: ask about
burrmuru, N: dragon fly
burunu, N: nest (in tree)
bururru, N: pubic hair
buwunyungu, N: black-nosed
   python
dadga+NGARRI, V: hang up
dagula, N: deep
dagurra+WU, V: go down
daliya+MA2, V: name
daliyba+RA2, V: call (refer to
   as__)
dalja+MA, V: grow up
dalja+NI, V: get big
dalja+WU2, V: rear
$dambalngu, N: place, camp
dangayba+RA2, V: assault
dangayga+WU2, V: hit, kill
danji, N: hard, strong
$danji, N: shell pubic cover
$daraga+NI, V: escape
darrali, N: whip snake
$darraman.ga+WU, V: sit down
dawungga+MA2, V: like
$debarra+$AUX, V: die
didiya+MA, V: chase
digulngara, N: crooked (road,
   etc.)

dinjili, N: navel, umbilical cord

dirrari, N: black cockatoo

dirrili, N: heavy

diyadiya, N: peewee

diyga+NGARRI,$birayla+RA+OBL, $birayla+$AUX, V: find

diyga+WU, V: find (a camping place)

dubarra+NI, V: dry out

$duduba+$AUX, V: follow

dug+RA2, V: pound, grind

dulu, N: heart

duluga+WU, V: die

dumbul+WU, V: go around, come around, avert

dumurru, N: chest

dungga+MA2, V: pierce

dungga+RA, V: burst

duwa+WU2, V: hit (H)

duwarrga+RA, V: be broken, break

duwarrga+YHA, V: break (i.e., cause to break)

$duwiya+$AUX, V: be burning (wood. etc.)

duwumbu, N: owl

gadjari, N: waterlily species (leaves arrow-shaped, flowers about 5-7 cm across)

gaj, $gay, INT: Come on!

galamuda, N: turkey bustard

galanganja, N: blacksoil plain

galangarri, N: wrong

galarra, N: widow, widower

galgala+MA, V: laugh

gali, N: returning boomerang type

galu, N: penis

galwaya, N: double-log raft

$gamalg+RA ... NP-DAT, V: ask for

$gamalg+RA(+OBL), V: tell, tell about, indicate

$gamalg+RA, V: speak

$gamalg+RA2, V: talk to

gaman(.ga/ba)+RA2, V: look for

gaman(ba)+RA, V: go hunting/foraging

gaman.ga+MA+OBL, V: look for

gambay+RA, V: yawn

gambinyi, N: egg

gambunu, N: ashes

gananganja, N: emu

gananyi, N: digging stick

ganaynggu buga, N: girl

ganba+RA2, V: follow

ganbararra, N: sand goanna

ganbarri, N: centipede

ganday, N: bad, old

gandiwali, N: tea tree species

gandiy, N: spinifex resin

gangan-gu, N: clapsticks (literally: 'for clapping')

ganjali, N: kite hawk

ganji, N: seed

garanya, N: earth oven

garra+NGARRI, V: throw, throw away

garra+RA/RA2, V: go throwing (e.g, fishing line)

garranggarrang, N: diver duck

garrawu, N: shin

garrga+WU2, V: leave

garri, N: armpit

garringga, N: river red gum tree

garriy, N: root of the garriy-ngarri water lily

garriy-ngarri, N: waterlily species with edible root

garruna, garrwuna, N: shield

garrwaru, ADV: afternoon

$garrwayla+$AUX, V: die

garuwa, N: water, grog

garwayla+RA, V: be dead

gawarra, N: sun

gawaru, N: anus, faeces

gawiy, N: fish (generic)

gawu, N: lungs

gayangurru, N: echidna ('porcupine')

gayga+MA2, V: cut (e.g., sugarbag)

gaygay(tha/ga)+RA2, V: cut

gijalu, N: raw, unripe

gilagi, N: father's father

gilandirri, N: big (used mainly of humans and animals)

gili, N: bindi-eye

gilili, N: shoulder blade

gilinymana, N: moon
gilinygiliny, N: galah
giliy, N: blood
gindili, N: grasshopper
ginyirriga+WU2, V: cuckold
ginyirriga+WU2, V: betray,
    double-cross, cuckold
girarra+RA/MA, V: crawl
$girili, N: tree, stick
giriywa, N: wind
girrabu, girrabungarri, N:
    long, tall
$girrajga+$AUX, V: fly
$girrbi+RA, V: start out
(balya+)girrgara+MA/RA, V:
    run, run away
$girribinyga+RA2, V: look for
giyga(/gijga)+NI, V: get up,
    wake up, come out, emerge
giygiyg+RA, V: keep getting up,
    waking up, coming out,
    emerging
guba, N: roundish, stocky,
    'nuggetty'
guda, N: belly, stomach, guts
gudaya+WU2, V: keep after, try
    in vain to persuade
gugunja, N: sheep
guji, N: chin
guju, N: bone
gula+RA, V: try, test (see
    §3.4.12b)
galadi, N: white clay
gulara, N: cuckoo
gulgu, N: waist
gulinyi, N: mosquito
$gulmun.ga+$AUX, V: put, put
    in place
gulmurr+RA2, V: vomit
guluma, N: bristle
gulwula, N: waterhole
gumani, N: knee
gumbarri, N: yellow ochre
gumbu, N: urine
$gumbulu, N: urine
$gumbuningarri, N: morning,
    tomorrow
$gumbuningga, ADV: yesterday
Gun.gunma, N: mother-in-law
    talk (see §5)

gunaga+NGARRI, V: (cause to)
    rotate
gunaga+WU, V: turn around,
    turn over
gunanggi, N: fig tree
gunda, N: male cross-cousin
gundawunda, N: kidney
gunduwa buga, N: boy
gunggala, N: fire drill, fire stick
gungulu, N: head
gungunu, N: black
gunygunyu, N: brain
gurama, N: man, person,
    Aborigine
gurama-ngarri wiyi, N:
    married (literally 'man-with')
    woman
gurarri, N: sulpher-crested
    cockatoo
gurra, N: stone axe
gurrad(ga)+RA, V: hop
gurrad(ga)+RA2, V: make
    jump, make hop
gurradga+WU, V: jump
gurraga+NI, V: cross over, ford
gurranda, N: brolga
$gurraya+$AUX/RA, V: call out
$gurrayga+$AUX, V: run, run
    away
gurrijga+RA2, V: hold on to
gurriranggul, N: butcher bird
gurrugurru, ADV: quickly,
    suddenly
guyhu, N: waterlily species
    (flowers about 15 cm across)
jabirri, N: shovel spear,
    fighting spear
jabiy, N: mother's father
jada, jadangurru, N: straight,
    right, proper
jadajada, N: (straight-REDUP)
    everyday Bunuba (as opposed
    to Gun.gunma 'mother-in-law
    talk')
jagula, N: shell pubic cover
jajal jajal, N: call of the
    crimson-winged parrot
jajalingga, N: crimson-winged
    parrot
$jalangana, N: big white

kangaroo species
$jalimanggurru, N: boomerang
jalmarra, N: wing feather
jalngga+MA2, V: heal or
    magically manipulate
    someone's body
jalnggangurru, N: Aboriginal
    'doctor'
jalungurru, N: good, gentle,
    quiet
jamayina, N: axe
jambala, N: hot
jaminyi, N: mother's father
$jamuniwa, ADV: yesterday
jamurrga+YHA, V: heap up
janda+MA2, V: pierce
jandamangurru, N: needle
jandangurru, N: boss, owner
$jangani+$AUX/RA2, V: eat
$jangani-ya+$AUX, V:
    swallow, drink, have a drink
jangga mayi, N: waterlily
    seedpod
janggurru, V: short necked
    turtle
jarinybara, N: crooked
    (boomerang, etc.)
jarraa, N: far away
jarrangarringga, N: other side
$jarrgambirri, N: foot
jarringgi, N: flying fox
$jarrnguri+RA, V: dance
jawawurru, N: kookaburra
jawiy, N: forehead
jawiy+RA2 V: tell, inform
jawula, N: marsupial mouse
jawulu, N: calf
$jayirriminyi, N: mouth,
    language, speech, story, name
jibilyugu, N: duck
jibirri, N: downstream
jilaj+RA2 V: carry underarm
jilya, N: green (branch, nut,
    etc.)
jimani, N: sugarbag (generic)
$jimara binjari-jangi, V:
    barbed spear (literally 'spear
    like a hook')
$jimara, N: spear
jimarri, N: mate

jimbila, N: bottle spear
jinali, $jimara, N: spear
    (generic)
jindili, N: vagina
jindiwirrinyi, N: willy wagtail
jingirri, N: lower arm
jira+WU, V: fall
jirali, ADV: before, for a long
    time, forever
jiraliga, N: old
jirigi, N: bird (generic)
jirragi, N: white frog
jirrbal+WU2 (with Obj. cross
    reference for experiencer), V:
    be in pain
jirri, N: wet
jirrin.gin, N: owlet nightjar
jirrmala+YHA, V: be shamed by
jiyani, N: night bird
jiyinjili, N: tea tree species
jiyirri, N: kingfisher
judiny+RA, V: crouch
judinyga+WU, V: bend over
jugu, N: son (man speaking),
    son or daughter (woman
    speaking)
jularrga, N: euro
julayi, N: black swan
julurr+WU, V: marry
julya+MA, V: squeeze
jumbulu, N: dry
jungunyi, N: mosquito, fruit fly
$jurrumbulu, N: dog
jurug+RA, V: bathe, swim
jurug+RA2, V: dive for (e.g.
    waterlily roots)
juruga+NI, V: go down into the
    water, drown
juwijbani, jurrguna, N: bower
    bird
juwumbu, N: elbow
juwurru, N: (male) subsection
    term
laari, N: sweet
lada, N: shallow
lajalaja, N: pocket country, i.e.,
    terrain with lots of pockets
lajini, N: grub
lalanggarra, N: fresh water
    crocodile

lalani, N: dreaming
lamajga+YHA, V: get (someone), take (someone) away
lamani, N: rib
lamburra, N: termite
langari, N: saliva
$langgula, N firewood
langulu, N: chin, jaw
lanygu, N: daytime
lanyi, N: freshwater eel
larrgari, N: boab tree
lawala, N: black duck
ligayhina, N: west (H)
ligi(wurra), N: west (L)
$liji, N: tooth
limba, N: policeman
limimiy, N: jaw
lingga+NI, V: wait
lingga+RA2, V: wait for
linygurra, N: saltwater crocodile
$lirra, N: fingernail, toenail
lirrba+MA2, V: tear up
lirrba+WU2, V: be angered by
$lirri+RA/$AUX, V: wait
lirriy, N: large intestine
lumbirayj+RA, V: float around
lun.ga, N: head louse
lunburru, N: king brown snake
lundu, N: tree, stick, wood
lunggura, N: bluetongue lizard
luwa+YHA, V: drive (cattle, etc.)
luwu, N: ankle
maali, N: creek
maangi, N: mate
maaningarri, ADV: morning, tomorrow
maaningga, N: night-time
mabilyi, N: little (one)
madari, N: heel
madija, ADV: really, truly, extensively
madjali, N: mother-in-law
madu, N: single-piece spear
majali, N: cicatricising stone
mal, V: Gun.gunma verbal auxiliary root (see §5.2.3)
$mala, N: belly, stomach, guts
malagalay, N: prickle
$malamala(ga)+$AUX, V: cut

malanyi, N: bad hunter
malawu, N: lip
malga+RA, V: dance
malmali, manmali, malngarri, N: white (literally 'red') person
malmali, manmali, N: red
malmurru, N: little wooden-tipped spear
malngirri, N: thunder, lightning
malwadja, N: mud
mamu, N: corpse, devil, ghost
mamulgu, N: sacred object
$man.ga, N: ear
mana, N: older brother
manay, N: older sister
manba, N: buttocks, rump
mandi, N: non-returning boomerang type, used for hunting
$mangarrinyi, N: vegetable food
manggay, N: wife
mangulu, N: shade
manja+MA2/RA2, V: make, build
manjimanji+RA, V: draw
$mantha dumurru, N: chest
manybu, N: fog
mariy, N: semen
marrira, N: leichhardt tree
marruli, marrul-ngarri, N: grey hair
matha+RA2, V: tell, tell about, indicate
mawurra, N: white ochre
mayada, N: pelican
mayaru, N: house
mayi, N: vegetable food
$mayinday, N: axe
midga+MA2, V: tie on, tie up
midmidmili, N: policeman (literally 'one who's always tying up [people]')
migili, $madu, V: single-piece spear
mila+RA, V: look around
mila+RA2+CTV, V: stare at
mila+RA2, V: see, look at
milalani, N: scorpion

miliy, N: liver

miljani, N: fingernail, toenail

miljidawurru, N: storm from the south

milnggi, N: antbed

milu+RA, V: be alive

milwa, N: angry, bad temper, trouble

milwirri, N: dove (red eyed)

mina+YHA V: roll up (swag, etc.)

min.ga, N: fat, marrow

minaluga, N: to here, in this direction

mindija+MA2, V: believe

mingali, N: hand, finger

minju, N: tooth

minthini, N: heavy

minybali, munybali, N: thin, skinny

$mirringga+$AUX, V: hold on to

mirriyhini, N: rainbow

mirrngi, N: face

$miyamburru, N: eye

miyanggu, N: fully initiated man

miyha, N: meat

miymiy, N: mother's mother

muba+WU, V: drown

muja+YHA, V: burrow into the ground

mula, N: ripe, cooked

mulu, N: eye

mulurru, N: catfish

mulurrug+RA, V: wander around

muraga, N: bloodwood tree

$murrag+RA, $murraba+RA, V: lie down

muthura, N: rotten

muway; $mangana, N: place, camp

muwurru, N: club (nulla nulla)

naa, nayha, N: a type of sugarbag found in trees, the bee that makes it (also used for English honey)

nada, N: short

nalija, N: tea

nangala, N: (female) subsection term

nangguraj+RA, V: limp

nawanu, N: hole in ground, cave

nayirri, N: sharp

nga(g)+RA, V: be burning (wood. etc.), eat

nga(g)+RA2, V: burn (of sun), eat

ngaala, N: another, some, any, different

ngabiy, N: daughter (man speaking)

ngada+RA2, V: make camp

ngadi, N: blind

ngaja, N: younger brother

ngajanyi, N: younger sister

$ngajarri, ADV: now, today

ngajirr+RA/MA, V: sneeze

ngalana, N: death adder

ngalany(ga)+MA2/RA2, V: sing someone (to seduce or make ill)

ngalany+RA, V: sing

ngalgurru, N: three, a few

ngalja, N: brown frog

ngaljarri, ngaljarri ganji, N: testicles

ngalmana+NI, V: be thirsty

ngalthirri, N: pandanus nut cluster

$ngambaj+$AUX, V: climb up

$ngambaj+NI, V: get up, wake up

ngamu, N: breast, milk

ngangga+YHA, V: give

nganhing+RA2, V: lick

nganhingga+MA, V: lick

nganja+MA2, V: bite

$nganthi gun.gunu, N: face

nganthi, N: body, trunk

nganybalgu, N: cheek, earlobe, temple (i.e., side of head)

$ngarangaraga+GG Aux, V: make, build

$ngarramili, N: stone, money

ngarranggani, N: Dreamtime

ngarranyi, N: mother, mother's sister

ngarrwali, N: sugarbag found in the ground, the bee that

makes it
$ngawagi, N: water
ngawalu, N: spear thrower,
woomera
ngawijiy, N: father's mother,
son's child
ngawiy, N: father's sister
ngawungu, N: father, father's
brother
ngāy, INT: yes, that's right
ngayag+RA2, V: ask
ngayaga+MA2, V: ask (for)
ngayi, $wumili, INT: no;
MODE PARTICLE: not
ngilamungga, N: east
ngilba+MA, V: spread around
(fire, etc.)
ngindangarringga, N: this side
ngirigangara, N: white
ngirrginyga+NI, V: be hungry
ngirrginyi, N: hungry, hunger
ngirri, N: spinifex with small,
sharp blades (cf. bininybalu)
ngirrilya, N: cold, cool
ngirrinyi, N: common fly
ngiyali, N: bohemia tree
ngiyamungga, N: south
ngulyba, N: soft
$ngumbana, N: husband
ngumurru, N: cloud
ngunybulu, N: black snake
ngurrubilinyalu, N: from that
side
ngurrungarriingga, N: other
side
$nguwanygula+YHA/$AUX, V:
break
nguyulu, N: sweat
nhungu, N: husband
nilamarra, N: brown snake
ninthila+MA2, V: pinch
nuna, N: smart
nurangarri, N: caterpillar
nyaanyi, N: mother's brother
nyaga+WU2, V: spear, stab
$nyajinda, N: meat
nyana, N: big
nyanangarri, N: many
nyanungga+NI, V: dive
nyawa, N: tail

nyawurru, N: (female)
subsection term
nyirali, N: stolen wife
nyirramiya, ADV: yesterday
nyiyidi, N: lower back
$nyumbayngga, N: woman
$nyumbayngga-ngarri baliya,
N: married (literally 'woman-
with') man
nyunba+YHA, V: paint
nyungga+MA2, V: be asleep
ramburra, N: fishing net
ranggumana, N: light (weight)
rarrgi, N: stone, money
rarriwalu, N: river gravel
rawuga+YHA/RA2, V: bury
rawurra, N: up, on top
rawurruga, N: upward
$rirra+$AUX, V: pull
rirrwa+RA2, V: pull
rirrwili, N: pebble
thada+RA2, V: scoop with hands
thalanyi, N: tongue
$thalirrgi, N: saliva
thalma+RA2, V: divide in half
(meat, etc.)
thamada, N: deaf
thamani, N: blunt
thandawa+RA, V: sit cross-
legged
thanggaltha+RA2, V: quarter
(meat, etc.)
thangani, N: mouth, language,
story, speech.
$thany+RA, V: sit, stay
$thanya+$AUX, V: be alive
tharra, N: dog
tharrga+NI, V: climb down, get
off
tharrga+RA2, V: put down,
lower
thatharra+WU, V: stand up
thawunu, N: ant
thawuru, N: beard
thaya+RA2, V: feed
thanybana, N: back, spine
thindijali, N: bush fowl
thinga, N: foot, footprint, track
$thingga+$AUX, V: defecate
thingga+WU2, V: lay an egg

thingi, N: cooking stone

thirridga+WU2, V: winnow, peel, strain

thiyila, N: tawney frogmouth

thubajga+RA2, V: push

thudga+MA2, V: pull up

thuninyi, N: dust

thurranda, N: two

thuruga+YHA/NGARRI, V: cover, bury

thuthulu, N: pheasant coucal

thuwan+MA, V: kick

$waandu mangana, N: hut, humpy

waandu, N: hut, humpy

wa(wa)+YHA/WU2, V: singe (the hair off a carcass)

wab+RA, V: smell (intr: 'it smells to me', etc.)

wabada, N: water goanna

wad(ga/ba)+RA2, V: take

wad+RA+ali(PROX), V: come

wad+RA, V: go, come

wadanyi, N: star

wadawiy, N: spotted nightjar (L)

wadba+MA2, V: get, catch

wajarri, N: boab nut

wala+RA, V: cry

walamba, N: big white kangaroo species

walanggala+WU2, V: lose, forget

walarri, N: ghost gum, snappy gum

$walawulu, N: son (man speaking), son or daughter (woman speaking)

walibirri, N: river

walimarrgu, N: butterfly, moth

walinggani, ADV: half way, partially

waliwali, N: sides

walyarra, N: sand

wal(y)ay, N: small, few

wambala, ADV: slowly, gradually

wanamindi, N: root

$wanbinyi, N: eyebrow

wandayga+MA2, V: pick up on to shoulder(s) and carry

wanday(ga)+RA2, V: carry on shoulder(s)

wandu, N: bough shade

wangarri, N: adolescent boy

wangay, N: wallaby species (black at the tip of his tail)

wanggu, N: bush potato

wanggura, N: crow

wangini, N: dead

wanjali, N: leaf

wanjirri, N: river kangaroo species

$wanyala+$AUX, V:

$wanyala+$AUX-OBL, V: leave (it) be, give to

$wanyala+NGARRI, V: throw

$wanyala+RA2, V: put, put in place

$wanyala+WU2/$AUX, V: get, catch

wanyay, N: small, few

wara+RA, V: stand

warara+RA, V: walk around

warirr+RA, V: itch

warirra+MA, V: scratch oneself

warij+RA2/MA2, V: kill

wariyga+WU, V: start out, start going, shift oneself

wariyga+WU2, V: start out for

warra, ADV: later, by-and-by

warrana, N: wedge-tailed eagle

warraynga, ADV: after a while

warrba+WU2, V: flog, pound

warrba, $jimara binjari-jangi, N: barbed spear (the Gun.gunma expression literally means 'spear like a hook')

warrgali, N: wattle tree

warrulu, warrwulu, N: coolibah tree

$warrwala+WU, V: fall

wathayga+WU, V: go in, enter

wathila, $malambarra, N: nearby

wawanyi, N: small goanna

wawili, N: frilled lizard

waya+MA, V: call out

waya+RA, V: be calling out, keep calling out

wayi+RA, V: be calling out

waywurru, N: long-necked turtle

wida, N bee (generic)

widigi, N: stick-insect

w idjal+RA2, V: jerk

wilagurru, INT: 'Alright', 'finished'

wina, N: any? (as in 'Is there any food for me?')

windi, N: charcoal

$winjala, N: head

winjarugu, N: soak

w i n j iy, N: rain

winthali, N: fire, firewood

winyi+RA2, V: hear, listen to

winyi, N: neck, throat

winyin.ga+NGARRI, V: hide

winyin.ga+NI, V: escape

wirama+RA2, V: forage, gather

wiriyirri, N: rock wallaby

wirray, N: big red hill kangaroo, male

wirrili, N: hair on head or body

wirrimalmal, N: eyebrow

wirrin.ga+RA2, V: scrape

wirriyga+MA2, V: dig

wirriyga+RA2, V: scratch

wirriywirriyga+MA2/RA2, V: write

wirruwu, N: flower

wiyi, N: woman

wiyi-ngarri gurama, N: married (literally 'woman-with') man

wiyidiy, N: dilly bag

wu(g)+RA2, V: cook

wuba+YHA, V: cook

wudjiga+RA2, V: throw spear at

$wuga+$AUX, V: cook

wula (la)+RA, V: talk at length

wula+MA, V: speak

wula+RA2, V: talk to

wulu, N: paper bark tree

wulug+RA, V: drink

wulug+RA2, V: drink, swallow

wuluga+MA, V: have a drink

wuluga+NGARRI, V: swallow

wulungarri, N: big mob, pack (of people, dogs, etc.)

wulwul+MA (with OBL cross reference for experiencer), V: be in pain

wumbarra, N: hip

wumbularri, N: hot coals

$wumilay, INT, ADV: no, not

$wumulu, N: hot coals

$wunbali, N: cheek, earlobe, temple (i.e., side of head)

wura, N: nose

wurrala+WU2, V: punch

wurrba+NI, V: sit down

wurrbinya, N: alone, by oneself

wurrga+YHA, V: put, put in place

wurrirali, N: brown blowfly

wuruga+RA2, V: take away, steal

yajili+RA2, V: dream (about)

$yalu, N: navel

yamadi, N: coolamon

$yambarra, N: hair on head or body

yanarri, N: town

yaninga, N: now

yaninggaya, N: new

yaningiya, $ngajarri, N: now, today

yaninja(wurru), $ngajarri(wurru), INT: O.K., all right

yarrara, ngalthirri-guda, N: pandanus tree

$yarrinyin, V: cry

yatha+RA, V: sit, stay

yathayatha-u, N: saddle (literally: 'for sit-sitting')

yawada, N: horse

yawurragi, N: dingo

$yilga+MA2, V: see, look at

yilngarri, ADV: altogether, for good, completely

yilngarri, ADV: altogether, for good, completely

$yimangali, N: small

$yimanjarri, N: one

$yimiyandi, N: two

$yinbarra+$AUX, V: hit, kill

yiningga, N: just like that

yingiy, N: name

yinnganay, N: yam species
yirabanggu, N: frightened,
    cowardly
yiriyirij(ga)+RA2/RA, V:
    straighten (spears) by heating
$yirrgi+YHA, V: give
$yirrimbali, N: good, gentle,
    quiet
$yiyuwurru, N: bad, old
yumburra wiyi, N: young,
    marriageable-aged woman
yungga+YHA, V: let go, send

ahead
yunggu, N: scrub
yungu, ADV:, ADV: sort of, a
    little bit
yuniya+MA2, V: show (L)
yura+WU2, V: fear
yurgula+WU2, V: pass by
yuwana, N: one
yuway, $yawu, INT: yes
yuwid+RA2, V: copulate with
yuwurra+MA, V: rush in,
    swarm

ACKNOWLEDGMENTS

For their help and friendship during my many trips to Fitzroy Crossing over the past twenty years I wish to thank to Banjo Wirrunmarra, George and Alice Brooking, Barbara Jones, Joyce Hudson, Eirlys Richards, Howard Coate, Johnny Marr, Molly Jalakbiya, William Leopold, Mona Oscar, Billy Oscar, June Oscar, and Casey Ross. For their valuable comments on the many drafts of this grammar, I thank Bob Dixon, Barry Blake, Bill McGregor, Francesca Merlan, Suzanne Kite and Emily Knight. The morphological analysis benefited especially from meticulous cross-checking and insightful comments on the penultimate draft by Suzanne Kite, and the word list in §7 from my collaboration with Kimberley Language Resource Centre linguist Emily Knight in 1995 on their book of Bunuba stories (KLRC forthcoming), and the exhaustive concordance she prepared for it. Thanks also to the KLRC for funding my travel expenses for that project, and to AIATSIS (then the Australian Institute of Aboriginal Studies) and Sydney University for funding my fieldwork on Bunuba in 1978 and 1979.

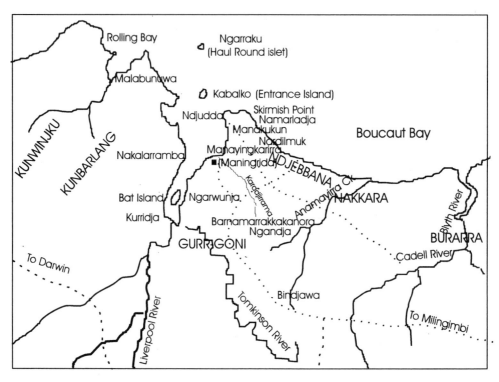

Map 3: Ndjebbana country

Ndjébbana
by Graham McKay

1. THE LANGUAGE AND ITS SPEAKERS

1.1 LINGUISTIC TYPE

Ndjébbana is a polysynthetic language which, in the Australian context, is a member of the non-Pama-Nyungan or prefixing group of languages. That is, it makes extensive use of both prefixes and suffixes for derivation and inflection, particularly with verbs.

The basic clause in the language consists simply of a verb complex, in which the core arguments subject and (where appropriate) object (or, for ditransitive verbs, indirect object) are marked by means of pronominal prefixes to the verb. Further affixes mark tense, mood and aspect. Optionally the pronominal core arguments may be expanded, elaborated or highlighted using independent nominals and pronouns. In fact such elaboration or highlighting is relatively uncommon in connected text in comparison with clauses containing simply a verb complex. The most commonly highlighted or elaborated arguments are the S and the O. Clauses may also contain further non-core elaboration by means of adverbs and so on.

Constituent order is based on pragmatic rather than syntactic considerations, with the most significant constituent occurring at the beginning of the clause and the remainder following in decreasing order of significance, often as 'afterthoughts' following the verb and providing elaboration.

Ndjébbana has very little case marking on nominals, having case suffixes only for ablative, purposive and the object of the hunt. The case roles of any independent nominals and pronouns which occur in the clause are primarily interpreted from context rather than being marked explicitly. There are two gender classes of nominals ('masculine' and 'feminine'). Ndjébbana has a complex system of marking possession on nominals which divides nominals into four 'possession classes'. These range from a more alienable type in which possession is marked using independent pronouns through to the most inalienable types which mark 'possession' (really identity of reference) using affixes.

Verbal morphology is rather complex. The system of pronominal prefixes is complicated, not least because Ndjébbana distinguishes seventeen separate pronominal person/number/gender category combinations which apply, with some neutralisations, to both subject (S and A) and object (O or IO) in partially analysable portmanteau pronominal prefix forms, combined with mood prefixes. Tense marking and some mood and aspect marking is by suffix. The present analysis shows that Ndjébbana verbs can be classified into eight conjugations on the basis of their tense/mood suffixes, if a total of 23 sub-conjugations is recognised. This leaves six known irregular verbs which do not fit the pattern of any of the eight conjugations. Reduplication is not used productively in Ndjébbana, unlike many languages of the area.

Ndjébbana is characterised by long, polysyllabic words and by complex patterns of stress shifting with resulting vowel reduction (together with some limited vowel harmony at the phonetic level). In rapid speech words are highly compressed, adding to the difficulty for the non-native speaker (and even, on occasion, for the native speaker).

1.2   TRIBAL AND LANGUAGE NAMES

Ndjébbana speakers themselves call their language Ndjébbana and claim that the term by which it is better known in the literature, 'Gunavidji', and its phonemically more accurate variant Kunibidji, is a name used by speakers of languages to the west (Kunbarlang, Kunwinjku and Maung) to refer to them. The Nakkara term for Ndjébbana is Ndjéya and the Burarra term is Gijiya. The term Ndjébbana (C. Coleman personal communication) is derived from the demonstrative djébba 'there', following a pattern that occurs with other language and dialect names in the area, particularly within the Burarra-speaking group. The term Kunibidji (C. Coleman personal communication) clearly follows the western Kunwinjkuan system of language names with the appropriate kun- prefix as used for language and country.

The term Ndjébbana refers only to the language. The people who speak the language refer to themselves as Ndjébbana njarrangúdjeya 'we who speak Ndjébbana' (also Ndjébbana barrangúdjeya 'those who speak Ndjébbana', etc.).

A significant unit of organisation is the yakkarrarra or bábburr, a patrilineal land-owning group. Details of the various Ndjébbana-speaking yakkarrarra are provided in Table 1.1 and discussed in §1.4.

Various 'tribal' names occur in association with different land-owning groups. The main terms encountered are the following: Márro people are those of the Kanduwúlka clan; Marlémarla people belong to the Karddúrra, Marlandjárridj and Wúrnal clans; and Mabárnad people belong to the Dukúrrdji and associated clans. This last term is currently being extended by some speakers as a general cover term for Ndjébbana speakers.

There is some variation in the language spoken by different clans in different areas. This variation has not been well studied but some indication of the types of differences noted is given in §1.4.

1.3   TERRITORY AND NEIGHBOURS

Ndjébbana speakers traditionally owned lands on the eastern side of the mouth of the Liverpool River in central Arnhem Land (upstream almost as far as Bat Island), the two islands in the mouth of the river, lands stretching along the coast of the Arafura Sea eastwards from the Liverpool River and some adjacent inland territories in the vicinity of Gudjerama Creek (Karddjirráma), Tomkinson River and Cadell River.

Their traditional neighbours were speakers of the following languages: Kunbarlang and dialects of Kunwinjku to the west and south-west; Kundjirrbara immediately upstream on the Liverpool River (this language has now given way to Ndjébbana and Gurrgoni); Gurrgoni (or Gungorrogone) to the south; Burarra (Gu-jingarliya (Gun-narda and Gun-narta) and Gunartpa or Gu-jarlabiya etc.) to the east and Nakkara to the north-east along the coast and the upper reaches of Gudjerama Creek.

Recent work on verb morphology by Green (1989) suggests that Ndjébbana, Nakkara, Burarra and Gurrgoni form a single subgroup, rather than separate language families as suggested by O'Grady et al. (1966) on the basis of lexicostatistical information. It is possible (in my view probable) that these languages are more distantly related to the Kunwinjkuan family of languages spoken to the west and south.

Though the languages bear some resemblance to one another linguistically it is probably true to say that they are not to any great degree mutually intelligible. On the other hand speakers of these languages tend to be able to use one another's languages to a greater or lesser degree as second languages, so that mutual interaction readily occurs, often involving code-switching by the various parties to a conversation or each speaker using his own language. See further discussion in §1.4.

1.4   SOCIOLINGUISTIC INFORMATION

[a] *Western Arnhem Land links.* Traditionally there was, and still is, a deep social division between the Aboriginal peoples of western Arnhem Land and those of eastern Arnhem Land. This traditional division cuts through the middle of the modern community of Maningrida, where Ndjébbana is now spoken. Anthropologists who have reported on this division have pointed to different social organisation patterns (western more matrilineal and eastern more patrilineal), different patterns of intermarriage and different trade links for the two groups (Armstrong 1967:11–14; cf. Elkin, Berndt and Berndt 1951, Berndt 1955, Hiatt 1965). People of the eastern Arnhem Land groups are circumcising while those of the western Arnhem Land groups are non-circumcising.

Within the Maningrida community itself there has been constant friction between people of the western and eastern Arnhem Land social groupings (Hiatt 1965:151–4; Armstrong 1967:15–22; McKay 1981d) and this was still observable in 1992.

The Ndjébbana-speaking people relate most closely to the western Arnhem Land bloc. Their closest relationships appear to be with Nakkara speakers, to the east, and with Kunbarlang (or Walang) speakers across the Liverpool River to the west. Both of these are classified by Armstrong (1967:11–13) among the 'Western Arnhem Land' group. Linguistically all of these languages are of the prefixing or non-Pama-Nyungan type.

In a self-report interview study of second language competence carried out in 1979 in connection with development of an orthography for Ndjébbana, McKay found that "...with the exception of Burarra, all the languages known by any significant number of [Ndjébbana] speakers interviewed are from the Western Arnhem Land group, the major ones being Gunbarlang and Gunwinjgu."(McKay 1981d:216) While a significant number of those interviewed in the study also spoke Burarra, a prefixing language of the eastern group, the speakers reported a rather lower level of competence in Burarra than in languages to the west (McKay 1981d:216). (This study does not claim to indicate actual levels of language competence but simply uses claimed competence as a broad indicator of attitudes towards the various languages.) Furthermore, though about half the marriages of Ndjébbana speakers over two generations were with Ndjébbana speakers, the remaining 'interlinguistic' marriages were almost exclusively with spouses from other western Arnhem Land groups (McKay 1981d:217; Armstrong 1967:12), though, by the beginning of the nineties this may be changing. This westward orientation was confirmed in the strong support of Ndjébbana speakers for an orthography modelled on that of one of the western Arnhem Land languages Kunwinjku or Maung (particularly the former), rather than on the locally developed orthography of the eastern language Burarra (McKay 1981d:217–18, 1982c). This westward orientation of Ndjébbana speakers continues to be confirmed by the broad pattern of travel, hunting activity, ceremonial life and so on, though there is also clear evidence of links across the east–west divide. In a couple of funerals held in 1992, for example, some of the singers 'booked' to participate were from eastern Arnhem Land groups (including Burarra) and photographs taken by photographer Axel Poignant in 1952 show Ndjébbana and Burarra speakers dancing together during a Rom ceremony on the west bank of the Liverpool River (R. Poignant personal communication).

In the day-to-day life of Maningrida, then, Ndjébbana speakers primarily associate amongst themselves and with members of other western Arnhem Land groups, while still interacting with their eastern neighbours, particularly on a more casual or a business footing. A large number of adult Ndjébbana speakers are also regular users of Kunbarlang and Kunwinjku and, to a lesser extent, of Nakkara and Maung.

[b] *Ndjébbana–speaking* yakkarrarra *or clans.* Each Ndjébbana speaker belongs to a specific yakkarrarra or bábburr. This affiliation with a land-owning group is inherited from a person's father and carries with it various responsibilities relating to the land itself and to the language and ceremonies linked with that tract of land from the 'beginning', when the natural order and the social system were set in place by the various creative beings. These yakkarrarra are exogamous.

TABLE1.1 *Ndjébbana-speaking yakkarrarra or clans*

Yakkarrarra	Moiety	Lang. type	Loc.	Country
Dukúrrdji	Y	Nj	L	Manayingkarírra
Djawándji	Y	Nj	L	Karddjirráma
Kanduwúlka	Dj	Nj	C	Nardílmuk
Karddúrra	Dj	Nj	C	Ndjúdda
Marlandjárridj	Dj	Nj	C	Ndjúdda
Naddjóddjarra	Y	Nj	W	Malabunúwa
Nakkuráduk	Y	M	I	Barnamarrákka--kanóra
Namanakarérrben	Y	Nj	L	Ngárwunja
Namidjbáli	Y	Nj	L	
Nganayerrebarála	Dj	M	I	Bíndjawa
Wárrkwarrk	Dj	M	I	Ngándja
Wúrnal	Dj	Nj	C	Ndjúdda, Kabálko, Ngarráku

Dj = *Djówanga*	Nj = *Njálkkidj*	C = *Coastal*
Y = *Yírriddjanga*	M = *Marndálangurrnga*	L = *Liverpool River*
		I = *Inland*
		W=*West of Liverpool R*

Table 1.1 sets out the names of the known yakkarrarra which have various forms of Ndjébbana as their language. Ndjébbana varieties are classified into two main types, described as njálkkidj 'soft' and marndálangurrnga 'hard'. The latter is associated with some of the more inland yakkarrarra. The traditional fish poisoning ceremony called lúrra, held at Kabálko (Entrance Island), is open only to men who speak njálkkidj forms of Ndjébbana and when a man first participates in this ceremony he has to display his ability to use this form of language to the 'old people', the spirits in charge of the place (cf. Armstrong 1967:71–2 and Text 7). Table 1.1 provides an indication of the location of the land of each clan. 'C' or Coastal' indicates land along the north coast, facing the Arafura Sea; 'L' or 'Liverpool' means along the east bank of the Liverpool River and the lower reaches of one of its tributary creeks; 'I' or 'Inland' refers to the areas south and east (i.e. inland) of the coastal and Liverpool areas.

Each yakkarrarra is associated with one of the two moieties Djówanga or Yírriddjanga (corresponding to the north-east Arnhem Land moieties Dhuwa and Yirritja). The same moiety affiliation applies also to the land and the religious and ceremonial responsibilities which go along with membership in a particular yakkarrarra. In the case of one yakkarrarra listed, an irregularity occurred a couple of generations back which has led to a mismatch between the moiety of the land and the responsibilities which go with it on the one hand and the individuals who own that land on the other. I refer to the Marlandjárridj group, which was traditionally Djówanga. When a man of that yakkarrarra married 'wrong', that is he married a woman who was Djówanga like himself, his children had to be in the opposite moiety to their mother. That is his children became Yírriddjanga, whereas if he had married correctly (into the opposite moiety to his own) his children would have been Djówanga like himself. Thus more recent generations of Marlandjárridj people are themselves Yírriddjanga, but the land and ceremonial matters which they have traditional links with are Djówanga, like the other groups with whom they share similar links.

The differences in language between the various yakkarrarra have not been studied. Nor has the distinction between njálkkidj language and marndálangurrnga language. The differences between various types of njálkkidj Ndjébbana which have been mentioned by speakers of the language largely fall into the category of lexical items but only a very small proportion of the lexicon is affected.

The examples which have been mentioned by speakers relate to the moiety division, where we find word equivalents such as the following:

Yírriddjanga	*Djówanga*	
yéna	yána	'earlier today'
yúya	ngálngarda	'fire'
kórnka, karrórnba	marnawarrínjba	'type of yam'

There are also some minor differences in verb inflections between the main Djówanga and Yírriddjanga speakers who have provided most of the information on which this grammar is based (Kanduwúlka and Dukúrrdji respectively). For instance the Djówanga speaker uses a suppletive future form -míba in the paradigm of the verb -rlúrrabayi (2B), while the Yírriddjanga speaker forms all tenses of this verb regularly on the same root -rlúrrabayi. The Yírriddjanga speaker had a slightly greater tendency to form the counterfactual using the infinitive with the counterfactual of the verb -yángka, while the Djówanga speaker tended to use more inflected forms for the counterfactual, while still recognising the other as legitimate. Thus, for instance we can hear both of the following forms, but the former is more likely to be used by the Djówanga speaker and the latter by the Yírriddjanga speaker:

kóma   nga-ya-rarraddja-ngóna
NEG   1MINA+3MINO-IRR-clean-CF
I didn't clean it.

```
kóma        na-rórrddja      nga-ya-ngka-yína
NEG         INFIN-clean      1MINA+3MINO-IRR-do-CF
I didn't clean it
```

[c] *Social organisation: Moieties and subsections.* All people, clans, tracts of land and most creatures are classified as members of one of two moieties. These are called Djówanga and Yírriddjanga and equate to the north-east Arnhem Land moieties Dhuwa and Yirritja respectively. The two moieties are in a balanced relationship of mutual dependence and mutual responsibility.

Each moiety is further divided into four 'subsections' or 'skins' and each person belongs to one of these by virtue of his or her birth, the determining factor being the subsection of his or her mother.

There are two levels of relationship between people in Ndjébbana-speaking society: that of blood relationships and that of classificatory or 'skin' relationships. That is, for instance, at the classificatory level a person calls all those who belong to the same subsection as himself 'brother' or 'sister', and all those who belong to his mother's subsection 'mother' or 'mother's brother' ('uncle'). Of all these classificatory kin, only a very restricted number actually bear blood relationships of these types to him.

According to the system, a person will be in the same moiety as his or her brothers, sisters, father and father's siblings and in the opposite moiety to his or her mother and mother's siblings. One normally must marry a spouse from the opposite moiety and doing otherwise completely disrupts the normal patterns of moiety membership (by putting one's children in the wrong moiety in terms of patrilineal norms). We will set out some of the basic kin relationships below as outlined in Eather (n.d.a).

Chart 1.1 (following Eather (n.d.a) which derives from Hiatt (1965: 49)) sets out the Ndjébbana subsection terms. The Djówanga subsections are plain and the *Yírriddjanga* subsections are italicised. The feminine forms of each subsection term has the feminine nja- prefix, the masculine term has one of the masculine prefixes (either n-, na- or zero). The paired masculine and feminine terms represent classificatory 'brother–sister' pairings. Thus a Kangíla man calls a Njakangíla woman 'sister' and she calls him 'brother'. Djábba is the term of address for 'older sibling' and karlamára for 'younger sibling'.

The adjacent positions joined by 'X' on the inner and outer circles represent the primary potential marriage relationships. These are across moieties. For instance a Kangíla man's first choice of wife is a Njabúlanj woman. Kangíla or Njakangíla men and women call any Búlanj or Njabúlanj person máma or kalikkali and vice versa.

The arrows indicate mother–child relationships with the arrow head pointing towards the child. Thus Búlanj and Njabúlanj are both children of a Njakamárrang woman and call her and all her sisters (real and classificatory) kíkka 'mother'. Mother's brother (in this example Nkamárrang) is called djádja 'uncle' and has a special protective role towards his sister's children, whom he calls ngákarda. (Note that a mother's 'skin' or subsection is the crucial determining factor for her child's skin, irrespective of the 'skin' of the father.)

CHART 1.1 *Ndjébbana subsections or 'skins'*

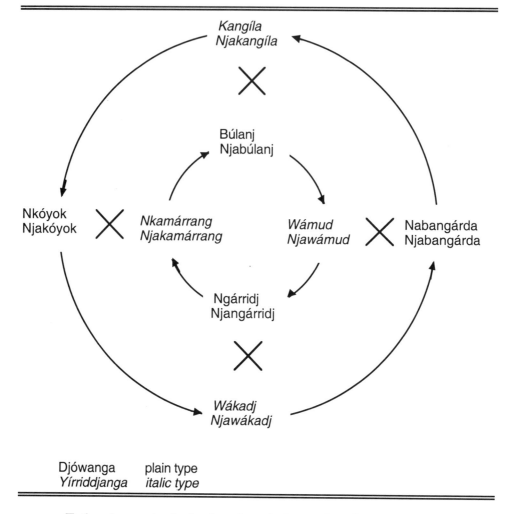

Djówanga   plain type
Yírriddjanga   *italic type*

Father is mother's husband and, in a classificatory sense, all his brothers. These are called bábba 'father'. In our example Búlanj and Njabúlanj's father is a Nkóyok man. Father's sisters, both real and classificatory (in this example Njakóyok) are called ngánja 'auntie'. Through one's father one inherits ownership links with land and ceremonial matters, while through one's mother one inherits managerial links with other land and ceremonies (in the opposite moiety classification).

A person has a special reciprocal relationship with people of his/her mother's mother's subsection. This is the subsection of the same moiety directly across the chart and linked by an upward sequence of two mother-child arrows. People in this relationship call one another kúdjala 'grannie' and can generally take liberties such as joking and swearing between themselves. Nkóyok/Njakóyok and Nabangárda/Njabangárda are grannies and call one another kúdjala.

A grannie's potential spouse (termed mámam) is one's 'second choice' spouse. Thus, for instance, a Wákadj/Njawákadj person's grannie is

Kangíla/Njakangíla and his/her mámam or alternative spouse is therefore Njabúlanj/Búlanj. If a man marries his second choice spouse (mámam) his children will be in a different subsection from what they would have been if he marries his primary potential spouse (though in the same moiety). This affects only blood relationships not classificatory relationships.

Two significant avoidance relationships are the brother–sister relationship and the djóngok '(poison–)cousin' relationship. Brothers and sisters, particularly biological brothers and sisters, may not give things or speak directly to one another, swear in front of one another or utter or hear one another's 'bush' names (Aboriginal names). They may certainly not marry.

Spouse's (or primary potential spouse's) mother, whether real or classificatory, is one's djóngok. One does not give things or speak directly to one's djóngok and marriage with such a person is out of the question because both are in the same moiety. For example the djóngok of Búlanj/Njabúlanj (Djówanga) is Nabangárda/Njabangárda (Djówanga).

To communicate with someone in one of these avoidance relationships one must address another person, either as an intermediary or simply to allow the real addressee to 'overhear'. Giving or receiving can be carried out through an intermediary (often a child) or by putting the item down and walking away so that the recipient can approach to pick it up.

[d] *Special language for taboo relations.* There are reports of a special form of Ndjébbana for use with people in various taboo relationships such as mother-in-law (djóngok) (C. Coleman personal communication) but this form of speech has not been studied.

[e] *Reference to various kin.* A special set of terms is available for referring to various kin in Ndjébbana. Many of these terms are verb complexes which are used as nominals. This terminology has not been studied in detail so only a few examples of these terms are given here. These terms do not refer to merely classificatory relations and are not terms of address. The terms are analysed in parentheses. For details of morphology see §3 below. See example (136).

njana-ramé-ra-yana   'my father (bábba)'
(3MINA+1MINO-hold-REM-3MINMASCDATA)

njana-ramé-ra-yángaya   'my auntie (ngánja)'
(3MINA+1MINO-hold-REM-3MINFEMDATA)

njana-má-nga-bba-yángaya   'my mother (kíkka)'
(3MINA+1MINO-get-REM-EXT-3MINFEMDATA)

njana-má-nga-bba-yana   'my uncle (djádja)'
(3MINA+1MINO-get-REM-EXT-3MINMASCDATA)

ka-má-nga-bba   'his mother'
(3MINA+3MINMASCO-get-REM-EXT)

nja-rra-nó-ra-nja (1UAFEMS-RE-sit-CTP-UAFEM)	'my wife'
nji-rri-rendjí-na (1UAMASCS-RE-stand-REM)	'my brother'
nja-rra-rendjí-na-nja (1UAFEMS-RE-stand-REM-UAFEM)	'my sister'
ngana-barrábarra-bba (2MIN-big-EXT)	'you are their mother'

A further set of dyadic kin terms refers to sets of individuals who bear certain classificatory relationships to one another. In the light of what is found in nearby languages it is likely that some of these terms used for referring to groups of classificatory kin vary according to speaker, addressee and the relationship of each to the persons being referred to. This terminology has not been studied so only a few examples are provided here. See also Text 25/80 and examples (125) and (136). In the list the pronominal prefix (which can vary with person and number) is set off by a hyphen.

birri-yáwaka	'two men who call one another djádja (uncle) and ngákarda (nephew) respectively'
birri-yurdunjmakkúkka	'two men who call one another kúdjala (grannie) reciprocally'
narra-mómardakka	'you (plural) brothers'
birri-kkúrrngkawa	'two men who are in the djóngok (poison–cousin) relationship'
birri-béyaka	'two men who call one another father and son respectively'

[f] *Death taboos on vocabulary items.* As is widely reported for Australian languages, the names of the recently deceased are subject to a taboo amongst Ndjébbana speakers. See example (170). Such a taboo usually applies for a number of years and alternative means of referring to the deceased individual are employed, particularly kin terms and yakkarrarra and subsection terms. In some cases publications of the bilingual education program have been withdrawn from circulation, at least temporarily, because of the fact that a deceased person's name was displayed on the cover (as author). In some cases where the name of a deceased person has appeared in the text of a publication or a photograph has appeared the name has been whited out or the photograph excised to allow the book to continue being used.

Such death taboos have some affect on the everyday vocabulary of the language but this is minimised by the fact that many personal names subject to such taboo are not everyday words but rather words from songs, ceremonies and the names of significant sites. Only a couple of specific examples are known of ordinary terms being tabooed in this way.

[g] *Contact with Macassans and English Speakers.* Entrance Island in the mouth of the Liverpool River was one of the sites visited regularly during the monsoon season by Macassan trepang fishermen from Makassar (Sulawesi) over a long period, ending early in the twentieth century (McKnight 1976). These visits provided earlier generations of Ndjébbana speakers with contact with speakers of Makassarese and related languages of what is now Indonesia. That relations were not always harmonious is shown by the name of one place on the river bank just south of the township of Maningrida called Balándabindibbónabba, which means literally 'where the white people (i.e. Macassans) killed two people (aborigines)'.

These Macassan visitors left a legacy, not only of potsherds and tamarind trees, of canoes and other tools, but also of words. Ndjébbana, in common with languages right along the north coast of Arnhem Land, numbers among its everyday vocabulary at least 43 items which can be traced to Makassarese or similar sources. Some of these are set out in Table 1.2 which draws on Walker and Zorc's study (1981) of Makassarese and similar borrowings into the Yolngu languages further east.

Contact with English–speaking Europeans began at an unknown date. A couple of tantalising clues to an early date for contact is a pair of words apparently borrowed from English, but not current in English of the recent past. These are the words budmánda for 'suitcase' and Budáwin for 'Darwin'. Budmánda probably comes from the English word 'portmanteau', which is not in current use, though clearly the source of the Queensland and New South Wales term 'porte' for the same item. Budáwin is clearly derived from the term 'Port Darwin', which is the name originally given (1839) to the harbour where the present city of Darwin is located. The town itself was first called Palmerston (1869) and then Darwin (1911). Additional early English borrowings could be the word for 'trailer', wáykin, clearly from 'waggon' and djilíbba 'thongs (sandal)' (<'slipper'). Alternatively it is possible that these words have been borrowed via another language.

Subsequently as mission stations were set up along the north coast of Arnhem Land the main points of contact with Ndjébbana speakers appear to have been at the Methodist missions at Goulburn Island and Croker Island. (In the interview study carried out in 1979, McKay (1981d:216 fn.6) found that the older generation of speakers interviewed (those born in about the twenties or thirties of this century) had all been to school, even if just for short periods, at Goulburn Island. This generation spent its younger years primarily 'in the bush', living off the land and maintaining ceremonies and other traditional practices. The speakers of the younger generation had all been to school at Maningrida itself.) Various coastal travellers, anthropologists, missionaries and patrol officers also had occasional contact with Ndjébbana speakers in the Liverpool River region. Finally the government settlement of Maningrida was set up on Ndjébbana speakers' traditional territory in 1957, partly to provide medical treatment for leprosy patients and partly to provide, within the area, some of the goods and services in search of which people were travelling (on foot and by boat) to

TABLE 1.2 *Macassan Loanwords in Ndjébbana*

Ndjébbana		Makassarese	
baddúmang	'swimming goggles'	*padómang*	'compass'
badjikkáli	'drum'	*bássi + kálling*	'iron + can'
balánda	'white man'	*balánda*	Hollander
bárra	'west wind'	*bára'*	'west wind, monsoon'
birráddja	'rice'	*bérasa'*	'milled rice'
budjúlung	'bottle'	*bótolo'*	'bottle'
djalwárra	'trousers'	*salúwara'*	'trousers'
djambákkang	'roofing iron'	*tambága*	'copper'
djárrang	'horse'	*járang*	'horse'
djúrrang	'paper, book', letter	*sura'*	'letter'
kabbála	'boat'	*káppala'*	'boat'
kalúkku	'coconut'	*kalúku*	'coconut'
kalúrru	'cigarette'	*kalúru*	'cigar, cigarette'
karrúrru	'sail'	*karóro'*	'sail, canvas'
kúli	'steering wheel, tiller'	*gúling*	'rudder'
Mángkaddjarra	'Macassan'	*Mangkásara'*	'Makassarese'
núna	'white woman'	*nóna*	'miss'
nganíddji	'grog, alcoholic drink'	*ánisi'*	'anisette'
rrubbíya	'money, coin'	*rupia*	'money'

Darwin. Some of these events are outlined by Kyle-Little (1957), Drysdale and Durack (1974), Hiatt (1965) and Armstrong (1967).

From the outset many people of other Aboriginal groups 'invaded' and settled on Kunibidji territory giving rise to a singularly multilingual township where up to a dozen quite distinct Aboriginal languages can be heard in use (Elwell 1977 and 1982a). The east-west conflict within the community (see above) has probably been a significant factor in preventing the rise of a lingua franca in the Maningrida township. A subsidiary factor in this is the lack of centralised adoption of a single language for use in the community at Maningrida, unlike the adoption of Kunwinjku by the Christian mission at Oenpelli, or that of Gupapuyngu by the Christian mission at Milingimbi. At Maningrida the authorities commenced operations much later, had a much shorter period of development before fragmentation into separate departments and, most importantly, used largely English, giving little practical recognition to the Aboriginal languages until the commencement of a bilingual program in the school in Ndjébbana in 1981 and in Burarra in 1986. This situation was no doubt exacerbated by the linguistic heterogeneity of the community.

1.5 PRESENT SITUATION

Ndjébbana is currently spoken by about 150 native speakers in and around Maningrida, central Arnhem Land, Northern Territory. Many children of Ndjébbana speaking parents are learning to speak Ndjébbana as their first language but some of the reported dialect differentiation appears to be disappearing among younger speakers. The most widely learned form of the language in the township of Maningrida is the Yírriddjanga form spoken by Mabárnad groups centred on that area. The specialised avoidance language is not used any longer and it is reported (C. Coleman personal communication) that, though basic natural species vocabulary is being transmitted to the younger generation, the more specialised vocabulary in this field is not being learnt by younger speakers because they spend a lot less time in the 'bush' environment with their elders, hunting and gathering only as weekend recreation rather than as a day-to-day means of subsistence.

In the light of these factors one would have to say that the language, though 'healthy/strong' in Annette Schmidt's (1990) terms (apart from perhaps not meeting the 'number of speakers' criterion), is clearly moving into her 'Stage 2' (Schmidt 1990:124) of language loss. Further evidence of this is the apparent development of some simplification/regularisation of the language amongst some younger speakers.

The Ndjébbana speakers suffer extensive alienation and social difficulty within the Maningrida community as a result of the invasion of their land by others. They are more likely to learn the language of some of the numerically dominant groups in the area than those people are to learn Ndjébbana. Over recent years, however, some of them have been more assertive about their rights as traditional landowners of the area.

A bilingual education program in Ndjébbana and English, involving initial literacy in Ndjébbana and the use of Ndjébbana-speaking assistant teachers in Ndjébbana-speaking classes began to be developed from 1975 with the appointment of a full-time linguist (McKay) to do background language research. A separate Ndjébbana-speaking class was set up with its own teacher and Ndjébbana-speaking assistant teacher in 1976, the orthography was approved in 1979, Ndjébbana-speaking literacy workers and assistant teachers were trained and the primary bilingual program formally commenced in 1981. This program is still running within the Maningrida Community Education Centre.

The development of the bilingual education program entailed the production of a range of materials for use in the classroom including beginning readers, alphabet books, children's dictionaries, Ndjébbana articles in the local 'newspaper', more advanced readers based on tape recorded traditional stories, translations of material in other languages, as well as the children's own writing. Production still continues through the Maningrida Literature Production Centre, which also produces materials for other languages of the area. Given the small number of speakers and thus the relatively small scale of the language group, the number of materials produced is relatively small and the majority of them are directed to the primary education levels.

The Ndjébbana orthography was deliberately modeled on the Kunwinjku orthography of western Arnhem Land to give readers access to print material in both languages. This mainly applies to adult readers.

Several speakers of Ndjébbana have undergone literacy worker or teacher training to various levels through the School of Australian Linguistics or Batchelor College.

1.6   PREVIOUS INVESTIGATIONS

The first published material on Ndjébbana was a page and a half under the name *Gunavidji* in a survey of Arnhem Land languages by Capell (1943:27–9). The survey nature and brevity of Capell's work makes it unsurprising that there was little analysis possible and that there are a number of inaccuracies, but the forms quoted are recognisable and it does provide the earliest brief overview of the language.

The next significant study involving Ndjébbana was Harris's comparative study of Gunwingguan languages (Harris 1969a). Gunaviji (Ndjébbana) was one of the nine languages studied. Unfortunately the comparative nature of the study and the number of languages involved meant that data collection was too superficial for accurate coverage of the language. Her overall conclusion, that Gunaviji diverged further from Gunwinggu than any of the other languages studied, can probably be justified on other grounds, but many of the details of her analysis are flawed simply because, as a result of the comparative format of her study, she clearly did not have an adequate body of data to provide material for analysis and checking.

For instance she claims that Ndjébbana has no reflexive because the -ya suffix she observed with many 'reflexive' clauses is homophonous with a number of other tense suffixes and the example clause she was given (p.82) is a non-reflexive (as she recognises), even though a reflexive version would have been available. Further analysis (beyond what was possible within her comparative study format and based on additional data) was necessary to show the real situation here. She further found that Ndjébbana had no 'ditransitive' construction (i.e. clauses with indirect objects). In fact her example clause (p. 80) wrongly glosses the indirect object pronoun form [yik]kóyanga as the clause object 'fruit', though it actually disproves her claim (p. 129) that a separate dative/benefactive pronoun paradigm does not exist. Finally she analyses certain forms (e.g. the locational/directional form wipa-ra [=wíbbara] (p.77)) which I have found unanalysable in the light of much more extensive data (e.g. there are no parallels for a -ra locational suffix, and the closest root is wíba not wíbba).

In short, though Harris and Capell provide some valuable pioneering Ndjébbana material it is now generally of little direct use, as a result of the fact that it is based upon study of insufficient depth (comparative surveys) which has now been superseded.

In 1975 McKay began a more in-depth study under the auspices of the Department of Education (first Commonwealth, later Northern Territory) in preparation for the development of a Ndjébbana–English bilingual education program in the school at Maningrida. McKay's fieldwork and analysis of Ndjébbana from 1975 to 1982 resulted in a number of published and unpublished papers on the language which have provided most of the basis for the present grammar. McKay made further field notes over a six-week period during 1992. Copies of most of McKay's original field notes, tapes and text transcriptions have been lodged in the library of the Australian Institute of Aboriginal and Torres Strait Islander Studies in Canberra.

Subsequent linguists in the Ndjébbana bilingual education program have been Eather and Coleman. They, like McKay, were heavily involved in consultative, editorial and advisory work with the Aboriginal and non-Aboriginal staff of the bilingual education program, resulting in the publication of classroom materials and notes for internal departmental use rather than linguistic articles. Eather, together with various Aboriginal and non-Aboriginal staff members, developed and taught an elementary unpublished course (Eather et al. n.d.). Coleman's main field of work has been in the lexicon, more specifically in the ethnoclassification of natural species (especially fish and plants to date) but this is, as yet, unpublished.

Specific anthropological studies of 'Gunavidji' people (Ndjébbana speakers) were carried out by Armstrong (1967, 1973). McKay's (1981d) background study for orthography development and his study of attitudes to literacy (1982a) are both more anthropological/sociological than linguistic.

1.7   SOURCES FOR THE PRESENT STUDY

The three principal sources of language data for the present study were as listed below. Initials are used here and in the body of the grammar, particularly for those who have died, out of respect for the taboo on the names of the dead. The names of the living have been treated the same way in order to avoid difficulties using the grammar in its published form at Maningrida in the event of any future deaths. A key to the full names is provided in the Appendix.

My Kúdjala, JB (Nabangárda Nayikkanduwúlka) who, at the time of writing, is probably in his late sixties.

My late Kalikkali, JM (Nkamárrang Nayikdukúrrdji) who was probably in his early sixties at the time of writing.

My late Ngákarda, JK (Wákadj Nayikmarlandjárridj) who would have been in his fifties when I last worked with him ten years ago.

All three men grew up in the Liverpool River area prior to the establishment of a settlement at Maningrida, though all three had early contact with white people at Goulburn Island, Croker Island and Darwin as well as with periodic visitors to their area. JB and his elder brother JN were amongst the most significant travel companions of patrol officer Syd Kyle-Little in the late forties (Kyle-Little 1957) and later worked with Kyle-Little and Jack Doolan in the establishment of a post at Maningrida. JM also had some contact with Kyle-Little during this period. JB seemed to have particular prominence in Drysdale and Durack's account (1974) of the establishment of the settlement at Maningrida in 1957.

Several other, mostly younger, speakers also provided information and assisted in various ways with the research into their language, though to a lesser degree than the senior men mentioned above. These included JB's daughter LDj (Ngalikkanduwúlka), PM and his brother the late DW (both Namanakarérrben), HDj, the late WDj, the late JBo and various others. It was HDj who acted as the native-speaker resource for the meeting of the Department of Education Orthography Committee which examined and approved the proposed Ndjébbana orthography in 1979.

Further sources of data were stories recorded on tape by various children in the bilingual education program and subsequently transcribed and published at Maningrida for use in the school.

2.   PHONOLOGY

2.1   PHONEMES AND THEIR REALISATIONS

Ndjébbana has sixteen consonant phonemes and five vowel phonemes. These are set out in Table 2.1 and Table 2.2, using the orthography approved for use in the Ndjébbana bilingual education program at Maningrida. This orthography will be used throughout this grammar to present Ndjébbana material, except where phonetic detail is being discussed, for which purpose phonetic symbols will be employed.

2.1.1 STOPS.   There is a single series of stops, though an areal controversy on this point will be discussed below. Stops normally have lenis and voiced allophones in syllable-initial position and fortis and voiceless allophones in syllable-final position. Word-final stops are frequently unreleased. When immediately following a (fortis) syllable-final stop within a word, a syllable-initial stop assimilates to it in fortisness and voicelessness. Thus both members of all medial stop clusters, whether hetero-organic or homorganic, are normally fortis and voiceless. Single fortis or voiceless stops not preceded or followed by a non-homorganic stop occur only syllable-finally, that is word-finally or word-medially only before a nasal or a semivowel. Prevocalic single stops, whether word-initial or word-medial, are always syllable-initial and therefore normally lenis and voiced. Put in other terms, a medial phonetically fortis stop which is not in a hetero-organic stop cluster either stands before another consonant (showing itself to be in syllable-final position) or, if intervocalic or between a liquid and a vowel, straddles a syllable boundary as a cluster of two identical stops, with the stop closure occurring at the end of one syllable and its release occurring only with the articulation of the vowel within the following syllable. Fortis or long prevocalic stops should on no account be considered a single segmental phoneme but rather a sequence of two phonemically identical stops, one closing a syllable and the next initiating the following syllable.

To clarify this we present the phonetic status and syllabic position of several occurrences of the phoneme /d/ in the following words. In both the orthographic and the phonetic representations the syllable boundaries are indicated by means of a full stop. Each orthographic d represents a single

TABLE 2.1 *Ndjébbana Consonant Phonemes*

	bilabial	apico-alveolar	apico-post-alveolar (retroflex)	lamino-palatal	dorso-velar
stop	b	d	rd	dj	k
nasal	m	n	rn	nj	ng
lateral		l	rl		
rhotic		rr	r		
semivowel	w			y	

TABLE 2.2 *Ndjébbana Vowel Phonemes*

	front (unrounded)	back (rounded)
high	i	u
mid	e	o
low	a	

phonemic /d/. (This means that a 'geminate' stop, dd, represents a sequence of two /d/ phonemes.)

dam.balk.ka	[dam.bálk.ka]	'sugar glider'
bud.mán.da	[bʊt.mán.da]	'suitcase'
n.djúd.da	[n.ɟút.ta]	'Juda Point'
djab.bú.lid	[ɟap.pú.lɪt]	'tarpaulin'

The /d/ phoneme in dambálkka is word-initial (and pre-vocalic) and thus syllable-initial. The lenis, voiced allophone [d-] is therefore used. The first /d/ phoneme in budmánda is syllable-final (and preconsonantal) and the appropriate allophone is thus fortis and voiceless (and somewhat long as is normal for fortis stops) [-t-]. This stop clearly cannot be syllable-initial because it is not immediately followed by a vowel, but rather by a syllable-initial nasal. The second /d/ phoneme in this word is syllable-initial because it is pre-vocalic. It is thus the lenis and voiced (and short) allophone [-d-]. In the word Ndjúdda the first /d/ phoneme is syllable-final (pre-consonantal) because it precedes a consonant (the second /d/ phoneme) and is thus the fortis, voiceless and long allophone [-t-]. The second /d/ phoneme is prevocalic and thus syllable-initial but because it immediately follows a phonetically voiceless fortis syllable-final stop the usual lenis and voiced allophone does not occur but assimilates to the preceding syllable-final stop in fortisness and voicelessness, so that both stops of the cluster are pronounced fortis and voiceless [-tt-]. Finally the /d/ phoneme of djabbúlid is word-final and syllable-final and therefore the fortis, voiceless allophone [-t] is used, often unreleased in this position.

The velar stop k very commonly has a voiced velar fricative allophone [ɣ] when followed by a vowel and preceded by a vowel or a liquid (l or rr). In rapid speech the articulation of this voiced velar fricative can be very slight between two vowels (-a- or -u-). This vowel-fricative-vowel sequence can sound very much like a long vowel. For example manakúkun '[place name]' is commonly pronounced [mʌnʌɣúːɣun] or even almost [mʌnʌɣúːn].

The bilabial stop b has a voiced bilabial fricative allophone [β] occasionally in intervocalic position. This is by no means as common as the fricative allophone of the velar stop.

The lamino-palatal stop, as in nearby languages (cf. Jernudd 1974), appears to be pronounced with the tongue tip behind the lower teeth and the blade of the tongue pressed against the teeth, the alveolar ridge and the palate.

Controversy over interpretation of apparent medial stop contrasts. The phonemic interpretation of stops has been a controversial matter in descriptions of a number of Arnhem Land languages from both the Pama-Nyungan (suffixing) and non-Pama-Nyungan (prefixing) groups. Controversy has hinged on whether the apparent stop contrasts in medial position should be interpreted as separate series of voiced (lenis or short) and voiceless (fortis or long) stop phonemes (the 'segmental' interpretation in Wood's (1978:100) terms) or as clusters of two identical stops (sometimes termed the 'geminate' interpretation). Thus, for instance, Ndjébbana has a contrast between the words kabála [gabála] 'he/she ate it' and kabbála [gappála] 'boat' as represented using the 'cluster' interpretation. If the segmental interpretation (two stop series) were to be adopted, these two words would read gabála and gapála respectively.

Significant differences between the two interpretations lie in the number of phonemes required, the implications for syllable structure and the position of syllable boundaries. Table 2.3 sets out a number of Ndjébbana words giving the two alternative interpretations: the 'cluster' interpretation as adopted in the practical orthography and the 'segmental' interpretation as adopted in the orthographies of neighbouring languages such as Burarra and Yolngu. The Ndjébbana orthography uses the voiced symbols for stop phonemes except for the velar stop, for which the voiceless symbol is used to leave ng completely unambiguous as the symbol for the velar nasal. Syllable boundaries are marked in this table by a full stop, though this is not a normal feature of the orthographic system.

Note that under the 'cluster' interpretation several closed syllables with final stops correspond to open syllables in the 'segmental' interpretation (e.g. in kabbála, bíbbo, kíkka and djubdjubbánda). Note, too, that apparent partial reduplication (historically only) within a word like djubdjubbánda as posited by the 'cluster' interpretation is denied by the 'segmental' interpretation, and that identity of syllables or of consonants as posited by the 'cluster' interpretation is also denied by the 'segmental' interpretation. See for example the initial and final stops of kurrámbalk and the two ba syllables of malabardídjbana.

TABLE 2.3 *Alternative Interpretations of Ndjébbana Stops*

'Cluster' Interpretation	'Segmental' Interpretation	Meaning
kab.bá.la	ga.pá.la	boat
ka.bá.la	ga.bá.la	he/she ate it
bíb.bo	bí.po	crab
kík.ka	gí.ka	mother
ku.rrám.balk	gu.rrám.balk	house
djub.djub.bán.da	djup.tju.pán.da	axe (with short handle)
ma.la.ba.rdídj.ba.na	ma.la.ba.rdítj.pa.na	woolly butt tree

The 'cluster' interpretation was first proposed for a language of the area by Glasgow and Glasgow (1967) for Ndjébbana's prefixing neighbour, Burarra, and for the suffixing Yolngu languages of north-east Arnhem Land by Schebeck (1972 and n.d.). Carefully argued discussions of the phenomenon in a number of languages of the area (such as McKay 1975 and 1984b, Wood 1978, Morphy 1983 and Walker 1984) show that there are both advantages and disadvantages for each of these proposed analyses when phonetic, phonemic, prosodic, morphophonemic, syllabic and comparative aspects are taken into account. There is also considerable variation from language to language in the weight of the arguments for and against each interpretation. Wood (1978:100) also proposed a third interpretation, the 'prosodic' interpretation under which the medial voiceless fortis stops are interpreted as phonetic variants of stop phonemes of a single series, conditioned by the presence of a preceding 'fortis syllable' (defined as containing an underlying glottal stop). Waters (1980) proposed that long fortis stops in Djinang are allophonic variants conditioned by a preceding primary-stressed syllable. In Ndjébbana (§2.4 below; McKay 1984b) stop gemination occurs in some verbal and nominal forms conditioned by a following stress. In short, though the existence of such a stop contrast is clearly an areal phenomenon, it is a phenomenon which must be studied separately for each language and it is not possible to reach a general conclusion on interpretation which is valid for all languages of the area.

In Ndjébbana the cluster interpretation has been adopted in the light of a number of factors:

[i] Word-medial prevocalic fortis voiceless stops are phonetically long (as observed from spectrographs) and clearly articulated with the stop closure occurring to close one syllable and the stop release (as the syllable-initial stop) leading directly into articulation of the vowel of the following syllable. In slow articulation the pause for the syllable boundary occurs during the stop closure, not before it.

[ii] In the course of orthography testing with four Ndjébbana speakers who were already literate in English, all four speakers clearly preferred the cluster interpretation to the 'segmental' interpretation, as the most accurate representation of the phonemic and in particular of the syllabic structure, in spite of the fact that their prior literacy in English could be expected to bias them in favour of the 'segmental' interpretation. Some subsequent difficulties with this aspect of the orthography within the school bilingual program at

Maningrida (beginning with a year in which there was no linguist in the program) appear to have resulted from a shift in literacy teaching from a focus on the syllable structure to a simple but quite inaccurate English-based rule of thumb: "If it sounds like 'b' put b; if it sounds like 'p' put bb". This rule gives quite the wrong results everywhere except in prevocalic position.

[iii] At least one other consonant, n, occurs in geminate clusters as in ngannawarrámaya 'you are skinny' (contrasting with nganawarrámaya 'he is skinny').

[iv] The phonetic rule required to render both stops of a medial geminate (i.e. homorganic) stop cluster voiceless and fortis is independently required to handle heterorganic stop clusters (such as in kúdjbarra [gúcpara] 'kangaroo' or kárddjurl [gátcʋ[] 'egret'), thus generalising the rule.

[v] The existence of clear medial contrasts between single and double (or short and long) stops (see §2.1.5), as well as the existence of exceptions to morphophonemic rules geminating and leniting morpheme-initial (but word-medial) stops (see §2.4) show that pre-vocalic long or geminate stops (i.e. homorganic stop clusters) in Ndjébbana are not phonetically determined variants such as found by Waters (1980) for Djinang.

[vi] The cluster interpretation of medial long stops does not require any additional syllable types.

2.1.2 LIQUIDS, NASALS, SEMIVOWELS. The two rhotics are an apico-alveolar flap or trill and a post-alveolar frictionless continuant. The two laterals and five nasals are voiced and match the corresponding stops in point of articulation. The two semivowels are a lamino-palatal and a labio-velar semivowel respectively. As is common for languages of the area, words having apparent initial high vowels i and u are interpreted as having initial CV sequences rather than initial vowels in the light of the syllable patterns otherwise found in the language even though the two semivowels are not always very clearly distinguishable word-initially before their corresponding high vowels (i.e. w before u and y before i).

2.1.3 VOWELS. Each of the five vowel phonemes has two major allophones as follows:

/i/ The basic allophone is the high tense vowel [i] which occurs in all positions except before an apical consonant (alveolar or post-alveolar), where a laxer allophone [ɪ] occurs.

/e/ The basic allophone is the lax, mid, unrounded [ɛ] which occurs in all positions and which is obligatory in word-final position. Sometimes the vowel has a tenser allophone [e] before a laminal consonant or semivowel but this is not obligatory.

/a/ The basic allophone is the low central [a], which occurs in all positions, and which is the only possibility when word-final and when lengthened. Word-final unstressed /a/ is often lost completely. After a laminal consonant (and especially when also before an apical or a laminal) a raised and fronted allophone [æ] is sometimes used.

/o/ The basic allophone is a lax, mid rounded [ɔ], which occurs in all positions, including word-finally. Sometimes in stressed position a closer allophone [o] occurs.

/u/ The basic allophone is the lax, high, rounded [ʋ], which occurs in all positions except word-final. In word-final position a closer allophone [u] always occurs. This closer allophone also tends to be used when the vowel is long and stressed.

All vowels have an [ɪ] offglide preceding a laminal consonant [ɛ¹ æ¹ ɔ¹ ʊ¹].

2.1.4 STRESS AND VOWEL LENGTH. The vowels of certain syllables of most Ndjébbana words are both long and strongly stressed. This stress/length (here simply stress) is represented in the Ndjébbana orthography by an acute accent as in makéddja 'turtle'. Minimal pairs establishing the phonemic status of vowel stress on the vowel a are given in §2.1.5. While no minimally contrastive examples of vowel stress on other vowels have been found, all the vowel phonemes have been found in stressed form and in unstressed form and speakers have little difficulty in indicating which syllable in a word bears the stress, irrespective of the vowel involved. The lack of contrasting pairs for stress on vowels other than a is presumably related to the relatively low frequency of these vowels.

The significance of vowel stress is highlighted by the fact that this stress shifts to different syllables in various forms of some verbs. In such cases the unstressed vowels are often neutralised to a as discussed in §2.3. The significance of the vowel length/stress phoneme is further supported by its function as the triggering factor for the stop gemination rule discussed in §2.4.

This phonemic feature of vowel length/stress in Ndjébbana involves, phonetically, both length and stress, neither of which can at present be shown to be primary. This phonemic vowel length/stress may be referred to in this grammar as 'length' (or 'long') or 'stress' (or 'stressed') but this is simply an abbreviation for the complex feature of length and stress.

2.1.5 CONTRACTION. Ndjébbana words generally have many syllables and are spoken rapidly and with considerable contraction of syllables. Speakers who attempt to pronounce words syllable-by-syllable may actually lose track of where they are up to in words which are normally highly contracted. In what follows we will exemplify some of the contractions which have been found to occur without providing a systematic analysis.

The realis prefix attached to a root with initial apico-alveolar -n- may be realised as a retroflexed nasal -rn-.

*ba-rra-nmarramarló-nga	>	barnmarramarlónga
3AUGS-RE-swim-REM		they swam

Sequences involving low vowels and the palatal semivowel can be collapsed into a smaller number of syllables with a raised vowel:

*ngá-ya-yarra	>	ngé-yarra
1MINS-IRR-go		I'll go

Rules 4, 5, 6 and 7 of the morphophonemic processes applying to verbs (§3.6.16) also have the effect of contracting verb forms, as do the zero forms of various verb prefixes (§3.6.5).

The very rapid nature of speech is evidenced by the four-syllable English form (*Maningrida*) of the six-syllable Ndjébbana place name Manayingkarírra. In the Ndjébbana form the second and fourth syllables in particular are usually pronounced so rapidly as to almost disappear, and this must be how the English speaking recorders of the name perceived it. Compare also the form in nearby languages: Manidjangkarirra.

2.1.6 MINIMAL PAIRS. The following minimal or sub-minimal pairs and sets demonstrate the contrast between various critical phonemes. The two apical stops do not appear to contrast in word-initial position, though some words appear to regularly have one and other words regularly the other.

Apical consonants
d/rd   djabbúlid 'tent' / bákkird 'flower'
n/rn/nj   ránba 'beach' / ngarnba 'perspiration' / ngánjbarl 'sneeze'
l/rl   nkála 'fork' / nkárla 'wet'

Rhotics and apical stops
rr/r/rd   djalwárra 'trousers' / njayára 'shoulder' / nabangárda '(subsection name)'
rr/d   nganabbárru 'buffalo' / nakkuráduk '(clan name)'

Medial stop contrasts
b/bb/k/kk káyakkabo 'he is tying it' / káyakabbo 'he will fall'
b/bb   yíbarda 'barramundi' / míbbarda 'bandicoot'; kabála 'he ate it' / kabbála 'boat'
rd/rdrd   nmardárda 'bone, shell' / buwárdrda (buwárdda) 'bush turkey, bustard'
dj/djdj   yídja 'man' / nakídjdjal (nakíddjal) 'new shoots'
k/kk   kakárra 'shade, leaf' / nakkárriyala 'Burdekin duck'; kayókaya 'sleep, night time, lizard' / yókkarra 'fish'

Vowels
i/e/a/o/u bákki 'tobacco' / yékke 'cold weather time' / kíkka 'mother' / mókko 'pubic covering, hair belt' / kalíkku 'cloth'
i/e/a/o/u djalakkíyak 'fish spear' / nakéyakayakka 'him first' / nakkáyala 'on foot, on the ground' / bayakóyabba '(go) past' / babukúyakka 'long ago'

Vowel length/stress
a/á   ngáyabba 'I' / ngayábba 'she'; wardawarda 'spear' / wardawárda 'goat's foot creeper'; barrabála 'they ate it' / bárrabala 'they are coming hither'; ngalawáya 'I know' / ngálawaya I am hanging it up'; ndjaráma 'heavy' / djárama 'you are holding it'; ngánawala 'your name' / nganáwarla 'different'; barrawála 'they went up' / bárrawala 'their names'.

2.2   PHONOTACTICS

2.2.1 SYLLABLE STRUCTURE. Four separate syllable types occur in Ndjébbana:

> C
> CV
> CVC
> CVCC

All four syllable types occur independently of the cluster interpretation of medial fortis stops, though this interpretation of these stops greatly increases the range of stops which is found to occur in syllable-final, word-medial positions.

2.2.2 INITIAL SEGMENTS OF SYLLABLE AND WORD. The syllable type which consists of a single consonant occurs only in word-initial position and always comprises a syllabic apico-alveolar nasal. In many cases this constitutes a third person singular masculine prefix on nominals of possession class D1 such as nbarrábarra 'big (3sgmasc)'. Compare feminine njabarrábarra. Table 2.4 sets out a number of further examples of words containing this syllable type. In some cases a minimally contrasting form without the initial syllabic nasal is given on the right. The initial syllabic nasal has only been found preceding stops and peripheral (i.e. labial and velar) nasals.

In general younger speakers omit this syllabic nasal completely producing forms like djúdda 'Juda Point' instead of ndjúdda, or bókka 'bad (masc)' instead of nbókka.

Syllables containing a vowel have only a single syllable-initial consonant. All consonants occur syllable- and word-initially except for the apico-post-alveolar stop, nasal and lateral. The contrast between two apical series of stops, nasals and laterals appears to be neutralised word-initially, but initial apical stops sometimes appear to be phonetically retroflexed.

In a prefixing language a significant number of lexical items cannot appear without a prefix. Table 2.5 sets out word-initial consonant frequencies based on a count of free lexical items in the interim dictionary prepared during 1981–1982 (McKay 1981a, 1981b, 1981c, 1982b), excluding those words which require an initial prefix. That is, excluding verbs and certain classes of nominals. The final count was based on just over six hundred lexical items.

The figures presented in Table 2.5 show that peripheral (labial and velar) consonants, particularly stops and nasals are the most common in word-initial position. Apical consonants, in particular the liquids, are the rarest in word-initial position. Stops and nasals are also the most common prefix-initial consonants occurring in word-initial position with bound lexical morphemes such as verbs and nominals.

Only one word is known with an initial vowel. This is arrabba, a conjunction meaning roughly 'and, but'. The vowel-initial form is a variant of a more common form of the conjunction with an initial velar stop: karrabba.

TABLE 2.4 *Word-initial syllabic nasal: syllable type C*

ndjarramáya 'thoracic spine (masc)'	njayarramáya 'thoracic spine (fem)'
ndjúdda 'Juda Point (Skirmish Point)'	
nmáma 'long harpoon spear for turtles'	máma 'brother-in-law'
nmódda 'fish type'	
nmalála 'bee'	malála 'mangrove type'
nmárdba 'skinny (fish type)'	márdba 'neck'
nkála 'fork'	kála 'ear'
nbirriwúna 'they (du) gave it to me/you'	birriwúna 'they (du) gave it to him'
nbarrawúna 'they (pl) gave it to me/you'	barrawúna 'they (pl) gave it to him'

TABLE 2.5 *Ndjébbana word-initial consonant frequencies (%)*

bilabial	apico-alveolar	apico-post-alveolar	lamino-palatal	velar	TOTALS	
b 12	d 1.7	rd	dj 10.8	k 18.7	stops 43.2	stops and nasals 82.4
m 17.4	n 5.3	rn	nj 6.2	ng 10.3	nasals 39.2	
	rr 0.8	r 2.4			rhotics 3.2	liquids 4.7
	l 1.5	rl			laterals 1.5	
w 7.4			y 5.5		semi-vowels 12.9	

labials (incl. w)	alveolars	post-alveolars		velars (excl. w)
36.8	9.3	2.4		29
	apicals		laminals	peripherals (labials and velars)
	11.7		22.5	65.8

TABLE 2.6 *Ndjébbana word-final phoneme frequencies (%)*

a	74.8	e	0.5	i	3	o	1.6	u	2.3
b	nil	d	1.4	rd	0.6	dj	1.5	k	3.7
m	0.6	n	2.5	rn	0.3	nj	0.8	ng	1.9
l	0.6	rl	0.6	r	nil	rr	2.7		
w	0.1					y	0.5		

2.2.3 FINAL SEGMENTS OF SYLLABLE AND WORD. An overwhelming majority of words in Ndjébbana have a final vowel. All verb forms have a final vowel and a dictionary count of words other than verbs showed that 81.7% of these words have a final vowel. Of these vowel-final words, 91.5% had the vowel a, representing 74.8% of the total final segments.

All consonants apart from b and r have been found to occur word-finally, the most common being the velars, followed by the apico-alveolars, as shown in Table 2.6.

2.2.4 FINAL CONSONANT CLUSTERS OF SYLLABLE AND WORD. The only consonant clusters so far found word-finally are rrng, rrk, lk and rlk, all involving an apical trill or lateral followed by a velar stop or nasal. A number of the other clusters predicted by this generalisation are not attested.

Word-medially, syllable-final consonant clusters show a wider range of consonants, as a result of the 'cluster' interpretation of medial long, fortis stops which takes such stops as straddling the syllable boundary, rather than being purely syllable-initial as in the 'segmental' interpretation (See §2.1.1). In non-final syllables syllable-final consonant clusters consist of a liquid or a laminal semivowel followed by a non-apical stop as set out in Table 2.7. rrk and lk are the only two syllable-final clusters which have been found to occur both word-finally and word-medially. In Table 2.7 all clusters apart from those marked with asterisks occur only as a result of the 'cluster' interpretation of medial long, fortis stops. Those with a single asterisk occur in both word-final and non-final syllables, those with a double asterisk occur in word-final syllables only.

2.2.5 INTERSYLLABIC CONSONANT CLUSTERS. Given the syllable structures listed in §2.2.1 Ndjébbana permits two and three-consonant intersyllabic clusters made up of a syllable-initial consonant preceded by a syllable-final consonant or two-consonant cluster. The following patterns apply:

[i] Intersyllabic clusters occur only when their final consonant, the initial of the following syllable, is a stop, nasal or semivowel. The greatest range occurs when this consonant is peripheral (p, k, m, ng, w).

[ii] Homorganic stop plus stop as well as nasal plus stop clusters are all possible. A number of heterorganic clusters also occur. Apical plus apical clusters are always fully homorganic.

TABLE 2.7 *Ndjébbana syllable-final two consonant clusters*

	b	dj	k	ng
rr	rrb	rrdj	rrk*	rrng**
r			rk	
l	lb	ldj	lk*	
rl	rlb	rldj	rlk**	
y			yk	

[iii] With the exception of the clusters bdj and md, when a heterorganic two-consonant cluster involves a peripheral consonant (stop, nasal, or semivowel), the peripheral consonant follows the non-peripheral.

[iv] In a two-consonant cluster the orders apical followed by laminal, apical followed by peripheral and nasal followed by stop occur but never the reverse with the only known exceptions being a peripheral-apical cluster in the word kómdudj 'initiand' and a stop-nasal sequence in the borrowed word budmánda 'suitcase' (from English *portmanteau*).

[v] With three exceptions, three-consonant clusters involve double (or geminate) stops preceded by a liquid. Such clusters would be converted to two-consonant clusters if the 'segmental' interpretation of medial long, fortis stops were adopted (§2.1.1). The three exceptions (which remain three-consonant clusters under either interpretation of medial stops) are lkb, rrkng, rrkw. In three-consonant clusters there are no double apical stops. The cluster rrkng exists only in the verb root -djórrkngaya 'run', which, for most speakers, takes the form djórrkkangaya, thus rendering this cluster somewhat marginal.

Table 2.8 sets out the attested two-consonant intersyllabic clusters and Table 2.9 sets out the attested three-consonant intersyllabic clusters.

2.3   STRESS, VOWEL ALTERNATIONS AND UNDERLYING FORMS

The phoneme of stress and vowel length shifts, in a number of verbal and nominal forms, to various positions within the prefix, root and suffix but may never occur in word-final position.

Note that all five vowel phonemes are clearly differentiated when stressed and long, but there is a tendency for all vowels to be reduced to a when not bearing the phonemic stress and length. This tendency is overridden by certain morphophonemic processes affecting vowels. These involve vowel harmony with certain prefix vowels and the shifting of an underlying stress to avoid word-final position.

The following verbs exemplify the pattern of stress shifting. Rules for the stress-conditioned alternations between root-initial b and bb (bo 'fall,

TABLE 2.8 *Intersyllabic two-consonant clusters*

bb			bdj							
	dd									
rdb		rdrd	rddj							
djb			djdj							
kb				kk					kw	
mb	md									
nb	nd		ndj	nk	nm	nn		nng		
rnb		rnrd		rnk	rnm			rnng		
njb			njdj	njk	njm			njng		
ngb				ngk						
lb				lk	lm		lnj	lng	lw	ly
									rlw	
rrb			rrdj	rrk	rrm	rrn		rrng	rrw	
rb									rw	
yb									yw	

TABLE 2.9 *Intersyllabic three-consonant clusters*

lbb	ldjdj	lkb	lkk		
rlbb	rldjdj				
rrbb	rrdjdj		rrkk	rrkng	rrkw
			rkk		
			ykk		

land') and between root-initial b, bb and w (biddabo 'follow, chase' §2.3.1) are given in §2.4.

bo 'fall, land'
bárra-bbo 'they are falling'	(pronominal prefix-initial)
barra-ba-ngóna 'they fell '	(suffix-initial/penultimate)
ba-ka-bbó-ngana 'he would have fallen'	(root-initial/root-final)

no 'sit'
ka-yá-ka-na 'he will sit'	(realis prefix)
ka-nó-ra 'he is sitting'	(root-initial/final)
ka-kó-na 'he sat'	(-ko- prefix)
ka-ya-na-rayína 'he would have sat'	(penultimate of suffix)

rimi 'grasp, hold, have'
ka-ya-ka-ríma 'he will grab it'   (root-initial)
ká-rama 'he is holding it'   (pronominal prefix)
ka-ya-ramí-ngana 'he would have grabbed it' (root-final)

2.3.1 STRESS SHIFTING AND UNDERLYING FORMS.

Certain forms of verbs and some nominals have a root-final phonemically stressed/long vowel when followed by a suffix, but this stress/length shifts to word-initial position when the root-final syllable is also word-final. In the case of verbs of conjugation classes 1B, 8C and 6A which have a root-final ó when a suffix follows, this root-final vowel becomes unstressed but remains phonetically [ɔ] (phonemically o) when the stress shifts to word-initial position. Other root-final vowels are reduced to unstressed a in this situation (see also McKay 1984a:131–4). The most common crucial examples involve minimal contrasting forms in the CTP, with and without the dual feminine suffix -nja or the third person minimal dative pronouns -yana and -yángaya as agent markers. Other suffixes and other uses of the dative suffix have also been found to have the same effect on the position of stress.

bo 'fall, land'
bárra-bbo 'they (pl) are falling'
barra-bbó-nja 'they (dufem) are falling'
bárri-bbo 'they (dumasc) are falling'

bakabinji 'dig'
bárra-bakabanja 'they (pl) are digging'
barra-bakabanjí-nja 'they (dufem) are digging'
bárri-bakabanja 'they (dumasc) are digging'

njembo 'waken'
njána-njabo 'you woke me'
njana-njabó-yana 'he woke me'

biddabo 'chase, follow'
njána-waddabo 'you are chasing me'
njana-waddabó-yana 'he is chasing me'

yiyi 'leave'
bárra-ya (<*bárra-yaya) 'they (pl) are leaving it'
barra-yayí-nja 'they (dufem) are leaving it'

balo 'come'
njarra-baló-bba 'we came'
njárra-balo 'we came'

ndabayi 'make bilabial pop sound'
ngá-ndabaya 'I made the bilabial pop sound'
nga-ndabayí-yana 'I made a bilabial pop sound to him'

-walá 'name'
bá-rra-wala 'their names (AUG)'
bá-rri-wala 'their names (UAUGMASC)'
ba-rra-walá-nja   'their names (UAUGFEM)'

In the light of examples of this type the underlying form of the root-final syllable in each case is interpreted as having stress and vowel quality matching those of the forms which have a suffix. When a root-final phonemically stressed vowel occurs in word-final position due to the lack of a suffix, the stress/vowel length shifts to word-initial position. The final vowel in this case is normally reduced to a but retains its distinctive quality if it is the vowel o.

2.3.2 VOWEL HARMONY. Limited patterns of vowel harmony appear to occur in which high vowels of certain prefix syllables harmonise phonetically with various other unstressed prefix- and root-initial syllables in the vicinity. In particular two prefixes are involved:

-rri-	unit augmented masculine realis prefix
-wu-	aversative

The copying of the high back vowel -u- of the aversative prefix -wu- onto preceding syllables (other than those with the high front vowel -i-) giving forms such as the following has been outlined and exemplified in §3.6.5. The corresponding contemporary form is given here in parentheses.

> bu-rri-wu-nó-ra
> (bi-rri-nó-ra)
> 3UAMASCS-RE-AV-sit-CTP
> lest they (two) sit

> bu-rru-wu-nó-ra
> (ba-rra-nó-ra)
> 3AUGMASCS-RE-AV-sit-CTP
> lest they (plural) sit

The unit augmented masculine form of the realis prefix -rri- always retains its high front vowel quality even when unstressed to distinguish it from the other numbers (see §3.6.5). This vowel quality is also adopted by a preceding unstressed single open syllable prefix with underlying -a-, though, when stressed the underlying vowel quality is realised. Compare the following verb forms which actually form a phrase with the main verb followed by an auxiliary.

bi-rri-njíndja-na	bá-rri-na
3UAMASCS-RE-cry-REM	3UAMASCS-RE-sit(+REM)
they (two) cried	they (two) sat

The realis prefix of both verb complexes consistently indicates unit augmented masculine by means of its high front vowel. This vowel copies onto the preceding prefix (*ba-) only when it does not bear the phonemic vowel length/stress which, in the case of bárrina, is shifted to word-initial position because it may not occur word-finally. The bi- (*ba-) of the main verb has only a secondary non-phonemic stress and therefore has undergone the harmony process.

With the verb root -kamíya- 'get up, set off' both the above vowel harmony processes affect also the root-initial syllable giving forms such as the following:

bi-rri-kkimíya   bu-rru-kkumíya
3UAMASCS-RE-get up(+CTP)   3AUGS-RE(+AV)-get up(+CTP)
they (two) are getting up   lest they get up

This might suggest that the unstressed root-initial -kV- on this verb is in origin a prefix as is suggested by other features as outlined in connection with the prefix -kó- in §3.6.5.

One additional partial harmony or assimilation process involves the pronominal prefix form ngaba- '1/2 person augmented' which, before bilabial root-initial consonants where the irrealis has a zero form, lenites the -b- to -w- and rounds the vowels giving ngowu- or ngow- as in:

ngow(u)-mayáwaya   ngow(u)-bbúdjeya
1/2AUGS(+IRR)-sing   1/2AUGS(+IRR)-call out
let's sing   we'll call out

2.4   STOP ALTERNATIONS

Phonemic vowel length/stress shifts to different positions in various forms of some verbs and nominals. See §2.3. In some cases this stress shifting gives rise to alternations in root-initial position between single stop, double stop and semivowel. (See also additional discussion in McKay 1984b.) Note that this root-initial environment is only one of many environments where the geminate stop clusters are found.

2.4.1 STOP GEMINATION AND LENITION RULES. The set of stop alternations can be described in terms of two rules:

Rule 1
   An intervocalic root-initial non-apical (peripheral (=labial or velar) or laminal) stop geminates before a vowel bearing the phonemic stress and vowel length, inserting a stop in final position in the preceding syllable.

There are no exceptions to this rule among the verbs for the laminal stops but there are some exceptions among the verbs for the peripheral stops and for all stops among the nominals (see §2.4.3 and §2.4.5).

Rule 2
   An intervocalic root-initial non-apical (peripheral or laminal) stop lenites to the corresponding semivowel when it precedes a vowel which does not bear the primary phonemic stress and vowel length.

Again this rule is without exception among the verbs for the laminal stops but there are exceptions to its application amongst verbs for peripheral stops and amongst nominals for both peripheral and laminal stops.

The existence of exceptions to the applications of the rules shows that the rules are not fully productive within the language as it is currently spoken, though the widespread applicability of the rules shows that they were probably productive in a relatively recent stage of the development of the language.

2.4.2 ROOT INITIAL ALTERNATIONS ON VERBS. The operation of these rules can be clearly seen only where stress shifting (§2.3) provides the various environments for the application of these rules within the paradigm of a single verb, at the same time giving rise to vowel alternations in the root (§2.3). Nevertheless the majority of verbs (in which stress does not shift) are found to be consistent with the output of at least Rule 1.

Where both rules apply, the underlying root-initial single stop never appears in the surface form unless the root can occur either word-initially (as with the infinitive form of verbs with root-initial unstressed dja-) or following a prefix-final consonant (only nginj-, a variant of ngana- '2minS' used with the verb djirrí 'to go'). An example of the former is provided by the forms of the verb djúwe 'be sick, suffer, die' while the only available example of the latter is provided by forms of the verb djirrí 'go':

CTP	ka-djdjúwa 'he is sick'	Rule 1 applies
REM	ka-yawé-la 'he was sick/died'	Rule 2 applies
INFINITIVE	djawé-la 'be sick/die'	Neither rule applies

CTP	ka-yirrí-ya 'he is going'	Rule 2 applies
REM	nginj-djirrí-ya 'you are going'	Rule 2 cannot apply

The root-initial consonant of the verb bíddabo 'follow, chase, track' can never appear word-initially so its underlying single root-initial stop never appears in surface form. It is always geminated or lenited:

FUTURE	nga-ya-bbíddaba 'I'll follow him'	Rule 1 applies
CTP	ngá-waddabo 'I'm following him'	Rule 2 applies
REM	nga-waddabé-ra 'I followed him'	Rule 2 applies

2.4.3 EXCEPTIONS AMONGST VERBS. Rule 2 does not apply in all cases where its structural description is met so that single root-initial peripheral stops do occur intervocalically as in:

CTP	ka-bbúdjeya 'he is shouting'	Rule 1 applies
REM	ka-badjí-na 'he shouted'	Structural description of Rule 2 met but Rule 2 does not apply

Verbs with invariant stress patterns are in the main consistent with Rule 1 in the sense that either a geminate stop cluster precedes a stressed vowel in the root-initial syllable or a single stop precedes an unstressed vowel in the root-initial syllable. The exceptions only involve the peripheral stops. The following are a number of examples of verb forms with invariant stress which are consistent with Rule 1 (on the left) and others which are not (on the right).

ka-karráwa-ra 'he looked around'	ka-kkamíya-na 'he got up'
ka-bbándja-nga 'he put it down'	ka-bíwa-ra 'he smelled it'
	ka-bíwa-ya-na 'he stank'
ka-bbó-na 'he hit it (REM)'	ka-bú-ya-na 'he hit himself (REM)'
ka-bbú-ra 'he hit it (CTP)'	ka-bú-ya 'he hit himself (CTP)'

An interesting set of cases are those quoted here with the verb bú 'hit'. Used in its basic form its forms are consistent with Rule 1 (kabbóna, kabbúra), but forms derived using the reflexive/reciprocal suffix -ya- are not consistent with Rule 1 (kabúyana, kabúya).

Clearly the existence of such exceptions suggests that the stop gemination and lenition rules, at least as formulated at present, are not entirely productive and, therefore, that geminate stops are not simply positional variants of single stops.

2.4.4 STOP ALTERNATIONS AMONGST NOMINALS.   Similar alternations between single stops, geminate stop clusters and semivowels occur with nominals of Class D which take the class prefixes, n- '3minmasc' and nja- '3minfem'. With the former prefix both rules are blocked, with the latter both may apply. Furthermore some nominals show stress shifting similar to that found with verbs. Examples of nominals consistent with the rules follow here, while other examples, not consistent with the rules, are given in §2.4.5.

Rule 1 applies in feminine form (Consistent)

n-bókka 'bad (masc)'	n-djídjabba 'same'	n-kódda 'skin'
nja-bbókka 'bad (fem)'	nja-djdjídjabba	nja-kkódda

Rule 1 does not apply because structural description not met (Consistent)

n-barrábarra 'big'	n-karrúmakkarra 'slippery'
nja-barrábarra	nja-karrúmakkarra

Rule 2 applies in feminine form (Consistent)

n-djaráma 'heavy'	n-djarramáya 'thoracic spine'
nja-yarráma	nja-yarramáya

Stress shifting nominal, structural description for Rule 1 not met (Consistent)

n-káro 'fat'	n-kárddja 'cooked, ripe'	n-kálakarra 'Aboriginal man'
njá-karo	njá-karddja	njá-kalakarra 'Aboriginalwoman'

Stress shifting nominal, Rule 2 applies (Consistent)

n-djárawarra 'young person, adolescent'
njá-yarawarra

2.4.5 EXCEPTIONS AMONGST NOMINALS. While after the masculine prefix n- Rules 1 and 2 predict a single root-initial stop, after the feminine prefix nja- these rules predict a root-initial geminate stop cluster if the syllable-initial syllable is stressed and a root-initial semivowel if the root-initial syllable is unstressed. Exceptions of various types occur as exemplified here.

Geminate stop cluster before unstressed vowel (Not consistent with Rule 1)
n-barlánga 'raw, unripe'
nja-bbarlánga

Single stop before stressed vowel (Not consistent with Rule 2)
n-kánkarra 'meat'   n-búlanj '(subsection name)'   n-kóyawa 'crooked'
nja-kánkarra   nja-búlanj   nja-kóyawa

Semivowel before stressed vowel (Not consistent with Rule 1 and Rule 2)
n-djínjawa 'alive'   n-djáwarlbba 'old person'
nja-yínjawa   nja-yáwarlbba

Again the exceptions to the rules, at least as formulated here and in the absence of an explanation for the exceptions, suggest that the processes summarised by Rules 1 and 2 are not completely general in the modern language, even if they might have had some historical validity. This shows that neither geminate stop clusters nor semivowels are simply phonetic variants of single stops, though where the rules do apply they form morphological variants.

2.5   DISCOURSE FEATURE OF VOWEL LENGTH FOR EXTENT

Particularly in narrative, Ndjébbana speakers express duration or extent as it applies to the content of a clause by considerably lengthening the final syllable of the clause and raising the pitch of the voice to a sustained sing-song for that syllable. I have observed this feature in the speech of speakers of several Arnhem Land languages from Kunwinjku to Rembarrnga to Ngandi, as well as Ndjébbana and its close neighbours. It is also used in Aboriginal English of the area.

In Ndjébbana the lengthening of a clause-final vowel in this way sometimes appears to lead to change of the word-final vowel to i as in Text 25/60. In example (1) and Text 25/60 this feature of raised pitch and lengthened syllable is indicated by means of a double colon following the vowel of the relevant syllable.

(1)   Njarra-nóra::.   Yeláwa   mudíkkang   karnayédjabba
            we-sat   then   vehicle   two
               warábbana   ka-karlábaya.
               one   it [= they]-descended
       We stayed there a long time before three vehicles came down [to the landing].
(XXV/77–8)

2.6   PRACTICAL ORTHOGRAPHY

In 1979, at a meeting of the Department of Education's Orthography Committee, a practical orthography was approved for use in the Ndjébbana bilingual education program at Maningrida. The background to this decision was the 'Djeebbana (Gunibidji) orthography proposal', which comprised six papers, two of which have subsequently been published, along with further material of relevance to the orthography (McKay 1981d, 1982a; see also 1982c).

2.6.1 ORTHOGRAPHIC MODEL.

The neighbouring Kunwinjku orthography used in the west of Arnhem Land was chosen as the model for the Ndjébbana orthography in the light of the preferences expressed by Ndjébbana speakers and of the ongoing traditional westward social and cultural orientation of Ndjébbana speakers (§1.4). This choice of a model was intended to reduce orthographic diversity in a region of considerable phonological similarity and to open up literature in Kunwinjku to Ndjébbana literates, most of whom speak Kunwinjku and other related languages of western Arnhem Land as second languages. It happened that the Kunwinjku orthography was the only established one in the vicinity which was based on the 'cluster' rather than the 'segmental' interpretation of medial fortis/long stops (§2.1.1). This interpretation of this phonological feature matched the preferences of emerging literates in Ndjébbana as determined during orthography testing. The only modifications required to adapt the Kunwinjku orthography to represent Ndjébbana phonemes were the dropping of h as the symbol for glottal stop, which does not occur in Ndjébbana, and the addition of the acute accent to symbolise phonemic stress/vowel length, which is not required in Kunwinjku. The use of the acute accent to symbolise stress/vowel length was selected by the majority of a group of Ndjébbana speakers after a trial of four alternatives during orthography testing.

2.6.2 ORTHOGRAPHIC CONVENTIONS (SPELLING RULES).

The orthographic symbols representing each phoneme have been set out in Tables 2.1 and 2.2, and are used throughout this grammar to represent Ndjébbana material.

Note that, though the voiced symbols (b, d, rd, dj) are used for most of the stops, the voiceless symbol is used for the velar stop (k) in order to avoid confusion between the velar nasal (ng) and the sequence of alveolar nasal plus velar stop (n+k which would otherwise be n+g).

The use of digraphs for the retroflex and laminal series of consonants as well as the apico-alveolar trill gives rise to consonant cluster symbols potentially six symbols long to represent three phonemes (e.g. -rrdjdj-). In order to reduce the length of these clusters in written material a convention was adopted of using the "modifying element" (r for retroflexes and j for laminals) only once in the case of homorganic clusters giving the following simplifications:

rnrd	$\rightarrow$	rnd	njdj	$\rightarrow$	ndj
rdrd	$\rightarrow$	rdd	djdj	$\rightarrow$	ddj
rldjdj	$\rightarrow$	rlddj	rrdjdj	$\rightarrow$	rrddj

The only simplified cluster which was thought to be likely to create ambiguity is ndj which could represent either nj+dj as in njínjdjabba 'you (sg)' or n+dj as in djándjana 'pelican'. The latter cluster is relatively rare and native speakers know which is appropriate from the spoken language. This written ambiguity has presented no problem.

The simplification conventions are adopted in general in this grammar but occasionally it may be necessary to spell out a cluster in full (as in the words quoted in the previous paragraph) in order to make it clear which consonants are involved. In the wordlist the clusters are spelled out to avoid ambiguity but users of the lists are at liberty to apply the simplification conventions themselves in spelling these forms.

One problem with these simplification conventions has emerged. This is linked to the importance of the syllable boundary in the teaching and early mastery of the orthographic system by native speakers. The simplification conventions mean that, on one side or the other of a syllable boundary separating homorganic clusters, the point of articulation of the cluster is symbolised inaccurately. Thus, for instance, the normal spelling of the word makédjdja 'turtle', incorporating the conventional simplification of the stop cluster, would be makéddja. This spelling, however, suggests to the new literate that there is a syllable-final apico-alveolar stop in the second syllable, followed by a syllable-initial laminal stop in the third syllable. This orthographic representation is at odds with the speaker's perception of their own articulation of a laminal stop in both positions. Treating the word as a whole, as a skilled reader would do, this is not a significant issue but for the learner who is approaching the stop clusters through syllabic analysis following articulatory practice, the orthographic simplifications create some uncertainty or confusion.

2.6.3 MORPHOPHONEMIC PROCESSES AND THE ORTHOGRAPHY. The stop alternations discussed in §2.4 and the vowel reduction linked with stress shifting (§2.3) are potential candidates for morphophonemic spelling in which the underlying form rather than the surface phonemic form is represented in writing. In all cases except one, the surface phonemic form has been used as the basis for the writing system. The one exception is that of verb root-initial laminal stops which geminate according to Rule 1 (§2.4.1). Because with verb roots gemination of laminal stops is without exception when the structural description of Rule 1 is met, the initial laminal stop is normally written singly, even when geminated by the rule. When Rule 2 applies, leniting the stop to a semivowel, the semivowel symbol is used. With non-verbal roots and non-laminal stops, geminate stops are spelled in full where they occur because in those cases the rules do not apply without exception.

This convention, too, has created some difficulty for beginning readers who are approaching stop clusters via syllable analysis and find that the orthography does not provide representation of the first (syllable-final) stop of the cluster.

2.6.4 THE ORTHOGRAPHY IN USE. The Ndjébbana orthography was approved in 1979 following its trial use by a small group of young

Ndjébbana speakers who were already literate in English. The Ndjébbana bilingual program was implemented in the Maningrida school from 1981. Ndjébbana-speaking literacy workers, teaching assistants and children involved in the preparation for and implementation of this program appeared to have no systematic difficulties with the orthography during the period until the first linguist's (McKay's) departure from Maningrida in mid-1982. Subsequently there was a period of at least a year without a linguist in the program, during which time a rather laissez faire approach to spelling Ndjébbana words appears to have developed. Problems in using the orthography were reported by subsequent staff of the bilingual program. These problems affected the medial stops (geminate clusters) and the rhotics in particular, as noted by Johnson (n.d.). It is probable that some of these problems arose from the development of a false, English-based approach to the orthography, particularly in connection with the medial stops. Certainly some of those providing guidance within the program have not clearly understood the important role the syllable structure plays in the interpretation of medial stop clusters (see §2.1.1). It is also likely that some of the problem lay with a general difficulty in using digraphs consistently. Reports of such difficulties have become fewer and the orthography has continued to be used without modification within the bilingual education program.

3.   MORPHOLOGY

3.1   PARTS OF SPEECH

The principal parts of speech in Ndjébbana are nominals, verbs, pronouns, demonstratives, adverbs, interrogative/indefinites and a small residue set of particles and interjections. These parts of speech are categorised using formal and functional criteria.

Verbs are marked directly with affixes for tense and mood and carry obligatory bound pronominal affixes to mark their principal arguments. Intransitive verbs mark only the intransitive subject S, while transitive verbs mark two arguments – in the case of ditransitive verbs the transitive subject or agent A and the indirect object IO, and in the case of ordinary transitive (i.e. monotransitive) verbs the transitive subject or agent A and the direct object O (see §3.3.3 and §3.6.3).

Nominals may function as head of a noun phrase, or as a predication within a verbless clause. Nominals may be marked with pronominal affixes for S or for agreement, but these are normally distinct in the third person minimal from the prefixes used to mark the S of verbs, being either zero for Class A or one of a variety of other prefixes or other forms for classes B, C and D (see §3.2.3). Nominals are not marked for tense/mood, unlike verbs.

3.2   NOMINALS

Nominals in Ndjébbana correspond to both nouns and adjectives in English. All can be used as predicates in verbless clauses. The formal class of nominals in Ndjébbana includes several subclasses (§3.2.2 and §3.2.3) and lexical items referring to concrete objects and individuals, qualities and characteristics are distributed among these. It would be true to say that nominals with 'noun-like' meanings predominate in the more alienably possessed Class A, while the nominals with more 'adjective-like' meanings predominate in Class D. Classes of nominals are based on gender (§3.2.2) and on the forms of possession marking (§3.2.3). Reduplication of nominals is unknown in Ndjébbana, probably due to the length of many morphemes and words.

3.2.1 CASE INFLECTIONS. Unlike many other Australian languages, case inflections are not a significant feature of Ndjébbana. Only two case affixes are used in Ndjébbana. These are -(k)kawa ABLATIVE (example (2)) and -ngána PURPOSIVE (example (3)). The ablative suffix has a single suffix-initial stop following a root-final stop or nasal (e.g. Madjárrkkadj-kawa) and a double stop following a vowel.

(2)   Ndjúdda-kkawa   ka-balála-nga.
        Juda.Point-ABL   3MINMASCS-come-REM
        He came from Juda Point. (II/26)

(3)   Makéddja-ngána   babbúya   ngirri-ngódjba-na.
        turtle-PURP   ironwood   1/2UAA+3MINMASCO-make-REM
        We made [harpoons] for turtles from ironwood. (VII/13)

The form wékkana-ngána ('night-PURP') means 'in the (early part of the) morning'.

The major participants in a clause (A, O, S, IO) are marked by pronominal affixes to the verb (§3.3.3) and, if also included as independent nominals and pronominals, are not marked for case. See (4),(5) and Text 25/95–6.

(4)   Karrddjúnja   njana-bá-la-yángaya.
        stingray   1MINO+MINA-bite-REM-3MINFEMA
        A stingray bit me. (XXIII/15)

(5)   Bábba   ka-bé-na   mámam
        father   3MINMASCS-go+REM   grandmother
                  bindi-wú-na   míbbarda.
                  3MINA+3UAIO-give-REM   bandicoot
        My father went and gave a bandicoot to my two grandmothers. (VII/45)

The object of the hunt (or gathering expedition) need not be specially marked (6), but can be marked with an immediately following namánja which is either a suffix, an enclitic or a postposition. Its status in this respect is not clear. See (7).

(6)   Ka-ddjórrkka   bárrbaya.   Bárrbaya
        3MINA+3MINMASCO-take   dog
           ka-ddjórrkka   nabbarlángkareya.
                            goanna
        He would take his dog(s). He would take his dog(s) [to get/when hunting
        for] goanna. (VII/37)

(7)   Ba-rra-bé-na   kúdjbarra   namánja.   / warakkála namánja.
        3AUGS-RE-go-REM   kangaroo   HUNTOBJ   long yam
        They went hunting kangaroos/to gather long yams.

3.2.2 NOMINAL CLASSES—GENDER. Ndjébbana has two grammatical
gender classes, which are labelled *masculine* and *feminine*. Most, if not all,
nominals of possession class A (see §3.2.3 below) have inherent gender
which is morphologically indicated only by means of agreement affixes on
the verb and on associated nominals of classes B, C and D, as seen in
examples (8) and (70) (=Text 25/17-19), in each of which every word agrees
with the subject nominal. The latter is discussed in more detail in §3.6.21.
Agreement affixes or possessor affixes are detailed in §3.2.3. In classes B, C
and D generally, nominals do not have inherent gender, but vary according to
the nominals they agree with. Many of such nominals refer to body parts or
correspond to adjectives in English.

(8)   Balawúrrwurr   ka-rakarawé-ra   yinjírra
        wind (MASC)   3MINMASCS-move-REM   1AUGDAT
           nga-namánda.
           3MINMASC-small
        A little bit of wind blew for us.

      In the verb pronominal prefix system the masculine-feminine contrast
applies only in the third person minimal (=singular) S forms and in the third
person minimal O forms when A is also third person. When A is non-third
person, gender of third person minimal O is neutralised. The gender contrast
is also neutralised in A position. See §3.3.3 and §3.3.4. The so-called unit
augmented feminine forms (dual feminine) constitute a separate phenomenon
and are used only with human referents except where animals of known sex
are clearly individuated as in Text 25/74–6 (see §3.3.2).
      The gender contrast is neutralised in the augmented (or plural) number
for nominals with human referents, while for nominals with multiple non-
human referents number may be neutralised and the gender contrast retained
if the number of referents is non-specific, as in the noun phrases below. If,
however, the plural non-human referents are individuated or enumerated (as
in Text 25/27–8, 74–6 etc.) the appropriate augmented or unit augmented
pronominal affixes are used. Finally number may be neutralised for human
referents when some sort of general/habitual statement is made without
specific referents in mind as in Text 7/35–41 in which the unit augmented
number is used for a series of general statements, or in (117), (150), (196)
and (203), in all of which the minimal number is used for a range of general

statements. See also (27) in which a minimal O form occurs referring to a non-specific/unindividuated, but apparently non-singular, object.

Contrast the nominal ngarráma 'woman' (which carries a number prefix and the extent suffix (§3.2.4) in the non-minimal number) with all the other nominals given here (which have invariant form). The only other nominals regularly marked like ngarráma in the non-minimal are (n-)karókaddja 'child' (barra-rókaddji-ba) and múya 'dead person, spirit' (barra-múyi-ba).

yídja n-barrábarra	yídja barra-karrówa
man 3MINMASC-big	man 3AUG-many
a big man	many men

ngarráma nja-barrábarra	barra-ngarrámi-ba barra-karrówa
woman 3MINFEM-big	3AUG-woman-EXT 3AUG-many
a big woman	many women

yókkarra n-barrábarra	yókkarra n-karrówa
fish 3MINMASC-big	fish 3MINMASC-many
a big fish/big fish	many fish

bíbbo nja-barrábarra	bíbbo nja-karrówa
crab 3MINFEM-big	crab 3MINFEM-many
a big crab/big crabs	many crabs

Note the minimal rather than augmented number forms (see §3.3.1) throughout sentence (9) for the semantically plural O. Feminine agreements are maintained wherever the necessary forms are available.

(9)   Njirri-ná-na   nja-múlbbum   karrddjúnja
        1UAA+3MINO-see-REM   3MINFEM-several   stingray
                yaka-yó-ra.
                3MINFEMS-lie-CTP
        We saw several stingrays there. (XXIII/5–6)

Both number and gender contrasts are neutralised with plural non-human mixed-gender referents. In the example (10) the S comprises both yókkarra (a masculine nominal) and bíbbo (a feminine nominal) and the two verbs both carry third person minimal S prefixes.

(10)   Yókkarra   njana   bíbbo   kóma   ka-kó-na
        fish   and   crab   NEG   3MINMASCS-kó-sit
                ka-yawarlakkayí-na
                3MINMASCS-run out-REM
        There's no fish and crab, they've run out.

There are homophonous word pairs which differ only in the gender agreements they command on associated nominals. Thus, for instance, the feminine noun makéddja appearing in Text 25/17–19 refers to the long-necked turtle, a specific species of freshwater turtle. There is another nominal makéddja, which is masculine in gender and is the generic term for turtle, including all species of freshwater and marine turtles.

In a rare text example grammatical gender overrules natural gender when a songman named after a feminine bird (kaddíkadda) is referred to using the third person minimal feminine pronoun ngayábba (XIV/210).

In the alphabetical wordlist the inherent gender of nominals is indicated where appropriate (and where known).

3.2.3 NOMINAL CLASSES—POSSESSION.

In Ndjébbana noun phrases, the marking of possession involves four quite different methods, depending on the nominal involved. These methods of possessor-marking form the basis of a further subclassification of nominals. This complex system of possession marking, first noted by Capell (1943:28), has been extensively explored by McKay (1995).

Possession class A involves marking possessor by juxtaposing the appropriate Cardinal Pronoun form (§3.3.2) to the nominal denoting the possessed item. This class is the most general, open class, and the possession relationship so marked is the most separable or alienable.

At the other, inalienable, extreme are nominals of possession classes C and D. 'Possession' marking on these nominals indicates referential identity of 'possessor' and 'possessed'. Class C marks possessor using a Possessive Pronoun (§3.3.2) suffixed to the possessed nominal, while class D marks possessor in the form of pronominal prefixes to the possessed nominal (cf.§3.3.3).

Class B comprises a type with an intermediate level of alienability, for which possessor is marked by the subject prefix of the accompanying verb réndjeyi 'to stand'.

In the alphabetical wordlist appended to this grammar known nominals of possession classes B, C and D are indicated. The remaining nominals apparently belong to the open class A.

[a] *Class A.*   Class A is an open class of nominals including some body-part terms, most kin terms and a range of non-possessed nominals. This seems to be the only class which receives borrowings. Some nominals of this class can not be marked as possessed (e.g. lárla 'trepang-like sea creature').

The Cardinal Pronoun form indicating the possessor is normally marked with a prefix agreeing in number and gender with the possessed nominal, though many younger speakers omit the third person minimal masculine prefix n-. In this construction the Cardinal Pronouns take prefixes as nominals of class D1 except when the pronoun-initial consonant is n-, which would be identical to the third person minimal masculine prefix. In these cases (second person unit augmented and augmented) the cardinal pronoun is treated as a nominal of class D2, with a third person minimal masculine prefix nga-. When the n- third person minimal masculine prefix (D2) is omitted, this pronoun is treated as a nominal of class D4, with zero third person minimal masculine prefix. The Cardinal Pronoun may precede or follow the possessed nominal. (The root -karókaddja 'child' loses the root initial   syllable   -ka-   in   the   non-minimal   number.)

bábba   n-ngáyabba
father   3MINMASC-1MINCARD
my father

nja-ngáyabba   kíkka
3MINFEM-1MINCARD   mother
my mother

barra-ngáyabba   barra-rókaddji-ba
3AUG-1MINCARD   3AUG-child-EXT
my children

barra-rókaddji-ba   barra-barrayabba
3AUG-child-EXT   3AUG-3AUGCARD
their children

marddúrddiba ngáyabba
heart   1MINCARD
my heart

njíndjabba   wíba
2MINCARD   camp/place/home
your place

The following examples show clearly the different third person minimal masculine prefixes used with different forms of the cardinal pronoun. When the pronoun has an initial n-.the nga- prefix of class D2 is used in order to avoid the word initial occurrence of geminate n-n-.

bárrbaya   n-ngúrrabba
dog   3MINMASC-1/2AUGCARD

bárrbaya   nga-núrrabba
dog   3MINMASC-2AUGCARD

There are homophonous sets of nominals in different possession classes which show that nominals of classes C and D are associated with more inalienable possession and with humanness when compared with nominals of class A. Possession class is given in parentheses after the gloss.

njamánja   nja-ngáyabba
mussels (A)   3MINFEM-1MINCARD
my mussels

njamánja-njabba
knee (C)-1MINPOSS
my knee

kánkarra   ngáyabba
meat/flesh (A)   1MINCARD
my meat [for eating]

nga-kánkarra
1MIN-meat/flesh (D)
my flesh [part of my body]

n-ngáyabba   ngalidjbínja
3MINMASC-IMINCARD   didgeridoo (A)
my didgeridoo

ngalidjbínja-njabba
throat/windpipe (C)-1MINPOSS
my throat/windpipe

nja-ngáyabba   ngalidjbínja
3MINFEM-1MINCARD   shotgun (A)
my shotgun

On the other hand, a number of apparently quite inalienable body parts and kin terms are class A nominals which mark the possessor using a cardinal pronoun. Examples are the words marddúrddiba 'heart', karnbilíbala 'blood', bábba 'father' and kíkka 'mother'.

[b] *Class B.* Class B is a closed class, containing a score of body-part nominals. Possessor is marked by means of the subject S prefix on the contemporary form of the accompanying verb réndjeyi 'to stand/be'.

bárnka	nga-réndjeya		míbba	ya-réndjeya
elbow	1MINS-stand+CTP		forehead	3MINFEMS-stand+CTP
my elbow			her forehead	

The body-part nominals forming class B tend to be nominals which refer to externally visible body parts, particularly in comparison with related body-part nominals in classes C and D.

márdba	nga-réndjeya	ngalidjbínja-njabba
neck (B)	1MINS-stand/be+CTP	throat/windpipe (C)-1MINPOSS
my neck		my throat/windpipe

djánama	nga-réndjeya	nga-bbúrrbba
belly (B)	1MINS-stand/be+CTP	1MIN-guts/innards (D1)
my belly [external]		my guts/innards

On the other hand, some externally visible body-parts are referred to by nominals which are not members of class B, but rather mark possessor by affixation (Class C or Class D). Examples include yúrnka- 'head (C)', díla- 'eye (C)', rakáya- 'finger-/toenail (C)', -móya 'sore, wound (D)', -(k)kódda 'skin (D)'.

Finally, one homophonous pair suggests that class B nominals are less associated with humanness than Class C.

kúdja	ka-réndjeya	kúdja-njabba
base (B)	3MINMASCS-stand/be+CTP	foot-1MINPOSS
its base [tree]		my hand/foot

[c] *Class C.* For nominals of this class the possessor is marked using the Possessive Pronoun (§3.3.2) suffixed to the possessed nominal. The class contains only 27 nominals, largely body-part terms such as the following:

marnákarna-njabba	yúrnka-ngaya
rib.bone-1MINPOSS	head-3MINFEMPOSS
my ribs	her head

With a very small number of nominals of this class the Possessive Pronoun suffix indicates identity of reference or agreement rather than possession. The English-based distinction in interpretation between agreement or inalienable possession depends on the meaning of the word. For example a body part, as in (13), is treated in English as possessed, while a quality or characteristic, as in (14), is treated in English as an adjective and the 'possession' marking in Ndjébbana appears more like agreement, as it does also in (11) and (12).

(11)   Nga-nó-ra   warábba-njabba.
         1MINS-sit-CTP   alone-1MINPOSS
         I am sitting by myself. / I am alone.

(12) yídja   karnayédjabba   warábba-baddabirra
      man   two   one-3AUGMASCPOSS
      three men

(13) lárla-baddana
      penis-3UAMASCPOSS
      their [two] penises

(14) lárla-baddana   birri-búlanj.
      male-3UAMASCPOSS   3UAMASCS-[subsection name]
      The two boys are both Búlanj.

Two nominals of class C appear to have inherent gender of their own. These are djakí 'speed' and wíba 'country'. Both are masculine and this is marked, for example, by the masculine prefix on the accompanying nominal in the following phrase. All other known nominals of this class refer to body parts or qualities and thus take the gender of their 'possessor'.

bíbbo   djakí-ngaya   n-bókka
crab (AFEM)   speed (CMASC)-3MINFEMPOSS   3MINMASC-bad
the crab is slow/goes slowly

Two nominals have been found in class C with which the Possessive Pronoun suffix marks neither a possessor nor agreement but rather the subject of a predication. That is, the Class C forms of these two nominals (with possessive suffixes) are consistently treated by speakers as clauses, not as noun phrases. Each of these nominals is homophonous with a nominal appearing in another class which is treated as a noun phrase when marked for possession ('my strength', 'my country'). See also example (55).

búrrbba-njabba   nga-bbúrrbba
strong (C)-1MINPOSS   1MIN-guts (D1)
I am strong   my guts

wíba-njabba   ngáyabba   wíba
country (C)-1MINPOSS   1MINCARD   country/home (A)
I belong to this country.   my country

[d] *Class D.* Possessor or agreement is marked on nominals of class D by means of pronominal verb prefixes to the nominal.

nga-kkódda   ngána-wala   barra-walá-nja
1MIN-skin   2MIN-name   3UAFEM-name-UAFEM
my skin   your name   their [two females] names

The last of these forms shows that the underlying stress of the root -walá- 'name' is on the root-final syllable and shifts to word-initial position when it would otherwise be word-final. It may occur root-finally only if a suffix prevents it being at the same time word-final, as here (§2.3.1). The third person minimal masculine form of this nominal has lost the root-initial syllable.

> ná-la   (<*ná-wala (D6))
> 3MINMASC-name
> his name

Another nominal with underlying root-final stress is (ká-)lakarra 'Aboriginal (man)' (D3).

> ká-lakarra   bárri-lakarra   barra-lakarrá-nja
> 3MINMASC-Aboriginal   3UAMASC-Aboriginal   3UAFEM-Aboriginal

The prefix form used with class D nominals is identical to the intransitive subject (S) prefix used with verbs as set out in Table 3.3 (§3.3.3), except that the 3 person minimal feminine prefix used on nominals does not vary with tense, but is always nja-, while the possession subclass D1 to D6 varies according to the 3 person minimal masculine form:

MASC.: D1 n-   D3 ka-   D5 ma-   FEM.: D1-D6 nja-
        D2 nga- D4 Ø-   D6 na-

The subclasses D1 to D6 are closed subclasses of nominals with the following numbers of known members: D1 42; D2 14; D3 3; D4 18; D5 1; D6 2.

In addition to a number of body-part nominals which are clearly possessed (see examples above) this class contains a wide range of other nominals, many of which refer to qualities and attributes rather than to possessions. The pronominal prefix does not so much refer to a possessor but rather identifies the referent of the pronominal with the referent of the nominal by way of agreement or even as the subject of a predication, though these and the possession examples are not formally distinguished.

Njirri-kóyok.
1UA-[subsection term]
We are both in the Kóyok subsection.

Nga-nawarrámaya.
1MIN-skinny
I am skinny.

ngalidjbínja   nja-mádjarna
shotgun (FEM)   3MINFEM-proper/real/genuine
proper guns

birri-yáwarlbba
3UAMASC-old person
two old men

This is true, too, of nominals referring to human beings and 'kin' terms in this class, as in the following noun phrases:

nja-karókaddja
3MINFEM-child (D1)
girl [not 'her child']

nga-ndjórrkkabba
3MINMASC-spouse (D2)
husband [not 'his spouse']

barra-múyi-ba
3AUG-spirit/dead person-EXT
dead people/spirits [not 'their spirits']

nja-ndjórrkkabba
3MINFEM-spouse (D2)
wife [not 'her spouse']

The referential identity marked by the 'possessor' prefix is clearly seen in the text example (15) in which the subject of the verb 'to get better' and the wound are both marked as first person minimal. The speaker's own translation is given first.

(15)   Nga-ngadjba-yí-na   nga-móya.
       1MINS-repair-REFL-REM   1MIN-wound/sore
       'I got better, my sore. / My wound healed.' (XX/239)

3.2.4 EXTENT SUFFIX. A general suffix indicating extent is used with nominals as well as with verbs and other classes of words. It has two phonological forms: -(i)-ba and -(V)-bba. Both forms are common with verbs but -(i)-ba is the more common with nominals. The vowel in parentheses in the citation form of the suffix indicates that the stem-final vowel is always i or the normal stem-final vowel (V) respectively. In the case of -(i)-ba this normally means that the vowel changes from its usual realisation (a) when the extent suffix is added. It is not clear whether there is any difference in meaning and function between the two forms, nor what are the determining factors in the use of one rather than the other. A couple of forms (one nominal, one verb) have been found to take both forms without apparent distinction.

This suffix apears to have a wide range of meaning including *plural*, *durative*, *habitual*, *iterative*, *intensive*. With nominals it is used, along with the augmented number prefixes of the appropriate person, in the formation of plural forms of three words, including múya in example (16) and the following:

ngarráma   barra-ngarrámi-ba   n-karókaddja   barra-(ka)rókaddji-ba
woman   3AUG-woman-EXT   3MINMASC-child   3AUG-child-EXT
woman   women   child [boy]   children

Compare the phrase ngarráma-bba yídja (woman-EXT man) meaning 'men and women' (XIV/207, 17ON), in which the other form of the extent suffix is used with the nominal ngarráma 'woman', apparently with 'additive' meaning.

Other uses of the suffix are found in examples (16) and (17). In the former the extent suffix is used on a nominal (obligatorily) to mark plurality and on a verb (optionally) to mark habitual aspect. In the latter example the extent suffix appears to have intensive meaning.

(16)   Ngandjúddama... barra-múyi-ba
       bark.canoe   3AUG-dead/ancestor-EXT
           barra-ngóddji-ba
           3AUGA+3MINO-call/name+CTP-EXT
       It was what our ancestors used to call ngandjúddama (a bark canoe). (VII/67)

(17)   ...ngundu-wu-bbú-ra-yana   wálangandjáyiba
         ...1/2AUGO+MINA-EVIT-hit-CTP-3MINMASCA   lightning
            malóya   n-barrábarra   wóndja   n-barrábarra-bba
            rain   3MINMASC-big   as.well   3MINMASC-big-EXT
         [If we light a fire at that dreaming place] lightning and rain will come upon
         us, very big rain. (XVIII/14–15)

The two different forms of the suffix are found on the verb nó 'to sit'
and yó 'to lie' in the meaning 'to reside (habitually)' in examples (203) and
Text 25/61.
        In example (18) the main verb is marked as habitual (future) using the
extent suffix and this is reinforced by the use of the auxiliary verb (§4.2.6),
while the verb phrase meaning 'eastwards' in example (19) also has the
extent suffix with habitual locational ('where...') meaning.

(18)   'Kanja   ngaba-yú-ka-ya-bba   ngaba-yú-ka-na'
         well   1/2AUGA+3MINO-IRR-kó-drink-EXT   1/2AUGS-IRR-kó-sit
         'Well, we'll always drink [here/this water].' (XIII/86–7)

(19)   Nja-rra-bé-na...   wárrwarra   ya-ka-rlúrrbayi-ba
         1AUGS-RE-go-REM   sun   3MINFEMS-kó-arrive-EXT
         We went eastwards ['sunrise way' lit. 'where the sun always rises']. (I/107)

The suffix -(i)-ba in combination with a prefix form (ba)na- (LOCative)
on a nominal is used to derive an expression meaning '(in/at) the/a place
where [nominal] is found', as in Text 25/86–8 and (20), each of which also
contains another instance of the extent suffix. In particular the extent suffix
on the last main verb of (20) indicates the full extent of the activity.

(20)   Máwala   yúya   ka-ngárawa-na
         paperbark.torch   fire   3MINA+3MINMASCO-ignite-REM
            ka-bé-na   ka-kkó-ya
            3MINS-go-REM   3MINMASCS-REM-lie/be
            na-waléykkarri-ba.   Marlémarla
            LOC-stone/rock-EXT   [fish poison plant]
            ka-wú-ni-ba   ka-bé-na.
            3MINA+3MINMASCO-give-REM-EXT   3MINMASCS-go-REM
         He lit the paperbark torch going along the rocky area. He applied the fish
         poison all along. (XVII/39-41)

Compare also the word bana-kkábbi-ba (<kábba 'water') which means
'littoral' or 'in the water' and na-kardárrmali-ba (<kardárrmala 'jungle') which
means 'in the jungle place'.
        The extent suffix is used derivationally to differentiate lexical items,
though it is not clear that it has an identifiable meaning in these cases.
Compare the following pairs of forms:

n-djídja	'old'	n-djídja-bba	'same'
bólkkarda	'in deep water, on the open sea'	bólkkarda-bba	'half way, on the way, part way'
naké-bba	3MINMASCCARD	naké-mala	3MINMASCEMPH
ba-rra-rawáya 3AUGS-RE- dance	'they [women] are dancing'	ba-rra-rawáyi-ba	'they are playing [of children, or of adults playing cards]'

Some lexical items have an obligatory extent suffix, even though in many cases there are no contrasting forms without it. For example:

> ba-rra-bbínbi-ri-ba   wálangandjáyi-ba
> 3AUGS-RE-write-CTP(-EXT)   lightning
> They are writing.

A significant function of the extent suffix is to mark certain time clauses (see §4.10.1).

3.2.5 OTHER NOMINAL AFFIXES.

There is a small range of other nominal affixes used in the language.

[a] *na- Location (LOC)* . This suffix means 'a place where...' or 'a place which is...' as in examples (20), Text 25/88 and (21). Other distinctions related to location (e.g. locative or allative case) are left unmarked.

(21)   Ya-rlabí-na   na-djówanga.
        3MINFEMS-descend-REM   LOC-[moiety]
        She went down to Djówanga country. (XII/104)

[b] *nayik- and ngalik- Clan member (CLAN)* . These two prefixes are used, as in a number of other languages of the area, only with the names of yakkarrarra or bábburr 'patrilineal clans', giving the meaning 'member of X clan'. Nayik- is a third person minimal masculine prefix, while ngalik- is a third person minimal feminine prefix. Thus:

> nayik-karddúrra   ngalik-karddúrra
> CLANMASC-[clan name]   CLANFEM-[clan name]
> Karddúrra man   Karddúrra woman

In Ndjébbana it appears that these prefixes can vary for other numbers as in Text 7/11, where the third person unit augmented masculine appears with the prefix birriyik- showing that the na- of nayik- is being treated as a third person minimal masculine prefix for nominals of class D6. The extent of such number variation is not known.

It appears that these clan prefixes are not used with yakkarrarra names commencing with the syllable na-.

[c] *-balóbala Entire/Entire Group (ENT).* This suffix (in fact the evidence for suffix status is not clear) is attached to a nominal or pronoun and indicates the completeness of a group or of an entity, as shown by examples (22) to (24). In (24) the use of balóbala seems to indicate that the speaker's father and the Macassans formed a 'complete' group, though 'with' is a better translation into English. In all known examples it is used in an 'afterthought', after the main clause.

(22)   Ba-rra-bakabanjé-ra,   biridjina-balóbala.
        3AUGS-RE-dig-REM   prisoner-ENT
        They dug [it], all the prisoners. (II/90–1)

(23)   Yawa-rra-má-nga   yaba-rra-yikkabé-ra
        3AUGA+3MINFEMO-RE-get-REM   3AUGA+3MINFEMO-REM-tie-REM
          njarakkíla,   nja-náwarla   nja-mardárda-balóbala.
          cockle.meat   3MINFEM-different/other   3MINFEM-shell-ENT
        [After shelling some of the cockles] They got [the cockle meat FEM] and tied
        it up [in paperbark], others [cockles] complete with shells. (VII/28–30)

(24)   Bábba   ba-rrú-ka-na   nakébba-balóbala.
        father   3AUGS-RE-kó-sit(+REM)   3MINMASCCARD-ENT
        [My] father was [there] with them. (II/58–9)

3.3   PRONOMINAL FORMS

The principal pronominal forms of Ndjébbana are bound forms, mainly prefixes (§3.3.3), obligatorily used with all verbs and with many nominal forms. These, though bound, function as full arguments and are not simply copies cross-referencing independent pronouns (see §4.1). On each verb complex up to two of the clause participants or arguments must be specified using bound pronominal forms (§4.1, §4.2.1). Independent or free-form pronouns (§3.3.2) sometimes occur elsewhere in the clause, in apposition to the bound pronominal forms. When the optional free-form pronouns do occur in the clause they normally carry some sort of contrastive, emphatic or focus significance (§4.2.2). In the same way, lexical nominals are, like independent pronouns, not obligatory in the clause, but when they do appear they serve to elaborate on or clarify the pronominal reference of the bound pronominal forms (§4.2.2, §4.2.3).

The pronominal categories used in this grammar are set out in §3.3.1. The analysis of the pronominal forms, both free and bound, is outlined in §3.3.4.

3.3.1 PRONOMINAL CATEGORIES. As in some other languages of Arnhem Land (e.g. Burarra (Glasgow 1964a, Glasgow 1984:15), Rembarrnga (McKay 1978), Kunwinjku (Carroll 1969; 1976:63–4)) the

TABLE 3.1 *Ndjébbana pronominal categories: cardinal pronoun forms*

Traditional categories

	singular	dual	trial	plural
1exc	ngáyabba	njirrikébba		njírrabba
1excfem		njarrayábbanja		
1inc		ngárrabba	ngirrikébba	ngúrrabba
1incfem			ngarrayábbanja	
2	njíndjabba	nirrikébba		núrrabba
2fem		narrayábbanja		
3masc	nakébba	birrikébba		barrayabba
3fem	ngayábba	barrayábbanja		

Modified categories used in this grammar

	minimal masculine	minimal feminine	unit augmented masculine	unit augmented feminine	augmented
1	ngáyabba		njirrikébba	njarrayábbanja	njírrabba
1/2	ngárrabba		ngirrikébba	ngarrayábbanja	ngúrrabba
2	njíndjabba		nirrikébba	narrayábbanja	núrrabba
3	nakébba	ngayábba	birrikébba	barrayábbanja	barrayabba

traditional person and number categories (as set out in Table 3.1) are not entirely appropriate for Ndjébbana. In this grammar the following person and number categories are used:

1 person	(+ speaker - addressee	=first person exclusive)
1/2 person	(+ speaker + addressee	=first person inclusive)
2 person	(- speaker + addressee	=second person)
3 person	(- speaker - addressee	=third person)

minimal number   (=singular for 1, 2, 3 person and dual for 1/2 person)

unit augmented number   (=minimal plus one, i.e. dual for 1, 2, 3 person, trial for 1/2 person)

augmented number   (=minimal plus two or more, i.e. three or four or more, depending on person)

It is the number categories which are non-traditional because (unlike the traditional number categories) each number category varies in its numerical reference depending on the person category. In particular the first person inclusive (1/2 person) does have a minimal number but traditionally would not be treated as singular.

Minimal number is defined as the minimal set of referents appropriate to the particular person category (generally one, but two in the case of 1/2 person). Unit augmented number means minimal-plus-one and varies from two to three, depending on person category. Augmented refers to a set larger than unit augmented, that is three or more or four or more, depending on person category.

A comparison of the Cardinal Pronoun forms in Table 3.1, set out according to both systems clearly shows that the analysis adopted here conforms more closely to the formal structure of the paradigm in Ndjébbana.

Unit augmented feminine.   Unit augmented feminine forms of both free and bound pronouns in Ndjébbana are formed, with some minor specific modifications, using the feminine suffix -nja with the augmented form. This is apparent in the forms of the cardinal pronoun given in the second half of Table 3.1, if it is noted that a vowel has its underlying quality only if bearing the main phonemic stress. Otherwise it is reduced to -a-.

The significance of the unit augmented feminine form for each person category is that the 'unit augment' is feminine. The unit augment is the single individual over and above the minimal set of individuals referred to by that person category. (See also McKay 1979 and 1990.)

The first person unit augmented feminine form njarrayábbanja, for instance, refers to the speaker (the minimal set for first person) plus one other individual, who must be feminine. If the speaker herself is female, then this unit augmented feminine form refers to a set of two female individuals (=dual feminine), but if the speaker is male, then this unit augmented feminine form refers to a mixed sex set of one male and one female.

Thus, for example, a man, when speaking to a third party, would use the unit augmented feminine form njarrayábbanja to refer to himself (the speaker) and his wife (the unit augment, i.e. the individual addition to the minimal set). His wife would use the unit augmented masculine form njirrikébba to refer to herself and her husband, because in this case the unit augment is male, given that the wife is the speaker.

3.3.2 INDEPENDENT AND SUFFIX PRONOUNS.

3.3.2 INDEPENDENT AND SUFFIX PRONOUNS. Ndjébbana has two types of independent pronouns which are clearly free forms: Cardinal pronouns and Emphatic Pronouns. Dative Pronouns and Possessive Pronouns, on the other hand, have some of the characteristics of suffixes in that they occur always in a fixed position immediately following the word they modify and some of the forms appear not to be phonologically fully independent (e.g. -na 3MINMASCPOSS and -ngka 2MINPOSS, the first because it is so short and has no stressed syllable and the last because its initial nasal is the final consonant of the preceding stem final syllable).

Furthermore the suffix -yana 3MINMASCDAT and its feminine counterpart -yángaya may be used as an agent marker with verbs and, with some of these, stress placement shows that the presence of one of these suffixes renders the root-final vowel no longer word final (§2.4.1), thus clearly showing the pronoun to be a suffix. The same stress-shifting

Table 3.2 *Ndjébbana independent and suffix pronouns*

	Cardinal Pronouns	Emphatic Pronouns	Dative Pronouns	Possessive Pronouns
1min	ngáyabba	ngáyamala	ngabúyanga	-njabba
1uamasc	njirrikébba	njirrikémala	yinjerrekéyanga	-njaddana
1uafem	njarrayábbanja	njarrayámalanja	yinjerreyánja	-njaddayúnja
1aug	njírrabba	njírramala	yinjírra	-njaddabirra
1/2min	ngárrabba	ngárramala	yingárra	-ngadda
1/2uamasc	ngirrikébba	ngirrikémala	yingerrekéyanga	-ngaddana
1/2uafem	ngarrayábbanja	ngarrayámalanja	yingarrayánja	-ngaddayúnja
1/2aug	ngúrrabba	ngúrramala	yingúrra	-ngaddabirra
2min	njínjdjabba	njínjdjamala	yikkóyanga	-ngka
2uamasc	nirrikébba	nirrikémala	yinerrekéyanga	-naddana
2uafem	narrayábbanja	narrayámalanja	yinerreyánja	-naddayúnja
2aug	núrrabba	núrramala	yinúrra	-naddabirra
3minmasc	nakébba	nakémala	-yana	-na
3minfem	ngayábba	ngayámala	-yángaya	-ngaya
3uamasc	birrikébba	birrikémala	yiberrekéyanga	-baddana
3uafem	barrayábbanja	barrayámalanja	yiberreyánja	-baddayúnja
3aug	barrayabba	barrayamala	yibérra	-baddabirra

phenomenon shows that the possessive pronoun forms are all suffixes but that only the third person minimal masculine and feminine dative pronouns are suffixes. The remaining dative pronoun forms are separate words, though they occur in a fixed position relative to the word they modify.

Table 3.2 sets out the Cardinal, Emphatic, Dative and Possessive Pronoun forms. Table 3.1 (§3.3.1) sets out the Cardinal Pronoun forms using the traditional pronoun categories for comparison with the categories used in this grammar.

[a] *Cardinal and Emphatic Pronouns.* The Cardinal and Emphatic Pronouns are used to express contrasts as exemplified in (25), (26), (79), (80), (86), (88), Text 7/16, 20, Text 9/31 and Text 25/22–3, 25, 95. See §4.2.2.

(25)   Barrayabba   yaláwa   barra-bala-yirrí-ya   yawúyakka...
        3AUG   then   3AUGS-hither-go-CTP   first
        nja-rra-yó-ra   bakkándja   nja-rra-wola-kkamíya.
        1AUGS-RE-sleep-CTP   later   1AUGS-RE-hither-depart
        They came on ahead. We camped there and came on later. (XXV/91–4)

(26)   Ngayámala   yi-bé-na   ngarráma   njana
        3MINFEMEMPH   3MINFEMS-go-REM   female   and
        nakémala   lárlana   ka-bé-na,   warábba.
        3MINMASCEMPH   male   3MINMASCS-go-REM   alone
        The female went away and the male went away, alone. (XXI/45–6)

These two types of pronouns are used to introduce new subjects or change of subject (a type of contrast) as in Text 7/20, Text 9/4, 13, 18, 22, 33 and Text 25/33, 41, 95. See §4.2.2.

The Cardinal and Emphatic Pronouns are also used as demonstrative adjectives qualifying a nominal as in the second sentence of example (27) and as in example (90). See §4.4.1.

(27)   Yaláwa   ka-rá-na.   Nakébba
        then   3MINA+3MINMASCO-spear-REM   3MINMASCCARD
        Mángkaddjarra   barra-rá-na.
        Macassan   3AUGA+3MINMASCO-spear-REM
        Well they murdered them [lit. 'he murdered him']. It was Macassans they murdered. (V/88)

The Cardinal Pronoun has a further major function: it is used to mark the possessor for nominals of class A (see §3.2.3). When used attributively in this function the Cardinal Pronouns are themselves nominals of Class D, taking a prefix to cross-reference person, number and gender of the possessed nominal as exemplified for possession class A (§3.2.3). First person minimal and 1/2 person augmented appear to belong to class D1 with minimal masculine prefix n-; second person non-minimal cardinal pronouns appear to belong to class D2 with minimal masculine prefix nga-; remaining cardinal pronouns belong to class D4 with zero minimal masculine prefix. See Text 25/61.

nja-ngáyabba   kíkka   birri-rókaddji-ba   birri-nirrikébba
3MINFEM-1MINCARD   mother   3UA-child-EXT   3UA-2UACARD
my mother   your (two) two children

The Cardinal Pronoun may also be used predicatively to mark the possessor (e.g. *This spear is mine/his*). The regular Cardinal Pronoun forms are used with the exception of the third person singular (minimal) for which a special predicative form is used: -nábba which is a nominal of Class D2. (Therefore with a third person singular masculine possessed object it would have the form nga-nábba.)

[b] *Dative Pronouns.* The Dative Pronoun has two functions. The first is to mark an indirect 'interest' in the verb, that is a non-subject interest other than that of direct object of any transitive verb or of (direct or) indirect object of a ditransitive verb (which objects are marked directly by pronominal prefix to the verb as with the ditransitive verb wu 'to give' in (28)):

(28)   Djabindi-wú-na
        2MINA+3UAMASCIO-give-REM
        You gave it to them.

With other verbs such an indirect interest may not be marked by the pronominal prefixes but is marked by means of a Dative Pronoun as in examples (29) (a) and (b) (speech), (30) and (31). See also example (77) and the first sentence of (99), Text 7/1, Text 9/17 and Text 25/22, 45, 48, 66, 78–9 and 81–2.

(29) (a)   'Yá-rakarawo,'   ka-ngúdjeya   ngabúyanga.   'Kóma.'
           1/2MINS(+IRR)-go/move   3MINMASCS-say   1MINDAT   no
           'Let's go', he said to me. 'No'. (XV/43–4)

(29) (b)   ...ngúdja   nga-marabí-na-yana   deksi.
           word/story   1MINS-enter/telephone-REM-3MINMASCDAT   taxi
           I rang a taxi.(LDj Njarrabéna Ngána Holiday Sydney p. 13)

(30)   Balawúrrwurr   ka-rakarawé-ra   yinjírra   nga-namánda.
       wind   3MINS-move-REM   1AUGDAT   3MINMASC-small
       A little bit of wind blew for us. [It got rid of the mosquitoes.] (XVIII/6)

(31)   Malóya   ka-rlarrabí-na   yinjírra   bólkkardabba.
       rain   3MINMASCS-arrive-REM   1AUGDAT   on.the.way
       Rain fell on us on the way there. (I/47)

The second function of the Dative Pronoun is to mark the person and gender of a minimal transitive subject A, thus disambiguating certain pronominal prefix combinations which would otherwise fall together. This can be seen by comparing the following two forms in which the prefix form actually fully specifies only the IO (as second person minimal) and specifies the minimal number but not the person of the A. Such dative suffixes will normally be glossed DATA, providing both a formal (DAT) and a functional (A) characterisation.

ngana-wú-na   ngana-wú-na-yana
MINA+2MINIO-give-REM   MINA+2MINIO-give-REM-3MINMASCDATA
I gave it to you   He gave it to you

Only the third person minimal dative suffix forms -yana 3MINMASC and -yángaya 3MINFEM disambiguate A in this way, though this occurs with a wide range of O and IO prefix forms (e.g. all those forms with minimal A in Table 3.4 and similar forms in Tables 3.5 and 3.6). Compare the text example (32). Elsewhere in this grammar prefix forms with minimal A which are ambiguous as to person of A will be glossed for person of A in the light of the accompanying dative suffix for clarity. The gender of third person minimal A will be glossed only on the suffix.

(32)   [Karrddjúnja]   njana-rá-na-yángaya.
       stingray [FEM]   MINA+1MINO-pierce/sting-REM-3MINFEMDATA
       A stingray stung/bit me. (XXIII/12)

[c] *Possessive Pronouns.* Possessive Pronouns perform two functions. The first is to mark agreement with or inalienable possession of nominals of Class C (§3.2.3). Most nominals in class C refer to body parts. In effect the Possessive Pronoun marks an identity relation between the referent of the nominal and that of the pronoun. See §3.2.3. See also Texts 9/16 and 25/27.

díla-ngaya
eye/seed/cartridge-3MINFEMPOSS
her eye/seed [FEM plant]/cartridge [shotgun FEM]

warábba-njabba
alone-1MINPOSS
[I am] alone/by myself

The second function of the Possessive Pronoun is to mark an indirect 'interest', as with the 'Dative of Interest' discussed above. The Possessive Pronoun is relatively less common than the Dative Pronoun in this function and it is not clear whether there is any other difference between the two in this. See examples (33), (34) and (35). See also Text 7/4, 7 and Text 25/42.

(33)   Bárriya   birri-mérba-ra-njabba
        3UA   3UAMASCA+3MINMASCO-hide-CTP-1MINPOSS
            birri-nó-ra.
            3UAS-sit-CTP
        Those two are hiding it from me. (VII/64–5)

(34)   Njáya   yi-bé-na-njabba.
        3MINFEMDEM   3MINFEM-go-REM-1MINPOSS
        She's deserted me. (XII/70)

(35)   Ka-badjí-na-njabba,   'Na-bangárda.
        3MINMASCS-call-REM-1MINPOSS   3MINMASC-[subsection]
            Dá-bala-yarra.   Yaláwa   balánda
            MINIMP-hither-go   well   white.man
            ka-bbúdjeya-ngka.'
            3MINMASCS-call-2MINPOSS
        He called to me, 'Nabangárda. Come here. A/the white man is calling for you.' (XIV/86–7)

3.3.3 PRONOMINAL PREFIX FORMS.

Each Ndjébbana verb bears a pronominal prefix form, as do many nominals. This form is normally a partly analysable portmanteau form which specifies person, number and gender of one or two core noun phrases associated with the verb as follows:

Intransitive verbs	S (subject)
Transitive verbs	A (subject) and O (direct object)
Ditransitive verbs	A (subject) and IO (indirect object)

Formally the pronominal prefixes used with (mono-)transitive verbs are identical to those used with ditransitives. The indirect object is marked instead of the direct object in the latter. In the tables of pronominal prefix forms O should be interpreted as referring to IO in the case of prefixes used with ditransitive verbs.

Table 3.3 sets out the S (intransitive subject) prefixes as well as the A and O prefix combinations (transitive subject and object) when O (IO in the case of ditransitives) is third person. Tables 3.4, 3.5 and 3.6 set out the A and O prefix combinations which occur when O is 1/2 person, 1 person and 2 person respectively. The forms given in the tables are those used with realis.

TABLE 3.3 *Intransitive S prefixes and transitive A and O prefixes with 3 person O*

A or S	S	O minimal	unit augmented	augmented
1min	nga-	nga-	ngabindi-	ngabanda-/ ngabana-*
1uamasc	njirri-	njirri-	njanbirri-	njanbirri-
1aug	njarra-	njarra-	njanbirri-	njanbirri-
2min	dja-/ngana-*	dja-	djabindi-	djabanda-/ djabana-*
2uamasc	nirri-	nirri-	nanbirri-	nanbirri-
2aug	narra-	narra-	nanbirri-	nanbirri-
1/2min	yV-/ka-*	yV-/(rr)ka-	nganbirri-	nganbirri-
1/2uamasc	ngirri-	ngirri-	nganbirri-	nganbirri-
1/2aug	ngabarra-	ngabarra-	nganbirri-	nganbirri-
3minmasc	ka-	ka- (O=masc) yaka- (O=fem)	bindi-	banda-/bana-*
3minfem	nja-/yV-*	ka- (O=masc) yaka- (O=fem)	bindi-	banda-/bana-*
3uamasc	birri-	birri- (O=masc) yibirri- (O=fem)	banbirri-	banbirri-
3aug	barra-	barra- (O=masc) yabarra- (O=fem)	banbirri	banbirri

TABLE 3.4 *Transitive A and O prefixes with 1/2 person O*

A	O minimal	unit augmented	augmented
3minmasc	nganda- -yana/ nganarra- -yana*	ngindi- -yana	nganda- -yana/ nganarra- -yana*
3minfem	nganda- -yángaya/ nganarra- -yángaya*	ngindi- -yángaya	nganda- -yángaya/ nganarra- -yángaya*
3uamasc	nganbirri-	nganbirri-	nganbirri-
3augmasc	nganbirri-	nganbirri-	nganbirri-

or non-future indicative verb forms, except where indicated in notes to the tables. The realis prefix -rrV-, where -V- is any vowel, is not strictly part of the pronominal prefix but is replaced in irrealis or future forms by one of the allomorphs of the irrealis prefix (§3.6.3, §3.6.4). In the tables unit

TABLE 3.5 *Transitive A and O prefixes with 1 person O*

A	O		
	minimal	unit augmented	augmented
2min	njanda-/njana-*	djabindi-	djabanda-/djabana-*
2uamasc	nbirri-	njanbirri-	njanbirri-
2aug	nbarra-	njanbirri-	njanbirri-
3minmasc	njanda- -yana/ njana- -yana*	njindi- -yana	njanda- -yana/ njanarra- -yana*
3uamasc	nbirri-	njanbirri-	njanbirri-
3aug	nbarra-	njanbirri-	njanbirri-

TABLE 3.6 *Transitive A and O prefixes with 2 person O*

A	O		
	minimal	unit augmented	augmented
1min	dja-/ngana-*	nindi-	nanda-/nanarra-*
1uamasc	nbirri-	nanbirri-	nanbirri-
1aug	nbarra-	nanbirri-	nanbirri-
3minmasc	dja-/ngana-*-yana	nindi--yana	nanda- -yana/ nanarra- -yana*
3uamasc	nbirri-	nanbirri-	nanbirri-
3aug	nbarra-	nanbirri-	nanbirri-

augmented feminine forms have been omitted. When both A and O are non-minimal (and the prefix therefore has the form njanbi-rri-, nganbi-rri-, nanbi-rri- or banbi-rri-) the unit augmented feminine is not distinguished from unit augmented masculine or augmented in either A or O. Where S, A or O is unit augmented feminine (and in the case of transitive prefixes, the other element is minimal in number) the appropriate form of prefix is that for the corresponding augmented, together with the suffix -nja. Thus, for instance we get the following sets of forms:

nirri-bé-na
2UAMASCS-go-REM
they (two) went

narra-bé-na
2AUGS-
they (plural) went

narra-bé-na-nja
2UAS-   -UAFEM
they (two) went

djabindi-wú-na
2MINA+3UAMASCIO-give-REM
you gave it to them (two, masculine)

djabana-wú-na
2MINA+3AUGIO-
you gave it to them (plural)

djabana-wú-na-nja
2MINA+3UAFEMIO- -UAFEM
you gave it to them (two, feminine)

In Tables 3.3, 3.4, 3.5, and 3.6 some sets of alternative forms are marked with an asterisk (*). In each of these cases the first alternative form of prefix is used with irrealis (including future) verb forms, the second alternative is used with realis (including non-future) verb forms. Note that the 3 person minimal masculine dative suffix -yana is given as accompanying certain prefix forms for which the A (transitive subject) is third person minimal masculine. In these cases the use of this suffix is obligatory to differentiate the total verb form from one with an identical prefix but no suffix, for which the A is non-third person. For third person minimal feminine A the third person minimal feminine dative suffix -yángaya replaces -yana. (See §3.3.2 Dative Pronoun.)

At the end of §3.6.5 details are provided of pronominal prefix forms in combination with the tense and mood affixes on different types of verb. Representative fully inflected verb forms are provided in Tables 3.8 to 3.17.

3.3.4 ANALYSIS OF PRONOMINAL PREFIX FORMS.

Pronominal prefixes in Ndjébbana operate in a global system in the sense that the overall shape of the transitive prefix depends on the identity of both the A and O elements and on the relationship between the two. Extensive analysis of the prefix forms has been carried out and the main points will be outlined here. For the role and form of the realis and irrealis prefix see §3.6.4 and §3.6.5.

Intransitive S prefixes are straightforward and parallel, in the main, those of the transitive A/O prefixes in which O is 3 person minimal masculine. Transitive prefixes mark two elements (A/O or A/IO), at most one of which is fully specified for person, number and gender. The other, usually the second, is either partially specified (e.g. number only) or unspecified (zero).

The following non-zero elements make up the various pronominal prefix forms:

1 minimal S and A	nga-	1 non-minimal	njV-
1 minimal O	nja-		
1/2minimal	yV-/ka-*	1/2 non-minimal	ngV-
2 minimal A	dja-	2 non-minimal	nV-
2 minimal S and O	dja-/ngana-*		
3 minimal masc.S	ka-	(3) non-minimal	bV-
3 minimal A	ka-		
3 minimal fem.S	nja-/yV-*		
3 minimal fem O	ya-		
'inverse' marker	-nd(V)-/-n(V)-*		
minimal number	-a-		
unit augmented number	-i-		
augmented number	-u- (neutralised to -a- when not bearing main stress)		
realis prefix	-ɽɽV- (de facto plural marker in most cases)		

The pairs of alternatives marked with a single asterisk are tense/mood based alternations, with the left hand form being used before the irrealis prefix (that is in future and counterfactual verbs) and the right hand alternative being used before the realis prefix. The masculine/feminine contrast is neutralised in 3 person minimal A and in third person minimal O where A is non-third person. The term 'inverse marker' is borrowed from Blake's (1979: 342 and 368) suggestion for a similar form in other languages of the area but the 'inverse' marker does not always have the function of marking an inverse combination (see below) in Ndjébbana. -bV- is given as (3) non-minimal because in many of the forms, where it represents the second of two elements, it is used to represent number only, person contrasts having been neutralised in second (non-initial) position. Furthermore in the 1/2 person augmented S form -ba- is added to nga- to distinguish it from the otherwise identical first person minimal form nga-.

A nominal hierarchy (cf.Silverstein 1976, Heath 1976) operates within the global conditioning which determines the form of the pronominal prefixes. This hierarchy is as follows (highest to left, lowest to right):

1 minimal > 2 minimal > 1 & 2 non-minimal > 3 non-minimal > 3 minimal

Direct combinations of prefix elements (following Heath 1976:177 and originally from works on Algonquian languages) are those in which A is higher on the hierarchy than O, *equipollent* combinations are those in which A and O are level on the hierarchy, and *inverse* combinations are those in which O is higher than A.

Complex patterns of ordering, neutralisation and use of the 'inverse' marker apply in the various forms to reveal patterns of relative markedness which are 'accusative' (i.e. O is more marked than A) in the case of direct A/O combinations and 'ergative' (i.e. A is more marked than O) for equipollent and inverse combinations. For instance the multiply ambiguous prefix form nanbirri- (Tables 3.3 and 3.6) is used for all combinations of non-minimal A (1 or 3 person) with 2 non-minimal O, and for all combinations of 2 non-minimal A with 3 non-minimal O. In all these combinations the first element na- marks 2 non-minimal A or O. This is followed by the 'inverse' marker -n-, which is clearly not a true inverse marker here because it marks not only inverse combinations but also equipollent and direct combinations. This, in turn, is followed by -bi–, which is a neutralised form marking non-minimal number only of the non-second person element (1 or 3 person), whether A or O. Order is significant. The 2 non-minimal A element stands initial when the A/O combination is direct (that is when the O is lower on the hierarchy than the 2 non-minimal A—only 3 non-minimal O). The 2 non-minimal O element stands initially when the combination is equipollent or inverse (that is when the A element is level with or lower than the 2 non-minimal O on the hierarchy—1 or 3 non-minimal). When there is an equipollent combination of 2 non-minimal A and 1 non-minimal O, it is the 1 non-minimal O form nja- which stands initially (njanbirri-), confirming this analysis. These multiply ambiguous prefix forms are normally unambiguous in context. Formal disambiguation in the sentence is not frequently required and is difficult to achieve due to the lack of case marking.

A most significant feature of the analysis of these pronouns is the form of 1 minimal and 2 minimal elements, which show a 'split-ergative' pattern. The 1 minimal form nga- marks both S and A, while a distinct form, nja-, marks O. This linking of S and A in contradistinction to O provides what is termed an 'accusative' pattern of marking. In the 2 minimal forms, however, S and O have the same pattern of tense/mood-determined variation between dja- and ngana-, while A has a single invariant form, irrespective of tense/mood. This linking of S and O in contradistinction to A is an 'ergative' pattern of marking.

3.4   INDEFINITE FORMS

The interrogative forms are dealt with in §3.4.1. In §3.4.2 there are three 'uncertainty' forms which are used to refer to something when the speaker cannot remember the correct term.

3.4.1 INTERROGATIVE/INDEFINITE FORMS   In common with many other Australian languages (Dixon 1980:372) Ndjébbana has a number of forms which are used to introduce questions and which can also be used as indefinites. Thus the Aboriginal English phrase 'Might be someone took 'im' translates a phrase which could equally be translated 'I don't know who took it'.

[a] *Kárnmawa 'where?'*. This interrogative form can be used with verbs, with demonstratives, or on its own to query a location or destination. It may be used with the ablative suffix -kkawa to give a form meaning 'where from?' Further examples of the use of kárnmawa are to be found in (167) and Text 9/16. The use of kárnmawa as an indefinite ('somewhere', 'anywhere') has not been clearly substantiated. If such use does occur it is very rare.

(36)   Yey!   Kárnmawa   ngana-kkamíya   ngin-djirrí-ya?
        Hey!   where   2MINS-depart+CTP 2MINS-go-CTP
        Hey! Where are you heading off to? (V/300)

(37)   Ka-ngadjiyí-na   'Jockey Bundubundu   karnmáwa
        3MINMASCS-say-REM   where
        ka-nó-ra?'
        3MINMASCS-live-CTP
        He said, 'Where does Jockey Bundubundu live?' (V/243)

(38)   Ka-wola-bé-na   kárnmawa?... Kabálko
        3MINMASCS-come.hither-go-REM   where   Entrance Island.
        He came to where was it?...to Entrance Island. (II/27)

[b] *Nangalayana 'How many? What time?'*   This invariant interrogative form is interchangeable with ngékayabba below.

(39)   Njirri-yirringabbabé-ra...   nangalayana   dina   wukúyawa.
         1UAA+3MINO-hoist.sail-REM   what.time.was.it   midday   perhaps
         We set sail at...what time was it?...maybe midday. (V/290–1)

(40)   Nangalayana   bádj   ka-ya-ka-wála?
         what.time?   barge   3MINS-IRR-kó-come ashore
         What time will the barge arrive?

[c] *Ngaléwara   'what?,   which?,   something,   anything'*.   This interrogative/ indefinite is used with non-human referents and with much more general significance. It can be used on its own or with a nominal. Further examples are found in Text 25/49 and (168).

(41)   ...djóya,   yókkarra,   njanabbardákka,...   ngaléwara...
         trumpet.shell   fish   trevally fish   anything
         [In his drag net] he would catch trumpet shells, fish, trevally,...any kind...
         (V/29–30)

(42)   Djíya   ngaléwara   mudíkkang?
         that   which   truck
         Which truck is that? (XVIII/54)

(43)   ...kabbála,   ngaléwara   nála?
          boat   what   3MINMASC+name
         ...the boat, what was its name? (V/11)

(44)   Njírrabba   nja-rra-bé-na   kóma   ngaléwara
         1AUGCARD   1AUGS-RE-go-REM   NEG   anything
         nja-ka-rá-yana.
         1AUGA+3MINO-IRR-spear-CF
         We went [hunting] but didn't catch anything.

[d] *Ngédja/ngádja   'what (activity)?,   anything (activity)'*.   This interrogative/in-definite is used in conjunction with the verb -yángka 'do' to inquire about activities. It may also be used with the negative particle kóma with the meaning 'nothing'.

(45)   Ngédja   dja-ka-yángka?
         what   2MINA+3MINO-IRR-do
         What are you going to do? (V/255)

(46)   Kóma   njirri-balábara   ngádja   njirri-yángka   kóma.
         NEG   1UAA+3MINO-hit+FUT   anything   1UAA+3MINO-do   NEG
         We don't hit it or do anything to it. (XVIII/27–8)

[e] *Ngékayabba   'how many?'*.   This invariant form is a very uncommon indefinite, having been recorded only once in spontaneous text material. It may also be used in reference to time with the meaning 'when?' or 'how long?', compare nangalayána above.

(47)   '[Mángkaddjarra]... yeláwa   bana-bbó-na,
          Macassan(s)   then   3MINA+3AUGO-kill-REM
            bindi-rá-na,   ngékayabba?   karnayédjabba?'
            3MINA+3UAO-shoot-REM   how many?   two
          'Bindi-rá-na   karnayédjabba.'
            3MINA+3UAO-shoot-REM   two
          '[The Macassans got wild] and killed them [pl]. They shot two [Aborigines].
          How many was it? Two?' 'Yes they shot two.' (V/80–1)

(48)   Ba-rra-rókaddji-ba   ngékayabba   djábana-rama.
          3AUG-RE-child-EXT   how many?   2MINA+3AUGO-have(+CTP)
          How many children have you got?

          [f] *Njúngkowara 'who?, someone, anyone'.* This interrogative/
indefinite form takes person/number/gender prefixes like nominals of Class
D4 (§3.2.3). It s used to refer to human entities and can be used with a
nominal such as nála 'name'. It is used as an indefinite in (129).

(49)   Njarra-rlarrabí-na-yibérra   Kunwinjku   drayb,
          1AUGS-arrive-REM-3AUGDAT   Kunwinjku   tribe
            barra-njúngkowara?
            3AUG-who
          We came to the Kunwinjkus - who were they all? (V/317–19)

(50)   Ngayábba   nja-njúngkowara   njá-wala?
          3MINFEMCARD   3MINFEM-who?   3MINFEM-name
          What's her name?

(51)   Ngalidjbínja   nja-mádjarna   kóma   babukúyakka
          gun (FEM)   3MINFEM-genuine/proper   NEG   long ago
            njúngkowara   nja-ya-ramí-ngana.
            anyone   1AUGA+3MINO-IRR-have/hold-PAST2NEG
          Long ago none of us had proper guns. (V/60)

          This personal indefinite is used in an idiom referring to death meaning
literally that the dead 'are not sitting'.

(52)   Kóma   njúngkuwara   ka-kó-na,   yaláwa
          NEG   anyone   3MINS-kó-sit(+NRN)   well
            ba-rra-múyawa-na   ba-rra-karrówa.
            3AUGS-RE-die-REM   3AUG-RE-many
          None of them are left, many [have] died. (III/31–2)

3.4.2 UNCERTAINTY INDEFINITES. These two forms are used in
cases where the correct term escapes the speaker. The main interrogatives can
be used similarly (e.g. example (38)).

[a] *Njánabba* *'what's-it?, thingummy, what's-its-name'.I* This indefinite form often co-occurs with the demonstrative djéya. See also Text 25/69–70.

(53)   Njana   ka-má-nga   njánabba   djéya...
        then   3MINA+3MINMASCO-get-REM   what's-it   DEM
        bángku.
        mangrove.bark
        Then he got some of that what's-its-name...mangrove bark [for dyeing
        trepang]. (V/41–2)

[b] *Yabanánaka* *'what's-the-place'.* This indefinite form is used while searching for the name of a place.

(54)   Ngáyabba   yeláwa   nga-bé-na...   yabanánaka   (Nála
        1MINCARD   then   1MINS-go-REM   what's.the.place name
        nganéyabba   ma-ngóddja   wíba...)   Djardúrra.
        that   MINIMP-call.name place   [place name]
        I went to...what's the place...(Tell me the name of that place...) Djardúrra.
        (V/222–4)

3.5   DEMONSTRATIVES

Ndjébbana has a wide variety of demonstrative words. There is some overlap between these words in terms of their function, meaning and use, but they appear to fall into a small number of groups.

Firstly there are groups of demonstratives based on two 'roots': djé 'that/there/this/here' and djí 'this/here'. Approximate meanings are listed with each word and exemplified below. It seems clear that though djí is restricted to the nearer meaning 'this/here', the meaning of djé can range over both nearer and further meanings.

djé   *djí*
djébba 'this/here'   djíbba 'here'
(n-)djéya 'that way'   djíya 'this/here (3MINMASC)'

djé   *djí*
djéyabba 'that'   djí(ya)kabba 'this way'
ndjékkawa 'from here'   djímandja 'at this time, nowadays'

Of these sets djíya 'this, here (3MINMASC)' is actually a single form from a fuller paradigm which can vary for number and gender within the third person, as follows. They seem in the main to be formed by the addition of third person prefixes to the base -yá, with word stress shifting, according to the normal phonological rule (§2.3.1), to the word-initial syllable, since the base syllable is word final. Stress in the third person unit augmented feminine does not fit this suggested pattern.

djíya	bárriya	bárreya
3MINMASC	3UAMASC	3AUG

njáya	barréyabbanja
3MINFEM	3UAFEM

Secondly there is a group of directional and locational demonstratives:

ngána/ngáni	'there' (final -i- pronounced only when lengthened for extent §2.5, otherwise -a)
yakanábba	'this/that way'
yakanádja	'this way'
yinganábba	'that way'

A third group of demonstratives, which refer to concrete objects or human beings, is formed on the base -néyabba with third person prefixes. The forms nganéya 'that one/there' and nanéyabba 'there' have also been attested.

nganéyabba	'that 3MINMASC'
njanéyabba	'that 3MINFEM'
birrinéyabba	'those 3UA'
barranéyabbanja	'those 3UAFEM'
barranéyabba	'those 3AUG'

The following exemplify a number of the demonstratives. See also example (42) and Text 25/1–2, 22–4, 55–6, 60.

(55) Djíbba   wíba-na   Ndjébbana
      here   country-3MINMASCPOSS [language]
      ka-ngúdjeya.
      3MINMASCS-speak+CTP
      He belongs to this country here [cf.§3.2.3 Class C] and he speaks Ndjébbana. (XVII/53)

(56) Yíbarda   ngí-yi-yarra   ngí-ya-ra
      barramundi 1/2MINS-IRR-go   1/2MINA+3MINMASCO-IRR-spear
      nganéyabba, wíba   ngána kabalakóra.
      there   place there island
      We'll go and spear barramundi there, that island place. (I/181)

(57) Ma-ngúdjeya-yibérra   bárreya   barra-kkúdja-nga
      MINIMP-tell-3AUGDAT   those 3AUG   3AUGS-be.in.group-REM
      You tell that mob sitting there. (V/282)

(58) Mámam   kómabba n-barélabba   ngurrarákka
      grandfather both   3MINMASC-younger   elder
      bi-yi-ngúdjeya, birrinéyabba yaláwa.
      3UA-IRR-talk   those 3UA   ok
      My two grandfathers, the younger and the elder, are going to tell the story, those two. (II/56–7)

3.6   VERB MORPHOLOGY

3.6.1 ELEMENTS OF THE VERB COMPLEX.

The verb complex in Ndjébbana constitutes the basic clause on its own. The basic additions to each verb root are a pronominal prefix complex and tense and mood affixes.

Intransitive verbs have a pronominal prefix (Table 3.3) which indicates the subject S of the clause. (See§3.3.1 for details of pronominal person and number categories.)

nga-wákka
1MINS-go.back
I (S) am going back.

ka-njíndja
3MINS-cry
He/it (S) is crying.

The pronominal prefix complex added to transitive verb stems indicates the subject A and direct object O of the clause, or, in the case of the small number of ditransitive verbs, the subject A and the indirect object IO, while, with these forms, the O is understood or inherent.

djabindi-nídja
2MINA+2UAO-await (TR)
You (A) are waiting for us two (O).

djabindi-wú-na
2MINA+2UAIO-give (DITR)-REM
You (A) gave [it (O)] to us (IO) two.

njana-kkóndja
2MINA+1MINO-cut (TR)
You (A) are cutting me (O).

njana-wú-na
2MINA+1MINIO-give-REM
You (A) gave [it (O)] to me (IO).

Further basic elements of the verb complex are the tense suffixes and the mood prefixes. The mood prefixes are inserted between the pronominal prefix and the verb stem, the simplest example being the use of the irrealis prefix (here -ya-/-ka-; see §3.6.5) without a tense suffix, to express the meaning 'potential' or 'future'.

nga-ya-wákka
1MINS-IRR-go.back
I will go back.

ba-ka-njíndja
3AUGS-IRR-cry
They will cry.

A realis prefix -rrV- occurs mainly (but not exclusively) with non-singular prefixes, replacing the irrealis prefix in these verb forms. This realis prefix has vowel -i- for unit augmented and vowel -a- for minimal number and for augmented number when unstressed. See §3.6.5 .

ba-rra-njéwa-nga
3AUGS-RE(AUG)-rest-CTP
They are resting.

ba-ka-njéwa
3AUGS-IRR-rest
They will rest.

bi-rri-ngidjí-na
3UAS-RE(UA)-talk-REM
The two of them talked.

bá-rri-na
3UAS-RE(UA)-sit/be+REM

In certain cases a third person minimal dative pronominal suffix is used to disambiguate the person and gender of the minimal transitive subject A of the verb complex:

njana-ná-na
MINA+1MINO-see-REM
You saw me

njana-ná-na-yángaya
MINA+1MINO-see-REM-3MINFEMDATA
She saw me

Finally a derivational affix such as the intransitivising reciprocal or reflexive suffix -ya- may be attached to the verb with corresponding effects on the other affixes (in this case converting from transitive to intransitive pronominal prefixes and changing tense suffixes). In the following example the addition of the reflexive suffix with the contemporary tense suffix is very straighforward. In the remote tense, however, various phonological rules related to the shifting of the main stress to the reflexive suffix make the verb root much more difficult to recognise. The stop (dj) at the beginning of the root is lenited to y and vowel changes occur.

nbarra-ddjáma
3AUGA+1 or 2MINO-wash+CTP
They washed me/you.

barra-ddjáma-ya (*nbarra-...)
3AUGS-wash-REFLEX+CTP
They washed. [i.e.themselves]

nbarra-ddjáma-nga
3AUGA+1 or 2MINO-wash+REM
They washed me/you.

barra-yama-yí-na (*nbarra-...)
3AUGS-wash-REFLEX+REM
They washed. [i.e.themselves]

Table 3.7 sets out the basic structure of the Ndjébbana verb complex and provides references to the sections where the various affixes are discussed in detail. Where two affixes are shown as alternatives within the formula by being shown in braces together (e.g. REalis and IRRealis) they may both be shown as 'obligatory'. This means that one or the other is obligatory in that position. They may not occur together. A number of the affixes have a zero form under specified conditions. Thus, for instance, the realis prefix usually has zero form with minimal number subjects. The absence of an overt irrealis form with minimal number subjects would indicate that the realis category applies.

3.6.2 TRANSITIVITY CLASSES. Ndjébbana has three transitivity classes of verbs, based on the number and type of arguments which occur obligatorily with the verb. The category listed as (Mono-)transitive is normally termed simply 'transitive'. Ditransitive verbs are, strictly speaking, also transitive in the sense that their use involves an obligatory A (transitive subject or agent) and O (direct object) as well as an IO (indirect object), though the former is not marked in the pronominal prefix.

Intransitive   S
(Mono-)Transitive   A O   } Transitive
Ditransitive   A O IO

TABLE 3.7 *Ndjébbana Verb Complex*

$$\begin{Bmatrix} \text{PRON PRFX} \\ \text{IMP} \end{Bmatrix} - \begin{Bmatrix} \text{RE} \\ \text{IRR} \end{Bmatrix} \text{-AV-baló-kó-} \sqrt{} \text{-REFL-TNS-EXT-UAFEM-} \begin{Bmatrix} \text{DAT} \\ \text{POSS} \end{Bmatrix}$$

Abbreviation	Morpheme	Reference	Optional/ Obligatory	May have zero form
PRON PRFX	Pronominal Prefix	§3.3.3	obligatory	Yes
IMP	Imperative	§3.6.5	obligatory	No
RE	Realis prefix	§3.6.5	obligatory	Yes
IRR	Irrealis prefix	§3.6.5	obligatory	Yes
AV	Aversative prefix	§3.6.5	optional	Yes
baló	Verb 'come hither'	§3.6.18	optional	No
kó	kó prefix	§3.6.5	obligatory/ optional	Yes
$\sqrt{}$	ROOT			
REFL	Reflexive/ Reciprocal/ Intransitiviser	§3.6.17	optional	No
TNS	Tense/aspect/mood suffix	§3.6.6	obligatory	Yes
EXT	Extent suffix	§3.2.4	optional	No
UAFEM	Unit augmented feminine suffix	§3.3.2, §3.3.3	optional	No
DAT	Dative pronoun suffix	§3.3.1	optional	No
POSS	Possessive pronoun suffix	§3.3.1	optional	No

The basic transitive (i.e. monotransitive and ditransitive) versus intransitive contrast is marked by the choice of the transitive (A/O) or intransitive (S) series of pronominal prefixes (§3.3.3) respectively. There are, in fact, no unique intransitive prefix forms, but there are numerous prefix forms which may only occur with transitive verbs of both types. Thus, for instance, while both transitive and intransitive verbs may be marked with the prefix form ngaba-rra- (which represents 1/2AUGA+3MINO/IO on a transitive/ditransitive verb or 1/2AUGS on an intransitive verb), the form djabindi- may occur only on transitive (including ditransitive) verbs with the meaning 2MINA+1MINO/IO or 3MINO/IO. In fact transitivity of verbs in the present grammar was usually tested by determining whether they could be used in a non-future realis tense with the prefix dja- 2MINA+3MINO, which can occur as S marker on intransitive verbs only in the future tense or irrealis mood.

While in a (mono-)transitive verb form the transitive pronominal prefix represents both A and O, in a ditransitive verb form the pronominal prefix represents the A and IO and the O is clearly understood to be an obligatory element of the sentence, though it may have no overt form at all. It can not be marked by the pronominal prefix form and, like the A and IO, it need not be represented by any free nominal or pronominal form (see §4.1). Only four ditransitive verbs are known in Ndjébbana: djébba (1A) 'deprive someone of something, take something from someone'; lémaye (1B) 'show something to someone'; mándja (1A) 'steal something from someone'; and wú (7A) 'give something to someone'.

We give examples of verb forms of the three transitivity classes:

Ditransitive

nga-djébba-nga
1MINA+3MINIO-deprive of-REM
I deprived him/her [of it].
I didn't give [it] to him/her.

ngabindi-djébba-nga   (1A)
1MINA+2UAIO-deprive of-REM
I deprived them (two) [of it].
I didn't give [it] to them (two).

Transitive

nga-yakkabé-ra
1MINA+3MINO-tie.up-REM
I tied him/her up.

ngabindi-yakkabé-ra   (6A)
1MINA+3UAO-tie.up-REM
I tied them (two) up.

Intransitive

nga-yawé-la
1MINS-get/be sick-REM
I was/got sick.

*ngabindi-yawé-la   (8A)
*1MINA-3UAO-get/be sick-REM

Note that transitivity of verbs in Ndjébbana does not always match that of the equivalent verb in English. For example the verb lakalá (5B) 'hear' is intransitive in Ndjébbana, though its English equivalent is transitive.

3.6.3 PRONOMINAL AFFIXES.   As outlined in §3.3.3 intransitive pronominal prefixes mark a single obligatory constituent of the clause, the intransitive subject or S, while the transitive pronominal prefix forms normally overtly mark a maximum of two obligatory consituents of the clause. These are the transitive subject (A) and the direct object (O) in the case of (mono-)transitive verbs, and the transitive subject (A) and the indirect object (IO) in the case of ditransitive verbs. With ditransitive verbs the obligatory direct object (O) can not be marked by means of a pronominal affix on the verb.

Certain transitive prefix forms provide an unambiguous marking of the O or IO only, leaving the identity of the minimal number A ambiguous between third and non-third person. This must be disambiguated by using the third person minimal masculine or feminine Dative Pronoun (§3.3.1) as a person and gender marking suffix to the verb complex when the A is third person. Without this suffix the A is interpreted as the relevant non-third person minimal (distinct from the O or IO).

ngana-wú-na
MINA+2MINIO-give-REM
I gave it to you (sg).

ngana-wú-na-yana
MINA+2MINIO-give-REM-3MINMASCDAT
He gave it to you (sg).

An additional non-obligatory 'indirect object' can be marked on a verb complex of any of the three transitivity classes (§3.6.2) using the dative pronoun suffixes as outlined and exemplified in §3.3.1. Such an indirect object is understood as having some sort of indirect 'interest' in the verb, that is an interest other than that characteristic of any of the obligatory arguments of the clause.

3.6.4   TENSE, MOOD AND ASPECT: AN OVERVIEW. Ndjébbana verb inflections distinguish the following forms:

Future	
Contemporary	} Indicative
Remote	
Counterfactual	
Non-Remote Negative	} Negative
Aversative	
Imperative	

These formal distinctions are made using various combinations of affixes, both prefixes and suffixes. Some of the distinctions are not made for certain groups of verbs but all are recognised in the paradigms of the majority of verbs.

We will first characterise the various distinctions in brief before setting out the various affixes involved in making the distinctions in detail in §3.6.5.

[a] *Future (FUT)*. The future indicative is marked by means of the irrealis or potential prefix and in most conjugations has no suffix (see Table 3.18 and §§3.6.7 to 3.6.15). The same irrealis prefix is used in the counterfactual form (there with a counterfactual suffix) but not in the remaining inflectional categories listed here. For some verbs the future has a unique root allomorph. The future form of the root is also used in the imperative and the non-remote negative, but in these the realis prefix is used. The future tense is used with adverbs such as barnómandja 'soon, later on', and wékanabba 'tomorrow'.

The future tense characterises a state or event as future in time and therefore as hypothetical or irrealis, because it has not yet been realised.

[b] *Contemporary (CTP)*. The contemporary indicative indicates an event which is currently in progress or which occurred in the recent past, prior to the day of the speech situation, or to a state which was in effect in one of those time frames. Thus it means roughly 'at the moment', 'yesterday' or 'recently' and it, unlike the remote tense, co-occurs with the Ndjébbana adverb of time ngabalóbala 'yesterday, recently'. Contemporary forms are marked by the realis prefix and by a contemporary verb suffix, as listed for each conjugation in Table 3.18 and further specified in §§3.6.7 to 3.6.15.

[c] *Remote (REM)*. The remote indicative refers to an activity or state, now completed, which occurred or was in effect earlier on the day of the speech situation or in the more distant past. The remote tense, but not the contemporary tense, co-occurs with the Ndjébbana adverbs of time wúrdeyak 'long ago', babukúyakka 'long ago', yéna 'earlier today'. Remote forms are marked by the realis prefix and by a remote verb suffix, as listed for each conjugation in Table 3.18 and as further specified in §§3.6.7 to 3.6.15.

The contrast 'contemporary' versus 'remote' was discussed, for the neighbouring language Burarra, by K. Glasgow (1964b:118). Green (1995: 183–4) follows Eather (1990) in naming this tense 'pre-contemporary'.

[d] *Counterfactual (CF)*. The counterfactual form refers to a hypothetical and unrealised action or state in the remote time frame. It corresponds to English verb forms such as 'should/would have (but did not)', 'was going to (but did not)' and is used in conjunction with the negative particle kóma to provide remote negative forms. The counterfactual form of any verb is of one of two specific types.

The inflectional or suffixal type involves the irrealis prefix (as used also in the future) and a counterfactual verb suffix as listed for the various conjugations in Table 3.18 and as further specified in §§3.6.7 to 3.6.15.

The auxiliary type of counterfactual involves the use of the infinitive form of the verb root together with a fully inflected counterfactual form of the auxiliary verb yángka 'do' (2A). The auxiliary verb carries the pronominal prefix combination which would be carried by the main verb if the inflectional counterfactual form were used. The counterfactual form of the auxiliary has the irrealis prefix and counterfactual suffix characteristic of the inflectional type of counterfactual form, but in these cases the main verb does not.

The inflectional type appears to be historically older than the other, or auxiliary type, because it involves a range of suffixes according to the various conjugations, while the auxiliary type involves an invariant infinitive form of the root and the use of inflected forms of just a single verb. The inflectional type appears to have given way to the auxiliary type in some conjugations and in some dialects. The inflectional type of counterfactual form is significantly more common in the speech of Djówanga informants from the Márro group from the northern coastal area, than it is in the speech of Yírriddjanga speakers from the river-based Mabárnad and Kanakána groups. Thus we find, for example, the following two forms being used side-by-side in the community by different speakers, the inflectional form by coastal Djówanga speakers and the auxiliary form by riverside Yírriddjanga speakers:

kóma   nga-ya-rarraddja-ngóna
NEG   1MINA+3MINO-clean-CF
I did not clean it.

kóma   na-rórrddja   nga-yangka-yína
NEG   INFIN-clean   1MINA+3MINO-do-CF
I did not clean it.

[e] *Non-Remote Negative (NRN)*. The non-remote negative is an infrequent form used together with the negative particle kóma to form negative sentences in the contemporary or future time frames. It uses the realis prefix (like the contemporary and the imperative but unlike the future or the counterfactual) and the suffix (or root) form characteristic of the future (rather than of the contemporary, where these are distinct). In fact, with minimal subjects (A or S), the non-remote negative is overtly characterised more by lack of the irrealis prefix than by presence of the realis plural prefix, which has overt form only with non-minimal subjects except in a very small number of imperative forms. Thus we find forms such as the following, in which first person minimal and third person augmented S or A (with third person minimal O) forms are given for the future, the non-remote negative and the contemporary, as well as the minimal imperative:

	warlékka 'use up, finish up' (7D)	*bá* 'bite, eat' (8C)	*má* 'fetch, get' (1C)
FUT	nga-ya-warlékka ba-warlékka	nga-ya-móya ba-ka-móya	nga-yá-ka-ma ba-yú-ka-ma
NRN	nga-warlékka ba-rra-warlékka	nga-móya ba-rra-móya	(Ø)-kó-ma ba-rrú-ka-ma

CTP	nga-warlékka-ya	ngá-ba	nga-má-ngka
	ba-rra-warlékka-ya	bá-rra-ba	ba-rra-má-ngka
MIN IMP	da-warlékka	da-móya	ma-rrá-ka-ma

In these forms the future form of bá 'bite, eat' is suppletive, and, in common with a small number of very common and usually monosyllabic verbs, certain forms of the verb má 'fetch, get' (in this case future, non-remote negative and imperative) use the additional prefix -kó- (or -ka- when unstressed) (see §§3.6.5, 3.6.7). Note the occurrence of the realis prefix in the minimal imperative form of má 'fetch, get', where the -kó- prefix also occurs (as -ka-).

Particularly noteworthy is the fact that in the non-remote negative a small number of verbs, mostly restricted to those which use the additional prefix -kó- in these forms, have a zero form of pronominal prefix for first person minimal S or first person minimal A (with third person minimal O), as does má 'fetch, get'.

[f] *Imperative (IMP)*. The imperative expresses a command that the addressee carry out (or bring to reality) the action or event specified by the clause.

da-bbíddaba   bi-rri-balákka   ba-rra-nídja
MINIMP-follow/chase   UAIMP-RE-return   AUGIMP-RE-wait.for
Follow him!   Come back!   Wait for him!

Utterances with imperative function can also be couched in the form of the future using a second person subject (A or S). The future is the normal form when the O or IO is other than third person minimal.

dja-ka-nídja   ni-yi-balákka
2MINA+3MINO-IRR-await   2UAS-IRR-return
Wait for him!   Come back!

njanda-ka-lémaya
2AUGA+1MINIO-IRR-show
Show it to me!

[g] *Aversative (AV)*. The aversative or evitative form of the verb is used to express the undesirability of some potential action or event. It can be translated into English using the auxiliary 'might' with the clear implication that the occurrence should be avoided, as in examples (59), (169), (171), (172) and Text 25/71–2. Aversative or evitative forms can be used with the particle kómalakka to express negative purpose (i.e. 'lest...', 'so that not...', 'otherwise...') as in examples (170) and (60). Some speakers (particularly younger speakers) use the aversative form instead of the non-remote negative in conjunction with the negative particle kóma to express a present or future negative. See example (60).

(59)   Ngu-rri-bbú-ra   balawúrrwurr
        1/2UAA+3MINO(AV)-RE(UA)-damage-CTP   wind
          kú-míba   n-barrábarra...
          3MINMASCS(AV)-arrive   3MINMASC-big
          We mustn't damage it [the djalákarra dreaming near Juda Point] or a big wind
          storm might come...(XVIII/23–4)

(60)   Kóma   warábba-na   nú-rru-wa-ya
        NEG   one-3MINMASCPOSS   3AUGA+2MINO-RE-AV-leave
          kómalakka   kóma   kándim
          otherwise   NEG   count (<English)
          bu-rru-nó-ra.
          3AUGA+3MINMASCO+AV-RE-sit/be-CTP
          [If there are, say, three names on the ballot paper you must put numbers 1, 2
          and 3.] You can't leave one number out, otherwise they won't count it [your
          ballot]. (XI/21–2)

As is apparent from these examples, the characteristic form of the
aversative mood is the occurrence of the vowel -u- in at least the first syllable
of the pronominal prefix and/or the use of the aversative prefix -wu- following
the realis prefix. The aversative form uses the contemporary form of the verb
root and suffix.

3.6.5 TENSE/MOOD INFLECTIONAL AFFIXES.   Tense and mood
categories in Ndjébbana are marked using a number of affixes. The most
significant and varied group of such affixes is the tense/mood suffixes. On
the basis of these suffixes the verbs can be classified into seven broad groups
of conjugations. These are set out in §§3.6.7 to 3.6.15.
    There are also three basic tense/mood prefixes, used in various
combinations with various tense/mood suffixes, and an additional prefix of
unknown significance (-kó-).
    Given the complexity of the interplay of the various combinations of
these prefixes and the pronominal prefixes with different types of verbs, this
section concludes with a series of tables setting out the attested combinations
and patterns (Tables 3.8 to 3.17).

    [a] *Irrealis and Realis.* A basic distinction which is normally marked
obligatorily on every verb is that between IRREALIS (unreal, hypothetical or
potential) and REALIS (a much broader and less easily definable category
covering non-irrealis). The irrealis prefix is used with future and
counterfactual forms (see §3.6.4) while the realis form is used with all other
forms. These two prefixes are mutually exclusive and occupy a position
immediately following the pronominal prefix elements. In Tables 3.3 to 3.6
the pronominal prefix forms have been cited with the realis prefix included,
because this element of the prefix correlates with certain number distinctions
in most verb forms.

    [b] *Number marking in Realis and Irrealis.* Both realis and irrealis
prefixes have underlying characteristic vowels to indicate the number of the
subject, though when unstressed many of the minimal and augmented forms

merge using the vowel -a-. Even in unstressed position, however, the unit augmented realis and irrealis prefixes never lose their vowel quality, though the unit augmented irrealis prefix -yi- may coalesce with a preceding -i- to be realised as a long -í-. Both prefixes have a zero form in certain positions.

Minimal	*-a-
Unit Augmented	*-i-
Augmented	*-u-

While the augmented vowel -u- in particular occurs rarely, the various vowels are exemplified most clearly in the imperative and future forms of some of the monosyllabic verbs, for example the following:

	wú 'give' (7A)	*djí* 'drink' (IRG)
MIN IMP	ma-rrá-ka-wa MIN IMP-RE-kó-give Give it to him.	ma-rrá-ka-ya MIN IMP-RE-kó-drink Drink it.
UA IMP	bá-rri-wo UA IMP-RE-give Give it to him.	bá-rri-ya UA IMP-RE-drink Drink it.
AUG IMP	ba-rrú-ka-wa AUG IMP-RE-kó-give Give it to him.	ba-rrú-ka-ya AUG IMP-RE-kó-drink Drink it.
1MINFUT	nga-yá-ka-wa 1MINA+3MINIO-IRR-kó-give I'll give it to him/her.	nga-yá-ka-ya IMINA+3MINO-IRR-kó-drink I'll drink it.
1/2UAFUT	ngí-ya-wa (<*ngí-yi-ya-wa) 1/2UAA+3MINIO+IRR-kó-give We'll give it to him/her.	ngí-ya-ya (<*ngí-yi-ya-ya) 1/2UAA+3MINO+IRR-kó-drink We'll drink it.
1/2AUGFUT	ngaba-yú-ka-wa 1/2AUGA+3MINIO-IRR-kó-give We'll give it to him/her.	ngaba-yú-ka-ya 1/2AUGA+3MINO-IRR-kó-drink We'll drink it.

[c] *Realis.* The realis prefix has the form -rrV- with non-minimal subjects and with certain non-singular objects, and Ø with minimal number subjects, except in the minimal imperative of the (mostly monosyllabic) verbs which take the prefix -kó-. In these imperative forms the -rra- form occurs. In combination with the varying vowel marking number discussed above, the realis prefix thus has the following allomorphs (ignoring stress):

-rra-   minimal number and unstressed form of augmented
-rri-   unit augmented number
-rru-   augmented number

In various languages of Arnhem Land and the Kimberley, an affix of
the form -rra- occurs. This has frequently been analysed as a plural marker
(e.g. Rumsey 1980a:16; Blake 1977:27, 1987:107). In Ndjébbana the fact
that this prefix is used in a few minimal imperative forms and the fact that it is
in direct contrast with the irrealis prefix shows that, at least in this language,
its primary function is as a mood marker. The fact that it has non-zero form
mainly with non-minimal subjects means that, in non-imperative forms, it has
the secondary de facto function of marking non-minimal number. It is
possible (though it cannot be proved) that the da- form of the minimal
imperative (see below §3.6.5) is in origin a word-initial form of the realis
prefix with no preceding overt pronominal imperative form.

[d] *Irrealis.*   The irrealis prefix has various allomorphs:

-yV-   {
before overt allomorphs of -kó-
after MIN S and A+3MINO not including 2nd person S/A
with UA S and A+3MINO
following -i-
}

Ø   before verb root (stem) with initial velar stop or nasal or with
         initial unstressed syllable (except where -yV- form is used)

-ka-   elsewhere

The vowel of the -yV- allomorph varies according to number as
outlined above (§3.6.5).
The following examples clarify the use of these various irrealis prefix
forms. (+IRR) in parentheses indicates the zero allomorph of the irrealis
prefix.

nga-yá-ka-ma
1MINA+3MINO-IRR-kó-get
I'll get it.

ba-yú-ka-ma
3AUGA+3MINO-IRR-kó-get
They'll get it.

nga-ya-ddjórrkka
1MINA+3MINO-IRR-take
I'll take it.

dja-ka-ddjórrkka
2MINA+3MINO+IRR-take
You'll take it.

bi-yi-ddjórrkka
3UAA+3MINO-IRR-take
They'll take it.

nanbi-yi-kkálawa
2AUGA+3AUGO-IRR-know
You'll think about/know them.

ba-ka-ddjórrkka
3AUGA+3MINO-IRR-take
They'll take it.

ba-bala-djórrkka
3AUGA+3MINO(+IRR)-come.hither-take
They'll bring it.

nga-ya-ma-ngána
1MINA+3MINO-IRR-get-CF
I would have got it.

ba-ma-ngána
3AUGA+3MINO(+IRR)-get-CF
They would have got it.

ba-ngúdjeya
3AUGS(+IRR)-talk
They'll talk.

ngaba-ka-nídja
1/2AUGA+3MINO-IRR-await
Let's wait for him. / We'll wait for him.

[e] *Imperative.* The imperative has special imperative pronominal subject forms for S and for A where O is third person minimal. For other A and O combinations the commands are normally expressed in the future form. The imperative form uses the future root and suffix form with the following pronominal prefixes together with the realis prefix (as marked in the non-minimal forms here). In most (but not all) minimal imperative forms the realis prefix has a zero form.

MIN IMP	da-	before a stem initial labial (b m w)
	ma-	elsewhere
UA IMP	bi-rri-	with male augment
	ba-rra-...-nja	with female augment
AUG IMP	ba-rra-	

The augmented and unit augmented imperative forms are thus the same as the non-remote negative forms with their combination of future root and suffix with realis plural prefix. Though addressed to a second person addressee, these non-minimal imperative forms use ostensibly third person pronominal marking for S and A (ba- and bi-). These 'third person' forms bV- can thus be seen to represent unmarked person forms in non-minimal number, as they do in other pronominal prefix forms (see §3.3.4). Compare subject deletion in the English imperative.

The form of the minimal imperative prefix depends on the stem-initial rather than the root-initial consonant, irrespective of whether this consonant is syllable-initial or syllable-final as in the following examples:

mé-yarra
MINIMP-go
Go!

ma-nmarabúya
MINIMP-bury
Bury it!

da-bbúdjeya
MINIMP-shout
Call out!

dá-bala-yarra
MINIMP-come.hither-go
Come here!

da-malónba
MINIMP-pick
Pick it [e.g. fruit]!

da-méraba
MINIMP-hide
Hide it!

With stress-shifting verbs, the verbs' normal patterns of stress placement occur. For instance in the singular imperative forms of -yirrí 'go' above, the underlying root-final stress shifts to word-initial position whenever it would otherwise fall word-finally. (For the vowel alternations in this type of root see Rule 3 §3.6.16.) See further examples of non-minimal imperative forms of -yirrí contrasted with non-minimal imperative forms of bú 'hit' which has constant stress placement on the suppletive future stem.

Unit augmented imperative masculine (with male unit augment)

bá-rri-yarra   bi-rri-balábara
UAIMP-RE-go   UAIMP-RE-hit
Go!   Hit it!

Unit augmented imperative feminine (with female unit augment)

ba-rra-yarrí-nja   ba-rra-balábara-nja
UAIMP-RE-go-UAFEM   UAIMP-RE-hit-UAFEM
Go!   Hit it!

Augmented imperative

bá-rra-yarra   ba-rra-balábara
AUGIMP-RE-go   AUGIMP-RE-hit
Go!   Hit it!

With verbs which take the -kó- prefix (discussed below), stress in the imperative form occurs on the pronominal prefix in the unit augmented masculine imperative (the only forms with realis prefix -rri-) and on the realis prefix in the minimal, the augmented and the unit augmented feminine imperative, as exemplified here.

Minimal imperative

ma-rrá-ka-ma   ma-rrá-ka-na
MIN IMP-RE-kó-get   MIN IMP-RE-kó-sit
Get it.   Sit.

Unit augmented imperative (masculine)

bá-rri-ma   bá-rri-na
UA IMP-RE-get   UA IMP-RE-sit
Get it.   Sit.

Unit augmented imperative (feminine)

ba-rrú-ka-ma-nja   ba-rrú-ka-na-nja
UAIMP-RE-kó-get-UAFEM   UAIMP-RE-kó-sit-UAFEM
Get it.   Sit.

Augmented imperative

ba-rrú-ka-ma   ba-rrú-ka-na
AUG IMP-RE-kó-get   AUG IMP-RE-kó-sit
Get it.   Sit.

[f] *Aversative.* The aversative prefix has the basic form -wu- which stands as the final inflectional prefix before the verb root. The vowel quality of this prefix, -u- is copied onto all preceding vowels of the pronominal prefix and of the realis prefix, except for the realis -i- vowel , which remains as -i-.

Finally, when the verb root begins with a labial consonant (b, m, w) or with an unstressed syllable, the -wu- itself is deleted, leaving the aversative marked only by means of one or more of the pronominal prefix vowels onto which the aversative vowel quality has been copied.

Aversative forms such as the following are found (with the corresponding non-aversative (i.e. contemporary) form in parentheses):

ngu-wu-ddjúwa (nga-ddjúwa)
1MINS-AV-be.sick
I might get sick.

ngunu-wu-ddjú-wa (ngana-ddjúwa)
2MINS-AV-be.sick
You might get sick.

ngú-bbo (ngá-bbo)
1MINS+AV-fall
I might fall.

ngú-wa-ya (<*nga-wu-yí) (ngá-ya)
1MINA+3MINO-AV-leave
I·might leave it.

njunu-wu-ná-dja-yana (njana-ná-dja-yana)
MINA+1MINO-AV-see-CTP-3MINMASCA
He might see me.

bú-rri-bbo (bá-rri-bbo)
3UAS-AV-fall
They (two) might fall.

ngunbi-rri-wu-kkóndja (nganbi-rri-kkóndja)
3AUGA+1/2MINO-RE-AV-cut
They might cut you and me.

búnbi-rri-lamaya (bánbi-rri-lamaya)
3AUGA+3AUGIO-RE-show
They might show it to them.

njunu-wuddubó-yana (njana-waddabó-yana)
MINA+1MINO+AV-follow-3MINMASCA
He/it might follow me.

nunu-rru-bá-yana (nana-rra-bá-yana)
MINA+2AUGO+AV-RE-bite-MINMASCA
Look out, he'll bite you! [of dog]

djubunu-wu-kkóndja (djabana-kkóndja)
2MINA+3AUGO-AV-cut
You might cut them.

nbi-rri-wu-kkóndja (nbi-rri-kkóndja)
2UAA+1MINO-RE-AV-cut
You (two) might cut me.

nbu-rru-wu-kkóndja (nba-rra-kkóndja)
2AUGA+1MINO-RE-AV-cut
You (plural) might cut me.

bu-rru-má-ngka (ba-rra-má-ngka)
3AUGA+3MINMASCO+AV-get-CTP
They might get it.

bu-rru-wu-ddjí-ndja (ba-rra-ddjí-ndja)
3AUGA+3MINMASCO-RE-AV-drink-CTP
They might drink it.

[g] *-kó-*. This prefix is of unknown significance but is used in a number of forms, especially the non-remote negative and the future, of

certain verbs, particularly of the irregular and monosyllabic verb roots. It is used optionally following the -ya- form of the irrealis prefix. The -kó- prefix has four overt forms distributed as follows and as exemplified below:

-kkó-   when stressed and non-word-initial in forms of the verb yó 'lie'

-kó-   when stressed elsewhere and when word-initial

Ø   {following a pronominal or realis prefix with final -i-
       following the irrealis prefix form -ka-

-ka-   when unstressed elsewhere

Placement of main stress is affected in the verb forms where -kó- appears obligatorily on one of the monosyllabic verb roots (but not when it occurs optionally with other verb roots). In summary, main stress occurs on the following syllables in these verb forms (FUT, REM, NRN, IMP) as in the example verb forms below:

In the Future

-kó- prefix   with all forms of verb yó 'lie'

Pronom. prefix initial   {overt minimal subject incl. 2nd person (2 or 1/2)
                            unit augmented subject

Pronom. prefix final   after pronominal prefix ending in -nda-

Realis/Irrealis prefix   elsewhere

In the Remote, Imperative, Non-Remote-Negative

kó- prefix   {with minimal subject prefix other than 2MINS
                with Ø- subject prefix (1MIN)
                with all forms of verb yó 'lie'

Pronom. prefix final   {overt 2nd person minimal S
                          unit augmented subject

Compounding verb -baló-

Realis/Irrealis prefix   elsewhere

The remote and non-remote negative second person minimal S prefix ngana- is the only two-syllable minimal subject prefix in this set. In the remote and non-remote-negative forms the placement of stress as listed above ensures that in all cases of minimal subject the main stress falls on the second syllable of the word (either on -kó- after a single syllable prefix or on the second syllable of a two-syllable prefix). The stress falls on the -kó- prefix even where the pronominal prefix is the second person minimal A (+3MINO) form dja-. The only exception is when the compounding verb -baló- occurs, because the main stress always falls on the final syllable of this verb preceding -ka- (<*-kó) (see example (67)).

The -kó- prefix is obligatory in certain forms of most of the monosyllabic verb roots including the irregular verbs nó 'sit, be', bó 'fall, land', djí 'drink', yó 'lie' as well as djó 'berate'(1C), má 'get, fetch'(1C), ná 'see'(7A), wú 'give'(7A), and rá 'spear, shoot, pierce'(7C). The presence of this prefix gives these verbs distinctive forms as outlined in §§3.6.7, 3.6.13, and 3.6.15 and exemplified here. Where, in a form of the verb yó 'lie', stress falls on the allomorph -kó- and this allomorph is not word-initial, Rule 1 (stop gemination §2.4.1) applies in the regular manner to give -kkó-. For all the other monosyllabic verbs which take the -kó- prefix the stop gemination rule does not apply in the expected manner, even when the main stress falls on this syllable.

nga-ya-kkó-ya
1MINS-IRR-kó-lie
I'll lie.

nga-yá-ka-ya
1MINA+3MINO-IRR-kó-drink
I'll drink it.

nganá-ka-na
2MINS-kó-sit(+REM)
You sat.

(Ø-)kó-na
(1MINS-)kó-sit(+REM)
I sat.

ya-kó-na
3MINFEMS-kó-sit(+REM)
She sat.

njá-rri-na
1UAS-RE-sit(+REM)
We (two) sat.

ngánbi-ya-wo
3AUGA+1/2UAIO-IRR(+kó)-give
They'll give it to us (three).

nga-yá-ka-na
1MINS-IRR-kó-sit
I'll sit.

ngaba-yú-ka-na
1/2AUGS-IRR-kó-sit
We'll sit.

djá-ka-na
2MINS-IRR-sit(+FUT)
You will sit.

njí-ya-na
1UAS-IRR(+kó)-sit
We (two) will sit.

nja-rrú-ka-na
1AUGS-RE-kó-sit
We (plural) sat.

ma-rrá-ka-ya
MINIMP-RE-kó-drink
Drink it.

bi-rri-baló-ka-na
3UAS-RE-hither-kó-sit(+REM)
(AUX) They did it coming this way.

The various allomorphs of -kó- are here exemplified using the verbs -yó- 'lie', -nó- 'sit' and djí 'drink'. The verb djí 'drink' forms future forms like nó and other similar verbs, using the unstressed allomorph of -kó- (=-ka-), because the main stress is placed on the preceding irrealis prefix. This is unlike yó 'lie', which uses the stressed form (-kkó-) throughout, because it has a fixed form and fixed stress placement throughout these tenses/moods. Only by this means are the otherwise homophonous future and non-remote negative forms of these two verbs distinguished, because the application of the morphophonemic Rules 2 (stop lenition §2.4.1) and 3 (unstressed vowel reduction §3.6.16) to the unstressed root renders the future forms of both roots identical (as -ya). A third verb which would also have a homophonous regular root form (-ya) in this position is djó 'to berate, be angry at', but the problem of homophones is avoided in the case of this verb by the use of a suppletive future stem, which is contrasted here with the regular contemporary form. The unattested regular future form would be as given in parentheses and would thus be homophonous with the regular, expected future forms of -yó- 'lie' (unattested) and djí 'drink' as discussed above.

ngá-ya-warrawo (*nga-yá-ka-ya)   nga-ddjó-ngka
1MINA+3MINO-IRR-berate   1MINA+3MINO-berate-CTP
I'll go mad at him.   I am going mad at him.

A most noteworthy feature is the zero or unmarked form of the first person minimal subject (S or A+3MINO) prefix when -kó- occurs without the realis or irrealis prefixes (i.e. minimal remote or non-remote negative) as in:

kó-na   kóma   kó-wa
(1MINS+)kó-sit(+REM) NEG   (1MINA+3MINIO+)kó-give(+NRN)
I sat.   I won't give it to him.

Two significant points should be noted here. One is that the negative particle kóma itself has the same form as the non-remote negative form of má 'get, fetch' with a zero first person minimal A and third person minimal O. Thus kóma kó-ma means 'I won't get it'. The other point of note is that five further verbs have been found so far to take this zero form of the first person minimal pronominal prefix in the non-remote negative. While the root form occurring in each of these forms is, with one exception, the same as in other forms of the respective verb, so that there is no evidence of analysability into -kó- prefix plus root, it may be significant that all these verbs have roots commencing with the syllable -kV-. This suggests that historically they may have developed from a combination of -kó- plus a shorter root, though this analysis does not hold for the modern language. The five verbs are given in the non-remote negative form following the negative particle kóma and with first person minimal subject (this form being identical to the simple root (with no prefix or suffix)):

kóma kákka   'I'm not pushing'(7D)(TR)
kóma karráwa   'I'm not looking, overseeing'(5A)(INTR)
kóma kamíya   'I'm not getting up'(2A)(INTR)
kóma kúrrngarna 'I won't stand CAUS, wear, name'(IRG)
kóma kálawa   'I don't know'(IRG) (CTP nga-lawá-ya 'I know')

The verb kóndja 'cut' has a special, shortened counterfactual root form (dja §3.6.7) which lacks the kó(nj), suggesting that it may also have links with this small group of verbs.

The -kó- prefix may occur optionally following the irrealis prefix form -ya- with most, if not all, verbs.   Thus we find forms such as the following side-by-side, with no apparent difference in meaning and with no effect on placement of main stress:

nga-ya-bbínbi-ba   nga-ya-ka-bbínbi-ba
1MINA+3MINO-IRR-write-EXT   1MINA+3MINO-IRR-kó-write-EXT
I'll write [it].   I'll write [it].

Though the unstressed allomorph of -kó- is formally identical to the -ka- allomorph of the irrealis prefix, the fact that the two are to be distinguished is shown by the possibility of the co-occurrence of -kó- with either the realis prefix -rrV- or the irrealis prefix (-yV-) as in forms like ma-rrá-ka-ya 'Drink it' and nga-yá-ka-na 'I'll sit'.

[h] *Verb prefix patterns.*   The interplay of the various mood prefixes with both the pronominal prefix forms and various types of verbs leads to a complex set of prefix paradigms.   In order to facilitate interpretation of the patterns set out above a series of tables (3.8 to 3.17) will now be presented giving full verb forms for all the main possible combinations of pronominal prefixes (§3.3.3), realis and irrealis prefixes (§3.6.5) and verb types.   The representative verb types exemplified in each table are as follows:

Future form (including irrealis prefix)
Regular verb with root-initial stressed syllable and root-initial non-velar consonant (nídja 'await' (1A TR), njíndja 'cry, weep' (2A INTR))
Regular verb with root-initial velar consonant or root-initial unstressed syllable (ngódja 'call, name' (1A TR), balákka 'come back' (2A INTR))
Monosyllabic, stress-shifting verb root (wú 'give' (7A DITR), nó 'sit' (IRG INTR))

Remote form (including realis prefix)
Monosyllabic, stress-shifting verb root (transitive and intransitive)
Regular verb root with constant stress (intransitive only)

In these tables the unit augmented feminine forms are indicated in parentheses with the corresponding augmented form. That is, the unit augmented feminine is formed by adding the parenthetical suffix -nja to the augmented form. In the heading the bracketed unit augmented feminine gloss should be understood as replacing the corresponding augmented gloss when the -nja suffix occurs.

TABLE 3.8 *Pronominal prefix and mood: 1st person minimal A*

	1MINA+2MINO	1MINA+2UAO	1MINA+2AUGO(3UAFEMO)
FUT	dja-ka-nídja	nindi-yi-nídja	nanda-ka-nídja(-nja)
FUT	dja-ngódja	nindi-yi-ngódja	nanda-ngódja(-nja)
FUT	djá-ka-wa	nándi-ya-wa	nandá-ka-wa(-nja)
REM	ngana-wú-na	nindi-wú-na	nana-rra-wú-na(-nja)

	1MINA+3MINO	1MINA+3UAO	1MINA+3AUGO(3UAFEMO)
FUT	nga-ya-(ka)-nídja	ngabindi-yi-nídja	ngabanda-ka-nídja(-nja)
FUT	nga-ya-ngódja	ngabindi-yi-ngódja	ngabanda-ngódja(-nja)
FUT	nga-yá-ka-wa	ngábindi-ya-wo	ngabandá-ka-wa(nja)
REM	nga-wú-na	ngabindi-wú-na	ngabana-wú-na(-nja)

TABLE 3.9 *Pronominal prefix and mood: 2nd person minimal A*

	2MINA+1MINO	2MINA+1UAO	2MINA+1AUGO(1UAFEMO)
FUT	njanda-ka-nídja	djabindi-yi-nídja	djabanda-ka-nídja(-nja)
FUT	njanda-ngódja	djabindi-yi-ngódja	djabanda-ngódja(-nja)
FUT	njandá-ka-wa	djábindi-ya-wo	djabandá-ka-wa(-nja)
REM	njana-wú-na	djabindi-wú-na	djabana-wú-na(-nja)

	2MINA+3MINO	2MINA+3UAO	2MINA+3AUGO(3UAFEMO)
FUT	dja-ka-nídja	djabindi-yi-nídja	djabanda-ka-nídja(-nja)
FUT	dja-ngódja	djabindi-yi-ngódja	djabanda-ngódja(-nja)
FUT	djá-ka-wa	djábindi-ya-wo	djabandá-ka-wa(-nja)
REM	dja-wú-na	djabindi-wú-na	djabana-wú-na(-nja)

TABLE 3.10 *Pronominal prefix and mood: Non-minimal A and 1st or 2nd person minimal O*

	UAA+1 or 2MINO	AUGA(UAFEMA)+ 1 or 2MINO
FUT	nbi-yi-nídja	nba-ka-nídja(-nja)
FUT	nbi-yi-ngódja	nba-ngódja(-nja)
FUT	nbí-ya-wo	nba-yú-ka-wa(-nja)
REM	nbi-rri-wú-na	nba-rra-wú-na(-nja)

TABLE 3.11 *Pronominal prefix and mood: 1/2 person A with 3rd person minimal O*

	1/2MINA+3MINO	1/2UAA+3MINO	1/2AUG(1/2UAFEM)A+3MINO
FUT	yi-yi-nídja	ngi-yi-nídja	ngaba-ka-nídja(-nja)
FUT	yi-yi-ngódja	ngi-yi-ngódja	ngaba-ngódja(-nja)
FUT	yá-ka-wa	ngí-ya-wo	ngaba-yú-ka-wa(-nja)
REM	(rr)ka-wú-na	ngi-rri-wú-na	ngaba-rra-wú-na(-nja)

Table 3.12 *Pronominal prefix and mood: Non-singular A and O*

	1st person	2nd person
FUT	njanbi-yi-nídja	nanbi-yi-nídja
FUT	njanbi-yi-ngódja	nanbi-yi-ngódja
FUT	njánbi-ya-wo	nánbi-ya-wo
REM	njanbi-rri-wú-na	nanbi-rri-wú-na

	1/2 person	3rd person
FUT	nganbi-yi-nídja	banbi-yi-nídja
FUT	nganbi-yi-ngódja	banbi-yi-ngódja
FUT	ngánbi-ya-wo	bánbi-ya-wo
REM	nganbi-rri-wú-na	banbi-rri-wú-na

TABLE 3.13 *Pronominal prefix and mood: 3rd person non-minimal A*
with 3rd person minimal O

	3UAA+3MINMASCO	3UAA+3MINFEMO
FUT	bi-yi-nídja	yibi-yi-nídja
FUT	bi-yi-ngódja	yibi-yi-ngódja
FUT	bí-ya-wo	yábi-ya-wo
REM	bi-rri-wú-na	yibi-rri-wú-na

	3AUG(3UAFEM)A+3MINMASCO	3AUG(3UAFEM)A+3MINFEMO
FUT	ba-ka-nídja(-nja)	yaba-ka-nídja(-nja)
FUT	ba-ngódja(-nja)	yaba-ngódja(-nja)
FUT	ba-yú-ka-wa(-nja)	yaba-yú-ka-wa(-nja)
REM	ba-rra-wú-na(-nja)	yaba-rra-wú-na(-nja)

TABLE 3.14 *Pronominal prefix and mood: 3rd person minimal A with 3rd*
person O

	3MINA+3MINMASCO	3MINA+3UAO	3MINA+3AUGO
FUT	ka-ya-nídja	bandi-yi-nídja	banda-ka-nídja
FUT	ka-ya-ngódja	bandi-yi-ngódja	banda-ngódja
FUT	ka-yá-ka-wa	bándi-ya-wo	bandá-ka-wa
REM	ka-wú-na	bindi-wú-na	bana-wú-na

	3MINA+3MINFEMO	3MINA+3UAFEMO
FUT	ya-ka-nídja	banda-ka-nídja-nja
FUT	nja-ya-ngódja	banda-ngódja-nja
FUT	nja-yá-ka-wa	banda-ka-wú-nja
REM	ya-wú-na	bana-wú-na-nja

TABLE 3.15 *Pronominal prefix and mood: 3rd person minimal A, non-3rd person O*

	3MINMASCA+1MINO	3MINMASCA+1UAO	3MINMASCA+1AUGO (1UAFEMO)
FUT	njanda-ka-nídja-yana	njindi-yi-nídja-yana	njanda-ka-nídja(-nja)-yana
FUT	njanda-ngódja-yana	njindi-yi-ngódja-yana	njanda-ngódja(-nja)-yana
FUT	njandá-ka-wa-yana	njindi-yi-wú-yana	njandá-ka-wa(-nja)-yana
REM	njana-wú-na-yana	njindi-wú-na-yana	njana-rra-wú-na(-nja)-yana

	3MINMASCA+2MIN0	3MINMASCA+2UAO	3MINMASCA+2AUGO (2UAFEMO)
FUT	dja-ka-nídja-yana	nindi-yi-nídja-yana	nanda-ka-nídja(-nja)-yana
FUT	dja-ngódja-yana	nindi-yi-ngódja-yana	nanda-ngódja(-nja)-yana
FUT	djá-ka-wa-yana	nándi-ya-wa-yana	nandá-ka-wa(-nja)-yana
REM	ngana-wú-na-yana	nindi-wú-na-yana	nana-rra-wú-na(-nja)-yana

	3MINMASCA+1/2MINO	3MINMASCA+1/2UAO	3MINMASCA+1/2AUGO (1/2UAFEMO)
FUT	kanda-ka-nídja-yana (nganda-)	ngindi-yi-nídja-yana	nganda-ka-nídja(-nja)-yana
FUT	kanda-ngódja-yana (nganda-)	ngindi-yi-ngódja-yana	nganda-ngódja(-nja)-yana
FUT	kandá-ka-wa-yana (ngandá-)	ngindi-yi-wú-yana	ngandá-ka-wa(-nja)-yana
REM	kana-rra-wú-na-yana (ngana-rra-)	ngindi-wú-na-yana	ngana-rra-wú-na(-nja)-yana

NOTES:

(i) In all forms given in this table the substitution of -yángaya for the final suffix -yana marks 3rd person minimal feminine A rather than 3rd person minimal masculine A.

(ii) With 1/2 person minimal O forms one (Djówanga) speaker uses forms with initial kan(d)a- while another (Yírriddjanga) speaker uses forms with initial ngan(d)a-.

TABLE 3.16 *Pronominal prefix and mood: Intransitive non-third person S*

	1MINS	1UAS	1AUGS
FUT	nga-ya-njínjdja	nji-yi-njínjdja	nja-ka-njínjdja
FUT	nga-ya-balákka	nji-yi-balákka	nja-balákka
FUT	nga-yá-ka-na	njí-ya-na	nja-yú-ka-na
REM	nga-njínjdja-na	nji-rri-njínjdja-na	nja-rra-njínjdja-na
REM	kó-na	njá-rri-na	nja-rrú-ka-na

	2MINS	2UAS	2AUGS
FUT	dja-ka-njínjdja	ni-yi-njínjdja	na-ka-njínjdja
FUT	dja-balákka	ni-yi-balákka	na-balákka
FUT	djá-ka-na	ní-ya-na	na-yú-ka-na
REM	ngana-njínjdja-na	ni-rri-njínjdja-na	na-rra-njínjdja-na
REM	nganá-ka-na	ná-rri-na	na-rrú-ka-na

	1/2MINS	1/2UAS	1/2AUGS
FUT	yi-yi-njínjdja	ngi-yi-njínjdja	ngaba-ka-njínjdja
FUT	yi-yi-balákka	ngi-yi-balákka	ngaba-balákka (ngawa-balákka)
FUT	yá-ka-na	ngí-ya-na	ngaba-yú-ka-na
REM	ka-njínjdja-na	ngi-rri-njínjdja-na	ngaba-rra-njínjdja-na
REM	ka-kó-na	ngá-rri-na	ngaba-rrú-ka-na

3.6.6   VERB CONJUGATION CLASSES—SUMMARY.   Ndjébbana verbs can be classified on the basis of the forms of the tense/aspect/mood affixes used with each. Such classification can only be rough because the variety of forms is very great. The verbs are classified into eight major classes on the basis of significant sharing of common features but within most of the eight classes there are a number of subclasses. A different grouping of subclasses and classes would have been possible if different features had been taken as significant. The total number of subclasses is 23, with a further seven irregular verbs. This section provides a summary statement of the verb classes and their suffixes, but it must be read in conjunction with §3.6.4, §§3.6.7 to 3.6.14, and §3.6.16.

   Table 3.18   summarises the verb conjugation classes and the tense/mood suffixes used with each. The future and counterfactual suffixes occur with the irrealis prefixes, while only the contemporary and remote suffixes may occur, where they are appropriate, with the realis (usually non-

TABLE 3.17 *Pronominal prefix and mood: Intransitive third person S*

	3MINMASCS	3UAMASCS	3AUGS
FUT	ka-ya-njínjdja	bi-yi-njínjdja	ba-ka-njínjdja
FUT	ka-ya-balákka	bi-yi-balákka	ba-balákka
FUT	ka-yá-ka-na	bí-ya-na	ba-yú-ka-na
REM	ka-njínjdja-na	bi-rri-njínjdja-na	ba-rra-njínjdja-na
REM	ka-kó-na	bá-rri-na	ba-rrú-ka-na

	3MINFEMS	3UAFEMS
FUT	nja-ya-njínjdja	ba-ka-njínjdja-nja
FUT	nja-ya-balákka	ba-balákka-na-nja
FUT	nja-yá-ka-na	ba-yú-ka-na-nja
REM	ya-njínjdja-na	ba-rra-njínjdja-na-nja
REM	ya-kó-na	ba-rrú-ka-na-nja

minimal) prefix -rrV-. In the table an asterisk against the subclass number indicates that the phonemic stress/vowel length shifts within the root or from root to affix with different forms. Of these the only stresses marked in the table itself are those which occur on the suffix and those which occur on the final syllable of the root, which are marked as an acute accent preceding the suffix dash. In some cases where it is fixed or modified the root-final vowel is given. If one of these root-final stresses occurs before a zero suffix form, that is if it occurs word-finally, it will shift by the regular rule to word-initial position (§2.3.1). Note that for many verbs, and particularly in the Yírriddjanga dialect, the counterfactual is formed using the infinitive of the verb with the counterfactual form of the auxiliary -yángka (conjugation 2A). The use of such forms for at least some verbs or by at least some speakers is indicated in the table by the symbol ¶ in the counterfactual row. Details should be checked in §§3.6.7 to 3.6.14. The infinitive form is available only for subclasses where the auxiliary construction is used for the counterfactual because it is normally only in this construction that the infinitive form is encountered. The infinitive is marked by the prefix na- unless the root begins with underlying unstressed dja- in which case the prefix is zero.

TABLE 3.18 *Ndjébbana verb conjugations – summary*

Conjugation 1	1A	1B*	1C*
FUT	-∅	-∅	-∅
CTP	-∅	´-∅	-ngka
REM	-nga	´-nga	-nga
CF	-ngóna	´-ngana	-ngóna
	-ngána		-ngána
	-ngéna		
	¶		
INFIN	∅-/na-		

Conjugation 2	2A	2B*	
FUT	-∅	-∅	
CTP	-∅	-∅	
REM	-na	í-na	
CF	-na	í-na	
	¶		
INFIN	na-		

Conjugation 3	3		
FUT	∅		
CTP	∅		
REM	∅		
CF	-na		
	¶		
INFIN	na-		

Conjugation 4	4A*	4B*	4C
FUT	-∅	-∅	-∅
CTP	-ra	-ra	-ra
REM	-na	-na	-∅
CF	-yóna	´-rana	¶
	¶		
INFIN	na-		∅-/na-

Conjugation 5	5A*	5B*	5C
FUT	-∅	-ya	-∅
CTP	-nga	-ra	-nga
REM	-ra	-ya	-na
CF	-róya	-róya	¶
	¶	¶	
INFIN	na-	∅- -ya/	∅-/na-
		na- -ya	

Conjugation 6	*6*A*	*6B**	*6C**		
FUT	-Ø	-njdja	-njdja		
CTP	´-Ø	´-Ø	´-Ø		
REM	é-ra	é-ra	´-ya		
CF	´-ngana	´-ngana	´-ngana		
INFIN					

Conjugation 7	*7A**	*7B**	*7C**	*7D*	*7E*
FUT	-Ø	-Ø	-Ø	-Ø	-ya
CTP	-dja	-ya	-ya	-ya	-ya
REM	-na	-na	-na	-ya	-nga
CF	-djéna	-yéna	-yana	´-yana	-yana
		¶		¶	
INFIN		na-		na-	

Conjugation 8	*8A**	*8B**	*8C**		
FUT	-Ø	-Ø	-Ø		
CTP	´-Ø	´-Ø	´-Ø		
REM	é-la	é-la	é-la		
CF	¶	¶	´-ngana		
INFIN	Ø-´-la/	Ø-´-la/			
	na-´-la				

Table 3.19 sets out the distribution of transitivity classes amongst the various conjugations, the monosyllabic verb roots found in each conjugation, and the characteristic root-final syllables (if any) in each conjugation. In the monosyllabic roots column the symbol Δ indicates that the roots listed are the sole members of that particular conjugation. In the root-final syllable column the symbol Δ indicates that the syllables listed are the only root-final syllables found in that particular conjugation. Further detailed information is provided in §§3.6.7 to 3.6.15. The numbers of verbs given in Table 3.19 are based on McKay (1980), as further annotated during the remainder of McKay's period of extended contact with speakers of Ndjébbana (and thus personal access to language data) up to mid-1982. This represents a total of 176 'regular' verbs (91 transitive, 4 ditransitive, 81 intransitive).

3.6.7   CONJUGATION 1. Conjugation 1 subclasses share the remote suffix -nga and counterfactual suffixes with the basic form -ngVna. With the exception of the contemporary suffix -ngka of class 1C, all subclasses of conjugation 1 have a zero suffix for both future and contemporary forms.

[a] *Conjugation 1A.*   The typical verb of conjugation 1A forms the counterfactual using an auxiliary with the infinitive. Rule 1 (stop gemination) and Rule 2 (stop lenition) (§2.4.1) apply to root-initial stops as appropriate.

TABLE 3.19 *Membership of Ndjébbana verb conjugations*

Conjugation	No. trans.	No. ditrans.	No. intrans.	Monosyllabic roots	Characteristic root-final syllables
1A	27	2	8		-(dj)dja- -(b)ba-
1B	4	1	1		-ma- -ye- -rlo-
1C	2	–	–	djó 'be angry with, berate' má 'get, fetch'	
1 Total	33	3	9		
2A	1	–	28		-ya-(<*yi)
2B	–	–	22		-yi-
2 Total	1	–	50		
3	4	–	2		
4A	13	–	–		-ba-(<*bu) Δ
4B	2	–	–	bú 'hit, kill'	-bú-
4C	1	–	5		-ba- -ya-
4 Total	16	–	5		
5A	9	–	2		-wa-
5B	–	–	6		
5C	2	–	–		(-wa-/-ba-)
5 Total	11	–	8		
6A	6	–	3		-bo- -wo-
6B	2	–	–		
6C	1	–	–	yí 'leave' Δ	
6 Total	9	–	3		
7A	1	1	–	ná 'see' wú 'give' Δ	

7B	1	–	1	(-ka-/-wa-)
7C	1	–	–	rá 'spear, shoot, pierce'
				Δ
7D	10	–	1	-ka- (-wa-)
7E	–	–	1	
7 Total	13	1	3	
8A	1	–	1	
8B	1	–	–	
8C	2	–	–	bá 'bite, eat'
8 Total	4	–	1	

The examples provided here have the pronominal prefix for 3AUGA+3MINMASCO or 3AUGS depending on transitivity. Rule 1 applies in all forms of bédja and djúbba, while Rule 2 applies in all forms of djarrárlma except for the infinitive.

	bédja 'heat in fire'	*djúbba* 'extinguish'	*yangádja* 'shut off, enclose'	*djarrárlma* 'grow up'
FUT	ba-ka-bbédja	ba-ka-ddjúbba	ba-yangádja	ba-yarrárlma
CTP	ba-rra-bbédja	ba-rra-ddjúbba	ba-rra-yangádja	ba-rra-yarrárlma
REM	ba-rra-bbédja-nga	ba-rra-ddjúbba-nga	ba-rra-yangádja-nga	ba-rra-yarrárlma-nga
INFIN	na-bbédja	na-ddjúbba	na-yangádja	djarrárlma

The three allomorphs of the counterfactual suffix are distributed as follows:

-ngóna is added to a root which has initial w- or contains an -o-
-ngána is added to a root which ends in -ma- or -ba- (cf. Conj.1C)
-ngéna is used elsewhere

The verbs of this conjugation listed below have been found to have an inflectional counterfactual form. Of the verbs listed those marked with an asterisk use the counterfactual suffix only in the Djówanga coastal dialect. Yírriddjanga speakers form the counterfactual of these verbs using the auxiliary construction. Verbs marked ¶ have both suffixal and auxiliary counterfactual forms as alternatives in one or both dialects. Some of the verbs have a special modified form of the root to which the counterfactual suffix is added. These modified root forms involve loss of a syllable in some cases, lenition to a nasal in others, and suppletion. This special root form is given in parentheses with the appropriate verbs. The selection of the correct counterfactual suffix depends on the characteristics of the main root for these verbs, not on the special, modified counterfactual form of the root. Thus the counterfactual form of kóndja 'cut' is (ba-)dja-ngóna because the full root of the verb contains an -o-, even though the truncated counterfactual root has a form (dja) which would normally give rise to the counterfactual suffix -ngéna.

Note that the intransitive verb kúndja 'to defecate, shit, lay (egg), give birth' is more common as part of a phrase with the verb rakarawo 'to move' (Conjugation 6A), the whole phrase meaning 'to run'. This verb kúndja has a special counterfactual form (full form including suffix given in parentheses in the list) linking it with the intransitive verbs of conjugation 2.

balála	'come in (tide)'	bándja (mandja)	'put'
djáma*¶	'wash'	kóndja¶ (dja)	'cut'
kúndja (mandji-yína)	'defecate, shit, give birth to, lay (egg)'	módja*	'pick up from ground'
ndabarlíndja	'turn (TR)'	nídja	'await, wait for'
ngáma¶ (marnama)	'carry on shoulder'	ngódja* (dja)	'name, call'
ngórraddja (rraddja)	'roast'	rórraddja*	'clean (TR), clear'
wála¶	'ascend, go up, go ashore'	wárrabba*	'take out (from hole or bag)'
wéndja	'climb (e.g. tree)'	wéra	'put in bag'

Thus we find inflected forms as in the following examples of Conjugation 1A verbs using the 3AUGA+3MINMASCO or 3AUGS prefix forms. Note that Rule 1 (stop gemination) applies in all forms of bándja and djáma apart from counterfactual, that Rule 2 (stop lenition) applies in the counterfactual form of djáma, and that Rule 6 deletes the underlying vowel from the second or third-last syllable of the word in all forms of rórraddja, but does not delete the vowel from this syllable in the counterfactual form because in this case the syllable is the fourth-last syllable in the word.

	bándja 'put'	*djáma* 'wash (TR)'	*rórraddja* 'clean (TR)'
FUT	ba-ka-bbándja	ba-ka-ddjáma	ba-ka-rórrddja
CTP	ba-rra-bbándja	ba-rra-ddjáma	ba-rra-rórrddja
REM	ba-rra-bbándja-nga	ba-rra-ddjáma-nga	ba-rra-rórrddja-nga
CF	ba-mandja-ngéna	ba-yama-ngána	ba-rarraddja-ngóna
INFIN		na-ddjáma	na-rórrddja

[b] *Conjugation 1B.* Verbs of conjugation 1B end in -ye- or -rlo-. They all have stress on the third-last syllable of the root in the future form and on the root-final syllable in the contemporary, remote and counterfactual forms. In the contemporary tense, since the tense suffix is zero, this underlying root-final stress is word final and so shifts regularly to prefix-initial position unless some other suffix (e.g. possessive or unit augmented feminine) is used (§2.3.1). All verbs of this conjugation have a regular counterfactual form using a suffix.

The first two syllables of each of the forms bárra-nmarramarla and barra-nmarramaló-nga usually collapse phonetically into one: bárn- and barn- respectively (see §2.1.5).

	lémaye 'show'	*rrókaye* 'carry in arms'	*nmarrímarlo* 'swim, bathe'
FUT	ba-ka-lémaya	ba-ka-rrókaya	ba-nmarrímarla
CTP	bá-rra-lamaya	bá-rra-rrakaya	bá-rra-nmarramarla
REM	ba-rra-lamayé-nga	ba-rra-rrakayé-nga	ba-rra-nmarramarló-nga
CF	ba-lamayé-ngana	ba-rrakayé-ngana	ba-nmarramarló-ngana

[c] *Conjugation 1C.* Conjugation 1C contains two monosyllabic verbs má 'fetch, get' and djó 'berate, be angry with', plus a third verb which is formed from the verb má using the extent suffix -(i)ba and which means 'lightning flash'. Stress shifts from the root to the suffix-initial syllable in the counterfactual form and the allomorphs of the counterfactual suffix follow exactly the same rule as for conjugation 1A above.

In the future and imperative forms of má, the -kó- prefix (§3.6.5) is obligatory and gives rise to the regular shifts in the position of stress (§3.6.5).

The future form of djó is suppletive, having the form -warrawó giving rise to the -Ø- form of the irrealis prefix. When word-final, the stress shifts to the word-initial position (see §2.4.1).

The following examples show the main forms of these two verbs:

	má 'get, fetch'	*djó* 'berate, be angry with'
FUT	ba-yúka-ma	bá-warrawo
CTP	ba-rra-má-ngka	ba-rra-ddjó-ngka
REM	ba-rra-má-nga	ba-rra-ddjó-nga
CF	ba-ma-ngána	ba-ya-ngóna
MINIMP	ma-rrá-ka-ma	

3.6.8   CONJUGATION 2. Conjugation 2 subclasses share the remote and counterfactual suffix -na, as well as a zero suffix for both contemporary and future.

The only transitive verb in this conjugation is the verb yángka 'do' when used as an auxiliary to form the counterfactual of transitive verbs. In this construction it has transitive pronoun prefixes. Used as a verb in its own right, yángka is intransitive.

Apart from four verbs in conjugation 2A which have final -ka- (balákka (<*balo+wákka) 'come back', béngka 'float, be in water', wákka 'go back' and yángka 'do'), all verbs of conjugation 2A and all verbs of conjugation 2B have final underlying -yi-, which is the reflexive/reciprocal/ intransitiviser suffix (§3.6.17). The difference between the two conjugations is that in conjugation 2A the major stress has a constant position in the root, while in conjugation 2B the major stress shifts to root-final position in the remote and counterfactual forms.

In conjugation 2A, where the principal stress never falls on the root-final syllable, this syllable always has the surface form -ya- (by Rule 3 §3.6.16), while in conjugation 2B the syllable has the form -yí- when bearing major stress and -ya- when not bearing this stress. The underlying identity of this derivational suffix in these two conjugations is established by the fact that intransitive verbs in each conjugation (2A and 2B) are derived from transitive verbs of other conjugations with exactly the same meaning correspondence, the only difference lying in the different stress patterning of conjugations 2A and 2B. In the examples, verbs of both conjugations, 2A and 2B, are cited with the underlying form of the reflexive suffix -yi-, though this is always realised phonetically as -ya- in conjugation 2A and in contemporary and future forms of conjugation 2A.

2A

bóraba-yi	'paint self'	<	bóraba	4A	'paint'
bíwa-yi	'stink'	<	bíwa	5A	'smell (TR)'
ná-yi	'meet, see each other'	<	ná	7A	'see'
yakkabí-yi	'get tangled, tie self'	<	djákkabo	6A	'tie'

2B

djáma-yi	'wash self'	<	djáma	1A	'wash'
méraba-yi	'hide (INTR), go inside'	<	méraba	4A	'hide (TR), put inside'
nangardórrddja-yi	'break (INTR)'	<	nangardórrddja	1A	'break (TR)'
ngódjba-yi	'get better (of sore)'	<	ngódjba	4A	'make, mend'

Only one known verb of conjugation 2 has a counterfactual form using the auxiliary construction. This is béngka 'float, be in water', for which both suffixal and auxiliary counterfactual forms have been found.

kóma   na-bbéngka ka-yangkayí-na.   kóma   ka-ya-bbéngka-na.
NEG   INFIN-float 3MINMASCS-do-CF   NEG   3MINMASCS-IRR-float-CF
It did not float.   It did not float.

The verb djáma-yi 'wash self' appears to be in conjugation 2A for Yírriddjanga speakers and conjugation 2B for Djówanga speakers from the north coast. One verb of conjugation 2A, yángka 'AUX', has a counterfactual form based on a variant root form in which the root-final syllable is stressed -yí-, like conjugation 2B. In addition, Yírriddjanga speakers use a counterfactual form of djámayi which is based on the regular form for conjugation 2A. In the counterfactual form of the lexical verb yángka 'do', the irrealis prefix -ya- is deleted by Rule 4 (§3.6.16) before the root-initial syllable. The remote-tense form of this verb is regular for conjugation 2A in that the suffix is added to a root with invariant root-initial stress.

	djámayi 'wash self'	*yángka* 'do, AUX'
CTP	nga-ddjámaya	nga-yángka
REM	∫nga-ya-ddjámaya-na ∖nga-yamayí-na	nga-yángka-na
CF	∫nga-ya-ddjámaya-na ∖nga-yamayí-na	∫nga-yángka-na ∖nga-yangkayí-na

For verbs of conjugation 2B for which the final syllables have the form -djVyi-, the unstressed vowel between the laminal stop and the laminal semivowel is normally reduced to -e- rather than -a- (e.g. ngúdjeyi 'speak', réndjeyi 'stand').

The root form of rlúrrabayi 'arrive' is the stem for all tenses in the Yírriddjanga dialect but coastal Djówanga speakers use a suppletive root míba 'arrive' to replace it in future and contemporary forms.

A number of verbs of conjugation 2B have special stem forms (usually shortened) to form the remote and counterfactual. These verb roots are listed with their special counterfactual stem forms in parentheses.

kónjdjeyi (njdjí)	'cut self, stop (rain)'	mayáwayi (mawayí)	'sing'
nangardórrddjeyi (nangarddjí)	'break (INTR), be broken'	ndabakkúrrngarna (ndabarakkayí)	'sit down (INCHO)'
rnawárrabayi (rnarrabayí)	'split (INTR)'	yawarnáwayi (yawarnayí)	'refuse'

The following examples of tense/mood forms of conjugations 2A and 2B show not only the patterns of affixation and stress shifting but also the application of various morpho-phonological rules (§2.4.1 and §3.6.16). All forms in this group of examples, with the exception of one verb, have the appropriate prefix for 3MINFEMS. The exception is the verb marlakkórlayi 'split up', which is exemplified using the prefix for 3AUGS. Rule 1 (Stop Gemination) applies to all forms of bórabayi 'paint self' and to the future and contemporary forms of búdjeyi 'shout, call'. In the remote and counterfactual forms of this latter verb the underlying root-initial single stop occurs because the main stress shifts to the root-final syllable, so that the conditions for application of Rule 1 are no longer met. Rule 3 (Vowel Reduction) applies in different syllables in each of the forms of each verb of conjugation 2B, as can be seen by comparing with the root form or with the other tense/mood forms. Each vowel has its underlying quality only when carrying the main stress. Rule 4 applies to delete one occurrence of the syllable -ya- in the remote and counterfactual forms of nmarabúyaya 'be buried', both of which forms have a non-zero suffix -na. Rule 4 does not apply when there is no non-zero suffix, as in the future and contemporary forms of the same verb. Rule 5 applies in the future and contemporary forms of ndamérabaya 'set (sun)', but is blocked from applying in the remote and counterfactual forms by the presence of the main stress in the second-last syllable. Rule 7 applies to shorten the root by deleting the sequence -Vy- from the remote and counterfactual forms of búdjeyi 'shout' and ndamérabayi 'set (sun)', but does not apply to the remote and counterfactual forms of marlakkórlayi 'split up' because it does not have a laminal stop -dj- immediately before this sequence, and the root is five − rather than three or four − syllables long.

2A	*bórabayi* 'paint self'	*nmarabúyaya* 'be buried'	*wákka* 'return, go back'
FUT	nja-ya-bbórbaya	nja-ya-nmarabúyaya	nja-ya-wákka
CTP	ya-bbórbaya	ya-nmarabúyaya	ya-wákka
REM	ya-bbórbaya-na	ya-nmarabúya-na	ya-wákka-na
CF	nja-ya-bbórba-ya-na	nja-ya-nmarabúya-na	nja-ya-wákka-na

2B	*búdjeyi* 'shout, call'	*marlakkórlayi* 'split up, separate'	*ndamérabayi* 'set (sun FEM)'
FUT	nja-ya-bbúdjeya	ba-marlakkórlaya	nja-ya-ndamérbaya
CTP	ya-bbúdjeya	ba-rra-marlakkórlaya	ya-ndamérbaya
REM	ya-badjí-na	ba-rra-marlakkarlayí-na	ya-ndamarabí-na
CF	nja-ya-badjí-na	ba-marlakkarlayí-na	nja-ya-ndamarabí-na

3.6.9   CONJUGATION 3.   Conjugation 3 verbs are unique in Ndjébbana in having zero suffixes for future, contemporary and remote forms.

Counterfactual forms use the auxiliary construction for most verbs of this conjugation, but there is a suppletive counterfactual root form for the verb djórrkka 'take'. A suffixal form of the counterfactual of the verb djórrkkangaya has been reported only by a Yírriddjanga speaker. Djówanga speakers have preferred the auxiliary form. With this suppletive counterfactual root form of the verb djórrkka it is uncertain where the division between root and suffix lies.

ba-rra-ddjórrkka
3AUGA+3MINMASCO-RE-take+CTP/REM
They took it.

ba-ndjayí-na
3AUGA+3MINMASCO(+IRR)-take-CF
They would have taken it.

ba-bala-ndjayí-na
   -come hither-take-CF
They would have brought it.

ba-ndjayí-na-ngaya (<djórrkkangaya 'run')
   -run-CF-run
They would have run.

3.6.10   CONJUGATION 4.   The principal common feature of verbs of Conjugation 4 is the contemporary suffix -ra in addition to a zero suffix for future in all three subclasses and the -na remote suffix in two of the three subclasses. Conjugation 4C's membership of conjugation 4 is the most tenuous, also in the light of the intransitivity of the verbs of this conjugation, but it is grouped with 4A and 4B on account of its contemporary suffix.

Conjugation 4A verbs all have the final syllable -ba-, which is the form which would normally be assumed by an underlying -bú- when it loses its stress. These verbs, then, can be considered to have developed historically as compounds of -bú- 'hit'. The same might be said of those verbs of conjugation 4C which have final -ba-, but there are other verbs of this conjugation which have final -ya-. Conjugation 4B comprises only the monosyllabic verb bú 'hit, kill' and one of its compounds, warrabú 'burn, be cooked, be hot', which retains the main stress on -bú-, unlike the compounds found in conjugations 4A and 4C.

Many verbs of conjugation 4A and all verbs of conjugation 4C use the auxiliary form for the counterfactual. A number of the verbs in conjugation 4A which have a suffixal form for the counterfactual have a special counterfactual root form or special counterfactual suffix forms. All known inflectional or suppletive counterfactual forms of conjugation 4A are listed here, showing root plus suffix where the division between the two can be established. The expected forms are marked with an asterisk. In these, stress shifts from the root to the suffix-initial syllable. The contemporary form of each verb is also listed for reference. In the list the pronominal prefix indicating 3AUGS or 3AUGA+3MINMASCO (ba(-rra)-) is used for all counterfactual forms. Note the application of morphophonemic Rule 5 in several of the contemporary forms, the application of Rule 1 in the contemporary forms of bóraba and djórraba and of Rule 3 in all the regular counterfactual forms. The verb wáraba 'sing' has an auxiliary counterfactual form.

	Contemporary	Counterfactual
bardórrbba 'crush, grind, punch, smash'	ba-rra-bardórrbba-ra	ba-mara-yóna
bóraba 'paint'	ba-rra-bbórba-ra	ba-njamíngana
djórraba 'cook'	ba-rra-ddjórrba-ra	ba-balangóna
méraba 'hide'	ba-rra-mérba-ra	⎰ba-maraba-yóna* ⎱ba-maraba-yóngana
rnarnawárraba 'cut off, split (turtle shell)'	ba-rra-rnarnawárrba-ra	⎰ba-rnarraba-yóna ⎱ba-rnarraba-yóngana
ngódjba 'cause, make, repair'	ba-rra-ngódjba-ra	ba-ngadjba-yóna*
wáraba 'sing (TR) (i.e.sorcery)'	ba-rra-wárba-ra	ba-waraba-yóna*

In the future forms bú itself has a suppletive form, and the main stress on future forms of both verbs in conjugation 4B is on the third-last syllable. In the remote forms of verbs of conjugation 4B the root-final vowel is lowered to -ó-. The verb warrabú 'burn, be cooked, be hot' (4B) has a shortened counterfactual stem. In the list of forms for both verbs the pronominal prefix indicating 3MINMASCS or 3MINA+3MINMASCO (ka-) is used. Note the application of morphophonemic Rule 1 (stop gemination) in all forms of bú except the future. (Compare non-application of Rule 1 in the corresponding forms of warrabú, where b is not root-initial.)

	bú 'hit, kill'	*warrabú* 'burn, be cooked, be hot'
FUT	ka-ya-balábara	ka-ya-wárraba
CTP	ka-bbú-ra	ka-warrabú-ra
REM	ka-bbó-na	ka-warrabó-na
CF	ka-ya-bbú-rana	ka-ya-rrabú-rana

In future forms of verbs of conjugation 4C, Rule 4 deletes one occurrence of the syllable -ya- when, after application of Rule 2, an underlying root-initial unstressed dja- is lenited to ya-. In the list of example forms the prefix form for 1MINS or 1MINA+3MINO (nga-) has been used. In the list, where Rule 4 does apply it is the irrealis prefix ya- which is shown as deleted.

	djanarrába 'sneeze'	*walédjba* 'paddle (in canoe)'
FUT	nga-yanarrába (<*nga-ya-yanarrába)	nga-ya-walédjba
CTP	nga-yanarrába-ra	nga-walédjba-ra
REM	nga-yanarrába	nga-walédjba
INFIN	djanarrába	na-walédjba

3.6.11   CONJUGATION 5. Subclasses 5A and 5B are included in conjugation 5 on account of their unique counterfactual suffix -róya, though this suffix is found with only one verb in conjugation 5A (the remaining verbs using the auxiliary construction or having suppletive forms for counterfactual). 5A and 5C are linked in Conjugation 5 on account of their common contemporary suffix -nga. Morphological patterns plus the transitivity patterns suggest that 5B is the odd one out in this group of conjugations.

With one exception the characteristic root-final syllable of verbs of conjugation 5A is -wa-. Conjugation 5C has one verb with -wa- and another with -ba-, but no pattern of root-final syllables is discernible for conjugation 5B.

All but two verbs of conjugation 5A use the auxiliary construction for the counterfactual form. Of the two verbs which do not use the auxiliary counterfactual construction, one (karráwa 'look for, etc.') has a suppletive counterfactual form and the other (míwa 'send') uses the counterfactual suffix listed for this conjugation but attached to a shortened stem. In the examples the prefix for 1MINA and 3MINO is used and a third verb provided for comparison. This uses the auxiliary construction for counterfactual, like the remaining verbs of this conjugation.

5A	*karráwa* 'look around, go hunting, look for, oversee, be boss'	*míwa* 'send'	*ndamáwa* 'tie up, tether'
FUT	nga-ya-karráwa	nga-ya-míwa	nga-ya-ndamáwa
CTP	nga-karráwa-nga	nga-míwa-nga	nga-ndamáwa-nga
REM	nga-karráwa-ra	nga-míwa-ra	nga-ndamáwa-ra
CF	nga-ya-lengéna	nga-ya-ma-róya	
INFIN			na-ndamáwa

The verb marláya 'put gum on' (conjugation 5A) loses its root-final syllable -ya- before the remote suffix (e.g. nga-marlá-ra REM, compare nga-marláya-nga CTP).

Only three of the six verbs of conjugation 5B have been reported to have auxiliary counterfactual forms. A Yírriddjanga speaker reported such a form for djarramá 'laugh' and a Djówanga speaker for rlakarlú 'bow head'. In each case a speaker of the opposite moiety reported an inflectional form. The third verb with an auxiliary counterfactual form is ngarraddjá 'be open'. Only one verb (warré 'jump over, be born, cross (creek)') has a fully regular suffixal counterfactual form. The remaining verbs either use the regular suffix on a modified stem or they have a suppletive counterfactual form or a different suffix. The root-final vowel of lawayó 'hang (INTR)' changes to -é- when the suffix has an initial -y- as in the future, remote and counterfactual forms. When the regular counterfactual suffix -róya occurs the major stress shifts from the root to the suffix. Here we give sample paradigms for two verbs and then a list of the remaining three verbs which use an inflectional counterfactual form, giving the counterfactual form in parentheses. In all cases the prefix for 1MINS is used:

5B	*djarramá* 'laugh'	*warré* 'jump over, be born, cross (creek)'
FUT	nga-yarramá-ya (<*nga-ya-yarramá-ya)	nga-ya-warré-ya
CTP	nga-yarramá-ra	nga-warré-ra
REM	nga-yarramá-ya	nga-warré-ya
CF	nga-ya-wa-róya	nga-ya-warra-róya
INFIN	djarramá-ya	

lakalá	(nga-ya-la-róya)	'listen, feel (i.e. perceive touch)'
lawayó	(nga-ya-lawayé-yana)	'hang (INTR)'
rlakarlú	(nga-ya-rlakarlú-yana)	'bow head'

Note the application of Rule 2 (§2.4.1) in all but the infinitive form of djarramá, of Rule 4 (§3.6.16) in the future form of djarramá and of Rule 3 (§3.6.16) in the counterfactual form of warré.

3.6.12 CONJUGATION 6. The common feature of subclasses 6A and 6B is the remote suffix -ra . Though 6C does not share this remote suffix it shares with 6B the unique future suffix -njdja. All three subclasses have a common contemporary suffix form (zero) and a common counterfactual suffix form -ngana following a root-final stressed syllable.

For all verbs in conjugation 6 (with the exception of the contemporary form of the verb yerrengábbabo 'hoist sail, lift up' (6A)) the underlying major stress is on the root-final syllable in the contemporary, remote and counterfactual forms. In these contemporary-tense forms, since there is no overt suffix, and when there is no additional suffix (e.g. unit augmented feminine), the root-final syllable would also be word-final. Therefore the major stress shifts phonetically to word-initial position, following the regular pattern (§2.3.1). For those verbs which have underlying root-final -o, this vowel quality is retained when the stress shifts to word-initial position. Other root-final vowels are reduced to -a by Rule 3 (§3.6.16) when the stress shifts to word-initial position. The exceptional verb yerrengábbabo retains its major stress on the middle syllable of the root in the contemporary form. The remote stem in conjugations 6A and 6B has final vowel -é before the suffix -ra. All verbs of conjugation 6 have inflectional counterfactual forms.

Certain verbs of conjugation 6A have variant phonetic root forms in different tenses/moods. Thus, for instance, the vowel of the root-initial syllable of various forms of bíddabo 'follow, chase, track' (6A), when unstressed, often has the quality of -o-, presumably under the influence of the preceding labial semivowel. Thus ngá-waddabo (1MINA+3MINO-follow+CTP) is usually pronounced ngá-woddabo. In the same way the unstressed root-initial vowel of various forms of djákkabo 'tie up' frequently takes on the quality of -i- from the preceding laminal semivowel. Thus nga-yakkabé-ra (1MINA+3MINO-tie up-REM) often sounds more like nga-yikkabé-ra. Vowel harmony (§2.3.1) may have some influence too.

Two verbs of conjugation 6A, rawo and rakarawo, have the last two syllables of the root (rawo) reduced to ro in the future form and the underlying root-final stress shifts to word-initial position. In the future forms of both verbs of conjugation 6B, the root-final syllable -yi- is lost. The verb bakabínji 'dig' in conjugation 6A frequently has, alongside its regular expected future stem form bakabínja, the alternative future stem form biyibínja resulting from consistent fronting or palatalisation of the first two syllables.

Sample paradigms are given here of selected verbs in the three conjugations of this group, using the prefix forms indicating 3AUGA+3MINMASCO or 3MINS. Note the application of Rule 1 (§2.4.1) in the future form and of Rule 2 (§2.4.1) in the remaining forms of bíddabo 'follow'. Rule 3 (§3.6.16) applies throughout, and it appears that Rule 4 (§3.6.16) applies in the contemporary form of yíyi 'leave' to delete one syllable from an underlying *bárra-yaya.

	bakabínji 'dig' (6A)	*bíddabo* 'follow, chase, track' (6A)	*nábo* 'dance, stamp, step' (6A)
FUT	ba-bakabínja/ ba-biyibínja	ba-ka-bbíddaba	ba-ka-nábba
CTP	bá-rra-bakabanja	bá-rra-waddabo/ bá-rra-woddabo	bá-rra-nabo
REM	ba-rra-bakabanjé-ra	ba-rra-waddabé-ra/ ba-rrawoddabé-ra	ba-rra-nabé-ra
CF	ba-bakabanjí-ngana	ba-waddabó-ngana/ ba-woddabó-ngana	ba-nabó-ngana

	rakarawo 'move' (6A)	*ndabúyi* 'lick, smack lips, kiss' (6B)	*yí* 'leave' (6C)
FUT	bá-rakaro	ba-ndabú-ndja	ba-ka-yí-ndja
CTP	bá-rra-rakarawo	bá-rra-ndabaya	bá-rra-ya
REM	ba-rra-rakarawé-ra	ba-rra-ndabayé-ra	ba-rra-yí-ya
CF	ba-rakarawó-ngana	ba-ndabayé-ngana	ba-ka-yí-ngana

3.6.13 CONJUGATION 7. The common feature of conjugation 7 is the occurrence of initial laminals (dj and y) on the contemporary and counterfactual suffixes (-dja/-ya and -djéna/-yVna respectively). Verbs of 7D form the counterfactual using an auxiliary so they have no counterfactual suffix, and do not fully meet this criterion for membership of conjugation 7.

All but one of the verbs in the most numerous conjugation in this group, 7D, have the characteristic final syllable -ka-. The remaining verb has root-final -wa-. Conjugation 7B (two verbs) has one each with final -ka- and -wa-.

The verbs of conjugations 7A and 7C, being the monosyllabic verbs of conjugation 7, like the monosyllabic verb má 'fetch, get' in conjugation 1C, have an obligatory -kó- prefix in the future and imperative forms with the appropriate stress shifts as outlined in §3.6.5.

In the counterfactual forms of verbs of conjugations 7A and 7B, the main stress shifts from the root to the initial syllable of the suffix. The verb ná 'see' in conjugation 7A has a reduced form of the root, -n-, in the counterfactual. Only one of the two verbs in conjugation 7B, ngárawa 'light a fire' has a suffixal counterfactual form. The remaining verb of conjugation 7B, mankawákka 'hurry', has an auxiliary counterfactual form, like all but one of the verbs of conjugation 7D. The one exception in 7D is the verb kálawa 'know, think about, worry about', which is irregular in the sense that the root-initial syllable is deleted when unstressed, that is in all forms except for the future.

The following paradigms, using the 1MINA+3MINO prefix, exemplify forms of conjugation 7 verbs:

	ná 'see' (7A)	*ngárawa* 'light fire' (7B)	*rá* 'spear, shoot, pierce' (7C)
FUT	nga-yá-ka-na	nga-ya-ngárawa	nga-yá-ka-ra
CTP	nga-ná-dja	nga-ngárawa-ya	nga-rá-ya
REM	nga-ná-na	nga-ngárawa-na	nga-rá-na
CF	nga-ya-n-djéna	nga-ya-ngarawa-yéna	nga-ya-rá-yana
MINIMP	ma-rrá-ka-na	ma-ngárawa	ma-rrá-ka-ra

	warlékka 'use up, finish up' (7D)	*kálawa* 'know, think about, worry about' (7D)	*warayéma* 'be afraid, frightened' (7E)
FUT	nga-ya-warlékka	nga-ya-kkálawa	nga-ya-warayéma-ya
CTP	nga-warlékka-ya	nga-lawá-ya	nga-warayéma-ya
REM	nga-warlékka-ya	nga-lawá-ya	nga-warayéma-nga
CF		nga-ya-lawá-yana	nga-ya-warayéma-yana
INFIN	na-warlékka		

3.6.14   CONJUGATION 8.

The common feature of verbs of conjugation 8 is the remote suffix -la (following the root-final mid front vowel é). These verbs also share zero suffixes for future and contemporary. All verbs of conjugation 8 shift the major stress to the root-final syllable in the remote and counterfactual forms. Major stress also shifts to root-final position in the contemporary forms of conjugations 8B and 8C, though, with a zero suffix, this underlying word-final stress is actually realised in word-initial position except when a suffix, such as unit augmented feminine, follows (§2.3.1).

Conjugations 8A and 8B share the use of the auxiliary form for the counterfactual, while conjugation 8C verbs have an inflectional counterfactual form.

In contemporary, remote and counterfactual forms of njémbo 'waken' (8C), the -m- is deleted from the root, while bá 'eat, bite' (8C) has a suppletive future form of the root: móya.

The following paradigms for three verbs of the various conjugations in this group are given using the prefix form for 3AUGS or 3AUGA+3MINMASCO.

	djúwe 'be sick' (8A)	*njémbo* 'waken, wake up (TR)' (8C)	*bá* 'eat, bite' (8C)
FUT	ba-ka-ddjúwa	ba-ka-njémba	ba-ka-móya
CTP	ba-rra-ddjúwa	bá-rra-njabo	bá-rra-ba
REM	ba-rra-yawé-la	ba-rra-njabé-la	ba-rra-bá-la
CF		ba-njabó-ngana	ba-ka-bá-ngana
INFIN	djawé-la		

3.6.15   IRREGULAR VERBS. Six verbs have been classed as irregular in
Ndjébbana because they have unique tense/mood inflections and do not fit the
patterns of any of the eight conjugations. Some of the listed subclasses or
conjugations of verbs (6C, 7C, 7E) contain only a single verb, with unique
inflectional patterns, but they are classed among the conjugations because of
their greater fit with the broad patterns within one of the eight conjugations.

Paradigms for the various irregular verbs will be given here using
the 1MINS or 1MINA+3MINO prefix. To clarify the patterns of affixes, zero
affixes will be indicated in parentheses.

	bó 'fall, land' INTR	*djí* 'drink' TR	*kúrrngarna* 'stand (CAUS), wear, name' TR
FUT	ngá-ya-ka-bbo(-Ø)	nga-yá-ka-ya(-Ø)	nga-ya-kkúrrngarna
CTP	ngá-bbo(-Ø)	nga-djdjí-njdja	(Ø-)kúrrngarna
REM	nga-ba-ngóna	nga-djdjí-njdja	nga-kkawúna
CF	nga-ya-bbó-ngana	nga-ya-né-ngana	nga-ya-ra-yóna

	nó 'sit, be' INTR	*djirrí* 'go' INTR	*yó* 'lie, be, sleep' INTR
FUT	nga-yá-ka-na(-Ø)	ngé-yarra(-Ø)	nga-ya-kkó-ya(-Ø)
CTP	nga-nó-ra	nga-yirrí-ya	nga-yó-ra
REM	(Ø-)kó-na(-Ø)	nga-béna	(Ø-)kó-ya(-Ø)
CF	nga-ya-na-rayína	nga-ya-bbóbbana	nga-ya- bardarrbbayína

The verb bó 'fall, land' has its underlying major stress shift from the
root-final syllable in the future, contemporary and counterfactual forms. In the
first two of these, this stress is realised in word-initial position when there is
no other suffix such as unit augmented feminine. Rule 1 (§2.4.1) applies to
the underlying form to geminate the root-initial stop in the future,
contemporary and counterfactual forms, but Rule 2 does not apply to the root-

initial stop in the remote form. This verb is most closely related to conjugation 1, differing from it only in the remote form. It would be possible to interpret the remote and counterfactual suffixes as identical in underlying form (-ngóna) but with vowel reduction (§2.3) applying in the absence of stress on the counterfactual suffix.

The verb djí 'drink' has no clear links with any conjugation, though it shares the use of the unusual suffix -njdja with 6B, 6C and 7A. The analysis of the counterfactual form of this verb listed above assumes a suppletive counterfactual root form -né- and a counterfactual suffix -ngana-, used with the irrealis prefix -ya-. Alternative interpretations could be suggested.

Note the zero first person minimal S prefix form in the contemporary form of kúrrngarna.

In both the future and contemporary forms of djirrí 'go' the underlying stress occurs on the root-final syllable, but in the case of the future this word-final underlying stress is realised in word-initial position unless a further suffix follows. The future and contemporary suffixes of djirrí 'go' can be compared to verbs of conjugation 7, but the remote and counterfactual forms are clearly suppletive, being cognate to verbs (bo/ba) meaning 'to go' found in the neighbouring languages Burarra, Nakkara and Gurrgoni (Green 1989:8). Rule 2 (§2.4.1) applies to the root djirrí in all forms except when it is immediately preceded by a consonant as in the form nginj-djirrí-ya '2MINS-go-CONTMP', where a special form of the pronominal prefix occurs. All monosyllabic pronominal prefixes have a special form when attached to the future root form yarra 'go'. This has the form of Cé- in the minimal and augmented and Cí- in the unit augmented, where C varies according to person: ngé- 1MINS, njé- 3MINFEMS, ngí- 1/2UAS, né- 2AUGS, bé- 3AUGS, and so on. The irrealis prefix -ya- is identical to the root-initial syllable in the future form so one of the two is deleted by Rule 4 (§3.6.16).

The verbs nó 'sit, be' and yó 'lie, be' both require the -kó- prefix (§3.6.5) in future and remote forms, though with yó the normal stress shifting with this prefix does not apply. In the remote forms of both nó and yó the first person minimal S has no overt representation. Apart from the 1MINS remote form, regular pronominal prefixes are used in the future and remote forms of yó. Remote forms of these two verbs and future forms of nó are given here to show all person and number possibilities for subject S.

Future	MIN	UA	AUG
1	nga-yá-ka-na	njí-ya-na	nja-yú-ka-na
1/2	yá-ka-na	ngí-ya-na	ngaba-yú-ka-na
2	djá-ka-na	ní-ya-na	na-yú-ka-na
3MASC	ka-yá-ka-na	bí-ya-na	ba-yú-ka-na
3FEM	nja-yá-ka-na	ba-yú-ka-na-nja	

Remote	MIN	UA	AUG
1	(Ø-)kó-na	njá-rri-na	nja-rrú-ka-na
1/2	ka-kó-na	ngá-rri-na	ngaba-rrú-ka-na
2	nganá-ka-na	ná-rri-na	na-rrú-ka-na
3MASC	ka-kó-na	bá-rri-na	ba-rrú-ka-na
3FEM	ya-kó-na	ba-rrú-ka-na-nja	

Remote	MIN	UA	AUG
1	(Ø-)kó-ya	nji-rri-kkó-ya	nja-rra-kkó-ya
1/2	ka-kkó-ya	ngi-rri-kkó-ya	ngaba-rra-kkó-ya
2	ngana-kkó-ya	ni-rri-kkó-ya	na-rra-kkó-ya
3MASC	ka-kkó-ya	bi-rri-kkó-ya	ba-rra-kkó-ya
3FEM	ya-kkó-ya	ba-rra-kkó-ya-nja	

3.6.16 MORPHOPHONEMIC PROCESSES OF THE VERB.

A number of morphophonemic processes apply within the verb system to derive surface phonetic forms after affixation. There appear to be some exceptions to the generality of all these rules, though reasons for the exceptions are not clear.

Two significant morphophonemic processes applying to verbs have already been presented in §§2.4.1 to 2.4.3. These are Rule 1 (Stop Gemination) and Rule 2 (Stop Lenition), both of which apply to root-initial underlying stops.   Further processes are presented here as additional rules.

Rule 3

> *Vowels which do not bear the major phonemic stress are normally realised by the unmarked vowel a.*

The application of Rule 3 is found with verb paradigms in which stress shifts position in different forms (§2.3). Exceptions to the application of the rule occur with word-final underlying stressed o, which retains its vowel quality when the stress shifts phonetically to word-initial position, with vowel harmony (§2.3.2) and with certain specific forms.

Rule 4

> *One of a pair of identical unstressed open (CV) syllables is deleted.*

A rule of rare application, such as in the contemporary form of the verb yiyi 'to leave' in which stress shifts to the prefix from underlying word-final position, both underlying root vowels neutralise to unstressed a and then one of the identical ya syllables is deleted. A further example is the verb balála 'come in (tide)', which itself seems to be derived from baló 'come hither' and/or wála 'ascend, go ashore'. In the counterfactual form the main stress shifts to the suffix, leaving a sequence of identical unstressed syllables, one of which is deleted. The root-initial stop lenites to a semivowel.

ngá-ya   (<*ngá-yaya <*nga-yayí)
1MINA+3MINO-leave
I am leaving it.

kóma   ka-ya-wala-ngóna   (<*ka-ya-balala-ngóna)
NEG   3MINS-IRR-come.in-CF
The tide didn't come in.

Rule 5
An unmarked vowel is deleted between a rhotic and a bilabial stop in the third-last unstressed syllable of a verb form provided no stressed syllable follows it within the word.

Thus (apart from the application of Rule 3 in neutralising the first vowel to a) the verb root méraba 'to hide (TR)' has its full number of syllables only in the counterfactual (where the syllable beginning with a rhotic is the fourth-last syllable of the word) or in the future (where the syllable in question is the second-last syllable of the word). In the contemporary or remote forms, where the suffix has only a single syllable, the vowel of the underlying third-last syllable of the word is deleted, reducing the number of syllables in the word.

nga-ya-maraba-yóna	nga-ya-méraba	nga-mérba-na
1MINA+3MINO-IRR-hide-CF	-IRR-hide	-hide-REM
I would have hidden it.	I will hide it.	I hid it.

This rule applies only to a group of verbs of Conjugation 4 and their intransitive derivatives in conjugation 2B, such as the intransitive or reflexive verb méraba-yi 'to hide (INTR)'.

nga-marabí-na	nga-mérbaya
1MINS-hide-REM	1MINS-hide(+CTP)
I hid/entered.	I am hiding/entering.

The verb bórba-yi 'paint oneself' in conjugation 2A is clearly derived from bóraba 'to paint' in conjugation 4A but has lost the underlying middle vowel in all forms, unlike méraba-yi 'hide' discussed above, because Rule 5 has apparently applied to the root, giving a constant form of the root, which is unaffected by stress shifting or other factors.

Rule 6
An unmarked vowel is deleted between the apical trill and a geminate stop cluster where the verb suffix is zero or unstressed CV, apparently to permit the major word stress to occur on the second-last syllable of the root, except when it must occur on the suffix.

For instance the full form of the root rórraddja 'to be clean, clear' occurs only in the counterfactual form, because here the suffix is two syllables. Even here all the root vowels are neutralised by Rule 3 because the stress shifts to the suffix. In the other forms of this verb Rule 6 applies:

nga-ya-rarraddja-ngóna	nga-ya-rórrddja	nga-rórrddja-nga
1MINA+3MINO-IRR-clean-CF	-IRR-clean	-clean-REM
I would have cleaned it.	I will clean it.	I cleaned it.

This rule applies only to certain verbs of conjugation 1A and to one verb of conjugation 7D.

Rule 7

In remote and counterfactual verb forms of conjugation 2B the sequence -Vy- is deleted immediately preceding the root-final vowel -í- (thus reducing the root by one syllable) when the consonant immediately preceding this sequence is -dj- or when the root is only three or four syllables in length with stress in the citation form on the root-initial syllable.

The following examples show the results of the application of this rule, with the final example (yawarlékkayi) showing the non-application of the rule because its structural description is not met. For each example the following forms are given: root, meaning, actual remote/counterfactual form (following application of Rule 7), postulated underlying remote/counterfactual form (prior to application of Rule 7 – starred form).

búdjeyi	'shout'	-badjí-na	<*-badjayí-na
rlábayi	'descend'	-rlabí-na	<*-rlabayí-na
ndabarlíndjeyi	'turn (INTR)'	-ndabarlandjí-na	<*-ndabarlandjayí-na
rníbayi	'go underground'	-rnabí-na	<*-rnabayí-na
mérabayi	'hide (INTR)'	-marabí-na	<*-marabayí-na
yawarlékkayi	'run out, finish, be used up'	-yawarlakkayí-na	<-yawarlakkayí-na

3.6.17 DERIVATIONAL AFFIXES.

Ndjébbana has only two clear derivational affixes used with verbs. In both cases the productivity of the affix is uncertain. A further formative seems to take the form of a prefix -nda- but the function of this apparent formative is not clear.

[a] *-yi- Intransitiviser/Reflexive/Reciprocal (REFL).* The reflexive/ reciprocal/ intransitiviser suffix, normally termed simply 'reflexive' and glossed REFL, is the characteristic formative of conjugation 2 verb (§3.6. an has the underlying form *-yi- which is actually realised as -yí- in the remote and counterfactual forms of verbs of conjugation 2B, in which the major stress falls on the root- or stem-final syllable. In the remaining forms of conjugation 2B and in all forms of verbs in conjugation 2A the major stress does not fall on this syllable, so the reflexive/reciprocal/intransitiviser suffix is realised as unstressed -ya-. It is possible that the Ndjébbana reflexive/reciprocal/intrans-itiviser suffix *-yi- is a reflex of the postulated proto-Australian reflexive/intransitiviser suffix *-DHirri-y (Dixon 1980:447–8).

It is unclear how productive this suffix is in Ndjébbana, and it is equally unclear on what basis intransitivised verbs are distributed between the patterns of conjugation 2A, with fixed stress placement, and conjugation 2B with shifting stress. Many of the verbs in conjugation 2 which are formed using the intransitivising suffix -yi- have transitive counterparts without the suffix in other conjugations. Examples of such verbs are listed in §3.6.7. There are, however, a number of intransitive verbs formed using this suffix for which no transitive counterpart is known in any other conjugation. These include such verbs as:

búdje-yi	'shout, call out'(2B)	kkamí-ya	'get up, set off'(2A)
rlába-yi	'descend'(2B)	mayáwa-yi	'sing'(2B)
ngawí-ya	'thunder'(2A)	ngúdje-yi	'speak'(2B)
réndje-yi	'stand'(2B)		

The few verbs of conjugation 2 with root- or stem-final -ka- and -dja- are still without explanation.

The -yi- suffix has a syntactic effect and a range of meanings which is characteristic of this type of suffix in many Australian languages (Dixon 1980:447–8; Blake 1987:57).

A verb derived using the -yi- prefix is intransitive and therefore takes an intransitive pronominal prefix marking the S of the sentence. It may not take a transitive prefix form, unlike the transitive or ditransitive verb it may be derived from, as in the following verb forms:

banda-mérba-ra	barra-mérba-ya	*banda-mérba-ya
3MINA+3AUGO-hide-CTP	3AUGS-hide-REFL(+CTP)	
He is hiding them.	They are hiding [themselves].	

dja-djáma-nga	ngana-djáma-ya-na/	*dja-djáma-ya-na/
2MINA+3MINO-wash-REM	ngana-yama-yí-na	*dja-yama-yí-na
You washed it.	2MINS-wash-REFL-REM	
	You washed [yourself].	

One of the principal functions of the reflexive suffix is to derive reflexive verbs. These are marked with an S pronominal prefix (either singular or plural), the referent of which functions simultaneously as A and O of the underlying transitive verb from which the reflexive verb stem is derived. Thus, for instance, the verb form ngana-djáma-ya-na above has a second person minimal S prefix which indicates that the agent (A) and the patient (O) of the act of washing were identical. Without the reflexive suffix, as in dja-djáma-nga, the agent and the patient are necessarily referentially distinct. See also the text examples (61) and (62), in which the reflexive and non-reflexive forms of the verb djákkabo 'tie up, bind' are compared.

(61)   Wékkana   ka-rlarrabí-na   bana-yakkabé-ra.
         night time   3MINS-arrive-REM   3MINA+3AUGO-tie/bind-REM
         He came during the night and handcuffed them [Aboriginal people]. (II/107)

(62)   Nganéyabba-kkawa   ka-wala-bé-na   kalíkku...
         there-ABL   3MINS-come.hither-go-REM   cloth
         njarra-yikkabí-ya-na
         1AUGS-tie/bind-REFL-REM
         Cloth arrived from there...We put on nagas [a piece of cloth passed between the legs and held up by knotting on each side at the waist]. (V/156–8)

     A further significant function of the reflexive suffix -yi- is to derive reciprocal verb forms. The (necessarily non-singular) S prefix of the derived reciprocal verb refers to a number of individuals who function as A and O (or IO in the case of a ditransitive verb) for a series of different acts or a complex act of some duration described by the underlying transitive verb. That is the reciprocal verb describes a situation of 'doing something to each other', as exemplified in (63) in which the base verb is djébba 'deprive someone of something, take something away from someone', a ditransitive verb with which the transitive prefix would mark the A and the IO. In the derived reciprocal verb form the S prefix marks the three players as functioning both as A and as IO towards one another in the struggle for the ball.

(63)   ...barra-ddjébba-ya   budborl.
         3AUGS-deprive.of-REFL+CTP   football
         They [one Kunibidji player and two Burarra players] are trying to get the ball [=are trying to deprive each other or prevent each other getting the football – in a description of a photograph of play].

     While the meaning is unambiguously reflexive when the S prefix of a derived reflexive verb refers only to a single individual, when the S prefix refers to more than one individual the reflexive verb is formally ambiguous between the reflexive and the reciprocal interpretations, though this may be contextually quite clear. Thus, for instance, in example (62) the final verb form could refer either to a situation in which the people each tied their own nagas (reflexive) or to one in which they tied nagas for each other (reciprocal) (or, indeed, to one in which both things occurred). There is no formal difference between the two in Ndjébbana. Example (64) is a further one in which both reflexive and reciprocal interpretations would surely be simultaneously valid.

(64)   Márru nála   ka-ngódja-ya-na.
         [name] name   3MINMASCS-call.name-REFL-REM
         They [lit. 'he'] called themselves Márru [people].   (II/81)

Finally the so-called reflexive suffix -yi- is used to derive intransitive verbs from transitives in cases where it is not really plausible to consider a reflexive or a reciprocal interpretation applicable. Verbs of reflexive form but without transitive counterparts (such as ngúdje-yi and others listed above) also fall within this category of formally reflexive verbs which do not have reflexive or reciprocal meanings. In such cases the -yi- suffix functions as a simple intransitiviser which converts the O of the base transitive verb into the S of the derived intransitive, simply omitting the A of the base transitive verb from the pronominal prefix complex of the derived intransitive verb in the process, as is evident from the following examples of intransitive verbs with their transitive counterparts. In some cases the English passive provides a good comparison in this respect. (Note that this intransitivising use of the reflexive suffix syntactically parallels the English passive and is distinct from the 'anti-passive' construction reported from a number of Australian languages in which the underlying A can be put into derived S position (Dixon 1980:445–8).)

With the derived intransitive verb yawarlékkayi 'use up, finish; die', the intransitive stem has an additional syllable ya- prefixed to the stem, when compared to the transitive root. The transitive warlékka is a verb of conjugation 7D for which the remote suffix is -ya and the future suffix -Ø (without the -ya). Contrast the derived intransitive for which the remote suffix is -na and the future -Ø, both retaining the -yi/-ya reflexive suffix. Rule 3 (unstressed vowel reduction §3.6.16) accounts for the vowel variation between the members of certain pairs of examples. See also example (16) (§3.2.3).

ka-nmarabúya -ya
3MINS-bury-REFL-CTP
He is buried [there].

ba-rra-nmarabúya
3AUGA+3MINO-bury+CTP
They are burying him.

ka-bíwa-ya
3MINS-smell-REFL+CTP
It [e.g. meat] stinks/smells.

ka-bíwa-nga
3MINA+3MINMASCO-smell-CTP
He/she can smell it [e.g. meat].

ka-ya-nangardórrddje-ya
3MINS-IRR-break-REFL
It will break.

ka-ya-nangardórrddja
3MINA+3MINO-IRR-break
He/she will break it.

ka-yawarlakka-yí-na
3MINS-use.up-REFL-REM
It ran out/was used up. / He died.

ka-warlékka-ya
3MINA+3MINO-use.up-REM
He/she used it all up

ka-ngadjba-yí-na
3MINS-get.better-REM
It [sore] got better.

ka-ngódjba-na
3MINA+3MINO-make/repair-REM
He/she repaired it/made it better.

[b] *Infinitive (INFIN)*.   The infinitive form of the verb for each conjugation has been described in §§3.6.6 to 3.6.16. The infinitive is indicated by a na- prefix to the verb root except when the root has initial underlying unstressed dja-. In this case there is no infinitive prefix. In all known cases, except for conjugations 5B and 8A, there is no suffix on the infinitive form (§3.6.6, Table 3.18).

In addition to being used in the auxiliary form of the counterfactual (its most widespread use), the infinitive form of the verb appears to be able to function as a nominal form. This is clear only with three verbs, the infinitive forms of which have been encountered being used as nominals. Of these the last two are clearly marked as nominals of possession class D2 by their agreement prefix (§3.2.3), given here in the third person minimal masculine form nga- prefixed to the infinitive prefix na-.

djarnarrába 'sneeze/cough' (V, 4C)
rárrma 'be white, clean' (V, 1)
warrámayi 'be skinny' (V, 2B)

djarnarrába 'cough/sneeze' (N)
nga-na-rárrma 'white, light' (N, D2)
nga-na-warrámaya 'skinny (no flesh)'
(N, D2)

See, for instance, example (65).

(65)   nga-na-rárrma   ngí-ya-wo
        3MINMASC-INFIN-be.white   1/2UAA+3MINO+IRR-kó-give
        Let's give it [large number of fish] to the white man [in exchange for money
        and goods]. (I/274)

Furthermore, the phrase ránba nga-na-rárrma, based on the nominal ránba 'beach', has been glossed as 'clean sand'.

[c] *-nda-*. The apparent formative -nda- occurs on a small number of verbs, very few of which have counterparts without such a formative. While one possible meaning for this formative is something like 'inceptive' or 'inchoative', this is not clearly established by the available evidence. The verbs involved are listed here with their meanings and with their counterparts which have no -nda- formative. The only evidence that this -nda- could be construed formally as an affix is provided by verbs which have counterparts without the -nda-, even though these verb pairs do not suggest a clear meaning for the affix.

nda-bakkúrrngarna	'sit (INCHO)'(2B)		
nda-barlíndja	'turn (TR)'(1)		
nda-barlíndje-yi	'turn (INTR)'(2B)		
nda-búyi	'lick, smack lips'(6B)		
nda-karlába	'immerse'(3)	karlába	'immerse'(3)
nda-káwa	'be ready to take turn/dance'(5A)		
nda-lakalóma	'straighten'(1)		
nda-máwa	'tether, tie up'(5A)	máwa	'tie'(5A)
nda-méraba-yi	'set (sun)'(2B)	méraba-yi	'hide (INTR), go inside or underneath'(2B)
nda-rraddjáddja	'stop (TR)'(1A)		
nda-rraddjáddja-yi	'stop (INTR)'(2A)		
nda-warré	'be high in sky (sun)'(5B)	warré	'jump, be born, cross (creek), take off (plane)'(5B)
nda-yárraba	'fling down, knock over'(4A)		

3.6.18   VERB COMPOUNDING WITH BALO.   The Ndjébbana directional verb baló 'come hither or this way' can be used as an independent verb but it is more frequently incorporated within the verb complex to form a compound verb. In (66) the independent form is followed by an auxiliary incorporating the directional verb. When incorporated this verb is glossed simply as 'hither'.

(66)   Bá-rra-balo   ba-rra-bala-yirrí-ya.
        3AUGS-RE-come.hither   3AUGS-RE-hither-go-CTP
        They were coming towards us. (XXV/49)

Used as an independent verb baló has underlying stress on its final syllable, so this moves to word-initial position when it would otherwise be word-final, as in (66). (Compare Text 25/26, where stress remains in position because the extent suffix follows.)

Incorporated into another verb complex, baló usually loses its own stress, unless stress occurs as a result of a following -kó- (see example (67)). Both vowels of the incorporated root reduce to a (-bala-), and if the main verb root of the complex has an initial labial stop or nasal the initial b of -bala- lenites to w, which, in turn, phonetically colours the following vowel to give a form written -wala- but usually pronounced as -wola-.

The meaning contribution of this incorporated compounding verb can be clearly seen by comparing the following pairs of verb complexes, with and without -bala-, in which the pronominal prefix is held constant:

ka-ddjórrkka   ka-bala-ddjórrkka
3MINA+3MINMASCO-take(+REM)   -hither-take(+REM)
He took it.   He brought it.

ka-bé-na   ka-wala-bé-na
3MINMASCS-go-REM   -hither-go-REM
He went.   He came. / He arrived.

The incorporated verb baló occurs in the verb complex following the realis or irrealis prefix and preceding the -kó- prefix, as shown by the following text form and one in (67).

nga-ya-bala-rlábaya
1MINS-IRR-hither-descend
I'll come down [from top camp].

Incorporated baló also follows the aversative prefix -wu-, but, because the incorporated verb has an initial labial stop, it causes the deletion of the aversative prefix, leaving only the copied -u- vowels in the pronominal prefix forms to mark the aversative.

See examples of the use of -baló- in Text 7/6–7, Texts 9/14, 35, 37–8, and Texts 25/26, 29, 45, 49, 54, 65, 67 and 92.

There are two verb roots which appear to derive from this compounding process but the deletion of a syllable -wa- from the original underlying main verb roots has obscured the derivation. Balákka 'return, come back' probably derives from an original compound of baló 'come hither' and wákka 'go back, return' (*bala-wákka), while balála 'come in (tide)' probably derives from an original compound of baló 'come hither' and wála 'ascend' (*bala-wála). The verb 'to dawn' is derived using -baló- 'hither' and nabo 'step, dance' to give -balanabo- (6A). See Texts 7/23 and 25/12.

3.6.19 PHRASAL VERBS. Ndjébbana has a significant number of phrasal verbs, which can be divided into two main types: particle phrasal verbs and dual phrasal verbs. Both types are largely idiomatic. A third type of 'phrasal verb' is also presented, the affix phrasal verbs. These verb complexes are single words but they have fixed affixes either preceding or following the affixes which would normally come word initially or finally.

    [a] *Particle phrasal verbs.* The first type, which we will term *particle phrasal verbs*, is formed using a non-verb word or particle (frequently invariant) followed by a fully inflected verb. Generally speaking the meaning of the phrase cannot be predicted from the meanings of its parts, though with some of the examples included here this is not strictly the case. The particle phrasal verbs encountered so far are listed, grouped according to the main inflected verb of each. The literal meaning of the inflected verb form is given

in each heading and the meaning of the 'particle' as it appears in other contexts is indicated where this is known.

bá 'eat, bite'   (*ka-bá-la 'he ate/bit it'*)
n-bókka ['bad'] ka-bá-la   ngaléwara ['what?'] ka-bá-la
He missed it [shooting]   What happened to him?

bándja 'put'   (*ba-rra-bbándja 'they put it'*)
márdba ('neck') nga-bbándja   márnabba-yinjírra ('our chests') ba-rra-bbándja
I like it.   They came towards us.

bú 'hit'   (*ka-bbó-na 'he hit it'*)
karlóykkarloy ka-bbó-na   márrmarr   ka-bbó-na
He split it [e.g.wood].   He was happy.

djórrkka 'take'   (*ka-ddjórrkka 'he took it'*)
bordolbbordol ka-ddjórrkka
He rubbed/rolled it [to make string or cigarette].

djuwé 'suffer'   (*ka-ddjúwa 'he is suffering'*)
ména ('hungry/hunger') ka-ddjúwa
He's hungry.

má 'get, fetch'   (*ka-má-ngka 'he is getting it'*)
djábbarda ('lip, brim, full(ness)') ka-má-ngka   djakí ('speed') ka-má-ngka
He is filling it.   He's walking quickly.

ngúdji-ba ('story+EXT') ka-má-ngka   wédda ka-má-nga
He's telling the story.   He went past him/it.

nabó 'step, stamp, dance'   (*ka-nabé-ra 'it stepped/danced'*)
lándiba ka-nabé-ra
It was calm (sea).

rdéddjeya 'spear (REFLEXIVE)'   (*ka-rdéddjeya 'he speared himself'*)
márnabba ('chest') ka-rdéddjeya
He raised [aimed] his gun.

rimí 'hold, grasp'   (*ka-ramí-ya-na 'he held himself REFLexive'*)
kúdja ('hand/foot') ka-ramí-ya-na
He finished the job.

rakarawo 'move'   (*ka-rakarawé-ra 'he moved'*)
kalábba   ka-rakarawé-ra
He forgot/lost it.

rawo 'throw'   (*ká-rawo 'he is throwing it', yá-ka-ro 'let us throw it'*)
djakóra ká-rawo   kánkarra ('meat') yá-ka-ro
He is smoking.   Let's hurry.

wákka 'return, go back'   (*ka-wákka-na 'he went back'*)
ka-wákka-na n-barrábarra ('MASC-big') (cf. barrábarra karéndjeya 'his backbone')
He reversed (in vehicle).

yángka 'do'   (*ka-yángka-na 'he/it did'*)
lérra ka-yángka-na   mayurd ka-yángka-na
It dropped out [of their hands].   It/he ran away.

na-wála ('INFIN-ascend') ka-yángka-na
He vomited.

Interestingly this particular type of construction is used to borrow English verbs. Rather than providing borrowed verb roots directly with Ndjébbana verbal affixes, the English verb is treated as an invariant particle and a fully inflected verb (normally nó 'sit') is used with it as in Text 25/1, Text 9/17 and (67) to (69). The various English verb forms encountered include the simple root (Text 25/1, Text 9/17), the -ing form (67), a nominalisation (68) and a form marked with the pidgin or creole transitiviser -im (69).

(67)   ...wékkana   wébba   drabling   nga-baló-ka-na
             night   ?   travelling IMINS-hither-kó-sit(REM)
          I travelled (this way) at night. (V/249)

(68)   Obréddjin   kó-na   djíya
          operation   (1MINS)-kó-sit(+REM)   here
          I had an operation here [pointing to area]. (JB)

(69)   Mákkim   ka-kó-na   ka-ná-na.
          mark   3MINMASCS-kó-sit   3MINA+3MINMASCO-see-REM
          He marked it out [site for drilling bores near airstrip]. (XIV/222)

In (67) note the incorporation of baló into what is otherwise a positional, not a motion verb; compounding with the invariant particle drabling is apparently not possible.

The particle phrasal verb construction is similar to the attributive clause type in which a nominal indicating some attributed quality is used with a positional verb as, for example:

          barakángka   nga-nó-ra
          worn.out   1MINS-sit-CTP
          I'm worn out.

[b] *Dual phrasal verbs.* The second type of phrasal verb, which we will term *dual phrasal verb*, is formed using two fully inflected verb forms. The meaning of the combination is different from the sum of the meanings of the verbs involved. Only two of these phrasal verbs have been encountered:

ka-kkúndja
3MINA+3MINO-defecate/lay(CTP)
he is running/moving fast

ká-rakarawo
3MINS-move(CTP)

ka-má-ngka
3MINA+3MINO-get-CTP
He's working.

ka-réndjeya
3MINS-stand(CTP)

Note that the A of the first (transitive) verb as marked in the pronominal prefix is identical to the S of the second (intransitive) verb, and that both verbs are identical in terms of tense, mood and so on.

The dual phrasal verb construction clearly involves idiomatic phrases formed in the manner of the regular auxiliary construction discussed in §3.6.20 and §4.2.6.

[c] *Affix phrasal verbs.* The type of verb termed here 'affix phrasal verb' has an obligatory affix (either prefix or suffix) attached to the verb complex outside the normal pronominal and tense affixes. In most cases the affix has not been found in other contexts and does not appear to have a separate meaning on its own. In one or two cases the extent suffix (§3.2.4) occurs. In the list which follows elements which are known to have a separate meaning outside the affix phrasal verb combination have that separate meaning listed alongside.

ka-bbínbi-ri-ba (-ba EXT)
3MINA+3MINMASCS-write-CTP-
he is writing

ka-ddjórrk(ka)-ngaya (-djórrkka 'take')
3MINMASCS-run-
he is running

ka-má-ngki-ba (-má- 'get'; -ba EXT)
3MINMASCS-lightning-CTP-
lightning is flashing

ka-yakkabo-ngódda (-djakkabo 'tie up')
3MINA+3MINMASCO-roll.up.swag(+CTP)-
he's rolling up his swag

kí-bi-rri-yángka (-yángka 'do')
-3UAMASCS-RE-say/tell+CTP)
they (two) are saying

[d] *Emotion and sensation phrases.* A number of phrasal expressions which deal with emotion, sensation and some bodily functions can be mentioned here. Of particular interest are those which involve a nominal referring to the emotion or sensation and the experiencer being marked as the O of the verb bú 'hit' or another transitive verb.

kayókaya   njanda-bbú-ra-yana
sleep(M)   3MINA+1MINO-hit-CTP-3MINMASCDATA
I'm sleepy.

djarramáya   njana-bbó-na-yana
laugh(INFIN)   3MINA+1MINO-hit-rem-3MINMASCDATA
He laughed at me.

ngánjbarl   njana-rawé-ra-yangaya
sneeze(FEM)   3MINA+1MINO-throw-REM-3MINFEMDATA
I sneezed.

warayéma   njana-ramí-yana
                 3MINA+1MINO-hold/grasp[CTP]-3MINMASCDATA
He made me ashamed.

This last phrase is claimed to be quite different in meaning from nga-warayémaya, which means 'I'm frightened'.

Other phrases of interest here, apart from those listed among the idiomatic phrasal verbs above, are the following (collected by Eather):

djánama   nga-warrabú-ra   nga-réndjeya
stomach   1MINS-burn-CTP   1MINS-stand
I'm angry.

djánama   nga-rnarrabayí-na
stomach   1MINS-split-REM
I got a shock, I'm frightened ["heart crack"].

mangúya   ka-ddjúwa   ka-nó-ra
throat   3MINS-suffer   3MINS-sit-CTP
I'm really sad.

yúrnka-njabba   ká-rawo
head-1MINPOSS   3MINA+3MINO-throw(+CTP)
I've got a headache.

3.6.20 VERB AUXILIARY CONSTRUCTION. Ndjébbana verbs frequently occur with a following auxiliary verb, which is normally a verb of position or motion. Both verbs are fully inflected for person, number, tense, mood and so on. This construction will be treated in more detail in the syntax chapter §4.2.6. The agreement required between main verb and auxiliary can be exploited to provide disambiguation of main verb pronominal prefixes (§3.6.21) and tense (§4.2.6).

3.6.21   AGREEMENT: PERSON, NUMBER, GENDER.   Agreement in person, number and gender is a prominent feature of Ndjébbana, serving to tie texts together and to provide disambiguation in certain cases. Gender classes, masculine and feminine, have been outlined and examples of agreement within noun phrases have been given in §3.2.2 and person and number categories have been outlined in §3.3.2.

Agreement is marked using pronominal verb prefixes (§3.3.3), independent and suffix pronouns (§3.3.1) and nominal affixes (§3.2.2 and §3.2.3). Agreement may encompass some or all of person, number and gender.

The agreement between the head nominal of a NP and other nominals in apposition to or qualifying it (e.g. in the manner of adjectives) is discussed in §3.2.2 and §3.2.3.

Two principal areas of agreement marking which affect verbs are:

[1] the agreement between a core argument marked on the verb (that is the subject (A or S) and/or object (O or IO) pronominal prefix of a verb) and any accompanying free-standing nominal or pronoun in apposition to it; and

[2] the agreement between the subject (A or S) of a verb and the subject (S) of an accompanying auxiliary verb.

Example (70) is an example of the first type of agreement marking, that between a verb complex and the associated core nominals.

(70)   Nja-rra-ná-dja   makéddja
         1AUGA+3MINO-RE-see-CTP   long-necked turtle (FEM)

         ya-rríkka   nja-nabarlámbarla,
         3MINFEMS-crawl(+CTP)   3MINFEM-freshwater

         nja-barrábarra. Nga-má-ngka...
         3MINFEM-big   1MINA+3MINO-pick.up-CTP
         We saw a long-necked turtle crawling along, the fresh water one, a big one. I
         picked it up... (25/17–19)

There is an agreement chain in this sequence based on the nominal makéddja 'long-necked turtle', which is a feminine noun and minimal in number, referring to a single animal. The first verb njarranádja is marked as having a third person minimal O (the turtle), but no gender distinction can be made in this prefix form. The second verb yarríkka is marked as having a third person minimal feminine S, referring to the turtle. The following two nominals njabarlámbarla and njabarrábarra are marked by prefix as agreeing with the third person minimal feminine nominal makéddja. In the following sentences of this text (Text 25/19–21), following the same pattern, the transitive verbs mark person and number but not gender of the nominal makéddja 'turtle' as O while the nominals agree with it in person, number and gender. See also examples (126), (127) and (128).

The second main type of agreement affecting the verb is when an auxiliary verb is used with a main verb (§4.2.6). In this case the pronominal subjects A or S of both verbs generally agree (as far as the morphology permits) in person, number and gender and the verbs agree in tense, aspect and mood, as in the two auxiliary constructions of example (71).

(71)   Ka-rakarawé-ri-ba   ka-kkó-ya
         3MINMASCS-move-REM-EXT 3MINMASCS-kó-lie/sleep(+REM)
         nji-rri-bbándje-ya-na   nji-rri-kkó-ya   dórdbalk.
         1UAS-RE-put-REFL-REM   1UAS-RE-kó-lie/sleep(+REM)   good
         When [the wind] was blowing (moving) we would sleep all right [without
         disturbance from mosquitoes]. (XVIII/11–12]

Both types of agreement affecting the verbs occur in the further example (72).

(72)   Nja-njárlkkidj   ya-warrabó-na   ya-kkó-ya
         3MINFEM-soft 3MINFEMS-cook-REM   3MINFEMS-kó-lie
         mandjébba   karrakanódjabba   ya-ngalddjáyiba-na.
         until   in.the.morning   3MINA+3MINFEMO-take.out-REM
         It [trepang (FEM)] would cook until it was really soft and next morning
         [they] would empty it out [of the *kawa* or cooking pot]. (V/49)

Agreement is marked even when the determining nominal is not actually overt within the same sentence. Thus in Text 7/27–31 the feminine nominal máwala is introduced at the beginning of the sequence but in the first few sentences the morphology does not permit the gender agreement to be marked explicitly. Finally in Text 7/30 the gender agreement is marked on the verb, even though the nominal no longer appears within the sentence.

When the main verb is transitive its pronominal prefix marks both A and either O or IO, depending on whether the verb is transitive or ditransitive. The S pronominal prefix on an accompanying auxiliary verb agrees with the A prefix on the main verb:

(73)   Bi-rri-ddjó-nga   bá-rri-na.
         3UAA+3MINMASCO-RE-berate-REM   3UAS-RE-sit
         They (two) went mad at him. (VII/76)

Some transitive pronominal prefixes are ambiguous and in these cases the S prefix on the accompanying auxiliary may well disambiguate the prefix on the preceding verb. (The auxiliary can also disambiguate the tense of the main verb as discussed in §4.2.6.)

Thus, for instance, the third person minimal A prefix form does not distinguish masculine from feminine, unlike the third person minimal S and O forms. In an example like (74), then, it is the S prefix on the auxiliary which alone clearly indicates that the subject (A and S) of the main verb preceding it is feminine.

(74)   ...díla-ngáya   mándjad   ka-ná-dja
         eye-3MINFEMPOSS   straight/true   3MINA+3MINMASCO-see-CTP
         ya-ka-yó-ra.
         3MINFEMS-kó-lie-CTP
         [The buffalo cow] looked straight at him [as he approached]. (25/52–3)

All transitive pronominal prefix forms in which both A and O are non-minimal are multiply ambiguous. These are the forms in which -nbi-(rri-) follows one of the non-minimal person markers nja-, nga-, na- or ba- (see §3.3.4). Thus the form njanbirri- in isolation could refer to any one of the following combinations of A and O: first person non-minimal A (i.e. 1UAMASCA, 1UAFEMA or 1AUGA) with third person non-minimal O (3UAMASCO, 3UAFEMO, 3AUGO) (see Table 3.3); or second person non-minimal A (2UAMASCA, 2UAFEMA, 2AUGA) with first person non-minimal O (1UAMASCO, 1UAFEMO, IAUGO) (see Table 3.5); or third person non-minimal A (3UAMASCA, 3UAFEMA, 3AUGA) with first person non-minimal O (1UAMASCO, 1UAFEMO, 1AUGO) (see Table 3.5).

These 27 possible combinations of A and O will normally be at least partially disambiguated by the context, as they are in Text 25/78–80 in which the preceding and following intransitive verbs disambiguate the A and the O respectively as both unit augmented masculine. In Text 25/40 the A of the prefix of the main verb (njanbi-rri-ná-dja) is disambiguated by the following auxiliary but, to disambiguate the O, reference must be made to the preceding context, which shows it to be third person augmented. Note, that the S pronominal prefix of a following intransitive auxiliary clearly specifies the A of the main verb by agreement. (It is only in the light of this agreement and of other contextual clues that it is possible to give such a specific gloss for the pronominal prefix njanbi-rri- rather than '1NON-MINA+3NON-MINO-RE-' or '2 or 3NON-MINA+1NON-MINO-RE-'.)

4.   SYNTAX

4.1   BASIC CLAUSE

The common concept of a clause as containing a verb plus certain essential core participants marked by separate noun phrases and with optional modifiers at either the clause or the NP level is not entirely suitable to describe the 'clause' in Ndjébbana. In spite of this we will continue to use the term 'clause' rather than attempting to introduce any new term. Syntax in Ndjébbana has been less well studied than morphology and future work will further refine the analysis presented here, which is based primarily on tape-recorded narrative and descriptive text.

In Ndjébbana the basic clause consists simply of the inflected verb complex (§3.6). Every verb complex in Ndjébbana (§3.6.1) contains within it the verb root plus pronominal affixes marking the core participants or arguments in the clause (§§3.6.2, 3.6.3, 4.2.1), as well as tense/aspect/mood modification (§§3.6.4 and 3.6.5). The structure of the verb complex is summarised in Table 3.7 (§3.6.1).

This basic clause may be further elaborated or modified, but such elaboration is not grammatically necessary and, indeed, is not common. Elaboration and modification occurs using independent pronouns, free nominals, adverbs, and so on. These elements are often 'tacked on' in apposition to the pronominal core arguments already included within the verb complex and these additional elements frequently form a separate intonation contour as 'afterthoughts'.

A count of a small amount of narrative text material shows that almost forty per cent of clauses contain only a verb complex. Almost ten per cent of clauses contain an intransitive verb complex plus an independent nominal or pronoun representing the intransitive subject S, and only about two per cent of clauses contain a transitive verb complex and independent nominals or pronouns representing both transitive subject or agent A and object O (or indirect object IO in the case of ditransitive verbs). Approximately a further ten per cent of clauses contain a transitive verb complex and an independent nominal or pronoun representing only one of the core participants, normally the O. In all these cases where independent nominals or pronouns occur, they are in apposition to the bound pronominal marking of S or A and O/IO, and provide elaboration, clarification, focus or contrast. Additional non-core elements may be included in the clause. The verb complex would always be a complete and grammatical utterance on its own.

A small number of clauses contain no verb at all but have nominal or other predicates.

4.2   VERB AS PREDICATE

The large majority of clauses have a verb complex as their main or only component.

To provide the basis for discussion of basic verb-based clause structure in the sections which follow we will use the first few lines of a recorded text narrating events on a hunting trip. Each unit with final falling intonation and pause is treated as a separate clause, except that a comma separates items which are 'tacked on' to the main clause either as afterthoughts or because they are added following a non-final intonation. Though the clauses are numbered separately for ease of reference in the discussion they actually form a connected sequence from the beginning of the text (Text XXXI). The text material provided in the appendix will provide further exemplification of these points.

(75)   Nji-rri-kkó-ya.
         1UAMASCS-RE-kó-lie(+REM)
         We slept.

(76)   Ka-bala-nabé-ra.
         3MINMASCS-come hither-step-REM
         Dawn came.

(77)   Ka-ngadjí-na   ngabúyanga   'Yí-yarra,
         3MINMASCS-speak-REM   1MINDAT   1/2MINS+IRR-go(+FUT)
            nganabbárru.'
            buffalo
         He said to me, 'Let's go [for] buffalo.'

(78)   Bálay   nji-rri-bé-na.
         afterwards, already   1UAS-RE-go-REM
         So we went.

(79)   Nakébba   ngalidjbínja
         3MINMASCCARD   shotgun(FEM)
            ya-ka-ddjórrkka.
            3MINA+3MINFEMO-kó-take(+REM)
         He took a shotgun.

(80)   Ngáyabba   dídjburrk   nga-ddjórrkka.
         1MINCARD   axe   1MINA+3MINO-take(+REM)
         I took an axe.

(81)   Nji-rri-rakarawé-ra   nji-rri-bé-na   namarnakkúrrkka.
         1UAS-RE-move-REM   1UAS-RE-go-REM   creek
         We went along [and came to] a creek.

(82)   Nji-rri-rakarawé-ra   nji-rri-bé-na,   djábbarnma
       1UAS-RE-move-REM   1UAS-RE-go-REM   'sugarbag'/wild honey
       nga-ná-na.
       1MINA+3MINO-see-REM
       We were going along [when] I saw some sugarbag [a wild beehive in tree].

(83)   Ka-ŋgadjí-na   ngabúyanga
       3MINMASCS-speak-REM   1MINDAT
       He said to me:

(84)   'Djádja   yi-wúnkarla,   djábbarnma.'
       uncle   1/2MINA+3MINO+IRR-cut (through)(+FUT)   sugarbag
       'Uncle, let's cut it, [the tree] [to get] the sugarbag.'

(85)   'Ma-yí-ndja.'
       MINIMP+3MINO-leave-CTP
       'Leave it.'

(86)   Nga-ŋgadjí-na   ngáyabba.
       1MINS-speak-REM   1MINCARD
       I said.

(87)   Nji-rri-nji-rri-bé-na.
       1UAS-RE-1UAS-RE-go-REM
       We kept on going.

4.2.1   TRANSITIVITY IN THE BASIC VERBAL CLAUSE.   Each
Ndjébbana verb belongs uniquely to one of three transitivity classes as
outlined in §3.6.2. These transitivity classes are based on the core arguments
obligatorily marked by pronominal prefixes to the verb complex as set out
below. (S means subject of intransitive verb, A means subject of transitive
verb (including ditransitive), O means direct object of transitive verb
(including ditransitive), and IO means indirect object of ditransitive verb.)

Intransitive   S
(Mono-)Transitive   A O
Ditransitive   A [O] IO   } Transitive

Intransitive prefix forms mark the S of an intransitive verb.
Transitive prefixes mark both the A and the O of a transitive verb or the A and
IO of a ditransitive verb. The O of a ditransitive verb, though not overtly
marked by the pronominal prefix, is clearly understood to be a core element in
the clause. This is why it is given above in brackets.
      In the example text the verbs of (79), (80), (84), (85) and the second
verb of (82) are transitive, the remaining verbs are intransitive. Further
examples are given in §§3.6.1–3.

As can be seen in examples like (75), (84) and (85), the pronominal prefix on the verb is quite sufficient and there is no need to use independent nominals or pronouns to refer to the core arguments. It is possible to use independent nominals or pronouns in apposition to the pronominal prefix to clarify or further specify the S as in (86) or the A and O as in (79) and (80).

4.2.2 EXPANDING CORE ARGUMENTS: INDEPENDENT PRONOUNS AND NOMINALS. The basic means of indicating the core arguments of the clause is the pronominal prefix attached to the verb. These pronominal prefixes may be expanded (that is elaborated on or further specified) if there is a need to do so from the pragmatic point of view. This is not necessary from the grammatical point of view.

Such expansion or elaboration of the core pronominal arguments is achieved by using independent pronouns, demonstratives or nominals. Of the example sentences, (79), (80) and (86) have core arguments expanded. In all cases the subjects (A or S) are expressed by means of an independent pronoun in apposition to the basic pronominal prefix reference. In the two transitive clauses the O pronominal reference is expanded using a free nominal.

Independent pronouns, as in these clauses, are normally used only to express some kind of contrastive identification. The pair of sentences (79) and (80) together expresses an explicit contrast. In clause (86) there is a contrast with clause (83), though only in (86) is the independent pronoun used to clarify the identity of the subject.

A similar, clearly contrastive example is (88). In this example the independent pronouns are further specified using nominals. The third clause is a verbless clause (§4.3).

(88)	Ka-wéndja-nga.		Ngayábba	ngarráma	kádja
	3MINMASCS-climb.up-REM		3MINFEMCARD	female	under
	ya-kkó-ya.		Nakébba	lárla-na	
	3MINFEMS-kó-lie		3MINMASCCARD	male-3MINMASCPOSS	
	málaya.	Ya-ramé-ra.			
	on.top	3MINA+3MINFEMO-hold/grasp-REM			

He [male turtle] mounted. The female was underneath and the male was on top. He mated with her. (XXI/37–8)

Further examples of the use of the cardinal and emphatic pronouns in this contrastive sense are (25) and (26) in §3.3.1 and Text 25/24, 95–6.

In example (89) and in Text 9/4, 13, 22 and 33, the independent pronoun could be seen as a 'new subject' or 'change of subject' marker. This is, of course, another form of contrastive use, marking a contrast with the subject of the preceding sentences. In (89) the new subject in the second sentence is included within the subject of the preceding sentence, but is 'new' and contrastive in the sense that the 'others' making up the original augmented subject remained behind. Compare example (124).

(89)   Mardbalk   nja-rrú-ka-na.   Ngáyabba yaláwa
        Goulburn Island   1AUGS-RE-kó-sit   1MINCARD then
        nga-wala-bé-na   yawúyakka.
        1MINS-come.hither-go-REM   first

We all stayed at Goulburn Island. I was the first to come back here. (V/202–3)

In example (90) the independent pronoun is used to mark a new focus of attention, but this time it represents the O (direct object) of the clause rather than the grammatical subject. Here the independent pronoun is used as a demonstrative adjective qualifying the nominal.

(90)   Ba-rrú-ka-na   nganéyabba   yaláwa.   Ngayábba
        3AUGS-RE-kó-sit   there   well   3MINFEMCAR
        djarríbbang   yaba-rra-kkóndja-nga.
        trepang(FEM)   3AUGA+3MINFEMO-RE-cut-REM

So they were there [Entrance Island]. That trepang, that's where they used to cut it up. (V/109)

'Change of subject' or 'new subject' need not be marked by an independent pronoun; a pronominal prefix is sufficient. See Text 25/50 and example (83) and the last sentence of (91). In this last example, however, a nominal afterthought clarifies the identity of the new subject.

Further specification of core participants in the clause can be by means of nominals as in (91), (92), (72) and Texts 25/17–19 and 21. In the last clause of (91) (following the cohesive repetition of part of the previous clause – §4.2.4) and in the first clause of (92), the nominal identifies or specifies the S and the O respectively. In the remaining clauses the nominal describes the O rather than identifying it. The nominal specification of the new subject is treated as an afterthought in the last clause of (91) and in (92) the two clauses have identical verbs and overall structure. In each of the two clauses of (92) a different nominal first identifies then describes the same referent, the O.

(91)   Bi-rri-kkimíya-na   bi-rri-ngórrddja-nga.
        3UAMASCS-RE-get.up-REM   3UAA+3MINMASCO-RE-roast-REM
        Bi-rri-ngórrddja-nga   ka-rlarrabí-na   yiberrekéyanga,
                               3MINS-arrive-REM   3UAMASCDAT
        djúrddjurd.
        eagle

The two of them got up and roasted it [kórnka 'yam']. He came up to them, the eagle did. (VII/57–8)

(92)   Kórnka   bi-rri-wú-na.
        yam   3UAA+3MINMASCIO-RE-give-REM
        N-bókka   bi-rri-wú-na.
        3MINMASC-bad   3UAA+3MINMASCIO-RE-give-REM

They gave him yams. They gave him bad ones. (VII/60)

For an example of elaboration of both A and O in a negative clause see (51), and for a series of identifying elaborations of S as afterthoughts see (136).

4.2.3 CIRCUMSTANTIAL MODIFICATION OF BASIC CLAUSE.
Clauses may be expanded in a variety of other ways to provide further circumstantial detail of the situations and events they describe, apart from the core participants. Such details can include time, manner and place, non-core participants and so on. They are expressed using adverbs, demonstratives, dative and possessive pronouns and nominals.

Given the almost total lack of case marking on Ndjébbana nominals (see §3.2.1), nominals used to modify the clause must be interpreted in context to determine their role within the clause as a whole. Thus in example (93) the nominal wúbbunj 'canoe' functions to express location, while in (94) the nominal burrúddjang 'rag' represents an instrument.

(93)   Wúbbunj   nba-rra-bbándja-nga.
        canoe   3AUGA+1MINO-RE-put-REM
        They put me into the canoe. (XXIII/18)

(94)   ...kúdja-njabba   ba-rra-yakkabé-ra   burrúddjang
            foot-1MINPOSS   3AUGA+3MINO-RE-tie-REM   rag
        ...they tied my foot up with a rag. (XX/99)

In the second sentence of (188), the time modification to the main clause appears to be in the form of a subordinate clause (the first two words) which itself contains a nominal (marráya 'dirty water') indicating location (§4.10.1).

In (95) the nominal kánbaya 'crocodile' indicates the object of hunting, which was the job undertaken by the speaker's group. The independent pronoun expresses a contrast with other groups performing different tasks.

(95)   Njírrabba   djíbba   nja-rra-má-nga
        1AUGCARD   here   1AUGA+3MINO-RE-get-REM
            nja-rra-rendjí-na   kánbaya.
            1AUGS-RE-stand-REM   crocodile
        Our group here worked [hunting for] crocodiles. (XXIII/29–30)

In (96) the modifier (the last two words) is a possessed body-part nominal phrase indicating location, the whole clause itself being a parenthetical comment on a preceding nominal phrase.

(96)   ...yókkarra   nmódda. Mankimánki   ká-rama
            fish   fish sp.   spine   3MINA+3MINO-have(+CTP)
            waláya   ka-réndjeya.
            tail   3MINMASCS-stand(+CTP)
        ...the nmódda fish. It's got spines on its tail. (XX/44)

In (97) and (98) we have examples with adverbial modification of time and degree.

(97)   Karrakanódjabba   nja-rra-wala-kkamíya-na.
        in.the.morning   1AUGS-RE-come.hither-set.off-REM
        In the morning we set off back here. (XX/6)

(98)   Barréyabba   nga-ya-njíndja-na.
        close   1MINS-IRR-cry-CF
        I almost cried [the wound from the stingray was so sore]. (XXIII/57)

A very common pattern in narrative discourse is for the clause to be uttered in its most basic verb-only form at first and subsequently to be repeated with elaboration. Such a pattern is found for example in Text 25/34–5 and a variant of it in Text 25/19–21 where the second of the two main verbs in 19–20 is repeated with elaboration of its object in clause 21. A special case of this repetition with elaboration is that of the bare main verb which is repeated in the next clause with auxiliary modification as exemplified in (117) and (121). See also Text 25/42–3 and example (6).

Frequently (the main parts of) a clause will subsequently be repeated and on each repetition a new elaboration or modifying element will be added or substituted for another (as in the first two clauses of (99)), or the ordering will be changed in order to focus on different elements of the sentence one after another (as in the last two clauses of (99)). Compare also (92) and Text 9/1–3.

(99)   Ka-nangarddjí-na   yibérra   Makbreyd.
        3MINMASCS-break+REFL-REM   3AUGDAT   ?McBride
            Ka-nangarddjí-na   Karrábbu.   Ka-wéndja-nga
                                    Junction Bay   3MINMASCS-climb-REM
            waléykkarra...   ...Nganéyabba   ka-nangarddjí-na,
            rock   ...there
            ba-rra-balákka-na   djíbba.
            3AUGS-RE-return-REM   here
            Ba-rra-ngódjba-na,   nganangórrddjeya.
            3AUGA+3MINO-RE-repair-REM   cypress.pine
            Nganangórrddjeya   ba-rra-ngódjba-na.
            cypress.pine   3AUGA+3MINO-RE-repair-REM
        Their [boat] the ?McBride was damaged on the rocks at Junction Bay. They came back here and repaired it with some cypress pine. (XIV/16–21)

4.2.4   COHESIVE REPETITION. A significant feature of discourse in Ndjébbana is the use of repetition of the main elements of a clause, in particular the verb complex, to provide a cohesive thread through a sequence of clauses. Typically this takes one of two forms.

[1] The main element(s) of the clause is repeated, adding a different elaboration or modifying element each time or replacing one such element with another. This has been discussed and exemplified at the end of §4.2.3 (examples Text 25/34–5, (92), (99)).

[2] When a sequence of actions is being described it is fairly common for the basic information from one clause (in the form of the verb complex) to be repeated at the beginning of the next sentence, with rising non-final intonation on the repetition before proceeding with the 'new' material of the sentence in the main clause, as in (91) where the 'new material' includes a subject change. Often the particle yaláwa 'finish, then, well, so' occurs at the end of the repetition as in example (100). Note the repetition of the preceding verb complex including the auxiliary in (100).

(100)	Yúya	na-yá-ka-ma.		Yaláwa
	fire/firewood	2AUGA+3MINO-IRR-kó-get		then
	ngaba-ddjórraba		ngaba-yú-ka-na.	
	1/2AUGA+3MINO(+IRR)		1/2AUGS-IRR-kó-sit	
	Ngaba-ddjórraba	ngaba-yú-ka-na		yaláwa,
				then
	ngaba-móya		ngaba-yú-ka-na	
	1/2AUGA+3MINO(+IRR)-eat		1/2AUGS-IRR-kó-sit	

Get some firewood and we'll cook it and [having cooked it we'll] eat it.

This repetition for cohesion is the direct opposite of the English use of ellipsis to mark cohesion.

Text examples of this feature will be found in the last two clauses of (105), in Text 25/8–9, Text 9/23–5, and Text 9/2 (with a change of order).

4.2.5 CONSTITUENT ORDER WITHIN THE CLAUSE. The obligatory core components of a Ndjébbana clause are all contained within the verb complex and their order is fixed by the morphology. Constituent order within the wider Ndjébbana clause, dealing as it does only with optional elaborations or specifications of the core components contained within the verb complex, appears not to be primarily grammatically determined, though there are some observable ordering tendencies. Pragmatic factors play perhaps the most significant role in ordering (cf. Mithun 1986, 1987) in the light of the fact that considerable flexibility in constituent order occurs without apparent grammatical consequences.

In almost half of all clauses the issue of order of the free-standing elaborations of core arguments does not arise because the clause consists simply of a verb complex, while many of the clauses which do have additional elaborative material contain only non-core items apart from the verb complex.

[a]*Significance of order.* Order appears to relate to prominence and focus. Initial position in the sentence is usually the most prominent and therefore the element which is to be made prominent is placed in that position. Following the verb, any words or phrases which occur are much less prominent, being largely tacked on as additional information, particularly if separated from the main intonation contour of the sentence. The most prominent element of a clause introduces a new item, action or topic to the discourse, indicates the focus of a contrast or specifies a significant time or place and so on (cf Mithun 1986:199). A clear example is the pair of clauses

in example (101) in which the focus of contrast is 'female' versus 'male'. See also (79), (80) and (88).

(101)   Ngarráma   kádja   ya-kkó-ya,   njana
          female   underneath   3MINFEMS-kó-lie(+REM)   and
          lárla-na   múnguy   ba-rra-bé-na-nja.
          male-3MINMASC   continuous   3UAFEMS-RE-go-REM-UAFEM
     The female was underneath and the male went with her all the time. (XXI/14–15)

[b] *Order of expansions of core arguments.* Independent nominals or pronouns elaborating on core arguments of the clause occur only when there is a need to indicate contrastive force or to highlight further specification. Such independent nominals or pronouns thus tend to occur early in the clause in a position of prominence. Hence S, A and O nominals or pronouns tend to occur before the verb more frequently than after it, but the opposite orders also occur, particularly if the independent nominal or pronoun is provided as an 'afterthought' giving additional information. References to examples of the various possible orders are set out here:

SV: Text 25/39, 40, 41   *VS:*   (86)

AOV: (79), (80), Text 25/95-96   *AVO:*   Text 25/100

OV: (82), Text 25/12, 21, 37, 58   *VO:*   (84), Text 25/19, 83

One good indicator that pragmatic rather than grammatical factors determine order in the clause is the sets of parallel clauses occurring in text in which a sentence is repeated with various orders to allow the various components in turn to be brought into focus at the beginning of the sentence, including examples such as (102) (two speakers), (103), (104) and the last two clauses of (99).

(102)   [A:] Ka-wala-bé-na   barnamarrákka.
                3MINS-come hither-go-REM   white clay [here=warriors/'soldiers']
          [B:] Barnamarrákka ka-wala-bé-na.
     [A:] Soldiers/warriors arrived. [B:] Soldiers arrived.

(103)   Kórnka   bi-rri-bbó-na   bá-rri-na.   (…)
          yam   3UAA-RE-hit/dig-REM   3UAS-RE-sit(+REM)
          Bi-rri-bbó-na   bá-rri-na   kórnka.
     The two of them were digging yams. (VII/51, 53)

(104)   Djérwarra.   Ka-bé-na   ka-kó-na
          young.people 3MINMASCS-go-REM   3MINMASCS-kó-sit(+REM)
          makéddja.   Makéddja   ka-bé-na   ka-kó-na.
          turtle
     The young people, they would go [hunting] turtles. Turtles, they would go for. (VII/148–9)

[c] *Non-core expansion.*   Independent words such as adverbs, demonstratives and nominals which provide non-core modification of the clause may come at the beginning of the clause or after the verb. Examples of each of these were given in §4.2.3 above.   See also (78), (81), (82), (101), Text 25/1, 2, 8 and the first clause of (188).

Again it is possible to find two different orderings (before and after the verb) for otherwise identical sentences which immediately follow one another as in (104). The auxiliary, however, always immediately follows the main verb, whether the main verb comes first or last in the clause (§4.2.6).

A dative pronoun marking a non-core indirect object always follows the verb, a fact which suggests that the dative pronoun is a suffix or a clitic, rather than a free form (see §3.3.1). See for instance (77) or the first clause of (99).   The indirect objects in these examples are considered non-core because the verbs are not ditransitive.

One element which occurs in initial position (but is not to be seen as especially prominent as a result) occurs with cohesive repetition (§4.2.4). Here the repeated component of the preceding sentence is put forward, marked by a non-final intonation, and then the first (most prominent) element of the main clause occurs.

A further type of constituent which appears to be always initial is the time clause marked with the extent suffix (§4.10.1).

One text passage which exemplifies some of these points is (105).

(105)   Njá-rra-na,   djalwárra   kóma.   Kalíkku   warábba-na
         1AUGS-RE-sit   trousers   NEG   cloth   one-3MINMASC
         ka-wala-bé-na.   Maránboy   ka-wala-bé-na
         3MINMASCS-come.hither-go-REM   Maranboy
         kalíkku.   Maránboy   ka-wala-bé-na   nganéyabba
                                                        there
         nja-rra-yakkabí-ya-na.   Nja-rra-náwarla   mókko
         1AUGS-RE-tie-REFL-REM   1AUG-RE-other   pubic covering
         nja-rra-kkawú-na.
         1AUGA+3MINMASCO-RE-wear-REM

We lived there, and we had no trousers. Cloth for nagas came from one place. It came from Maranboy [later corrected to Mainoru]. [When it came from Maranboy] we tied nagas on ourselves. Others of us [still] wore traditional pubic coverings [made of things like pandanus or possum hair]. (XIV/3–6)

In the second clause the S nominal kalíkku 'cloth' stands first because it presents a contrast with 'no trousers' in the first clause. In the third clause the location stands first because, having already mentioned that cloth had arrived, the focus of attention is now being directed to where it came from. The subject nominal is tacked on after the verb in this clause because it is no longer so prominent. The fourth clause commences with a cohesive repetition (§4.2.4) of the main elements of the third clause, before moving on to the new information about putting nagas on. (A naga is a strip of cloth of body-width passed between the legs, and knotted either side at the waist, worn by men.) The final sentence contrasts with the one before it both in A and in O. Hence the appearance of independent nominals for both A and O, with A prominent in initial position.

4.2.6 AUXILIARY CONSTRUCTION.

The auxiliary construction is widely used in Ndjébbana discourse, though more by some speakers or in some contexts than others. In examining the auxiliary construction I have benefited a great deal from the suggestions made by Eather (n.d.b) about the significance of a similar construction in Nakkara.

[d] *Form*. The auxiliary construction involves an auxiliary verb, fully inflected with pronominal prefixes and tense/aspect/mood affixes, following a main verb which is also fully inflected. The auxiliary verb is one of the three position verbs nó 'sit', yó 'lie' and réndjeyi 'stand' or one of the two general movement verbs djirrí 'go' or rakarawó 'move'. The subject (S) of the auxiliary verb must agree with, or include, the subject (A or S) of the main verb. The auxiliary must also agree with the main verb in tense/aspect/mood inflection. This is illustrated in examples (16), (81), (106) and (107).

(106)   Dílkarra   ba-rra-ná-na-nja
         moon   3UAFEMA+3MINMASCO-RE-see-REM-UAFEM
         ba-rrú-ka-na-nja.
         3UAFEMS-RE-kó-sit(+REM)-UAFEM
         They [male and female turtle] looked at the moon. (XXI/21)

(107)   Ma-ngúdjeya   ma-rrá-ka-na   yaláwa.
         MINIMP-speak   MINIMP-RE-kó-na   well.
         Tell the story now. / Go on telling the story now. (V/46)

Further discussion of the agreement of auxiliary verbs with main verbs, together with additional examples, is presented in §3.6.21, where it is shown that the fact that all the auxiliary verbs are intransitive allows the pronominal prefix marking on the auxiliary to disambiguate some of the pronominal prefix forms used with transitive main verbs.

The auxiliary may occasionally disambiguate the tense/aspect of the main verb (C. Coleman, personal communication). For instance it is only the auxiliary which distinguishes tense/aspect in ka-ddjórrkngaya ka-bé-na 'he was running (REM)' and ka-ddjórrkngaya ki-yirrí-ya 'he is running (CTP)'.

The S of the auxiliary verb may not only agree with the S or A of the main verb but may go beyond that to incorporate the O or some other participant(s) as well. Thus in (108) the S prefix of the auxiliary verb includes both the A and the O of the main verb.

(108)   Dja-kkáma   ní-ya-na!
         2MINA+3MINO(+IRR)-fuck   2UAS-IRR-sit
         Fuck yourselves/each other! [lit. You fuck him, you two sit.] (IX/71)

In example (109) the S prefix of the auxiliary verb incorporates both the S of the main verb and the indirect object.

(109)   Ba-rra-njíndja-na   ngabúyanga   nja-rrú-ka-na.
         3AUGS-RE-cry-REM   1MINDAT   1AUGS-RE-kó-SIT(+REM)
         They were all crying for me [bitten by shark]. (XX/73)

In the text example (25/75) the S of the auxiliary verb includes the S of the preceding main verb (the young buffalo) plus an additional participant who does not otherwise appear in the clause (the mother buffalo).

[e] *Choice of position auxiliary.* Choice of position auxiliary relates partly to the characteristic posture of the subject for the particular activity, which may differ between subjects. Thus in Text 25/44 the auxiliary used with the verb bá 'eat' is réndjeyi 'stand' when the subject is buffaloes but in (115) the same verb is used with the auxiliary nó 'sit' when the subject is human. The auxiliary verb nó 'sit' in particular is the unmarked auxiliary and is normally used without reference to, or rather in spite of, its lexical meaning as in (110) or in (104).

(110)   ...ka-ddjórrkngaya   ka-kó-na   nakébba   kúdjbarra
         3MINMASCS-run   3MINMASCS-kó-sit   3MINMASCCARD   kangaroo
         ...it ran away, that kangaroo.

It is possible for the main verb and the auxiliary to be homophonous.

(111)   Dílkarra   ngí-ya-na   ngí-ya-na.
         moon   1/2UAA+3MINO-IRR-see   1/2UAS-IRR-sit
         Let's look at the moon [to determine timing[. (XXII/22)

[f] *Negation with auxiliary.* In a negative clause one occurrence of the negative particle kóma is sufficient to negate the verb complex plus auxiliary as in example (112).

(112)   Ka-ndakarlába   kóma
         3MINA+3MINMASCO-immerse(+REM)   NEG
          ka-ya-ka-bbéngka-na   ka-ya-bardarrbbayí-na.
          3MINMASCS-IRR-kó-float-CF   3MINMASCS-IRR-lie-CF
         He put it [log] in the water but it didn't float. (IX/45–6)

[g] *Auxiliary to mark aspect.* The significance of the auxiliary construction is not clear but it appears to be aspectual.

In general, the addition of a positional auxiliary to a verb indicates some kind of imperfective, progressive, continuous or habitual meaning, that is, it indicates an activity which has some extent.

Some indication of this comes in the contrast between the verbs of (113) and (114), given as Ndjébbana translations of the English forms below them.

(113)   Nga-lawáya   nganéyabba.
         1MINA+3MINO-know/think about(+CTP)   3MINMASCDEM
         I know that man.

(114)   Nga-lawáya   nga-nó-ra.
         1MINA+3MINMASCO-know/think about(+CTP)   1MINS-sit-CTP
         I'm worrying about him [that man].

In the examples (71), (115) and (116) the progressive ('in progress')
or continuous meaning of the auxiliary construction is apparent.

(115)   Nga-ná-dja   ká-ba
         1MINA+3MINO-see-CTP   3MINA+3MINMASCO-eat(+CTP)
         ka-réndjeya.
         3MINMASCS-stand(+CTP)
         I saw them drinking. (XXV/35)

(116)   Ba-rra-bé-na   ba-rra-rá-na
         3AUGA+3MINMASCO-RE-go-REM   3AUGA+3MINO-RE-go-REM
         warábba-na,   Márdbalk
         one-3MINMASCPOSS   Goulburn Island
         ka-nmarabúya-ya   ka-yó-ra.
         3MINMASCS-bury-REFL(+CTP)   3MINMASCS-lie-CTP
         They went and speared only him, and now he's buried at Goulburn Island.
         (II/85–6)

Motion verb auxiliaries appear to be used to express meanings in the
range durative, iterative, distributive (widespread) and extensive, as can be
seen from examples (117), (118), (119), (120) and Text 9/9, while in Text
7/13 the motion auxiliary appears to have general 'in progress' significance.
In example (117) the subject is marked as minimal though it is actually a
generalised reference to a group of people.

(117)   Ya-rayé-ra.   Ya-rayé-ra ka-bé-na.
         3MINA+3MINFEMO-tear-REM   3MINMASCS-go-REM
           Ya-rayé-ra   ka-bé-na,   ya-rayé-ra   ka-bé-na   ka-bé-na
           ka-bé-na   ka-bé-na.   Yaláwa   ya-yikkabé-ra.
                               then   3MINA+3MINFEMO-tie.up-REM
         [They] would tear up [the fish poison plant]. [They] would tear it all up and
         then tie it in a bundle. (XVII/20–1)

(118)   Karrówa   duram   ka-rendjí-na   ka-bé-na.
         many   drum   3MINMASCS-stand-REM   3MINMASCS-go-REM
         There were many drums standing there.

(119)   Marlémarla   ka-wú-ni-ba   ka-bé-na.
         fish.poison   3MINA+3MINMASCO-give-REM-EXT   3MINS-go-REM
         He applied fish poison right through the water [by dragging]. (XVII/40–1)

(120)   Ba-rra-njúngkuwara?   ngabanda-ngódja
         3AUG-RE-who?   1MINA+3AUGO(+IRR)-call name
           ngé-yarra.
           1MINS(+IRR)-go
         Who were they all? I'm going to give all their names... (V/318–19)

In (121) the verb 'to bury/cover with sand' is introduced first with no auxiliary, aparently giving a bald mention of the next action. Then the verb is repeated with an auxiliary to provide aspectual elaboration, apparently indicating the extended scooping of sand involved in covering the roasting emu with sand. This pattern of introducing the bare verb first and then elaborating with an auxiliary upon repetition of the verb is relatively common in texts (cf. §4.2.3). The verb 'to cook' has an auxiliary from the outset. The cooking is a lengthy process during which the hunters turned their attention to looking for 'sugarbag' or wild honey.

(121)   Nji-rri-yalóla-nga   nganawúna,
          1UAA+3MINO-RE-cover.with.paperbark-REM   type.paperbark
             nji-rri-nmarabúya-nga.   Nji-rri-nmarabúya-nga
             1UAA+3MINO-RE-bury-REM   1UAA+3MINO-RE-bury-REM
             nji-rri-bé-na,   ya-warrabó-na   ya-kkó-ya
             1UAS-RE-go-REM   3MINFEMS-cook-REM   3MINFEMS-kó-lie
          We covered it with paperbark and then covered that with sand. We covered it completely and [the emu(FEM)] cooked. [We went off looking for wild honey ('sugarbag').] (XXXI pp. 4–5)

4.2.7 REPETITION FOR DURATION AND EXTENT.
In Ndjébbana, unlike many Australian languages, reduplication is not a productive process, though there is evidence of the use of reduplication in word formation in the language's past (e.g. njélnjel 'late afternoon' is clearly connected with njél 'cool'). In fact the only example of possible reduplication found so far in the research leading to this grammar is (87). Its significance is not clear.

Though morphological reduplication is not available to indicate some of the things frequently marked in other languages by reduplication (such as plurality, durative, iterative or broad extent), repetition of full verb forms can be used with these types of significance.

[a] *Durative.* Repetition of the verb complex or of a longer sequence can be used to express a general durative meaning when the verb represents an activity without a defined end point as in examples (122), (117) and Text 25/89–90.

(122)   Njírrabba   nja-rra-bé-na   ngána   nakkáyala.
          1AUGCARD   1AUGS-RE-go-REM   there   on.foot
             Nja-rra-wala-bé-na   nja-rra-wala-bé-na   nja-rra-wala-bé-na
             1AUGS-RE-come.hither-go-REM
          We were walking along on foot. We walked and walked...

Alternative means of expressing duration involve the use of motion auxiliaries (§4.2.6) or the extensive lengthening of the final syllable of a sentence together with a rise in pitch (§2.5).

[b] *Iterative.* If the verb is interpreted as one representing an action or activity with a defined end point, repetition of the verb or of a longer sequence can represent repeated occurrences of the action or activity (that is iteration) as in (184). The number of repetitions frequently represents the

actual number of occurrences, as in (123), taken from a child's story
transcribed from tape and published for the Ndjébbana bilingual education
program. Text 25/90–1 shows the iteration of a complete short sequence of
actions.

(123)   'Ni-rrikébba   ní-yarra   budborl?'
          2UACARD   2UAS(+IRR)-go   football
           Nji-rri-yángka-na   'I.'   Nja-rra-kkó-ya,   nja-rra-kkó-ya,
          1UAS-RE-say/do-REM   yes   1AUGS-RE-kó-sleep/lie
           nja-rra-kkó-ya,   nja-rra-kkó-ya,   yaláwa
                                                               then
           nja-rra-wala-bé-n   kúl.
          1AUGS-RE-come hither-go-REM   school
          'Would you like to go to the football?' [the teacher said.] We said, 'Yes'. Four
          days later [lit. 'we slept, we slept, we slept, we slept', four times] we came to
          school...

4.2.8 REFLEXIVE/RECIPROCAL CLAUSES.

Reflexive/reciprocal verbs
are derived using the reflexive/reciprocal/intransitiviser suffix -yi-.
Morphology and syntax of these verb forms is outlined in §3.6.17. In terms
of the use of independent nominals and pronouns and of the use of adverbs
and so on, reflexive clauses are like any other intransitive clause. Apart from
those given in §3.6.17, examples of reflexive clauses are (116) and Text
25/4, 7 and 48.

4.2.9 TO ACCOMPANY, COLLABORATE OR DO IT 'WITH' SOMEONE.

In Ndjébbana there is no comitative or proprietive ('having') affix, such as one
would find in many other Australian languages to mark the person
accompanying another or doing something 'with' that person. Ndjébbana
speakers use the resources of the verb pronominal prefix forms to express this
type of meaning as in example (124).

(124)   Ngáyabba   yí-yarra?
          1MINCARD   1/2MINS(+IRR)-go(+FUT)
          Can I go with you? [literally perhaps 'I, can you and I go?']

In this example the independent pronoun is used to focus on the one
who wishes to accompany and the verb is marked with an S pronominal prefix
which includes both that person and the other (the addressee) who is to be
accompanied. That is, the pronominal prefix to the verb specifies the whole
group which is going, including the person making the request to join the
group. It is the partial overlap between the reference of the independent
pronoun and the (more inclusive) pronominal prefix which expresses the
notion of accompaniment. See also examples (191), (192) and (125).

(125)   Ka-ngadjí-na   yibérra,   'Ngábi-yarra
          3MINMASCS-speak-REM   3AUGDAT   1/2AUGS(+FUT)-go
           yaláwa   narra-mómardakka   narra-kkúrrkkurk.'
          then   2AUG-brothers RECIP   2AUG-cousins RECIP
          He said to them, 'Come with us you [who call each other] brothers and
          cousins'. (XII/39–40)

A further example of this feature is the second clause of example (101). See also examples (108), (109) and Text 25/75, discussed in §4.2.6, in which the pronominal prefix on an auxiliary is more inclusive than that on the main verb it goes with.

4.2.10 EXISTENTIAL CLAUSES.   Existential clauses in Ndjébbana ('there is...', 'there was...') are formed using the positional verbs nó 'sit', réndjeyi 'stand' and yó 'lie', depending on the item being referred to. See examples (126), (127), (128) and Text 9/9, 10.

(126)   Nganéyabba   yaláwa   djarríbbang   ya-kkó-ya.
        there   now   trepang (FEM) 3MINFEMS-kó-lie
        [The Macassans anchored at Entrance Island.]   That was where the trepang
        was. / There was trepang there. (V/36–7)

(127)   Djawalárra   ka-yó-ra.
        spike.rush   3MINMASCS-lie-CTP
        There are spike rushes there. (V/227–8)

(128)   Warábba-na   middjin   ka-rendjí-na
        one-3MINMASCPOSS   mission   3MINMASCS-stand-REM
        Márdbalk.
        Goulburn Island.
        There was one/a mission at Goulburn Island. (V/132)

Existential clauses can also be formed with a non-verbal predicate (§4.3.1), both positive and negative, as in (129) and (130). The two clauses of (129) exemplify both types, non-verbal and verbal. See also (213), Text 9/8 and the negative existential clause (148).

(129)   Nakéyakayakka   balánda   kóma.   Kóma   njúngkuwara
        at.first   white.man NEG NEG   anyone
        ka-ya-na-rayína.
        3MINMASCS-IRR-sit-CF
        At first there were no white people. No one was [here] [except Aborigines].
        (XIV/1–2)

(130)   ...yókkarra   karrówa   nganéyabba   yaláwa.
        fish   many   there   'finish'
        [We'll go back to that place] where there are a lot of fish. (I/255)

The use of a dative pronoun with an existential clause marks general possession as in example (131).

(131)   Mardayin   warábba-na   yinjerrekéyanga.
        ceremony   one-3MINMASCPOSS   1UAMASCDAT
        [We (general) have different languages but] we've got a single Mardayin
        ceremony. [Lit. 'There is to us a single Mardayin.'] (XII/130)

4.3   NON-VERBAL PREDICATE

Clauses expressing an equative or predicative relation, in which the subject is described, identified or qualified using a nominal or adverb, are expressed in Ndjébbana using the nominal or adverb as the predicate. Such clauses are expressed in Ndjébbana without the use of a copula unless a non-contemporary (non-present) tense has to be marked. The subject and the predicative nominal are simply juxtaposed in the clause and all appropriate agreements are marked. Normally the subject (S) stands before the predicate when it is a separate word. The subject can take the form of a pronominal prefix only.

There are two main forms a clause with a nominal predicate can take, depending on whether the predicate nominal takes affixes to mark a subject or not.

[a] *Uninflected nominal predicate.*   Example (132) has a simple invariant nominal yírriddjanga as predicate and (206) has uninflected rdórdbalk 'good' as the whole main clause (consequent) with a non-referential subject (= 'it would have been good').

(132)   Njanabbárdakka   yírriddjanga.
         trevally (fish)   Yírriddjanga.
         The trevally is Yírriddjanga [moiety]. (XXI/3)

[b] *Inflected nominal predicate.*   The second type involves as predicate a nominal which takes affixes to indicate the subject (S) as in (133) and (202).

(133)   Na-rra-búlanj-nja.   Lárla-baddana
         2UAFEMS-RE-[subsection]-UAFEM   male-3UAMASCPOSS
         bi-rri-búlanj.
         3UAMASCS-RE-[subsection]
         You two girls are njabúlanj. The two boys are búlanj too.

[c] *Non-nominal predicates.*   Other types of words can be used as predicates such as adverbs, cardinal pronouns (as possessor marked with a prefix to agree with the possessed item (§3.3.2)) and the negative particle. These, too, tend to follow the subject S as in Text 9/33 and in (129), (130) and the third clause of (88).

[d] *Tense-marked equative clauses.*   When the equative or copulative relationship is to be marked as being in a non-contemporary (non-present) tense, one of the three positional verbs is used to carry tense as in (134), (135) or the second clause of (88).

(134)   Nga-namánda   ka-kó-na.   Dja-ná-na
         3MINMASC-small   3MINS-kó-sit   2MINA+3MINO-see-REM
         ka-yarrárlma-nga.
         3MINMASCS-grow-REM
         He used to be small but you've seen him he's grown now. (XVII/53–5)

(135)   N-karrakárramardba   ka-rendjí-na.
          3MINMASC-long   3MINMASC-stand-REM
            Ka-nangarddjí-na   yaláwa.
            3MINMASCS-break (REFL)-REM   that's it.
          It [stone dreaming] used to be tall. It's broken now. (XVIII/37–8)

4.4   NOUN PHRASE

The basic realisation of a core argument in Ndjébbana is the bound pronominal prefix (§3.3.3). This can be expanded using independent nominals, pronouns, demonstratives and so on (§4.2.2).

These expansions of bound pronominal core arguments may be made up of more than one word, and it is these combinations of optional independent nominals, pronouns and demonstratives, as well as similar phrases in non-core roles (e.g. location), which we will discuss here under the term noun phrase.

4.4.1 NOMINAL PLUS QUALIFIER PHRASES.

A nominal may be qualified using another nominal, a numeral or a pronoun used as a demonstrative adjective.

[a] *Nominal-nominal phrases.* The modifier nominal is most likely to follow the head nominal and to be one of the (attributive) nominals from nominal classes C and D (§3.2.3), which are inflectionally marked for agreement with the head. The head nominal may also follow its modifier in a nominal phrase. See also Text 25/29.

nbalóyara   n-barrábarra
well   3MINMASC-big
a big well (VIII/6-7)

wíba   nga-náwarla   nga-náwarla   wíba
place   3MINMASC-other/different   3MINMASC-different   place
a different place (I/168–9)   a different place (VII/6–7)

ngalidjbínja nja-mádjarna   nja-múlbbum karrddjúnja
gun   3MINFEM-genuine   3MINFEM-many   stingray
real guns (V/60)   many stingrays (XXIII/56)

This same basic structure could form a whole clause on its own in the form of subject followed by predicate. Thus, for instance, the first of these examples could be used as a nominal phrase meaning 'a big well' or as a clause meaning 'the well is big'.

[b] *Nominal-numeral phrases.* The two numerals are regular attributive nominals which usually follow the head nominal (but see Text 25/3) and which may be combined. In the case of warábba 'one' the numeral must agree with the head in person, number and gender.

kayókaya	warábba-na	nganabbárru	karnayédjabba
night	one-3MINMASC	buffalo	two
one night (XXV/80)		two buffaloes (Text 25/81)	

For combinations of numerals marking 'three' and 'four', especially agreement marking with 'three', see example (12) and Text 25/27–8. The numeral and the nominal may, rarely, be separated by another word as in Text 9/10.

[c] *Pronoun demonstrative and nominal phrase.* The cardinal or emphatic pronouns (§3.3.1) may be used as demonstrative adjectives, usually (but not always) preceding the nominal, as in the following noun phrases. Such phrases are used to highlight and clarify, linking back to previous discourse.

ngayábba	marnúbbarr	nakébba	bárrbaya
3MINFEMCARD	magpie.goose	3MINMASCCARD	dog
those geese [that goose] (I/69)		that dog [subject of the story]	
			(VIII/11)

yókkarra	nakébba
fish	3MINMASCCARD
'that fish' [in context: 'and fish too'] (I/31)	

Further examples, using both the cardinal and the emphatic pronouns, are (26), (27) and Text 9/13.

4.4.2 POSSESSION PHRASES.

A specialised type of expanded noun phrase involves the marking of possession. The morphology of possession marking is outlined in §3.2.3.

With nominals of possession class A, the possessor is marked using a cardinal pronoun form juxtaposed to the (possessed) nominal and marked to agree with it in number and gender. The pronoun indicating the possessor usually follows the nominal marking the possessed item as in the following noun phrases and Text 25/60.

bárrbaya	n-ngúrrabba	bíbbo	nja-barrayabba
dog	3MINMASC-1/2AUGCARD	crab	3MINFEM-3AUGCARD
our dog		their crab	

With nominals of possession class B, the possessor is marked by pronominal prefix as the S on the contemporary form of the verb réndjeyi 'stand' which always follows the possessed noun. This class of nominals contains only body-part terms.

Nominals of possession classes C and D mark 'possessor' by means of an affix: in the case of class C the possessive suffix, and in the case of class D a pronominal prefix. In these cases the possessor and the possessed are combined within a single word.

With nominals of classes B, C and D, the relationship termed here 'possession' is really one of identity of reference between 'possessor' and 'possessed'. When the 'possessed' nominal is a body part or similar item, English treats the relationship as one of possession but when the 'possessed' nominal refers to a quality or to a class of being, English is more likely to translate with an adjective or a specific noun. Compare the following sets of phrases, noting the formal similarities whether or not the English equivalent is expressed as possession.

kála   nga-réndjeya
ear   1MINS-stand(+CTP)
my ear

kúdja-njabba
foot/hand-1MINPOSS
my foot

nga-méyameya
1MIN-(head) hair
my hair

ba-rra-walá-nja
3UAFEM-RE-name-UAFEM
their names [two females]

nja-ndjórrkkabba
3MINFEM-spouse
wife

warábba-njabba
one/alone-IMINPOSS
[I ạm] alone, only me

nga-karókaddja
1MIN-child
I [am] a child

ba-rra-múyi-ba-nja
3UAFEM-RE-spirit-EXT-UAFEM
spirits / dead people [two females]

In a couple of these cases ('child' and 'spouse') the fully inflected nominal form can then be treated as a nominal of possession class A with a juxtaposed possessor inflected for agreement as in the following:

bi-rri-rókaddji-ba   bi-rri-ngáyabba
3UAMASC-RE-child-EXT   3UAMASC-RE-1MINCARD
my two children

A few can be interpreted more than one way in different contexts, as in the following examples.

lárla-na   ngarráma
male / penis-3MINMASC   female / woman
male / a male / his penis female / a female / a woman

Finally in covering 'possession' it is pertinent to mention a small set of immediate kin terms which are actually verbal in form. They can appear in a clause to elaborate one of the pronominal arguments (e.g. subject). The 'possession' aspect (from an English point of view) is handled by means of the pronominal prefix form as in the following examples:

ngáyabba   nja-rra-nó-ra-nja
1MINCARD   1UAFEMS-RE-sit-CTP-UAFEM
my wife [lit. 'I, she and I sit together']

ngáyabba   njana-ramé-ra-yana
1MINCARD   3MINA+1MINO-hold/grasp-REM-3MINMASCDATA
my father [lit. 'me, he held/grasped me']

The phrase for 'my uncle' in example (136) is a text example of this type of 'possession' phrase.

(136)   Ka-ngadjí-na   ngárridj,   djádja,   ngáyabba
          3MINMASCS-speak-REM   [subsection]   uncle   1MINCARD
          njana-má-nga-bba-yana,   kaláddjarr.
          3MINA+1MINO-get-REM-EXT-3MINMASCDATA   deaf
          ka-ngadjí-na   bárriya   bi-rri-yurdunmakkúkka.
                    3UAMASCDEM   3UAMASC-RE-'grannies together'

He said, [that's] Ngárridj, uncle, my uncle (=my mother's brother), the deaf [man]. He said to those two who call each other grannie... (XX/84–7)

4.5   NEGATION AND THE COUNTERFACTUAL

In this category we include both clause and nominal phrases that indicate things that do/did not happen or do/did not exist in reality or in fact. The principal means of expressing this meaning are the negative particle kóma and the combination of the irrealis verb prefix with the counterfactual suffix (§3.6.5). The irrealis or unreal prefix is used also in the future tense because things which are still in the future have not been realised (have not become real) yet. We will not be discussing the future in this section. (See §3.6.5.)

4.5.1 CLAUSE NEGATION.   Clauses are negated using the negative particle kóma plus the negative form of the verb appropriate to the time-frame of the clause: the counterfactual (CF) form in the remote time frame and the non-remote negative (NRN) in the contemporary and future time-frames (§3.6.4). The negative particle usually stands somewhere before the verb and frequently occurs at the beginning of the clause. All verbs within the scope of the negation, both main and auxiliary verbs, are marked with the appropriate negative form. Some (mainly younger) speakers appear to use the aversative form (§3.6.5) instead of the counterfactual after the negative particle kóma.

The examples (137) to (140) show the use of the negative particle in a variety of positions in the clause. The most common text examples are in the remote time frame and use the counterfactual form.

(137)   Ba-rra-kábbuli-ba   kóma
          3UAS-RE-old.person-EXT   NEG
               ba-lawáya-na   balánda.
               3AUGA+3MINMASCO(+IRR)-know-CF   white.man
The old people didn't know/understand white people. (XX/161–2)

(138)   Lárla-na   kóma   ka-ya-la-ngéna.
          male-3MINMASC   NEG   3MINMASCS-IRR-look-CF
She [female turtle] didn't even look at the male. (XXI/17)

(139)   Kóma   karrabba   bakkándja   ka-ya-balákka-na.
          NEG   and/like   again   3MINMASCS-IRR-come.back-CF.
[After some of them were killed the Macassans] did not come back again.
(V/105)

(140)   Kóma   kálawa.
    NEG   (1MINA+3MINO+RE)-know(+NRN)
    I don't know. [Also means 'I don't know him'.] (V/291)

A single negative particle kóma can include within its scope two verbs, either a main verb and an auxiliary as in example (112), or a main verb and its complement as in (141). The main verb itself is a particle phrasal verb (§3.6.19).

(141)   Ngáyabba   barakángka   kó-na...
    1MINCARD   weak/worn out   (1MINS+)kó-sit(+REM)
      Kóma   márdba   nga-ya-mandja-ngéna
      NEG   *'want'   1MINA+3MINO-IRR-*put-CF
      nga-ya-ka-rá-yana   yókkarra.
      1MINA+3MINO-IRR-kó-spear-CF   fish
    I was feeling weak... I did not want to spear fish. (XX/34–6)

The negative particle kóma can also be used together with an indefinite word as in examples (51) and (129).

The negative possibility (NEGPOSS) particle kóndjalabba introduces a clause (with a contemporary realis verb) which seems to emphatically deny the possibility of some action as in example (142).

(142)   Djíya   kóndjalabba   ngana-kkúwa-nga.   Djíya
    this   NEGPOSS   1MINA+2MINO-deceive-CTP   this
      yaláwa   n-bamúmawa   nga-ngúdjeya   yikkóyanga.
      now   3MINMASC-true   1MINS-speak   2MINDAT
      Kóma   ngana-kkúwa.
      NEG   1MINA+2MINO-deceive(+NRN)
    I can't lie to you. This is true, what I'm telling you. I'm not lying to you. (XXI/97–100)

Negative imperative. The negative imperative is formed using the negative particle kóma and the non-remote negative form of the verb with a second person subject as in examples (143), (161) and (162).

(143)   Kóma   ngana-kkamíya.
    NEG   2MINS(+RE)-get.up(+NRN)
    Don't get up! (V/120)

4.5.2 NOMINAL PHRASE NEGATION. Nominal phrases may be negated using the negative particle kóma. The negative particle usually follows the nominal it negates and is intonationally linked with it in a phrase. That the scope of the negation includes only the nominal is shown by the fact that such negative nominal phrases may be used with non-negative verbs as in example (144). Contrast (145) in which the counterfactual verb form shows that the scope of the negation includes the verb, which, in line with the pattern for a negative clause, follows the negative particle. Here kóma is intonationally linked with the following verb rather than with the preceding object nominal.

(144)   Yaláwa   djíya   djadjórla   kóma   nja-rrú-ka-na.
       well   here   house   NEG   1AUGS-RE-kó-sit(+REM)
       We lived without houses here [then]. (XXIII/43–4)

(145)   [Mídjiyang]   yindjin   kóma   ka-ya-ramí-ngana
       prau   engine   NEG   3MINA+3MINMASCO-IRR-have-CF
         njana   wóndja   karrúrru.
         but   only   sail.
       [The Macassan praus] had no engine but only a sail. (II/30–1]

See also the negative nominal phrases and negative clauses in (146) and (147), in particular the position of the negative particle after the nominal in a negative nominal phrase and before the verb in a negative clause.

(146)   Mabbúlarr   ka-kó-na,   balawúrrwurr   kóma.
       calm   3MINMASCS-kó-sit   wind   NEG
       It was calm—no wind. (XX/18)

(147)   Djéyabba   ngúdja   kóma.   Kóma   ka-ya-ngadjí-na.
       that.one   speech   NEG   NEG   3MINMASCS-IRR-speak-CF
         Marnbúrrba   kóma   nji-rri-bé-na   wúrdeyak.
         naga/cloth   NEG   1UAS-RE-go-REM   long.ago
         Bákki   kóma   djakóra   njí-rawó-ngana.
         tobacco   NEG   *to smoke   1UAA+3MINO+IRR-*throw-CF
       That man [initiand] [uttered] no words, he did not speak. In the old days we went around with no clothes and we didn't smoke tobacco. (VII/152–4)

[a] *Negative existential and non-verbal predicate.* Negated nominal phrases may be used as negative existential clauses as in example (148) (nominal phrase negation). In example (149) the negated non-verbal predicate is a cardinal pronoun indicating possession (clause negation).

(148)   Djíya   wurrámbalk   kóma.
       here   house   NEG
       There were no houses here. (XXIII/69)

(149)   Ngandjúddama   kóma   njíndjabba.
       bark.canoe   NEG   2MINCARD
       The bark canoe does not belong to you/is not yours. (IX/86)

[b] *Contrastive or corrective nominal phrase negation.* The negative particle kóma together with the conjunction njana is used to express a contrast of the form 'not x but y', as in (150) or to make a contrastive correction as in example (151).

(150)   Syuka   kóma   njana   djungkúrlu   ka-bá-la
         sugar   NEG   but   [name]   3MINA+3MINMASCO-eat-REM
         ka-kó-na.
         3MINMASCS-kó-sit(+REM)
         [The Macassans] didn't have sugar, but djungkúrlu [?sugar cane]. (II/13–14)

(151)   Nji-rri-má-nga   wúbbunj.   Wúbbunj   kóma
         1UAA+3MINO-RE-get-REM   canoe   dugout.canoe   NEG
         njana   ngandjúddama.
         but   bark.canoe
         We got canoes. Not dugout canoes but bark canoes. (VII/9–10)

[c] *Negative particle as utterance.* The negative particle kóma can be used as a single word utterance meaning 'nothing' in the sense of 'Nothing was there', 'There was no response', 'Nothing happened' and so on, as in example (152) and Text 9/15, 45.

(152)   Ka-badjí-na.   Kóma.
         3MINMASCS-shout-REM   NEG
         He called out. Nothing. / [There was] No reply. (XII/15)

The negative particle kóma also functions as a complete utterance ('No.') to reject a suggestion as in (213) and Text 25/57, to deny a claim or to refuse a request/instruction. See example (158).

4.5.3 COUNTERFACTUAL CLAUSES. Hypothetical but unrealised activities or situations in the remote time-frame are expressed using the counterfactual mood form (§3.6.4). See also example (206). The desiderative (DESID) particle kóndjala may introduce this type of clause when it refers to what 'should have been'. In (153) the speaker has substituted a version of the English form 'should be' (swíbi) for kóndjala.

(153)   Swíbi   nganéyabba   yaláwa   mángkaddjarra
         should.be   that(3MINMASC)   now   Macassan
         nála   ka-ya-rendjí-na
         3MINMASC+name   3MINMASCS-IRR-stand-CF
         The name [of the place Balándabindibbónabba] should have been Mángkaddjarra... (Macassan...) [instead of Balánda... (white man)]. (V/91–2)

Again with or without the particle kóndjala the meaning can be more like 'was going to/would have, but did not', as in (154) or (98).

(154)   Nganéyabba   yaláwa,   njélnjel,   nga-rlarrabí-na.   Kóndjala
         there   well   late.afternoon   1MINS-arrive-REM   DESID
         nja-nabó-ngana,   djangkúrrinj,   njana   bakkándjamandja
         3AUGS(+IRR)-dance-CF   [song type]   but   instead

ba-rra-rlarrabí-na...
3AUGS-RE-arrive-REM

I arrived there in the late afternoon [with the young men]. We were going to dance the djangkúrrinj [a song from Oenpelli] but [some others] arrived [so we left it]. (V/230–2)

The desiderative particle kóndjala can also be used with a nominal to express mistaken identity ('I thought it was...') as in (155).

(155)   Kóndjala   barrábarra   yókkarra   njana   barrábarra   djabbarnbókka
           DESID   big   fish   but   big   shark
           ka-nabíya.
           3MINMASCS-lie/be(+CTP)

I thought [it was] a big fish but it was a big shark.

4.6   IMPERATIVE CLAUSES AND OTHER INSTRUCTIONS

Instructions, commands and requests in Ndjébbana are expressed using the imperative or the future form (§§3.6.4, 3.6.5), or using one of a small number of imperative interjections.

4.6.1   SINGLE WORD IMPERATIVE INTERJECTIONS.
Ndjébbana has a number of single-word imperatives which are not recognisable as inflected forms. These are listed below.

Báb	'Sit down!'	Djóbo	'Shoo!'
Djáddji	'Come here!'	Kalábbuk	'Shut up!' 'Be quiet!'

These forms are most commonly used alone but can be combined with other imperatives as in Text 25/71. Djóbo is usually addressed to animals, the remaining three are addressed to children and to other people with whom the speaker has a relatively close relationship. In situations of less familiarity full verbal imperative forms would normally be used.

In a sense the 'goodbye' expression used by Ndjébbana speakers has a similar function, though clearly recognised as an inflected form:

Ngana-wúyakka.
2MINS-go first
Goodbye. / Off you go. [lit. 'You go first.']

There are also certain paralinguistic signals which have imperative function. Examples of this are the voiceless bilabial 'pop' sound meaning 'Stop!' which is mentioned in Text 25/44 and the hand signal for 'Come here!' (flat hand, palm facing down, fingers together, pointing toward addressee, four fingers bend down and back to close against palm in a single move).

4.6.2 IMPERATIVES. The imperative prefixes to the verb complex have been discussed in §3.6.5. Frequently an imperative verb complex occurs on its own as in (156) and (157), both heard shouted to children around the camp. See also example (85). Text 25/45 is an example with two simple imperative verbs, while (107) is an imperative made up of a main verb and an auxiliary.

(156)   Ma-ddjáma-ya.
          MINIMP-wash-REFL
          Wash yourself.

(157)   Ma-rlábaya.
          MINIMP-descend
          Climb down [from tree].

An imperative clause can also be elaborated in the same ways as any other clause (§4.2), for pragmatic reasons such as contrast, as in example (158). The negative particle kóma is used to refuse to comply.

(158)   'Kí-nga-yángka-na-yana,   búlanj,
          kí-1MINS-say-REM-3MINMASCDAT   [subsection]
            'Njíndjabba   ma-nmirrímarla..   Baddúmang
            2MINCARD   MINIMP-swim   goggles
            djá-ka-ra   yókkarra, njana
            2MINA+3MINO(+IRR)-kó-spear(+FUT) fish   because
            ngáyabba   nga-ddjúwa.'   'Kóma...'
            1MINCARD   1MINS-be sick(+CTP)   NEG
          I said to Búlanj, 'You swim and spear fish with the goggles, because I'm not well'. 'No [you do it].' (XX/37–40)

4.6.3 FUTURE AS IMPERATIVE. Future tense forms are frequently used with imperative force, particularly when the object (O or IO) is not third person minimal. An example of this occurs in (158) alongside an ordinary imperative form. Example (159) has two future tense verbs as imperatives while (160) has future imperative main verb and auxiliary.

(159)   'Yéy.   Ní-bala-yarra   nbi-yi-bbándja...'
          Hey!   UAIMP-RE-hither-go   2UAA+1MINO-IRR-put
          [I came to the surface and called to them] 'Hey! Come and pick me up' [in your canoe]. [A shark has just bitten me.] (XX/59)

(160)   Walákka   dja-ngúdjeya   djá-ka-na.
          slowly   2MINS(+IRR)-speak   2MINS(+IRR)-kó-sit
          Speak slowly. (V/3)

4.6.4 NEGATIVE IMPERATIVE. To express negative instructions the negative particle kóma is used with the non-remote negative form of the verb as in examples (161) and (162). Example (162) also contains an ordinary imperative.

(161)   Djébba   balánda   kóma
         this   English   NEG
         ngana-ngúdje[ya]-yana.
         2MINS(+RE)-speak(+NRN)-3MINMASCDAT
         Don't speak English to him [this white man]. (V/147]

(162)   Kóma   dja-móya,   karrddjúnja.'
         NEG   2MINA+3MINO-eat-(NRN)   stingray
         'Kóma.   Nba-rrú-ka-wa.
         NEG   AUGIMPA+1MINIO-RE-kó-give
         Nga-ya-móya,   ména   nga-ddjúwa.'
         1MINA+3MINO-IRR-eat(+FUT)   hunger   1MINS-suffer(+CTP)
         [They said to me,] 'Don't eat [any], it's stingray.' 'No. No. Give me some.
         I'm going to eat it. I'm hungry.' [Speaker had just been bitten by a
         stingray.] (XXIII/58–60)

It is possible that an aversative clause (§4.8) such as (60) can be taken in
context as having the force of an instruction.

4.6.5 HORTATIVE CLAUSES. The term 'hortative' is used here to refer
to utterances which function as suggestions or instructions in which the
speaker is included. These would frequently be translated into English as 'let
us...'. These verbs have 1/2 person subject prefixes and future tense verb
forms. Examples include (77), (84), Text 9/28–32 and Text 25/86.

4.7   QUESTIONS

Questions are of three basic types: yes/no questions, tag questions
and information questions (equivalent to English WH questions).

4.7.1 YES/NO QUESTIONS. Yes/No questions in Ndjébbana are formed
by using a rising question intonation on a regular clause (whether verbal or
nominal predicate) as in the examples (123), (124) and (163) to (165).

(163)   Ngáyabba   nga-ngadjí-na   yibérra,   'Kayl Lidil   djíya
         1MINCARD   1MINS-say-REM   3AUGDAT   Kyle-Little   here
         ka-nó-ra?'   'Ngawa.'
         3MINMASCS-sitCTP   yes
         I said to them, 'Is Kyle-Little here?' 'Yes.' (XX/167)

(164)   'Na-rra-lawá-ya,   JB?'   'Ngaw.'
         '2AUGA+3MINO-RE-know-CTP   [name]   yes
         'Do you know JB..?' 'Yes.' (XIV/81)

(165)   Ka-ngadjí-na,   'Yaláwa?'   'Ngaw.'...   'Máwala
         3MINMASCS-say-REM   enough   yes   paperbark
         nja-karrówa?'   'Wúrdayak.'
         3MINFEM-much   long ago/already
         He said, 'Is that enough?' 'Yes.'... 'Is there a lot of paperbark?' 'Plenty [lit.
         already]' (XXII/91)

4.7.2 TAG QUESTIONS. Ndjébbana has an invariant tag question particle ya? (TAGQ), which follows an ordinary clause or phrase as in example (166). These tag questions are a type of yes/no question. The tag question particle may be used on its own as a general question about something which is clear in the context of situation or with the meaning 'What do you think?' used to lead into a more specific question.

(166)   'Djabbarnbókka   njana-bá-la-yana.'
        shark   3MINA+1MINO-bite-REM-3MINMASCDATA
          'N-barrábarra   búlkkidj,   ya?'   'Ngawa.   Búlkkidj.'
          3MINMASC-big   big.wound   TAGQ   yes
        'A shark's bitten me!' 'Badly hurt, are you?' 'Yes.' (XX/60)

4.7.3 INFORMATION QUESTIONS. Information questions are formed using the interrogative/indefinite words discussed and exemplified in §3.4.1. While the interrogative particle frequently stands first in the clause it does not need to. These questions are the equivalent of WH questions in English and normally ask for details of one constituent of the clause to be supplied. The reply requires specific information of the questioned constituent, not just a yes or no. See examples (167), (168), (120) and Text 9/16, 18.

(167)   Nga-karráwa-ra   nga-ngadjí-na,   'Djíya   kárnmawa?'
        1MINS-look-REM   1MINS-say-REM here where?
        I [came to and] looked around and said, 'Where's this?' (XX/92)

(168)   Nga-ngadjí-na-yana,   'Yey!   Djalakkíyak   djíya
        1MINS-say-REM-3MINMASCDAT   Hey!   fish.spear   this
          ngaléwara   yá-ka-ra?'
          what?   1/2MINA+3MINO(+IRR)-kó-spear(+FUT)
        'Ma-yí-ndja.   Wánarda   yá-ka-ra
        MINIMP-leave-FUT   paddle   1/2MINA+3MINO-kó-spear
        yá-ka-na.'
        1/2MINA+3MINO-kó-sit
        I said to him, 'What are we going to kill them [stingrays] with?/What spear are we going to use? [i.e. 'We haven't got a spear.']' 'Leave it. We'll spear them with the paddle.' (XXIII/87–9)

4.8   AVERSATIVE CLAUSES

The aversative form of the verb expresses the undesirability of some possible action or event and the need to avoid it if possible. The element of avoidance within the meaning sometimes gives it a negative imperative force dependent on the context of situation. Details of forms are provided in §3.6.5 and some examples of use are provided under *Aversative* in §3.6.4.

Example (169) shows the 'intent to avoid' meaning clearly, expressing the reasons behind suggestions for action expressed by what we have called hortative verbs (§4.6.5) in the future tense.

(169) Nja-rra-ngúdjeya,   'Ngábi-yarra.   Kábba
       1AUGS-RE-say(+CTP)   1/2AUGS(+IRR)-go(+FUT)   water/tide
       ka-yó-ra.   Bakkándja   ku-wu-kkádja.'
       3MINMASCS-lie-CTP   later.on   3MINMASCS-AV-go.out [tide]
       'Yaláwa,   ngábi-yarra.'   Bakkándja   malóya
       ok   later on   rain
       njundu-bbú-ra-yana...
       3MINA+1AUGO+AV-hit-CTP-3MINMASCDATA
       We said, 'Let's go. The tide is still in, but it will go out soon [and beach the
       boat].' 'OK. Let's go.' The rain was going to get us too later on [so we
       left]. (XXXII/35–7)

Example (170) provides an action to be avoided followed by a reason
in the remote indicative because it is something which has already happened.
The aversative clause is marked with the aversative (AV) or negative purpose
particle kómalakka which requires the aversative verb form to follow it.

(170) His name [nála]   kómalakka   ngu-wu-má-ngka,
       [3MINMASC+name]   AV   1MINA+3MINO-AV-get-CTP
       njana   ka-yawé-la.
       because   3MINMASC-die-REM
       I can't use his name because he has died. (XIV/135)

Further examples are provided in (171) and (172), the latter being
taken from a child's story, transcribed and published as a reader.

(171) Djalákarra   ngu-rri-yirrí-ya,
       [dreaming place]   1/2UAS+AV-RE-go-CTP
       mábbarda   ngú-rri-warrawo...
       (bush/grass) fire   1UAA+AV-RE-light.fire
       ngundu-wu-bbú-ra-yana
       1/2AUGO+MINA-AV-hit-PAST1-3MINMASCDATA
       wálangandjáyiba   malóya   n-barrábarra...
       lightning   rain   3MINMASC-big
       If we go to the Djalákarra dreaming place or light a grass fire through there,
       lightning and big rain will come upon us [and this is something to be
       avoided if possible]. (XVIII/14–15)

(172) 'Na-ka-djórrkkangaya,   karrabba   nunburru-yí-ndja.'
       2AUGS-IRR-run   and   3AUGA+2AUGO+AV-leave-FUT
       'Run or they might leave you behind.' (*Banakúdjabba njarrabéna búdborl*)

Text examples of the aversative are Texts 25/72 and 77. The latter
does not appear to signify a desire to avoid the action because it expresses an
unsuccessful attempt. No parallels to this example have been found.

4.9   COORDINATION

4.9.1   CLAUSE LINKING. Most commonly, clauses are simply placed in sequence with no overt marker of coordination, as shown by many of the clauses in the texts accompanying this grammar.

There are, however a small number of overt markers of coordination, each of which tends to have a range of functions. Each of these will be treated in turn.

[a] *njana.* The conjunction njana appears to function as a fairly general link between clauses, usually having some sort of contrastive/comparative or adversative sense, or marking a consequence.

The contrastive meaning is apparent in examples (173) to (175), in example (26), in Text 7/16, 36 and in Text 9/27, 31.

(173)   [Ngámangarda   djówanga.]   Nakébba   njana
         [fish]   [moiety]   3MINMASCCARD   and/but
         kalalmúkkayana   djówanga.
         [fish]   [moiety]
         [?Trevally is Djówanga] and mullet, too, is Djówanga. (XXI/5–6)

(174)   [Ngaríbba]   Narrúrri-ba   ka-réndjeya   njana
         [palm dreaming] in.open-EXT   3MINMASCS-stand(+CTP)   and/but
         kádja   ka-réndjeya.
         inside
         [The Ngaríbba dreaming palm at Ndjúdda.] It grows in the open and also inside [the small patch of jungle] there. (XVIII/34–5)

(175)   [Ndjérwarra]   Makéddja ka-bé-na   ka-kó-na
         young people   turtle   3MINMASCS-go-REM   3MINMASCS-kó-sit
         njana, bi-rri-yáwalbbi-ba   yaláwa
         and/but 3UAMASC-RE-old person-EXT   then, well, on the other hand
         bá-rri-na.
         3UAS-RE-sit(+REM)
         [The young people] went off [hunting] turtles while the old people stayed behind [in the camp]. (VII/150)

A more adversative link between clauses occurs in examples (145) and (155) while njana expresses a more general linkage in examples like Text 9/6, 11, 41 and Text 25/77, 97. See also §4.9.2.

The consequence meaning occurs in (176) while njana marks a reason in example (170).

(176)   [Kénkarla]   Ya-ba-ngóna   njana   barnómandja
         pandanus nuts (FEM)   3MINFEMS-fall-REM   and/but soon
         nja-ya-ka-wála.
         3MINFEMS-IRR-kó-come ashore(+FUT)
         When the pandanus nuts have fallen [the female turtle] will come ashore soon [to lay her eggs]. (XXI/55-6)

[b] *yaláwa*. The word yaláwa on its own has a meaning something like 'that's that', 'that's enough', 'the end', 'that's all right'. Compare example (165). It is frequently used as a connective between clauses with the general sense that the activity covered by the first clause is complete and that the action then moves forward to that covered by the second clause. Yaláwa occurs either at the end of the first clause or at the beginning of the second of a pair of clauses. Thus yaláwa is the equivalent of English 'and then' or 'when...then...' and so on as exemplified in (177) to (179), in Text 7/38, Text 9/2, 6 and in Text 25/9, 36, 37, 76, 86 and 99.

(177)   Karrabba   rénjmarla   ka-ya-kkó-ya,   yaláwa
         and   new moon   3MINMASCS-IRR-kó-lie   then
         barrúra   yaláwa   nja-ya-kkúndja.
         egg   then   3MINFEMS-IRR-lay eggs(+FUT)
When the new month comes she'll lay her eggs [turtle]. (XXI/58–9)

(178)   Ya-yikkabé-ra   ka-bé-na.   Yaláwa
         3MINA+3MINFEMO-tie-REM   3MINMASCS-go-REM   then
         kúdja   ka-ramí-ya-na.   Yaláwa
         *hand/foot   3MINMASCS-*hold-REFL-REM   then
         ka-kkádja-nga.   Yaláwa   ka-rlabí-na
         3MINS-tide go out-REM   then   3MINMASCS-descend-REM
         ka-bardórrbba-na   marlémarla.
         3MINA+3MINMASCO-crush-REM   poison berry
[They] kept on tying up [the bundles of paperbark into torches] until they finished. Then when the tide went out they came down and crushed the poison berries. (XVII/24–9)

(179)   Ka-nangarddjí-na   yaláwa,   kíddjal
         3MINMASCS-break+REFL-REM   then   new shoots
         ka-míba   múlbbum.
         3MINMASCS-arrive   several
The main [ngaríbba dreaming palm] got broken and now several new shoots are emerging. (XVIII/37–8)

[c] *karrabba*. The basic meaning of karrabba involves comparison: 'similarly', 'likewise' (§5.1.1). It, too, can be used to conjoin clauses or noun phrases but differs from njana, even if only slightly, in its focus on similarity rather than contrast. See also §4.9.2. Examples (180) to (184) and Text 7/6, 12 show the use of karrabba as a linker of clauses, though (183) suggests contrast, not similarity. Perhaps the meaning is 'both according to need'.

(180)   ...warakkála,   karndóya,   njandakalábarna.
         long.yam   round.yam   lily.root
         Ngindi-wú-na-yángaya,   karrabba
         3MINA+1/2UAIO-give-REM-3MINFEMDATA   and.similarly
         ngirrikémala   ngi-rri-wú-na.
         1/2UAMASCEMPH   1/2UAMASCA+3MINIO-RE-give-REM
[The women went gathering] long yams, round yams and lily roots. They would give us [these foods] and [in the same way] we would give them [some turtle].   (VII/16–17)

(181)   N-kárddja   bi-rri-bá-la   nawála
          3MINMASC-cooked   3UAA+3MINMASCO-RE-eat-REM   *vomit
          bi-rri-yángka.   Karrabba   bakkándja
          3UAS-RE-do(+REM)   and   again
          bi-rri-ngárawa-na   wébba.
          3UAMASCA+3MINO-RE-light fire-REM   same
          They ate it cooked and vomited. Once again they lit a fire [and tried cooked
          fish with the same result]. (VII/91–3)

(182)   Wékkana   ya-ka-má-nga.
          at night   3MINA+3MINFEMO-kó-get-REM
          ka-má-nga   ka-rendjí-na   wékkana,
          3MINA+3MINO-*get-REM   3MINMASCS-stand-REM   at.night
          karrabba   djadjírra   ya-ka-má-nga.
          and   daytime   3MINA+3MINFEMO-kó-get-REM
          [The Macassans] got [trepang (FEM)] at night. They worked at night and
          they also got it in the daytime [hot part of the day]. (V/113–14)

(183)   Ngarráma... kalíkku   karrakárramardba,   karrabba   yídja
          woman   cloth   long   and   man
          ka-ndarládja.
          3MINMASC-short
          The women [got] long pieces of cloth, and the men got short ones. (V/274–5)

(184)   Kúdja-ngaya   ya-ka-wákka-na,   karrabba
          tracks-3MINFEMPOSS   3MINFEMS-kó-go.back-REM   and
          ya-balákka-na,   karrabba   ya-wákka-na,
          3MINFEMS-come.back-REM   karrabba   ya-wákka-na,
          karrabba   ya-balákka-na,   n-djídjabba   wébba...
                                           3MINMASC-same   same
          She went this way and that leaving many tracks all over the place [to confuse
          the husband she was deserting, and then she set off...] (XII/66–9)

4.9.2 NOMINAL PHRASE COORDINATION.

Nominal phrases are usually coordinated simply by listing them next to one another in Ndjébbana, as in example (180) and Text 7/20. Nevertheless the words njana and karrabba are used to link nominal phrases in the same way as they link clauses. Njana occurs in a contrastive function such as in examples (150), (151) and (155).

Karrabba is the more general conjunction between nominals as in Text 7/11 and in (185).

(185)   ...djábbarnma   nakébba,   ngárrabbakaddawórna
          sugarbag [wild honey] 3MINMASCCARD   [type sugar bag]
          karrabba   barlúya   wára.
          and   [type sugar bag]   too
          ...sugar bag, both ngárrabbakaddawórna and barlúya. (I/152–3)

4.10   SUBORDINATION

Clause subordination is rarely overtly marked in Ndjébbana and therefore is not clearly distinct from coordination. The core grammatical relationships in a clause are expressed within the verb complex and any additional material in the clause provides specification and elaboration of this. We will use the term 'subordinate clause' here for clauses which appear to provide such elaboration within another clause.

Subordinate clauses contain backgrounded information and, in common with other languages of the area (e.g. Rembarrnga, McKay 1988), it appears that Ndjébbana does not clearly distinguish specific types of subordinate clause from one another (e.g. time clause, relative clause, reason clause etc.). The sections which follow set out some uses of clauses within clauses, without attempting to provide a definitive analysis at this stage. In the following sections the putative subordinate clauses in the Ndjébbana text are enclosed in parentheses .

4.10.1 TIME CLAUSES WITH EXTENT SUFFIX.   An unusual subordinate clause type, because it does have overt marking, is a time clause which is marked using the extent suffix (§3.2.4) attached to the verb. The significance of this type of clause seems to range from 'when...' (indicating sequential actions) (e.g. (188) and Text 25/78)) to 'while...' (indicating an action in progress when the main clause action takes place) (e.g. (186) and (187)).

(186)   (Nga-wála-nga-bba)   nja-rra-bé-na
        1MINS-come.ashore-REM-EXT   1AUGS-RE-go-REM
          na-rra-lawá-ya   ngána   middjin
          1AUGA+3MINO-RE-know-CTP   there   mission
          Mangkulálkkudj.
          Croker Island
        [I didn't stop long at Goulburn Island.]   As soon as I landed [there] we went to – you know that mission – Croker Island. (XX/253)

(187)   (Nja-rra-baló-bba)   njanbi-rri-bbándja-nga.
        1AUGS-RE-come.hither(+CTP)-EXT   3AUGA+1AUGO-RE-put-REM
        When we arrived there they dropped us off. (XXV/95–7)

(188)   Marráya   ya-marabí-na.   (Marráya ya-marabí-na-bba)
        dirty water   3MINFEMS-enter-REM   -EXT
        njana-rá-na-yángaya.
        3MINFEMA-1MINO-jab-REM-3MINFEMDATA
        [The last stingray I was trying to spear] went into murky water. When it went into the murky water it bit me. (XXIII/10–11)

4.10.2 COMPLEMENT CLAUSES. The term 'complement clauses' is used here to cover clauses which provide a clausal object or complement to perception verbs (or which elaborate on the objects of perception verbs).

Verbs with such complements include lakalá 'to hear or feel', lémaye 'show' and the phrasal verb márdba ka-bbándja 'like'.

There is no overt marking of any complement status, with the complement clause following the main verb. The tense of perception verb and complement usually matches, as in examples (189) and (190) and Text 25/19,41, 62, 79. One exception is example (9).

(189) N-bárdbana   nja-rra-bé-na,   nga-ná-na
      3MINMASC-shallow   1AUGS-RE-go-REM   1MINA+3MINO-see-REM
      ka-kkó-ya.
      3MINMASCS-kó-lie(+CTP)
      We went into shallow water and I saw [a dugong (múrnun)] lying [in the water eating grass]. (XXIII/81)

(190) Nga-lakalá-ya   djíya   baddúmang,   nga-lakalá-ya
      1MINS-feel-REM   here   goggles   1MINS-feel-REM
      ka-ramí-ya-na.
      3MINS-hold-REFL-REM
      I felt my goggles here tightening. (XX/49–50)

After verbs like 'like' and 'show' complements may take the same tense as the main verb as in example (191) and in the negative example (141) or a tense marking a subsequent time as in (192) and (193).

(191) Mudíkkang   márdba   dja-ka-bbándja
      vehicle   *neck   2MINA+3MINO-IRR-*put(+FUT)
      yí-yarra   djá-ka-na...
      1/2MINS(+IRR)-go   2MINA+3MINO-IRR-see
      Would you like to take me [in your] truck to see... / [If] you like to take me with you [in your] truck you can see [the dreaming place, I'll show it to you...]. (XVIII/32–4)

(192) 'Márdba   nja-rra-bbándja-yana
      *neck   1AUGA+3MINO-RE-*put(+CTP)-3MINMASCDAT
      ká-ya-bala-yarra   njé-yarra
      3MINMASCS-IRR-hither-go(+FUT)   1AUGS(+IRR)-go(+FUT)
      Manayingkarírra.'
      Maningrida
      'We'd like him to come and go with us to Maningrida.' (XIV/83–4)

(193) 'Djíya   yaláwa   njá-rra-lamaya
      this   now   1AUGA+3MINIO-RE-show(+CTP)
      ka-ya-balába   yókkarra.'
      3MINA+3MINMASCO-IRR-hit(+FUT)   fish
      'We are showing this man how to catch fish [using the scoop net at the lúrra fish poisoning place]. (XVII/56)

4.10.3 CLAUSE AS NOUN PHRASE OR QUALIFIER. A clause, in particuar a verb complex, without any special marking, may occur to elaborate on one of the core arguments of the clause pronominally marked on the verb complex or to provide circumstantial modification of the clause (cf. §§4.2.2, 4.2.3).

Example (194) contains a non-verbal clause functioning to specify the S of the main clause. Compare Text 7/6, 9.

(194)   (Barrayabba   Márdbalk   wíba-baddabirra)
          3AUGCARD   Goulburn Island   country-3AUGPOSS
          ba-rra-bala-kkamíya-na   warábba-na.
          3AUGS-RE-hither-get up-REM   one-3MINMASCPOSS

          The people of Goulburn Island ('those whose country is Goulburn Island) went after that one [man]. (II/88–9)

Examples (195) and (142) contain non-restrictive relative clauses, while (196) and Text 7/2 contain restrictive relative clauses. The extent suffix appearing on the verb of the subordinate clause of (196) indicates habitual aspect (§3.2.4).

(195)   Nganéyabba   dengk   nga-namánda   yaláwa
          3MINMASCDEM   tank   3MINMASC-small   now
          ka-rawé-ra,   (njirrikébba
          3MINA+3MINMASCO-discard-REM   1UACARD
          nji-rri-kkawú-na).
          1AUGA+3MINO-RE-set up-REM

          They took down/got rid of that little tank which we had erected [and Forestry erected the big one which is there now]. (XIV/35)

(196)   Djíya   ka-malawédja-nga   djadjórla,   (Búnji
          this/here 3MINA+3MINMASCO-build-REM   house   Father
          Lódda   ka-yó-ra-bba).
          Latu   3MINMASCS-lie-CTP-EXT

          They built this house, where Bábba ['Father'—Búnji is a Maung word] Latu lives now [Rev. Mosese Latu, the Tongan missionary who was United/Uniting Church minister at Maningrida from 1972]. (XIV/40)

4.10.4 TIME AND PLACE CLAUSES. Clauses can be used to provide circumstantial modification of another clause, particularly giving details of time and place. Again, the subordinate clauses are not marked in any way for specific function. Examples (197) and (198) each contain the same time clause with a different function. Cohesive repetition (§4.2.4) also involves a time clause ('after having   -ed...then...').

(197)   Ngawa-balákka   (malóya   ka-ya-kkóndje-ya).
          1/2AUGS+IRR-come.back   rain   3MINMASCS-IRR-cut-REFL
          We'll come back when the rain finishes. (I/131–2)

(198)   Ngaba-yú-ka-na   (malóya ka-ya-kkóndje-ya).
         1/2AUGS-IRR-kó-sit rain   3MINMASCS-IRR-cut-REFL
         We'll stay until the rain stops. (I/150)

Examples (199) and (200) could both be seen as made up of coordinated clauses, (199) (from conversation) with no connective and the clauses of (200) joined by njana. It appears that, in context, one of the clauses in each example is backgrounded to the other.

(199)   (Ka-ya-balákka)   nga-ya-ngáwa.
         3MINMASCS-IRR-come back   1MINA+3MINO-IRR-ask
         When he comes back I will ask him.

(200)   '(Mábbarda   ka-ya-ka-wárraba),   njana
         grass fire   3MINMASCS-IRR-kó-burn   and
            nga-ya-ka-míba.'
            1MINS-IRR-kó-arrive
         'At "burnt grass time" I will come. (lit. 'When the grass burns..'] (XIV/68–9)

Example (201) contains a sequence of pairs of clauses which are coordinated using njana and yaláwa but which, in context, appear to contain backgrounded time clauses and main clauses.

(201)   (Kénkarla   ya-ba-ngóna)   njana   barnómandja
         pandanus.nut   3MINFEMS-fall-REM   and   soon
            nja-ya-ka-wála...   Karrabba (rénjmarla
            3MINFEMS-IRR-kó-come ashore   and   new moon
            ka-ya-kkó-ya),   yaláwa   barrúra... nja-ya-kkúndja.
            3MINMASCS-IRR-kó-lie   then   egg   3MINFEMS-IRR-lay
         When the pandanus nuts have fallen it won't be long before she [female turtle] will come ashore... when the new moon comes she [female turtle] will lay her eggs. (XXI/55–9)

In example (202), the subordinate clause could be taken either as a time specification or as a relative clause qualifying the indirect object of the main clause.

(202)   Ka-ngadjí-na   ngabúyanga   (nga-yarrárlma-nga
         3MINMASCS-speak-REM   1MINDAT   1MINS-grow-REM
            yaláwa),   (nga-ngurrarákka   yaláwa).
            then   1MIN-adult   then
         [My father] told me about this when I had grown up, when I was an adult. (II/71–2)

Examples (203), (204) and Text 25/35, 60 contain clauses which function as specifiers of place or destination. In each case the extent suffix -ba or -bba has a specific function other than the marking of subordination. In Text 25/35 the extent suffix on the word ngarakáya 'pandanus' indicates an area where many pandanus trees grow, while in each of the remaining examples it indicates 'habitual' aspect on the verb (§3.2.4).

(203)   (Balánda   ka-nó-ra-bba)   ngi-yi-wákka.
         white man   3MINMASCS-sit-CTP-EXT   1/2UAS-IRR-go back
         Let's go back to the white settlement.   [lit: 'to where the white man
         lives/where the white men live']   (I/244)

(204)   Nganéyabba   (wurrámbalk   ka-réndjeya-bba)
         there   house   3MINMASCS-stand(+CTP)-EXT
         ngi-yi-wákka.
         1/2UAS-IRR-go back
         Let's go back there where the houses are.   (I/249)

4.10.5 CONDITIONAL CLAUSES.   There is no specific marker of
conditional clauses. A number of the examples found so far (e.g. (171) use
the aversative mood. Others have future tense consequents as in (191) and
(205), while others are clearly hypothetical comments on past situations as in
example (206) from conversation.

(205)   Márdba   dja-ka-bbándja   djé-yarra
         *neck   2MINA+3MINO-IRR-*put   2MINS(+IRR)-go(+FUT)
         dja-kkóndja,   mardírrbala
         2MINA+3MINO(+IRR)-cut(+FUT)   mosquito
         dja-ka-mó[ya]-yana.
         3MINA+2MINO-IRR-bite(+FUT)-3MINMASCDATA
         If you want to go and cut it [dreaming place] mosquitoes will bite you.
         (XVIII/49–51)

(206)   Nga-ya-bbóbba-na   Bráydey   rdórdbalk.
         1MINS-IRR-go-CF   Friday   good
         [If] I had gone on Friday [it would have been] all right [but now it's too late].
         (JB June 1992)

5.   SEMANTICS

Comment will be made on just two areas of Ndjébbana semantics in this
chapter. These are comparison and gender class assignment in relation to
processing and technology. A major comparative ethnosemantic study of
natural species in Ndjébbana and other languages of western Arnhem Land
has been carried out by C. Coleman but has not yet been prepared for
publication. A further semantic topic, that of alienability of possession and
identity, has been discussed in connection with possession classes of
nominals (§3.2.3; McKay 1995).

5.1   COMPARISON

Under comparison we will include forms which express similarity, translating terms such as 'like' and 'same', as well as comparison relative to a norm.

5.1.1 SAMENESS OR SIMILARITY.   Apart from its use to conjoin clauses (§4.9.1) karrabba, usually used as a preposition and often combined with the postposition wébba, is used to express similarity, as in examples (207), (208) and Texts 25/60 and 70.

(207)   Djalákarra...   balawúrrwurr   ka-ngódjba-ra
         stingray dreaming   wind   3MINA+3MINMASCO-make-CTP
           malóya—   karrabba   ngaríbba   wébba.
           rain   like   dreaming palm   like
         The stingray dreaming makes wind and rain, just like the ngaríbba palm dreaming [does]. (XVIII/3-4)

(208)   Ngaríbba — karrabba   djéyabba   kalúkku   méyameya   —
         dreaming palm like   that   coconut   leaf
           ka-réndjeya.
           3MINMASCS-stand/be(+CTP)
         The ngaríbba palms—their leaves are like coconut leaves—are there. (XVIII/1)

Karrabba can also be used to compare in the sense 'me too', as in (209), though Karrabba ngáyabba would be the more usual order if 'Me too' were to be expressed as an utterance on its own.

(209)   "Alf Wilson?" "Nganéyabba   nga-lawáya."
         (name)   3MINMASCDEM   1MINA+3MINMASCO-know(+CTP)
           "Nganéyabba   nga-lawáya   ngáyabba   karrabba"
                                            1MINCARD   like/too
         "Alf Wilson?" "I know the man you mean." "I know him too." [lit. I know him, me too.] (JN)

Similarity of appearance can also be expressed using the reflexive form of the verb bú 'hit' coupled with the extent suffix.

(210)   Bi-rri-bú-ya-bba.
         3UAS-RE-hit-REFL(+CTP)-EXT
         They look like one another.

5.1.2 SAMENESS OR IDENTITY.   To express identity of reference and its opposite, the nominals djídjabba (D1) 'same' and náwarla/náworrkala (D2) 'different' are used. The postposition wébba may be used with djídjabba. See (211), (184) and Text 7/18, 25/69.

(211)   Naméwaya   ngí-ya-ma   djídjabba   wébba.
         net   1/2UAA+3MINO-IRR-get(+CTP)   same   same
         We'll get the same net. (I/170)

5.1.3 GRADABLE COMPARISON.

Ndjébbana gradable adjectives do not have morphologically marked comparative and superlative forms but it appears that the simple form of the adjective may be used to express implied comparison with a norm or reference point. See (212) and (213).

(212)   Wukúyawa   nga-namánda.
         perhaps   3MINMASC-small
         Perhaps it's too small. (Comment on finding a cork which might be used as a
         plug for the speaker's boat.) (JB)

(213)   "Djé-yarra?"   "Kóma.   Ba-rra-karrówa."
         2MINS(+IRR)-go   no   3AUGS-RE-many.
         "Are you going?" "No. There are too many people already." (i.e. the boat is
         already overloaded) (JB)

5.2   TECHNOLOGY AND GENDER CLASSES

There is slight evidence in Ndjébbana for an association between the feminine gender class (cf.§3.2.2) and modern western technology and processing. The evidence comes from gender class assignment with two forms which also have homophonous forms with masculine gender class assignment.

kánkarra (D1) 'meat' normally agrees in gender class with the nominal referring to the animal from which the meat is taken. On the other hand the masculine form n-kánkarra is used as a generic term for fresh (or frozen) meat when a specific source animal is not being referred to. In reference to 'sausages', however, the generic term is the feminine form nja-kánkarra.

Similarly (cf.§3.2.3) the nominal ngalidjbínja, apart from its class C form meaning 'throat or windpipe', has two homophonous class A forms, the masculine one meaning 'didgeridoo or dronepipe', the feminine one meaning 'shotgun or rifle'.

This may be no more significant than that, the masculine gender already being used for one category in each case, the feminine form was the only remaining form available to mark a distinct (borrowed) category not previously needed.

5.3   ALIENABILITY AND POSSESSION MARKING

The four distinct methods of marking possession or identity on nominals in Ndjébbana correlate iconically with a cline of alienability as outlined in §3.2.3. Simple juxtaposition of separate words, nominal and possessor (marked by cardinal pronoun) in class A represents the most alienable form of possession marking, while at the other end of the scale identity of reference or inalienable possession is marked by pronominal suffixes or prefixes on the nominal as in classes C and D respectively.

6. TEXTS

The three texts provided here are transcriptions of tape recorded narratives, one from each of the three main speakers who provided the information upon which the grammar is based. Each text is an extract or a series of extracts from a larger discourse, Text 7 being a procedural narrative, Text 9 a traditional story and Text 25 a description of recent personal experience. They provide rich exemplification of material presented in the grammar as well as some connected discourse to complement the isolated sentences used in the grammatical exposition. * in glosses marks idiomatic phrases.

6.1   TEXT 7

JM 7 April 1976

The lúrra is a ceremonial fish poisoning held at Entrance Island. Only men who are speakers of the njálkkidj form of Ndjébbana are permitted to participate. People from many different groups gathered at Ndjúdda (Juda Point) to help eat the huge catch. The participants made their way across to the island in bark canoes (ngandjúddama) and, at the appropriate time dragged bags of crushed poison berries through the water at the lúrra pool., scooping up the stunned fish with nets. This very brief outline concentrates primarily on the preparations for lúrra and on its nature as a cooperative occasion shared by many groups.

1	Lúrra		ka-bbándja-nga		yinjírra,
	[place for fish poisoning]		3MINA+3MINMASCO-put-REM		1AUGDAT
2		njírrabba	Ndjébbana	nja-rra-ngúdjeya...	
		1AUGCARD	[language]	1AUGS-RE-speak(+CTP)	

The lúrra [fish poisoning place/ceremony at Entrance Island] was given to us speakers of Ndjébbana... (VII/122)

3	Bárriya		bábba	bá-rri-na	
	3UAMASCDEM		father	3UAS-RE-sit(+REM)	
4	bi-rri-badjí-na-baddana.			Nganéyabba	
	3UAS-RE-call-REM-3UAMASCPOSS			there	
5	bi-rri-rlibí-na		Ndjúdda	ba-rrú-ka-na...	
	3UAS-RE-go down-REM		Juda Point	3AUG-RE-kó-sit(+REM)	

My two fathers called to those two and they all went and gathered at Ndjúdda... (VII/126)

6	Karrabba	bá-rri-na	Namarládja	bi-rri-baló-ka-na
	and	3UAS-RE-sit	[place]	3UAS-RE-hither-kó-sit
7	bi-rri-bidjí-na-baddana			bi-rri-wala-bé-na
	3UAS-RE-sing out-REM-3UAPOSS			3UAS-RE-hither-go-REM
8	nganéyabba	warábba-na	wébba	nja-rra-kkúdja-nga.
	there	one-3MINMASC		1AUGS-RE-group-REM

9 Bá-rri-na   Karddjirráma   warábba-na   wébba   nja-rra-kkúdja-nga
   3UAS-RE-sit   [place]
10 Ndjúdda.
   Juda Point

And the Namarládja people were there. They sent out the call to them and they came and we all gathered at the one place. And the Karddjirráma people joined us there at Ndjúdda. (VII/127)

11 Bárriya   bi-rri-yik-Karddúrra,   karrabba Wúrnal
   3UAMASCDEM   3UAMASC-RE-CLAN-[clan name]   and   [clan name]
12 bi-rri-bidjí-na.   Karrabba   bárriya   birrikémala
   3UAS-RE-sing out-REM   and   3UAMASCEMPH
13 (ngá-waddabo   ngi-yirrí-ya)   Kanduwúlka,
   1MINA+3MINO-follow(+CTP)   1MINS-go-CTP   [clan name]
14 bi-rri-bidjí-na   marnákarna...
   stick frame for scoop net

Those two Karddúrra men, and the Wúrnal men sent out the call. And those two...(I'm just trying to think of their clan name...) Kanduwúlka sent out the call [with] a scoop net. (VII/131)

They sent the call this way (towards Manayingkarírra) and that way (towards Namarládja) and in between (towards Karddjirráma) using the sticks from a scoop net or bits of the poison bush (Diospyros maritima) as a signal.

15 Yaláwa   ránba   nji-rri-rlabí-na   kómabba.   Marlémarla
   then   beach   1UA-RE-descend-REM   all   poison bush (berries)
16 ba-rra-malónba-na-nja.   Njana   njirrikémala
   3UAFEMA+3MINO-RE-pick-REM-UAFEM   and   1UAMASCEMPH
17 naméwaya.   Máwala.   N-djárwarra
   scoop net   paperbark 3MINMASC-adolescent
18 ka-rawé-ra.   Nga-náwarla   barrangúdja
   3MINA+3MINMASCO-throw-REM   3MINMASC-other   game (turtle)
19 bi-rri-bé-na.
   3UAS-RE-go-REM

[In response to the call] we all went down to the beach [at Ndjúdda]. The women picked the berries of the poison bush (strychnine bush) and we [men looked after] the nets. Some of the young men got paperbark from the trees [the very stringy paperbark from the small paperbarks growing around the saltpan behind the mangroves]and others went [hunting] turtle. (VII/137)

20 Barrayámalanja   múlil   njandakalábarna,   warakkála   karndóya
   3UAFEMEMPH   feast   lily root   long yam   cheeky yam(FEM)
21 yaba-rra-karlába-nja,   kuyángba
   3UAFEMA+3MINFEMO-RE-immerse(+REM)-UAFEM   roasted cheeky yam
22 yika.   Ya-kkárdda   ya-kkó-ya   karrakanódjabba
   as well 3MINFEMS-under water   3MINFEMS-kó-lie   next morning
23 ka-balanabé-ra   yaláwa   nja-rra-bé-na.
   3MINMASCS-dawn-REM   then   1AUGS-RE-go-REM

The women [gathered food for the] feast: lily roots, long yams, and round cheeky yams. They soaked some of the cheeky yams in water and others they sliced and roasted. Early the next morning we set off. (VII/141)

24 Nja-rra-bé-na   ránba   nganéyabba   djúlumukkiyirriya   ngáni::.
   1AUGS-RE-go-REM   beach   that   point   there
25   Warakkála-n-karrówa-ka-réndjeya.   Nja-rra-wála-nga.
      yam-3MINMASC-many-3MINMASCS-stand   1AUGS-RE-go ashore-REM
26   Máwala   nja-rra-bbándja-nga.
      paperbark   1AUGA+3MINO-RE-put down-REM

We went [from] the beach at that point over there [pointing with lips to Ndjúdda] and went ashore at Warakkálankarrówakaréndjeya [on Entrance Island] where we piled up the paperbark. (VII/143)

27 Máwala   nja-rra-bbándja-nga.   Máwala   nja-rra-bbándja-nga.
   paperbark   1AUGA+3MINO-RE-put-REM
28   Bi-rri-yáwalbbi-ba   njanbi-rri-bbándja-nga.
      3UAMASC-RE-old person-EXT   1AUGA+3UAO-put-REM
29   Bi-rri-yáwalbbi-ba   njanbi-rri-bbándja-nga
      3UAMASC-RE-old person-EXT   1AUGA+3UAO-put-REM
30   yibi-rri-nídja-nga   bá-rri-na.
      3UAA+3MINFEMO-RE-wait for-REM   3UAMASCS-RE-sit(+REM)
31   Yibi-rri-rayé-ra   bá-rri-na   máwala...
      3UAMASCA+3MINFEMO-RE-tear up-REM   3UAMASCS-RE-sit(+REM)   paperbark

We put the paperbark there and we left the old people to attend to it. They tore the paperbark up [into pieces which were later bound together to make long torches]. (VII/145)

32 N-djárwarra   kómrdudj   njanbi-rri-má-nga
   3MINMASC-adolescent   initiand   1AUGA+3UAMASCO-RE-get-REM
33   karnayédjabba,   nangalayana   warábba-na
      two   how many?/maybe   one-3MINMASCPOSS
34   Djéyabba ngúdja   kóma.   Kóma   ka-ya-ngadjí-na.
      that one   speech   NEG   NEG
      3MINMASCS-IRR-speak-CF

We might have one or two 'new men' [at the lúrra] and they were not allowed to speak. (VII/151)

35 Marnbúrrba   kóma   nji-rri-bé-na   wúrdayak.   Bákki   kóma
   cloth   NEG   1UAS-RE-go-REM   long ago   tobacco   NEG
36   djakóra   njí-rawó-ngana.   Njana   wóndja
      *smoke   1UAA+3MINO+IRR-*throw-CF   but   only
37   marnákarna   njana   yókkarra   yaláwa.
      net(stick frame)   and   fish   that's it.

In the old days we got around with no clothes and we didn't smoke tobacco. [We only had] nets and fish, that's all. (VII/153)

38 Njélnjel   ka-kó-na,   yaláwa   nji-rri-bé-na
   late afternoon   3MINMASCS-kó-sit(+REM)   then   1UAS-RE-go-REM

39	njá-rri-na.		Nji-rri-bé-na	njá-rri-na
	1UAS-RE-sit(+REM)		1UAS-RE-go-REM	1UAS-RE-sit(+REM)
40	nganéyabba	lúrra		nji-rri-djórrba-na,
	there	fish poisoning place		1UAA+3MINMASCO-RE-cook-REM
41	ránba.	Nji-rri-djórrba-na,		wékkana.
	beach	1UAA+3MINMASCO-RE-cook-REM		night time.

When late afternoon came we would go there to the lúrra place. [When we had caught all the fish holding our torches and poisoning the water then scooping up all the stunned fish in our nets] we would cook them on the beach at night. (VII/155)

42	Nji-rri-balála-nga		múlil,	nji-rri-rendjí-na.
	1UAS-RE-come back-REM		party/feast	1UAS-RE-stand-REM
43	Nganéyabba	yaláwa	nji-rri-múyawa-na.	
	there	then	1UAS-RE-finish-REM	

We would come back to Ndjúdda (Juda Point) and have a great feast [of the fish and the food which the women had collected before]. And then we were finished. (VII/158)

44	Marlémarla	karrabba	djíya	yaláwa,	malóya	njáya	yaláwa
	poison bush	like	this	now	rain	3MINFEMDEM	that's it
45		balarrírra,	nganéyabba	yaláwa	nji-rri-múyawa-na.		
		new grass	that	that's it	1UAS-RE-finish-REM		

The poison bush [is fruiting] this time now. [We wait for] the rain and the new green grass. Then we have finished. (VII/159)

6.2   TEXT 9

JB 11 October 1977

The story begins with Djawándja having fed Kángkarlangarda, the white breasted sea eagle, and Djambalówa, the brahminny kite with the yam marnawarrínjba (Djówanga name) or karrórnba (Yírriddjanga name). He plans to leave them with the bark canoe they have just finished while he goes to get more yams. When he gets back they will all go off in the bark canoe to Manakúkun, a spike rush place which existed at that time between the present Kabálko (Entrance Island) and Ndjúdda (Juda Point or North East Point).

1	'Méd	nbi-yi-nídja.		Nbi-yi-nídja	nga-ya-balábara
	not yet	2UAA+1MINO-IRR-wait			1MINA+3MINO-IRR-hit
2		marnawarrínjba	karrórnba.	Karrórnba	nga-ya-balábara	yaláwa,
		cheeky yam	cheeky yam			'finish'
3		ngi-yi-móya		ngí-yarra.'	
		1UAMASCS-IRR-eat		1UAMASCS(+IRR)-go	

'Wait a bit for me. Wait for me [while]I go and get more of these yams, then we can eat them and go [to Manakúkun]. (IX/29)

4	'Ngawa.' Ka-kkamíya-na.		Ka-bé-na.		Birrikébba
	yes	3MINMASCS-leave-REM	3MINMASCS-goREM		3UAMASCCARD

5   birrikébba karnayédjabba,   bi-rri-ndakalába.
      two   3UAA+3MINO-RE-put in water(+REM)

6   Bi-rri-bbándja-nga   bana-kábbi-ba   yaláwa,   njana
      3UAA+3MINO-RE-putREM   LOC-water-EXT   'finish' and

7   bi-rri-walédjba   bi-rri-bé-na.
      3UAS-RE-paddle(+REM)   3UAS-RE-go-REM

'Yes,' [they said.] He went off and the two of them put the canoe in the water and
started paddling. (IX/31)

8   Bi-rri-rakarawé-ra   bi-rri-bé-na::::.   Ngána djíya karlakárrbba.
    3UAS-RE-moveREM   3UAS-RE-go-REM(+DUR)   there there river

9   Yanakkábba   ka-rendjí-na   ka-rakarawé-ra   yakanádja
      dry land   3MINS-stand-REM   3MINS-move-REM   this side

10   ngána.   Warábba-na   djíya   karlakárrbba
      there   one-3MINMASCPOSS   there   river

      ka-rendjí-na   ka-rakarawé-ra.
      3MINS-stand-REM   3MINS-move-REM

Off they went. Over on that side [to the west of Entrance Island] there was the river,
but on this side [east of Entrance Island] there used to be dry land right across. There
was only one river channel [in those days]. (IX/33)

11 Ka-waledjba   ka-rakarawé-ra.   Njana bi-rri-rakarawé-ra
    3MINS-paddle(+REM)   3MINMASCS-move-REM   and   3UAS-RE-move-REM

12   bi-rri-bé-na,   bi-rri-wála-nga,   Kabálko.
      3UAS-RE-go-REM   3UAS-RE-go ashore-REM   Entrance Island

They paddled all the way and went ashore at Kabálko [Entrance Island]. (IX/36)

13 Nakémala   Djawándja,   ka-kó-na.
    3MINMASCEMPH   Djawándja   3MINMASCS-kó sit(+REM)

14   Ka-balákka-na   ka-bala-rakarawé-ra.
      3MINS-return-REM   3MINMASCS-come hither-move-REM

15   Ka-karráwa-ra.   Kóma.
      3MINMASCS-look around-REM NEG

Djawándja came back and looked around. [He saw] nothing [i.e. noone]. (IX/37)

16 'Kárnmawa   ni-rri-bé-na?   Bábba-naddana   ka-yawé-la.'
    where?   2UA-RE-go-REM   father-2UAMASCPOSS 3MINS-die-REM

17   Swéya   ka-kó-na   yiberrekéyanga.
      swear   3MINMASCS-kó-SIT(+REM)   3UAMASCDAT

'Where have you gone, you bastards? He swore at them. (IX/39)

18 'Kárnmawa   ni-rri-bé-na   karnayédjabba?   Ngáyabba
    where?   2UA-RE-go-REM   two   1MINCARD

19   nindi-wú-na.   Marnawarrínjba   ni-rri-bá-la,
      1MINA+2UAIO-give-REM   yam   2UAA+3MINO-eat-REM

20   karrórnba. Nindi-wú-na. Dórdbalk   kómabba ni-rri-bá-la.
      yam   good   both   2UAA+3MINO-eat-REM

21   Djaráma   ni-rri-nibí-ya-na.   Nbi-rri-wérangarda.'
        *heavy   2UAS-RE-*step-REFL-REM   2UAA+1MINO-RE-leave behind
'Where have you gone, [you] two? I gave you [yams] and you ate them. You both ate
well [until] you were full, and now you've [gone and] left me behind.' (IX/40)

*He set to to find a log which could serve him instead of a canoe. After trying several
different types of log, all of which sank, he found that the nbókka log would bear his
weight and he set off paddling in pursuit. Meanwhile...*

22 Birrikémala   bi-rri-kkimíya-na   bi-rri-rakarawé-ra
    3UAMASCEMPH   3UAS-RE-set off-REM   3UAS-RE-move-REM
23   yókkarra,   ngayaméla.   Bi-rri-rá-na.
        fish (MASC)   mullet(FEM)   3UAA+3MINMASCO-RE-spear-REM
24 Bi-rri-rá-na bi-rri-balákka-na.   Bi-rri-ddjórrba-na.
     3UAS-RE-return-REM   3UAA+3MINMASCO-roast-REM
25   Bi-rri-ddjórrba-na   bi-rri-bá-la   bá-rri-na.
        3UAA+3MINO-roast-REM   3UAA+3MINO-eat-REM   3UAS-RE-sit(+REM)
26   Na-wála   bi-rri-yángka.
        INFIN-rise 3UAS-RE-do
Those [other] two went [hunting for] fish–mullet. They speared some, came back and
cooked it. Then they ate it. They vomited. (IX/63)

27 Na-wála   bi-rri-yángka.   'Yé.   Djéyabba   n-kárddja   njana
    INFIN-rise 3UAS-RE-do   Hey!   this   3MINMASC-cooked but
28   méd   yí-wákka   bakkándja   yá-ka-ra
        not yet 1/2MINS+IRR-go back   again   1/2MINA+3MINO-IRR-spear
29   yá-ka-na.   Yídja   ngána   n-kálakarra,
        1/2MINS-IRR-sit   man   that   3MINMASC-person/Aboriginal
30   ka-yi-ka-móya   n-kárddja.
        3MINA+3MINMASCO-IRR-kó-eat+FUT   3MINMASC-cooked
31   Njana   ngárrabba   yí-yarra   n-barlánga   méd
        and   1/2UACARD   1/2UAS+IRR-go   3MINMASC-raw   still
32   yí-móya.'
        1/2MINA+3MINO+IRR-eat+FUT
They vomited. 'Hey! This is cooked. Let's go back and get some more [fish]. Let
people eat cooked [fish], but you and I will eat raw [fish].' (IX/67)

33   Nakémala   barréyabba.
        3MINMASCEMPH   close
[Djawándja] was nearly there... (IX/70)

*He swore at them again (including example (108)). They carried on cooking fish, unaware
of his approach*

34 Ka-walédjba.   Ka-kkúndja-nga   ka-rakarawé-ra.
    3MINMASCS-paddle   3MINA+3MINO-*defecate-REM   3MINS-*move-REM
35   Ka-bala-rakarawé-ra   ka-wala-bé-na.
        3MINMASC-come hither-move-REM   3MINS-come hither-go-REM
36   Kóma   ngaléwara.   Kábba   djíya,   ngúlmardirdi.
        NEG   anything   water   there   big wave/rough sea

He paddled like mad and got there. [He tried to get hold of the bark canoe but could do]
nothing [because of] the water there, the huge waves. (IX/72)

37 Ka-kkúndja-nga   ka-bala-rakarawé-ra.
    3MINS-*defecate-REM   3MINS-come hither-*moveREM
38   Ka-bbó-na.   Ka-bala-kkákka-ya,
        3MINA+3MINMASCO-hit-REM   3MINA+3MINO-hither-push-REM
39   hábwey.   Bakkándja.   Ka-méymayéya-na.
        half way   again   3MINS-be ready-REM

He rushed [it again] and bumped [the canoe on the shore]. He pulled it half way. [He
tried] again. He managed it... (IX/73)

*Meanwhile the other two were busily trying fish cooked and raw and did not notice him at
first. When they saw him they rushed to try and stop him.*

40 Rúrr   ka-ddjórrkka-bba.   Ka-rlabí-na,
    whoosh   3MINA+3MINMASCO-take(+REM)-EXT   3MINMASCS-descend-REM
41   njana   djúrrk   ka-warré-ya.
        and   hop   3MINMASCS-jump-REM

Whoosh! he pulled [the bark canoe] down [into the water] and hopped into it.

*They swore at him and accused him of stealing a canoe which did not belong to him.   They
rushed at him.*

42 Bi-rri-ramé-ra.   Kóma.   Ngawa.   Ka-warré-ya.   Ngána
    3UAA+3MINO-RE-grab-REM   NEG   yes   3MINS-jump-REM   there
43   ka-walédjba   ka-rakarawé-ra.   Bakkándja
        3MINS-paddle(+REM)   3MINMASCS-move-REM   again
44   bi-rri-kkúndja-nga   bi-rri-bala-rakarawé-ra.
        3UA-RE-*defecate-REM   3UAS-RE-hither-*move-REM
45   Bi-rri-ramé-ra,   kóma.   N-bókka
        3UAA+3MINO-RE-grab-REM   NEG   3MINMASC-*bad
46   bi-rri-bá-la.
        3UAA+3MINO-RE-*eat-REM

They grabbed at him. Nothing. Well he hopped on and paddled [away]. Again they
rushed and [tried to] grab him. They missed. (IX/88)

*Djawándja paddled off and split and sank the land between Ndjúdda and Kabálko, opening up
a second river channel to the sea on the east of Kabálko, turning it into an island and
stranding the other two there.   The former spike rush place Manakúkun was submerged
under the salt water which rushed in.   Djawándja went ashore and established himself at
Karddjirráma (Gudjerama Creek).*

6.3   TEXT 25

JK 21 May 1981

*This text deals with a typical hunting trip only a few days before the date of
recording. The narrator JK was accompanied throughout these episodes by JB who, in
1992, after JK's death, was able to clarify a number of points regarding the original
transcription and translation. JK was a regular, skilled and successful hunter, especially on
the sea.*

1	Braydey,	sdád	nja-rra-nó-ra		Braydey,	djíbba.
	Friday	start	1AUGS-RE-sit-CTP		Friday	here
2		Nja-rra-yó-ra		djíya	ránba.	Nja-rra-yó-ra
		1AUGS-RE-lie-CTP		this	beach	1AUGS-RE-lie-CTP
3		warábba-na		kayókaya.	Nja-rra-kkamíya,	léndin.
		one-3MINMASCPOSS		night	1AUGS-RE-depart(+CTP)	landing
4		Nja-rra-bbándja-ya.	(GMcK:)		Kárnmawa	lénding?
		1AUGS-RE-put-REFL(+CTP)			where?	landing
5		(JK:)	Kurrídja.			
			[place name]			

We started on Friday, here. We camped one night at the beach here and then we left
and camped at the landing. (GMcK) Where's the landing? (JK) Kurrídja. (XXV/1)

6	Nji-rri-bbándja-ya		nja-rra-nó-ra.		Nji-rri-yirrí-ya
	1UAS-RE-put-REFL(+CTP)		1AUGS-RE-sit-CTP		1UAS-RE-go-CTP
7		njélnjel. Nji-rri-yirrí-ya	njélnjel	yaláwa	kóma.
		late afternoon		okay	nothing
8		Nji-rri-balákka.	Nji-rri-balákka.	Warábba-na	
		1UAS-RE-return(+CTP)		one-3MINMASCPOSS	
9		lárla-na	nji-rri-ná-dja,		nbúrla.
		male-3MINMASCPOSS	1UAA+3MINO-RE-see-CTP		bull
10		Ka-rá-ya.	Nbók[ka]	ká-ba.	
		3MINA+3MINMASCO-shoot-CTP	*bad	3MINA+3MINO-*bite(+CTP)	

We camped there. We [the two men of the party] went out [hunting] in the late
afternoon, but got nothing. We came back. We saw one male buffalo, a bull. He
[my nephew] took a shot at it and missed. (XXV/4)

11	Nji-rri-balákka	nji-rri-yó-ra	ya-ndamérbaya.
	1UAS-RE-come back(+CTP)	1UAS-RE-lie-CTP	3MINFEM-set
	(sun)(+CTP)		

12 Nji-rri-yó-ra   wékkana-ngána   ká-bala-nabo.
    1UAS-RE-lie-CTP   night-PURP   3MINMASCS-come.hither-step(+CTP)

13   Nji-rri-ddjí-ndja   dí   brekbis,   bálay   nja-rra-yirrí-ya.
       1UAA+3MINO-RE-drink-CTP   tea   breakfast   then   1AUGS-RE-go-CTP

We went back to sleep and the sun went down. In the morning dawn came, we drank
tea and [ate] breakfast and then we went. (XXV/7)

14 Njá-rra-rakarawo   nja-rra-yirrí-ya.   Namarnakkúrrkka
    1AUGS-RE-move(+CTP)   1AUGS-RE-go-CTP   creek

15   nja-rra-warré-ra,   nabarlámbarla.   Kúdja-baddabirra
       1AUGS-RE-cross-CTP   freshwater   track-3AUGPOSS

16   njanbi-rri-ná-dja.
       1AUGA+3AUGO-RE-see-CTP

We were going along and we crossed a freshwater creek, when we saw the tracks of
some buffaloes. (XXV/10)

17 Nja-rra-ná-dja   makéddja
    1AUGA+3MINO-RE-see-CTP   long necked turtle (FEM)

18   ya-rríkka   yi-yirrí-ya   nja-nabarlámbarla,
       3MINFEMS-crawl(+CTP)   3MINFEMS-go-CTP   3MINFEM-freshwater

19   nja-barrábarra.   Nga-má-ngka
       3MINFEM-big   1MINA+3MINO-pick up-CTP

20   nga-ddjórrkka   nji-rri-yirrí-ya.
       1MINA+3MINO-take(+CTP)   1UAS-RE-go-CTP

21   Nja-yínjawa   nga-ddjórrkka
       3MINFEM-alive   1MINA+3MIN0-take(+CTP)

We saw a long-necked turtle crawling along, the freshwater one, a big one. I picked it
up and took it with me. I carried it live [by the neck]. (XXV/15)

22 Nga-réndjeya.   Nji-rri-ngúdjeya   yiberrekéyanga, 'Nirrikébba
    1MINS-stand(+CTP)   1UAS-RE-speak(+CTP)   3UAMASCDAT   2UACARD

23   ndjéya   bá-rri-yarra,   njirrikébba   nji-yi-wákka,
       this way   UAIMP-RE-go   1UACARD   1UAS-IRR-return(+FUT)

24   yakanádja   nji-yi-wákka   njí-yarra.'   Njanbi-rri-míwa-nga
       that way   1UAS-IRR-return   1UAS+IRR-go   1UAA+3UAO-RE-send-CTP

25   Yakanábba   bi-rri-yirrí-ya   njirrikébba   nji-rri-balákka
       this way   3UAS-RE-go-CTP   1UACARD   1UAS-RE-come back+CTP

I stopped. We said to them, 'You two go this way [west] and us two, we'll go back
that way [east].' We sent them off. They went this way and we came back.
(XXV/18)

26 Nji-rri-baló-bba   nji-rri-bala-yirrí-ya
    1UAS-RE-come hither-EXT   1UAS-RE-hither-go-CTP

27   njanbi-rri-ná-dja   kúdja-baddabirra,   káw,   karnayédjabba
       1UAA+3AUGO-RE-see-CTP   track-3AUGPOSS   cow   two

28   karnayédjabba.   Ba-rra-wála   ba-rra-yirríya.
       two   3AUGS-go up(+CTP)   3AUGS-RE-go+CTP

We were walking up when we saw their tracks [buffaloes], a cow [and three calves],
four of them [four fingers raised]. They were going up.

29 Ba-rra-bala-yirrí-ya   nabarlámbarla   namarnakkúrrkka
   3AUGS-RE-hither-go-CTP   freshwater   creek

30   ba-rra-warré-ra.   Njá-rri-rakarawo   nji-rri-yirrí-ya   kúdja-baddabirra
      3AUGS-cross-CTP   1UAS-RE-move   1UAS-RE-go-CTP   track-3AUGPOSS

31   kúdja-baddabirra.   Ba-rra-réndjeya   ba-rra-kkamíya
      track-3AUGPOSS   3AUGS-RE-stand(+CTP)   3AUGS-RE-depart(+CTP)

32   Bá-rra-rakarawo   ba-rra-yirrí-ya.
      3AUGS-RE-move(+CTP)   3AUGS-RE-go-CTP

They came to a freshwater creek and crossed it. The two of us moved along
[following] their tracks. They stopped, they set off again and moved along. (XXV/24)

33 Njá-rri-rakarawo   nji-rri-yirrí-ya.   Njá-rri-rakarawo   nji-rri-yirrí-ya.
   1UAS-RE-move   1UAS-RE-go-CTP

34   Djakí   nji-rri-má-ngka   kúdja-baddabirra.
      speed   1UAA+3MINO-RE-get-CTP   track-3AUGPOSS

35   Kúdja-baddabirra   nji-rri-warré-ra.   Nji-rri-rlábaya.
      track-3AUGPOSS   1UAS-RE-cross-CTP   1UAS-RE-descend(+CTP)

We hurried along, following their tracks. We crossed [the creek] and went down.
(XXV/27)

36 Nji-rri-rlábaya   ngarakáyi-ba   ba-rra-réndjeya.
   1UAS-RE-descend(+CTP)   pandanus-EXT   3AUGS-RE-stand-CTP

37   Ba-rra-réndjeya   yaláwa   wárrwarra   yaláwa   njáya
                        well   sun (FEM)   well   3MINFEMDEM

38   ya-rlúrrbaya,   ya-ndawarré-ra.
      3MINFEMS-arrive(+CTP)   3MINFEMS-be high in sky-CTP

39   Ba-rra-rlábaya   yaláwa   kábba   ba-rra-ddjí-ndja.
      3AUGS-RE-descend   so   water   3AUGA+3MINO-RE-drink-CTP

40   Njanbi-rri-ná-dja   nji-rri-réndjeya.
      1UAA+3AUGO-RE-see-CTP   1UAS-RE-stand(+CTP)

We went down to where they were standing among the pandanus. They were standing
around [because] the sun was high in the sky [pointing with lips][mid to late
morning]. So they had gone down and were drinking water. We saw them. (XXV/30)

41 Nakébba   ka-kkamíya.   Nakébba
   3MINMASCCARD   3MINMASCS-set off(+CTP)   3MINMASCCARD

42   yawúyakka-njabba   ki-yirrí-ya.   Ngáyabba   nga-réndjeya.
      first-1MINPOSS   3MINMASCS-go-CTP   1MINPOSS   1MINS-stand

43   Nga-wákka   nga-yirrí-ya.   Nga-ná-dja
      1MINS-return   1MINS-go-CTP   1MINA+3MINO-see-CTP

44   ká-ba   ka-réndjeya
      3MINA+3MINMASCO-eat(+CTP)   3MINMASCS-stand(+CTP)

[Actually] he went off. He went before me. I stopped and went back. I saw them
eating [while their mother was lying in the water]. (XXV/33)

45 Nga-bbúdje[ya]-yana   'Ma-kkúndja   dá-bala!'
   1MINS-shout(+CTP)-3MINDAT   MINIMP-*defecate   MINIMP-come hither

46   Nga-bbúdje[ya]-yana   nga-yirrí-ya   kóma
     1MINS-shout(+CTP)-3MINDAT   1MINS-go-CTP   NEG

47   ka-lakalá-ya,   deb   ka-nó-ra,   kaláddjarr.
     3MINMASCS-hear-NRN   deaf   3MINMASCS-sit-CTP   deaf

I called out to him, 'Come here!' but he didn't hear. He was deaf [because of the rustling grass]. (XXV/35)

48   Nga-ndabayí-yana   π π π
     1MINS/A-make a bilabial sound(+CTP)-3MINDAT   [bilabial 'pop' sound]

49   'Dá-bala-yarra!'   'Ngaléwara?'   'Bárreya   ba-rra-réndjeya.'
     MINIMP-hither-go   what?   3AUGDEM   3AUGS-RE-
                                                          stand(+CTP)

I signalled to him to stop [by popping with my lips]. 'Come back!' 'What is it?' 'Here they are.'

50   Ngayábba   nja-barrábarra-bba   ya-ka-bbándje-ya
     3MINFEMCARD   3MINFEM-big-EXT   3MINS-kó-put-REFL(+CTP)

51   ya-ka-yó-ra.   Ya-karráwa-nga   ya-ka-yó-ra.
     3MINFEMS-kó-lie-CTP   3MINFEMS-look around-CTP   3MINFEMS-kó-lie-CTP

The mother one was lying down looking around. (XXV/38)

52   Ka-rríkkaya   ka-yirrí-ya.   Ká-rakarawo   ka-yirrí-ya.   Díla-ngaya
     3MINS-creep   3MINSgo-CTP   3MINS-move   3MINSgo-CTP   eye-3MINFEMPOSS

53   mándjad   ka-ná-dja   ya-ka-yó-ra.
     straight   3MINA+3MINO-see-CTP   3MINFEMS-kó-lie-CTP

54   Ya-bala-karráwa-nga   ya-bala-ka-yó-ra.
     3MINFEMS-hither-look-CTP   3MINFEMS-hither-kó-lie-CTP

He was creeping up [towards her]. She was looking straight at him. (XXV/40)

55   Márnabba   ka-rdéddjeya.   Djíya
     *chest   3MINMASCS-*spear+REFL(+CTP)   here

56   yaka-rá-ya.   Mayurd   ba-rra-yángka
     3MINA+3MINFEMO-shoot-CTP   *run   3AUGS-RE-*do(+CTP)

He raised his gun/took aim. He shot her here [indicating left armpit]. They ran away. (XXV/42)

57   'Yá-rakarawo,'   ka-ngúdjeya   ngabúyanga.   'Kóma.'   'N-bókka
     3MINFEMS-move   3MINMASCS-say   1MINDAT   no   3MIN-*bad

58   nga-bá-la.'   Karnbilíbala   nji-rri-ná-dja.
     1MINA+3MINO-*bite-REM   blood   1UAA+3MINO-RE-see-CTP

59   'Ya-ka-djáwa-nga   ya-yirrí-ya.'
     3MINFEMS-kó-bleed/flow-CTP   3MINFEMS-go-CTP

'She's getting away,' he said to me. 'No.' 'I missed.' We saw blood. 'She's bleeding.' (XXV/43)

60   Bá-rra-rakarawo   karrabba   djíbba   njana   ngáni::,   njíndjabba
     3AUGS-RE-move   like   here   to   there   2MINCARD

61   ngana-yó-ri-ba,   djadjórla   njíndjabba.   Nganéyabba
     2MINS-live-CTP-EXT   house   2MINCARD   there

62   yaláwa   ba-rra-réndjeya.   Nji-rri-mankawákka-ya.
      just   3AUGS-RE-stand   1UAS-RE-hurry-CTP
63   Njanbi-rri-ná-dja   bárreya   ba-rra-réndjeya.
      1UAA+3AUGO-RE-see-CTP   3AUGDEM   3AUGS-RE-stand
They moved off as far as from here to there, where you live, to your house [about four
hundred metres]. They stopped there. We hurried along and saw them standing.
(XXV/45)

64 Márnabba   ka-rdéddjeya.   Rdów.   Yaka-rá-ya-bba.
    *chest   3MINS-*spear+REFL   bang!   3MINA+3MINFEMO-shoot-CTP-EXT
65   Bá-rra-bala   ba-rra-bala-yirrí-ya.
      3AUGS-RE-come hither(+CTP)   3AUGS-RE-hither-CTP
66   Márnabba   yinjerrekéyanga   ba-rra-bbándja.
      *chest   1UADAT   3AUGS-RE-*put
67   Ba-rra-bala-yirrí-ya-bba   karrabba   djíbba
      3AUGS-RE-hither-go-CTP-EXT   like/too   here
68   ya-ka-rá-ya-bba   yá-ka-bbo
      3MINA+3MINFEMO-kó-shoot-CTP-EXT 3MINFEMS-kó-fall(+CTP)
69   njáya   nja-náworrkala,   háb   nja-ngurrarákka,
      DEMFEM   3MINFEM-different   half   3MINFEM-grown up
70   karrabba   njánabba   nganabbárru   ngána   Bobo.
      like   what's it   buffalo   that   [name]
He raised his gun. Bang! He shot her. They [calves] were coming straight towards
us. As they came he shot another female, half grown, like that–what's-it?–that buffalo
Bobo [pet buffalo calf in Maningrida]. (XXV/48)

71 'Djobo   mé-yarra!'   'Mé-yarra   bakkándja
    shoo   MINIMP-go   MINIMP-go   later
72   nbu-rri-wu-rá-ya!'   Nji-rri-kkúwa-nga
      1UAMASCA+2MINO-RE-AV-shoot-CTP   1UAA+3MINO-RE-deceive-CTP
73   nji-rri-yirrí-ya.
      1UAS-RE-go-CTP
'Shoo! Off you go!' 'Off you go or we might shoot you too.' We tried to frighten it
away. (XXV/53]

74 Kóma   ba-rra-yarrí-bba-nja.   Ya-ka-rá-ya
    NEG   3UAFEMS-RE-go-EXT-FEM   3MINMASCA+3MINFEMO-kó-shoot-CTP
75   Yá-nabo   ba-rra-yó-ra-nja.
      3MINFEMS-step(+CTP)   3UAFEMS-RE-lie-CTP-FEM
76   Ba-rra-ddjúwa-nja.   Yaláwa   nji-rri-kkóndja.
      3UAFEMS-re-die(+CTP)-FEM   well   1UAA+3MINO-RE-cut(+CTP)
They [two females] didn't go away. He shot her and she fell on top of her mother.
They both died and we cut [the meat] up. (XXV/54)

77 Nji-rri-kkóndja   njana   kóndjala   ngu-wu-bbúdjeya.
    1UAA+3MINO-RE-cut   and   try unsuccessfully   1MINS-AV-call out(+CTP).

78   Nji-rri-bbúdjeya   yaláwa.   Nji-rri-bbúdji-ba
     1UAS-RE-call out   ok   1UAS-RE-call out(+CTP)-EXT

79   njanbi-rri-ná-dja   bi-rri-míba   yinjerrekéyanga,
     1UAA+3UAO-RE-see-CTP   3UAMASCS-RE-arrive   1UADAT

80   D bi-rri-yáwaka.
     T 3UA-RE-'uncles together'/uncle and nephew

We cut it up and I tried to call out [to the others].   We called out and while we were
calling out we saw them [two] approaching us, T and his nephew. (XXV/56)

81   Bi-rri-míba   nji-rri-ngúdjeya,   'Nganabbárru   karnayédjabba
     3UAS-RE-arrive(+CTP)   1UAS-speak(+CTP)   buffalo   two

82   yaláwa   yingúrra.'   'A: n-káro   ey,   bed kaw.'
     well   1/2AUGDAT   3MINMASC-fat   eh   fat cow

83   Nja-rra-kkóndja   nga-ngárawa-ya   yúya.
     1AUGA+3MINO-RE-cut   1MINA+3MINO-light fire-CTP   fire

84   Nja-rra-ddjórrba-ra   djanímarra.
     1AUGA+3MINO-RE-cook-CTP   coals

85   Njá-rra-ba   nja-rra-nó-ra::.
     1AUGA+3MINO-RE-eat(+CTP)   1AUGS-RE-sit-CTP(DUR)

They came up and we said, 'We['ve got] two female buffaloes.'   'Ah, lovely fat ones,
eh–fat cows.'   We cut it up and I lit a fire.   We cooked some [meat] in the coals and ate
it. (XXV/60)

86   Yaláwa   nja-rra-ngúdjeya,   'Ngábi-yarra.'   Mayórli-ba
     then   1AUGS-RE-speak(+CTP)   1/2AUGS(+IRR)-go   carry on shoulder-EXT

87   nja-rra-yirrí-ya.   Njá-rra-rakarawo   nja-rra-yirrí-ya::.
     1AUGS-RE-go-CTP   1AUGS-RE-move   1AUGS-RE-go-CTP(DUR)

88   Nja-rra-rlábaya   ránba.   Na-máwali-ba   nja-rra-nó-ra.
     1AUGS-RE-descend   beach   LOC-paperbark-EXT   1AUGS-RE-sit-CTP

Then we said, 'Let's go.'   We set off, carrying [the meat] on our shoulders.   We went
along, went down to the beach [should have said makábbin 'plain' - JB] and rested
amongst the paperbarks. (XXV/64)

89   Nja-rra-nó-ra.   Nja-rra-nó-ra.   Nja-rra-nó-ra.   Nja-rra-kkamíya.
     1AUGS-RE-sit-CTP   1AUGS-RE-get up

90   Nja-rra-yirrí-ya.   Nja-rra-ndabakkúrrngarna.   Nja-rra-yirrí-ya.
     1AUGS-RE-go-CTP   1AUGS-RE-sitINCHO(+CTP)

91   Nja-rra-ndabakkúrrngarna.   Nja-rra-yirrí-ya. Nja-rra-ndabakkúrrngarna.
     1AUGS-RE-sitINCHO(+CTP)

We rested.   We got up, went on further then sat down [to rest] again.   We did this a
couple more times. (XXV/67)

92   Nja-rra-bala-yirrí-ya   mudíkkang.   Kalakórrbba
     1AUGS-RE-come hither-go-CTP   truck   road//bank

93   nja-rra-rakarawó-bba   nja-rra-yirrí-ya
     1AUGS-RE-move(+CTP)-EXT   1AUGS-RE-go-CTP

94	Njanbi-rri-ná-dja.		'Nganabbárru!' Nja-rra-míba.		Duram
	3AUGA+1AUGO-RE-see-CTP		buffalo	1AUGS-RE-arrive	drum
95	ba-rra-ddjórrba-ra,		djanímarra.	Ngáyabba	
	3AUGA+3MINMASCO-RE-cook-CTP		coals	1MINCARD	
96	makéddja	nga-ddjórrba-ra.			
	turtle	1MINA+3MINO-cook-CTP			

We reached the truck and went by road. They saw us [and called] 'Buffalo!' We arrived. They cooked [the buffalo] in a drum and [the ribs] on the coals, while I cooked the turtle. (XXV/69)

97	Njá-rra-ba		nja-rra-nó-ra.	Njana	mudíkkang
	1AUGA+3MINO-RE-eat(+CTP)		1AUGS-RE-sit-CTP	then	truck
98	ka-míba.		Njanbi-rri-wú-dja		
	3MINMASCS-arrive(+CTP)		1AUGA+3AUGIO-RE-give-CTP		
99	yaláwa	ba-rra-ddjórrkka,		Namokardábu,	kánkarra.
	then	3AUGA+3MINFEMO-RE-take		[place]	meat
100	SK	ka-ddjórrka		n-kánkarra...	
	[name]	3MINA+3MINMASCO-take		3MINMASC-meat	

We ate some meat. Then a truck arrived. We gave them some meat to take back to Namokardábu. SK took the meat... (XXV/73)

7.   VOCABULARY

7.1   SEMANTIC FIELDS WORDLIST

The following list contains as many as possible of the Ndjébbana words included in the standard five hundred-word list used by the editors of this series for comparative purposes. This list, however, did not include many of the most characteristic words used amongst speakers of Arnhem Land languages, especially those whose life centres around the sea, like the speakers of Ndjébbana. To the standard items, therefore, have been added a selection of additional words in order to make the semantic fields list not simply a list with a comparative linguistic purpose but also a list which typifies in some measure the life and environment of Ndjébbana speakers. The additional words will provide comparative material especially relevant to languages of the Arnhem Land region. Much of this list is derived from the field notes of Graham McKay but these have been augmented, particularly in the field of natural species, by the work of Carolyn Coleman. In cases where there is a discrepancy in the forms recorded by the two fieldworkers McKay's records have usually been given preference. In the matter of semantics and species identifications Coleman's lists are much more recent, accurate and comprehensive, so her lists have been given precedence.

The following abbreviations give word class and related information as far as this can be determined

N	nominal	V	verb
A,B,C,D1-D6	nominal class	1A-8C	verb class
m	masculine	IRG	irregular
f	feminine	DEF	defective
Dj	Djówanga	tr	transitive
Y	Yírriddjanga	intr	intransitive
dy	dyad	ditr	ditransitive
sp.	species		
VOC	vocative	Prn	pronoun
REF	referential	Prt	particle

Nominals not marked as belonging to classes A, B, C, or D belong in most cases to nominal class A and are marked for gender and moiety where known. Nominals of classes D1-6 are arranged alphabetically by root, without the prefix (in the third person minimal masculine: n- D1, nga- D2, ka- D3, ma- D5 and na- D6), while nominals of the remaining class (D4) have zero third person minimal masculine prefix and therefore are listed under the root initial consonant.

A. *Body Parts*

yúrnka NC head

njakkórdba NC brain

méyameya ND4 hair of head, plumage, feather, leaf of palm tree; part that grows out the top

míbba NB forehead

díla NC eye; seed; cartridge (for gun); small round-shaped object

mangúya NB nose; face

yírda NC nose (bridge/bone)

kála NB ear; parts that stick out on opposite sides

rénjmarla NB cheekbone; upper jaw; crescent shaped object

ramalówandja/ramorolówanja NB lower jaw; jawbone

mangalówarra ND1 jaw

djábbarda NB lips; mouth; rim of container

mandjamándja NC whiskers, beard

rídda NB tooth, blade (e.g. of axe)

djangórna NB tongue

kárla NC neck (front of)

márdba NB neck (front of)

ngalidjbínja NC throat (internal); aesophagus; long, hollow, cylindrical object

djaréya NB nape of neck

njayára NC shoulder

yakára NC shoulder

marnakkúrrkka NB arm

wánba NB arm

wánja N arm (of turtle)

bárnka NB elbow

kúdja NC hand, finger, foot, toe

rakáya NC fingernail, toenail

kalórla NC breast (female); flower

márnabba NB chest; lungs
djarramáya NC chest; rib-cage
marnákarna NC rib bone
marlúkarla ND4 hip
ngalkkúnda NC hip (bone)
manbáma NC waist, side
djánama NB stomach; belly
   (external)
djangéra NB navel
djúrddjurd NA heart
marddúrddiba NAm heart (?CC—
   NC)
marnawarrínjba NC kidney
ngardabbámba ND4 liver
búrrbba ND1 guts
barrábarra NB back; spine
djúya NC buttocks, bottom;
   (fish)tail; base of an object
mémarla NB thigh
njamánja NC knee
njakkárla NC calf, shin, lower leg
waláya NB lower leg (human); tail
   (kangaroo, stingray); back leg
   (turtle)
kúdja NC foot, hand, finger, toe
lárla NC penis; male; man/boy
lékka NB testicles
ngawálirr N semen
yalangaló NC pubic hair
rárra NC vagina
kúnja N faeces
bórdanja NA urine; NC bladder
múraka ND4 body or limb hair,
   fur
kódda ND1 skin
mardárda ND1 bone; shell; bark
   (tree); pod (seeds)
karnbilíbala NA blood
karó ND1 fat (noun)
ngárnba NA armpit sweat,
   perspiration
búrrbbarra N perspiration, sweat
   (brow, body, general)
móya ND4 open sore, ulcer,
   wound
djína N boil

labalúya V4C swell, come up in a
   lump
rínja NA sickness, bad cold,
   fever, influenza
karléngarla N tears
ndakabbírda ND5 right hand(ed)
báymala/bímala ND1 left hand(ed)

B. Human Classification

lakarrá ND3 person, Aborigine
yídja NA man
ngarráma ND4 woman, female
   (plural also has EXT suffix -(i)-
   ba (§3.2.4))
karókaddja ND1 child, boy, girl
karókaddja njálkkidj ND1 newborn
   baby (lit. "soft child")
djárwarra ND1 young person,
   adolescent, boy, girl (post-
   puberty)
komrdudj NA initiand
kábburla ND1 old person, old
   man, old woman (lit. "blind")
djáwarlbba ND1 old person, (n-
   djáwarllbba old man, nja-
   yáwarlbba old woman)
njadjákka NAf girl, young woman
   (mature, but has not yet given
   birth)
kamarriyúkun Nmf widower;
   widow
nabaláma ND2 sorcerer; healer;
   "clever" man
mankárni NAm Aboriginal
   'doctor'
barnamarrákka N warrior (=
   "white clay" because smeared
   on body)
balánda NAm white person, man
núrna NAf white woman
warríwarra N policeman; "cheeky"
   or dangerous one
múya ND4 ghost, spirit, dead
   person
barrómaya ND1 spirit, ghost
ngórdo ND6 leper
walá ND1 name (nála 3MINM)

yakkarrárra NA patrilineal descent group; clan

C. *Kinship*

kíkka NAf mother (VOC)

njabarrábarrabba N matriarch (REF)

ngálinga N mother's sibling (REF)

bábba NAm father (VOC)

ngánja NAf father's sister (VOC)

kúdjala NA mother's mother, mother's mother's brother/ sister; woman's daughter's child; man's sister's daughter's child; person two generations up or down the matriline

mámam NA mother's father and his brother and sister; man's daughter's child; womans brother's daughter's child

máwa NA father's father

mákka N father's mother and her sister and brother; woman's son's child; man's sister's son's child

wórlngara N sibling

djábba NAm/f older brother/ sister (VOC)

ngurrarákka ND1m/f older brother/sister (REF)

karlamára NAm/f younger brother/sister (VOC/REF)

njarrarendjínanja my sister (REF) (lit. "we two (m & f) stood") (cf §1.4)

yarrá ND man's child; woman's brother's child; person one generation down in the patriline

ngákarda ND woman's child; man's sister's child; person one generation down in the matriline

kála NC older sister's child

ngangába NC husband; brother-in-law

njangába NC wife; sister-in-law

njdjórrkabba ND2m/f spouse (the husband/wife of a couple)

njarranóranja my wife (REF) (lit. "we two (m & f) sit") (cf §1.4)

kárrddjiya NC mother-in-law; son-in-law (actual, not classificatory)

nganjíba N father/son-in-law (of woman)

njanjíba N mother/daughter-in-law (of man)

bérrkkawa Ndy brothers-in-law (cf §1.4)

D. *Mammals*

barrangúdja NA animal (large, usu. edible incl. mammals, lge game birds; reptiles, amphibians); rainbow

djúrnmarra NA rodent (generic), mouse (incl. marsupials)

ngandjérrarobarrábarra NA quoll

kalamíndja(rra)barrábarra NAfDj echidna, 'porcupine'

míbbarda NAmDj bandicoot

márlarra NAmDj brushtail possum

kúdjbarra NAm kangaroo/ macropod (generic); agile wallaby (species n.)

nganawombálma NAmY antilopine kangaroo (male)

njanabarnúma/njanabunúma NAfDj antilopine kangaroo (female).

kálkberd NADj northern·black wallaroo

wólerrk NADj agile wallaby

bálkkidj NA agile wallby (large male)

mérlbbe agile wallaby (adult female)

nganangádjaya NAY dingo (wild dog)

bárrbaya NAm/fY dog (tame)

djawukkaléla NA bat (generic); little red flying fox

dambálkka NA sugar-glider

ndjaráma N big black flying fox

wárlan N ghost bat

djárrang NA horse; donkey; mule

bulíkkang NA bullock

bedkaw NA cow; female bullock
   or buffalo
nganabbárru NA buffalo
karrúmakkarra NAmDj dolphin
múrnun NAmDj dugong

E. Reptiles

kánbaya NAmY crocodile
   (estuarine)
kalamómo NADj Johnson
   crocodile (freshwater)
kumúken NADj Johnson
   crocodile (freshwater)
makéddja NAm turtle (generic);
   freshwater turtle (generic)
makéddja NAfY long-necked
   freshwater turtle
marládja NAmDj green turtle
ngárd NAfDj short-necked
   freshwater turtle
yúrnkankáya NAmY loggerhead
   turtle
djénkardibakábakanóra NAmY
   bluetongue lizard (lit. "he feeds
   in the snail place.")
bádjborro NA dragon-lizard
   (rocks); ring-tailed dragon
ngárrabba NAmDj frilled necked
   lizard
mayáya NA spotted tree goanna
nabbarlángkareya NAmY ground
   goanna
káddawórnandjérreyarra big ground
   goanna (V. panoptes)
ngayidjúrna NA mangrove goanna
djárrkka NA freshwater goanna
karówalaya NAm snake (generic);
   whip snake (specific)
djanímarradjamungúya NA black-
   headed python (lit. "charcoal
   face")
náwaran NA olive python
bémurrkka NA carpet python
djárladjarladjábbarda NA file snake
nalyóra NA banded tree snake
   (night tiger)

njakkárla NA bockadam;
   mangrove snake
mélkkarda NA death adder
njakékkayanjamalára NA taipan
ngaléngkarnakabulúyara NADj
   king brown snake

F. Birds

djúrrka NA little birds (generic);
   smaller honeyeaters (specific)
barrúra NAm/f egg
ngániba N nest
bálbbala NC wing (feathers)
njanamarlábbana NAfY emu
kábukkurdurrk NAfDj brolga
nganakayúla NAmY jabiru
djándjana NAmDj pelican
marnúbbarr NAfDj magpie goose
buwárdda NAfDj bustard, plains
   turkey
kórnda NAfY orange-footed
   scrub fowl
karlóddod NA dove/pigeon
   (generic); diamond/peaceful
   dove (specific)
kalamúya NAf Torres Strait
   imperial pigeon
njanakkarlóddjanama NAfY
   peewee
kúlakalakórrbba NA pied
   butcherbird
nganjónganja NAmDj crow
   (also="black")
kawudjábbarda NA cuckoo-shrike
kárarra NAfDj northern blue
   winged kookaburra; kingfisher
   (generic)
njakkála AfDj blue-faced honey
   eater
djékkardadjékkarda NA willy
   wagtail
njanangalórrma N cuckoo
   (generic), small cuckoos
mandabírlbirl N channel-billed
   cuckoo
nganangalórrma N pheasant
   coucal

ngarrangálangalérnkarna NAmY
white (sulphur crested)
cockatoo

bángkararrk NAmY black
cockatoo (red-tailed)

djakalíkala NAfDj galah

rángka NAfDj red-collared
lorikeet

rákarra N birds of prey (generic);
osprey (species n.)

lúrrbba N brown falcon

kángkalangardanganangórrdjiba-
lélekanóra N wedge-tailed
eagle

kángkarlangarda NAmDj white
breasted sea eagle

mardárdibakakkákkaya N whistling
kite (lit. "he shoves bones
around/shoves amongst bones")

djúrddjurd NA Brahminny kite

djamalakakardíddja/djamalararrídja
NAmY spoonbill

njanayerléya NAfY cormorant;
shag

kárddjurl NAmY egret

kalabángarra NAfDj white ibis

njánaborrk N duck, goose, grebe
(generic); whistling duck
(specific)

ngárnkul N teal; black duck

nakkárriyala NAmY radjah
shellduck

malamalárra NAmDj sea birds
(generic); tern (specific)

njanabórnakanadja NAfDj gull
(generic); silver gull (species
n.)

G. Fishes

yókkarra NAm fish (generic)

bókala N reef fish (generic)

karlédda NAfDj freshwater
catfish

djínbarra NAmY fishtailed catfish
(generic); blue catfish (species
n.)

karrarábba N eel-tailed catfish
(generic); freshwater eel-tailed

catfish (generic); Rendahl's
catfish (species n.)

yíbarda NAmY barramundi (giant
perch)

nkanúnga N juvenile barramundi;
sand bass

ngérdamúkkayangaya NDj
saratoga (northern spotted
barramundi)

njamíbbarda N freshwater (pike)
eel

karóyiba N shark/stingray
(generic); stingray (generic)

mangarángkad N river stingray
(generic); yellow-brown river
stingray (species n.)

marnandjúbba N sea stingray
(generic); cowtail stingray
(species n.)

djabbarnbókka NAmDj shark
(generic); lemon shark (species
n.)

djabayéna N sawfish

kalabólkkarra N billfish/tuna/
mackerel (generic)

njanabbardákka N trevally/
queenfish etc. (generic); giant
silver trevally (specific)

yakawírrbara Nf archer fish (lit.
"she spits")

H. Insects, Crustaceans
etc.

baríyala NAm antbed; termitalia

ngérda N green ant

djíddirirrin N wasp sp. (large)

makarrúnbala N wasp sp. (small)

nganánanj NAm beeswax

djábbarnma NAm sugarbag,
honey (generic)

barlúya N honey type (from
ground/rock)

káddeyana N honey type (from
hollow trees)

karónmanja N honey type (from
roots of trees)

yindidjbórna N scorpion

njanarrabarrábarra N centipede;
  millipede
nganamukkúkkaya NA maggot
mabbunúna N blowfly
mandjimíndja N bushfly
barrúkala NAfY march fly
mardírrbala NAmY mosquito
wóngorlwongorl N winged insect;
  butterfly; moth; dragonfly
balíndja N hairy caterpillar
warrángala N witchetty grub
naméwayakaráyakanóra Nm spider
  (lit. "he spins nets")
wúya N earthworm
kangódjbaya NAmY mangrove
  worm
karnáya NA leech
róngkarra NAf prawn (large,
  saltwater)
njakkódda NAf crustacea
  ("husked") (generic); 'long'
  crustacea (generic); freshwater
  yabby (specific)
bíbbo NAfDj crab; 'round'
  crustacea (generic); mud crab
  (specific)
djénkarda NAfDj snail (land)
mardárda ND1 shell, bone
njamánja NAf mud mussel
  (mangroves)
barrakkalámadja N freshwater
  mussels
yéya NAmDj oyster (generic);
  milky oyster (specific)
wénjngala NAfDj small sand
  clams; Veneridae
njáyarrayarra N cockles
njanamáya N bailer shell
warramarléla N Trochus shell
kalburárra N sea urchin
djómi N brittle-star
bárdbarrarra NAm frog
njanabbúrnda NAm grasshopper;
  locust
minuwarrúrru N termite
kádda N flea; tick; body lice
kakarrakarráwanga N headlice

njakkárla N sandfly
nmalála N native bee
ngárrabbakaddawárna N wasp
  type; European honey bee

I. Language, Ceremony etc.

ngúdja N language, speech, story
walá (nála 3MINM) ND1 name
ngalabíba N cicatrice
njabólarra NA red ochre (bright)
kambúkka NAmDj red ochre
  (dull)
njabbarlánga NAY yellow ochre
barnamarrákka NAmDj white clay/
  ochre

J. Artefacts etc.

karlikárli NAmDj boomerang
nganabakabínja N digging stick
díbbarra NAf spear (generic)
láma N shovel nose spear
djarnábu NAfDj fighting spear,
  bamboo spear
bárddi N fighting spear (wooden
  head, serrations point back)
djalakkíyak NAm multipronged
  fish spear
nmáma N harpoon shaft (for
  dugong/turtle)
nganamakéddja N harpoon prong
  (for turtle)
djurddjurd N harpoon warp (short
  rope)
bardíwanga NA string; rope
yírndidj NAf spear thrower,
  woomera
márkka NAm stone axe
nganawébba NAm stone knife
njalárla (ra) NAm (Vtr7C)
  firestick. fire drill
naméwaya NAm fishing net
marnákarna N hinged scoop net
nganjdjúddama NAm bark canoe
bamakkánba N bark canoe
wúbbunj NAm dugout canoe
wánarda NA paddle

barlangúnngun NAmDj string
   dilly bag
béya NAmDj pandanus dilly bag
njamádja NAfDj water bag/ honey
   bag (close woven from
   pandanus)
kolónkolon N paperbark water
   dish
rrubbíya NAmY money
waléykkarra NA rock, stone; coin
   money
nganawúna NA paperbark; paper;
   paper money
djúrra(ng) N paper; letter
ngalidjbínja NAm didgeridoo
ngalidjbínja NAf gun (long
   barrelled), shotgun
nganamayáwaya NA clapsticks
babbúya N large flat grinding
   stone (mortar)
dérrederr N spherical grinding
   stone (pestle)
mókko N man's pubic covering

K. Fire, Food, Water

kánkarra ND1 meat, flesh (food
   type incl. animals, birds,
   fishes, crustacea)
barrangúdja NAm 'game' animal
yalába NAm vegetable food,
   'tucker' (food type)
djóya ND1m/f tuber; root
   vegetable (food type)
rakkíyala ND1m/f shellfish (food
   type)
djábbarnma NAm sugarbag,
   honey (generic) (food type)
yúya NAm fire, firewood (Y
   dialect word)
ngálngarda NAm fire (Dj dialect
   word)
djúrlu NA matches
djanímarra NAmDj charcoal
njarrawarrówarra NA ashes
walangánjdjarra NAm smoke
   (thick)
djakóra N smoke (thin, wispy)

yúya djangórna karéndjeya flame
   (lit. "tongue of fire")
mábbarda N bushfire
kábba NAmY water (generic)
nabarlámbarla ND2 freshwater
kalakalóddjarra NA fresh/sweet (of
   water)
namanerrbálmiba N salt (of water)
warríwarra NA salt (of water)
namarnakkúrrkka NAm intertidal
   creek
kalakárrbba N river
nganalakárrbba N oxbow lake
malóya NAm rain; rainstorm; wet
   season; year
ngúrldjarr N heavy rain (as at the
   start of a storm)
njílanjila N light rain (as at the end
   of a storm)

L. Celestial, Weather

wárrwarra NAfY sun; time
   (=o'clock), clock/watch
kakárra NAm shade
dílkarra NAmDj moon
búkkulurl N full moon
dílkarra rénjmala kayóra N crescent
   (new) moon
njananábba NAf star
njákarddja N morning star
wékkana N dark, at night
nmárnabba N cloud
kunngadja cloud
róya mist; fog
balawúrrwurr NAm wind (generic)
bárra NA northwest wind
djímurru NA southeast wind
mabbúlarr Adv calm (no wind)
wálangandjáyiba NAmDj thunder
ngawíya V2A thunder
má- -ba V1C lightning
yékke NA cold weather
wárlirr NAm hot weather

M. Geography

wíba NAm/C place, country
karlakórrbba NAm path, road

djadjórla NA house; humpy

káyala NAm ground, dirt, earth, sand

ránba NAm beach, sand

namarnebálbiba beachfront, shoreline

kádjarna NAf mud

wéddawa NA mud

nakábbirriba NA mud (generic)

namarlúkarla N deep mud in estuary, mangrove creeks

barnamarrákka NAmDj white clay; warrior (because normally smeared with white clay)

djarramarrákkiba N claypan; dry mud

yúlbbur N dust

djerrebalódjiba N dry forest; country without water

waléykkarra NA rock, stone

nganawaléykkarra 'stone country' (Arnhem Land Escarpment)

kábbal NA floodplain

kúdjam N escarpment; outlier (big rock)

makábbin N floodplain (black soil)

malírra N sub-coastal bog (black soil)

djúlumukkiyirriya NAm point (of land)

kabalakóra NAm island

nabarlámbarla NAm freshwater billabong, waterhole (in river)

banakkábbiba littoral, under/in/ through water

karnangarrónarra inland, dry land, ashore, overland

yanakkábba NAm dry land

N. *Arboreal*

kúrla NAm tree, stick woody plant (generic) (Y dialect word)

nganabaláma NAm tree, stick woody plant (generic) (Dj dialect word)

kakárra NAm leaf (except palm type), shade; shady bough shelter; plant (generic)

méyameya ND4 leaf of palm tree, head hair, plumage, feather

kála ND1 fork (of tree)

kídjal N new growth, shoots

kalórla NC flower and fruit (of the kind that have an edible part budding out of the flower)

makkúkka NAm grass (generic, incl. all grasses, sedges, herbs with non-woody stems); small grasses with feathery flower heads (specific)

djamándjalk N spear grass (Sorghum intrans)

balarrírra N bladey grass type (Sehima nervosum)

kalbarárra NAfY waterlily seed

njanakarráwa NAY stem of waterlily

njandakalábarna NAY root of waterlily

wankarrídja NAmDj bloodwood

djawála NAfDj coastal she-oak (Casuarina equisetifolia)

malabardidjbana N woollybutt (Eucalyptus mineata)

bamakkánba NAfDj stringy bark tree (Eucalyptus tetrodonta)

yárlk N bark of stringy bark tree

kárnangandja N Eucalyptus bleeseri

malála NAmY mangrove (generic); Rhizophora stylosa (specific)

ngalóla NAf mangrove sp.

kádjbarl N wattle tree (generic); black wattle (Acacia auriculiformis) (specific)

wardangínjbana NAmY paperbark tree (generic); big paperbarks growing in stands (specific); bark (Y. dialect)

nganakúna NAm paperbark tree (generic); big paperbarks growing in stands (specific); bark (Dj. dialect)

warakkála NAmDj long yam
(Dioscorea transversa)

karndóya NAfDj round 'cheeky'
yam (Dioscorea bulbifera)

ngarakáya NAm pandanus
(generic); Pandanus spiralis

njarakáya NA Pandanus aquaticus

kalamínjdjiba NAfY cycad, xamia
palm

nganangórrddjeya NAmY cypress
pine, Callitris intratropica

babbúya N ironwood
(Erythrophleum chlorostachys)

njadjéngka NAfDj banyan, Ficus
virens

djárlabarrakéyanga N red apple
(Syzigium suborbiculare)

djalákarra N white apple
(Syzigium eucalyptoides
bleeseri)

nganarraddjéngka N green plum
(Buchanania obovata)

lékka N green plum (Terminalia
ferdinandiana)

djawalárra N spike rush
(Eleocharis dulcis)

kadárrmala N climbing vines
(generic); native jasmine
(Jasminum didymum)(specific)

nakardárrmaliba in the jungle vine
thicket

kíyirrkiyirr N palm (generic);
Hydriastele wendlania (specific)

O. Adjectives

warábba NC one; alone; single;
only

karnayédjabba NA two; paired

karnayédjabba warábbabaddabirra
N three (3rd person unit
augmented (dual) masculine—
varies with person and gender)

múlbbum ND4 clustered;
grouped; several

kúdja warábbana N a few, five; 'a
handful' (lit. 'one hand')

karrówa ND1 many

nganjónganja ND1 black; (blue);
dark; dull; dirty; crow

narárrma ND2 white; bright;
shiny; clean

rárrma V1A be white

barrábarra ND1 big, fat

namánda ND2 little, thin

karrakárramárdba ND1 long

ndarládja ND3 short

káya ND1 fat; distended; big

nawarrámaya ND2 skinny

djárreyarra ND1 wide (eg river);
dispersed (eg spots)

nakkúrrngarnawa ND2 straight

kóyawa ND1 crooked

ngarídda NA cold (feeling)

kárla ND1 wet

kádja ND1 dry

marndálangurrnga ND4 hard

njálkkidj ND4 soft; weak;
vulnerable

djaráma ND1 heavy; black flying
fox

djawukkaléla ND1 light (weight);
leavened (bread); red flying fox

rárrangala ND2 sharp (point/
blade)

mabbúrla NA blunt (point/ blade)

warríwarra NA salty, bitter,
poisonous, dangerous,
'cheeky', wild

nabbórla ND2 harmless, tame,
not dangerous

ngówolk ND1 harmless

kékkaka ND1 new

djídja ND1 old

dórdbalk N good

bókka ND1 bad, no good

mádjarna ND1 authentic, real,
proper; hale, healthy; whole;
complete; sound

búrrbba NC strong

djínjawa ND1 alive

barlánga ND1 raw (meat), unripe
(fruit)

kárddja ND1 cooked (meat), ripe
(fruit)

nabbórnba ND2 rotten, stinking, dead (animal)

djuwé V8A be sick, suffer, die

bar(ak)ángka NA lazy, tired

ména (-djuwé) N (V8A) hungry (be, suffer)

kaláddjarr NA deaf, mad, crazy

kábburla ND1 blind

yúrnkana mardárda he is bald (lit. "his head is a shell/bone")

yúrnkana narrúrra karéndjeya he is bald (lit. "his head is exposed/bare")

bamúmawa ND4 (-w-) truth; true; honest

kárdda ND3 immersed in water, submerged

bárdbana ND1 shallow

karrúmakkarra ND1 smooth, slippery

barráma ND3 (-bb-) sore, aching

VERBS

P. Motion

djirrí VintrIRG go (to)

rakarawó Vintr6A move (along)

balayirrí (= baló + djirrí) Vintr6A come

baló VintrDEF come, hither

mérabayi Vintr2B go in, enter; hide (intrans.); set (of sun)

rlúrrabayi Vintr2B come out, emerge; arrive; rise (of sun)

balákka Vintr2A come back, return

wákka Vintr2A go back (there), return

ndabarlínjdja Vtr1A turn around (trans)

ndabarlínjdjeyi Vintr2B turn around (intrans.)

biddabó Vtr6A follow, chase

wédda má Vtr1C pass, go past

rríkka Vintr7D crawl, slither

warré Vintr5B jump (across), be born; take off (bird or plane)

nabó Vintr6A dance (of men), stamp, tread; stand on (?tr)

nabíya Vintr2B become; turn out to be

rawáya Vintr2A dance (of women), play (of children); twist, sway

djórrkkangaya Vintr3 run

bó VintrIRG fall, land (of aeroplane)

wénjdja Vtr1A climb (tree); go up onto

wála Vintr1A climb (slope), ascend; move away from water

rlábayi Vintr2B climb down, go down, descend

nmarrímarlo Vintr1B swim, bathe, 'bogey'

djáwa Vintr5A flow

walédjba Vintr4C paddle

Q. Rest

nó VintrIRG sit, stay, be (settled on a base)

kkamíya Vintr2A get up, stand up, rise, set out, depart (from)

kkúrrngarna VtrIRG stand (tr), put standing

rénjdjeyi Vintr2B stand (position), be standing, be (vertical)

yó VintrIRG lie (position), sleep, be (horizontal)

bbándjeya Vintr2A lie down (inchoative)

lawayé Vintr5B be hanging, hang (intr)

bbéngka Vintr2A float (in water), be in water

R. Induced Position

bánjdja Vtr1A put down

lawayé Vtr1B hang up (tr)

má Vtr1C pick up, fetch, get

módja Vtr1A pick up

rimí Vtr6A hold in hand, grab, grasp, have, knead

rrókaye Vtr1B carry on arms, nurse

ngáma Vtr1A carry on shoulder (person O)

djórrkka Vtr3 take

baladjdjórrkka Vtr3 bring

yiyí Vtr6C leave (it) be

bala-kkákka Vtr7D pull (towards self)

djárrdjdja pull (down)

kákka Vtr7D push

ndabarlínjdja Vtr1A turn (tr)

rawó Vtr6A throw, discard, lose

marnawákka Vtr7D throw (spear)

méraba Vtr4A hide (tr), put inside, put away

mérabayi Vintr2B hide (intr), be inside, go inside, go underneath, enter; put on/wear (clothes); ngúdja mérabayi ring up/telephone (recipient DAT)

wéra Vtr1A put in bag

wú Vditr7A give

djébba Vditr1A deprive s.o. of sth.

míwa Vtr5A send

S. *Affect*

bú Vtr4B hit

bardórrbba Vtr4A punch

rá Vtr7C pierce

bakabinjí Vintr6A dig

kónjdja Vtr1A cut

wankarló Vtr1B cut through or across (not lengthwise); make a cutting (e.g for railway)

riyí Vtr6C scratch, tear into small pieces

nangardórrdddjeyi Vintr2B be broken, break (intr)

nangardórrddja Vtr1A break (tr)

djórraba Vtr4A cook (tr); start (of engine)

ngórrddja Vtr1A roast in ground oven

warrabú Vintr4B be burning

ngárawa Vtr7B light fire

djúbba Vtr1A extinguish (e.g. fire, light); turn off (light)

djákkabo Vtr6A tie, bind

ndamáwa Vtr5A tether, attach

máwa Vtr5A tie together, assemble by tying

bóraba Vtr4A paint

bórbaya Vintr2A paint self

wírrba Vtr4A wet (tr), splash; spit on; have (place) as 'mother' country

bínbi-...-ba Vtr4A write

ngódjba Vtr4A make, repair, assemble

malawédja Vtr1A build

T. *Attention*

níbba Vtr1A not know, be ignorant of

kálawa VtrIRG know, think/worry about

nídja Vtr1A wait for, await

ná Vtr7A see, look at

karráwa Vintr5A look around (for), oversee, be awake

lemayé Vditr1B show

lakalá Vtr5B hear, listen to, feel (touch)

márdba bánjdja Vtr1A desire, like; love (object DAT)

yéma Vtr1A dislike, not want

warayémaya Vintr7E Be anxious, be afraid (of sth DAT)

U. *Talking etc.*

ngúdjeyi Vintr2B speak, talk, tell a story

yángka Vintr2A say, do

yawarnáwayi Vintr2B refuse

ngáwa Vtr8A ask

ngáwaya Vintr2A think about, consider (lit. ask oneself)

karlíndja V answer; reply (intr)

búdjeyi Vintr2B shout, call out

mayáwayi Vintr2B sing (intr)

wáraba Vtr4A sing (tr) (sorcery)

djó Vtr1C berate, be angry with, abuse, swear at
kúwa Vtr5A deceive, lie to

V. *Corporeal*
bá Vtr8C eat, bite
núkka Vtr7D swallow
djí VtrIRG drink
nawála -yángka Vintr2A vomit
njéwa Vintr5A have a rest/spell
bíwa Vtr5A smell (tr)
bíwaya Vintr2A smell (intr), stink
ndabuyé Vtr6B lick, kiss
káma Vtr1A copulate with
kúnjdja Vintr1A defecate, lay (egg), give birth to
djarrárlma Vintr1A grow up
djuwé Vintr8A be sick/ill, suffer, be sore, ache; die
njínjdja Vintr2A cry, sob, weep
djarramá Vintr5B laugh

W. *Adverbial*
kónjdjala Prt try to do
múyawa Vtr(?)5C finish, die

X. *Location*
wálem south
kardówarra south
bólkkarda centre, middle, deep, north
bólkkardabba in deep water
barréyabba near, close by
karrakárriba far away
málaya up, outside, on top
kádja down, inside, underneath, below
nanákawa other side (of creek/river)
wíbbara at home
banakúdjabba Adv to/in town

Y. *Time*
ngabalóbala yesterday, recently
yéna/yána earlier today
djímanjdja up to now, until now
djíyalawa now (immed. future); nowadays
barnómanjdja later today; soon
wékanabba tomorrow
wékkana at night
wékkanangána early in the morning
karrakanódjabba in the morning
njélnjel late afternoon (sun low)
wúrdeyak/babukúyakka long ago
naka later on, afterwards; at first

Z. *Interjection*
ngawa yes (agreement)
kóma no, nothing (denial)
wukúyawa I don't know, perhaps maybe
aydju I don't know (uncertainty)
ma ok, do it (exhortation or agreement to action)
nganéyabba yaláwa well, that's it (ends conversation/topic)
worro sorry, poor thing (sympathy)
rdów Bang! (gunshot)
djóbo Shoo!
kalábbuk Shut up!
méd Wait! Just a minute!
yey Hey! (preface to question or hortative)

7.2   ALPHABETICAL WORDLIST

The following list contains all lexical items and free pronoun forms found in the grammar, the examples and the texts as well as a small number of additional items, including homophonous forms. It does not include all the items from the semantic fields list. The abbreviations used are to be found at the head of the semantic fields list.

bá Vtr8C: eat, bite

báb 'Sit down!'

bábba NAm: father

bábburr N: clan

babbúya NmY: ironwood

babukúyakka long ago

baddúmang N: goggles (swimming)

badjikkáli N: drum

bakabinjí Vintr6A: dig

bakkándja again, once more, later

bakkándjamandja instead

bákki Nm: tobacco

bala-kkákka Vtr7D: pull (towards self)

bala-nabó Vintr6A: dawn

balába V: scoop, catch with scoop net

balábara Vtr: See bú

baladjdjórrkka Vtr3: bring

balákka Vintr2A: come back, return

balála Vintr1A: come in (tide), come back

balánda NAm: white man, English language

balarrírra Nf: spear grass

balawúrrwurr NAm: wind

bálay afterwards, already, then

balayirrí (= baló + djirrí) Vintr6A: come

bálbbal NAm/f: wing

baló VintrDEF: hither, come hither

bamakkánba NAfDj: stringy bark tree, Eucalyptus tetrodonta

bamúmawa true

bángkararrk NAmY: black cockatoo

bángku Nm: mangrove bark

bánjdja Vtr1A: put, put down

bánjdjeya Vintr2A: lie down (inchoative)

bara(ka)ngka NA: lazy, tired

barakángka...-nó VintrIRG: be tired, worn out

bardarrbbayí Vintr: See yó

bárdbana ND1: shallow

bárdbarrarra NAm: frog

bardórrbba Vtr4A: crush, grind, pound, punch, smash

barélabba (n-barélabba) ND1: younger

baríyala NAm: antbed

barlánga ND1: raw (meat), unripe (fruit)

barlangúnngun NAmDj: string dilly bag

barlúya NmDj: wild honey sp.

barnamarrákka NAmDj: white clay, warrior

bárnka NB: elbow

barnómandja soon, later today

bárra NmDj: northwest wind

barrábarra NB: back

barrábarra ND1: big

barráma ND3: sore, aching

barranéyabba those 3AUGDEM

barranéyabbanja those 3UAFEMDEM

barrangúdja NAm: game, quarry, turtle (excl. fish, crab, shark)

barrayabba Prn: 3AUGCARD

barrayábbanja Prn: 3UAFEMCARD

barrayamala Prn: 3AUGEMPH

barrayámalanja Prn: 3UAFEMEMPH

bárrbaya NAm/fY: dog (tame)

bárreya 3AUGDEM

barréyabba close, near, almost

barréyabbanja 3UAFEMDEM

bárriya 3UAMASCDEM

barrúkala NAfY: fly

barrúra NAm/f: egg

bé Vintr: See yirrí

bédja Vtr1A: heat in fire

béngka Vintr2A: float , be in water

béya NAmDj: pandanus dilly bag

béyaka Ndy: father and son

bíbbo NAfDj: mud crab

bíddabo Vtr6A: follow, chase, track

bínbi-...-ba Vtr4A: write

birráddja NmY: rice

birrikébba Prn: 3UAMASCCARD

birrikémala Prn: 3UAMASCEMPH

birrinéyabba those 3UAMASCDEM

bíwa Vtr5A: smell (tr)

bíwayi Vintr2A: smell (intr), stink

bó VintrIRG: fall, land (of aeroplane)

bókka ND1: bad, no good

bólkkarda in deep water, on the open sea

bólkkardabba on the way, part way

bóraba Vtr4A: paint

bórbayi Vintr2A: paint oneself

bórdanja NA: urine

bordolbbordol...djórrkka Vtr3: rub, roll

bú Vtr4B: hit, kill, dig (yams)

Budáwin N: Darwin

búdjeyi Vintr2B: shout, call out

budjúlung Nm: bottle

budmánda Nm: suitcase

Búlanj ND1Dj: subsection name

bulíkkang NA: cow, bullock

búlkkidj big/serious wound

búrrbba NC: strong

búrrbba ND1: guts, innards

burrúddjang Nm: rag

buwárdda NAfDj: bustard, plains turkey

díbbarra NAf: spear (generic)

dídjburrk Nm: axe

díla NC: eye, seed, cartridge

dílkarra NAmDj: moon

dina at midday

djábba NAm/f: older brother/ sister

djábbarda NB: lip; djábbarda má Vtr1C: fill

djabbarnbókka NAmDj: shark

djábbarnma NAm: 'sugarbag' (bee's nest), wild honey (generic)

djáddji 'Come here!'

djádja Nm: uncle

djadjírra in the hot part of the day

djadjórla Nm: house

djakalíkala NAfDj: galah

djakí NCm: speed; djakí...-má Vintr1C: hurry

djákkabo Vtr6A: tie, bind

djákkabo...-ngódda Vtr6A:roll up swag

djakóra...-rawó Vintr6A: to smoke

Djalákarra NfDj: dreaming place name; stingray sp.

djalakkíyak NAm: multipronged fish spear

djalwárra Nm: trousers

djáma Vtr1A: wash

djáma-yi Vintr2A: wash self

djamalakakardíddja NAmY: spoonbill

djambákkang Nm: roofing iron

djánama NB: belly (external)

djándjana NAmDj: pelican

djangkúrrinj N: song type

djangórna NB: tongue

djanímarra NAmDj: embers, hot coals, charcoal

djaráma ND1: heavy

djaréya NB: nape of neck

djarnábu NAfDj: fighting spear, bamboo spear

djarnarrába Vintr4C: sneeze/ cough

djarramá Vintr5B: laugh

djarramáya N(INFIN): laugh

djárrang NAm/f: horse

djarrárlma Vintr1A: grow up

djárrdjdja pull (down)

djarríbbang Nf: trepang

djárwarra ND1: young person, boy, girl

djáwa Vintr5A: flow, bleed

djawála NAfDj: Casuarina sp.

djawalárra NmDj: spike rush

Djawándji NY: clan name

djáwarlbba ND1: old person, (n-djáwarllbba old man, nja-yáwarlbba old woman)

djawarlékka-yi Vintr2B: run out, be used up

djawukkaléla ND1: light (weight)

djébba this/here
djébba Vditr1A: deprive someone
   of something, take something
   from someone
djénkarda NAfDj: snail (land)
djénkardibakábakanóra NAmY:
   bluetongue lizard
djérwarra ND1: young person,
   adolescent
djéya that way
djéyabba that, that one
djí VtrIRG: drink
djí(ya)kabba this way
djíbba here
djídja ND1: old
djídjabba ND1: same (again)
djilíbba Nm: thongs (i.e.sandal)
djímandja at this time, nowadays
djímurru NA: southeast wind
djínbarra NAmY: saltwater catfish
djínjawa ND1: alive
djirrí VintrIRG: go
djíya 3MINMASC, here, this
djó Vtr1C: berate, be angry with
djóbo 'Shoo!'
djóngok N: (poison-)cousin
djórraba Vtr4A: cook (tr)
   (generic); start (of engine)
djórrkka Vtr3: take
djórrkka-ngaya Vintr3: run
Djówanga moiety name
djóya Nm: trumpet shell
djúbba Vtr1A: extinguish (e.g.
   fire, light)
djúlumukkiyirriya NAm: point (of
   land)
djúrddjurd NA: Brahminy kite
djúrddjurd NA: heart
djúrrang NmDj: paper, book, letter
djuwé Vintr8A: be sick/ill, suffer,
   be sore, ache; die
djúya NC: buttocks, bottom
dórdbalk N: good
Dukúrrdji NY: clan name
ka-kárdda ND3: under water,
   submerged

ka-ndarládja ND3: short
ka-ndarládja ND3: short.
kabalakóra NAm: island
Kabálko NDj:Entrance Island
kábba NAmY: water (generic),
   tide, beer
kabbála NmY: boat
kábburla ND1: old person, old
   man, old woman
kábukurdurrk NAfDj: brolga
kaddíkadda NfDj: pied oyster
   catcher
kádja down, inside, underneath,
   below
kádja Vintr1A: tide go out
kádjarna NAf: mud
kakárra NAm: shade
kákka Vtr7D: push (tr)
kála NB: ear
kála ND1: fork (of tree)
kalabángarra NAfDj: white ibis
kalábba...-rakarawó Vintr6A: forget,
   lose
kalábbuk 'Shut up!' 'Be quiet!'
kaláddjarr NA: deaf, mad, stupid
kalakalóddjarra NA: fresh (of
   water)
kalakarrá ND1: Aboriginal person
kalalmúkkayana NmDj: fish sp.
kalamíndjarrabarrábarra NAfDj:
   echidna, 'porcupine'
kalamínjdjiba NAfY: cycad, Cycas
   sp.
kalamómo NADj: Johnson
   crocodile (freshwater)
kalamúya NAf: pheasant coucal
kálawa Vtr7D: know, think about,
   worry about
kalbarárra NAfY: waterlily seed
kalíkku Nm: cloth
kálkberd NADj: northern black
   wallaroo
kalórla NC: breast (female)
kalúkku NfY: coconut
kalúrru N: cigarette
káma Vtr1A: copulate with

Kamárrang ND1Y: subsection name

kambúkka NAmDj: red ochre (dull)

kamíya Vintr2A: get up, set off, depart, leave, stand up, rise

kánbaya NAmY: crocodile (estuarine)

Kanduwúlka NDj: clan name

Kangíla ND1Y: subsection name

kángkarlangarda NAmDj: white breasted sea eagle

kangódjbaya NAmY: mangrove worm

kanja well...

kánkarra ND1: meat, flesh

kánkarra...-rawo Vintr6A: hurry

kárarra NAfDj: northern blue winged kookaburra

kárdda ND3: immersed in water, submerged

kárddja ND1: cooked (meat), ripe (fruit)

kárddjurl NAmY: egret

Karddúrra NDj: clan name

kardówarra south

kárla NC: neck (front of)

kárla ND1: wet

karlába Vtr3: immerse

karlakárrbba Nm: river

karlakórrbba NAm: path, road

karlamára NAm/f: younger brother/sister

karlamára Nm/f: younger sibling

karlédda NAfDj: freshwater catfish

karlikárli NAmDj: boomerang

karlóykkarloy...-bú Vtr4B: split

karnáya NA: leech

karnayédjabba NA: two

karnayédjabba warábbabaddabirra N: three (3UAM)

karnbilíbala NA: blood

karndóya NAfDj: round 'cheeky' yam

kárnmawa? where?

karó ND1: fat (noun)

karókaddja ND1: child, boy, girl

karówalaya NAm: snake (generic)

karrabba like, and, and similarly

karrabba...wára both...and

Karrábbu NDj: Junction Bay

karrakanódjabba in the morning, next morning, tomorrow

karrakárramardba ND1: long, tall

karrakárriba far

karráwa Vintr5A: look around, go hunting, look for, oversee, be boss, be awake

karrddjúnja NfDj: stingray

karrórnba N: yam sp.

karrówa ND1: many

karrúmakkarra NAmDj: porpoise, dolphin

karrúmakkarra ND1: smooth, slippery

karrúrru Nf: sail.

kawúna VtrIRG: See kúrrngarna

káyala NAm: ground, dirt, earth, sand

kayókaya Nm: sleep, night's sleep; lizard sp.

kékkaka ND1: new

kénkarla N: nut of Pandanus spiralis

kí-...-yángka Vintr2A: say, tell

kíddjal Nm: new shoot (plant)

kíkka NAf: mother

kódda ND1: skin

kóma NEG, No, nothing

kómabba both, all

kómalakka AV lest, so that not, otherwise

kómrdudj ND4: initiand

kóndja Vtr1A: cut

kóndjala DESID, try unsuccessfully

kóndjalabba NEGPOSS

kónjdja Vtr1A: cut

kónjdje-yi Vintr2B: cut self, stop (rain)

kórnda NAfY: scrub fowl

kórnka NmY: yam sp.

kóyawa ND1: crooked

Kóyok ND1Dj: subsection name

kúdja NB:base, foot

kúdja NC: foot, hand, finger, toe, tracks

kúdja Vintr1A: group, be in group

kúdja warábbana N: a few, five (lit. 'one hand')

kúdja...-ramí-ya Vintr2A: finish

kúdjala NA: mother's mother, mother's mother's brother, 'grannie'

kúdjbarra NAm: kangaroo (generic)

kúli N: steering wheel, tiller

kumúken NADj: Johnson crocodile (freshwater)

kúndja Vintr1A: defecate, shit, lay (egg), give birth

kúndja...-rakarawó Vintr6A: run

kúrla NAm: tree, stick (generic) (Y dialect word)

kúrrkkurk Ndy: cousins

kúrrngarna VtrIRG: stand (tr), put standing, wear, name

kúrrngkawa Ndy: cousins

kúwa Vtr5A: lie to, deceive

kuyángba N: soaked and roasted (i.e. non-toxic) cheeky yam

labalúya V4C: swell, come up in a lump

lakalá Vintr5B: hear, listen, feel (i.e. perceive through touch)

lakarrá N: See kalakarrá

lándiba...-nabo Vintr6A: be calm (sea)

lárla NC: male, boy, penis

lawá Vtr: See kálawa

lawayé Vtr1B: hang up (tr)

lawayó Vintr5B: be hanging, hang (intr)

lékka NB: testicles

lémaye Vditr1B: show something to someone

lérra...-yángka Vintr2A: drop out of hand

lúrra N: fish poisoning ceremony, place for same on Entrance Island

má Vtr1C: pick up, fetch, get

má-...-ba Vintr1C: lightning flash

ma-ndakabbírda ND5 right handed

má...-réndjeyi Vintr1C...2B: work

mábbarda Nm: bushfire, grass fire

mabbúlarr calm

mabbúrla NA: blunt (point/ blade)

mádjarna ND1: authentic, real, proper, genuine

makéddja NAfY: long-necked freshwater turtle

makéddja NAm: turtle (generic)

makkúkka NAm: grass (generic)

malála NAmY: mangrove

malamalárra NAmDj: tern, gull

malawédja Vtr1A: build

málaya up, outside, on top

malónba Vtr4A: pick fruit (from plant)

malóya NAm: rain

mámam NA: mother's father, grandfather, grandmother, grannie's (potential) spouse

Manayingkarírra NY: Maningrida

manbáma NC: waist, side

mándja Vditr1A steal something from someone

mándjad straight, true

mandjamándja NC: whiskers, beard

mandjébba until

mangalówarra ND1: jaw

Mángkaddjarra Nm: Macassan

Mangkulálkkudj N: Croker Island.

mangúya NB: nose

mankárni NAm: Aboriginal 'doctor'

mankawákka Vintr7B: hurry

mankimánki Nm: spines

mardárda ND1: bone, shell

mardayin N: ceremony

márdba NB: neck (front of)

márdba...-bándja Vintr1A: like, want

Márdbalk N: Goulburn Island

marddúrddiba NAm: heart

mardírrbala NAmY: mosquito

márkka NAm: stone axe

marládja NAmDj: green turtle

marlakkórlayi Vintr2B: split up

Marlandjárridj NDj: clan name

márlarra NAmDj: possum

marláya Vtr5A: put gum on

marlémarla NmDj: fish poison berry/bush

marlúkarla ND4: hip

márnabba NB: chest

márnabba...-bbándja Vtr1A: come towards

márnabba...-rdéddje-yi Vintr2B: raise gun/ take aim

marnákarna NC: rib bone

marnákarna Nm: stick frame for scoop net

marnakkúrrkka NB: arm

marnawákka Vtr7D: throw (spear)

marnawarrínjba NC: kidney

marnawarrínjba NmY: yam sp.

marnbúrrba Nm: naga, cloth

marndálangurrnga ND4: hard

marnúbbarr NAfDj: magpie goose

marráya N: murky/dirty water

márrmarr...-bú Vintr4B: be happy

Márru NDj: group of clans

máwa NA: father's father

máwa Vtr5A: tie together, assemble by tying

máwala Nf: paperbark sp., paperbark torch

mayáwayi Vintr2B: sing (intr)

mayórla carry on shoulder

mayurd...-yángka Vintr2A: run away

méd not yet, still

mémarla NB: thigh

ména hunger, hungry; ména - djuwé V8A: be hungry

méraba Vtr4A: hide (tr), put inside, put away

méraba-yi Vintr2B: hide (intr), be inside, go inside, go underneath, enter, put on/wear, set (of sun)

méyameya ND4: hair of head, plumage, feather, leaf of palm tree

méymayéya Vintr2A: try out, be ready

míba Vintr: See rlúrrabayi

míbba NB: forehead

míbbarda NAmDj: bandicoot

mídjiyang N: prau

míwa Vtr5A: send

módja Vtr1A: pick up from ground

mókko Nm: pubic covering

mómardakka Ndy: brothers

móya ND4: sore, wound

móya Vtr: See bá

mudíkkang Nm: motor vehicle, truck

múkka Vtr7D: swallow

múlbbum ND4: many, several

múlil N: feast

múnguy continuously, all the time

múraka ND4: body hair, fur

múrnun NAmDj: dugong

múya ND4: ghost, spirit, dead person

múyawa Vintr5C: finish, die

ná Vtr7A: see, look at

na-Bangárda ND6Dj: subsection name

ná-yi Vintr2A: meet, see each other

nabarlámbarla NAm: billabong, waterhole (in river)

nabbarlángkareya NAmY: goanna

nabbórla ND2: harmless, tame, not dangerous

nabbórnba ND2: rotten, stinking, dead (animal)

nabíya Vintr2A: lie, (turn out to) be

nabó Vintr6A: dance (of men), stamp, tread, step

Naddjóddjarra NY: clan name

nakábbirriba NA: mud (Dj dialect)

nakébba Prn: 3MINMASCCARD

nakémala Prn: 3MINMASCEMPH

nakéyakayakka at first

nakkárriyala NAmY: Burdekin duck

nakkáyala on foot

Nakkuráduk NY: clan name

nakkúrrngarnawa ND2: straight

nála ND1: See walá

Namanakarérrben NY clan name

namarnakkúrrkka NAm: creek

naméwaya NAm: butterfly net

Namidjbáli NY: clan name

nanákawa other side (of creek/river)

nangalayana How many? What time?

nangardórrddddje-yi Vintr2B: be broken, break (intr)

nangardórrddja Vtr1A: break (tr)

narrayábbanja Prn: 2UAFEMCARD

narrayámalanja Prn: 2UAFEMEMPH

narrúrra N: naked, open place

nawála -yángka Vintr2A: vomit

nbalóyara Nm: (water) well, soak

nbókka...-bá Vtr8C: miss (shooting/ spearing)

nbúrla Nm: bull

ndabakkúrrngarna Vintr2B: sit down (INCHO)

ndabarlínjdja Vtr1A: turn (tr)

ndabarlínjdje-yi Vintr2B: turn around (intrans.)

ndabúyi Vintr6B: lick, smack lips. make bilabial sound, kiss

ndakarlába Vtr3: immerse, put in water

ndakáwa...-POSS Vintr5A: be ready to take turn/dance

ndalakalóma Vtr1A straighten

ndamáwa Vtr5A: tie up, tether

ndaméraba-yi Vintr2B: set (sun)

ndarraddjáddja Vtr1A: stop (tr)

ndarraddjáddja-yi Vintr2A: stop (intr)

ndawarré Vintr5B: be high in sky (sun)

ndayárraba Vintr4A: fling down, knock over

ndjékkawa from here

Ndjúdda NDj: 'Juda Point', North East Point

nga-nabarlámbarla ND2: freshwater

nga-namánda ND2: small, little, thin

nga-narárrma ND2 white, light

nga-náwarla ND2: other, different

nga-nawarrámaya ND2: skinny (no flesh)

nga-náworrkala ND2: See náwarla

nga-ndjórrkkabba ND2: spouse

nga-rakkíla ND2: shellfish meat

ngabalóbala yesterday, recently

ngabúyanga Prn: 1MINDAT

ngadjba-yi Vintr2B: get better (of sore)

ngákarda N: sister's child, nephew, niece

ngalddjáyiba Vtr4A: take out (of pot, fire)

ngaléwara what?, which?, something, anything

ngalidjbínja NAf: gun (long barrelled), shotgun

ngalidjbínja NAm: didgeridoo

ngalidjbínja NC: throat (internal), windpipe

ngálngarda NAm: fire (Dj dialect)

ngalóla NAf: mangrove

ngáma Vtr1A: carry on shoulder (person O)

ngámangarda NmDj: fish sp.

ngána there

nganabaláma NAm: tree, stick (generic) (Dj dialect word)

nganabbárru NAmDj: buffalo

nganakayúla NAmY: jabiru

nganamayáwaya NA: clapsticks

nganamukkúkkaya NA: maggot

nganánanj NAm: beeswax

nganangádjeya NAY: dingo (wild dog)

nganangórrddjeya NAmY: cypress pine, Callitris intratropica

nganawambálma NAmY: antilopine kangaroo (male)

nganawébba NAm: stone knife

nganawúna NAm: paperbark sp.

Nganayerrebarála NDj: clan name

ngandjúddama NAm: bark canoe

nganéyabba 3MINMASCDEM there, that

nganíddji N: grog, alcoholic drink

ngánja NAf: aunt, father's sister

ngánjbarl Nf: sneeze

nganjónganja NAmDj: crow (also=black)

ngarakáya NAm: Pandanus spiralis

ngárawa Vtr7B: light fire, ignite

ngárd NAfDj: short-necked freshwater turtle

ngardabbámba ND4: liver

Ngaríbba NDj: palm dreaming place

ngarídda NA: cold (feeling)

ngárnba NA: sweat, perspiration

ngárrabba NAmDj: frill-necked lizard

ngárrabba Prn: 1/2MINCARD

ngárrabbakaddawórna NmDj: wild honey sp.

ngarraddjá Vintr5B: be open

Ngarráku NDj: Haul Round Islet

ngarráma ND4: woman, female

ngárramala Prn: 1/2MINEMPH

ngarrangálangalérnkarna NAmY: white (sulphur crested) cockatoo

ngarrayábbanja Prn: 1/2UAFEM CARD

ngarrayámalanja Prn: 1/2UAFEM EMPH

Ngárridj ND4Dj: subsection name

ngawa yes

ngáwa Vtr8A: ask

ngawí-ya Vintr2A thunder

ngayábba Prn: 3MINFEMCARD

ngáyabba Prn: 1MINCARD

ngayámala Prn: 3MINFEMEMPH

ngáyamala Prn: 1MINEMPH

ngayaméla Nm: mullet

ngédja/ngádja what (activity)?, anything (activity)

ngékayabba how many?

ngirrikébba Prn: 1/2UAMASCCARD

ngirrikémala Prn: 1/2UAMASCEMPH

ngódja Vtr1A name, call

ngódjba Vtr4A: cause, make, repair, mend, assemble

ngórdo ND6: leper

ngórraddja Vtr1A: roast (under paperbark and sand)

ngówolk ND1: harmless

ngúdja Nm: language, speech, story

ngúdjeyi Vintr2B: speak, talk, tell a story

ngúlmardirdi N: big wave, rough sea

ngúrrabba Prn: 1/2AUGCARD

ngúrramala Prn: 1/2AUGEMPH

ngurrarákka ND4: adult, grown up, big, elder

níbba Vtr1A: not know, be ignorant of

nídja Vtr1A: wait for, await

nirrikébba Prn: 2UAMASCCARD

nirrikémala Prn: 2UAMASCEMPH

nja-barrábarra-bba Nf: mother one

njabbarlánga NAY: yellow ochre

njabólarra NA: red ochre (bright)

njadjákka NAf: girl, young woman (mature, but has not yet given birth)

njadjéngka NAfDj: banyan, Ficus virens

njakkála AfDj: blue-faced honey eater

njakkárla NC: calf, shin, lower leg

njakkódda NAf: prawn (freshwater)

njakkórdba NC: brain

njalárla (ra) NAm (Vtr7C): firestick. fire drill

njálkkidj ND4: soft

njamádja NAfDj: water bag/ honey bag (close woven from pandanus)

njamánja NAf: mussel

njamánja NC: knee

njana and, because, but, then

njanabarnúma NAfDj: antilopine kangaroo (female).

njánabba what's-it?, thingummy, what's-its-name?

njanabbárdakka/njanabbardákka NfY: trevally fish

njanabbúrnda NAm: grass-hopper

njanabórnakanadja NAfDj: seagull

njanakarráwa NAY: waterlily stem

njanakkarlóddjanama NAfY: peewee

njanamarlábbana NAfY: emu

njananábba NAf: star

njandakalábarna NAY: waterlily root

njanéyabba that 3MINFEM

njarakáya NA: Pandanus aquaticus

njarrawarrówarra NA: ashes

njarrayábbanja Prn: 1UAFEMCARD

njarrayámalanja Prn: 1UAFEMEMPH

njáya 3MINFEMDEM

njayára NC: shoulder

njél cool

njélnjel late afternoon

njémbo Vtr8C: awaken, wake up

njeneyerléya NAfY: cormorant

njéwa Vintr5A: have a rest/spell

njínjdja Vintr2A: cry, sob, weep

njínjdjabba Prn: 2MINCARD

njínjdjamala Prn: 2MINEMPH

njírrabba Prn: 1AUGCARD

njírramala Prn:1AUGCARD

njirrikébba Prn: 1UACARD

njirrikémala Prn: 1AUGEMPH

njúngkowara who?, someone, anyone

nmalála N: native bee

nmarabúya Vtr1A: bury

nmarabúya-yi Vintr2B: be buried

nmárnabba N: cloud

nmarrímarlo Vintr1B: swim, bathe, bogey

nmódda NmY: fish species

nó VintrIRG: sit, stay, be

nó-...-bba VintrIRG: live, reside

núna NAf: white woman

núrrabba Prn: 2AUGCARD

núrramala Prn: 2AUGEMPH

rá Vtr7C: spear, shoot, pierce

rakarawó Vintr6A: move

rakáya NC: fingernail, toenail

ramalówandja NB: jaw

ramé Vtr: See rimí

ránba NAm: beach

rángka NAfDj: red-collared lorikeet

rárra NC: vagina

rárrangala ND2: sharp (point/ blade)

rárrma Vintr1A: be white/clean

rawáya Vintr2A: dance (of women), play (of children)

rawáya...-ba Vintr2A: play

rawó Vtr6A: throw, discard, lose

rdórdbalk See dórdbalk.

rénjdjeyi Vintr2B: stand (position), be standing, be

rénjmarla NB: cheekbone

rénjmarla Nm: new moon

rídda NB: tooth, blade (e.g. of axe)

rimí Vtr6A: hold in hand, grab, grasp, have, knead

rínja NA: sickness, bad cold

riyí Vtr6C: scratch, tear into small pieces

rlába-yi Vintr2B: descend, go/climb down

rlakarlú Vintr5B: bow head

rlarrabí Vintr: See rlúrrbayi

rlúrraba-yi Vintr2B: come out, emerge, arrive, rise (of sun)

rnarnawárraba Vtr4A: cut off, split (turtle shell)

rnawárraba-yi Vintr2B: split

rníbayi Vintr2B: go underground

róngkarra NAf: prawn (saltwater)

rórraddja Vtr1A: clean, clear

rríkka Vintr7D: crawl

rrókaye Vtr1B: carry on arms,

rrubbíya NAmY: money, coin

waddabó Vtr: See bíddabo

Wákadj ND4Y: subsection name

wákka Vintr2A: go back, return

wákka...nbarrábarra Vintr2A:
    reverse(vehicle/engine)

walá (nála) ND1: name

wála Vintr1A: ascend, go up, go
    ashore, land

walákka slowly

wálangandjáyiba NAmDj: thunder;
    lightning

walangánjdjarra NAm: smoke

waláya NB: lower leg (human);
    tail (kangaroo, stingray, fish,);
    back leg (turtle)

walédjba Vintr4C: paddle

wálem south

waléykkarra Nm: stone, rock

Wámud ND4Y: subsection name

wánarda Nm: paddle

wánba B: arm

wánja N: arm (of turtle)

wankarrídja NAmDj: bloodwood

wáraba Vtr4A: sing (tr) (sorcery)

warábba NC: one, alone

warakkála NAmDj: long yam

warayéma Vintr7E: be afraid,
    frightened

wardangínjbana NAmY:
    paperbark (bark)

warlékka Vtr7D: use up, finish up

wárlirr NAm: hot weather

wárrabba Vtr1A: take out (from
    hole or bag)

warrabú Vintr4B: burn, be cooked,
    be hot

warrámayi Vintr2B: be skinny

warrawo Vtr: See djó

warré Vintr5B: jump, be born,
    cross (creek),take off (plane)

warríwarra NA: salt (of water),
    bitter, dangerous, 'cheeky'

Wárrkwarrk NDj: clan name

wárrwarra NAfY: sun

wáykin Nm: trailer

wébba same

wédda má Vtr1C: go past

wéddawa NA: mud

wékanabba tomorrow

wékkana N: dark, night, at night

wékkana-ngána in the early
    morning

wénjdja Vtr1A: climb (eg tree)

wénjngala NAfDj: cockle

wéra Vtr1A: put in bag

wérangarda Vtr: leave behind

wíba NAm: place, home, camp,
    country

wíba NC: belong to country

wíbbara at home, (to) home

wólerrk NADj: agile wallaby

wóndja but only, only

wú Vditr7A: give something to
    someone

wúbbunj NAm: dugout canoe

wukúyawa I don't know, perhaps
    maybe

wúnkarlo Vtr1B: cut through

wúrdayak/wúrdeyak long ago

Wúrnal NDj: clan name

wurrámbalk Nm: house

ya Vtr: See djí

ya? TAGQ,'What do you think?'

yabanánaka what's-the-place

yakanábba this/that way

yakanádja that/this way, this side

yakára NC: shoulder

yakkabíyi Vintr2A: get tangled, tie
    self

yakkarrárra NA: patrilineal clan

yalába NAm: vegetable food,
    'tucker'

yalangaló NC: pubic hair

yaláwa OK, that's it, then

yalóla Vtr1A: cover with paperbark

yána See yéna

yanakkábba NAm: dry land
yangádja Vtr1A: shut off, enclose
yángka Vintr2A/AUXtr: do, say
yarra Vintr: See djirrí
yarrárlma Vintr1A: grow up
yáwaka Ndy: uncle and nephew
yáwarlbba N: See djáwarlbba
yawarlékkayi Vintr2B: run out, finish, be used up
yawarnáwayi Vintr2B: refuse
yawé Vintr: See djúwe
yawúyakka first
yékke NA: cold weather
yéna/yána earlier today
yerrengabbabó Vtr6A: hoist sail, lift up
yey! Hey!
yéya NAmDj: oyster
yí Vtr6C: leave
yíbarda NAmY: barramundi (giant perch)
yibérra Prn: 3AUGDAT
yiberrekéyanga Prn: 3UAMASCDAT
yídja NA: man
yika as well
yikkóyanga Prn: 2MINDAT
yinerrekéyanga Prn: 2UAMASCDAT
yinerreyánja Prn: 2UAFEMDAT

yinganábba that way
yingárra Prn: 1/2MINDAT
yingarrayánja Prn: 1/2UAFEMDAT
yingerrekéyanga Prn: 1/2UAMASCDAT
yingúrra Prn: 1/2AUGDAT
yinjerrekéyanga Prn: 1UAMASCDAT
yinjerreyánja Prn: 1UAFEMDAT
yinjírra Prn:1AUGDAT
yinúrra Prn: 2AUGDAT
yírda NC: nose (bridge/bone)
yírndidj NAf: spear thrower, woomera
yirrí Vintr: See djirrí
Yírriddjanga moiety name
yiyí Vtr6C: leave (it) be
yó VintrIRG: lie (position), sleep, be, camp
yó-...-(b)ba VintrIRG live, reside
yókkarra NAm: fish (generic)
yurdunjmakkúkka NDy: grannies
yúrnka NC: head
yúrnkankáya NAmY: loggerhead turtle
yúya NAm: fire, firewood (Y dialect)

7.3   LIST OF AFFIXES

The following list contains all affixes mentioned in the grammar and associated examples and texts, with the exception of pronominal verb prefixes (§3.3.3) and tense/aspect/mood suffixes (§3.6.6). These two categories of affix have too great a variety of forms to be usefully presented in this list.

-ba/-bba EXT §3.2.4
-baddabirra 3AUGPOSS §3.3.2
-baddana 3UAMASCPOSS §3.3.2
-baddayúnja 3UAFEMPOSS §3.3.2
-bala- See -baló-
-baló- VCompound: hither §3.6.18
-balóbala Entire/Entire Group (ENT) §3.2.5

bana- See na- LOC
da- Minimal imperative MINIMP §3.6.5
-ka- Irrealis (IRR) §3.6.5
-ka- See -kó- §3.6.5
ka- 3MINMASC NclassD3 §3.2.3
-kkawa ABL §3.2.1
-kkó- See -kó- §3.6.5

-kó- §3.6.5

ma- 3MINMASC NclassD5 §3.2.3

ma- Minimal imperative MINIMP §3.6.5

-mala EMPH §3.3.2

n- 3MINMASC NclassD1 §3.2.3

na- INFIN §3.6.17

na- Location (LOC) §3.2.5, §3.2.4

-na 3MINMASCPOSS §3.3.2

-naddabirra 2AUGPOSS §3.3.2

-naddana 2UAMASCPOSS §3.3.2

-naddayúnja 2UAFEMPOSS §3.3.2

-namánja HUNTOBJ §3.2.1

nayik- Clan member (CLANMASC) §3.2.5

-nda- §3.6.17

-ngadda 1/2MINPOSS §3.3.2

-ngaddabirra 1/2AUGPOSS §3.3.2

-ngaddana 1/2UAMASCPOSS §3.3.2

-ngaddayúnja 1/2UAFEMPOSS §3.3.2

ngalik- Clan member (CLANFEM) §3.2.5

-ngána PURP §3.2.1

-ngaya 3MINFEMPOSS §3.3.2

-ngka 2MINPOSS §3.3.2

nja- 3MINFEM NclassD1-D6 §3.2.3

-nja UAFEM §3.3.2, §3.3.3

-njabba 1MINPOSS §3.3.2

-njaddabirra1AUGPOSS §3.3.2

-njaddana 1UAMASCPOSS §3.3.2

-njaddayúnja 1UAFEMPOSS §3.3.2

-rrV- Realis (RE) §3.6.5

-wu- Aversative (AV) §3.6.5

-yana 3MINMASCDAT §3.3.2

-yángaya 3MINFEMDAT §3.3.2

-yi- Intransitiviser/ Reflexive/ Reciprocal (REFL) §3.6.17

-yik- CLAN §3.2.5

-yV- Irrealis (IRR) §3.6.5

ACKNOWLEDGEMENTS

I wish to thank a number of people who have helped me by providing information and comment which has helped to make the final version of this grammar as good as possible. The most significant are the Ndjébbana speakers, listed in §1.7, who taught me their language, starting in 1975, especially JB, †JK, and †JM. They were very patient with a rather slow learner who found their language fiendishly complicated. Additional data was provided by my successors in the position of linguist in the Ndjébbana bilingual education program, Bronwyn Eather and Carolyn Coleman. Others who have commented on or contributed to the various drafts of the grammar are Barry Blake, Carolyn Coleman, Bob Dixon, Diana Eades, Nicholas Evans, Kevin Ford, Rebecca Green, Eric Vasse, Cecily Willis and Peter Cooke. Immeasurable improvements have resulted from the input of these people, though they should not be held to blame for any remaining shortcomings, because I stoutly resisted some of their attempts to persuade me of the merit of further improvements. Even in these instances, they initiated a beneficial rethinking process. Peter Cooke provided essential information for the map from his recent researches, drawing in part also on early notes from Gowan Armstrong.

I wish to acknowledge the support of the Australian and then the Northern Territory Department of Education, who employed me as a linguist to work on the establishment of the Ndjébbana bilingual education program from 1975 to 1982. And I wish to thank Edith Cowan University and the Institute of Applied Language Studies, who, between them, sponsored my 1992 fieldwork at Maningrida.

I would like to express my gratitude to Alison, Duncan, Alastair, Megan and Hamish — my wife and children — who put up with a great deal of neglect and sacrifice during my absences on fieldwork and during periods of analysis and writing, but who continually supported me in my endeavours.

Finally I wish to thank the whole community of Ndjébbana speakers who welcomed me and my family into their homes and families, who supported me in my work and who have continued to make use of some of it in their ongoing bilingual education program (1981 to the present). I hope that this grammar will be a useful contribution to maintaining and developing your language at Maningrida. I am sorry that it has been such a long time in the writing, but I encourage you to work together for many more generations of Ndjébbana speakers. Look up things in this grammar, by all means, but it's better to talk to the old people, who know so much more than I could write down here, and to keep speaking Ndjébbana amongst yourselves.

APPENDICES

APPENDIX 1   KEY TO PERSONAL NAMES

DW	†Don Waybananga	JN	Johnny Nalíba
HDj	Helen Djimbarrwála	LDj	Lena Djabíbba
JB	Jockey Bundubundu	PM	Peter Marralwanga
JBo	†Jimmy Bóborrk	WDj	†Willy Djárrkkarla
JK	†Johnny Karddáwarr	SK	Stephen Káwulkku
JM	†Joseph Mangkúdja		

APPENDIX 2   NDJEBBANA AND EASTERN ARNHEM LAND SUBSECTION NAMES

Ndjébbana subsections and their eastern Arnhem Land equivalents

Ndjébbana Subsections (m/f)	*Eastern Arnhem Land equivalents (e.g. Rembarrnga) (m/f)*
Djówanga	*Duwa*
Búlanj/Njabúlanj	Kela/Kalidjan
Nkóyok/Njakóyok	Wamud/Wamuddjan
Ngárridj/Njangárridj	Balang/Belinj
Nabangárda/Njabangárda	Kamarrang/Kamanj
Yírriddjanga	*Yirridjdja*
Kangíla/Njakangíla	Bulanj/Bulanjdjan
Wámud/Njawámud	Kodjok/Kodjdjan
Wákadj/Njawákadj	Ngarridj/Ngarridjdjan
Nkamárrang/Njakamárrang	Bangardi/Bangɥ rn

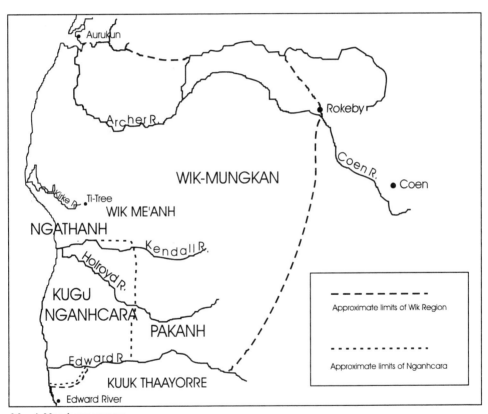

Map 4: Nganhcara country

Kugu Nganhcara
by Ian Smith and Steve Johnson

DEDICATION

This grammar is dedicated to Gwen Johnson and to the memory of Kathy Smith.

1. THE LANGUAGE AND ITS SPEAKERS

Kugu Nganhcara is a Middle Paman language of the Cape York peninsula in North Queensland. The majority of its 250 to 300 speakers are located at Edward River and Aurukun, on the west coast of the peninsula, the inland town of Coen and various outstations.

1.1 LINGUISTIC TYPE

Phonologically, Kugu Nganhcara departs from the predominant Australian pattern in its contrasting voiced/voiceless stop series, glottal stop, single rhotic and five vowel system. It also has a few unusual consonant clusters and a typologically less frequent reduplication process which places the reduplicated syllable to the left of its model.

Morphologically, the language is exclusively suffixing. Pronouns are typical for Australia in distinguishing singular, dual and plural numbers and first, second and third persons, with a further inclusive/exclusive distinction for first person dual and plural. They are unusual, however, in having reflexive forms. Verbs mark such common Australian categories as present, past, irrealis, and imperative. Obligatory subject-concord is a less usual characteristic. Two major verb conjugations are distinguished on the surface level, with membership determined by the rather un-Australian feature of a stem-final thematic vowel. Causative is the only valence-changing derivational category.

Syntactically, the language has a common type of Australian split case-marking system with pronouns displaying nominative/accusative marking and non-pronominal NPs ergative/absolutive marking. Enclitic cross-referencing pronouns also function in a nominative/accusative system. The syntax of these bound pronouns is the most significant aspect of the language for linguistic theory: they are positioned with respect to one syntactic constituent (the verb) but may encliticise to a different constituent: that which precedes the verb, irrespective of its identity. Such clitic behaviour has received considerable scholarly attention and was unique when first reported (Smith and Johnson 1979); it has since been found in a very few other languages, such as Kwakwala (Anderson 1984) and Djinang/Djinba (Waters 1989). A second set of enclitics serves to mark the case categories of noun phrases, a phenomenon which is to our knowledge unique in Australianist literature. The comitative case is also of particular interest: this category is an Australian areal feature, and conventional wisdom treats it as derivational in nature, but in Nganhcara, as part of the case system, it is clearly inflectional. Finally, the existence of a single case category covering ablative and genitive functions is typologically unusual.

In the lexicon, 'generics' (as they are referred to in Australianist literature) are one focus of interest, since they constitute a system of noun classifiers in Kugu Nganhcara. The RESPECT lexicon (see 5.5) also has some interesting features. Finally, many Australian groups use complex systems of directionals which often go unreported; the Nganhcara system is sketched in 5.4.

1.2   SOCIAL GROUP AND LANGUAGE NAMES

Despite its small size, Nganhcara society is highly complex. As an initial approximation, we may note that there are two main units of social organisation: the land-owning PATRICLAN (patrilocal descent group) and the RESIDENCE GROUP (actual on-the-ground land-using camp group). Each (patri)clan is associated with a clan-lect, which we call a PATRILECT (Smith and Johnson 1986), since no existing term can be appropriately used (see 1.4.3). Note, however, that the number of patrilects is much smaller than the number of clans, so that a given patrilect may not be exclusively ascribed to one clan.

The language name Kugu Nganhcara (kugu 'language' nganhcara 'our (1plexcDAT/ABL)') covers six closely related patrilects spoken between Kendall River and Moonkan Creek by groups that share many cultural features and have a high degree of interaction (see J. von Sturmer 1978). The people themselves, however, have no common name for the speech varieties described here. They normally use the names of the patrilects: Kugu Muminh (Mm), Kugu Uwanh (Uw), Kugu Ugbanh (Ug), Kugu Mu'inh (M'), Kugu Yi'anh (Yi), and Wik Iyanh (Iy). (A further name, Kugu Mangk, is likely an alternative label for Kugu Yi'anh, although some speakers apparently claim they are distinct (J. von Sturmer 1978:171); the differences may be minor ones that are emphasized for political purposes; see discussion of sub-patrilectal variation in 1.4.2. The name 'half-Iyanh' also crops up in the literature, but we cannot confirm its existence.)   In each

instance, kugu or wik means 'language', and is followed by the verbal noun
for 'go' in the particular patrilect (except for mangk, whose etymology is
unclear). The description here is based primarily on Kugu Uwanh, with
notes on any significant differences in the other patrilects, especially Wik
Iyanh.

Although these are the terms most often used for the patrilects,
others are also heard. For example, the name of the principal totem of a
patriclan may be used with kugu/wik as a designation for both the group and,
less commonly, its language; e.g. kugu pangku 'wallaby clan; wallaby
language', kugu tooto 'barramundi clan; barramundi language', kugu yome
'possum clan, possum language'. These totemic names, however, do not
map one-for-one onto the patrilectal names: different clans affiliated with the
same patrilect usually have different totems and the same totem may be shared
by clans affiliated with different patrilects.

The term Kugu Nganhcara (or Wik Nganhcara) appears to have
arisen among the Wik peoples to the north of the Kugu Nganhcara territory,
and as D. von Sturmer notes (1980:27), 'is often used in a pejorative sense to
insinuate that people from the area are still living like the "wild bush blacks"
did before the missionaries arrived, and that they are exponents of practices
long since given up by their northern neighbours'. It surfaces in the
anthropological literature as e.g. Wik-nantjara (McConnel 1930), Wik
Ngantjera (Sharp 1939, Scheffler 1972), Wiknantyara (McConnel 1939,
1940), Ngandjara (Capell 1963) and Kugu Nganychara (J. von Sturmer
1978). Among the Cape Keerweer people, the term Wik Ngenycharr is also
partly a geographical term applying only to the nearby speakers of Nganhcara
patrilects and excluding those from more distant areas (Sutton 1991:51). J.
von Sturmer's work is important in delineating the groups to which the term
properly applies as a purely linguistic label. We shall use both Kugu
Nganhcara and Nganhcara to refer to the language and THE (Kugu)
Nganhcara to refer to the people.

The relationship between land, language and land-users in the region
is a complex one. Having done no field investigation of this question
ourselves, we rely heavily on the thorough anthropological work of Sutton
on the coastal people of the Cape Keerweer region, which abuts the
Nganhcara territory on the north, and of J. von Sturmer on the people of the
Nganhcara region (Sutton 1978, J. von Sturmer 1978, Sutton and Rigsby
1979, Sutton 1991).

Our use of the term PATRICLAN mirrors Sutton's (1978) use of
CLAN; J. von Sturmer uses the term LAND CORPORATION, since
(PATRI)CLAN, as used in the anthropological literature, is not strictly
appropriate here. (Patri)clan usually denotes an enduring corporation whose
membership does not depend on remembered genealogy, the latter typically
being shallow among Australian groups; the Wik area '(patri)clans',
however, are more fissile and for the groups of the Nganhcara region von
Sturmer notes, 'In the vast majority of cases, all individuals with primary
rights in the same sites are genealogically linked at *no more* than two
generations (sic) degree of removal. In short, all individuals share a common
FF.' (1978:281, italics original). Both Sutton and von Sturmer point out two
other difficulties in defining land 'ownership' in terms of patrilineal descent
groups. (Also at issue is whether 'ownership' is the appropriate term, but

this question need not concern us here.) Such a group:
- may not include ALL the individuals that stand in patrilineal descent from a male forebear, as some members may have split off
- may contain subgroups that have no clear patrilineal links to each other.

The first anomaly arises because political authority in a patriclan normally resides with the structurally senior male (the FOCAL male) and is passed on to his eldest son. Ambitious junior brothers and sons of junior brothers may seek to escape the dominance of a senior male by establishing their independence. Various avenues are available for such an enterprise; for example men hold subsidiary rights to the territory of their M, FM and MM which in the right circumstances may serve as the basis for a claim to 'ownership'. Given the shallow genealogical depth of most patriclans such schisms must occur in the normal course of events. The second anomaly may arise if a smaller clan joins forces with another on a permanent basis and the two come to be considered one clan; ·alternatively if remembered genealogies are shallow, it may be possible for distant relationships to be forgotten as one generation is replaced by the next. For such composite clans among the Nganhcara, all components speak the same patrilect. Sutton paints a similar picture for the Cape Keerweer area, 'All surviving clans claim linguistic unity within themselves, but clan 1 [now extinct - IS] ... is said to have "had two languages, Wik-Paacha and Wik-Ngathàrra"; this may have been a case where two lineages affiliated to separate dialects claimed the same country' (1978:59).

As noted earlier, the number of patriclans is much greater than the number of patrilects; consequently a given patrilect may be ascribed to more than one patriclan. We can see how such a situation can arise through clan schism, although it cannot be proven that all cases of multiple ascription have arisen through this mechanism. We deal in 1.4.2 with the question of whether patriclans evolve distinctive sub-varieties of a patrilect.

Patriclans, particularly those belonging to a single riverine system, may be linked in a COMPANY relationship, marked by contracting of marriages among the groups, joint exploitation of resources, joint ownership of some of their territory and/or recognition of subsidiary rights .in each other's territory.

Major differences exist between coastal and inland zones: the coastal area is more varied ecologically and presents a wider variety of food resources than the relatively uniform inland zone; the coastal area is also more severely affected by annual flooding (January to July). Consequently, the coastal area supports a higher population density than the inland zone and imposes immobility on its residents for a considerably longer period. The coastal/inland division had social correlates as well: the Wik Iyanh patriclans, whose estates were all inland, were somewhat peripheral to the Kugu patriclans, whose estates lay in the coastal zone.

Although he presents no statistics on marriage patterns, J. von Sturmer observes a 'relatively high level of regional endogamy' (1978:406). He also notes that there are few hard and fast rules regarding marriage partners, although there are restrictions on marriage with very close kin ('M, MZ, FZ, Z etc.' 1978:404). Nor is there any 'notion of corporation [i.e. our patriclan - IS] or totem exogamy' (1978:406). Nevertheless, he concedes that 'Where residential groups are small and comprise mostly close kin, the search for sexual partners must inevitably lead elsewhere.' (1978:408). More important for our purposes is the question of patrilect exogamy, which he does not address. Sutton finds that approximately three-quarters of a sample of 291 marriages in the Cape Keerweer area were between individuals of different dialects or languages (1978:110). This figure, if applicable to the Nganhcara, would, against the background of regional endogamy observed by J. von Sturmer, mean that a preponderance of Nganhcara marriages are between speakers of different Nganhcara patrilects, a conclusion that also accords with our own impressions. Von Sturmer states that 'Marriages are contracted freely between the coastal and the inland divisions' (1978:406), but Sutton notes a strong tendency for endogamy within coastal and inland divisions of the Cape Keerweer region. For example only 13% of women married by men of coastal patriclans came from the inland zone (1978:115). The apparent contradictions between Von Sturmer's remarks and Sutton's data are best resolved by interpreting the former as seeking to establish precise limitations on marriage (or rather the lack of limitations) and the latter as investigating actual practice. In short, the tendencies to regional endogamy (including coastal area endogamy) and patrilectal exogamy exist in practice, if not in law.

We now turn to the composition of RESIDENCE GROUPS, the actual land-using camp groups. These centre on a focal male and other members of a patriclan together with others associated by kinship, marriage, or company relationship. Residence groups are more fluid in their membership than patriclans: company people may be present only for the exploitation of a seasonal food resource; newly married men usually leave to reside for a time in their wife's territory; arguments may result in departures; there may be refugees from hostility elsewhere; people may leave or arrive temporarily to visit relatives or for a variety of other reasons. The shifting alliances and schisms at the level of the residence group play a large role in the evolution of longer term changes at the clan level. From the linguistic point of view, the most salient feature of residence groups is their intrinsically polylectal nature: the preponderance of patrilect exogamy implies that an individual's affinal kin likely speak other patrilects, and unrelated people present in the group are likely not to speak the patrilect of the focal male.   As Sutton remarks 'Multilingualism is an integral part of everyone's social competence.' (1978:xiii).

1.2.1 PATRILECTAL CHARACTERISTICS.   The six patrilects are identical in syntax and exhibit only minor phonological and morphological differences; substantial lexical differences are found, however.

[1] *Phonology.*   The six patrilects have identical phonological inventories (see 2.1).   Three types of phonological differences occur: systematic, semi-systematic and idiosyncratic.   Only a few systematic phonological differences are found, and these are all quite minor.   For example, alveolar obstruents tend to be retracted in Mu'inh and Iyanh. In Muminh the contrast between long and short vowels (generally restricted to initial syllables) is neutralised to a long vowel before /g/ (2.1.1[1]). There are a few semi-systematic phonological differences. In certain words, Uwanh, Ugbanh and Muminh have an intervocalic /r/ following a long vowel where

Mu'inh, Yi'anh and Iyanh have an /n/ following a short vowel; for example Uw, Ug, Mm iiru 'this', aara 'that' versus M', Iy, Yi inu and ana; Uw, Mm thaaranamu 'their' (3plABL), Yi thananamu, Iy thananam (corresponding forms in other patrilects unrecorded). Yi'anh has lost a nasal before [-cor] voiced stops in some words; thus Yi wojeń nga 'gather', muga 'eat', kaagu 'bandicoot', pibeń nga 'float'; Uw wonje, mungga, kaanggu, pimbi, but also Yi, Uw kumbi 'shift', nhumba 'rub', yinjenga 'wet', wangga amba 'fine fishing net'. Finally there are a great many idiosyncratic differences in the phonemic make-up of the same lexical item in different patrilects. Examples follow (in some items not all patrilects have words from the same root):

ego's mother	Uw, Ug, M' ngathidhe; Mm ngathadhe; Yi ngathidha; Iy ngatha
small	Uw mepen; Mm mapan; Ug madhadhi; M' mangaya; Yi mangengkon; Iy wayaya
hairy round yam (dioscoria sativa var. rotunda)	Uw, Ug kungba; Mm kungkuwa; M' kungguwa; Iy ka'ara; Yi wanci
knife spear	Uw, Ug, Yi, M' cawara; Mm, Iy thawara
cry	Uw, Ug, Yi, M' paabi; Mm paawi; Iy paayi

[2] *Morphology*. Wik Iyanh has a number of features that isolate it somewhat from the Kugu patrilects, for example:

- It lacks a distinction between dual and plural first person exclusive: in the Kugu patrilects ngana 'we (duexc)' contrasts with nganhca 'we (plexc)', while Iyanh has the one form ngana 'we (exc)' for dual and plural.

- There is only one conjugation for all verbs, compared with the two major and two minor conjugations of the other patrilects (3.4).

- Many of the oblique pronoun forms have a unique structure, and show greater regularity than in the other patrilects (3.3).

These differences reflect the fact that Iyanh speakers are somewhat peripheral to the Nganhcara group (see above). We have found no morphological differences among the Kugu patrilects, apart from the phonological realisation of one or two grammatical morphemes.

[3] *Lexicon*. It is in the lexicon that the majority of differences among the patrilects are to be found. Figures on cognate lexicon given in 1.3 (Table 1.1) indicate that interlectal differences are on the order of 15% - 25%. Note, however, that these figures would be higher if phonological differences in cognate items were also taken into account. It is also clear from the data in Table 1.1 that the greatest lexical differences are between Wik Iyanh and the Kugu patrilects. This is again in keeping with Iyanh's peripheral status. Work in progress indicates that some areas of the lexicon (such as mammals that serve as a source of food) are more differentiated than others. We may note that no area seems to be immune from differentiation: even grammatical

morphemes are involved. For example the comitative case marking enclitic appears as M', Iy, Mm -nhja; Uw -ra; and Yi, Ug -la; the most common causative suffix appears as -nha in Iy and -nga in the Kugu patrilects.

1.3   TERRITORY AND NEIGHBOURS

The Wik region, of which the Nganhcara territories form part, traditionally extended from the Watson River in the north to Moonkan Creek in the south, and as far inland as the upper reaches of the Archer. Ironically, the three focal points of European-initiated settlement where Wik peoples are found today, Aurukun, Edward River and Coen, lie just outside traditional Wik territory, but can be taken to mark the extreme limits of influence at the present time.

Kugu Nganhcara lands form most of the southern part of the Wik region, from the Kendall River to Moonkan Creek. Generally, the Kugu patriclans own estates in the coastal region and Wik Iyanh estates predominate in the immediate inland region. While the Wik Iyanh estates form a more-or-less continuous block, the territory owned by coastal patriclans sharing the same patrilect is often separated by land owned by groups speaking other patrilects. For example one group of Uwanh speakers own an estate north of the King River while another group's estate is south of the Thuuk River (known officially as Hersey Creek). Between these two rivers is an estate belonging to a group of Muminh speakers, which is itself isolated from estates of other Muminh groups south of the Holroyd River (known officially as Christmas Creek) (J. von Sturmer 1978: Map 3). Indeed, von Sturmer notes that even the land owned by a single patriclan 'may consist of a number of non-contiguous sites.' (1978:316).

The largest share of the Wik region was occupied by Wik-Mungkan speaking clans, who traditionally lived in the inland region north of the Kendall River. However, it would be wrong to assume they constituted a majority of Wik speakers. Settlement was much denser along the coast than in the inland areas owned by the Mungkan. The northern Wik coastal strip, from the Kendall to the Archer, was inhabited by speakers of Wik Ngathan, Wik Ngatharr and Wik Alkanh, three very closely related patrilects. (According to Sutton 1978:38, the latter two refer to the same variety.) Other little-known peoples lived at the mouth of the Archer and along the Watson River. Although some of them bear a Wik label, not much more is known, except that some of the languages they spoke were Northern rather than Wik. One other language, Wik Me'anh — also known as Wik-Ep or Wik-Iit (Sutton 1978:87) — is definitely a separate Wik language, and still has a handful of speakers. It was traditionally spoken a little way inland north of the Kendall River, but little is known about its traditional sociolinguistic relationships. McConnel (1939:63) remarks that the Me'anh 'appear to be culturally one with their *Wik* neighbours, with whom they regularly intermarry - as do all the *Wik* tribes'. In the extreme southeastern corner of the Wik area, another little-known language, Pakanh, was spoken. A short interview with a speaker in 1979 indicates that it is likely a Wik language, but certainly not one of the Nganhcara group. Other probably extinct languages which, according to Sutton (1978) may have belonged to the Wik group include Wik Ompom, Wik Paach, Ayapathu and Wik Keyangan.

The languages spoken to the north of the Archer were designated by the Wik Mungkan as Wik Waya (difficult to understand), partly because they are phonologically quite different from Wik languages, and partly because they were spoken on the other side of a cultural boundary. South of Moonkan Creek, below the Edward River, Thaayorre was spoken, and although this language bears evidence of considerable lexical borrowing from its Wik neighbours, few Thaayorre words came north. Again there were considerable cultural as well as linguistic differences. To the east lay Kaanchu.

Of the surrounding languages, only Wik Mungkan is closely related to Nganhcara (Sutton 1978 chapter iv gives lexico-statistical evidence to support this view). This relationship is demonstrated in Table 1.1 (adapted from Sutton 1978:178). These figures are based on a list of 100 common items, attributed to Kenneth Hale. If it were not for the considerable phonological and morphological differences between Mungkan and the Nganhcara patrilects, one would be tempted to regard them as one language on lexical grounds.

TABLE 1.1 - *Percentages of Close Cognates Shared by Wik-Mungkan and some Nganhcara Patrilects*

Mungkan				
75	Iyanh			
77	88	Mu'inh		
63	74	87	Uwanh	
61	74	81	84	Muminh

As noted in 1.2.1, Wik Iyanh is slightly more distinct from the Kugu patrilects than they are from one another. It shares much vocabulary — e.g. wik 'language', iya 'go' and mungka 'eat' — with Wik Mungkan of which it has sometimes been taken to be a sub-variety. Genealogically, however, Iyanh is clearly closer to the Kugu Nganhcara patrilects. Unlike Wik Mungkan and the other more distantly related neighbouring languages, all Nganhcara patrilects participated in a major phonological innovation whereby the loss of contrastive vowel length brought about contrastive voicing in the stops via secondary split (2.1.1[1]). All also share the subsequent reestablishment of a vowel length contrast and the development of phonetic labial-velars (2.1.1[3]). They all retain a five-vowel contrast in final open syllables (2.1.2) which Wik Mungkan and other languages have lost. They all exhibit alternations in verb stems with high thematic vowels (3.4.2, 3.4.3), which Wik Mungkan and other languages lack. Finally, they have identical case systems, and differ in only minor details in their morphology (1.2.1[2]).

It should be noted that the terms WIK and KUGU do not reflect any deep-seated linguistic or cultural cleavages in the region. For example the Kugu patrilects are much more closely related to Wik Munkan than they are to Kuuk Thaayorre (kuuk being cognate with kugu). All we can say is that varieties spoken along the coast south of the Kendall River use a version of kugu instead of wik. Some speakers of Kugu patrilects resident in Aurukun have taken to using Wik under the influence of Wik Mungkan speakers. (Thus Hale 1976a, based on data collected in Aurukun, refers to 'Wik Muminh'.)

1.4   SOCIOLINGUISTIC SITUATION

1.4.1   PATRILECT AS SOCIAL REALITY.   Many aspects of Nganhcara society reflect patrilineal organisation. One's patrilect is constantly on display as a marker of one's descent and hence as a marker of other patrilineally inherited characteristics; e.g. patriclan membership; rights to land (of prime importance as a means of survival); ownership of sacred places, rights to perform ceremonies and ownership of songs, dances and stories (all factors that enhance the individual's prestige and political power); and finally totems, which are an integral part of one's identity. Patrilect as a marker of one's patrilineal descent is thus an important symbol of social identity.

A clear indication of the significance of patrilects is the fact that the Nganhcara do not have a single generally recognised name for themselves as a people or for their language.   What they use are terms referring to patriclans, clan estates, riverine companies, residence groups, focal males and, as mentioned above, the names of the patrilects.

The patrilectal heterogeneity of the residence group (1.2) means that conversations commonly take place among people each speaking their own patrilect, but at least receptively competent in the other patrilects being spoken. Speakers of Nganhcara sometimes marry outside the orbit of their own language and are often multilingual in Mungkan, Thaayorre, Ngathan or other languages of the region. A further dimension to this complexity is added by RESPECT vocabulary, a parallel lexicon used in certain social situations, such as in the recounting of myths or when speaking to people in mourning or to certain categories of kin (see 5.5). The fact that the patrilects remain distinct in such an environment is further testimony to their social importance.

As noted above, marriage among the Nganhcara is most frequently between speakers of different patrilects. Thus most speakers of Nganhcara have competence in two patrilects, although it is their father's language that they normally regard as theirs. Many have also learnt the language of their mother's mother, or other people who have been present in the residence group. The fact that fathers are not generally primary care-givers must make the acquisition of one's patrilect a challenge. Our fieldwork was mostly of the formal elicitation interview type, which allowed us to uncover a large part of the grammatical system in a short period, but which taught us little about such areas as discourse structure or language acquisition.   Sutton, who carried out extensive participant-observation in the Cape Keerweer area provides some important insights:

> For the children, most of the waking hours are spent
> with members of their peer groups or with women, not
> with adult men. Their exposure to formal narrative,

> however, is frequently in the evenings when both men and women (but more commonly men; wives are very quiet when their husbands are around) often tell stories. In present-day settlements peer-groups of children are quite large. In such conditions the people from and with whom one acquires language are somewhat of the same categories as in an urban society. In pre-settlement times, however, it is certain that residential groups were commonly smaller, at least for a good part of each year, and the influence of older kin on the acquisition of language by children may be assumed to have been greater. (1978:98)

> Women bringing up children will tend to play the strongest role in their early linguistic education, and they do not simply speak to children in their own personal dialects. Even today, they will often address a child in the patri-dialect of the child's father. Whether or not they speak it well depends on their own socialisation and adult contact with that dialect. (1978:161)

Despite the existence of some individual variation (see below) there appears to be general community agreement on the linguistic features of each patrilect, and, as Sutton indicates, considerable trouble is taken to make sure that children acquire the appropriate patrilect. For example, our chief Uwanh consultant reported having switched to her deceased husband's patrilect, Mu'inh, at home in order to provide her children with the correct model. (We observed that in providing Uwanh examples she occasionally made lexical substitutions from Mu'inh, particularly for function morphemes). In our 1979 fieldwork we found that we each became associated with the patrilects of our first collaborators (Smith with Kugu Uwanh, Johnson with Kugu Muminh) and were often corrected by speakers of various patrilects for using words inappropriate to 'our' patrilects. These corrections were generally consonant with the vocabulary we elicited from our main Uwanh and Muminh collaborators.

1.4.2   INDIVIDUAL AND CLAN-LINKED VARIATION. With such a complex situation forming the background for the Nganhcara child's acquisition of language, strong pressures exist to promote borrowing. This results in a vocabulary pool being available to all Nganhcara speakers, from which they can select their own words; informants from the same patrilect sometimes differ in their preferred vocabulary, and an unmarked word in one patrilect may be used by the speaker of another for special effect (cf. 5.5). We noticed that within some patrilects different groups display variation in vocabulary; the name 'half-Iyanh' referred to above (1.2) may be an indication that Iyanh in particular can be subdivided. We also were often told, or noted ourselves, that a particular speaker's Muminh, Yi'anh or Uwanh was different from that of our main consultants. Such sub-patrilectal differentiation is fuelled by two cultural factors. First is the need to express the distinctness of patriclans which share a single patrilect:

Each clan is said to have its own way of speaking, although a few dialect [i.e. our patrilect - IS] names are used to subgroup this variety. The subgrouping is made basically on what Westerners would consider objective linguistic criteria, although there is room for politicking. The ideology says, however, that dialects were left county-by-country [i.e. our estate - IS] to individual clans, and were not left *en bloc.* (Sutton 1978: 138)

Informants are apt to make remarks such as "Those people from country _____ speak *Kugu-Ugbanh,* but it is a little different *Ugbanh* from that other mob". ... There may be differences - greater or smaller - between the way in which a particular language (or dialect) is spoken by members of two different estate corporations [our patriclans - IS], or even within a particular estate corporation. ... It can be hypothesized that each estate corporation moves in the direction of linguistic distinctiveness. (J. von Sturmer 1978:325-326)

Second is the emphasis placed on the distinctness of the individual:

Emphasis on personal style characterises the whole of social ideology at Cape Keerweer. Intense egoism is reflected in an acceptance of rather wide variations of idiolect. ... my impressions accord with the local view that individual speech styles are as easily recognisable as individual footprints. (Sutton 1978:161)

Within the coastal division of the [Kugu Nganhcara] region, diversity is not only tolerated, it is actively sponsored. In matters of language or dialect, people point to and base distinctions on the slightest variations imaginable; and as I hypothesized elsewhere (...p. 326) each local group - and, refining the hypothesis further, each "big man" - moves in the direction of linguistic distinctiveness. I have noted elsewhere ... that there is a strong stress on individual rights and on individuation. This is reflected in phenomena other than language, e.g., nowadays it is expressed in the singular and distinctive shapes into which "cowboy hats" are moulded, and the elaboration of decorative details: bands, studs, badges, personal names and printed epithets ... the idiosyncratic is the norm, not the exception. The guiding principle is "style" - i.e. developing one's own distinctive persona or image. (J. von Sturmer 1978: 345-346).

Our general impression is that intra-patrilectal variation is relatively minor but of great social significance. However, until the real extent of such variation is examined through further study (especially quantitative study) it is important to identify the source of information on any particular patrilect. Most of our information for a given patrilect came from a single speaker; where the source of a particular example is other than our main consultant for that patrilect, an indication is made.   Sources are identified in the acknowledgements section following chapter 7.   To avoid offending any member of the community who may read this grammar, however, we have refrained from referring to individuals by name in the body of this work, in case one of those named has passed away — a distinct possibility, given the age of our fieldwork.

1.4.3   DIALECT, SOCIOLECT AND PATRICLAN.   In the above sections we have seen that the Nganhcara patrilects are significant social categories and that they are linguistically differentiated. It should come as no surprise that social groups as important as the Nganhcara patriclans are marked linguistically.   The fact that in such a linguistically heterogeneous environment the lexicon plays by far the greatest role in distinguishing among the patrilects is reminiscent of the example of Urdu/Marathi/Kannada contact discussed by Gumperz and Wilson (1971). The main difference seems to be that the latter is clearly a product of convergence and diffusion, while there is no evidence of prior convergence among the Nganhcara patrilects.

  We have used the term PATRILECT to describe the different socially significant language varieties in Kugu Nganhcara primarily because existing terms — in particular the terms SOCIOLECT and DIALECT — seem to be inappropriate.

  The term SOCIOLECT denotes the speech variety of a social group; however, it cannot be appropriately applied to the Nganhcara patrilects, since it implies a hierarchy of stratified groups not present here.   In addition the group hierarchy is matched by a prestige ranking among the speech varieties which is also lacking.   Finally, the Nganhcara patrilects are more clearly delineated than typical sociolects, which generally grade into one another seamlessly, though this difference may be a function of the fact that most studies have been carried out in modern urban environments where stratified groups are not discrete.

  The term DIALECT can be differentiated from PATRICLAN on two counts.   First, DIALECT implies a close nexus between on-the-ground land-using group and language-using group, which does not obtain here. Second, dialect affiliation is generally derived from the region in which one lives or has lived, and the dialect affiliation of an individual may change over time; patrilect affiliation on the other hand is ascribed on the basis of lineage and cannot generally be changed.   Finally, dialectal differences arise through linguistic changes that do not spread through the entire territory in which a language is spoken.   Such a mechanism clearly cannot underlie the differentiation of the Nganhcara patrilects, given the heterogeneous nature of the residence groups.

1.5   PRESENT SITUATION

Church missions were founded in the area earlier in this century
(Presbyterian at Aurukun, 1904, Anglican at Edward River, 1936), but the
Nganhcara were largely undisturbed until the fifties.   J. von Sturmer
summarises the situation as follows (1978):

> South of the Love River, life continued largely
> uninterrupted in the bush.   Certainly contact had been
> made with sandalwooders and with pearling luggers
> along the coast. A few men were recruited to the lugger
> trade directly from the bush as far south as the Kendall
> River.   And south of the Kendall, entire bands were
> engaged in cutting sandalwood. Payment was in food,
> tobacco and tomahawks. Moreover, treks were made
> inland to the cattle stations, to visit relations and to
> obtain European goods, especially tobacco. Visits were
> also made to the mission at Aurukun. Nevertheless, the
> intensity of interaction was never high; and populations
> remained stable in number, and socially integrated. (40)

> In general ... the *Kugu Nganychara* did not move out
> of the bush systematically until the late 1950s, though
> mission contact had been established with the area in
> 1928 and some children were taken into the dormitories
> at Aurukun after this date. (178)

D. von Sturmer recounts one Nganhcara speaker's recollection of
the efforts to remove children from their parents to 'educate' and Christianise
them in the missions in the 1930s:

> ...Old Archie [a well-known 'native missionary'
> working for the European missionaries at Aurukun]
> come from mission to back Holroyd, keep teasing
> people, stopping people fighting.... people still spear
> one another. Old McKenzie come with boat, took
> children. He paid for children with sugar, flour,
> tobacco. People worry and cry for children, I keep
> running away. McKenzie saw me small time [as a
> child], keep coming up with boat, with horse till easy
> time picking up children, keep pushing people to
> mission' (1980: 29-30, interpolations original).

Despite these abductions, at the time of our fieldwork most mature
adults had been born in the bush into the traditional way of life, although
some traditional practices, such as cremation battles and mummification of the
dead were already in decline or discontinued. Some elderly people had no
knowledge of English; for others it was quite limited. Most of the Nganhcara
return to their lands when they can, so that even today young children spend
some time in a traditional environment away from the settlements and the

influence of English and White society. These groups return to Aurukun and Edward River for various purposes, such as accessing shopping facilities and government services, visiting friends and relatives, and participating in meetings and cultural events. Nganhcara is spoken today chiefly at Edward River and Aurukun, though it is not possible to state with accuracy the population figures for each patrilect. Kilham (1974:70) gives the Nganhcara population at Aurukun in 1972 as shown in Table 1.2. For Edward River we obtained the approximate figures in Table 1.3. These figures do not take into account fluctuations in population caused by the constant arrivals and departures to and from other settlements and towns. Even allowing for these and other inaccuracies, it is clear that Iyanh, Muminh, Uwanh and Mu'inh have relatively large numbers of speakers, while Ugbanh and Mangk/Yi'anh are poorly represented. While the two communities have similar total numbers of Nganhcara speakers, their very different language situations have already produced contrasting prognoses for the survival of the language. We have no information on the state of affairs at Coen.

TABLE 1.2 - *Nganhcara Population at Aurukun (1972)*

Iyanh	40	Mu'inh	7
Uwanh	40	Ugbanh	6
Muminh	31	Mangk	1

TABLE 1.3 - *Nganhcara Population at Edward River (1979)*

Iyanh	41	Yi'anh	10
Mu'inh	35	Uwanh	3
Muminh	10	Ugbanh	2

1.5.1 AURUKUN. As Aurukun lies at the northern coastal extremity of the Wik region, the dominant peoples of the area, before the founding of the mission, would likely have been speakers of Northern languages, although the linguistic affiliations of Wik Paach and Wik Thinta, two local extinct languages, are unclear. Nevertheless, it was Wik Mungkan, spoken by people drawn to the community from up the Archer River, that came to predominate (Johnson and Smith 1987).

As a numerically minor group of latecomers to the mission, the Nganhcara have experienced strong community pressures to conform in matters of language. In addition to being the lingua franca of the community, Wik Mungkan is officially supported by the establishment: schooling at Aurukun is partly in the language (Sayers 1982), a dictionary (Kilham et al. 1986) and Bible translation have been published, and since early times Wik Mungkan has been the one Aboriginal language European mission workers have considered worthwhile learning. Moreover, as Kugu Nganhcara and Wik Mungkan are very closely related and share a large amount of cognate vocabulary (1.3), it is easy for features of one language to slip into speech in the other. The nature and degree of accommodation may of course vary with individual and context. Smith (1986) found that the Kugu Muminh of two younger adult speakers he investigated was heavily influenced by Wik Mungkan, even in an elicitation situation, where interference might be expected to be minimised by the focus on language. For example they had adopted the distinctive Mungkan intonation pattern, dropped final syllables extensively, and used a mixed morphology.

1.5.2   EDWARD RIVER.   The Edward River settlement lies at the northern edge of Thaayorre territory, and the people who settled there were originally all speakers of Kuuk Thaayorre and closely related languages. As noted above, Kugu Nganhcara speakers from the north began to come into the settlement in numbers in the 1950s. The present physical division of the community reflects group origins: 'Mungkan-side' is the northern half of the village, 'Thaayorre-side' the southern. As the earlier arrivals, the Thaayorre have until recently enjoyed social precedence. J. von Sturmer (1973:5) noted: 'The Thaayorr group regards itself as a cut above the Mungkans; they are more achievement oriented, they see themselves as more responsible; and their view of their rival group is shared by the white staff. There is a simple hierarchy operating: white staff — Thaayorr-side — Mungkan-side (descending order).' Bible translation and the subsequent literacy programme were both in Kuuk Thaayorre. Eventually the school added a few Nganhcara passages to its cyclostyled reading materials, but the languages of instruction continued to be Thaayorre and English.

During the eighties, the political situation and social standing of the Nganhcara improved, due to faster-increasing numbers that gave them a numerical majority, and to a strong and committed involvement in the political and economic life of the settlement. The school bilingual programme was halted in 1985, partly as a result of their strong opposition to Nganhcara children being taught in Thaayorre rather than their own language.

Wik Mungkan is not spoken at Edward River and the Nganhcara spoken there shows none of the recent influence evident at Aurukun. Nor has there been any accommodation towards the already-established Thaayorre. The Nganhcara's vigorous resistance to assimilation together with the cultural and linguistic distance between them and the Thaayorre have insured that their language has survived up to the present. The main threat to the future of the language is English. Given their low numbers, the introduction of even a small population of English speakers in the area could have a devastating effect on both the culture and the language. Fortunately, there is little reason for immigration at present: the land behind the coastal ridges is flooded during the wet season and thus of little use for agriculture, and no useful mineral or oil deposits have been discovered in the vicinity. Nevertheless, the inexorable advance of communications are increasingly bringing the Nganhcara into contact with English as a purveyor of White Australian society. Whatever the eventual outcome of the growing exposure to English, the main concern is whether the Nganhcara will be well-enough informed to chart their own course or whether they will find themselves following a path not of their own making.

1.6   PREVIOUS WORK

There is little published linguistic work on Kugu Nganhcara. The pioneering anthropologist, Ursula McConnel included a list of kin terminology in 'Wik Ngantjara' and other Wik languages in McConnel 1934; Hale 1976a described developments in phonology in Kugu Muminh and other Wik languages; the present writers have several papers devoted exclusively to Kugu Nganhcara (Smith and Johnson 1985, 1986; Smith 1986; Johnson 1988, 1991). Considerable unpublished work exists: word lists have been collected most prominently by Kenneth Hale and by John von Sturmer; texts are to be found in cyclostyled materials from the Pormpuraaw State School Bilingual Programme, Edward River; von Sturmer (1980) contains ethnolinguistic analysis as well as a brief phonological statement and many lexical items; Sutton (1978) deals primarily with the Cape Keerweer people but often touches on adjacent Nganhcara patrilects. Our own unpublished work (Johnson 1984; Johnson and Smith 1986, 1987; Smith and Johnson 1979) is largely superseded by this publication. Finally, R.M.W. Dixon (p.c.) reports manuscripts by Aguas, Martin and Sayers, Bos, Hale, Rigsby and West, held at the Australian Institute of Aboriginal and Torres Straight Islander Studies.

1.7   THIS STUDY

The primary basis for this study is a nine-week field trip to Edward River and Aurukun undertaken by both authors in January-March 1979, and data from a previous short visit to Edward River by Steve Johnson in 1974. Our corpus, collected with the assistance of nine principal speakers (see ACKNOWLEDGEMENTS), consists of approximately 425 pages of elicited vocabulary and sentences and approximately 150 pages of texts. A significant component of the study was the systematic elicitation of about two thousand lexical items from one or two speakers for each patrilect. Speakers of a particular patrilect were in all but one case identified with that patrilect by virtue of their patriclan membership. For Yi'anh no such speaker was available and we had to settle for a speaker whose own patrilect was Uwanh, but whose mother's patrilect was Yi'anh. Speakers were selected on the basis of four factors: age, availability, willingness to work with us, and aptitude for linguistic work. The majority of our speakers were middle-aged; none was younger than 25. This was to ensure that they had adequate linguistic and sociolinguistic competence. We made no attempt to get a random representative sample: this would have ben absurd, given the small population and the complex relationships between kinship and language. The only way to get a really representative sample in this community would be to interview all its members. Nor did our field projects have the resources to study variation in the usage of individual speakers. On would expect that such variation might occur, particularly as a result of shifting political alliances (cf. Sutton 1991). Consequently, what we have recorded as the characteristics of a a particular patrilect represents more a stereotype that observation of contextual use.

Steve Johnson made several subsequent trips to the region, primarily to work on Wik Munkan; unfortunately, any Kugu Nganhcara data from these excursions has not been located since his death.

2. PHONOLOGY

2.1 PHONEMES AND THEIR REALISATION

Table 2.1 displays the phoneme inventory of Nganhcara in the practical orthography we have developed for the language. J. von Sturmer (1978:30) lists two additional segments for which we find no evidence: /h/ (used to break up long vowels, as in thaha (our thaa) 'mouth') and an apical continuant /R/. He also uses /./, presumably as in some Wik Munkan orthographies to represent a reduced vowel (often realized as syllabicity of the following consonant), e.g. oynych.n (our oncon) '"dry-wet" season (Mar-Jul)', kay.man (our kayiman) 'dry season (Jul-Oct)'; we have not observed such reduced vowels or syllabic consonants except in some younger speakers resident at Aurukun who show other signs of Wik Munkan influence (Smith 1986:517).

A few orthographical conventions used here need mentioning. First, we have followed Australianist tradition in using h to indicate dental articulation; thus th = IPA [t̪], dh = [d̪] and nh = [n̪]. We also use the common Australianist convention of indiciating the palatal nasal as ny (= IPA [ɲ]), but we depart from the conventional digraphic representation of palatals in our use of c (= [c]) and j (= [ɟ]), the latter symbols being both simpler and closer to IPA than conventional ty and dy. We further simplify by writing n for both nh and ny in clusters with following homorganic stops. Thus nth = nh+th (IPA [n̪t̪]), ndh = nh+dh (IPA [n̪d̪]), nc = ny+c (IPA [ɲc]) and nj = ny+j (IPA [ɲɟ]), as in puntha 'arm, wing', pindha 'top of head', anci 'hole' and punji 'tawny frogmouth'. This abbreviation causes no confusion, as apico-alveolars do not co-occur in clusters with laminals (2.2.1[2]); it also avoids such visual monstrosities as nydy and nhth. In this work, the apico-alveolar nasal in clusters with following velars is written ń . Thus ń g = n+g, ń k = n+k and ń ng = n+ng, as in ań gu 'bustard', wań ki 'return' and kukuń ngu 'golden bronze cuckoo'. This convention is necessary only to distinguish the cluster ń g from the velar nasal ng; ń k and ń ng are used for the sake of consistency. In writing designed exclusively for speakers of the language, the diacritic could be omitted if speakers desire. Finally, in this description, we shall place an exclamation point (!) at the beginning of words belonging to the respect lexicon (5.5), e.g. !kikudha 'arm, wing'.

TABLE 2.1 - *Nganhcara Phoneme Inventory*

CONSONANTS

	bilabial	apico-alveolar	lamino-dental	lamino-palatal	dorso-velar	glottal
vl. stop	p	t	th	c	k	'
vd. stop	b	d	dh	j	g	
nasal	m	n	nh	ny	ng	
lateral		l				
tap		r				
glide	w			y		

VOWELS

	short front	short back	long front	long back
high	i	u	ii	uu
mid	e	o	ee	oo
low	a		aa	

2.1.1   CONSONANTS.

[1] *Voicing Contrasts.* Nganhcara has a contrast between voiced and (unaspirated) voiceless stops, an unusual feature for an Australian language. Minimal pairs for this contrast are listed below.

bilabial:	umpi	cut	umbi	jewfish
dental:	watha	water rat	wadha	crow
alveolar:	!thatu	ear	thadu	top of hip
palatal:	thuci	small bird	thuji	crawl
velar:	aku	skin	agu	place

Historically the voicing contrast arose via secondary split. Originally a single series of stops had voiced allophones following long vowels and voiceless allophones following short vowels. Then the vowel length contrast was lost, while the voicing distinction was retained (Hale 1976a). This innovation distinguishes the Nganhcara patrilects from nearby closely related languages, which preserve the original vowel length contrast (and lack contrastive voicing). Cf. Wik Munkan ak 'skin', aak 'place'; Wik Pakanh aaku 'skin', wika 'language'. Contrastive vowel length has subsequently been restored to initial syllables in Nganhcara by the introduction of new long vowels (cf. 2.1.2[1]). The voicing contrast is found in all positions except word initially.

Stops in initial position are usually voiceless, and we have thus assigned them to the voiceless phonemes. However, within a phrase, a word-initial stop may have voiced allophones; cf. 2.4.2. Similarly, in compounds an initial stop in the second element frequently undergoes voicing, even in careful style. E.g. thaa+thutha / thaa+dhutha (thaa 'mouth', thutha 'pluck') 'pull out'. Whenever such variation has been observed or whenever the second element is known as a free form we regularise the representation of such compounds by consistently using the voiceless stop; thus for example we shall consistently write thaa+thutha. When, however, the second element has not been observed as a free form and a voiceless pronunciation has not been observed, we use a voiced stop in our representation, as for example in thaa+bama 'yawn'.

Only a few words have voiceless consonants following long vowels or in third (and subsequent) syllables, some of these are clearly of recent origin, or are lexicalised compounds. Examples are: kuuku 'brush turkey' (also manonponum), ceeceng 'honeyeater', !ngaapa 'vagina', ciici (Mm, Ug) 'land rat', puutu 'boat', poothera 'bullock', kupatha 'land rat', thatata 'rough', puranci 'humpy' (anci 'hole'), ngathukpe 'mother's elder sibling' (ngathu 'me (1sgDAT)', pukpe 'child'), ngathepe 'elder sister', ngathake 'younger brother'. The scarcity of voiceless stops in these positions provides further insight into the earlier allophonic distribution of stops. Prior to the development of contrastive voicing they were likely voiceless initially and in second syllable onsets following a short-vowelled initial syllable and voiced in all other environments.

The voiced stops /b dh g/ have fricative allophones [β ð ɣ] in two environments: following a long vowel, as in paabi 'cry', kaagi 'dance, play', thaa+benga 'goatshead burr', and in third and subsequent syllables following vowels and non-nasal consonants, as in yakalba 'red kangaroo', ngathidhe 'mother', kothcogo 'willy wagtail', kaa+dhabadha 'wasp'. When preceded by a nasal, /b dh g/ are always realised as stops, as in nguuyumba 'butterfly', nhumeń ganh 'stonefish', waliń go 'gecko'. In Kugu Muminh, vowel length was not lost (or has redeveloped) before intervocalic /g/, which is thus always a fricative; e.g. kiiga (Mm) 'back' (Uw kiga), yaagi (Mm) 'tendon' (Uw yagi).

[2] *Laminal vs. Apical.* As is common in Australian languages, dental, alveolar and palatal points of articulation correlate with an equally important distinction between 'laminal' and apical tongue settings, where LAMINAL is used loosely to include frontal (anterodorsal) articulation. For laminals there are contrasting dental and palatal points of articulation. Apicals are generally articulated in the alveolar region, although in some speakers, the tongue tip is quite retracted and may give the impression of being retroflexed. However, there is no alveolar-retroflex contrast in any of the Nganhcara patrilects. Phonotactically, laminals and apicals belong to different classes: laminals can occur in clusters only with other laminals, while apicals may combine only with non-laminal consonants (2.2.1[2]). The contrast between apical and laminal articulations is illustrated by:

watha	green ant	wata	little sugarbag
pindha	top of head	pinda	lick, suck
ngaanha	sand	ngaana	person's shadow

The contrast between dental and palatal laminals is illustrated by:

thuthi	be broken	thuci	small bird
kodhe	bush celery	koje	straight
nganhca	we (1plexcNOM)	nganca	taboo, 'poison'
anhci	fall	anci	hole

[3] *Labial-velars.* The stops /p/ and /b/, when occurring as the final member of heterorganic clusters with nasals or stops, are phonetically bilabial-velars with weak velaric suction, as in: patpa 'kite hawk', wudbi 'channel-billed cuckoo', munpa 'little land rat', pinba 'rainbow lorikeet', pukpe 'child', yagbi 'peewee', ungpa 'break', kungba 'round yam'.

[4] *Glottal Stop.* Nganhcara is unusual among Australian languages in possessing a glottal stop. It occurs only ·between the first and second syllables, either alone or following a liquid, as in kor'o 'brolga', pal'a 'turtle sp.'. Minimal sets are:

wu'a	blow	wutha	shark sp.	wura	(name)		
nga'a	fish	ngaka	water	ngatha	shut (V)		
ma'a	hand	maa	pick up	mata	ascend		
tha'u	foot	thaku	left	thadu	top of hip	!thatu	ear

[5] *Rhotic.* The presence of only one rhotic is rare for an Australian language, as is the fact that it is a tap. It occurs only in intervocalic position, either alone or as the first element of a cluster (2.2.1[2]). When alone, following the first syllable, it is most frequently preceded by a long vowel (15 out of 18 examples in our data), but one minimal pair exists to show that this is not conditioned: kurawu 'dragonfly', kuurawu 'yellow ochre'. Minimal and sub-minimal sets for /r/ are:

kaaram	Dreamtime	kaanam	glider possum		
wura	(name)	wutha	shark sp.	wudu	old mán (Iy)
kaarin	short	kaagi	dance		
kuurulu	bent	kuuyi	tern		
poorowo	light (A)	!poolom	hand		

[6] *Gemination.* All consonants except /r/ have geminate allophones optionally in intervocalic position following a short first syllable vowel Gemination is very common in careful speech and less common in allegro style. When an intervocalic consonant is involved in reduplication (2.3), gemination applies either to the occurrence of the consonant following the SECOND vowel, or to both occurrences (or, of course, to neither). Thus:

yaka	cut	[jaka jakka]
yakaka	cutREDUP	[jakaka jakakka jakkakka]

2.1.2   VOWELS. Nganhcara has a five vowel system with distinctive length. The full set of contrasts exists in all syllables. The presence of contrastive mid-vowels, which is not common in Australian languages, can be demonstrated by the following minimal pairs:

i - e	ngaci	father	ngace	snake
e - a	peba	wind	paba	breast
	wage	white gum	waga	small spotted possum
e - o	woye	fig tree	woyo	throwing stick
u - o	kuce	two	koce	lizard
ii - e e	ngiing	I hear	ngeeng	I heard
aa - oo	waadhan	they scold	woodhan	they argue RECIP
	maa	hold	moo	body

[1] *Length.* Long vowels are acoustically twice as long as short vowels. Short vowels are on average 120 msec in initial syllables and 100 msec in second syllables, while long vowels average 240 msec (Johnson 1974). All monosyllables, other than grammatical particles, have a long vowel. Only a few minimal pairs for long versus short vowels have come to light:

paba	breast	paaba (Iy)	big
putu	Eucalyptus sp.	puutu	boat
ngana	we (1duexcNOM)	ngaana	persons shadow

The scarcity is not surprising, since long vowels are much less frequent than their short counterparts. This is due to the historical loss of vowel length in initial syllables referred to earlier (2.1.1[1]). Examples of long vowels are: ngiing 'I hear', iiru 'this', yee 'wave', ceeceng 'honey eater', waa 'tell', kaaram 'Dreamtime', moo 'body', loorom 'sea turtle', puu 'cabbage tree', thuuyu 'flounder'.

Vowel length is not contrastive when a high vowel is followed by the corresponding glide, as in muwa 'grey-haired', uwa 'go', uwi 'see', wiya 'other', iyanh 'Iyanh'. Wik Iyanh tends to have long /aa/ before w, where Uwanh and other patrilects have short /a/, thus: Iy kaawa, Uw kawa 'south'; Iy thaawa, Uw thawa 'say'.

[2] *Diphthongs.* Before palatal consonants, all vowels have a noticeable palatal off-glide. This unremarkable fact deserves mention only because the off-glide serves as the primary auditory clue (to English speakers' ears) differentiating palatals from dental plus palatal clusters (2.2.1[2]). There is no reason to treat such off-glided vowels as diphthongs. When the sequences ay uy oy ooy are followed by a non-palatal, as for example in: puypune 'wood duck', poykolo 'catfish sp.', thaympa 'boxwood', a case might be made to treat them as diphthongs. Distributional considerations, however, do not favour such an analysis. Putative diphthongs would be much rarer than other vowels (ooy has been found in only one word: yooyko 'hill') and restricted to initial syllables preceding velars and labials. Such restrictions are better expressed as limitations on the distribution of the consonant /y/, which do not differ markedly from limitations on other consonants (see 2.2.1). Johnson (1974) mentions in

passing that measurements from sound spectrograms show that such V+y sequences are no longer than short vowels, but this fact does not constitute evidence for the diphthongal analysis, since vowel length may be affected by the nature and number of following consonants. In summary, we conclude that diphthongs do not have phonological status in Nganhcara.

2.2   PHONOTACTICS

The majority of Nganhcara roots are bisyllabic. Monosyllabic and trisyllabic roots and, rarely, roots of more than three syllables are also found. The generalisations below are based on a lexicon of over 1200 lexemes; which, when different patrilectal and respect forms are counted, amounts to well over 3000 roots. While we are confident that the statements made are essentially valid, some details have doubtless been missed. In particular, additional triconsonantal clusters likely remain to be discovered.

2.2.1   CONSONANTS.

[1] *Single Consonants.* Examples of consonants in initial, medial and final position are given in Table 2.2. All consonants occur word-initially except for the voiced stops (as discussed in 2.1.1[1]), the glottal stop and the tap. However, alveolars and the palatals /c/ and /ny/ are uncommon in this position. All consonants occur intervocalically, with the restriction that /c j ny/ are rarely followed by /u/. Word-final consonants are limited to the nasals; /ny/ is very rare. The glide /y/ also appears finally in the interjection woy 'hey, cooey', which we treat as non-linguistic. The presence of the peripheral nasals /m/ and /ng/ in final position is areally unexpected (Dixon 1980: 244). Non-inflectional final /ng/ is uncommon in Nganhcara, except in Mu'inh and Iyanh, in which final /ng/ often appears where other patrilects have no final consonant, however no general rule can be formulated. Examples: muń kaye (Uw, Yi, Mm) muń kayi (Ug), muń kaying (Iy, M') 'Torres St. Pigeon, Myristicivora spilorrhoa'; puypun (Yi, Ug), puypune (M'), puypuneng (Iy) 'Australian little grebe, Podiceps novaehollandiae' (Uw punthigunh); kuja (Uw, Yi, Ug, Mm), kujang (M', Iy) 'grey kangaroo Macropus giganteus' All roots ending in /ng/ denote birds, fishes and turtles. We have no explanation for this apparent lexical restriction.

[2] *Consonant Clusters.* Initial clusters are found only in the Muminh word ndhaa 'see' (a monosyllable), Ugbanh cwaa 'possum sp.' (cf. Mm cawanha), and Iyanh nhyeen 'fly' (cf. Uw nheen) and nhyaara 'swift, swallow'. Intervocalic clusters are common, but there are strong restrictions on permitted combinations. No final clusters occur.

Medial clusters are biconsonantal or, more unusually, triconsonantal. The possible biconsonantal clusters are exemplified in Table 2.3. Homorganic clusters are restricted to nasal plus stop.

TABLE 2.2 - *Consonants Occurring Initially, Intervocalically and Finally*

p	pintili	smooth	thapa	forked stick		
t	tothcon	bark container	thatata	rough		
th	thintha	injured	athatpa	shallow		
c	caka	large wader sp.	mucalin	knotted bag		
k	kanti	salt	uku	lg. bark container		
			pu'an	shield		
b			kabi	mix		
d			wadanga	miss		
dh			pidhanda	feral		
j			wojenga	fold		
g			thagan	lg. house		
m	mompo	placenta	mama	hold	itam	slowly
n	nina	you (2sgACC)	ngaana	shadow	thayayan	curly
nh	nhukan	blackboy tree	wanhaga	dolphin	wakanh	of land
ny	!nyilka	fall for	thulokonye	goshawk	!kanykany	(Iy) bat
ng	ngaji	sneeze	winga	hop	kuypang	bream
l	loto	legume sp.	yilim	again		
r			opere	medicine		
w	woloma	have authority	ketewe	necklace		
y	yaki	tear (int)	nhaya	string		

The most common heterorganic clusters are stop+stop, nasal+stop and nasal+nasal. Of lower frequency, we find clusters of /l/, /r/ or /y/ + a stop or nasal. For the heterorganic clusters the following generalisations can be made: (a) for laminals, the only permitted combination is dental+palatal; (b) for non-laminals, there are three main possibilities: alveolar+labial, alveolar+velar and velar+labial; clusters involving /r/ and /l/ have the additional possibility of glottal stop as second element. The palatal glide /y/, which fits none of these schema as first element of a cluster, combines with labials and velars; the labial glide /w/ is not found as first element of clusters. We have found single examples of six clusters not conforming to these patterns: pw, mw, mth, mdh, mng and ly: yapwang (Iy) 'pee-wee' (cf. Uw yagbi, Ug yagbwi), !waanumwi (Iy) 'hit' (which may involve the inchoative suffix -wi), pindhamthe 'finch sp.', kapi pugamdhe 'new moon', !wocomngo 'pull'; ngathalye 'koel'.

Heterorganic dental+palatal clusters are a rarity in the world's languages and deserve special mention. The following examples illustrate the contrast between these and homorganic dental and palatal clusters as well as with single dental and palatal consonants, which may be phonetically geminate (2.1.1[6]).

nganhca	We (1plincNOM)	nganca	taboo	thaa+ngantha	tongue
anhci	fall V	anci	hole	panthiyanh	darter
kunhji	sibling, cousin	punji	frogmouth	kondhe	moth
thathce	sand goanna	ngace	snake	ngathepe	elder sister
madhji	meat hungry	waji	sing	thadhi	hide
nhanhnyi	dirt	panyi	dig out	minha	animal, meat

While the contrast with homorganic dental clusters and geminates is easy for English speakers to hear, the contrasts with homorganic palatal clusters and with geminates are more problematic. Auditorily the distinctive element is a transitional palatal glide present before homorganic palatal clusters and geminates (2.1.2[2]) but not before dental+palatal clusters. (Thus J. von Sturmer (1978) distinguishes fairly consistently between 'nych' (= nhc) and 'ynych' (= nc) following /a/.) Articulatorily, dental+palatal clusters are characterised by a forward initial position of the tongue for the dental element followed by a lowering of the blade of the tongue between the dental and palatal elements; palatal clusters and geminates on the other hand have a slightly further back initial position of the tongue, which does not change until the cluster or geminate is released into the following vowel. The distinction is readily observed by visual inspection, with the transitional lowering of the tongue (or lack thereof) being more salient than initial tongue position.

TABLE 2.3 - *Biconsonantal Clusters*

HOMORGANIC

mp	pimpa	speargrass tree	mb	thamba	obstruct
nt	yenta	spear V	nd	wanduwa	legume sp.
nth	mentho	pretty	ndh	kondhe	moth
nc	thence	handsome	nj	wonje	gather (int)
ngk	thangku	deep	ngg	yengganga	undo

HETERORGANIC

tp	matpam	engraver	db	wudbi	nut
np	munpa	fish trap	nb	pinba	rainbow lorikeet
nm	thinhanmala	dugong			
ń k	puń ku	bamboo pipe	ń g	nhumeń ganh	rock cod
ń ng	kukuń ngu	cuckoo sp.			
thc	pathcal-nga	clean V	dhj	padhja	hog V˙
nhc	anhcupan	fish sp.	nhj	koyenhji	water snake sp.
nhny	anhnyi	bail, pour			
kp	ngukpa	water snake sp.	gb	yagbi	peewee
ngp	kaje wungpa	lg. cattle egret	ngb	yengbe	lady apple
lp	ingk+alpiya	white-necked heron	lb	molbe	fish sp.
lm	!alman	body hair			
lk	walka	ray sp.	lg	thulga (Ug/Mm)	brolga
lng	!kukulnga	(Iy) brave			
l'	pal'a	tortoise sp.			
rp	ngurpu (Iy)	bark (Uw ngutpu)			
rm	thaa wa'erma	(Iy) yawn			
rk	kathcarka	scrape	rg	!wirgin	(Iy) white
r'	kor'o	brolga			
yp	puypune	duck sp	yb	puybe	bee sp.
ym	!nhuuyma (Iy)	bathe (Uw !nhuuma)			
yk	poykolo	catfish sp.	yg	oygo	big lagoon

The few triconsonantal clusters we have found mostly consist of / l / or /y/ + nasal + homorganic stop; they are illustrated in Table 2.4. The sole exception is ntr in M' pintri 'smooth' (cf. Uw pintili) and Iy yintran 'itchy'.

TABLE 2.4 - *Triconsonantal Clusters*

lmp	thalmpo (Iy)	salt	lmb	walmbi (M')	swamp turtle sp.
			lnd	wagalnda	caterpillar
lngk	malngkayim	bush pipe			
ymp	thaympa	boxwood?			
yngk	koyngkon (Iy)	cabbage tree palm	yngg	thaa+oynggo	vomitus

2.2.2   VOWELS.

[1] *Vowel quality.* All five vowel qualities can be found in any syllable, subject to the co-occurrence restrictions set out in [3] below. They can all occur word-initially and word-finally, e.g.:

i	ingki	shoulder	mini	good
e	eka	shell	othe	sated, full
a	aku	skin	punha	soft
o	olko	dillybag	wotho	screw palm
u	unggu	long, tall	uthu	dead

[2] *Vowel length.* All short vowels can occur in any syllable. Long vowels are generally restricted to initial syllables. They may also be found in both first and second syllables, when an initial syllable is reduplicated (2.3). In Iyanh long vowels also occur in some verb suffixes because of the historical loss of intervocalic consonants (3.4.7). As mentioned earlier (2.1.2[1]) all lexical monosyllables have long vowels.

[3] *'Metaphony'.* In monomorphemic roots the back mid vowel / o / co-occurs only with other mid-vowels in adjacent syllables, e.g.:

kono	ear	yewo	whale	ekondo	dollar bird
ko'ele	three	yome	grey possum	kothcogo	willy wagtail
okonhnye	hibiscus				

We know of only one exception: waliń go 'gecko'; since trisyllabic morphemes are rare, this may eventually turn out to be bimorphemic and thus not exceptional.

The front mid vowel /e/, when it is in the first syllable, allows only /a/ and /o/ in following syllables. In non-initial syllables /e/ may follow any vowel. Examples:

initial:	eka	shell	yengan	hair	yega	tendon
	thepa	lower face	thepanda	taipan		
non-init:	pukpe	child	ngate	bone	pinye	FB+

When /o/ represents the reciprocal suffix (see 3.4.9), it may follow high vowels without affecting them, but it raises a preceding /a/ to /o/, as in patha 'bite', recip: potho. The same process has occurred in ngothope '(my) FM', from *ngath+ope, cf. ngathide '(my) M' and nhingope '(other's) FM'. The raising and rounding of /a/ to /o/ is, however, not a completely general process: it is not triggered by the change of the final vowel of a word to /o/ in vocatives used for hailing (3.2.1[8]). Thus thako '[Hey] lefty' from thaku 'left-hander'.

2.3   REDUPLICATION

Reduplication as a phonological process occurs in all parts of speech. In polysyllabic words, the initial vowel and immediately following consonant(s) are reduplicated, according to the following formula:

$$(C_1) \, V_1 \, C_2 \, V_2 \ldots \Rightarrow (C_1) \, [V_1 \, C_2] \, V_1 \, C_2 \, V_2 \ldots$$

Accent placement indicates that the reduplicated segments are placed to the left of the root segments they copy rather than to the right (see 2.5). Examples follow:

munji	swim	munjunji
yumpi	do	yumpumpi
mungga	eat	munggungga
thena	stand	thenena
ngaya	I (1sgNOM)	ngayaya
iiru-ma	here-EMPH	iiriiru-ma

When C_2 is a non-homorganic cluster whose second element is a labial (phonetically a labial-velar - 2.1.1[3]), it usually undergoes reduction in the reduplicated stretch. In heterorganic stop+labial stop clusters, the labial does not appear in the reduplicated cluster:

| pukpe | child | pukukpe |
| wegbe | keep | wegegbe |

In heterorganic nasal+labial stop clusters, the labial in the reduplicated cluster is replaced by a stop homorganic with the nasal:

nunpa	run	nuntunpa
thanpa	cough	thantanpa
wunpa	gather, get	wuntunpa
ungpa	break	ungkungpa

Although this reduction normally takes place, it is optional (e.g. ungpa 'break' may also be reduplicated regularly as ungpungpa).

Reduplication in monosyllabic roots does not follow the above schema; instead, the root is repeated in its entirety:

thii-ng   I throw   thiithii-ng
    waa-dhan   they told   waawaa-dhan

2.4   SANDHI PHENOMENA

2.4.1   FINAL VELAR NASAL REDUCTION. In final position /ng/ optionally deletes, causing the preceding vowel to undergo nasalisation and optionally compensatory lengthening, as seen below. The nasalisation may be quite light, and as a result the ergative marker and 1sg verbal concord suffix (both -ng) are easily missed.

uwa-ng   I go / went   [uw̃ã   uw̃ãː]

2.4.2   INITIAL STOP LENITION. As seen above, there is no voicing contrast in word-initial position (cf. 2.1.1[1]). In citation forms, stops in this position are always voiceless. However, in context they may lenite to voiced stops. In addition, /p th k/ may further lenite to the corresponding voiced fricatives following a vowel-final word (i.e. when they are intervocalic: cf. the fricative allophones of intervocalic /b dh g/, section 2.1.1[1]). Lenition occurs with high frequency in close-knit phrases and compounds and in allegro speech. The following examples are taken from recordings of elicitation sessions in which speakers were asked to repeat phrases.

[ṯ]ana umpedhan [ṯ/ḏ]aaranmala
They cut themselves

nhinta minha [p/β]angku mancancingan
You are cooking the wallaby.

[p]ula nhaya [k/ɣ]aagiń nga
They are playing with the string.

ngaya minha [p/β]angku [p]ama+[ṯ/ð]umu ngathurumu-wu
mancingang
I am cooking the wallaby for my husband.

[ṯ]ana yuku [k]anhnyim [ḏ]aa+[β]oyedhan
They are jumping over the log.

[p]ula [β]ama [k/g]uce-ng [k]eka-la wanta
The two men are leaving their spears.

2.4.3   APOCOPE. Final /a/ optionally drops before a vowel-initial following word. In allegro speech this is a common phenomenon. Final /a/ regularly drops in compounds and often in generics. Enclitics commonly lose final /a/ even when a consonant-initial word follows. In the following examples, parentheses indicate possible apocope.

nga'(a) umbi	jewfish
kek(a) aara	that spear
pula kek(a) ungpa	They broke the spear.
ag(u)+ukewe-ngu	was born to her (T7)
kuyu wo'omb(o) agawu	to that woman who has given birth (T25)
pula nga'a-l(a) kalalo	They are carrying the fish.

In allegro speech apocope occasionally also affects other vowels:

-l(i) umpi	afterwards cut (153)

2.4.4   EPENTHESIS. Whenever the addition of a case marker to a word would create an inadmissible cluster, epenthetic /u/ appears optionally. In our transcriptions epenthetic /u/ is arbitrarily placed before the boundary. One example will suffice here. (Further examples can be readily found in chapter 4 and in the texts): pukpe mepen 'small child'; ERG: pukpe mepenu-ng; DAT: pukpe mepenu-wu (cf. pukpe yoko 'big child'; ERG: pukpe yoko-ng; DAT: pukpe yoko-wu).

2.5   ACCENT AND SYLLABLE TIMING

Phonological accent falls non-distinctively on initial syllables. In short-vowelled initial syllables, this accent is realised as optional gemination of the following consonant (2.1.1[6]) and a 20% lengthening of the vowel (Johnson 1974). In reduplication of polysyllabic stems, the accent falls on the second syllable rather than the first. This fact can be most easily accounted for by assuming that reduplicated segments are placed BEFORE the root material (2.3) and either that reduplicated material is extrametrical or that reduplication operates after accent placement.

Nganhcara is a syllable-timed language, rather than accent-timed: all syllables following the first are of approximately equal duration and stress, except of course, for syllables containing long vowels (cf. 2.1.2[1]).

3.   MORPHOLOGY AND MORPHOPHONEMICS

The structuralist distinction between morphology and syntax is not always the most effective basis for the presentation of a grammar. For Nganhcara in particular an ideal organisation is one in which related syntactic and morphological phenomena are presented together. We nevertheless follow the *Handbook's* presentation guidelines here, in the interests of maintaining comparability among descriptions of different languages. Even so, a fair amount of syntax has leaked into the present chapter. For the reader's orientation, we begin with a brief overview of clause structure.

Nganhcara clauses are normally verb-final, but the order of other main constituents is relatively free; within the noun phrase, however, word-order is fixed (4.4.). Like many Australian languages, Nganhcara may omit non-verbal constituents which the speaker judges to be information shared with the addressee. We follow the usual Australianist practice of distinguishing between three core syntactic functions:

> A subject of a transitive clause
> O object of a transitive clause
> S subject of an intransitive clause

The role of an NP within a clause may be marked in four ways:

- obligatory case marking on the NP, which is carried by the final element of the NP (4.4.3)
- (for non-pronominal NPs marked A, O, S, dative or ablative) an optional associated free pronoun having the same referent; such an associated pronoun is usually adjacent to the NP and bears the corresponding pronominal case marking
- (for NPs marked A, O, S, dative or ablative) an optional bound pronoun in the appropriate case form; bound pronouns are encliticised to the last pre-verbal constituent, or to the verb itself (3.3.3)
- (for subject NPs, viz. A or S) obligatory verb agreement

As is common in Australian languages, Nganhcara has a split case-marking system, with non-pronominal NPs inflecting for ergative (ERG), marking A, and ABSolutive, marking O and S, while pronouns inflect for NOMinative, marking A and S, and ACCusative, marking O.

These various phenomena are seen in the transitive sentence (1), where the role of the subject NP kuyu is indicated by its ERG case marker, the NOM pronoun thana and by the tense/agreement suffix -dhan, and the role of the object NP pama is indicated by its ABS case signified by no overt marker, the ACC pronoun nhunha and the ACC bound pronoun -nha. For comparison the intransitive sentences (2) and (3) have ABS subject NPs and NOM associated subject pronouns. Verb agreement with subject NPs is overt only for 1sg, 2sg and 3pl; thus no agreement marker is seen in (3). The marking of A, S and O is summarised in Table 3.1.

(1) thana   kuyu-ng   nhunha pama-nha   pigo-dhan
     3plNOM   woman-ERG 3sgACC manABS-3sgACC hit-3plPAST
     The women hit the man.

(2) thana   kuyu   waa+wununa-yin
     3plNOM   womanABS   sleepREDUP-3plPRES
     The women are sleeping.

(3) nhila   pama   puyu   uwa
     3sgNOM   manABS   away   go
     The man went away.

TABLE 3.1 - *Marking of A, S and O*

	A	S	O
case marking (obligatory):	ERG	unmarked	unmarked
associated pronoun (optional):	NOM	NOM	ACC
bound pronoun (optional):	NOM	NOM	ACC
verb agreement (obligatory):	yes	yes	no

Non-pronominal NPs also inflect for six other cases — dative, ablative, comitative, privative, locative, and vocative — whose functions will be discussed below and in the following chapter. Pronouns inflect for all these categories except vocative. Case markers for non-pronominal NPs are enclitics attached to the last element of the NP. In addition to the cases marking subject and object, NPs which may be cross-referenced by bound pronouns are dative and ablative.

3.1   PARTS OF SPEECH

3.1.1   NOUN. A noun has a fixed position within an NP and functions as its head. A subclass of nouns function as 'generics' classifier-like elements which often accompany their hyponyms in NPs (4.2, 5.2). For example, in (4) yuku 'THING; tree, stick' is the generic for pinci 'crocodile', and agu 'PLACE, TIME' is the generic for muci 'bank'. (The verb mata in this example is intransitive, thus taking an absolutive subject NP.) Generics are always NP-initial. Nouns functioning as generics will be glossed in upper case.

(4)   yuku   pinci   aara   agu   muci-ng mata
         THING   crocodile   thatABS   PLACE   bank-LOC climb
         That crocodile climbed the bank.

3.1.2   PRONOUN. Pronouns form a closed class of words which occupy an entire NP slot. Nganhcara has first, second and third person pronouns in singular, dual and plural numbers. In addition, there is a distinction between inclusive and exclusive in the first person dual and plural.

3.1.3   ADJECTIVE. In many Australian languages purely grammatical criteria distinguishing adjectives from nouns are difficult to find. Although Nganhcara has no inflectional distinction, it has a clear syntactic distinction by virtue of the fact that noun-adjective word order is fixed. For example:

         pukpe mepen   peba yoko
         child   small   wind big
         small child   big wind

The head slot of an NP can only be filled by a noun. The head of an NP may be omitted if it is clear from the context, leaving the adjective as possibly the the sole surface constituent of the NP, as for example in (5).

Because the head is recoverable, an adjective in such a headless NP is still in the attributive slot. Although we do not have the requisite data, the behaviour of adjectives with respect to generics (5.2) is likely to provide confirmation of this analysis. A noun normally occurs with only one generic, but an adjective should be able to combine in such headless NP constructions with the full range of generics. Thus for example pinci 'crocodile' occurs only with the generic yuku 'thing', but yoko 'big' should be able to occur with any generic in a headless NP.

(5)   tawun pala kungke-ni mepen epa-dhu
        house hither north-SUB little AFF-MAY
        To the north of the house, the little [hut] is probably [still there]. [Speaker is discussing what may remain of her camp after a recent cyclone.]

    Finally, note that uninflected nouns may also function attributively within the NP, but they normally PRECEDE the head noun, as for example minha thuci kuna ('ANIMAL bird faeces') 'bird droppings'. Such N+N combinations may all be compounds. In post-nominal position, attributive NPs occur, but they must be inflected (4.4), as for example:

        weń ko kungke-m
        side   north-ABL
        the north side

    Some items are recorded only as predicates in non-verbal sentences (4.2) and the decision as to whether these are nouns or adjectives may be difficult. In the glossary (7.2) these are assigned to a word class on the basis of semantics where possible; in case of doubt, they are coded as Adj?.

3.1.4   QUANTIFIER. Quantifiers form a closed class consisting of the numerals thono 'one', kuce 'two', and ko'ele 'three', and words such as uyu 'much, many' and kopo 'lots of' (countable or uncountable). They have a fixed slot in the NP. Example:

        nga'a mepen thono
        fish   small   one
        one small fish

3.1.5   DEMONSTRATIVE. The demonstratives are a closed class of three deictics (and their various case forms given in 3.2.2 below): iiru speaker-proximal, nhaaru addressee-proximal, and aara distal (i.e. not near the speaker or addressee). nhaaru is also used as a discourse anaphoric. Thus:

      yuku iiru   'this tree by me'
      yuku nhaaru   'that tree by you; that tree referred to'
      yuku aara   'that tree yonder'

Demonstratives are always NP-final, as seen in (79) and (80). Demonstratives also function as locational and temporal adverbials (38), (97), (98).

3.1.6   VERB. Verbs are characterised by their clause-final position, the fact that they serve as the locus for bound pronouns and other enclitics, and their inflectional paradigm (3.4).

3.1.7   ADVERB. Adverbs are (normally not subcategorised) elements of the VP that specify manner, spatial orientation, time, etc. Examples are *puyu* and *itam* in the sentences below. Our data do not provide evidence to address the issue of whether adverbs form a closed or open class.

(6)   nhila   ku'a   puyu   nhunpa
        3sgNOM   dog   away   run
        The dog ran away.

(7)   nhila   kuyu+waya   itam   thenene-n
        3sgNOM   OLD WOMAN   slowly   walkREDUP-PRES
        The old woman is walking slowly.

3.1.8   PARTICLE. A number of modal and aspectual particles and enclitics occur in pre- or postverbal position (4.12); in verbless clauses particles and enclitics are usually in final position. For example, the AFFirmation particle *epa* (see 4.12[5]) and the enclitic *-dhu* 'MAY' (see 4.12[4]) are seen in (5). A few other enclitics are not confined to pre- or post-verbal position (4.13).

3.1.9   INTERJECTION. A few non-predicative interjections are found, such as *apowu* 'good-bye' and *itharko* 'oh gosh' (4.14).

3.2   CASE MARKING AND NOUN MORPHOLOGY

Case marking for an NP in Nganhcara is carried by its final constituent. The order of constituents in non-pronominal NPs is invariant:

Generic - Noun - Adjective - Quantifier - NP - Demonstrative

where the embedded NP is a possessive (DATive or ABLative), PRIVative or COMitative element; for examples of embedded NPs, see (42), (117) - (119). In actual usage, the inclusion of all possible elements would be highly unusual.

For non-pronominal NPs which do not end in demonstratives, case markers are enclitics, while distinct case forms are found for demonstratives. Pronouns have distinct nominative, accusative, dative and ablative case forms; for other cases the case-marking enclitics are added to the nominative. Case marking in Nganhcara is thus a mix of syntax and morphology, reminiscent of the English possessive. The case enclitics are discussed in 3.2.1; forms of demonstratives and pronouns will be presented in 3.2.2 and 3.3 respectively.

3.2.1   CASE-MARKING ENCLITICS. The enclitic case markers for non-pronominal NPs are listed in Table 3.2. The functions of each case are discussed below. COM and PRIV are not usually considered to be case categories in Australian languages. Their inflectional status in Nganhcara is justified in 4.4.6.

TABLE 3.2 - *Case-marking Enclitics*

ABSolutive	(unmarked)
ERGative	-ng(u)
DATive	-wu/-na
ABLative	-m/-nam
COMitative	-ra
PRIVative	-yi
LOCative	-ng(a)/-n
VOCative	-n

[1] *ABSolutive*. As is common in Australian languages, absolutive case is characterised by an absence of other case marking in Nganhcara. Absolutive is used to indicate intransitive subject (S), transitive object (O), and equational predicate in verbless clauses (8). Physical and psychological states are commonly expressed by attributive absolutive NPs in verbless clauses (9). Absolutive demonstratives function as locational adverbials (38), (40), (97). 'Floating' absolutive NPs also occur in a variety of adjunctive roles in both verbal and verbless clauses (4.1.5 and 4.2.4)

(8)   iiru   thata. iiru   thata-m. iiru   thata-m.
       thisABS frog   thisABS frog-EMPH thisABS frog-EMPH
       yuku   nhilarum thata
       THING   all   frog
       [Looking at a set of pictures of different frog species] This is a frog. This is a frog too. This is a frog too. They all [lit. all the THINGs] are frogs.

(9)   nhinta   nhingurum ka'i ngangka wada
[Mm]   2sgNOM   3sgABL   NEG   stomach bad
       Don't you worry about him.

The category S includes subjects of verbless clauses (4.2, 4.3), which necessarily lack objects. Subjects (A, as well as S) are typically animate and definite, although other types are quite possible, as is seen in (10), (11), (84). We have insufficient data to determine whether there are constraints on the type of subject which may be cross-referenced, but for objects it is clear that no restriction exists; for example, the cross-referenced object is human definite in T13-T16; it is inanimate definite in (11), T11, T77; indefinite cross-referenced objects appear in (12), (180). Nevertheless, an O is more likely to be cross-referenced if it is higher on the animacy hierarchy.

(10)   thaa aara   peba-ng   ngatha
        door thatABS   wind-ERG   shut
        The wind shut the door.

(11)   mayi-ku   ngaka-ng-dhu-ran   pekeka
        food-EXCL rain-ERG-MAY-3plACC hitREDUP
        Rain may have hit the foodstuffs. (i.e. The food may have got rained on.)

(12)   ngaya   angan   yuku+thupi pakem ngaari-nh
        1sgNOM   thatLOC tree   under   anything-3sgACC
           uwe-ng
           see-1sg
        I saw something there under the tree.

    [2] *ERGative*. The ERGative marker is normally -ng, which often reduces to nasalisation of the preceding vowel (2.4.1); the form -ngu also appears in a few examples (T47). In addition to transitive subject (A), ergative marks the role instrument. Although not morphologically different, A and instrument can be differentiated syntactically: An A governs verb agreement (3.4.2, 3.4.4) but an instrument, being a VP adjunct, does not. Further, while an A may be cross-referenced by a bound pronoun; it appears that an instrument may not. But since As are typically animate and instruments typically inanimate, the cross-referenceability of both A and instrument may actually depend on some kind of animacy/empathy hierarchy, as is true with dative ([3] below). Unfortunately, we lack diagnostic examples to settle the issue. Examples of instruments appear below and in T94.

(13)   nhila   pukpe-ng   nhunha   kuyu   yuku   muka-ng-nha
        3sgNOM   child-ERG   3sgACC   woman   THING   stone-ERG-3sgACC
           peka
           throw at
        The child threw a stone at the woman.

(14)   nhila pama yuku   kantu-ng   thenene-n
        3sgNOM man THING stick-ERG   walkREDUP-PRES
        The man walks with a stick.

(15)   nhila   nganyi ma'a-ng pigo
        3sgNOM 1sgACC hand-ERG hitPAST
        He hit me with his hand. (cf. 88)

(16)   nhila   nganyi keka ilung-nyi   yenta
        3sgNOM 1sgACC spear thisERG-1sgACC spear
        He speared me with this spear. / He threw this spear at me.

    [3] *DATive*. Kinship terms and proper names take the dative marker -na; otherwise the allomorph is -wu. Within the NP and as a predicator in verbless clauses, dative and ablative both mark the possessive function (4.6).

The functions covered by dative in verbal clauses are recipient, beneficiary, goal, and purpose; in verbless clauses they are beneficiary and purpose. These are illustrated below. (Dative is also used in the ethical dative construction, 4.13[3]). It is possible, as in (22), for more than one dative, with different functions, to appear in the same clause.

(17) ngaya   nga'a nhingu kuyu agawu-ngu   waa-ng
      1sgNOM fish 3sgDAT woman thatDAT-3sgDAT give-1sg
      I gave the fish to that woman.

(18) ngaya   ngalin   mayi   tiya manci-nga-ng
      1sgNOM   1duincDAT VEG   tea   boil-CAUS-1sg
      I'm making tea for us.

(19) ngaya   mayi tiya-wu   ngaka manci-nga-ng
      1sgNOM   VEGtea-DAT water   boil-CAUS-1sg
      I'm boiling water for tea.

(20) ngaya   wa'a-wu uwa-ng
      1sgNOM river-DAT go-1sg
      I'm going to the river.

(21) keka+thu'u minha   pangku-wu
      thu'u+spear ANIMAL   wallaby-DAT
      A thu'u spear is for wallaby.

(22) ngaya   agawu   nga'a-wu uwa-ng
      1sgNOM   thatDAT fish-DAT go-1sg
      I'm going there for fish.

Only humans and dogs may be cross-referenced by dative bound pronouns. (Domesticated dogs have special status in Nganhcara society, standing in the relationship of son or daughter to their owners (J. von Sturmer 1978:329).) Thus (23) is ungrammatical if -ngu is taken to cross-reference ngaka-wu, and (24) has no grammatical reading (assuming no beneficiary is intended). Since recipient and beneficiary roles tend to be filled by humans, and purposive and goal functions tend to be filled by non-humans, it follows that purposive and goal are not usually cross-referenced by bound pronouns. However, (25) illustrates that when humans do occasionally fill these roles they may be cross-referenced as usual. Consequently, it seems that the four functional relationships (recipient, beneficiary, purposive and goal) cannot be distinguished syntactically.

(23) ngaya   ngaka-wu-ngu   uwa-ng
      1sgNOM water-DAT-3sgDAT go-1sg
      I'm going for water [for someone].

(24)   *   ngaya   wa'awa-wu-ngu uwa-ng
           1sgNOM   river-DAT-3sgDAT   go-1sg

(25)   ngaya   ngaci$\begin{Bmatrix} -\acute{n} \\ -wu \end{Bmatrix}$ -ngu uwa-ng
           1sgNOM   father-DAT-3sgDAT   go-1sg
           I'm going to/for father.

The dative marker -wu may also attach to an infinitive to mark a purposive subordinate clause (4.7.2[1]).

   [4] *ABLative.* The ablative marker for proper names is -nam; for kinship terms both -m and -nam are found, though some speakers strongly prefer the latter; for other NPs -m is most frequently used, but -nam is always possible.
   Apart from its role as marker of possessive within noun phrases and as a possessive predicator in verbless clauses (4.6), the ablative has two functions. The more common use, found in both verbal and verbless clauses, is to indicate a range of relations which are centred on the notion of source. Such relations include point of origin for a verb of motion, material from which something is made, and cause. Examples:

(26)   nhinta keka iiru   wayi-nam ekanga-n
           2sgNOM spear thisABS who-ABL   get-2sgPAST
           Who did you get this spear from?

(26)   nhila   pukpe puranci-m uwa
           3sgNOM child   humpy-ABL   come
           The child came from the humpy.

(28)   nhila   pama aara   ngaci-m-ngurum wań ke-n
           3sgNOM man   thatABS father-ABL-3sgABL   return-CNC
           That man is returning from father.

(29)   ngaya   ma'a-m yuku   thutha-ng
           1sgNOM   hand-ABL splinter pluck-1sg
           I pulled the splinter from my hand.

(30)   yuku nganhca   engka-m   yumpumpe-n
           thing   1plexcNOM bark-ABL   makeREDUP-CNC
           We make them out of bark.

(31)   ku'a-m thaaranam pukpe uyu   agu+ukewi-yin
           dog-ABL 3plABL   child   many be born-3plPRES
           Dogs have a lot of young.

(32)   nhila   nga'a-m yiwama
           3sgNOM fish-ABL   get offended
           She got offended because of the fish.

(33)   nhila   minha   pangku   ngaari$\begin{Bmatrix} -m \\ -wu \end{Bmatrix}$yenta

3sgNOM   ANIMAL wallaby   what-$\begin{Bmatrix} ABL \\ DAT \end{Bmatrix}$ spear

Why did he spear the wallaby? (Note that both DAT and ABL are possible in this example — see 3.3.3.)

(34)   pu'u+thaa   ngatha, me'e-m
[Mm]   door   close   mosquito-ABL
        Close the door — because of the mosquitoes.

In non-verbal clauses, it is often impossible to distinguish between the source and possessive marking functions of an ablative NP predicate:

(35)   kuna   iiru   ku'a-m.   minha   pangku-m   ya'a
        excrement thisABS\ dog-ABL. ANIMAL wallaby-ABL   NEG
        These droppings are dog's (from a dog), not wallaby's (from a wallaby)

The other relationship indicated by ablative is that of pragmatic patient; i.e. an animate entity that is not an actual patient of the predicate, but which is (usually adversely) affected by it, as in (36), (37), (132). In most varieties of English the preposition *on* can mark a similar relationship, as in *They drank all the beer on me.* This function of the ablative differs from the ethical dative (4.12[3]), in that the latter is not construed as a patient.

(36)   nhila   agu-thurum   anhce
        3sgNOM   down-1sgABL   fallPAST
        [I hit him and] He fell down on me.

(37)   thuma   athanga-ng   ngula   uthu-ma-thurum
        fire   light-1sg   then   dead-VBLSR-1sgABL
        I lit a fire; then it died on me.

Both non-possessive functions of the ablative may be cross-referenced by bound pronouns, as is seen in several of the examples above. It appears that inanimate ablatives cannot be cross-referenced. There does not appear to be any way of distinguishing syntactically between the pragmatic patient and the source functions mentioned above. Consequently all these functions will be subsumed under the single case relation ablative. Possessive is a syntactically distinct case relation since it may also be encoded by the dative case (3.2.1[3], 4.6) and since it cannot be cross-referenced. (All apparent counterexamples can be interpreted as pragmatic patient, e.g. (63), (64), T134. In any case, as an NP-internal constituent, a possessively marked NP should, on universal grounds, be unavailable for cross-referencing.)

[5] *COMitative.* The comitative marker -ra is unique to Uwanh; Iyanh has -nta; Ugbanh and Yi'anh have -la; and Muminh and Mu'inh have -nhja, a form our main Uwanh speaker also frequently used (42), (141).

Note that there is also a derivational comitative suffix -dha found in all patrilects (3.2.3[1]).

The comitative signals the inverse of the possessive, i.e. that the comitative NP accompanies or is possessed by another N or NP. It occurs within the NP (37), as a predicator in non-verbal clauses and as an adjunct in verbal clauses (40). Because of V-final word order, ambiguous structures arise. Thus in (40) thuma-ra might be a constituent of the subject NP or of the VP. In the intended meaning, however, it must be taken as a VP adjunct, since it is not predicated of thana thuma-ra that they are returning, but rather of thana that they are returning with firewood.

> pama thuli-ra
> man woomera-COM
> the man with a woomera.

(38) ngaya iiru yuku yinje-ra
1sgNOM thisABS THING wet-COM
Here I am with wet clothes. / Here I've got wet clothes.

(39) mayi ngaka kancari-nhja mungba-ng
[Mm] VEG water [tea] sugar-COM drink-1sg
I drink tea with sugar.

(40) thana thuma-ra nhaaru-pala waṅ ki-yin
3plNOM firewood-COM thatABS-HITHER return-3plPRES
There they are returning this way with firewood. / There those with firewood are returning this way.

[6] *PRIVative.* The privative signals the negative of the comitative, i.e. that the privative NP is lacked by some other N or NP, A privatively marked N is often reduplicated, particularly if the sole constituent is the head noun. Like comitative, privative occurs within an NP as well as in verbal and non-verbal clauses. We have referred to this case in other work as ABESSIVE, but use PRIVATIVE here to conform to the Handbook's guidelines. Examples follow, see also (100), (102), (114), (196), (182)

> pama kananu-yi
> man toothREDUP-PRIV
> the man without teeth

(41) ngaci nhingkurum kekeka-yi
father 2sgABL spearREDUP-PRIV
Your father hasn't got any spears.

(42) kuyu kananu-yi-ng nhila nga'a nhingu kuyu
woman toothREDUP-PRIV-ERG 3sgNOM fish 3sgDAT woman
kanu-nhja-wu-ngu waa
tooth-COM-DAT-3sgDAT give
The woman without teeth gave the fish to the woman with teeth.

The privative marker -yi also combines with an infinitive to mark a privative subordinate clause (4.7.2[2]).

[7] *LOCative.* Uwanh and Muminh have -n and -ng as locative enclitics in apparent free variation, while Iyanh has only -ng; information on the other patrilects is lacking. The variant -nga also occurs in a very few examples (T129), and the more common -ng may simply be a phonological reduction of this (2.4.3). Locative -ng(a) is thus different from ergative -ng(u); the demonstratives also show a clear morphological difference between locative and ergative (3.2.2), thus the two are distinct cases, even in Iyanh, which lacks the -n allomorph.

Locative indicates the location of the subject NP in verbless clauses and of the state or event expressed in verbal clauses. Examples of locative NPs are seen in (43), (98), (133) and (184). Adverbial phrases of location may also take a locative suffix (4.1.7).

(43) nhila   pama aara   puranci$\begin{Bmatrix} -n \\ -ng \end{Bmatrix}$ wunune-n
      3sgNOM   man   thatABS humpy-LOC   liveREDUP-PRES
      That man lives in the humpy.

[8] *VOCative.* For hailing over a long distance, the vocative marker, -n, is accompanied by a change in the last vowel of the host to /o/ or /oo/. Vocatives are used for address and hailing, their function overlapping with the interjections wooy and awe 'hey; cooey'. Examples follow:

(45) ngathidhe(e)-n
      mother-VOC
      [Hey] mother!

(45) kuyu+waya   ngothopo(o)-n
      OLD WOMAN   FM-VOC (cf. NOM ngothope)
      [Hey] grandma!

(46) thaku-n / thako-n
      lefty-VOC
      [Hey] lefty!

(47) thaa+ngantha yoko-n
[Ug] tongue   big-VOC
      [Hey] big tongue!

3.2.2 DEMONSTRATIVES. Nganhcara has three sets of demonstratives: speaker-proximal ('this near me'), addressee-proximal ('that near you'), and distal ('that over there'). The addressee-proximal forms also function as anaphorics ('that referred to'). Since demonstratives are constituents of non-pronominal NPs, their case marking is ergative/absolutive. However, their declension is somewhat irregular. Table 3.3 lists the unpredictable forms; comitative and privative cases of the demonstratives are formed by adding the regular case-marking clitics to the absolutive stem.   The demonstratives have no vocative forms; the nominative is used instead (48), (49).

TABLE 3.3 - *Demonstrative Declension: Distinctive Forms*

	1prox	2prox	dist
ABSolutive	iiru	nhaaru	aara
ERGative	ilung	nhalung	alang
DATive	iguwu	nhaguwu	agawu
ABLative	imun	nhamun	aman
LOCative	ingun	nhangun	angan

(48)   nhipa   pama kuce nhaaru pala   uwa-wu
       2duNOM   man   two   thatABS HITHER come-2duIMP
       You two men there, come here.

(49)   nhinta pama koyowo aara   pala   uwa
       2sgNOM man   behind thatABS HITHER come
       Man there behind, you come here.

The absolutive forms in Table 3.3 are found in Uwanh, Ugbanh and Muminh. The forms in Iyanh, Mu'inh and Yi'anh are inu, nhanu and ana. The correspondence between long vowel + /r/ and short vowel + /n/ is not regular but is seen occasionally elsewhere in the grammar. For example it exists as an alternation in the 3pl pronoun forms in some Kugu patrilects: thana NOM vs. thaarana ACC/DAT. It is also found in etymologically related forms such as thono 'one' / thoorong 'together' (see also 3.4.10[1]). Correspondences and alternations between /n/ and /r/ without the attendant difference in vowel length are also found, e.g. in the pronoun declension (3.3.1). While Uwanh has free demonstratives in /r/, bound demonstrative stems in /n/ are found in directionals (5.4.2), e.g. in+ungke (this+north) 'this place nearby in the north'. Since analogical change usually proceeds from free forms to bound forms, it is unlikely that the Uwanh distribution could have led by analogy to the uniform use of the n-stems seen in Iyanh, Mu'inh and Yi'anh. Consequently, the Uwanh, Ugbanh and Muminh forms in /r/ likely represent an innovation.

Muminh has the alternate ergative form alangan for alang. The dative forms above are found in all the Kugu patrilects, but Iyanh has forms with -k- in the place of -g-: ikuwu, nhakuwu and akawu.

If stem allomorphy is ignored, the absolutive, ergative, dative, comitative and privative forms are regular. Ergative -l- and dative -g- are remnants of earlier case-marking suffixes (cf. Dixon 1980:311). The ablative and locative have probably developed via metathesis from the regular formations *inu-m, *inu-ng etc., further evidence that the absolutive stems in /r/ are more recent than those in /n/.

3.2.3   DERIVATIONS. Only one nominal derivational affix occurs in our data. Much of the derivational work found in other Australian languages is done syntactically in Nganhcara (See e.g. 3.2.1[6] Privative.).

[1] -dha 'HAVing. The 'having' suffix -dha derives adjectives from nouns and is the derivational counterpart of comitative case marking (3.2.1[5]). Thus X-dha has the meaning 'having X' or 'with X'. It is not productive and there are only a few examples in our data. Note that there is a homophonous unrelated verb-deriving suffix -dha (3.4.10[3]). Examples are pu'u-dha 'female' from pu'u 'vagina', winhnyi-dha 'frightened' from winhnyi 'fear'

3.3   PRONOUNS

Like many Australian languages, Nganhcara has both free pronouns and a set of bound cross-referencing pronouns. Nganhcara bound pronouns are enclitics derived transparently from the free pronouns, which agree in person and number with subject, object, and dative and ablative NPs. They have some unusual syntactic properties which are rare or unreported for Australian languages and which have proved interesting for theoretical work on clitics.

3.3.1   FREE PRONOUN DECLENSION. The distinct case forms of the pronouns for Uwanh are given in Table 3.4. The person and number categories are commonplace on the continent. No patrilect distinguishes between dative and accusative in dual and plural forms. Like the demonstratives, pronouns have no separate vocative forms, and nominative forms are used in vocative expressions (48), (49). Comitative, privative, and locative cases of the pronouns are formed by adding the appropriate enclitic (Table 3.2) to the nominative form.

TABLE 3.4 - *Pronoun Declension: Distinct Forms*

	NOM	ACC	DAT	ABL
1sg	ngaya	nganyi	ngathu	ngathurumu
1duinc	ngale		ngalina	ngalinamu
1duexc	ngana		nganana	ngananamu
1plinc	ngampa		ngampara	ngamparamu
1plexc	nganhca		nganhcara	nganhcaramu
2sg	nhinta	nina	nhingku	ngingkurumu
2du	nhipa		nhipana	nhipanamu
2pl	nhiya		nhiyana	nhiyanamu
3sg	nhila	nhunha	nhingu	nhingurumu
3du	pula		pulana	pulanamu
3pl	thana		thaarana	thaaranamu

The forms of Table 3.4 are also found in Muminh. Yi'anh has the following differences:

3sgABL	nhingurumu/nhingunumu
3plACC/DAT	thanana
3plABL	thananamu

Mu'inh has similar forms to Yi'anh, but lacks the nhingunum variant.

    Pronouns have reflexive forms created by replacing the -mu of the ablative with -mala. Normally either the penultimate or antepenultimate vowel is dropped. For example, the 1sg form is ngathurmala in free variation with ngathurumla. Reflexive pronouns occur frequently as O of a transitive clause, as in (50) - (52). As in many languages no formal distinction is made between reflexive and reciprocal pronouns, but since Nganhcara has morphologically distinct reciprocal and non-reciprocal verb forms (3.4.9, 4.5.1), these determine the interpretation of the pronouns. Compare, for example, (52) and (123).

(50)   ngaya   ngathurumala umpe-ng
               1sgNOM 1sgREFL   cut-1sg
               I cut myself.

(51)   nhila   pama-ng ngathurum nhingurumala putpi-nga
               3sgNOM man-ERG 1sgABL   3sgREFL   hide-CAUS
               That man hid himself from me.

(52)   pula   pama kuce alang   pulanmala-la   yenta
               3duNOM man   two   thatERG 3duREFL-3duNOM spear
               Those two men speared themselves.

    The Iyanh declension is sufficiently different from that of the other patrilects to warrant the separate listing which appears in Table 3.5. The Iyanh forms exhibit a number of similarities to Wik-Mungkan and other related languages to the north, a fact suggesting contact-induced change: (a) syncretism of dual and plural in the first person exclusive forms (b) the accusative suffix -ng, (c) the ablative singular forms in -aCam, instead of -uCum, and (d) the reflexive forms; Wik-Mungkan has two formations, one in -akam(a), which is probably related to Iyanh -aama and one in -amang which is probably related to Iyanh -mang.

3.3.2   BOUND PRONOUNS I: FORM. The forms of the bound pronouns are listed in Table 3.6. In the sections that follow we discuss the external syntax of the bound pronouns (i.e. where they occur in a clause) and their internal syntax (the ordering relationships among them).

    There are two gaps in the paradigm: it is not possible to cross-reference a 1sg or 3pl subject. All bound pronouns are derived from the corresponding free pronoun by truncation of the initial consonant plus vowel, thus for example ngathurum '1sgDAT' yields -thurum.   Forms beginning with a nasal + stop

TABLE 3.5 - *Wik Iyanh Pronoun Declension: Distinct Forms*

	NOM	ACC	DAT	ABL	REFL
1sg	ngaya	nganyi	ngathu	ngatharam	ngathumang
1duinc	ngale	ngaling		ngalinam	ngalimang
1duplexc	ngana	nganang		ngananam	nganaama(ng)
1plinc	ngampa	ngampang		ngamparam	ngampaama
2sg	nhinta	nina	nhingku	nhingkaram	nhingkumang
2du	nhipa	nhipang		nhipanam	nhipaama
2pl	nhiya	nhiyang		nhiyanam	nhiyaama
3sg	nhila	nhunha	nhingu	nhinganam	nhingumang
3du	pula	pulang		pulanam	pulaama
3pl	thana	thanang		thananam	thanaama

TABLE 3.6 - *Bound Pronouns*

	NOM	ACC	DAT	ABL
1sg	-	-nyi	-thu	-thurum
1duinc	-le	-lin		-linam
1duexc	-na	-nan		-nanam
1plinc	-mpa	-mpara		-mparam
1plexc	-nhca	-nhcara		-nhcaram
2sg	-nta	-na	-ngku	-ngkurum
2du	-pa	-pan		-panam
2pl	-ya	-yara		-yaram
3sg	-la	-nha	-ngu	-ngurum
3du	-la	-lan		-lanam
3pl	-	-ran		-ranam

cluster drop the nasal when the host to which they are encliticised ends in a consonant. The patrilectal differences in the free pronouns outlined in the last section also extend to the bound pronouns.

Although bound pronouns in preverbal position are always followed by the verb, it is not possible on phonological grounds to treat them as proclitics to the verb. Certain consonants and consonant clusters which begin some of the clitics are inadmissible in word-initial position in Nganhcara. Others are extremely rare. Specifically:

- the nasal plus stop clusters /nt mp nhc ngk/ do not occur word-initially
- /r/ never occurs word-initially
- to our knowledge /l/ occurs initially in only one word
- /ny/ and /n/ are rare word-initially.

For an additional argument, see the following section. Bound pronouns are illustrated in (53) - (64). To aid the presentation, bound pronouns appear in **boldface**. Note that in general a cross-referenced NP need not itself be present in the surface string (55), (56), (59), (60).

(53)   nhila   pama-ng nga'a-**la**   yenta
         3sgNOM   man-ERG fish-3sgNOM   spear
         The man speared the fish.

(54)   nganhca   nga'a-**nhca**   yenta
         1plexcNOM fish-1plexcNOM   spear
         We speared the fish.

(55)   nhaguwu-**nhca**   wico
         thatDAT-1plexcNOM   travel
         We travelled to that place.

(56)   nhaguwu-**mpa**   wico
         thatDAT-1plincNOM   travel
         We travelled to that place.

(57)   nhila nga'a yupa-**nha**   yenta
         3sgNOM fish   FUT-3sgACC spear
         He will spear the fish.

(58)   nhila nganyi yupa-**nyi**   yenta
         3sgNOM 1sgACC FUT-1sgACC   spear
         He will spear me.

(59)   me'e-ng-**nyi**   pathatha
         mosquito-ERG-1sgACC biteREDUP
         Mosquitoes are biting me.

(60)   me'e-ng-**pan**   pathatha?
         mosquito-ERG-2duACC biteREDUP
         Are mosquitoes biting you?

(61)   nhila   pama-ng nhingu   pukpe-wu ku'a-**ngu** waa
         3sgNOM   man-ERG 3sgDAT   child-DAT   dog-3sgDAT give
         The man gave a dog to the child.

(62)   nhila   pama-ng ngathu   ku'a-**thu**   waa
         3sgNOM   man-ERG 1sgDAT   dog-1sgDAT give
         The man gave me a dog.

(63)   ngaya   ku'a nhingurum   ka'im-**ngurum** kala-ng
         1sgNOM   dog   3sgABL   NEG-3sgABL   take-1sg
         I didn't take his dog.

(64)   ngaya   ku'an hingkurum   ka'im-**ngkurum** kala-ng
         1sgNOM   dog   2sgABL   NEG-2sgABL   take-1sg
         I didn't take your dog.

3.3.3   BOUND PRONOUNS II: EXTERNAL SYNTAX.   There are two syntactic positions in which bound pronouns occur. The favoured position is encliticised to the last element before the verb, as in the examples above; less commonly, they occur encliticised to the verb itself, (65), (165), T97. Post-verbal position is mandatory in clauses containing no pre-verbal elements. This is additional evidence for treating the bound pronouns in pre-verbal position as enclitics to a pre-verbal element rather than proclitics to the verb: if they were proclitics, they should be able to occur before the verb in sentences such as (66), T43 (second clause).

(65)	nhila	pama-ng	nhingu	pukpe-wu	ku'a	waa-ngu
[cf. 61]	3sgNOM	man-ERG	3sgDAT	child-DAT	dog	give-3sgDAT

The man gave a dog to the child.

(66)   waa-ngu
          give-3sgDAT
          Give [it] to him.

It is important to distinguish enclitic cross-referencing pronouns from verbal concord suffixes (3.4.3, 3.4.4). For example the -ng in kalang in (63), (64) is a concord suffix, not an enclitic. Concord suffixes differ from enclitics in three respects:

• they are obligatory

• they are always attached to the verb and never appear preverbally

• they precede any encliticised material — in particular, they precede the clitics discussed in 4.12, while bound pronouns follow these.

When two bound pronouns occur in the same clause, it is possible for one to occur pre-verbally and the other post-verbally, T77. As a result of the relatively free constituent order in Nganhcara, any constituent may occur in preverbal position and thus serve as a host for cross-referencing pronouns. Other possibilities for (61) and (65) are:

(67)   nhila pama-ng ku'a nhingu pukpe-wu-ngu waa
[cf. 61,   nhila pama-ng ku'a pukpe-wu nhingu-ngu waa
65]   ku'a nhingu pukpe-wu nhila pama-ng-ngu waa
           ku'a nhingu pukpe-wu pama nhila-ng-ngu waa

The external syntax of the bound pronouns in Nganhcara is of an extremely rare type, although its existence is predicted by the general typology of cliticisation (Klavans 1985). Cliticised cross-referencing pronouns are, of course, a common typological trait in Australia and many Australian languages have such bound pronouns in pre-verbal position. However, according to Blake (1987:103-4) these are always one of three types: (1) they attach to the verb or to an auxiliary; (2) they directly follow the first constituent of the clause, and in some languages encliticise to it; (3) they are encliticised or affixed to an auxiliary particle that follows the first constituent of the clause.   The closest approximation to the Nganhcara situation is made by Walmatjari (Hudson 1978) where it appears that the auxiliary and the bound pronouns together make up a free form in preverbal position, which may, under certain rhythmic conditions, encliticise to the previous word. In some of the languages of type (2) above, bound pronouns may cliticise onto any type of constituent, but in all cases it is to the first constituent of the clause. Klavans (1985) characterises the Nganhcara bound pronouns as having 'dual citizenship'; that is they are syntactically a member of one constituent but are phonologically attached to another. The particular combination of preverbal position and the ability to cliticise freely to a variety of constituents was unknown before the Nganhcara data were reported (Smith and Johnson 1979). Note, however, that the possibility of a clitic occurring in either of two positions is not strange in Australia or generally.

Historically the Nganhcara bound pronouns have likely developed from a situation in which unstressed but unreduced cross-referencing pronouns could occur in pre- or postverbal position. The present system may have arisen quite recently: the bound pronouns are transparently derived from their unreduced counterparts, and even in modern Nganhcara it is possible to substitute an unaccented but unreduced pronoun for a bound pronoun (80). Moreover, bound pronouns do not occur obligatorily in Nganhcara as they do in many Australian languages. Nor has the use of free pronouns been diminished by bound pronouns. Indeed, as can be seen from the examples, free pronouns frequently occur alongside their bound counterparts in the same clause: often one finds a free pronoun in apposition to a non-pronominal NP as well as the corresponding bound pronoun.

3.3.4   BOUND PRONOUNS III: INTERNAL SYNTAX.   Turning to the internal syntax of the bound pronouns, we find another interesting situation. As in other Australian languages, when more than one NP in a clause can be cross-referenced it is possible for combinations of bound pronouns to occur. (There is also the possibility mentioned above, of avoiding a combination of two bound pronouns by putting them on different sides of the verb.) However, cross-referencing is optional in Nganhcara, and in practice only one or, less commonly, two NPs in a clause are cross-referenced. Speakers do not object to combinations of three bound pronouns, but none have been observed in natural speech; combinations of four bound pronouns are not considered grammatical. It would be interesting to know what, if anything, determines: (a) whether a particular NP will be cross-referenced and (b) which of several eligible NPs will be selected for cross-referencing. The animacy hierarchy is likely to be relevant. However, it would appear that stylistic or discourse factors are also involved, and the problem needs more fieldwork before a satisfactory statement can be made. Sequences of bound pronouns from spontaneous speech are illustrated below; see also T16, T137, T146.

(68)   nganhca   nhingu   nga'a waa-ngu-nhca
          1plexcNOM 3sgDAT   fish   give-3sgDAT-1plexcNOM
          We gave him a fish.

(69)   nhila   pama-ng ku'a nhingurum pukpe-m
         3sgNOM man-ERG dog   3sgABL   child-ABL
         kantu-ng-ngurum-nha   pigo
         stick-ERG-3sgABL-3sgACC hitPAST
         The man hit the child's dog with a stick.

(70)   nhinta   pama nhaaru pulan   kuce pala-lan-nan
         2sgNOM man   thatABS 3duACC   two hither-3duACC-1duDAT
         yengka
         send
         You send those two men to us.

　　　　We have no spontaneous examples of combinations of more than
two bound pronouns. The examples below were suggested to our main
Uwanh consultant, who repeated them and assented to their validity. She
would not repeat examples containing combinations of four bound pronouns
which were suggested to her. Thus a cline of grammaticality appears to exist
as far as combinations of bound pronouns are concerned, with two being
clearly grammatical, four being clearly ungrammatical and three of unclear
status.

(71)   ?pula   nhunha ngathu yupa-thu-nha-la   yengka
         3duNOM 3sgACC 1sgDAT   FUT-1sgDAT-3sgACC-3duNOM send
         They will send him to me.

　　　　When two or more bound pronouns combine, they may occur in any
order. Thus other versions of (68)-(71) are as follows:

(72)   nganhca nhingu nga'a waa-nhca-ngu
         nhila pama-ng ku'a nhingurum pukpe-m
            kantu-ng-nha-ngurum pigo
         nhinta pama nhaaru pulan kuce pala-nan-lan yengka
                                   ⎧-nha-thu-la⎫
         ?pula nhunha ngathu yupa ⎨-nha-la-thu⎬ yengka
                                   ⎩-la-thu-nha⎭

These examples are particularly interesting because in most Australian
languages having bound pronouns, when these combine, they do so only in
fixed order (cf. Dixon 1980:362), thus conforming to Perlmutter's (1971:48)
proposed universal on clitic ordering: 'in all languages in which clitics move
to a particular place in the clause, there are surface structure constraints on the
relative order of clitics.' The Nganhcara situation is a counterexample to both
these hypotheses. Note, however, that bound pronouns always follow other
types of clitics (4.12) in the same group. Jeffrey Heath (p.c.) notes that
Ritharngu also shows variability in clitic order when the 3sgACC clitic -a is
involved. Thus X-napu-a or X-a-napu, with the 1plexc subject clitic napu.
　　　　More generally, given that clitics are transitional between syntax,
where the free order of elements is one typological possibility, and
morphology, where fixed order prevails universally, the existence of freely

ordered clitics should not come as a surprise. Perlmutter may have identified a universal TENDENCY: clitics develop a fixed order as they become more integrated into their host. Free order might be expected when, as in Nganhcara, clitics are in the early stages of development. Similarly, when one preferred order gives way to a new one, as happened in Old Italian (Santangelo and Vennemann 1976), a transitional period where either order is acceptable seems mandatory.

3.3.5 INTERROGATIVES (INDEFINITES). As is standard in Australian languages, interrogatives in Nganhcara also function as indefinites. The interrogative roots are as follows:

wayi	who; someone, anyone
ngaari	what; something, anything
wantanda	how; somehow, anyhow
wantu	where; somewhere, anywhere; when; sometime, anytime

The interrogatives take the regular case-marking clitics; thus: wayi-ng 'who-ERG'; wayi-n 'who-DAT'; wayi-nam 'who-ABL, from whom, whose'; wantu-n 'where-DAT, where to'; wantu-m 'where-ABL, where from'. A few specialised forms are worth mentioning: ngaaraari 'how many' ('whatREDUP'), agu ngaari(-n) 'when' ('TIME/PLACE what(-DAT)'), ngaari-wu/ngaari-m 'why' ('what-DAT'/'what-ABL'. The following examples illustrate the use of interrogatives. The form wantanda also functions as a pro-form when the speaker has had a mental lapse 'what's-it, where was it now'; cf. also wayinda 'what's-his-name' (79), ngaarinda 'what's-it'.

(73) nga'a nhingku wayi-ng waa?
      fish 2sgDAT   who-ERG give
      Who gave you the fish?

(74) nhila   aara   wayi wunune-n?
      3sgNOM thatABS who   sleepREDUP-PRES
      Someone is sleeping there. / Who is that sleeping?

(75) ngaci wantu?
      father where
      Where is father?

(76) nhinta thaa+panci nhaaru   agu ngaari-pa umpi-ngan?
      2sgNOM beard   thatABS TIME what-FUT   cut-2sgPRES
      When are you going to shave off (lit. cut) your beard?

(77) nhinta wantu-m thangke-n?
      2sgNOM where-ABL arrive-CNC
      Where did you come from?

(78)   mayi pungga iiru   yuku wantu-m?
        VEG   fruit   thisABS   tree   which-ABL
        Which tree is this fruit from?

(79)   pama wayinda   nhaaru-n-ngu   thawa-ng.
        MAN   what's-his-name thatABS-DAT-3sgDAT   tell-1sg
          aa! X-n-ngu
          ah! X-DAT-3sgDAT
        I told what's-his-name. [Suddenly remembering:] Ah! X.   [Given the
        unusual case marking, nhaaru is probably functioning as a locational deictic
        here (3.1.5), rather than as a determiner.]

3.4   VERB MORPHOLOGY

The verb in Nganhcara is unusual among Australian languages in taking
obligatory subject-agreement (in both transitive and intransitive clauses).
Only Wik-Mungkan, its northern neighbour, is reported to have a similar
concord system.

3.4.1   TRANSITIVITY. Of roughly 1250 plain register vocabulary items
(not counting patrilectal differences), 20% were verbs. Half of these were
either monomorphemic or compounds of a noun + monomorphemic root not
occurring alone; we shall refer to these as primary verbs.   Approximately
40% of primary verbs are intransitive and 60% transitive.   Four of the
transitives are ditransitive, with the two subcategorised objects usually
differing in their position on the animacy hierarchy.   Generally, only the
object which is higher on the scale may be cross-referenced by a bound
pronoun. Thus in (80), nganyi is cross-referenced and yuku keene is not.

(80)   pula   pama kuce alang nganyi   yuku
        3duNOM man   two   thatERG 1sgACC   THING
          keene-nyi-pula   kaakaa
          tobacco-1sgACC-3duNOM   promiseREDUP
        Those two men promised me tobacco.

    Other ditransitive verbs are padhja 'deny [someone something that
should be shared]'; and piya 'take [something (from) someone]'. As is the
norm for Australian languages, verbs are strictly either transitive or
intransitive. Corresponding pairs of intransitive and transitive verbs may
have completely different forms, as thuthi T149 / ungpa 'break' T148, anhci
'fall, sneeze' / pupu 'fell', anca 'smell' / nhudha 'sniff, smell', or they may
be morphologically related. Morphologically related pairs are often based on
a common root; the intransitive member may have an inchoative suffix
(3.4.11) or intransitive-forming suffix (3.4.12), while the transitive member
generally carries a causative suffix (3.4.10); thus: minji / minji-nga
'finish', miyal-wi / miyal-nga 'cheer up', poje-ma / poje-dha-nga 'dry',
yerga-ma / yerga-dha 'scatter'.   Rarely, such a pair differs only in
conjugation class, as wanji / wanja 'hang'.

3.4.2   CONJUGATION.   Two major and two minor conjugations exist, although their differences can be minimised through morphophonological analysis.   They are distinguished by the stem-final thematic vowel or vowel-alternation.   The thematic vowel is always short, except in monosyllablic stems, where it is always long. (Monosyllables belonging to each class are listed in full below.)   Conjugation I contains stems with non-high thematic vowels (e, o, a), e.g. waa 'give', maa 'pick up, collect, buy', mungga 'eat', pithca 'burst (int)', uwa 'go, come', odh-o 'give to each other, share'.   Nearly 60% of primary verbs (3.4.1) belong to this conjugation, and they are nearly all a-stems; more than twice as many primary a-stems are transitive as intransitive. All o-stems result from the presence of the reciprocal suffix -o, e.g. yent-o 'spear each other/one another', from yenta 'spear'.   Reciprocals are productively formed, but are excluded from the primary group, which includes only monomorphemic stems.   Only five e-stems are found in our primary group: eke 'get up', wegbe 'keep, retain', thaa+poye 'jump', ente 'ask for' and enje 'singe'.   Conjugation II stems have high thematic vowels (i, u), which alternate with corresponding mid vowels, e.g. ngii, 'hear', thii 'throw, chuck', uwi 'see', wań ki 'return', yumpi 'do, make', pigu 'hit', nutpu 'bark'.   Nearly 40% of primary verbs are second conjugation, the overwhelming majority being i-stems; only three primary u-stems have been found and they are also rare outside the primary group.   Primary i-stems are equally divided between intransitives and transitives.   Conjugation III comprises thawa 'speak, say' and five intransitive verbs ending in -na: nhiina 'sit', thana 'stand', thena 'walk', mangalana '(lightning) flash', and wuna 'camp, stay', in which the thematic vowel changes to /e/ in a single form.   Conjugation IV has only the transitive verb, kali 'carry', characterised by a i/u/a alternation.

There are two concord systems.   One, which we shall refer to as the central system, operates in the two indicative tenses, present and past, and optionally in the irrealis.   A second system operates only in the imperative. There is one other finite form, the historic, which exhibits no concord.   The irregular verb kali aside,   stem vowel changes are limited to the central concord system.

3.4.3   CENTRAL CONCORD SYSTEM.   The pronominal system (see 3.3.1) has eleven distinct person/number categories (ten in Iyanh), but only four forms are found in the central concord system.   Three categories are distinguished uniquely: first person singular, second person singular and third person plural, while a fourth 'UNMarKeD' form does duty for all the other categories. Third person subjects that are low on the animacy hierarchy take unmarked agreement, even when plural (59), (60), (105), (184).

[1] *Surface forms.*   The affixes are listed in Table 3.7.   Except for the UNMKD:PRES form, the affixes are the same for all four conjugations. Affixes marked with an asterisk trigger lowering of the thematic vowel in conjugation II.   Examples of conjugation I and II verbs are given in Tables 3.8 and 3.9

TABLE 3.7 - *Central Concord Affixes*

	PRESent		PAST		IRRealis	
	I / IV	II / III	I / IV	II / III	I / IV	II / III
1sg	-ng	-ng	-ng	-ng*	-ng	-ng*
2sg	-ngan	-ngan	-n	-n *	-nhun	-nhun
3pl	-yin	-yin	-dhan	-dhan*	-nhin	-nhin
UNMKD	∅	-n *	∅	∅*	-nha	-nha

TABLE 3.8 - *Conjugation I: non-high thematic vowel* (a, e, o)

patha 'bite'	PRESent	PAST	IRRealis
1sg	pathang	pathang	pathang
2sg	pathangan	pathan	pathanhun
3pl	pathayin	pathadhan	pathanhin
UNMKD	patha	patha	pathanha
eke 'get up'			
1sg	ekeng	ekeng	ekeng
2sg	ekengan	eken	ekenhun
3pl	ekeyin	ekedhan	ekenhin
UNMKD	eke	eke	ekenha
odho 'giveRECIP'			
	(RECIProcal verb - no singular forms)		
3pl	odhoyin	odhodhan	odhonhin
UNMKD	odho	odho	odhonha

TABLE 3.9 - *Conjugation II: high thematic vowel* (i, u)

wa'i 'dig'	PRESent	PAST	IRRealis
1sg	wa'ing	wa'eng	wa'eng
2sg	wa'ingan	wa'en	wa'inhun
3pl	wa'iyin	wa'edhan	wa'inhin
UNMKD	wa'en	wa'e	wa'inha
pupu 'fell'			
1sg	pupung	pupong	pupong
2sg	pupungan	pupon	pupunhun
3pl	pupuyin	pupodhan	pupunhin
UNMKD	pupon	pupo	pupunha

    First person singular forms may end in either -ng (as in Table 3.7)
or in -nga; forms in -ng are subject to optional sandhi loss of this final
consonant with nasalisation of the preceding vowel (2.4.1). The unmarked

irrealis form in -nha has also been generalised, and provides an alternative for the first and second singular and third plural forms in the table. When an enclitic such as -dhu 'MAY' (4.12[4]) or -monh 'NONFACTual' (4.12[7]) attaches to the generalised form of the irrealis, the final /a/ drops, as e.g. thangke-nh-monh (arrive-SUBJ-NONFACT) 'would have arrived'.

It is interesting to note that the first conjugation verbs distinguish between past and present only in the second person singular and third person plural. In the second conjugation all past and present forms are distinguished by vowel alternation or by suffix. In both conjugations first person past and irrealis are the same.

Conjugation III verbs differ from conjugation I in only one form, and could be considered irregular members of that class. The irregular form is the unmarked present, which has the suffix -n, as in conjugation II, and the thematic vowel /e/. A sample paradigm is given in Table 3.10.

TABLE 3.10 - *Conjugation III:* a/e *verbs*

nhiina 'sit'	PRESent	PAST	IRRealis
1sg	nhiinang	nhiinang	nhiinang
2sg	nhiinangan	nhiinan	nhiinanhun
3pl	nhiinayin	nhiinadhan	nhiinanhin
UNMKD	nhiinen	nhiina	nhiinanha

Conjugation IV has only one verb, whose paradigm is seen in Table 3.11. The suffixes are as for the first conjugation verbs, but the forms exhibit a thematic vowel alternation between /a/, /u/, and /i/.

TABLE 3.11 - *Conjugation IV*

kali 'carry'	PRESent	PAST	IRRealis
1sg	kalung	kalang	kalang
2sg	kalungan	kalan	kalinhun
3pl	kaliyin	kaladhan	kalinhin
UNMKD	kalu	kala	kalinha

In the interlinear morph-by-morph glosses of verbs, we indicate the meaning of the stem and any grammatical categories which are unambiguously represented. For example, wa'i-ng is glossed as 'dig-PRES1sg', but wa'e-ng only as 'dig-1sg' since this form is common to both past and irrealis. Similarly wa'e-n is 'dig-CoNCord', since the same form is found in the unmarked present and 2sg past. The unmarked concord category is never glossed, thus wa'e is 'digPAST'.

The past indicative indicates exclusively past events and states; the present, however, might be more appropriately named nonpast; it indicates not only present events and states but also those of the future (in conjunction with the particle (yu)pa, 4.12[2]) and those with no specific timeframe. (e.g. Wallabies eat grass.)

The irrealis is used in conjunction with the particle waya to mark desideratives (4.12[6]) and is obligatory in clauses containing the nonfactual enclitic -monh (4.12[7]).

[2] *Morphophonological analysis.* The differences in thematic vowels can be accounted for by a neat morphophonological analysis based on a suggestion by Bob Dixon (p.c.). If we take the underlying representations of the affixes to be those in Table 3.12, most surface forms can be derived with the two rules given below.

TABLE 3.12 - *Underlying Central Concord Affixes*

	PRESent	PAST	IRRealis
1sg	-ng	-ang	-ang
2sg	-ngan	-an	-nhun
3pl	-yin	-adhan	-nhin
UNMKD	*(see text)*	-a	-nha

Lowering: $V \longrightarrow [-hi]/\ \_a$

Elision: $V \longrightarrow \emptyset\ /\ a\_$

The essence of this analysis is to represent suffixes that trigger thematic vowel lowering in conjugation II with an initial -a, which is subsequently deleted. The UNMKD:PRES affix will still need to be specified as -a (or $\emptyset$) following a non-high thematic vowel (conjugation I) and -an following a high thematic vowel (conjugation II). The UNMKD:PRES forms of the five known verbs of the third conjugation also need to be specified, as do the irregular forms of kali 'carry'.

3.4.4   IMPERATIVE. Imperative forms exist for all persons except first person singular, and dual and plural exclusive. The second person singular is expressed by the bare stem; the other forms by stem plus suffix. The third person forms are undifferentiated for number, and are the same as the second person dual form. The verb kali has the irregular imperative stem kala. No other irregularities occur. The imperative suffixes are listed in Table 3.13. Sample paradigms are given in Table 3.14. For examples see (48), (49), (145), 4.11, 4.13[2], 4.13[4]

TABLE 3.13 - *Imperative Suffixes*

	singular	dual	plural
1incl	—	-li	-mu
2	-$\emptyset$	-wu	-dha
3	-wu	-wu	-wu

TABLE 3.14 - *Imperative Paradigms*

	singular	dual	plural
waa 'give' (I)			
1incl	—	waali	waamu
2	waa	waawu	waadha
3	waawu	waawu	waawu
munji 'bathe' (H)			
1incl	—	munjili	munjimu
2	munji	munjiwu	munjidha
3	munjiwu	munjiwu	munjiwu
pupu 'fell' (II)			
1incl	—	pupuli	pupumu
2	pupu	pupuwu	pupudha
3	pupuwu	pupuwu	pupuwu
nhiina 'sit' (III)			
1incl	—	nhiinali	nhiinamu
2	nhiina	nhiinawu	nhiinadha
3	nhiinawu	nhiinawu	nhiinawu
kali 'carry' (IV)			
1incl	—	kalali	kalamu
2	kala	kalawu	kaladha
3	kalawu	kalawu	kalawu

3.4.5   HISTORIC. The historic is an invariant verb form, formed with the suffix -nhum for all persons and numbers. The function of the historic is not well understood. It is used frequently in story telling and can usually be interpreted duratively. Examples follow; see also T21, T23, T24, T28, T32 - T34, T71, T87, T95.

(81)   nganhca   thaaran   thangki-nhum
       1plexcNOM 3plDAT   arrive-HIST
       We used to go and visit them.

(82)   ngaya   ngaka   uyu mungga-nhum
       1sgNOM water [alcohol] much drink-HIST
       I had a big drink / I was drinking a lot.

(83)   ngaya   nga'a mungga-nhum
       1sgNOM fish   eat-HIST
       I used to eat fish.

3.4.6   DURATIVE / ITERATIVE. Verbs can reduplicate in all tenses and aspects to indicate continuous (or repeated) action. See for example T43, T64, T71. (For discussion of the phonology of reduplication, see 2.3).   The verbs ngii 'hear, listen' and thii 'throw' have the irregular reduplicated forms ngaangii and thaathii as well as the expected ngiingii and thiithii. The reduplication rule is applied after the tense and person inflection; thus for example the regular reduplicated past of ngii is ngeengee, not *ngiingee.

3.4.7   WIK IYANH FORMS. Wik Iyanh exhibits interesting differences from the system presented above, which are exemplified in Table 3.15 (where no entry is made, the forms do not differ). All verbs take an - n suffix in the third person singular; the stem vowel alternations of other patrilects are fully represented in conjugations I - III, but the verb   kala 'carry' (cf. Uw kali) is a regular conjugation I verb and Iyanh thus has no conjugation IV. Two suffixes have a different form in Iyanh: 3plPAST -an, and 2plIMP -ye. The loss of dh in the 3plPAST has led to the juxtaposition of two vowels, a phenomenon otherwise not seen in Nganhcara. When the verb is an a-stem the two like vowels coalesce to yield long aa. When the verb is an o-stem or u-stem, the suffix vowel assimilates to the stem final -o and long oo results. Because of these phonological changes, Iyanh has long vowels (aa and oo) in final syllables. Thus long vowels enjoy a slightly wider distribution in Iyanh than in the other patrilects. Finally, a-stems have their thematic vowel raised to e by initial y of the 3plPRES and 2plIMP suffixes.

TABLE 3.15 - *Comparison of Verb Forms: Wik Iyanh vs. Kugu Patrilects*

	a-stems		i-stems		u-stems	
	Kugu	Iyanh	Kugu	Iyanh	Kugu	Iyanh
UNMKD:PRES	patha	pathan				
3plPRES	pathayin	patheyin				
3plPAST	pathadhan	pathaan	wa'edhan	wa'ean	pupodhan	pupoon
2plIMP	pathadha	patheye	wa'idha	wa'iye	pupudha	pupuye

3.4.8   INFINITIVE. The infinitive, formed by the suffix -nh is a nominalised form of the verb which has a restricted distribution. Its main function is to head a subordinate clause, where it carries the case-marking enclitics -wu or -yi (4.7.2). It can also be used alone, e.g. kugu uwanh 'the language (which uses) uwa-nh (= to go)'.

3.4.9   RECIPROCAL. Reciprocals are formed by substituting / o / for the stem thematic vowel; all reciprocals are thus first conjugation verbs. Reciprocals also exhibit a restricted form of vowel harmony in that the reciprocal suffix assimilates an / a / in the preceding syllable. Examples of the reciprocal are:

peko	throw at each other	from peka	throw [missile] at
potho	bite each other	from patha	bite
yengko	send to each other	from yengka	send
odho	share	from adha	give

woo	argue	from waa	give; scold
wico	travel together	from wice	pull, draw

The semantic connection between reciprocal and non-reciprocal forms of the same root is usually clear, though sometimes the English gloss may at first obscure this — as for example with odho and woo (which was first translated to us as '[have] a tongue-bang'.)   However, some reciprocal forms, such as wico have gone their own way semantically.

Finally note that reciprocal verbs, by their nature, are formed only from transitive stems and cannot take a singular subject. Even semantically opaque reciprocals, such as wico, retain this latter characteristic. See 4.5.1 for discussion of the syntax of reciprocals.

3.4.10 CAUSATIVE.   The causative derivational suffixes -nga, -nha, -dha, -ya, -yinha and -dhani convert nouns, adjectives, quantifiers, adverbs and verbs into transitive verbs; thus thangki-nga 'send back' from thangki 'return'.

Causatives derived from transitive verbs do not generally occur. Compare, for example, the verbs mata 'climb' and kabanhji 'step over'. The former is intransitive, taking a locative complement, and has the causative mata-nga. The latter is transitive and has no causative.

There is considerable morphophonemic irregularity in the formation of causatives as well as some variation among the patrilects. Our data are deficient in Mu'inh examples. The various suffixes are examined separately below.

[1] -nga. The most common causative suffix in the Kugu patrilects is -nga. In general when -nga is added to stems of more than two syllables, the third and subsequent syllables are deleted; thus: pintil-nga 'make smooth' from pintili 'smooth', kuthir-nga 'make cold' from. kuthcira 'cold'.   There is at least one clear example in which truncation of the stem does not take place: winhnyi-dha-nga 'frighten' from winhnyi-dha 'frightened'.

A few verbs display an intrusive - n - between the stem and suffix: paabiń -nga 'make cry' from paabi 'cry', umuń -nga 'meet' from umu 'chest' and wogoń -nga 'cause to cross [a river] by swimming with a log' from wogoma 'cross [a river] by swimming with a log. In this last example - n- appears in place of the intransitive suffix -ma.

Quantifiers and a few adjectives display intrusive - l - between the stem and suffix; often this - l - is optional: thonol-nga / thono-nga 'join' from thono 'one', kucel-nga 'divide in two' from kuce 'two', uyul-nga / uyu-nga 'divide up' from uyu 'many', uthul-nga 'kill' from uthu 'dead', mica(l)-nga 'soften' from mica 'soft', poorol-nga 'lighten' from poorowo 'light', thintha-nga 'blunt' from thintha 'blunt', ungul-nga (Mm, cf. Uw unguń -nga) 'lengthen' from ungu 'long'.   Note that in porol-nga the linking -l- appears in place of the deleted third syllable.

Two pairs exhibit the sporadic alternation between short vowel +

/n/ and long vowel + /r/ (3.2.2): thaara-nga 'stand (tr)' from thana 'stand (int)', thooroń -nga / thooro(l)-nga 'join' (optional causative form from thono, cf. thono(l)-nga above). The alternation th/thc is unknown in Nganhcara outside the pair kuthir-nga / kuthcira above; the -r- in the causative form here is a further irregularity, since the root is usually truncated immediately after the second vowel when -nga is added.

One verb has intrusive -m- before the suffix -nga: winhnyim-nga / winhnyi-dha-nga 'frighten' from winhnyi 'fear(?)' / winhnyi-dha frightened'

Kugu Yi'anh uses intrusive -n- more frequently than the other patrilects. Yi'anh also employs the mid-vowel alternant of conjugation II verbs before intrusive -n-, while other patrilects use the high vowel alternant. Yi paceń -nga Uw paci-nga 'cause to sing out' from paci 'sing out', Yi wipań -nga Uw wipa-nga 'cause to be caught' from wipa 'get caught', Yi unpeń -nga Uw umpi-nga 'light [a fire]' from umpi 'cut', Yi karkeń -nga Uw karki-nga 'cause to hurry' from karki 'hurry'.

[2] -nha. In Wik Iyanh the causative suffix is usually -nha, instead of -nga, and this suffix occurs occasionally in the other patrilects as well, particularly in the respect register (5.5). Examples: Iy thangki-nha Uw thangki-nga 'send back' from thangki 'arrive', Iy mata-nha Uw mata-nga 'cause to climb' from mata 'climb', Iy munci-nha Uw munji-nga 'bathe (tr)' from Iy munci Uw munji 'bathe (int)', Iy Ug karki-nha Uw karki-nga 'cause to hurry' from karki 'hurry', Uw Ug !mudba-nha 'cause to run' from !mudba 'run', Uw Ug Iy !wadhi-nha 'send back' from !wadhi 'return', Ug Iy !munja-nha Uw !munja-nga 'burst (tr)' from !munja 'burst (int)', Mm ema-nha Uw ema-nga 'grow, raise' from ema 'grow (int)'.

[3] -dha. Wik Iyanh occasionally uses -dha to form causatives. Most examples are in the respect register (5.5). In some cases the -dha is used together with -nga. Often the non-causative itself ends in -nga; in such cases the Uwanh respect register causative and non-causative are often identical. Some Wik Iyanh examples follow: !wagunga-dha Uw !wagunga 'cause to climb' from !wagunga 'climb', !kuncunga-dha Uw !kuncunga 'cause to descend' from kuncunga 'descend', !nhuu(y)manga-dha Uw !nhuumanga 'bathe (tr)' from Iy !nhuuyma Uw !nhuuma 'bathe (int)'.

There are also one or two examples of -dha in the Iyanh plain register, and in the other patrilects: Iy ema-dha Uw ema-nga 'grow, raise' from ema 'grow (int)', Uw !pala-dha 'call over' from pala 'hither'. In one example -nga follows -dha: Uw poje-dha-nga 'dry (tr)' from poje 'dry (adj)'.

Note that there is a homophonous adjective-deriving suffix (3.2.3[1]) which should not be confused with causative -dha.

[4] -ya. In Wik Iyanh respect register the causativising suffix -ya is occasionally found, particularly when the corresponding plain register term uses the same root with the suffix -nha. Usually -ya replaces -nha, but

occasionally -nha is retained. E.g. Wik Iyanh !nhiina-ya 'cause to sit' (plain nhiina-nha) from nhiina 'sit', !ema-ya 'grow, raise' (plain ema-dha) from ema 'grow (int)', !parka-nha-ya 'warm' (plain parka-nha) from parka 'get warm', !minci-nha-ya 'finish (tr)' (plain minci-nha) from minci 'finish (int)'. We have only one clear example of -ya in another patrilect: Uw !nguca-ya (cf. Ug !nguca-nha) 'cause [fire] to catch` from !nguca '[fire] catch

[5] -yinha. The Wik Iyanh suffix -yinha occurs only a few times in our data. Like -ya it is restricted to the respect register. Examples: !mudba-yinha (Uw !mudba-nha) 'cause to run' from !mudba 'go, run', !parka-nha-yinha / !parka-nha-ya 'warm (tr)' from parka 'get warm'.

[6] -dhani. The suffix -dhani occurs only once in our data, in wanhci-dhani 'be sore' from wanhci 'sore'. As Iy has wanhci-dha, -dhani is likely bimorphemic.

3.4.11 INCHOATIVE. The derivational suffix -wi creates inchoatives, as is seen in: thaa+thayan-wi 'become tired' from thaa+thayan 'tired', ka'im-wi 'run out of' from ka'i(m) 'NEGative', kuurul-wi 'become bent' from kuurulu 'bent', kugu-yi-wi 'become quiet' from kugu-yi 'quiet', uke-wi 'be born' from uke 'exposed'. Verbs so formed belong to the second conjugation by virtue of the high vowel in the suffix.

3.4.12 INTRANSITIVE -ma. The derivational suffix -ma sometimes appears in the stem of intransitive verbs. In a few examples it is clearly added to an adjective to form an intransitive verb and has an inchoative sense: poje-ma 'dry (int)' from poje 'dry', nhoco-ma 'get quiet' from nhoco 'quiet'. In some of our examples the stem is not a known free form: yerga-ma 'scatter (int)'. The suffix -ma never co-occurs with the causative suffixes (3.4.10), which of course forms transitive stems. E.g. yerga-dha 'scatter (tr)', cf. yerga-ma 'scatter (int)'; poje-dha-nga 'dry (tr)', cf. poje-ma 'dry (int)'; nhoco-nga 'quieten (tr)', cf. nhoco-ma 'get quiet'; me'etha-nga 'steal', cf. me'etha-ma 'hide (int)'.

3.4.13 TRANSITIVE VERBALISER (ENGLISH LOANS). Examples of verbs based on English loans include: rayt-(i)madha 'write', pee-madha 'pay', taat-imadha 'start' (transitive), wos-imadha 'wash', miks-madha 'mix', cak-imadha 'stand [someone] down, fire [someone]' cf. Eng chuck, loen-imadha / leen-imadha 'teach' cf. Eng learn All our examples are transitive verbs with the suffix we have analysed as -(i)madha. The -(i)m(a) in these verbs is undoubtedly the well-known transitive marker of Aboriginal English. It is possible that -dha is connected with the causative suffix (3.4.10[3]). In their phonological form these loans are variably assimilated. Thus /oe/ in 'teach' represents the vowel of English learn; some speakers nativise this to /ee/.

4. SYNTAX

A clause consists of a subject NP and a predicating constituent. Clauses in Nganhcara can be categorised according to whether or not they contain a verb. Verbless clauses may be further sub-categorised as existential and non-existential.

Constituents, including the subject NP and occasionally even the verb, which the speaker judges to be information shared with the addressee are frequently omitted. Such omitted constituents or other explanatory material may then be included in a coda (or postscript) to the clause. For examples of codas see T2, T3, T5, T20, etc. Although they may carry the appropriate case marking, codas appear to be afterthoughts rather than part of the speaker's clausal plan: they fall outside the intonation contour of the preceding clause. Consequently, we will continue to treat Nganhcara as strictly verb-final, while including clause codas in our examples.

The basic elements of clause structure, case-marking, and constituent order were outlined in the introduction to chapter 3. Here we investigate further aspects of Nganhcara syntax: clause structure, NP structure, subordination, coordination and various particles and enclitics.

4.1 VERBAL CLAUSES

In this section we survey the major constituents of verbal clauses. Particles and enclitics are omitted and are covered instead in 4.12 and 4.13.

4.1.1 CONSTITUENT ORDER. The verb, together with its attached enclitics (if any) is nearly always the final constituent of the verbal clause, although an embedded clause, particularly if it is heavy, often follows the verb of its matrix clause (4.7). The order of the other major constituents is relatively free. However, the elements within a single constituent such as an NP cannot usually be separated (as in some Australian languages) and have a fixed order (4.2).

4.1.2 CORE CONSTITUENTS: S, A, O. By definition, intransitive verbs take an S, while transitive verbs require an A and O. Ditransitive verbs are further subcategorised for a second object (3.4.1). Because pronouns have nominative/accusative case marking and non-pronominal NPs ergative/ absolute case marking, the three syntactic functions S, A, and O are clearly distinguished. Word order provides no information as to which NP in a transitive clause is A and which is O, since their relative positions are not fixed.

4.1.3 NON-CORE NP. Case-marked NPs may play a variety of roles, as discussed and illustrated in 3.2.1. These are summarised in Table 4.1. Only dative and ablative non-core NPs may be cross-referenced by bound pronouns; in particular, ergative indicating instrument may not be cross-referenced (3.2.1[2])

TABLE 4.1 - *Roles of Case-Marked Nps*

DATive	recipient, goal, beneficiary, purpose
ABLative	source, cause, interested party
COMitative	accompanied, possessee
PRIVative	absentee
LOCative	location
ERGative	instrument

4.1.4 ADJECTIVE PHRASE. Adjectives in intransitive clauses refer to the subject, e.g. T86; those in transitive clauses refer to the object, as in (84), (85).

(84) mayi+waya peba-ng uke-dhu puge
food etc.   wind-ERG bare-MAY uncoverPAST
The food and stuff may have been uncovered bare by the wind.

(85) nhila   pama-ng nhunha kuyu uthu-nh   pigo
3sgNOM man-ERG 3sgACC woman dead-3sgACC hitPAST
The man struck the woman dead.

4.1.5 FLOATING ABSOLUTIVE NP. Absolutive NPs bearing no clear syntactic relation will be termed FLOATING. Often these appear to bear the same semantic relation to the verb as the intransitive subject or transitive object, as in (86) - (88). In contrast to absolutive NPs bearing S or O relations, floating absolutive NPs may not be cross-referenced by bound pronouns. Thus in (88) pulan kuce, semantically a stimulus, is the object of ngee-ng and is cross-referenced by the bound pronoun -lan; kugu is also a stimulus but it is not syntactically encoded as an object of ngeeng and cannot be cross-referenced. Floating absolutive NPs may also bear a much looser relationship to the event, as in (89), (144). It is likely that many noun-verb compounds in Nganhcara have developed from this type of quasi-constituent.

(86) ngaya   kempa thaa+thayan-wi-ng
1sgNOM flesh   get tired-INCHO:PRES-1sg
I'm getting tired. / My flesh is getting tired. [Lit: I flesh am getting   tired.]

(87) nhila   nganyi ma'a pigo
[cf. 15] 3sgNOM 1sgACC hand hitPAST
He hit my hand. / He hit me on the hand.

(88) ngaya   pulan   kuce kugu-lan   ngee-ng
1sgNOM 3duACC two   speech-3duACC hear-1sg
I heard them two talking. [Lit: I heard them two speech.]

(89) nhila   pama-ng nhunha kuyu   kamu-nh   pigo
3sgNOM man-ERG 3sgACC woman blood-3sgACC hitPAST
The man hit the woman [and drew] blood.

4.1.6   ADVERBIAL. This is a functional rather than a formal category which includes adverbs such as yilim 'again' (189), karkila 'quickly' and directional adverbs (5.4.4, 5.4.5) as well as absolute demonstratives signifying time or place (38), (40), T47 and directional nouns (5.4.1, 5.4.2, 5.4.3). Absolute demonstratives and nouns functioning adverbially may only occur alone, full NPs with similar function appear in locative case.

4.1.7   ADVERBIAL PHRASE. An adverbial phrase is composed of an adverbial operator and a noun phrase. In the majority of such phrases the operator is a location nominal, and the entire adverbial phrase may take a locative case enclitic. Often the NP may either precede or follow the adverbial operator, as with koyowo in (91). The operators putha 'front; in front of' and weń ko 'side; beside' may similarly precede or follow their arguments. However, with some operators, one or the other position is preferred. For example, in (92) the NP may not be moved after kanhnyim. An NP preceded or followed by thinthu 'near' takes dative case marking, as in (93).

(90)   yuku muka pakem-ung   putpe
          THING stone below-LOC   go inPAST
          [It] went in under the stone.

(91)   yuku koce muka koyowo-ng   wunune-n
          THING lizard stone   behind-LOC   stayREDUP-PRES
[Also:]   yuku koce koyowo muka-ng wunune-n
          There's a lizard behind the stone.

(92)   yuku koce aara   muka kanhnyim(-ung)
          THING lizard   thatABS stone   on top(-LOC)
              wunune-n
              stayREDUP-PRES
          There's a lizard there on top of the stone.

(93)   nhila yuku   koce aara   thinthu muka-wu-ng
          3sgNOM THING lizard thatABS   near   stone-DAT-LOC
              wunune-n
              stayREDUP-PRES
[Also:]   nhila yuku koce aara muka-wu thinthu(-ng) wunune-n
          There's a lizard there near the stone.

An adverbial phrase of manner, meaning 'like NP' may be formed using waya (see 4.12[6]) as operator. An NP associated with waya takes dative case marking, as seen in (94). A functionally equivalent (but syntactically different) formation uses the negative ka'i as operator; see 4.10.

(94)   nhila pama aara   waya pukpe-wu paabe-n
          3sgNOM man thatABS LIKE child-DAT   cry-CNC
          That man is crying like a child.

4.2   NON-EXISTENTIAL VERBLESS CLAUSES.

Non-existential verbless clauses consist of an absolutive NP or nominative pronoun subject and a non-verbal predicate. A floating absolutive NP may also occur. The predicate is always the final constituent and may be one of several types. These are covered in the following subsections.

4.2.1   CASE-MARKED NP.   Case-marked NPs have a variety of predicative functions related to the roles they may encode.   These are summarised in Table 4.2. For illustration, see 3.2.1 and 4.6

TABLE 4.2 - *Predicative Function of Case-Marked Nps*

ABSolutive	equational, attributive
DATive	purposive beneficiary, possessive
ABLative	source, cause
COMitative	accompanied, possessee
PRIVative	absentee
LOCative	location

4.2.2   ADJECTIVE PHRASE OR QUANTIFIER.   Adjectival predicates are illustrated in (95) - (96). A quantifier predicate occurs in T42.

(95)   yengan   nhingu   unggu   moo
             hair   3sgDAT   long   more
             His hair is very long.

(96)   wa'awa   poje
             river   dry
             The river is dry.

4.2.3   LOCATIONAL OR TEMPORAL EXPRESSION.   As in verbal sentences, locational or temporal expression may be a locative NP, a locative or absolutive demonstrative, an adverb, or an adverbial phrase.   Examples follow.

(97)   mayi   suga   iiru
             VEG   sugar   thisABS
             The sugar is here. / Here is the sugar.

(98)   ngaka biya aara   yuku   jaga ngamparamu-ng
             water beer   thatABS   THING jug   1plincABL-LOC
             The beer was there in our jug

4.2.4   FLOATING ABSOLUTIVE NP.   Syntactically isolated absolutive NPs complements as constituents of verbal clauses are discussed in 4.1.5. These are also occasionally found in verbless clauses.   Compare (99) with (86).

(99)   ngaya   moo thaa+thayan
                1sgNOM body tired
                I'm tired.

4.2.5   VERBLESS CLAUSES AS BASIC CLAUSE TYPE. It would be possible to derive some of the clause types listed above from underlying structures containing verbs such as wuna 'live', nhiina 'sit', thana 'stand', or thena 'walk', especially as these verbs are occasionally used with little semantic content, as in (100), T110. However, it is not possible to find a suitable verb when the subject is inanimate (96) - (98). Moreover, verbless clauses seem to form a distinct class with respect to negation. They mostly form negatives with ya'a, while verbal clauses form negatives with ka'i (4.10) (ka'i does occur in verbless clauses, but only as a marker of the 'like NP' construction).

(100)   nhila   kaba   wiya-m   kaba   wiya-m   kaba
            3sgNOM summer other-EMPH summer other-EMPH summer
            wiya-m   kugu-yi   thenene-n
            other-EMPH speech-PRIV walkREDUP-PRES
            She goes without talking [to her daughter-in-law] year after year after year.

4.3   EXISTENTIAL CLAUSES

The only obligatory element of an existential clause is the absolute NP whose existence is affirmed or denied. In vacuo expressions of existence being rare, however, at least one modifying element is normally also present. For example (5) contains an expression of modality (101) a temporal expression and (183) a negative respectively.

(101)   manu+ngunhca   peba yoko
            morning   wind big
            There was a big wind this morning.

4.4   NOUN PHRASE

The basic structure of NPs was outlined in 3.2. Here we further investigate the structure of simple and complex non-pronominal NP, including prepositional phrases and the like. Recall that a non-pronominal NP in Nganhcara consists of one or more of the following elements in fixed order:

Generic - Noun - Adjective - Quantifier - NP - Demonstrative

where the embedded NP is a possessive (DAT or ABL), comitative or privative element. The elements of an NP are never separated by other sentential constituents, except occasionally by an associated pronoun (4.4.1). The last element of the NP carries the case marking for the whole NP. Nganhcara is thus quite different from one common type of Australian language (cf Dixon 1980:270) which allows the elements of an NP to be scattered in any order throughout the clause and which, marks every word in the NP for case. In impromptu speech, however, it is possible to find examples such as (102), (153) and (203) that are suggestive of this more common Australian type. In such examples, an appositive NP, adds information which might have been included in the original NP. Such an appositive NP carries its own case marker, and its structural relationship to the 'original' NP appears to be no different from that of the more common associated pronouns (4.4.1).

(102)   ngaya   keka nhingurum pama aman
           1sgNOM spear 3sgABL   man   thatABL
            kananu-yi-m   kala-ng
            toothREDUP-PRIV-ABL take-1sg
            I took that toothless man's spear. [Lit: I took that man's - the one without teeth's spear]

The majority of Nganhcara nouns can be preceded by a 'generic' noun (3.1.1, 5.2). The generic is usually present on first mention of the head noun (or when vocabulary is being elicited) but generics such as yuku 'THING' and agu 'PLACE, [POINT IN] TIME' are frequently absent. First person kinship terms (5.3), body parts and many words for items of material culture lack generics. We adopt the term GENERIC here for the sake of consistency among handbook descriptions. Grammatically, however, they are similar, in both syntactic position and semantics, to the numeral classifiers of languages of Asia and Central America. The main difference lies in the fact that they do not enter into any special syntactic construction with quantifiers, as is the case for the great majority of noun classifier languages which have been described up to the present. Other classifier languages, however, are like Nganhcara in possessing a system that does not interact with quantifiers in any restricted way, for example Jacaltec (Craig 1977, 1986). We regard Nganhcara as a classifier language, but not one belonging to the subset of such languages which includes those with numeral generic constructions. We have no examples of possessives cooccurring with the comitative or privative elements within the same NP; however, the possibility cannot be ruled out entirely. Note that these elements are NPs embedded within larger NPs. When they occur finally within the matrix NP, the case marker of the matrix NP follows the case marker of the embedded NP (4.4.4).

4.4.1   ASSOCIATED PRONOUN. In association with a non-pronominal NP is often found a free pronoun with the same referent. Such an associated pronoun most frequently occurs at the beginning of the NP. Less frequently it follows the NP, and occasionally it is detached from it. Examples follow:

(103)   nhila   kuyu   alang   nga'a   nhingu   pama
        3sgNOM woman thatERG fish   3sgDAT   man
          iguwu-ngu   waa
          thisDAT-3sgDAT give
       That woman gave a fish to this man.

(104)   thana   kuyu-ng   nhunha pama pigo-dhan
         3plNOM woman-ERG 3sgACC man   hit-3plPAST
         The women hit the man.

4.4.2   NUMBER. Although number is not marked on the non-pronominal
NP itself, the number of many NPs is indicated in the morphosyntax of the
clause by associated pronouns (3.3.1), cross-referencing pronouns (3.3.2) or
verbal concord. (3.4.3, 3.4.4). As noted in 3.4.3, NPs low on the animacy
hierarchy do not trigger plural verb agreement (59), (60), (105), (184); they
may, however, be cross-referenced by bound pronouns that reflect their
number (106).

(105)   yuku watha-ng   pudha yumpumpe-n
[Mm]   THING green ant-ERG nest   makeREDUP-CNC
         Green ants build nests.

(106)   yuku watha-ran   pigo-ng
[Mm]   THING green ant-3plACC hitPAST-1sg
         I hit the green ants.

4.4.3   CASE MARKING I: CLITICS AS CASE MARKERS. The form
and function of case marking in Nganhcara were discussed in 3.2. Here we
examine its morphosyntax. The purpose of this first section is to provide
evidence that the case markers in Nganhcara are in fact clitics. The use of
clitics to mark case is rarely reported, not only in studies of Australian
languages, but also in the wider general literature on clitics. In some
instances this may be due to a reluctance to analyze case markers as clitics, or
because of the ambiguous status of case markers - an element which is
always found at the end (beginning) of an NP can often be analysed as either
a postposition (preposition) or as an enclitic (proclitic). It is therefore of
considerable theoretical interest that in Nganhcara there is a set of case
markers which are unequivocally enclitics. Certainly the marking of case by
enclitics should not be considered an unnatural or unexpected phenomenon.
The common diachronic development of case affixes from prior adpositions
implies an equally common transitional clitic phase. Indeed, as we have
seen, the transition to morphology has already taken place with the
Nganhcara demonstratives (3.2.2 see also further discussion in 4.4.5 below).
        Examples (107) - (110) demonstrate that the ergative and dative case
markers -ng and -wu   attach to the last element of their noun phrase.
Because of the optionality of most constituents of the NP, the last element of
an NP does not belong to any fixed syntactic class: in (107) -ng and -wu
attach to nouns, in (108) to adjectives, in (109), to quantifiers and in (110) to
possessive (embedded ablative) NPs. Since these case markers do not
consistently follow words of any one syntactic class, they are not formally
suffixes. Their syntactic position is defined relative to the entire NP, rather
than to one of its constituents (such as the head), but they cannot be treated as
full independent words, since they are not phonologically independent: -ng
and -wu are not possible word-shapes in Nganhcara. As phonologically
dependent forms whose syntactic position is defined relative to a constituent

larger than a word, they are clitics, in particular enclitics, since they cliticise
to the end of their host.

(107)   nhila pama-ng nhingu pukpe-wu ku'a-nguwaa
      3sgNOM man-ERG 3sgDAT child-DAT dog-3sgDAT give
      The man gave a dog to the child.

(108)   nhila pama yoko-ng nhingu pukpe mepenu-wu
      3sgNOM man big-ERG 3sgDAT child little-DAT
       ku'a-ngu waa
       dog-3sgDAT give
      The big man gave a dog to the little child.

(109)   pula pama yoko kuce-ng thaaran pukpe mepen
      3duNOM man big two-ERG 3plDAT child little
       ko'ele-wu ku'a-ran waa
       three-DAT dog-3plDAT give
      The two big men gave a dog to the three little children.

(110)   pula ngathunye kuce nhingkurumu-ng thaaran pukpe
      3duNOM B+   two 2sgABL-ERG   3plDAT child

       mepen ko'ele ngathurumu-wu ku'a-ran waa
       small three 1sgABL-DAT   dog-3plDAT give
      Your two elder brothers gave my three little children a dog.

   Exactly the same arguments, mutatis mutandis, can be used to
establish that the other regular case markers in Nganhcara are also enclitics.
Thus in (111) the ablative marker -m appears on both a noun and an adjective
(in two separate NPs), and in (112) it is attached to an adverbial operator
(4.1.7). Similarly, the privative marker -yi appears on a (compound) noun
in (113) and on a possessive in (114). Finally, in (115) the comitative
marker -ra appears on a quantifier, while in (116) it is attached to an
adjective.

(111)   nhila pama-ng nhunha ku'a nhingurum pukpe
      3sgNOM man-ERG 3sgACC dog 3sgABL   child
       mepenu-m puranci-m waka
       little-ABL-ABS humpy-ABL chase
      The man chased the little child's dog from the humpy.

(112)   yuku koce yuku muka yoko pakemu-m
      THING lizard-ABS THING rock big under-ABL
       thape
       come outPAST
      The lizard came out from under the big rock.

(113) nhila kuyu mayi+minha-yi nhiiniine-n
       3sgNOM woman-ABS vegetable+meat-PRIV sitREDUP-PRES
       The woman is sitting without any food.

(114) nhila ku'a nhingurumu-yi uwa
       3sgNOM dog 3sgABL-PRIV go
       He went without his dog.

(115) nhila pama ku'a uyu-ra uwa
       3sgNOM man-ABS dog many-COM go
       The man went with many dogs.

(116) nhila pukpe yuku yinje-ra putpe
       3sgNOM child-ABS clothing wet-COM come inPAST
       The child came in with wet clothing.

4.4.4 CASE MARKING II: SEQUENCES OF CASE-MARKING ENCLITICS.
Consider the following two facts (3.2, 4.4):
- case marking appears on the last element of an NP
- the structure of an NP provides for an embedded NP carrying case marking for possessive (DAT or ABL), comitative or privative

Now consider the situation in which an embedded NP is the last element of the matrix NP. We should expect to find a sequence of two case-markers, the first marking the relationship of the embedded NP to its matrix, the second marking the syntactic role of the NP in a larger construction. This is indeed what we find; in (117) for example, the dative marker -wu, belonging to the matrix NP whose head is pukpe, encliticises to the ablative marker -mu, which marks the embedded noun kuyu as a possessor. The structure of the complex NP is as follows:

[NP pukpe [NP kuyu]NP -mu]NP -wu.

More generally, we expect to find sequences of case markers in which the first is DAT, ABL, COM or PRIV, and the second is unrestricted. Some of the possibilities are seen in (42), (117) - (120), (102).

(117) pama-ng pukpe kuyu-mu-wu ku'a-ngu waa
       man-ERG child woman-ABL-DAT dog-3sgDAT give
       The man gave a dog to the woman's child.

(118) pama keka puganhum-nhja-ng minha thuthamba
[Mm]   man-ERG spear new-COM-ERG ANIMAL wallaby
          yeta
          spear
       The man with the new spear speared the wallaby.

(119) nhila pama ku'a pukpe-m-yi uwa
       3sgNOM man dog child-ABL-PRIV go
       The man went without the child's dog.

(120)   yuku koce thiinthu muka-wu-ng nhiiniine-n
           THING lizard near   rock-DAT-LOC   sit-PRES
           The lizard is sitting near the rock.

4.4.5   CASE MARKING III: THE IRREGULAR DEMONSTRATIVE FORMS.

The irregular forms of the demonstratives (3.2.2) may favour a morphological treatment of case-marked demonstratives; in particular the following would be problems in a purely syntactic treatment.

- the stem alternants iiru/ilu-/igu- etc. in the absolutive, ergative and dative.
- the metathesised ablative and locative forms imun, ingun etc.

Case markers attached to other constituents of NPs may, however, still be treated as enclitics. There is no requirement that the form of a given morpheme be always a separate word, always an affix or always a clitic, and the languages of the world provide many instances of morphemes which have different formal realisations depending on context. In general, contractions involve such formal ambivalence, and contracted forms often involve special allomorphs of the combining morphemes. For example, the English morphemes combined in the morphological formation *won't* can be realised as the separate words *will* and *not*.

4.4.6   CASE MARKING IV: IMPLICATIONS FOR THE STATUS OF PRIVATIVE AND COMITATIVE.

The equivalents of the comitative and privative in other Australian languages (comitative is often called PROPRIETIVE or 'HAVING') have generally been assumed to be 'derivational' in nature and thus distinct from the case system. (Thus for example one of the sessions of the 1974 conference on 'Grammatical Categories in Australian Languages' (Dixon 1976) was entitled 'The derivational affix "having"'. The same view is put forward in Dixon 1980:324f., and the guide for contributors to the *Handbook* lists them (n.d. 20-21) as 'two derivational affixes that occur in almost all languages of the continent'.) Our analysis of the corresponding Nganhcara forms as inflectional, first put forward in Smith and Johnson 1979, proved controversial. It is therefore necessary to provide justification for our treatment here.

Much ink has been expended on the problematical nature of the derivational/inflectional distinction, and we will not belabour the issue here more than to repeat the two most salient points. First, the distinction as seen by the classical grammarians is in some respects arbitrary. Second, no matter how one attempts to draw the line, there will be intermediate cases. Most modern writers take the position that the traditional distinction should be scrapped (or reinterpreted) in favour of a less arbitrary one between lexical and grammatical.

The Nganhcara comitative and privative are clearly grammatical rather than lexical for the following reasons.

- As enclitics, they are a priori grammatical units and not part of the lexical derivation of a word
- They are part of the (grammatical) system of case markers which exhibit identical properties: (i) phonological dependency; (ii) common syntactic position (at the end of their NP); (iii) common function, viz. to mark the

- role of the NP in a larger construction (iv) productivity; and (v) semantic regularity.

In addition to these two general arguments, a more specific argument flows from consideration examples in which the comitative and privative morphemes attach to an element other than the head noun of the NP they are marking, as in (38), (118), (119), (121), (122), (141). In such examples, it is clear that they express the syntactic role of the entire NP, not just of the element to which they attach. In other words, their function is a syntactic one — to signal the relationship of an NP within a larger construction — rather than a lexical one of deriving a new lexical item from an adjective, inflected pronoun, quantifier etc.

(121)   pama aara   ku'a uyu-ra
          man   thatABS dog   many-COM
          That man has many dogs.

(122)   ngaya   minha   keńke pi'an-yi
[Mm]   1sgNOM   ANIMAL fish   big-PRIV
          I haven't got any big fish.

These arguments stand in spite of the possibility that in a few instances, an expression involving a privative or comitative affix has become lexicalised and derivational affixes may be added to it, in apparent violation of the 'inflection outermost' principle, as in English *gutsy, artsy, ballsy*. The only such example we know of in Nganhcara is the inchoative kugu-yi-wi 'become quiet', based on the lexicalised kugu-yi (voice-PRIV) 'quiet'.

In their examination of the larger issue of the status of multiple case-marking in Australian languages, Dench and Evans (1988) argue that productivity, semantic regularity and phrasal scope establish the inflectional status of case-markers followed by other case-markers. From a broader typological perspective, the possibility of sequences of inflectional case-markers is nothing strange, as the papers in Plank (1988) attest.

4.5   WORD-LEVEL DERIVATIONS

A number of derivational affixes affect the subcategorisation frame of verbs in Nganhcara. The reciprocal affix removes one argument from the frame; the various causative affixes on the other hand introduce a new argument into the subcategorisation frame. Causative affixes also attach to a variety of non-verbal stems to create transitive verbs; inchoatives do the same to create intransitive verbs. Nganhcara lacks passive or antipassive constructions. Free word order and the optional omission of constituents allows Nganhcara to achieve the discourse functions of these formations without morphological apparatus, nor does the language possess the constraints on coordination or subordination which in some languages require their use.

4.5.1   RECIPROCAL. The formation of reciprocal verbs is discussed in 3.4.9. A reciprocal verb is sufficient to mark the clause as reciprocal, but a reflexive pronoun (3.3.1) may also optionally be present. In many Australian languages reciprocal verbs are always intransitive (Blake 1987:57) and the same is usually true in Nganhcara. Essentially, the addition of the reciprocal affix removes one of the arguments of the predication. Usually the removed argument is the one that is encoded as O (e.g. patient), so that an intransitive verb results, even when a reflexive pronoun is used. Compare, for example, the reciprocal and non-reciprocal pairs in (123)/(124), (125)/(126), and (127) /(128); (123) may also be compared with (52). With some verbs, however, the removed argument is not the one encoded as O, and in this case the resultant reciprocal is transitive, as in (129). Similarly a reciprocal derived from a ditransitive verb is monotransitive, since only one of the arguments encoded as O is removed; compare (130) and (80).

(123)   pula   pama kuce pulanmala-la   yent-o
          3duNOM   man   two   3duREFL-3duNOM spear-RECIP
          Those two men speared each other.

(124)   pula   pama kuce-ng minha   pangku-la   yenta
          3duNOM   man   two-ERG ANIMAL   wallaby-3duNOM spear
          Those two men speared a wallaby.

(125)   thana   ku'a   ko'ele aara   (thaaranmala)
          3plNOM   dog   three   thatABS   3plREFL
              pothoth-o-dhan
              biteREDUP-RECIP-3plPAST
          Those three dogs were biting each other.

(126)   thana   ku'a   ko'ele-ng nhunha pathatha-dhan
          3plNOM   dog   three-ERG   3sgACC biteREDUP-3plPAST
          Those three dogs are biting him.

(127)   ngana   yuku   muka-ng-na   pek-o
          1duNOM   THING   stone-ERG-1duNOM   throw at-RECIP
          We hit each other with stones. / We threw stones at each other.

(128)   pukpe-ng yuku   muka-ng   kuyu-nha   peka
          chile-ERG   THING stone   woman-3sgACC   throw at
          The child hit the woman with a stone. / The child threw a stone at the woman.

(129)   pula   kuyu   kuce alang   yengan-la   umpump-o
          3duNOM   woman   two   thatERG   hair-3duNOM cutREDUP-RECIP
          Those two women are cutting each other's hair.

(130)   pula   pama alang yuku   keene-la
          3duNOM   man thatERG THING tobacco-3duNOM
          kookoo,   pulanmala
          promiseRECIP:REDUP   3duREFL
          Those two men promised each other tobacco.

4.5.2   INCHOATIVE. The structure of inchoatives is described in 3.4.11. Inchoatives are intransitive verbs derived from adjectives (86), (131), or more rarely case-marked nouns (217), particles (132) or quantifiers (133).

(131)   keka kuurul-we
          spear bent-INCHO:PAST
          The spear got bent.

(132)   keene kana-thurum ka'im-we
[Yi]   tobacco PERF-1sgABL NEG-INCHO:PAST
          I've run out of tobacco. [Lit. The tobacco has run out on me.]

(133)   ngula yamang-ni   iiru   nganhca   kuwa+yi'i-ng-nhca
          then thus-SUBORD thisABS 1plexcNOM   beach-LOC-1plexcNOM
          thooron-we
          one-INCHO:PAST
          Then we used to gather here on the beach.

4.5.3   CAUSATIVE. The structure of causatives is described in 3.4.10. the various causative affixes derive transitive verbs from nouns (134), adjectives (135), adverbs (136), quantifiers (137) and intransitive verbs (138). When a causative suffix is added to an intransitive verb, it produces a transitive verb, whose O normally corresponds to the S of the intransitive. This is not always the case, however, as in nhunpa-nga 'run with [something]', T128, from nhunpa 'run'.

(134)   ngaya   thaaran   umuń -nga-ng
          1sgNOM   3plACC   chest-CAUS-1sg
          I met them.

(135)   thana   minha uthul-nga-dhan
          3plNOM   animal dead-CAUSE-3plPAST
          They killed the animal.

(136)   ngaya   nhunha pala-nga-ng
          1sgNOM   3sgACC hither-CAUS-1sg
          I made him come here.

(137)   thana   minha kucel-nga-dhan
          3plNOM   meat   two-CAUS-3plPAST
          They divided the meat in two.

(138)   ngaya   mayi kana   minji-nga-ng
        1sgNOM   food   PERF   finish(int)-CAUS-1sg
        I finished the food.

4.6   POSSESSION

No distinction is made between alienable and inalienable possession. The ablative is used most frequently within an NP and the dative most frequently as a predicate (4.2.1). Examples follow.

thuli $\left\{\begin{matrix}\text{nhingurum}\\\text{nhingu}\end{matrix}\right\}$ ngaci $\left\{\begin{matrix}\text{nhingkurum}\\\text{nhingku}\end{matrix}\right\}$

woomera   3sg$\left\{\begin{matrix}\text{ABL}\\\text{DAT}\end{matrix}\right\}$ father   2sg$\left\{\begin{matrix}\text{ABL}\\\text{DAT}\end{matrix}\right\}$

his woomera   your father

(139)   ku'a K-n-ngu
        dog   K-DAT-3sgDAT
        The dogs are K's.

Possession may also be signalled by means of a predicative comitative NP, as in (140), (141).

(140)   minha   thuthamba   mulu-nhja
[Mm]   ANIMAL   wallaby   tail-COM
        Wallabies have tails.

(141)   X,nhila   ku'a-ra, ku'a uyu-nhja
        3sgNOM   dog-COM   dog many-COM
        X, she has dogs — [she] has many dogs.

4.7   SUBORDINATION

Nganhcara, like some other Australian languages, is not richly endowed with subordinating devices; rather it makes extensive use of parataxis to convey what in other languages might be expressed by means of subordination. Some examples follow. In the idiomatic glosses of these examples we give first a clause-by-clause translation, then one or more complex-sentence translations.

(142)   ngaya   ngangka+wayaya-ma.   mayi, yuku, ngathurum
        1sgNOM   sadREDUP-EMPH   FOOD THING 1sgABL
           ngaya   wanta-nga. ngaya   ngangka+wayaya-ma
           1sgNOM   leave-1sg   1sgNOM   sadREDUP-EMPH
        [Context: A cyclone has recently passed by, and the speaker is worried that a cache of food and belongings she left at a distant camp may have been destroyed.] I am really sad. I left my food and belongings. I'm really sad. /

I'm really upset about having left my food and belongings. [Note that the SECOND element of ngangka+waya undergoes reduplication.]

(143)   ngaya   kanana-m   ka'im-ngu   thawa-ng.
        1sgNOM PERF:REDUP-EMPH   NEG-3sgDAT tell-1sg
           nhila   mayi waya+mini-monh
           3sgNOM   FOOD   goods-NONFACT
           uwi-nh-monh-cara
           see-IRR-NONFACT-1plexcABL
[Context: as above; one of the speaker's relatives had left on a trip that morning and would be passing the camp referred to.] I didn't tell him! He could have looked at our food and belongings. / I should have told him to check on our food and belongings!

(144)   pukpe mapan kugu   paawaawe-n.
[Mm]   child   small   voice   cryREDUP-CNC
           nhila   angge+nhala
           3sgNOM   tired
The small child is crying [because] it is tired.

(145)   thawa-ngu. nhila   pala-ku uwa-wu
        tell-3sgDAT 3sgNOM   hither-IMP come-IMP
Tell him. Let him come this way. / Tell him to come here.

(146)   ngaya   ngonggolo. nhila   agu ngaari thangke
[Mm]   1sgNOM don't know   3sgNOM time what   arrivePAST
I don't know. What time did he arrive? / I don't know what time he arrived.

(147)   nhila   keka yumpe.   nhila   minha   pangku
        3sgNOM spea r makePAST 3sgNOM   ANIMAL wallaby
           waya-pa yenta-nha
           LIKE-FUT spear-IRR
He made a spear. He wanted to spear a wallaby. / He made a spear so that he could spear a wallaby. / He made a spear because he wanted to spear a wallaby.

(148)   ngaya   pama-nh   uwe-ng.   (nhila) nga'a yenta
        1sgNOM man-3sgACC   seePAST-1sg 3sgNOM   fish   spear
I saw the man. (He) speared a fish. / I saw the man spear a fish.

(149)   ngaya   ngate nhala-thu   thangke. ngaya   nhingu
        1sgNOM bone   tired-1sgDAT arrivePAST 1sgNOM 3sgDAT
           kububi-ng
           waitPRES:REDUP-1sg
I'm fed up. [Lit: I bones tiredness arrived to me.] I'm waiting for him. / I'm fed up with waiting for him.

In the sections which follow we survey the various types of complex sentences in Nganhcara.

4.7.1 GENERAL SUBORDINATE CLAUSE WITH -ni. Nganhcara has a general-purpose subordinate clause which is marked by the subordinator -ni, a pre/post-verbal enclitic. The function of a -ni clause is to indicate any kind of background information. It is often only a sentence fragment, equivalent to a postscripted coda. The English equivalent may range from a syntactically separate parenthetical remark to a fully integrated subordinate clause such as a relative, purposive, or temporal. A similar type of multi-purpose subordinate clause is found in many Australian languages (cf. Hale 1976b).

We note in passing that -ni also occurs in the idiomatic combinations ngula nhaaru-ni (lit. then thatABS-SUBORD, cf. 4.1.6) and ngula nhamun-ni (lit. 'then thatABL-SUBORD). Both may be translated as 'and then...'. Examples are frequent in Text 1.

[1] -ni *Clause as Relative Clause.* One common function of the -ni clause is as a relative clause (modifying an NP). This type of -ni clause is the most syntactically integrated into its matrix clause. The following general characteristics of the relative -ni clauses can be observed:

- It is positioned directly after the NP it modifies.
- Within the -ni clause the coreferential NP is absent or pronominalised.
- In the part of the matrix clause which follows the relative -ni clause, the head NP is repeated, usually as a resumptive pronoun or demonstrative.

In the following illustrations, the relative -ni clauses are enclosed in square brackets; for further examples see T11, T49, T128.

(150)   pama [kuyu ngaya-n-ngu   wanta-ng] nhaaru
[=T136] man woman 1sgNOM-SUBORD-3sgDAT leave-1sg   thatABS
         nhunpa
         run

That man, who I left a woman to, ran up [to us]. I.e. My son-in-law came running up.

(151)   nhaaru nhila   pukpe puyawa   nhunpa, agawu,   agawu
[=T150] thatABS 3sgNOM   child eastward run   thatDAT thatDAT
         [pama+muwa L-n   wunune-n]
         OLD MAN   L-SUBORD live-PRES

Then the boy ran off to the east, to there, to where old man L lives.

[2] *Other* -ni *Clauses.* Non-relative -ni clauses are less syntactically integrated than relative -ni clauses. They occupy no particular syntactic slot in their matrix clauses, interrupt their matrix clauses less frequently, and are usually placed directly before or after them. As mentioned above, a wide variety of functions are served by -ni clauses. (152) - (155) illustrate temporal -ni clauses; we continue the practice of bracketing the -ni clause. For further exemplification, see T4, T8, T11. (154) may be interpreted either temporally or causally. In many languages

temporals may be used to express conditions and this is also true in Nganhcara (155). For another conditional formation, see 4.8.3. The -ni clauses in (156) and (210) have the status of parenthetical remarks, and their syntactic ties with their hosts are not strong; cf. also T17, T41, T88, T112.

(152)   [ngaya nga'a-wu-n   uwa-ng] ngaya
          1sgNOM fish-DAT-SUBORD go-1sg   1sgNOM
            pama ko'ele-ran   uwe-nga
            man   three-3plACC seePAST-1sg
          When I went fishing [lit. for fish] I met [lit. saw] three men.

(153)   [ngaya puyu-n   uwa-ng] nhinta
          1sgNOM away-SUBORD go-1sg   2sgNOM
            thepa+panci nhaaru nhingkurum-l umpi, koyowo
            beard   thatABS 2sgABL-THEN cut   after
          After I go, cut [i.e. shave off] your beard.

(154)   ngaya   kanana-m-nha   pigo-ng
          1sgNOM PERF:REDUP-EMPH-3sgACC hitPAST-1sg
          [nganyi ngula patha-ni]
          1sgACC then   bite-SUBORD
          I hit it [a mosquito] before it [could] bite me. / I hit it because it was going to bite me.

(155)   [nhila puyu-m-ni-pa   mume-n] epa ngaya
[Mm]   3sgNOM away-EMPH-SUBORD-FUT go-PAST   AFF 1sgNOM
          ngangka+wada
          sad
          If/When he goes away, I'll really be sad.

(156)   ngathunye ya'a [ngaya-n   ma'a-ma]. ngathake
          B⁺   NEG 1sgNOM-SUBORD more-EMPH B⁻
          Context: [One of the authors had told the speaker that he had met her elder brother while on a visit to Aurukun.] Not [my] elder brother. I'm older. Younger brother!

    In order to achieve a more unitary analysis of -ni clauses, it would be possible to view them all as parenthetical remarks giving background information. The position of relative -ni clauses could be predicted from pragmatic considerations: they contain information germane to a single constituent, rather than to the entire host clause. Note too that the head NP and the relative -ni clause are generally found either at the beginning of the clause, or else in a postscript. In the former position, the remainder of the host clause is in any case an independent syntactic unit because of the repetition of the head NP. Finally the pronominalisation or omission of the coreferential NP within the -ni clause is predictable from the general tendency in Nganhcara to omit constituents which are clear from the context .

4.7.2   INFINITIVAL SUBORDINATE CLAUSES.   A second type of subordinate clause in Nganhcara is constructed by attaching a case marker to a clause containing an infinitive (3.4.8).   Only dative and privative marked infinitives occur in our data. We deal with each of these in turn.

[1] *DATive Infinitival Clause.*   A dative infinitival clause has several functions, which correspond to functions of dative NPs (3.2.1[3]). (157) - (161) illustrate a purposive function.   When the dependent clause consists of the infinitive alone, it may come before the matrix verb, while heavy dependent clauses tend to follow it. As (159) shows, the subject of the embedded clause need not be the same as the subject of the matrix clause. We have no clear examples in which the subject of the embedded infinitive is expressed overtly. For example, the fact that ngampara in (159) is dative makes it more likely to be beneficiary adjunct of yenta than the subject of mungga-nh; in (160) it is not clear whether nhila is the subject of the matrix clause or of the embedded clause.   Pre/post-verbal enclitics in infinitival clauses must attach preverbally, rather than to the infinitive; however, such enclitics belonging to the matrix clause may, as in (160) attach to the inflected infinitive of the embedded clause, provided it is in the appropriate position. If nhila is the subject of the matrix clause in (160), we have the very interesting situation in which an enclitic (-nyi) is attached to an element which is not a constituent of the same clause.   Certain adjectives may take a purposive dative infinitival clause as a complement, as in (161)

(157)   ngaya   thuca-nga   mayi   yampim wa'i-nhu-wu
[Mm]   1sgNOM bend over-1sg VEG   yam   dig-INF-DAT
           I'm bending over to dig up yams.

(158)   ngaya   munji-nh-wu uwa-ng
           1sgNOM bathe-INF-DAT   go-1sg
           I'm going to bathe.

(159)   nhila   ngampara   mungga-nh-wu yenta
           3sgNOM 1plincDAT   eat-INF-DAT   spear
           He speared [it] for us to eat.

(160)   nhila-nyi   uwi-nh-wu-thu   thangke
           3sgNOM-1sgACC   see-INF-DAT-1sgDAT   arrivePAST
           He came to see me. (Lit. He arrived to me [in order] to see me.)

(161)   mayi pungga yuku imun   wanthi mungga-nhu-wu
           VEG   fruit   tree   thisABL good   eat-INF-DAT
           The fruit of this tree is good to eat.

The second function of the dative infinitival clause, illustrated in (162) - (164) is to serve as (non-purposive) complement of certain verbs and predicative adjectives. The dependent clause normally follows the verb or adjective.

(162)   nhila   ngathu thawa   nhunha   pigu-nhu-wu
[Mm]   3sgNOM   1sgDAT tellPAST   3sgACC   hit-INF-DAT
        He told me to hit her.

(163)   ngaya   ngonggolo   minha   wici-nhu-wu
[Mm]   1sgNOM   don't know   fish   catch-INF-DAT
        I don't know how to catch fish.

(164)   ngaya   kanggu   ka'i   (ngaya)   ingun-ma   nhiina-nh-wu
        1sgNOM   want   NEG   1sgNOM   thisLOC-EMPH   sit-INF-DAT
        I don't want to stay here.

Note that (162) may also be rendered paratactically as (165). However, it is not clear whether the two sentences are precise equivalents: it may be, for example, that the second implicates that I intend to hit her while the first does not. When the verb is thawa 'tell', a further paratactic possibility is available, using the IMPerative particle (ma)ku (4.13[4]) as in (145). Again, the precise difference between this and the other two constructions is not clear.

(165)   nhila   ngathu thawa   ngaya   nhunha
        3sgNOM   1sgDAT tellPAST   1sgNOM   3sgACC
           pigu-ng-pa-nha
           hitPRES-1sg-FUT-3sgACC
        He told me he would hit her. [Lit: He told me. I will hit her.]

[2] *PRIVative Infinitival Clause.* The privative marker -yi may attach either to the infinitive or to the bare stem of the verb, with no apparent difference in meaning. When the infinitive is used, elision of the final vowel of the infinitive marker -nha (3.4.8) yields the cluster nh-y, which optionally assimilates to nh-j. When the bare stem of the verb is used, this possibility does not arise. These alternatives are illustrated in (166). Note that clausal negation within the infinitival clause is obligatory when the privative marker is present. A privative infinitival clause may fill the slot of a privative NP both in verbal sentences (166) and in non-verbal sentences (167). A verbless sentence containing a privative infinitival clause may function as a negative imperative (168).

(166)   ngaya   pala   mayi ka'i   mungga-nh$\begin{Bmatrix} \text{-y i} \\ \text{-j i} \end{Bmatrix}$ uwa-ng
        1sgNOM   hither   food   NEG   eat-INF-PRIV   come-1sg
        I came without eating.
[Also:]   ngaya   pala   mayi ka'i mungga-yi uwa-ng

(167)   ngaya   minha   pangku   ka'i   yenta-nh-ji
        1sgNOM   ANIMAL   wallaby   NEG   spear-INF-PRIV
        I've never speared a wallaby.

(168)   minha   thuthamba ka'i   umpi-nh-ji
[Mm]   ANIMAL wallaby   NEG   cut-INF-PRIV
          Don't cut up the wallaby.

4.8   COORDINATION

4.8.1   CONJOINED NPs. Conjunction of NPs, is achieved by simply including both NPs in the sentence (they need not be together) along with the appropriate pronoun for the conjoined NP.   This pronoun is optionally repeated before each constituent (non-pronominal) NP of the conjunction, as in the first example below.   When one of the constituents of the conjunction is predictable from the pronoun representing the conjoined NP, it need not be represented explicitly, as in (170) - (171).   In (170), for example, the dual pronoun subsumes both ngathunye and the unexpressed nhinta '2sgNOM'. Note that the ethical dative construction (4.13[3]) also yields structures which may be glossed as conjoined NPs.

[Yi]   pula   X   pula   Y
          3duNOM X   3duNOM Y
          X and Y

(169)   ngaya   nga'a-wu pama kunhji nhingurum   ngana
          1sgNOM fish-DAT   man   brother 3sgABL   1duexcNOM
                   uwa
                   go
          His brother and I are going for fish. / I'm going fishing with his brother.

(170)   ngathunye puranci-wu nhipa   wico
          B+   humpy-DAT   2duNOM go
          [My] elder brother and you are going to the humpy. / [My] elder brother is going to the humpy with you.

(171)   agu iiru   nganana   ngathidhe ngathurumu-wu
          land   thisABS   1duexcDAT mother   1sgABL-DAT
          This land belongs to me and my mother.

4.8.2   CLAUSAL CONJUNCTION. Simple conjunction and disjunction at the clausal level is traditionally achieved by parataxis alone, as seen in (172) - (174). An innovative alternative construction for disjunction uses the borrowed English conjunction, oo 'or', T11.   Note that English often uses conjunction to encode   sequential events.   In Nganhcara such temporal sequence may, as in (173) - (174) be indicated by the inclusion of an adverb such as ngula 'then, afterwards' or the preverbal enclitic -li (4.12[9]).

(172)   nhila   nganyi muka-ng peka.   nganyi
[Mm]   3sgNOM 1sgACC stone-ERG   throw at 1sgACC
                   walunga-nyi
                   miss-1sgACC
          He threw a stone at me [but] he missed me.

(173)   nhila   pama aara   ingun   thangke.   (ngula)
          3sgNOM   man   thatABS   thisLOC   arrivePAST   then
          puranci kadhja. ngula nhila   iiru-ma
          humpy   build   then   3sgNOM   thisABS-EMPH
          wunune-n
          liveREDUP-PRES
          That man came here and built a humpy and now he's living here.

(174)   nhila   pama ingun   thangke.   (ngula) kuyu   ilung
          3sgNOM   man   thisLOC   arrivePAST   then   woman   thisERG
          pindh+eka-nha pigo
          head-3sgACC   hitPAST
          The man came here and the woman hit him on the head.

4.8.3   CONDITIONALS.   Conditional sentences as a functional class do
not constitute a homogeneous structural type.   Implicational relationships
between clauses may be expressed using a -ni clause (4.7.1), as in (155), or
the relationship may be expressed paratactically, as in (175).   However, two
formations — future conditions and irrealis conditions — are structurally
unique.

(175)   nhinta   thuli   nhingurum-pa   kalu-ngan;   nhila
          2sgNOM   woomera   3sgABL-FUT   take-2sgPRES   3sgNOM
          takake-n-pa
          get angryREDUP-CNC-FUT
          You will take his woomera; he will get angry. / If you take his woomera, he
          will get angry.

          [1] *Future Conditions.*   The FUTure particle (yu)pa   (4.12[2])
augmented by the EMPHatic enclitic -ma   (4.13[1]) in the protasis (condition
clause) yields a future condition, as in the examples below.   Although
(yu)pa-ma has no other use, future conditions do not require it, and may be
rendered with the future particle alone: compare (176) with (175).

(176)   nhinta   thuli   nhingu-pa-m-ngu   kalu-ngan,
          2sgNOM   woomera   3sgDAT-FUT-EMPH-3sgDAT   take-2sgPRES
          nhila   koyowo-li-pa   takake-n
          3sgNOM   afterwards-THEN-FUT   get angryREDUP-CNC
          If you take his woomera, then he'll get angry afterwards.

(177)   nhila   pala-pa-m   wań ke-n, nhila
[Mm]   3sgNOM   hither-FUT-EMPH   return-CNC   3sgNOM
          ngangka+wada
          sad
          If he comes back, she'll be sad.

(178)   ngaka ka'im yupa-m   anhce-n, ngampa   biya-wu
           rain NEG   FUT-EMPH fall-CNC 1plincNOM beer-DAT
           wico-mu
           go-1plIMP
           If it doesn't rain, let's go for beer.

[2] *Irrealis Conditions and Results.* An irrealis protasis is marked by the NONFACTual enclitic -monh (4.12[7]) accompanied by waya 'LIKE' (4.12[6]) and an irrealis verb. An irrealis apodosis (result clause) contains -monh plus an irrealis verb.

(179)   nhinta thuli   waya-dhu-monh-ngurum   kali-nhun,
           2sgNOM woomera LIKE-MAY-NONFACT-3sgABL take-2sgIRR
           ngula nhila   takaki-nh-monh
           then 3sgNOM   get angryREDUP-IRR-NONFACT
           If you had taken his woomera, he would have got angry.

4.9   POLAR INTERROGATIVES

In both verbal and verbless clauses, polar interrogatives are distinguished from affirmative sentences by rising versus falling intonation alone. Thus the structure of (180) - (181) is that of the corresponding affirmatives; see also (60). Since indefinites also function as interrogatives (3.3.5), polar questions containing indefinites must be distinguished from WH-questions. The AFFirmation particle epa (4.12[5]) usually appears in the former, (180).

(180)   nhinta pama wiya wayi epa-ran   uwe-n?
           2sgNOM man other anyone AFF-3plACC see-CNC
           Did you see anyone?

(181)   ngaci nhingku iiru?
[cf. 97]   father 2sgDAT   thisABS
           Is your father here?

4.10   NEGATION

Verbal sentences are negated with the particle ka'i(m),   placed before a verb (182), T73. The optional -m is likely a reduced form of the EMPHatic enclitic -ma   (4.13[1]).   The particle ya'a negates verbless sentences, as in (35), (183); ya'a is also found with the meaning 'nothing' and as a interjection meaning 'no'; this last function is shared with the form ka'e.   Exceptionally, certain verbless clauses expressing physical and emotional states are negated with ka'i (9), (164).

(182)   nhila   nga'a ka'im yenta. nhila   nga'a'a-yi   yupa
        3sgNOM fish NEG spear 3sgNOM fishREDUP-PRIV FUT
        wań ke-n
        return-CNC
        He didn't spear any fish. He'll come back without any fish.

(183)   nga'a ya'a
        fish   NEG
        There aren't any fish.

A second common function of ka'i is as an NP operator meaning 'LIKE'. The semantic connection between the two meanings of ka'i is that if X is merely LIKE Y, then X is NOT Y. An NP modified by ka'i retains the case-marking appropriate to its syntactic role in the clause. For example, in (184) the NP fishing+neta is locational and thus takes the locative case. In this behaviour, ka'i contrasts with the operator waya (4.12[6]). Note that this function of ka'i is used even in verbless clauses (187), (188), which form their negatives with ya'a.

(184)   ngula nhaaru nga'a nhangun wipa.
        then thatABS fish thatLOC get caught.
        ka'i fishing+neta-ng wipipa
        LIKE fishing net-LOC   get caughtREDUP
        Then the fish get caught in that [a traditional fish trap]. They get caught like in a fishing net.

(185)   nhila   pukpe ka'i pama   yumonh   kuli-wu
        3sgNOM child LIKE man   thus   anger-DAT
        thawawe-n
        seekREDUP-CNC
        The boy is looking for a fight like a man. [I.e. the boy is trying to act like a man by going around picking fights.]

(186)   ngaya   ka'i pama   pala   uwa-ng
        1sgNOM   LIKE man   hither go-1sg
        I'd like to be a man.

(187)   yuku iiru   buk ka'i ngathurum
        THING thisABS book LIKE 3singABL
        This book looks like mine.

(188)   yuku kantu nhaaru ka'i weenga
        THING stick thatABS LIKE boomerang
That stick looks like a boomerang.

4.11   IMPERATIVES

Imperatives are characterised by an imperative verb (3.4.4). Third person imperatives (i.e. jussives) require the particle (ma)-ku, which may also optionally appear with first person imperatives (hortatives).   (See 4.13[4] for examples).   Otherwise the HORTative enclitic -tho frequently appears with first person subjects.   (See 4.13[2] for examples).   In other respects imperatives have the same structure as verbal indicative clauses, in particular they form their negative with the negative particle ka'i (4.10).   A privative infinitival clause (4.7.2[2]) may also function as a negative imperative (168).

(189)   (nhinta) yilim   thawa
       2sgNOM   again   say
       Say it again.

(190)   nhinta nga'a nhaaru ka'im-ngu   waa
       2sgNOM fish   thatABS NEG-3sgDAT   give
       Don't give him that fish.

4.12   PRE- AND POST-VERBAL PARTICLES AND ENCLITICS

A number of temporal, modal and aspectual particles occur as free forms immediately preceding or following the verb.   Enclitics are attached either to the last preverbal constituent (which may be a particle), or to the verb itself.   Some morphemes have both particle and enclitic forms.   When more than one particle or enclitic occurs, some may be in preverbal position and others in postverbal position.   In verbless sentences particles and enclitics are usually in final position.   In combinations involving modal/aspectual particle/ enclitic(s) and bound pronoun enclitic(s), the bound pronoun(s) normally occur last; however, the negative ka'i(m) may also follow bound pronoun(s), as in (191).

(191)   nhila   pama aara   ngaci   nhingkurum-um-ngurum
       3sgNOM man   thatABS father 2sgABL-ABL-3sgABL
        wań ke-n   ngaci   ngathurum-um
        return-CNC father 1sgABL-ABL
        ⎰ka'im-ngurum ⎱
        ⎱-ngurum ka'im⎰ wań ke-n
        NEG-3sgABL   return-CNC
       That man is returning from your father; [he's] not returning from my father.

[1] ya'an/yaan *JUST*. The negative ya'a 'no; not' occurs in the idiomatic adverbial expression ya'a-n (often abbreviated to yaan) 'pointlessly, for nothing, in vain'. The -n here may be the subordinator -n i (4.7.1). It is unlikely to be the locative marker -n or dative marker -na, since ya'a does not occur with other case markers, and -na is restricted to kinship terms and proper names. We shall use the interlinear gloss JUST, but idiomatic English translations will vary. For further examples, see T73, T78, T88.

(192)   puga   ngaya   ya'an kubube-ng   nhinta
               yesterday 1sgNOM JUST   waitREDUP-1sg 2sgNOM
                 pala   ka'im   uwa-n
                 hither NEG   come-2sgPAST
                Yesterday I waited for nothing; you didn't come.

(193)   thana   nhunha yaan-nha   pigo-dhan.
               3plNOM 3sgACC JUST-3sgACC   hit-3plPAST
                 agudhaa+ya'an-nha pigo-dhan
                 nothing-3sgACC   hit-3plPAST
                They just hit him. They hit him for no reason.

(194)   ngaya   nga'a iiru   yaan yenta-ng.
               1sgNOM fish   thisABS   JUST spear-1sg
                 ngaya   iiru   thuma   uthula
                 1sgNOM thisABS firewood   lacking
                I speared this fish in vain. Here I haven't any firewood.

(195)   ngaya   nga'a kana   yaan-pa   yenta-ng
               1sgNOM fish   PERF   JUST-FUT   spear-1sg
                I'm just going to try and spear a fish.

[2] yupa/-pa *FUTure*.   The variant yupa occurs as a free form particle, -pa as an enclitic. The latter tends to occur in unstressed position in allegro style or when preceded by another particle or enclitic. For further examples, see (76), (178), (182), (195), T74. For waya + (yu)pa marking a desiderative, see [6] below.

(196)   nhila   minha   pangkangku-yi   ya'a-pa   wań ke-n
               3sgNOM ANIMAL wallabyREDUP-PRIV nothing-FUT return-CNC
               He will return without any wallabies.

[3] kana *PERFective*. Completed action (198) or a change of state (199), (57), T100 or action which is about to begin (197), (200) or has begun, T95, T102 is indicated by kana. kana also appears as an interjection meaning 'it's over/finished', T62.

(197)   ngana   kana wań ke-n. apowu
               1duexcNOM PERF return-CNC goodbye
               We're going back [home] now; goodbye.

(198)   ngaya   kana munje-ng
               1sgNOM PERF bathe-1sg
               I've already had a bath.

(199)   ngaya   kana wanthi
               1sgNOM PERF good
               I'm OK now. [Said after a sneezing fit.]

(200) thana   puyu kana-pa   uwa-yin
       3plNOM away PERF-FUT   go-3plPRES
       They are about to go away.

[4] -dhu *MAY*. The enclitic -dhu indicates a degree of uncertainty on the speaker's part; it can usually be translated by English 'may', 'might' or 'must have'. Examples follow; see also T41.

(201) nhila   ngula X nhaaru pala-m-dhu-pa   wań ke-n
       3sgNOM   then X thatABS hither-EMPH-MAY-FUT   return-CNC
       Then X may come back this way.

(202) nhila   X   pala-dhu   uwa.
       3sgNOM   X   hither-MAY come
         nhila   thangke-dhu   nhingu   Y-na.
         3sgNOM   arrivePAST-MAY 3sgDAT   Y-DAT
         pula   kugu   waya-la   thawawe-n
         3duNOM   speech LIKE-3duNOM   speakREDUP-UNMKD
       X must have come over here. He must have arrived at Y['s]. [Y lived next
       door.] It sounds like they are talking. [They could be heard through a
       common wall.]

[5] epa *AFFirmation*. The particle epa marks an affirmative proposition that is in contrast to some other proposition in the context. Examples follow; see also (5), T107, T156. T47 is atypical in that no contrast is apparent.

(203) mayi yuku imun   pungga   epa wanthi
       VEG tree thisABL fruit   AFF good
         mungga-nh-wu.   mayi yuku pungga wiya-m nhaaru
         eat-INF-DAT   VEG   tree fruit other-ABL thatABS
         waya
         bad
       The fruit of this tree is good to eat; the fruit of the other tree there is bad.

[6] waya *LIKE*. The main function of waya seems to be to mark a proposition which the speaker cannot confirm by direct experience, but which he or she assumes to be true, as in (202), (204) and T41. This function of waya borders on that of -dhu ([4] above), and the two often occur together. A more grammaticised function of waya is to mark a desiderative; in this case it is accompanied by the future particle (yu)pa ([2] above), and the verb is irrealis, (147), (205).

(204) nhiya   uthu waya
       2plNOM dead LIKE
       [We thought] you would be dead.

(205)   ngaya   mayi tiya waya-pa   mungga $\begin{Bmatrix} \text{-ng} \\ \text{-nha} \end{Bmatrix}$
          1sgNOM VEG tea   LIKE-FUT   eat-1sgIRR
          I want to have some tea.

Another grammaticised function of waya is to accompany the nonfactual marker -monh ([7] below; see examples there and in 4.8.3[2]). In this use, waya seems to be optional unless the clause is an irrealis condition. Finally waya also occurs as an adjective meaning 'bad, old' and as an adverbial operator meaning 'like' (4.1.7).

[7] -monh *NONFACTual*. The enclitic -monh marks past contrary-to-fact clauses of all types, including irrealis conditions and results. The verb in a clause in which -monh appears is obligatorily irrealis. monh is often accompanied by waya ([6] above), epa ([5] above), and/or -dhu ([4] above). It is not clear what conditions the appearance of these elements, except that waya is obligatory in irrealis conditions. (206) - (209) illustrate the use of -monh. The variants in (208) were given in response to the same prompt.

(206)   nhinta ngathu yuku keene-monh   waa-nhun.
          2sgNOM 1sgDAT THING tobacco-NONFACT give-2sgIRR
             nhinta   ngathu   thawa-n   yuku   keene ngathu
             2sgNOM   1sgDAT   say-2sgPAST THING   tobacco 1sgDAT
             waa-nhu-wu
             give-INF-DAT
          You were supposed to give me some tobacco — You told me you would
          give me some tobacco.

(207)   ngaya   miitingu-wu-dhu-monh   uwa-ng
          1sgNOM   meeting-DAT-MAY-NONFACT   go-1sg
          I was supposed to go to the meeting.

(208)   ngaya   thantam   waya (epa)-dhu-monh.
          1sgNOM   knowing   LIKE AFF-MAY-NONFACT
             ngaya   yupa-dhu-ngu   thawa-ng-monh.
             1sgNOM   FUT-MAY-3sgDAT   say-1sg-NONFACT
             thawa-ng   waya(-dhu)-monh-ngu.
             say-1sg   LIKE-MAY-NONFACT-3sgDAT
             ngula nhila   pala (waya)-dhu-monh uwa-nha
             then   3sgNOM   hither LIKE-MAY-NONFACT come-IRR
          If I had known [that you wanted to see him], I could have told him, then he
          could have come this way.

(209)   ngaya   ngaka   uyu mungga-nh-dhu-monh
          1sgNOM   drink   much drink-IRR-MAY-NONFACT
          I could have had a lot of drink.

[8] -ya *You Know*. The enclitic -ya marks a proposition which the speaker feels the addressee should already know. It is thus somewhat emphatic and often contrastive.

(210)   mayi   pungga iiru   yuku-m ya'a-ya. kangka-m-ni
           VEG   fruit   thisABS   tree-ABL NEG-YK   bush-ABL-SUB
           This fruit isn't from a tree, you know. [It's] from a bush.

(211)   nhila   nhadhu-ya-dhu   uwa
           3sgNOM   away-YK-MAY   go
           He must have gone away, of course.

[9] -li *THEN* . The enclitic -li is not well recorded in our data. Its function seems to be to indicate that its host sentence is temporally subsequent to the preceding discourse. It is thus an enclitic equivalent of ngula 'then'. It often occurs in the result clause of a conditional sentence. The use of -li is illustrated in (153), (176), (212), T55, T58.

(212)   ngaya   ngaka uyu kana   mungga-ng. ngaka ya'a-li
           1sgNOM   water much PERF drink-1sg   water NEG-THEN
           I've drunk a lot of water. Now there is no water.

[10] -(pa)la *HITHER*, -(pu)yu *THITHER*. The directional adverbs pala and puyu, indicating movement toward or away from the speaker, may encliticise in pre-verbal position and optionally reduce to -la and -yu respectively. The full forms, when encliticised, are rapidly articulated and unstressed. Examples follow; see also (40).

(213)   X nhadhu-puyu   uwa
           X away-THITHER go
           X has gone away.

(214)   ngana   puga   yupa-la-n   wań ke-n
           1duexcNOM   tomorrow   FUT-HITHER-1duexcNOM   return-CNC
           We will come back tomorrow.

4.13   OTHER SENTENTIAL PARTICLES AND ENCLITICS

In this section we deal with sentential enclitics which are not limited to pre/postverbal position.

[1] -ma *EMPHatic*. The enclitic -ma (often reduced to -m, cf. 2.4.3) has as its scope a single constituent. In all our examples the emphasised constituent is placed immediately before or immediately after the verb (except for particles and enclitics). Reduplication, which in non-verbs is another emphatic device, often cooccurs with -ma. Examples are (8), (154), (155), (156), (201), (215), T78, T88, T112.

(215) ngana   nga'a-wu   nganana-m-na
       1duexcNOM   fish-DAT   1duexcNOM:REDUP-EMPH-1duexcNOM
       uwa
       go
       We went fishing by ourselves.

[2] -tho *HORTative.* A hortative subject, viz. ngale (1duincNOM) or ngampa (1plincNOM), may optionally be marked with -tho., as in (216), T68.

(216) ngampa-tho   puyu   uwa-mu
       1plincNOM-HORT away   go-1plIMP
       Let's go away.

[3] *Ethical dative.* The ethical dative is marked by a dative bound pronoun attached to the free-form pronoun representing the subject (A or S), which is usually the first element in the clause. The bound pronoun represents associates of the A or S who are present, but often unconnected with the action. The construction is seen in (217) - (219), T90, T91, T96, T107. Because of their syntactic position, ethical dative pronouns will normally be clearly distinguishable from other bound pronouns, which appear in pre- or post-verbal position and in particular from dative bound pronouns signalling beneficiary. Note that the ethical dative does not mark a pragmatic patient, for which the ablative is used (3.2.1[4]).

(217) pama pula-lin   wantu-la
       man 3duNOM-1duincDAT what's up-3duNOM
       kugu-yi-we
       voice-PRIV-INCHO:PAST
       What's up - those two mates of ours have gone quiet!

(218) ngaya-ngku   kumpu-wuuwa-ng
       1sgNOM-2sgDAT   urine-DAT   go-1sg
       [Excuse me] mate, I'm going for a leak.

(219) nhinta-thu   mayi tiya ngalin   manci-nga
       2sgNOM-1sgDAT   VEG   tea   1duincDAT   boil-CAUS
       Make some tea for us [while I sit here].

[4] (ma)-ku *IMPerative (hortative/jussive).* The particle maku, which also occurs as an enclitic -ku, is usually preverbal. It obligatorily accompanies third person imperatives (i.e. jussives), as in (145), (220), (221).

(220) uke (ma)-ku   wunha-wu
       open IMP   stay-IMP
       Let it stay open.

(221)   nhila   X   maku   yumpi-wu
        3sgNOM   X   IMP   make-IMP
        Let X make [tea].

[5] -ku *EXCLamation.* The enclitic -ku is not well represented in our data. Its function appears to be to indicate material which is contrary to presupposition or expectation. It would thus seem to have no connection with the -ku of [4] above. Examples follow; see also T101.

(222)   nga'a   !nhangki nganhca   wambambanga-nhum.
[Uw:MGW]   fish   game   1plexcNOM   stalkREDUP-HIST
            yuku   gana-ku-ni   iiru   puguga
            THING   gun-EXCL-SUBORD thisABS   recentlyREDUP
            thangke
            arrive-PAST
            We used to stalk fish and game - the gun arrived here very recently!

(223)   thana   nganhca   nga'a kamba. minha   piki-ku
[M':GTH]   3plNOM   1plexcNOM   fish kapmari ANIMAL pig-EXCL
           They and we kapmaried fish, and even pig too!

4.14   INTERJECTIONS (INCLUDING VOCATIVES)

Some common interjections are listed below. Some of these are best treated as non-linguistic, as they involve non-phonemic sounds (the post-alveolar fricative in she) or unusual phonotactics (the final /y/ in wooy). Vocatives (3.2[8]) may also be included under this rubric, since their function overlaps with the hailing interjections wooy and awe.

yee	yes	ya'a	no
ka'e	no	awe	come here [hailing]
apowu	good-bye	itharko	oh gosh
wooy	hey, cooey	she	get lost [to dogs]

5.   SEMANTICS AND THE LEXICON

5.1   COMPOUNDS

Compounding is a common derivational process in nouns and verbs. Nominal compounds are noun-noun or noun-adjective formations, while verbs are noun-verb combinations.

5.1.1   NOMINAL COMPOUNDS. Compounding is frequent in detailed anatomical terminology, as in thaa+panci (mouth+hair) 'beard', thaa+aku (mouth+skin) 'lips', pu'u+thaa+aku (vagina+mouth+skin) 'vulva', thanta+thuka (eye+ball) 'eyeball' Semantically more opaque forms include: pindha+eka+waba (head+shell+frog) 'brain', kono+waba (ear+frog) 'eardrum'. Compounding is also common in terms for material culture, flora and fauna: watha+kumpu (green:ant+urine) 'cicada', kaa+kuthu+kimpu (face+nose+kookaburra) 'kingfisher', pinci+mepen (saltwater:crocodile+little) 'seahorse'. Body part terminology is used extensively in artefact vocabulary: thuma+pupi+pu'u (fire+matchwood+vagina) 'hole in firestick for twirling to make fire', thuli+kaa+kuthu (woomera+face+nose) 'peg in throwing end of woomera, heart'. Compounds composed of modifier and head normally have the same constituent order as NPs: nominal modifiers precede their heads and adjectival modifiers follow their heads. The only known exception to this rule involves a nominal modifier following its head: kunci+yuku (penis+stick) 'erect penis'.

Noun-noun compounds may be distinguished from generic constructions (5.2) three ways:

- A generic is superordinate to its head noun, whereas no such necessary relationship exists between the elements in compounds where the relationship is usually modifier-head.

- A generic is usually predictable from its head unlike the first element in a compound. (Exceptionally, trees and their fruits and shells and their edible contents use the same hyponym with different generics; see 5.2.2, 5.2.3)

- The meaning of a generic construction is fully predictable from its parts, in fact usually from the head alone, but the meaning of a compound is not predictable from the meanings of its components.

For example, in the generic construction minha pangku (ANIMAL wallaby) 'wallaby', minha is a superordinate term for pangku, and is predictable as pangku denotes a source of edible meat; the meaning of minha pangku is the same as pangku. In the compound tha'u+pukpe (foot+child) 'toe', on the other hand, tha'u is a modifier, not a superordinate term for pukpe, nor is tha'u predictable on the basis of pukpe; finally, the meaning of the compound is only suggested by the meanings of its parts, but is not fully predictable.

Phonologically, most compounds have no special characteristics. A small number of nominal compounds, however, are formed by deleting the final vowel, if any, of the first element and the initial consonant, if any, of the second element. For example, ngalampa 'namesake (term of address for members of the same patriclan)' (from ngale 'we (1duincNOM)' + nhampa 'name'). Whether this formation is still productive is not clear. It is particularly common in kin terminology (5.3) and directionals (5.4).

5.1.2 VERBAL COMPOUNDS. Verbal compounds consist of an uninflected noun immediately followed by a verb. These constructions are only rarely interrupted by another element. The noun is not the object of the verb and cannot be cross-referenced. Examples are: kaa+ungpa (face+break) 'turn, change direction', kaa+kulu+ungpa (face+??+break) 'fold, roll, twist', moo+thuthi (body+break) 'stretch oneself', thaa+poye (lower:face+??) 'jump', waa+wuna (sleep?+stay) 'sleep', agu+ukewi (place; ground+become:uncovered) 'be born'. Many compounds are formed with kaa 'upper face' and thaa 'lower face'.

5.2 'GENERICS' (CLASSIFIERS)

The syntactic properties of 'generics' have been briefly discussed in 3.1.1 and 4.4. There are only a small number of generics, but the great majority of nouns in Nganhcara can occur with one. The generic is normally given along with the noun when vocabulary is being elicited or discussed, but may not be present when the noun occurs in a sentence, especially when it has already been mentioned in the discourse. The semantics of each of the principal generics is discussed in turn below. For more extensive exemplification of the range of individual generics, see the alphabetical vocabulary (7.2) under the various generic headings.

5.2.1 minha 'ANIMAL (MEAT)'. Used as a noun, minha refers to any edible meat, except fish, molluscs and crustaceans (5.2.2). As a generic minha is used with all animals and birds which represent potential sources of food, including aquatic mammals, such as minha wanhaji 'dolphin', and reptiles, such as minha loorom 'sea turtle'.

Any animal which is not eaten for any reason is classified by yuku (5.2.5). Exceptionally birds are always classified by minha whether eaten or not. Small birds, which are not a usual food source, because too small to catch, are classified by thuci in combination with minha, for example, minha thuci kodhe 'wren' and minha thuci caka 'sandpiper'; minha thuci by itself means 'small bird'. There are various reasons as to why some seemingly potential sources of food are classified as yuku: yuku yewo 'whale' is too large and remote to catch, yuku pinci 'saltwater crocodile' too dangerous (the smaller minha kanhe 'freshwater crocodile' is eaten), yuku munpa 'little land rat' is too small and quick, while yuku mali 'insectivorous bat' has an unpleasant taste due to its diet, unlike minha woole and minha mukum, the two fruit-eating bat species.

5.2.2 nga'a 'SEAFOOD'. nga'a occurs with all fish, molluscs and crustaceans; it is not used for aquatic mammals or reptiles. Aquatic creatures which are not eaten are classified by yuku, which is also used to refer to the shellfish when regarded as shells rather than source of food. The generic nga'a does not occur in Kugu Muminh; in this patrilect minha includes seafood, and fish are generically referred to as minha kengke.

5.2.3 mayi 'VEGetable'. This generic is used for all edible roots, tubers, shoots, flowers and fruits. By extension, it also occurs in mayi keene 'tobacco' and mayi ngaka (VEGetable water) 'beer', and the synonymous mayi kumpu (VEGetable urine), cf. Australian English *piss*. Less semantically transparent is the use of mayi with bees and their products; honeycomb (mayi wuṅ ga 'large sugarbag' and mayi wata 'little sugarbag'), which is collected typically from trees, is so classified, and the use of this generic with bees themselves, e.g. mayi puybe 'little yellow bee' and mayi pudhi 'large bee', would appear to be as a result of their association with honey production. mayi puci 'beeswax' is a further extension of this semantic association. All other insects are classified by yuku.

The specific term denoting a fruit is used with the classifier yuku to denote the tree which bears it. E.g. mayi yengbe 'lady apple (fruit)', yuku yengbe 'lady apple (tree), Eugenia suborbicularis'. Edible underground roots and tubers, however, may have a different specific name from their aboveground shoots, for example mayi panten 'bullgru root', but waka pudhi 'bullgru shoots'.

5.2.4   waka 'GRASS'.   All grasses and inedible shoots come under this classification, for example the spiky grass used for nose and ear inserts, waka wincin, seaweeds waka madhja, and goatshead burr waka thaa benga.

5.2.5   yuku 'THING, TREE'.   Inedible flora and fauna, artefacts and animated natural phenomena are classified by yuku. We examine each of these three areas in turn.

[1] *Inedible Flora and Fauna.* All trees are classified by yuku, as are all insects, worms, etc. (except for bees and their products — 5.2.3). Animals and fish which are not eaten are also used with this generic (5.2.1, 5.2.2). Shells regarded as such and not with respect to their (edible) contents are classified with yuku also.

[2] *Artefacts.* Most items of material culture occur with this generic, such as yuku thonhe 'bark canoe' and yuku olko 'dilly bag', while some others are never classified. A few, such as (yuku) weenga 'boomerang' and (yuku) woyo 'throwing stick' are found occasionally with yuku. Also included are non-human artefacts, e.g. yuku pi'i 'termite nest, antbed', yuku maara 'web', and yuku pudhi 'nest'.

[3] *Animated Natural Phenomena.* Included under this rubric are items such as yuku nhaayu 'lightning', yuku wamara 'willy willy', and yuku yi'i 'falling star'.

5.2.6   agu 'PLACE'.   As a noun, agu means 'location in space or time; ground'. As a generic it classifies specific places and regions, for example agu pipi 'claypan', agu memolo 'Memolo', agu thupi 'bora, ceremonial ground', as well as periods of time, for example agu kaaram 'Dreamtime', agu pengge 'twilight', agu pungam 'daytime'.

5.2.7   pama 'MAN', kuyu 'WOMAN', pukpe 'CHILD'.   These three words classify the various stages of childhood and adulthood, and also kinship terms. The generic pukpe makes no sexual distinction, although the specific noun may refer to a specific sex, for example, pukpe pu'udha 'girl (lit. child with vagina)'and pukpe koncenh 'boy'. Both pama and kuyu are used with kinship terms when they do not refer to the speaker's own relations (see 5.3), for example, kuyu nhingadhe 'mother' and pama nhingale 'mother's younger brother, father-in-law'. kuyu+waya and pama+muwa, 'OLD WOMAN' and 'OLD MAN' respectively, are used as compound generics for grandparents, including one's own grandparents, for example, kuyu+waya ngathame 'my mother's mother', kuyu+waya nhingame 'any other mother's mother'.

5.2.8   kugu 'SPEECH'. This generic classifies all languages and patrilects, as in kugu uwanh 'the language which uses uwanh as the verb "to go"'.

5.2.9   UNCLASSIFIED WORDS. There are some categories of nouns that do not take a generic: kinship terms referring to the speaker's own relations (except for those words noted above in 5.2.7), all body parts, natural phenomena - such as punga 'sun' and thoko 'smoke', some words referring to material culture - such as keka 'spear' and matpam 'engraver', generics themselves, and the word ku'a 'dog' (see 3.2.1[3] on the special status of dogs). ku'a, keka, wangga 'fishing net', ngaka 'water, liquid' and some other words referred to here, are possibly also generics, but our collection of vocabulary is not sufficiently extensive to allow us to decide in every instance. For example, ku'a probably functions as a generic for domestic animals in the neologisms ku'a maara 'horse' and ku'a othogo 'cat'.

5.3   KINSHIP TERMS

Kinship terms commonly replace personal names in speech; the latter are avoided as terms of address for kin. Nganhcara possesses two parallel sets of kin terms, one for talking to or about the speaker's own relatives, and one for other people's relatives. In the majority of cases, forms are compounds in which the initial element ngath- (from ngathu 'my (1sgDAT') contrasts with nhing- (from nhingu 'his/her (3sgDAT'). The non-first person form occurs with a generic, kuyu or pama as appropriate. The terms for grandparents are always classified by kuyu+waya or pama+muwa, even when referring to the speaker's own grandparents. Examples follow:

	ego's kin	alter's kin
younger brother	ngathake	pama nhingake
elder sister	ngathepe	kuyu nhingepe
mother's father	pama+muwa ngathunge	pama+muwa nhingunge
mother's mother	kuyu+waya ngathame	kuyu+waya nhingame

The terms for kin of the generation below the speaker do not have alternative forms, e.g. pukpe nhengka 'children of F/B' and neither does pinye 'FB⁺'.

Compounds generally use the special nominal compound formation (5.1.1), e.g ngathame is from ngathu + *kame 'MM'. Other phonological idiosyncracies are found, such as the irregular vowel alternation in ngathidhe - nhingadhe 'mother' and the metaphony in ngothope (from *ngath-ope) 'FM' (2.2.2[3]).

5.4   DIRECTIONALS

Like many Australian languages, Nganhcara possesses a complex set of directionals. The parameters of the system include compass points as well as 'top', 'bottom' and 'outside'; the three demonstratives and nhadhu 'away'; and orientation of movement with respect to speaker's location. The data for this section are incomplete, as only a preliminary analysis was done in the field.

5.4.1   CORE DIRECTIONALS. The basic elements of the set of directionals are the cardinal points of the compass; 'above' and 'below'; and 'inside' and 'outside'. There is a semantic neutralisation of 'below' and 'inside', so that only seven distinct forms are found. The four cardinal compass points combine to give the four secondary points. We shall refer to these eleven forms, which are listed in Table 5.1, as the core directionals. The core directionals are identical in all patrilects, except that Iyanh has a long vowel in kaawa 'east' and the compounds based on it.

TABLE 5.1 - *Core Directionals*

kungke	north	kungke+kawa	northeast
yibe	south	kungke+kuwa	northwest
kawa	east	yibe+kawa	southeast
kuwa	west	yibe+kuwa	southwest
kanhnyi	top, above		
pake	bottom, below; inside		
koye	outside		

5.4.2   BASIC DEMONSTRATIVE-DIRECTIONALS. A further forty-four forms (plus phonological variants) are created by combining the eleven core elements with the three demonstratives (3.2.2) and with nhadhu 'off, away'. For example, nhath+ungke 'away in the north'. The compounds use the special nominal compound formation (5.1.1). The demonstrative elements are derived from earlier inu (speaker-proximal), nhanu (addressee-proximal) and ana (distal) rather than from the innovative Uwanh forms iiru, nhaaru and aara. (3.2.2). The /dh/ of nhadhu devoices to /th/ in compounds. This may indicate that the initial consonant of the directional element was earlier present in the compounds and caused assimilation of the /dh/ to /th/; thus for example *nhadh+kungke > *nhath+kungke > nhath+ungke. Only yibe does not begin with a voiceless stop, and nhath+ibe must result from analogy.

A number of other phonological idiosyncracies are found, and will be dealt with as they occur. The remaining three compounds formed from kungke 'north' are given below These forms refer to specific places, while nhathungke does not. The second /k/ of kungke usually voices to /g/, a fact in keeping with the preponderance of voiced stops in third and subsequent syllables (2.1.1[1]). In the remainder of the chapter we regularise to the form with /k/.

inungke/inungge	there (nearby) in the north
nhanungke/nhanungge	there (near addressees place or place referred to) in the north
anungke/anungge	there (distal) in the north

The full set of basic demonstrative-directionals is given in Table 5.2, where the gaps represent deficient data. A number of new morphological and phonological irregularities appear in these forms. The second element of a compound core directional is reduced to its last syllable, except for kuwa which retains the /u/ as well. This maintains the distinction between compounds on kuwa and those on kawa which have the same final syllable. Final vowels of kungke and yibe are deleted before -uwa. The combining form of koye is -aye rather than expected -oye. The combining form of pake is -aage; expected -ake is reportedly found in Mu'inh and Iyanh. Following /n/, the combining form of kuwa is -duwa. Finally, when yibe, yibekawa and yibekuwa are preceded by a nasal, /y/ becomes /j/ instead of being deleted. The only other instance of this process is in the abessively marked infinitive (4.7.2[2]). Apico-alveolar /n/ in the demonstrative bases is replaced by lamino-dental /nh/, since apical+laminal clusters are not permitted (2.1.1[2]).

TABLE 5.2 - *Basic Demonstrative-Directionals : Absolute Forms*

	inu	nhanu	anu	nhadhu
kungke	inungke	nhanungke	anungke	nhathungke
yibe	inhjibe	nhanhjibe	anhjibe	nhathibe
kawa	inawa	nhanawa	anawa	nhathawa
kuwa	induwa	nhanduwa	anduwa	nhathuwa
kanhnyi	inanhnyi	nhananhnyi	ananhnyi	nhathanhnyi
pake	inaage	nhanaage	anaage	nhathaage
koye	inaye		anaye	nhathaye
kungkekawa	inungkewa		anungkewa	
kungkekuwa	inungguwa			
yibekawa	inhjibewa			
yibekuwa	inhjibuwa			

All of the demonstrative-directionals are nouns, and the forms in Table 5.2 are absolute. Of the other cases, only dative, ablative and locative have been recorded — the roles marked by other cases may not be possible for a location. The inflection demonstrative-directionals is unusual in that the demonstrative is inflected within the compound; for the dative the DATive enclitic -wu is attached to the end of the compound rather than to the dative stem of the demonstrative. The case forms of the demonstrative-directionals based on kungke 'north' are shown in Table 5.3. As usual, kungke loses its initial consonant, and in the dative and ablative forms it may optionally further reduce to its final syllable. An alternative agakewu for agungkewu is built using the first two syllables of the dative demonstrative agawu and the last syllable of the directional kungke and the DATive enclitic -wu. No other forms of this type are recorded.

TABLE 5.3 - *Demonstrative-Directionals : Inflection Illustrated*

1proxDAT	igungke-wu	to that nearby place in the north
2proxDAT	nhagungke-wu	to addressee's place in the north; to that place mentioned in the north
distDAT	agungke-wu	to that distant place in the north
1proxABL	imunungke/imuń ke	from/of that nearby place in the north
2proxABL	nhamuń ke	from/of addressee's place in the north; from/of that place mentioned in the north
distABL	amunungke/amuń ke	from/of that distant place in the north
1proxLOC	ingunungke/inguń ke	in that nearby place in the north
2proxLOC	nhangunungke	in addressee's place in the north; to that place mentioned in the north
distLOC	angunungke/anguń ke	in that distant place in the north

Other forms of this type are listed in Table 5.4. Some of the ablative and locative forms show additional phonological idiosyncracies; in particular, a regressive vowel harmony operates on the second vowel. Note also that the vowel in -aage may shorten, particularly in third and later syllables. No examples are recorded involving the secondary compass points.

TABLE 5.4 - *Demonstrative-Directionals: More Inflectional Forms*

		DAT	ABL	LOC
from yibe:	1prox	igibe-wu	iminibe	inginibe
	dist		aminbe	
from kawa:	1prox	igawa-wu	imanawa	inganawa
	dist		amanawa	
from kuwa:	1prox	iguwa-wu	imunduwa	ingunduwa
from kanhnyi:	1prox	iganhnyi-wu	imananhnyi	inganhnyi
from pake:	1prox	igaage-wu	imanaage	inganage
	2prox			nhanganage
from koye:	1prox	igaye-wu	imanaye	inganaye

A few instances or regularised inflectional forms have also been recorded, in which the standard case-marking enclitics (3.2.1) are attached to the nominative forms of the demonstrative-directionals, e.g. the ablative forms anungke-m, nhanungke-m.

5.4.3 SIDE. Forms denoting a particular side of an object or larger locational context can be formed on the pattern pal + core directional + suffix. The suffix is usually -o (which replaces the final vowel of the core directional); however, 'eastern side' has the suffix -ra; no suffix appears for 'top' and 'bottom'. It is likely that the initial element pal- derives from pala 'this way, hither', although there is no obvious semantic connection. The only recorded forms in this set are:

palungko	north side
palibo	south side
palawara	east side
paluwo	west side
palanhnyi	top
palawaage	bottom

5.4.4 DIRECTION OF MOTION. Adverbs indicating direction of motion are formed by combining yama(ng) 'thus, like that, that way' and puyu 'away' with the core directional nouns according to the usual pattern. The recorded forms are listed below. The only new phonological idiosyncracy here is the long vowel in puyaawa. No forms based on the secondary compass points are recorded.

yamungke	puyungke	northward
yamibe	puyibe	southward
yamawa	puyaawa	eastward
yamuwa	puyuwa	westward
yamanhnyi	puyanhnyi	upward
yamaage	puyaage	downward, inward
yamaye	puyaye	outward

Three additional forms indicating direction of motion are built on the demonstratives:

inang	this way
nhanang	your way / that way referred to
anang	that way

5.4.5 MOTION TOWARDS AND AWAY FROM A REFERENCE POINT. The suffix -la, from pala 'this way, hither', may be added to any of the nominative or ablative forms in 5.4.2 to indicate motion from the point specified towards (but not necessarily to) a reference point, often the speaker's location. Similarly, the suffix -yu, from puyu 'away', may be added to the nominative demonstrative-directionals to indicate motion away from a reference point toward the place specified. We have also recorded a few examples of -yu affixed to an ablative stem, apparently indicating motion from the place specified. Some of these forms are illustrated in (224), (225). Note that motion TO (rather than TOWARD) the point in question is indicated by the dative forms listed in 5.4.2. There are no new phonological irregularities in these forms. For kungke 'north' the following forms are recorded:

inungkela/imuń kela/imunungkela	this way from there (nearby) in the north
nhanungkela /nhamunungkela	this way from there (your place or the place referred to) in the north
anungkela/amuń kela/amunungkela	this way from there (distant) in the north
(not recorded)	this way from off in the north
inungkeyu	away toward there (nearby) in the north
nhanungkeyu	away toward there (your place or the place referred to) in the north
anungkeyu	away toward there (distant) in the north
nhathungkeyu	off toward the north
imuń keyu/imunungkeyu	away from there (nearby) in the north
(not recorded)	away from there (your place or the place referred to) in the north
amunungkeyu	away from there (distant) in the north
(not recorded)	away from off in the north

(224) iminibela   uwa. palibo uwa. puyungke. ...
       this way from nearby S   go   S side   go   northward
          inhjibela   uwa,   inungkeyu
          this way from nearby S   move   away toward nearby N
       He is coming this way from just south of here. He is moving on the south side (of the house), northward. He is coming this way from just south of here, away towards the nearby north. (He is not coming to the speaker's location).

(225) ngaya   thidhji-m-ni   ngaya
       1sgNOM   Breakfast Creek-ABL-SUBORD   1sgNOM
          nhanhjibeyu   uwa-nga manupaa-wu
          away toward that place in S   go-1sg   Moonkan Creek-DAT
       nhaguwu
       thatDAT
       From Breakfast Creek I went away toward that place south (of there), Moonkan Creek. (Both locations are north of the speaker's location.)

    Other recorded forms in this paradigm are as follows. No examples are recorded involving the secondary compass points.

from yibe:	inhjibela/iminibela	nhanhjibela	anhjibela	
		nhanhjibeyu	anhjibeyu	nhathibeyu
from kawa:	inawala/imanawala			
	inawayu/imanawayu			nhathawayu
from kuwa:	induwala/imunduwala	nhanduwala		nhathuwala
				nhathuwayu
from kanhnyi:	inanhnyila	nhananhnyila	ananhnyila	
				nhathanhnyiyu
from pake:	imanaagela	nhanaagela		
		nhanaageyu		nhathaageyu
from koye:	inayela/imanayela	nhanayela	anayela	nhathayela
	inayeyu	nhanayeyu	anayeyu	nhathayeyu

5.5   RESPECT REGISTER

For many lexical items there exists an alternative form which may be used in certain styles of language often referred to in the literature as avoidance or mother-in-law language. These styles include what is referred to by Nganhcara speakers as 'side talk' and 'big' language in English. Certain kinfolk e.g. mother-in-law, are said to be nganca 'poison' and may be spoken to only indirectly (hence 'side-talk'). Eye contact with the addressee is avoided, and in some cases communication is made through the intermediary of a dog, both parties subscribing to the fiction that they are addressing the dog rather than one another. Respect vocabulary is mandatory, and often a slow, deliberate manner of delivery and a low voice are used. In important situations, talking about customs and giving instruction on ceremonial matters, for example, the heightened nature of the speech event is emphasised by the use of respect words. Respect vocabulary is also prescribed in culturally difficult situations such as speaking to someone in mourning. Respect register differs from plain register in lexicon only; its morphosyntax is identical.

A word that belongs to the respect register in one patrilect may be the plain register form in another. For example, in Uwanh !nhangki !thuthamba is the respect form of minha pangku 'wallaby', while minha thuthamba is the plain form for the same animal in Muminh. Muminh and Iyanh both have the plain form minha moń ke 'bandicoot', for which Uwanh has minha kaanggu, replaced in Uw respect register by !nhangki !moń ke. The Iyanh respect form is again different: !nhangki !kalbenji.

Respect forms are morphologically unrelated to their plain counterparts, and are available to replace a large part of the vocabulary. In general, the more common a word, the more likely it is to have a respect counterpart. Among nouns, respect forms occur infrequently for flora and fauna, but are common for body parts, material culture and natural phenomena. Quantifiers and generics all have respect equivalents as do most non-causative verbs and many adjectives and adverbs.

Plain register nouns having no distinct respect equivalents can be used in respect register with the appropriate respect generic, which, as mentioned above, all have distinct respect equivalents. Examples are: minha,

!nhangki 'ANIMAL'; agu, !mań gum 'LOCATION'; yuku, !ngunja 'THING'; waka, !mepam 'GRASS'; ngaka, !unyulu 'WATER'.

Compounds are calqued piecemeal into respect register; thus: thanta+panci, !wuthca+!alman (eye+hair) 'eyelash; eyebrow'; thaa+thutha, !thandhu+!wuraya (mouth+pluck) 'pull out; take out; take off'. More frequent in our data, are partial calques, where only one of the elements of the compound takes the respect form: thuma+thanta, thuma+!wuthca (fire+eye) 'live coal' (cf. !wukinh 'fire'); thaa+panci, thaa+!alman (mouth+hair) 'beard' (cf. !thandhu 'mouth'). We have also recorded some examples in which either the partial or the full respect calque can be used: thuma+pupi, !wukinh+pupi, !wukinh+!kunina (fire+firestick) 'firesticks'; thaa+aku, !thandhu+aku, !thandhu+!pe'en (mouth+skin) 'lips'. It is likely that this optionality is always present when both elements have respect forms; obviously, when only one of the elements has a distinct respect form, the partial calque is the only possibility. Sutton reports similar flexibility for Ngathanh (1978:223).

For the most part, the morphological structure of respect vocabulary is not distinctive. Respect verbs, however, are frequently derived by means of a suffix. The most common suffix is -nga, but -nye and -ya are also found. The first and last of these form causatives (3.4.10) in plain register verbs, but may function simply as verbalisers in respect register. For example, !thandhuń -nga 'eat' (from !thandhu 'mouth'), !kuncu-nga 'go' and !wura-ya 'pluck' are not causative, nor even transitive in the case of 'go'. Derived causatives can, however, be produced for some respect verbs in the same way as for plain verbs, thus !nhuuma-nga 'bathe (tr)' from !nhuuma 'bathe'. See 3.4.10 for additional examples.

Generally, plain register words having no respect equivalents may be used in respect register, since the discourse will certainly contain other items which do have respect equivalents. However, some items, such as kuna 'excrement' and kumpu 'urine', have no respect equivalents and are avoided in respectful speech.

6.   TEXTS

These texts are monologues collected in a fieldwork situation, with the fieldworker and cassette recorder as sole audience. Even so, they have a spontaneous feel to them, and Text 3 in particular is quite animated. The speaker in texts 1 and 3 is a middle-aged woman, that of text 4 a middle-aged man (see acknowledgements). The recordings were transcribed with the assistance of the speaker. Transcription being a laborious process, only a few texts were fully transcribed during our short time in the field, and our choice of material to present here is fairly limited. The selection of texts for transcription focussed on variety of genre rather than on the illustration of grammatical points. In order to properly convey narrative style, the texts are presented as recorded, without editing to remove false starts and sudden breaks (indicated by #) or repetition.

6.1   SOME CUSTOMS SURROUNDING CHILDBIRTH

This text describes the traditional practices surrounding pregnancy and childbirth, practices which have fallen into abeyance since the late 1960s as a result of a government policy requiring births to take place under hospital supervision at Cairns (J. von Sturmer 1978:331, 360). The monologue, recorded in 1974, was given as a commentary on a series of photographs in Thomson 1936. According to Thompson (who worked with the neighbouring Mungkan) the special status of the parents-to-be, and particularly of the mother, is marked in a number of ways. They are both subject to numerous food taboos, some of which are not lifted until the child is able to speak well. At the onset of labour, the father moves to a single men's camp and the woman to a 'shelter place', where she is attended by female relatives. She may not be seen by men until the child is ceremonially presented to the father. The practice of assigning a navel name, referred to in the text, is described by Thomson as follows:

> After the birth of the child ... the midwife takes the umbilical cord in her hand and shakes it, at the same time calling aloud names of various relatives of the child. The name called at the moment the placenta is delivered is the name of the baby. The umbilical cord is cut a few inches ... from the navel and is left until it dries and falls off. It is then encased in beeswax and carried as a token or charm by the individual whose name the child has taken. ... The relatives whose names may be called are the father and father's brothers and sister, the child's actual brothers and sisters, mother's brothers and sisters, but not the mother herself, father's father or mother's father, as well as many other relatives of a similar order, actual or classificatory. Thenceforth a special relationship exists between the baby and the one whose name it has taken... (380)

J. von Sturmer reports that among the Nganhcara the MB's name is favoured as the navel-name (1978:358), a preference confirmed in our text. After its skin has become pigmented and its umbilical cord has fallen off, the baby is painted with red ochre and white clay, adorned with mother of pearl ornaments and presented to the father.

The text refers to the 'giving of smell' (rubbing of axillary sweat), a gesture that protects the anointee from ritual danger. Finally, the thodhjo tree referred to may be the same as what J. von Sturmer records for M' as 'thocon ... unidentified tree sp. burnt to produce charcoal which is rubbed on corpses' (1978:644).

1. nhila   pukpe nhila#
    3sgNOM child   3sgNOM
    The child#

2.
    nhila   kuyu   nhingadhe thupin-ni   thenena
    3sgNOM woman   mother   pregnant-SUBORD walkPAST:REDUP
    nhila   agu   nhakun-ung-nhapi'i'a,   pama pibi
    3sgNOM PLACE camp-LOC-3sgACC keepREDUP MAN father
When the mother was pregnant, he kept her in the camp, the father.

3.
    pula   kuyu   pama-la   wunune-n,   nhakun-ung
    3duNOM woman man-3duNOM stay:REDUP-PRES camp-LOC
The two of them, the man and the woman stay [together], in the camp.

4.
    ngula nhamun pukpe-n-ngu   mangka+wań ke
    then   thatABL child-SUBORD-3sgDAT   cause back painPAST
    kuyu   nhila   puyaye   uwa
    woman 3sgNOM away   go
Then when the child gave her pain, the woman went away.

5.
    agu   koye   nhiina, pukpe# pukpe agawu
    PLACE   outside sitPAST child   child   thatDAT
She waited outside — for that child.

6.
    pukpe mangka+wań ke
    child   cause back painPAST
The child gave her pain.

7.
    ngulapukpe# pukpe agu+ukewe-ngu
    then child   child   be bornPAST-3sgDAT
Then the child# The child was born to her.

8.
    ngula pukpe agu+ukewe-n-ngu,   ngula pukpe m#
    then   child   be bornPAST-SUBORD-3sgDAT then   child
    pukpe   mompo-ni#   pukpe+kudin-nha
    child   afterbirth-SUBORD navel name-3sgACC
    waawaa-dhan
    sayREDUP-3plPAST
Then when the child was born to her, then the after# When the afterbirth#
They would be saying the navel names.

9.
    pama nhingale-wu nhingu   pukpe+kudin-ngu thangke
    man   MB⁻-DAT   3sgDAT   navel name-3sgDAT arrivePAST
The navel name came from the mother's younger brother.

10.
    pama nhingale-wu kudin-ngu   thangke
    man   MB⁻-DAT   navel name-3sgDAT   arrivePAST
The navel name came from the mother's younger brother.

11.   ngula nhaaru kuyu+waya# nhingame-ng ∞ kuyu+waya
        then   thatABS OLD WOMAN   MM-ERG   or OLD WOMAN
        nhingope-ng, pula   kuce-kuce-ng# mangka
        FM-ERG   3duNOM two-two-ERG   back
        thambamba-n,   pula   kuyu   aara-ni,
        restrainREDUP-SUBORD   3duNOM woman   thatABS-SUBORD
        pukpe   agu+uke+we-ni,   ngula nhaaru-ni
        child   be bornPAST-SUBORD then   thatABS-SUBORD
        pukpe   uke-ni,   kudin-nha   pula   umpe
        child   born-SUBORD   cord-3sgACC 3duNOM cutPAST

Then the mother's mother or father's mother [of the woman giving birth] —
the two who held her back [i.e. helped the mother give birth] — those
women, when the child was born, then when the child was born, they cut the
umbilical cord.

12.   ngulanhamun-ning# ngaka-ng   ngula
        then then-SUBORD w# water-ERG/LOC   then
        ma'a+kaa+nhiina
        wash

Then# then they wash him with/in water.

13.   ngaka-ng-nh   pula   munji-nga
        water-ERG/LOC-3sgACC 3duNOM   wash(int)- CAUS

They wash him/her with/in water.

14.   ngula ngaka-ng-nha   pula   munji-nga
        then water-ERG/LOC-3sgACC 3duNOM   wash(int)- CAUS

Then they wash him/her with/in water.

15.   ngulam # wunpa-nh-pula
        then   put-3sgACC-3duNOM

Then# they put him down.

16.   poje-dha-nga-nha-la
        dry(Adj)-CAUS-CAUS-3sgACC-3duNOM

They dry him.

17.   yuku   thuuyu-ng-ni   pula   wunpa
        THING bark-LOC-SUBORD   3duNOM put

They put him on bark, you know.

18.   yuku blengkita ya'a-m-ya
        THING blanket   NEG-EMPH-YK

No blankets, of course.

19.   ngula yuku   thuuyu pake-m   nhingu-la   wunpa
        then THING bark   down-ABL? 3sgDAT-3duNOM put

So they put down bark for him.

20.   ngulanhamun-ni#   pukpe pula   pi'i'a-nha,
           then   then-SUBORD   child   3duNOM   keepREDUP-3sgACC
               koye kuyu   nhingade-ng kuyu+waya   nhingope-ng
               outside WOMAN   M-ERG   OLD WOMAN   FM-ERG
               kuyu+waya   nhingame-ng
               OLD WOMAN   MM-ERG
           And then# they keep the child — outside [the camp] — the mother, father's
           mother and mother's mother.

21.   nhila   pama pibi nga'a minha nhila   yenta-nhum
           3sgNOM MAN father fish   game   3sgNOM   spear-HIST
           The father would spear fish and game.

22.   ngula yengka-nhum-la
           then   send-HIST-3sgNOM
           Then he would send [it to his wife].

23.   kuyu+waya   nhingadhe nhingurum-wu-ngu
           OLD WOMAN   mother   3sgABL-DAT-3sgDAT
               yengka-nhum
               send-HIST
           He would send it to the old mother [of the woman giving birth].

24.   ngulanhingadhe nhingurum-wu nga'a minha kali-nhum
           then mother   3sgABL-DAT   fish   game   carry-HIST
           So she would take the fish and game to the mother.

25.   waa-nhum-ngu,   kuyu   wo'ombo   agawu
           give-HIST-3sgDAT   WOMAN woman who has given birth   thatDAT
           She would give it to her — to the woman who had given birth.

26.   nhila   kuyu   wo'ombo#
           3sgNOM WOMAN   woman who has given birth
           The woman who has given birth#

27.   ngula nhaaru-ni   nhila#
           then   thatABS-SUBORD   3sgNOM
           Then he/she#

28.   pama yama nga'a   minha-wu-la   uwa-nhum
           man   thus   fish   game-DAT-3sgNOM go-HIST
           Like that, the man would go for fish and game.

29.   ngula thana   pukpe-wu m #ngandaaru#
           then   3plNOM   child-DAT   what's-it?
               yuku   thodhjo-n   thana   mama-nhum
               TREE   thodhjo-SUBORD   3plNOM   take-HIST
           Then they would take a — what's it's name — a thodhjo tree, you know —
           for the child.

30.   thodhjo nganhca#   thana-ni#   yuku   speshaltrii
       thodhjo   1plexcNOM   3plNOM-SUBORD tree
       thaarana
       3plDAT
      Thodhjo we# You know they# It was special tree for them.

31.   yuku nhila-nhila,   yuku thodhjo
       tree   3sgNOM-3sgNOM tree   thodhjo
      It was a special tree, the thodhjo.

32.   thuma   thana   mancinga-nhum
       fire   3plNOM   make-HIST
      They would make a fire.

33.   ngula!ukulu-ng thana   punca-nga-nhum
       then   water-ERG 3plNOM   wet-CAUS-HIST
      Then they would wet it [i.e. the ashes] with water.

34.   ngula thodhjo nhalung thana   mamama-nhum, pukpe
       then   thodhjo thatERG 3plNOM   rubREDUP-HIST   child
       mepen
       small
      Then they rub it with that thodhjo [ash], the baby.

35.   pukpe mepen   aara   kiga+kalidhan+wań ke
       child   small   thatABS   grow bigPAST
      Then that baby grew big.

36.   ngula kuman   yengk-o-dhan
       then   messenger send-RECIP-3plPAST
      Then they sent each other messengers.

37.   kuyu+waya   nhingope thangke,   pala pukpe
       OLD WOMAN FM   arrivePAST   hither child
       agawu-ngu
       thatDAT-3sgDAT
      The father's mother arrived — over here for the child.

38.   pukpe aara   kana-ku-nh   mama-wu,
       child   thatABS PERF-IMP-3sgACC hold-IMP
       pama pibi-ngu
       MAN father-ERG
      [and said] 'Now let the father take the child.'

39.   ngula nhamun-ni nhila   kuyu+waya nhingope
       then   then-SUBORD 3sgNOM OLD WOMAN FM
       koye-m   wań ke
       outside-ABL returnPAST
      So the old woman returned from outside [the camp].

40.   ngula thana# pama   pibi# manthayan# pama   pibi ngula
       then   3plNOM MAN   father senior   MAN   father then
       kuyam#
       junior
       Then they [referring to the picture]: the senior, [classificatory] father, then
       the junior [classificatory] father...

41.   nhila   pama# nhingake   akanda-ng   monhem-ung
       3sgNOM MAN   YB   middle brother-ERG middle-LOC
       waya-dhu wunpa pukpe aara-ni
       LIKE-MAY   put   child   thatABS-SUBORD
       He's the younger brother [of the natural father] — the middle brother [sitting]
       in the middle probably fathered the child.

42.   ngula kuyu   pinhnyi thana   uyu-ma
       then   WOMAN   aunt   3plNOM many-EMPH
       Then the aunts, they are many indeed!

43.   nhiiniina-yin.   kububi-yin-ngu
       sitREDUP-3plPRES waitREDUP-3plPRES-3sgDAT
       They are sitting and waiting for him.

44.   ngula pukpe   aara   thangke-rana
       then   child   thatABS   arrivePAST-3plDAT
       Then the child reached them.

45.   pukpe mama-dhan-nha
       child   hold-3plPAST-3sgACC
       They held the child.

46.   (repeats 45)

47.   ngulaaara   pukpe awal-nga-yin epa   kuyu   pi#
       then thatABS child   sweat-CAUS   AFFIRM WOMAN
       pama pibi-ngu   kuyu   pinhnyi-ngu
       MAN father-ERG   WOMAN   aunt-ERG
       Now here they are giving the child their smell [by rubbing their axillary
       sweat on it], the a# the father and the aunts.

48.   nhila   pukpe kuyu   awal-nga
       3sgNOM child   woman sweat-CAUS
       He gives his smell to the child and his wife.

49.   pama alang nhila   kuyu pi'a-ni
       man thatERG 3sgNOM   woman keep
       The man who is married to the woman.

50.   (repeats 48)

51.   pukpe nhila   mama
            child   3sgNOM hold
            He holds the child.

52.   pukpe awal-nga
            child   sweat-CAUS
            He gives the child his smell.

53.   kuyu   aara   mama
            woman thatABS hold
            He holds the woman.

54.   kuyu   thangke-ngu
            woman arrivePAST-3sgDAT
            The woman went over to him.

55.   awal-nga-li
            sweat-CAUS-THEN
            Then he gave her his smell.

56.   ngulanhaaru-ni   agu   nhakun-wu#   wico-yin
            then   thatABS-SUB   PLACE camp-DAT   travel-3plPRES
            Then they go to the camp.

57.   kana-li
            PERF-THEN
            Finished now.

58.   nhakun-ung-lipi'a pama alang
            camp-LOC-THEN keep   man   thatERG
            Then he keeps [her] at the camp — that man.

59.   ma'an+putpa
            together
            [They stay] together.

60.   kana
            PERF
            Finished.

61.   pula   wune-n   thooron
            3duNOM stay-PRES together
            They live — together.

62.   kana
            PERF
            Finished.

6.2   CURLEW AND CROW (A DREAMTIME STORY)

Stories recounting the activities of totemic heroes (kamwaya) are abundant in the Archer River area. These stories often account for the origin of some natural feature, phenomenon, cultural item, etc. At the end of these narratives, the heroes 'go down' — descend into particular geographic locations with which they are henceforth linked (awa). As J. von Sturmer finds this genre 'totally absent from the coastal division' of the Kugu Nganhcara territory (1978:352), it is possible that the following piece is imported from the north by the speaker (MGW) who spent part of his life at Aurukun. The text was recorded in 1979.

63.   kaaram   minha   wiiwii pula   minha   wadha
       Dreamtime ANIMAL   curlew 3duNOM   ANIMAL   crow
       pula   nga'a-wu-la   !wothcomngu
       3duNOM   fish-DAT-3duNOM   travel
       In the Dreamtime Curlew and Crow go for fish.

64.   nga'a-la   pipipa
       fish-3duNOM   catchREDUP
       They caught fish.

65.   pecele#   kalala-la
       fishing line carryREDUP-3duNOM
       They carried the fishing line.

66.   nhacin# !wunggam#   pathala   kumudhu
       heavy   barramundi   catfish   big-headed catfish
       It was heavy: barramundi, catfish, big-headed catfish.

67.   kalala-la
       carryREDUP-3duNOM
       They carried [them/it].

68.   ngale-tho   wiba ingun
       1duincNOM-HORT   shade thisLOC
       'Let's [stop]: here is some shade.'

69.   ngale   pupi   mama-li
       1duincNOM firestick hold-1duIMP
       'Let's twirl the firesticks [i.e. make a fire].'

70.   pupi   kana-la   mama nger nger nger nger nger
       firestick PERF-3sgNOM hold   (sound made by firesticks)
       He [Curlew] twirled the firesticks: whirr whirr whirr.

71.   nhila   wadha-la   thangkangki-nhum
        3sgNOM   crow-3sgNOM   laughREDUP-HIST
         kaa kaa kaa kaa kaa kaa kaa
          (sound of Crow laughing)
        Crow was laughing: 'Caw, caw, caw.'

72.   nhila   wiiwii-la   thawa
        3sgNOM   curlew-3sgNOM   sayPAST
        Curlew said,

73.   nhinta   yaan   ka'i   thangkangki
        2sgNOM   JUST   NEG   laugh
        'Don't laugh too much.'

74.   ngale   madhji-pa-le   uthuma
        1duincNOM   hunger-FUT-1duincNOM   die
        'We'll die of hunger.'

75.   kana   mama-la
        PERF   hold-3sgNOM
        He twirled them.

76.   kana mama-la
        He twirled them [again].

77.   pupi-nh   mama-la   nger nger nger nger nger
        firestick-3sgACC hold-3sgNOM   (sound of firesticks)
        [Again] he twirled the firesticks: whirr whirr whirr.

78.   ya'an-ma
        JUST-EMPH
        In vain.

79.   (Repeats 76)

80.   (Repeats 76)

81.   pupi   ka'im-lan   anhce
        firestick   NEG-3duDAT   lightPAST
        The firesticks wouldn't light for them.

82.   ya'a
        Nothing.

83.   nhila   wadha thangkangki-nhum
        3sgNOM   crow   laughREDUP-HIST
        Crow laughed.

84.   nhinta   yaan   ka'i   thangkangki
        2sgNOM   JUST   NEG   laughREDUP12
        Don't laugh too hard.

85.   (Repeats 84)

86.   ngale   madhji uthuma-pa-le
        1duincNOM   hungry   die-FUT-1duincNOM
        'We'll die of hunger.' [lit. We'll die hungry.]

87.   kana   pula   mama-nhum   nger nger nger nger nger
        PERF   3duNOM   hold-HIST   (sound of firesticks)
        They twirled [them again]: whirr whirr whirr.

88.   pupi-n   ya'an-ma
        firesticks-SUBORD JUST-EMPH
        But the firesticks were useless.

89.   nhila-la   mama-nhum   nger nger nger
        3sgNOM-3sgNOM   hold-HIST   (sound of firesticks)
        He [Curlew] would twirl them: whirr whirr whirr.

90.   nhila-ngu-la   kaa kaa kaa kaa
        3sgNOM-3sgDAT-3sgNOM   (sound of Crow laughing)
            thangkangki-nhum   wadha-ni
            laughREDUP:HIST   crow-SUBORD
        He would laugh at him: 'Caw caw caw.' - Crow, that is.

91.   ngulanhila-ngu   ngangka+kuli-ngu   thangke   !wabi
        then   3sgNOM-3sgDAT   anger-3sgDAT   arrivePAST   curlew
        Then he got angry - Curlew.

92.   pupi   mama nger nger nger nger nger
        firestick   hold   (sound of firesticks)
        He twirled the firesticks.

93.   !wuthca-nha   !kengga
        eye-3sgACC   burn
        And burnt [Crow's] eye.

94.   !wuthca-nha   !kengga   pupi-ng
        eye-3sgACC   burn   firestick-ERG
        He burnt out his eye - with the firestick.

95.   kana-la   thaa+poyi-nhum
        PERF-3sgNOM   hop-HIST
            cang cang cang cang cang cang cang cang cang
            (sound of Crow hopping)
        He began to hop around: hip hop hip hop.

96.   nhila-ngu   pupi   mama
        3sgNOM-3sgDAT   firestick hold
        He took the firesticks.

97.   pungku-nha pigo
        knee-3sgACC   hitPAST
        And hit him on the knees.

98.   kana
        PERF
        That's it.

99.   minha pula   kaawe
        animal 3duNOM   'go down'PAST
        They went down.

100.   nhila   kana   kaawi-nhum   waa waa waa waa
        3sgNOM   PERF 'go down'-HIST   (sound of Crow)
        He [Crow] went down: 'caw caw caw.'

101.   nga'a-ku   yetha   mungga
        fish-EXCL   raw   eat
        He eats fish raw!

102.   nhila   kana   thenena
        3sgNOM   PERF walkPAST:REDUP
        He [Curlew] started to walk.

103.   wii wii wii wii minha-wu-la   kaawe
        (sound of Curlew)   animal-DAT-3sgNOM   'go down'PAST
        'Wii wii wi', he became an animal.

104.   kaaram   pula   pama-la   wicico
        Dreamtime 3duNOM man-3duNOM   travel togetherREDUP
        In the Dreamtime, those two men were travelling together.

105.   ngula pupi   ya'an-la   mamama
        then   firesticks JUST-3duNOM   holdREDUP
        Then they twirled the firesticks in vain.

106.   ngale   madhji
        1duincNOM   hungry
        'We're hungry.'

107.   nhila-ngu   epa mungga
        3sgNOM-3sgDAT   AFF eat
        He [Curlew] went and ate anyway.

108.   nhila   kana ya'a
              3sgNOM PERF NEG
              He wasn't well.

109.   yuku pongkobo# yuku   ngaari# thala-la
              THING grasshopper THING what   centipede-3sgNOM
                munggungga-nhum
                eatREDUP-HIST
              He ate grasshoppers and what's-its-name - centipedes.

110.   madhji waya aara-la   thenena-nhum
              hungry   bad   thatABS-3sgNOM walkREDUP-HIST
              He was awfully hungry.

111.   wii   minha-wu-la   kaawe
              (sound of Curlew) animal-DAT-3sgNOM   'go down'PAST
              'Wii,' he turned into an animal.

112.   nhila-ngu   yama-ma, wadha-ni,
              3sgNOM-3sgDAT   thus-EMPH crow-SUBORD
                minha-wu   kaawe
                animal-DAT   'go down'PAST
              And he in the same way - Crow that is - he became an animal.

113.   kaaram-ni
              Dreamtime-SUBORD
              In the Dreamtime.

6.3   FIGHTING

The Nganhcara, like other people of the area are very individualistic
(1.4.2). In such a society, conflict is inevitable as individuals seek to
command the resources of power and prestige. Conflict is often negotiated
verbally, but violence is not uncommon. In this narration, a middle-aged
woman relates how she and others managed to prevent an incident between
two youths from escalating into a more serious conflict. The text was
narrated spontaneously during a 1979 fieldwork session, the morning after
the events described.

114.   nhila   pukpe aara,   pukpe J, nhila   kuli-nhja
              3sgNOM child   thatABS   child   J 3sgNOM   anger-COM
                nuntunpa
                runREDUP
              That boy, J, got angry [lit. ran with anger].

115.   pukpe nhila   ngaka   mungga
              child   3sgNOM   water [here: beer] drink
              The boy had drunk beer.

116.   nhila   ngaka mungga
        3sgNOM water drink
        He had drunk beer.

117.   ngulanhila   drangk   umpe
        then 3sgNOM   drunk   cutPAST
        Then he got drunk.

118.   ngula nhila   kuli-nhja nhingu K-n-ngu   nhuntunpa
        then   3sgNOM anger-COM 3sgDAT K-DAT-3sgDAT runREDUP
        Then got angry with K.

119.   ngula nhila   pama uthu waawaa
        then   3sgNOM man   dead callREDUP
        Then he 'called a body' [called out the name of a dead person, here K's father].

120.   nhampa-nha   waawaa
        name-3sgACC   callREDUP
        He called out the name.

121.   ngula nhila   K # ngangka+kuli-ngu   thangke
        then   3sgNOM K   anger-3sgDAT   arrivePAST
        Then K got angry.

122.   pukpe aara   pigo-nha
        child   thatABS hitPAST-3sgACC
        He hit that boy.

123.   nhila   pukpe aara# J kamu yejo   nuntunpa
        3sgNOM child   thatABS J blood bleeding runREDUP
        That boy ran [off] bleeding (?)

124.   nhila   keka-wu nhunpa.
        3sgNOM spear-DAT run
        He ran for a spear.

125.   ngula keka aara   eka-nga
        then   spear thatABS   get up-CAUS
        Then he got that spear.

126.   keka-wu, keka-wu m # ngandaaru# naayf
        spear-DAT spear-DAT   what's-it   knife
        For a, for a — what's-it — knife-spear.

127.   keka nhaaru eka-nga
        spear thatABS get up-CAUS
        He got that [kind of] spear.

128.   nhunpa-ng#   agu   ngathu   ngaya-n   wununa-ng
        run-CAUS   PLACE 1sgDAT 1sgNOM-SUBORD   live-1sg
        He ran with it by my place, where I live.

129.   kawa-nga nhana-ng nhunpa
        east-LOC   that-LOC   run
        He ran by the east [of the house].

130.   yupa-dhu-monh   nhunpa-nh
        FUT-MAY-NONFACT run-IRR
        He might have run [away].

131.   ngaya   keka   aara   m # putpam-ngurum   mama-ng
        1sgNOM spear   thatABS   ?tight-3sgDAT   hold-1sg
        [But] I held the spear tight.

132.   nhila   thakake
        3sgNOM get angryPAST:REDUP
        He got angry.

133.   keka wegegbe
        spear retainPAST:REDUP
        He tried to pull the spear off me.

134.   ngaya   keka   aara-ngurum   mań kań ke-nga.
        1sgNOM spear   thatABS-3sgABL   clingREDUP-1sg
        I held on to that spear of his. [-ngurum = pragmatic patient (3.2.1[4])]

135.   mań kań ke-nga
        clingREDUP-1sg
        Kept on holding on.

136.   nhilali, pama kuyu ngaya-n-ngu   wanta-nga
        then   man   woman 1sgNOM-SUBORD-3sgDAT leave-1sg
        nhaaru nhunpa
        thatABS run
        Then my son-in-law [lit. the man to whom I left a woman] ran there [i.e. over to us].

137.   keka ngana   kucuce-ng-ngurum-nha mań kań ke
        spear 1duexcNOM   two-ERG-3sgABL-3sgACC   clingREDUP
        The two of us held on to that spear of his.

138.   keka+thuli   ngana#nhingurum
        spear+woomera 1duNOM 3sgABL
        mań kań ke-nha
        clingPAST:REDUP-3sgACC
        We kept on holding on to that spear and woomera of his.

139.   mań kań ke
        clingPAST:REDUP
        We kept on holding on.

140.   nhamun nhila   pama pibi thangke
        then   3sgNOM MAN   father arrivePAST
        Then [his] father arrived.

141.   nhila   pama pibi thawa
        3sgNOM MAN father sayPAST
        His father said:

142.   nhila   pukpe wayi-ng-nha   pigo
        3sgNOM child   who-ERG-3sgACC hitPAST
        'Who hit [my] boy?'

143.   ya'a. ngaya   keka iiru   mań kań ki-nga
        No. 1sgNOM   spear thisABS   clingPRES:REDUP-1sg
        No [i.e. not me]. I'm holding on to this spear.

144.   nhamun koye   puyaye   striitu-wu-la   thape
        then   outside   outward   street-DAT-3duNOM go   outPAST
        Then they went away outside into the street.

145.   koye nhila# pama m# kuyu   ngaya-n-ngu
        outside 3sgNOM man   woman   1sgNOM-SUBORD-3sgDAT
          wanta-ng nhalung-la-nha   mań kań ke
          leave-1sg   thatERG-3sgNOM-3sgACC clingPAST:REDUP
        Outside my son-in-law kept on holding on.

146.   keka+thuli-la-nha   mań kań ke.
        spear+womera-3sgNOM-3sgACC cling:PAST:REDUP
        He kept on holding on to that spear and woomera. Kept on holding on.

147.   mań kań ke.
        clingPAST:REDUP
        Kept on holding on.

148.   keka nhaaru# ungkpa-dhan
        spear thatABS break-3plPAST
        They broke the spear.

149.   keka thuthe
        spear breakPAST
        The spear broke.

150. nhaaru   nhila   pukpe   puyawa   nhunpa, agawu,   agawu
     thatABS 3sgNOM   child   eastward run   thatDAT thatDAT
       pama+muwa   L-n   wunune-n
       OLD MAN   L-SUBORD   live-PRES
     Then the boy ran off to the east, to there, to where old man L lives.

151. nhaguwu   nhunpa
     thatDAT   run
     He ran there.

152. ka'i pukpe aara-monh-nha   pigu-nha
     NEG   boy   thatABS-NONFACT-3sgACC   hit-IRR
     He could have hit that boy [i.e. K, but he didn't].

153. nganhca   nhilarum   angan-nhca   wonje
     1plexcNOM   all   thatLOC-1plexcNOM   gatherPAST
     We all gathered there.

154. nhangun   woo-nhca.   woo-nhca
     thatLOC   argueRECIP-1plexcNOM   argueRECIP-1plexcNOM
     There we argued and argued.

155. ya'a-m   ka'impung#   kamu+punga-nh
     NEG-EMPH   NEG   bloody?-3sgACC
       pek-o-dhan
       hit-RECIP-3plPAST
     [But] they didn't fight (and draw blood) [again].

156. nhunha   pukpe thono   aara   epa-nh   pigo,   J
     3sgACC   child one   thatABS   AFF-3sgACC hitPAST J
       nhunha kamu nhila   K-ng
       3sgACC blood 3sgNOM   K-ERG
     Only that boy got hit; K [hit] J drawing blood.

7.   VOCABULARY

The first two sections of this chapter list basic Kugu Uwanh vocabulary by semantic field and by alphabetical order. The third section contains an alphabetical list of grammatical morphemes. All of the items here were collected during our 1979 fieldwork.   For nouns, the appropriate generic (classifier) is given. Because generic use is optional, some of the nouns we recorded without an associated generic may, in fact, have one; particularly suspect are time expressions in section X, many of which probably take the generic agu 'TIME, PLACE'. Grammatical status is indicated exhaustively in the second and third sections and as necessary for clarity in the first section. The following abbreviations are used:

Adj	Adjective
Adv	Adverb
Clit	(En)clitic
Gen	Generic (Classifier)
Vint	Intransitive verb
Vtr	Transitive verb
Vditr	Ditransitive verb
Int	Interjection
N	noun
Pcl	Particle
Pro	Pronoun
Dem	Demonstrative
Q	Quantifier
Sfx	suffix

In some cases we do not have examples of contextual use to determine the appropriate classification; in such cases an educated guess followed by a question mark, e.g. Vint?, is given. Loans from English are indicated by the annotation (<Eng).

7.1   VOCABULARY BY SEMANTIC FIELD

This section provides Kugu Uwanh forms for the list supplied by the *Handbook*'s editors. A few items are omitted where the Uwanh term is nonexistent or unknown, and a few additional items have been included in areas where Uwanh vocabulary is richer than the general list (e.g. sea creatures).

NOUNS

A - body parts
pindha+eka, head, skull
pindha+eka+waba, brain
yengan, head hair
muwa, grey-haired, old
ngulu+ngangka, forehead
kaa+thanta, face
thanta, eye
kaa+kuthu, nose
kono, ear
walu+manta, cheek
walu+koko, jaw

thepa, chin
thaa, mouth
thaa+aku, lip
thaa+panci, beard
kanu, tooth
thaa+ngantha, tongue
thaa+kati, saliva, spittle
manu, front of neck
manu+manha, throat
muci thaa, back of neck
ingki, shoulder
yiwan, armpit
puntha, arm
punti, elbow
ma'a, hand
ma'a+nhingadhe, thumb
ma'a+eka, fingernail
ma'a+pukpe, finger
tha'u+eka, toenail
paba, breast
umu, chest
wa'a+munthu, rib
pilu, side of hip
thadu, top of hip
ngangka, belly
kudin, navel
thupi, stomach, guts
thuli+kaa+kuthu, heart
kongom, kidney
yega, lungs
kogom, liver
kiga+ngangka, back
munu, buttocks
munu+anci, anus
kuman, thigh
pungku+pindha, knee
wanya, back of knee
konto, lower leg
konto+mila, ankle
tha'u, foot
kanda+munu, heel
kunci, penis
kunci+untu, scrotum
kunci+untu+thuka, testicle
kunci+pipu, semen
yi'i panci, pubic hair

pu'u, vagina
pu'u thaa aku, vulva
kuna, excrement
kumpu, urine
moo, body
panci, body hair, fur
aku, skin
ngate, bone
kamu, blood
nhepe, pulse
yi'i, fat
kimpi, sweat
wanhci, sore
thici, pus
ngaana, shadow of person

B - human classification
pama, person, man
kuyu, woman
pukpe kandha, newborn child
pukpe, child
pukpe mepen, baby (=little child)
pukpe koncenh, boy
pukpe mongkom, young lad
pama manthayan, young man
pama kompo, mature man
pama+muwa, old man
kuyu+waya, old woman
pukpe pu'udha, girl
kuyu mucami, widow
pama kigabe, widower
kiithana, white person
waypela, white person
pliisman, policeman

C - kinship
ngathukpe, mother's elder brother / sister
ngathale, mother's younger brother, father-in-law
ngathidhe, mother, mother's younger sister
pinye, father's elder brother
ngaci, father, father's younger brother
pama pibi, father of someone else

ngathinye, father's sister, mother-in-law

kuyu+waya ngathame, mother's mother

pama+muwa ngathunge, mother's father

kuyu waya ngothope, father's mother

pama+muwa ngathake, father's father

ngathunye, elder brother

ngathake, younger brother

ngathepe, elder sister

ngathule, younger sister

kunhji, sibling, cousin

pukpe nhengka, children of male/brother

pukpe othom, children of female/sister

pama pocon, husband

kuyu+thumam, wife

pama muuyu, brother-in-law

kuyu muuyu, sister-in-law

D - mammals

minha kompo kigande, echidna

minha watha, water rat

minha kupatha, land rat

yuku munpa, little land rat

minha cingka, native cat

minha kaanggu, bandicoot

minha kaanam, glider possum

minha muduwa, ring-tailed possum

minha yome, grey possum

minha pukawanh, cuscus

minha waga, small spotted possum

minha pangku, wallaby

minha yakalba, red kangaroo

minha kuja, grey kangaroo

mulu, tail

ku'a, dog, dingo

minha woole, yellow flying fox (fruit bat)

minha mukum, black flying fox (fruit bat)

yuku mali, insectivorous bat

ku'a maara / yaruman, horse

minha poothera, bullock

minha piki, pig

yuku yewo, whale

minha wanhaji, dolphin

minha waala, long-nosed dolphin

minha thinhanmala, dugong

E - reptiles

yuku pinci, saltwater crocodile

minha kanhe, freshwater crocodile

minha loorom, sea turtle

minha wanhci, short-necked swamp turtle

minha pal'a, short-necked tortoise

minha wali, blue-tongue lizard

minha thunta, frilled lizard

yuku koce waliń go, gecko

minha monge, spotted tree goanna

minha thathce, sand goanna

yuku ngace, snake (generic)

minha yangki, python

minha thepanda, taipan

yuku ngace thuli, seasnake

F - birds

minha thuci, small bird (generic)

minha thuka, egg

yuku pudhi, nest (of bird or insect)

thuthu, feather

minha nhampi, emu

minha kor'o, brolga

minha monte, jabiru

minha madhe, pelican

minha ko'on, magpie goose

minha koone, Burdekin duck

minha kulawi, stone curlew

minha ań gu, bustard

minha thukan, scrub turkey

minha nguyumba, black swan

minha ngathalye, koel

minha thuci yika, green bower-bird

minha pinba, rainbow lorikeet

minha punji, tawny frogmouth

minha thuci yagbi, peewee

minha ekondo, dollar bird

minha wadha, crow

minha thuci yaayang, cuckoo shrike

minha kimpu, kookaburra

minha thuci kothcogo, willy wagtail

minha kukuń ngu, golden bronze cuckoo

minha wudbi, channel-billed cuckoo

minha muwa, white cockatoo

minha nganthan, black cockatoo

minha kalime, galah

minha nhompo, hawk

minha patpa, kite hawk

minha wincin, yellow-billed spoonbill

minha kaabila, royal spoonbill

minha umele, pied cormorant

minha nguma, black cormorant

minha panthiyanh, darter

minha thampe, black duck

minha puypune, wood duck

minha pupu, pheasant coucal

minha miji, silver gull

minha kuuyi, tern

minha thuci nhaara, swallow, swift

minha thuci ceeceng, honeyeater

G - fishes

nga'a, fish, seafood

nga'a migu, broadmouthed freshwater catfish

nga'a poykolo, sharpnosed freshwater catfish

nga'a muka, forktailed saltwater catfish

nga'a tooto, barramundi

nga'a molbe, grunter

nga'a wiinganh, queenfish

nga'a lutu, sleepy cod

nga'a umbi, jewfish

yuku nhumeń ganh, stonefish

yuku upun, eel

nga'a patpa, anglerfish

nga'a maykun, riflefish

nga'a kuypa, freshwater bream

nga'a thupulu, garfish

nga'a thuuyu, sole, flounder

nga'a miji, fish sp. (small oval)

yuku thoyowo, hammerhead shark

nga'a pu'an, grey nurse shark

nga'a kampanyi, sawfish

nga'a manyire, butterfly ray

nga'a thawanha, eagle ray

nga'a ngome, gummy shark

H - insects, etc.

yuku pi'i, antbed

yuku mecom, little black ant

yuku watha, green ant

yuku kaadhabadha, wasp

mayi puci, beeswax

mayi wuń ga, big sugarbag

mayi wata, little sugarbag

yuku kunci, scorpion

yuku thala, centipede

yuku patpu, maggot

yuku wuuyuwuya, cockroach

yuku wolo, blowfly

yuku nheen, fly

yuku me'e, mosquito

yuku inye, sandfly

yuku nguuyumba, butterfly

yuku kondhe, moth

yuku wagalnda, caterpillar

yuku kapan, hairy caterpillar

yuku ngadha, spider

yuku maaya, web

yuku waawi, earthworm

nga'a ngancalan, prawn

yuku wa'i, jellyfish

nga'a puuya, mudcrab

nga'a ngoole, sandcrab

eka, shell

yuku wele, bailer shell

yuku yeban, bivalve shell

yuku thuci, mother of pearl

yuku punga, nautilus

nga'a yigu, goose barnacle

yuku peba, cuttlefish

yuku thata, frog

yuku muduwa, cricket
yuku kurawu, dragonfly
yuku pongkobo, grasshopper
yuku pinci, preying mantis, stick
    insect
yuku wongbo, Christmas beetle,
    Rhinoceros beetle
yuku mema, firefly
yuku kupan mukum, tick
yuku kupan, head louse
mayi pudhi, European bee
mayi puybe, little yellow bee
yuku thawa, native bee

I - language, ceremony etc.
kugu, language, speech
nhampa, name
aka, cicatrice
wu'u, red ochre
kuurawu, yellow ochre
agu thupi, bora, ceremonial
    ground
nganagu, company land

J - artefacts, etc.
(yuku) weenga, boomerang
(yuku) woyo, throwing stick
(yuku (kantu)) woyodho, nulla
    nulla, fighting stick
kacin, yamstick
muuyu, bullroarer
keka, spear
keka thu'u, wallaby spear
keka yikan, long (fighting) spear
keka cawara, knife spear
pitha+caka, multi-pronged fish
    spear
thuli, woomera
pu'an, shield
thayan+muka, stone axe
thuma+pupi, fire stick
thuma+thaji, torch
thuma+muntha, charcoal
wangga amba, fine mesh fishing
    net
wangga miji, broad mesh fishing
    net

yuku pecele, fishing line
munpa, fish trap
yuku thone, bark canoe
yuku olko, dilly bag, basket
yuku uku, big bark container
matpam, engraver
puranhci, hut, humpy
thagan, large summer house
yuku wutpa, sleeping platform

K - fire, food, water
minha, meat, animal, bird
mayi, vegetable, fruit
thuma, fire, firewood
ngu'unji, grass fire, bushfire
thoko, smoke
puthca, hot ashes
thuma+thanta, flame, light from
    fire, live coal
ngaka, water, rain
ngaka yee, flood
ngaka kanti, saltwater
wa'awa, creek, river

L - celestial, weather
punga, sun
agu pungam, daytime
wiba, shade
kapi, moon
thunpi, star
agu ngunhcan, nighttime
yuku ngaayu, rainbow
ngunyin, sky
yuku ngunyin, cloud
peba, wind
yuku wamara, willy willy, twister
thepanda, thunder, lightning

M - geography
agu, place, time
ngaka thempo, ocean
yipipi, low coastal ridge
ngalaman, wide open place
agu kulam, path, road
nhanhnyi, dirt
ngaanha, sand
kancari, river sand

pipi, mud, clay
wogo, dust
anci, hole, cave
agu palngka, plainland
agu pambe, swampland
yooyko, hill, elevation
(yuku) muka, rock, stone, pebble

N - arboreal, etc.
yuku, thing, stick, tree
kangka, bush
enga, leaf
agu kuga, scrub
agu thathca pii, mangrove swamp
yuku tha'u kuman, root
yuku wati, bark
waka, grass
waka thaabengga, goatshead burr
mayi ongkon, waterlily (Nymphaea
    gigantea)
mayi panten, bullgru (Heleochario
    sphaelata)
mayi kodhe, bush celery, waterlily
    stem
mayi munhnyim, bush turnip
    (Typhonium Brownii)
mayi po'olo, Nonda plum
yuku putu, Eucalyptus sp: ghost
    gum (E. papuana) or
    bloodwood (E. terminalis)
yuku thaympa, boxwood
yuku wooyodho, she oak
    (Casuarina)
yuku pupi, matchwood
mayi thantu, black mangrove
    (Bruguiera Rheidii)
yuku thampi, lancewood (Acacia
    Rothii)
yuku thumbudhu, paperbark tree
    (Melaleuca leucadendra)
yuku wage, white gum
yuku woye, fig tree (Ficus
    infectoria)
yuku nhukan, blackboy grass tree
yuku okonhnye, hibiscus
    (Hibiscus tiliaceus)
yuku ponthe, stringybark

(Eucalyptus tetradonta)
yuku yengbe, ladyapple tree
    (Eugenia suborbicularis)
yuku wotho, screw palm
    (Pandanus spiralis)
yuku thuuyu, ti-tree
mayi mugam, long yam (Dioscorea
    trversa)
mayi kungba, round yam
    (Dioscorea sativa, var.
    rotunda)

O - ADJECTIVES
[1] - quantifiers
thono, one
kuce, two
ko'ele, three
uyu, some, many

[2] - adjectives
ngunhca, black
pathca, white
ngolpolintha, red
yoko, big, fat
mepen, little
unggu, long, tall
kaarin, short
koje(nh), straight
wumpa, bent
kuurulu, twisted, bent
thumuma, hot (temperature)
kuthcira, cold (temperature)
yinje, wet
poje, dry
punha, soft, weak
nhacin, heavy
poorowo, light
thanta+pungga, blunt
puganhum, new
waya, old, bad, useless
mini, good
ngangka+kuli, anger, bad-temper
    (N)
ngangka+kuli   waya,
    unagressiveness (N)
winhnyidha, frightened
wendho, deaf, insane

uthu, dead
yethala, alive
yetha, raw, unripe
panci, get cooked (of meat) (Vint)
mancin, cooked (of vegetable), ripe
manpanh, rotten
nhala, tired
thagi, hungry (for meat)
madhji, hungry
ngaka+anca, be thirsty (V)
othe, full (of food), sated
athatpa, shallow
thangku, deep
thaku, left
mala, right
pintili, smooth
thatata, rough
ngangka+thayan, braveness (N)
ngangka+anci, sadness (N)

VERBS

P - motion
uwa, go, come
wico, travel in company
putpi, go in, enter
thapi, come out
thangki, arrive
wanta, leave
wań ki, return
nguthca, go out early in morning
kaa ungpa, turn, change direction
waka, chase; follow (tr)
icing+wanta, overtake
thuji, crawl; ford a river
thaa poye, jump
kaagi, dance; play
nhunpa, run; fly
kambi, disappear; run out; be away
anhci, fall; sneeze
mata, ascend; climb up
uka, descend, go down
munji, bathe, swim
wogoma, cross river by swimming with a log

Q - rest
wuna/e, stay, camp
nhiina/e, sit
eke, get up
thana/e, stand (intr)
thaaranga, put standing (tr)
waa wuna, lie down, sleep
pimbi, float

R - induced position
wunpa, put; gather
wanja, hang (tr)
wanji, hang (intr)
maa, pick up
mama, grasp, hold; manipulate
pi'a, keep, hold on
wegbe, retain, refuse (so. sg.)
kali/a/u, carry, take, bring
yengka, send, swallow
thutha, pluck
thaa thutha, take out ; pull out; take off
wici, pull, drag, draw
unca, push down
thii, throw
thadhi, hide, put inside (tr)
adha, give (as obligation)
waa, give, tell, scold

S - affect
pigu, hit
peka, throw missile at
akintha, poke
intha, squeeze, pinch
pithcanga, stab
wa'i, dig
panyi, dig out (with hand); take out
uga, scrape
thuthi, break (intr)
yaka, cut up
umpi, cut
ungpa, break (tr)
pithca, burst, smash (intr)
mancinga, cook, boil (tr)
enje, cook, singe

ngaga, cook in ashes
panci, get cooked, catch fire
yenganga, untie, undo
nhumba, rub
awalnga, smear with sweat
rayt-(i)madha, write
pee-madha, pay
kamba, cover, bury, kapmari, extinguish (fire) by burying
yumpi, make, do
kadhja, build
minji, finish

T - attention
kubi, wait
uwi, see, look at, find
yidhja, stare
thawi, look for, search
ngii, hear, listen

U - talking, etc.
thawa/e, speak, talk, tell (tr)
ngateko, chat (RECIP)
ente, ask, request
kumba, call out (in joy)
paci, call, sing out
waji, sing
aka, swear at

V - corporeal
mungga, eat, drink
patha, bite, toke
kandhi, vomit
pithi, dream
thaa+bama, yawn
nhudha, smell (tr)
wu'a, blow (tr)
pinda, lick, suck
thaa+thunda, kiss
pu'u aci (M'), copulate
agu ukewi, be born
ema, grow (intr)

wanhcidhani, be sore, ache
uthu-ma, die
paabi, cry

X - LOCATION

kungke, north
yibe, south
kawa, east
kuwa, west
thinthu, near
kaci, far
nhadhu, away
kanhnyi, up
pake, down
puyu, thither
pala, hither
weń ko, side

Y - TIME

puga, yesterday, tomorrow
pugaman, day before yesterday
yama-ng, now, thus
wa'ala, today
ngula, later, afterwards
manu+ngunhca, morning
yi'i thaa kuthcanh, afternoon
agu pengge, twilight
agu kaaram, Dreamtime
oncon, 'dry-wet' season (Mar-Jul)
kayiman, dry season (Jul-Oct)
thutpam, hot dry season (Oct-Dec)
kabam, wet season (Dec-Mar)

Z - INTERJECTION

yee, yes
ya'a, no
ngonggonggo, don't know (Adj.)
apowu, goodbye
ka'i, not, like (Pcl.)

7.2   ALPHABETICAL VOCABULARY

The words of the thematic vocabulary are listed in alphabetical order below. Standard alphabetical order is followed, with /'/ preceding /a/.

adha, Vditr: give (as obligation)
agu, N: place, time
agu kaaram, N: Dreamtime
agu kuga, N: scrub
agu kulam, N: path, road
agu ngaka thaa, N: littoral zone
agu ngunhcan, N: nighttime
agu palngka, N: plainland
agu pambe, N: swampland
agu pengge, N: twilight
agu pungam, N: daytime
agu thathca pii, N: mangrove swamp
agu thupi, N: bora, ceremonial ground
agu ukewi, Vint: be born
aka, N: cicatrice
aka, Vtr: swear at
akintha, Vtr: poke
aku, N: skin
anci, N hole, cave
anhci, Vint: fall
apowu, Int: goodbye
athatpa, Adj: shallow
awalnga, Vtr: smear with sweat
eka, N: shell
eke, Vint: get up
ema, Vint: grow
enga, N: leaf
enje, Vtr: cook, singe
ente, Vtr: ask, request
icing+wanta, Vtr: overtake
ingki, N: shoulder
intha, Vtr: squeeze, pinch, choke
ka'i, Pcl: not, like
kaa+kuthu, N: nose
kaa+thanta, N: face
kaa+ungpa, Vint: turn, change direction
kaagi, Vint: dance, play
kaarin, Adj: short
kabam, N: wet season (Dec-Mar)
kaci, Adj: far
kacin, N: yamstick

kadhja, Vtr: build
kali/a/u, Vtr: carry, take, bring
kamba, Vtr: cover, bury
kambi, Vint: run out, be absent
kamu, N: blood
kancari, N: river sand
kanda munu, N: heel
kandhi, Vint: vomit
kangka, N: bush
kanhnyi, N: up
kanu, N: tooth
kapi, N: moon
kawa, N: east
kayiman, N: dry season (Jul-Oct)
keka, N: spear
keka cawara, N: knife spear
keka thu'u, N: wallaby spear
keka yikan, N: long (fighting) spear
kiga+ngangka, N: back
kiithana (<Eng), N: white person
kimpi, N: sweat
ko'ele, Q: three
kogom, N: liver
koje(nh), Adj: straight
kongom, N: kidney
kono, N: ear
konto, N: lower leg
konto+mila, N: ankle
ku'a, N: dog, dingo
ku'a+maara, N: horse
kubi, Vint?: wait
kuce, Q: two
kudin, N: navel
kugu, N: language, speech
kuman, N: thigh
kumba, Vint call out (in joy)
kumpu, N: urine
kuna, N: excrement
kunci, N: penis
kunci+pipu, N: semen
kunci+untu, N: scrotum
kunci+untu+thuka, N: testicle
kungke, N: north

kunhji, N: sibling, cousin
kuthcira, N: cold (temperature)
kuurawu, N: yellow ochre
kuurulu, Adj: twisted, bent
kuwa, N: west
kuyu, N: woman
kuyu mucami, N: widow
kuyu muuyu, N: sister-in-law
kuyu+thumam, N: wife
kuyu+waya, N: old woman
kuyu+waya ngathame, N: mother's mother
kuyu+waya ngothope, N: father's mother
ma'a, N: hand
ma'a+eka, N: fingernail
ma'a+nhingadhe, N: thumb
ma'a+pukpe, N: finger
maa, Vtr: pick up, get, buy
madhji, Adj: hungry
mala, Adj?: right
mama, Vtr: grasp, hold
mancin, Adj: cooked (of vegetable), ripe
mancinga, Vtr: cook, boil
manpanh, Adj: rotten
manu, N: front of neck
manu+manha, N: throat
manu+ngunhca, N: morning
mata, Vint: ascend
matpam, N: engraver
mayi, N: vegetable, fruit
mayi kodhe, N: bush celery, waterlily stem
mayi kungba, N: round yam (Dioscorea sativa, var. rotunda)
mayi mugam, N: long yam (Dioscorea transversa)
mayi munhnyim, N: bush turnip (Typhonium Brownii)
mayi ongkon, N: waterlily (Nymphaea gigantea)
mayi panten, N: bullgru (Heleochario sphaelata)
mayi po'olo, N: Nonda plum
mayi puci, N: beeswax

mayi pudhi, N: European bee
mayi puybe, N: little yellow bee
mayi thantu, N: black mangrove (Bruguiera Rheidii)
mayi wata, N: little sugarbag
mayi wuń ga, N: big sugarbag
mepen, Adj: little
minha, N: meat, animal, bird
minha ań gu, N: bustard
minha cingka, N: native cat
minha ekondo, N: dollar bird
minha kaabila, N: royal spoonbill
minha kaanam, N: glider possum
minha kaanggu, N: bandicoot
minha kalime, N: galah
minha kanhe, N: freshwater crocodile
minha kimpu, N: kookaburra
minha ko'on, N: magpie goose
minha kompo kigande, N: echidna
minha koone, N: Burdekin duck
minha kor'o, N: brolga
minha kuja, N: grey kangaroo
minha kukuń ngu, N: golden bronze cuckoo
minha kulawi, N: stone curlew
minha kupatha, N: land rat
minha kuuyi, N: tern
minha loorom, N: sea turtle
minha madhe, N: pelican
minha miji, N: silver gull
minha monge, N: spotted tree goanna
minha monte, N: jabiru
minha muduwa, N: ring-tailed possum
minha mukum, N: black flying fox (fruit bat)
minha muwa, N: white cockatoo
minha nganthan, N: black cockatoo
minha ngathalye, N: koel
minha nguma, N: black cormorant
minha nguyumba, N: black swan
minha nhampi, N: emu
minha nhompo, N: hawk

minha pal'a, N: short-necked tortoise

minha pangku, N: wallaby

minha panthiyanh, N: darter

minha patpa, N: kite hawk

minha poothera, N: bullock

minha piki, N: pig

minha pinba, N: rainbow lorikeet

minha pukawanh, N: cuscus

minha punji, N: tawny frogmouth

minha pupu, N: pheasant coucal

minha puypune, N: wood duck

minha thampe, N: black duck

minha thathce, N: sand goanna

minha thepanda, N: taipan

minha thinhanmala, N: dugong

minha thuci, N: small bird (generic)

minha thuci ceeceng, N: honeyeater

minha thuci kothcogo, N: willy wagtail

minha thuci nhaara, N: swallow, swift

minha thuci yaayang, N: cuckoo shrike

minha thuci yagbi, N: peewee

minha thuci yika, N: great bower-bird

minha thuka, N: egg

minha thukan, N: scrub turkey

minha thunta, N: frilled lizard

minha umele, N: pied cormorant

minha waala, N: long-nosed dolphin

minha wadha, N: crow

minha waga, N: small spotted possum

minha wali, N: blue-tongue lizard

minha wanhaji, N: dolphin

minha wanhci, N: short-necked swamp turtle

minha watha, N: water rat

minha wincin, N: yellow-billed spoonbill

minha woole, N: yellow flying fox (fruit bat)

minha wudbi, N: channel-billed cuckoo

minha yakalba, N: red kangaroo

minha yangki, N: python

minha yome, N: grey possum

mini, Adj: good

minji, Vint: finish

muci+thaa, N: back of neck

mulu, N: tail

mungga, Vtr: eat, drink

munji, Vint: bathe, swim

munpa, N: fish trap

munu, N: buttocks

munu anci, N: anus

muuyu, N: bullroarer

muwa, Adj: grey-haired, old

nga'a, N: fish, seafood

nga'a kampanyi, N: sawfish

nga'a kuypa, N: freshwater bream

nga'a lutu, N: sleepy cod

nga'a manyire, N: butterfly ray

nga'a maykun, N: riflefish

nga'a migu, N: broadmouthed freshwater catfish

nga'a miji, N: fish sp (small oval)

nga'a molbe, N: grunter

nga'a muka, N: forktailed saltwater catfish

nga'a ngancalan, N: prawn

nga'a ngome, N: gummy shark

nga'a ngoole, N: sandcrab

nga'a patpa, N: anglerfish

nga'a poykolo, N: sharpnosed freshwater catfish

nga'a pu'an, N: grey nurse shark

nga'a puuya, N: mudcrab

nga'a thawanha, N: eagle ray

nga'a thupulu, N: garfish

nga'a thuuyu, N: sole, flounder

nga'a tooto, N: barramundi

nga'a umbi, N: jewfish

nga'a wiinganh, N: queenfish

nga'a yigu, N: goose barnacle

ngaana, N: shadow of person

ngaanha, N: sand

ngaci, N: father, father's younger brother

ngaga, Vtr: cook in ashes

ngaka, N: water, rain

ngaka+anca, Vint: be thirsty

ngaka kanti, N: saltwater

ngaka thempo, N: ocean

ngaka yee, N: flood

ngalaman, N: wide open place

nganagu, N: company land

ngangka, N: belly

ngangka+anci, N: sadness

ngangka+kuli, N: anger, bad-temper

ngangka+kuli waya, N: unagressiveness

ngangka+thayan, N: braveness

ngate, N: bone

ngateko, Vint, RECIP: chat

ngathake, N: younger brother

ngathale, N: mother's younger brother, father-in-law

ngathepe, N: elder sister

ngathidhe, N: mother, mother's younger sister

ngathinye, N: father's elder sister, mother-in-law

ngathukpe, N: mother's elder brother/sister

ngathule, N: younger sister

ngathunye, N: elder brother

ngii, Vtr: hear, listen to

ngolpolintha, Adj: red

ngu'unji, N: grass fire, bushfire

ngula, Adv: later, afterwards

ngonggonggo, Adj: don't know

ngulu ngangka, N: forehead

ngunhca, Adj: black

ngunyin, N: sky

nguthca, Vint: go out early in morning

nhacin, Adj: heavy

nhadhu, Adv: away

nhala, Adj: tired

nhampa, N: name

nhanhnyi, N: dirt

nhepe, N: pulse

nhiina/e, Vint: sit

nhudha, Vtr: smell

nhumba, Vtr: rub

nhunpa, Vint: run, fly

oncon, N: 'dry-wet' season (Mar-July)

othe, Adj: full (of food), sated

paabi, Vint: cry

paba, N: breast

paci, Vint: call, sing out

pake, N: down

pala, Adv: hither

pama, N: person, man

pama kigabe, N: widower

pama kompo, N: mature man

pama manthayan, N: young man

pama+moo, N: body

pama muuyu, N: brother-in-law

pama+muwa, N: old man

pama+muwa ngathake, N: father's father

pama+muwa ngathunge, N: mother's father

pama pibi, N: alter's father

pama pocon, N: husband

panci, Vint: get cooked, catch fire

panci, N: body hair, fur

panyi, Vtr: dig out (with hand); take out

patha, Vtr: bite

pathca, Adj: white

peba, N: wind

peka, Vtr: throw missile at

pee-madha (<Eng), Vtr: pay

pi'a, Vtr: keep, hold on to

pigu, Vtr: hit

pilu, N: side of hip

pimbi, Vint: float

pinda, Vtr: lick, suck

pindha+eka, N: head, skull

pindha+eka+waba, N: brain

pintili, Adj: smooth

pinye, N: father's elder brother

pipi, N: mud, clay

pitha caka, N: multi-pronged fish spear

pithca, Vint: burst, smash

pithcanga, Vtr: stab

pithi, Vint?: dream

pliisman, N: policeman

poje, Adj: dry

poorowo, Adj: light (of weight)

pu'an, N: shield

pu'u, N: vagina

pu'u+aci (M'), Vtr?: copulate (with?)

pu'u+thaa aku, N: vulva

puga, N: yesterday, tomorrow

pugaman, N: day before yesterday

puganhum, Adj: new

pukpe, N: child

pukpe kandha, N: newborn child

pukpe koncenh, N: boy

pukpe mongkom, N: young lad

pukpe nhengka, N: children of male/brother

pukpe othom, N: children of female or sister

pukpe pu'udha, N: girl

punga, N: sun

pungku+pindha, N: knee

punha, Adj: soft, weak

puntha, N: arm

punti, N: elbow

puranhci, N: hut, humpy

puthca, N: ashes, hot

putpi, Vint: go in, enter

puyu, Adv: thither

rayt-imadha (<Eng), Vtr: write

tha'u, N: foot

tha'u+eka, N: toenail

thaa, N: mouth

thaa+aku, N: lip

thaa+kati, N: saliva, spittle

thaa+ngantha, N: tongue

thaa+panci, N: beard

thaa+poye, Vint: jump

thaa+thunda, Vtr: kiss

thaa+thutha, Vtr: take out, pull out

thaa+bama, Vint: yawn

thaara-nga, Vtr: put standing

thadhi, Vtr: hide inside

thadu, N: top of hip

thagan, N: large summer house

thagi, Adj: hungry

thaku, Adj?: left

thana/e, Vint: stand

thangki, Vint: arrive

thangku, Adj: deep

thanta, N: eye

thanta+pungga, Adj: blunt

thapi, Vint: come out

thatata, Adj: rough

thawa/e, Vint: speak, talk

thawi, Vtr: look for, search

thayan+muka, N: stone axe

thepa, N: chin

thepanda, N: thunder, lightning

thici, N: pus

thii, Vtr: throw

thinthu, Adj: near

thoko, N: smoke

thono, Q: one

thuji, Vint: crawl, ford a river

thuli, N: woomera

thuli kaa kuthu, N: heart

thuma, N: fire, firewood

thuma+muntha, N: charcoal

thuma+pupi, N: fire stick

thuma+thaji, N: torch

thuma+thanta, N: flame, light from fire, live coal

thumuma, Adj: hot (temperature)

thunpi, N: star

thupi, N: stomach, guts

thuthi, Vint: break

thuthu, N: feather

thutpam, N: hot dry season (Oct-Dec)

uga, Vtr: scrape

uka, Vint: descend

umpi, Vtr: cut

umu, N: chest

unca, Vtr: push down

unggu, Adj: long, tall

ungpa, Vtr: break

uthu, Adj: dead

uthu-ma, Vint: die
uwa, Vint: go, come
uwi, Vtr: see, look at, find
uyu, Q: some, many
wa'a+munthu, N: rib
wa'ala, N: today
wa'awa, N: creek, river
wa'i, Vtr: dig
waa, Vtr: give, tell, scold
waa+wuna, Vint: sleep
waji, Vtr?: sing
waka, Vtr: follow, chase
waka, N: grass
waka thaabengga, N: goatshead burr
walu+koko, N: jaw
walu+manta, N: cheek
wangga amba, N: fine mesh fishing net
wangga miji, N: broad mesh fishing net
wanhci, Adj: sore
wanhcidhani, Vint: be sore, ache
wanja, Vtr: hang
wanji, Vint: hang
wanta, Vtr: leave
wanya, N: back of knee
waya, Adj: old, bad, useless
wań ki, Vint: return
waypela (<Eng), N: white person
wegbe, Vtr: retain, refuse
wendho, Adj?: deaf, insane
weń ko, side
wiba, N: shade
wici, Vtr: pull, drag, draw
wico, Vint: travel in company (RECIP)
winhnyidha, Adj: frightened
wogo, N: dust
wogoma, Vint: cross river by swimming with a log
wu'a, Vtr: blow
wu'u, N: red ochre
wumpa, Adj: bent
wuna/e, Vint: stay, camp
wunpa, Vtr: put, gather

ya'a, Int: no; N: nothing
yaka, Vtr: cut up
yama-ng, Adv: now, thus
yaruman, N: horse
yee (<Eng?), Int: yes
yega, N: lungs
yengan, N: head hair
yenganga, Vtr: untie, undo
yengka, Vtr: send, swallow
yetha, Adj: raw, unripe
yethala, Adj: alive
yi'i, N: fat, border
yi'i+panci, N: pubic hair
yi'i+thaa+kuthcanh, N: afternoon
yibe, N: south
yidhja, Vtr?: stare (at?)
yipipi, N: low coastal ridge
yinje, Adj: wet
yiwan, N: armpit
yoko, Adj: big, fat
yooyko, N: hill, elevation
yuku, N: thing, stick, tree
yuku inye, N: sandfly
yuku kaadhabadha, N: wasp
yuku kapan, N: hairy caterpillar
yuku koce waliń go, N: gecko
yuku kondhe, N: moth
yuku kunci, N: scorpion
yuku kupan, N: louse, head
yuku kupan mukum, N: tick
yuku kurawu, N: dragonfly
yuku maaya, N: web
yuku mali, N: insectivorous bat
yuku me'e, N: mosquito
yuku mecom, N: little black ant
yuku mema, N: firefly
yuku muduwa, N: cricket
(yuku) muka, N: rock, stone, pebble
yuku munpa, N: little land rat
yuku ngaayu, N: rainbow
yuku ngace, N: snake
yuku ngace thuli, N: seasnake
yuku ngadha, N: spider
yuku ngunyin, N: cloud
yuku nguuyumba, N: butterfly

yuku nheen, N: fly

yuku nhukan, N: blackboy grass tree

yuku nhumeń ganh, N: stonefish

yuku okonhnye, N: hibiscus (Hibiscus tiliaceus)

yuku olko, N: dilly bag, basket

yuku patpu, N: maggot

yuku peba, N: cuttlefish

yuku pecele, N: fishing line

yuku pi'i, N: antbed

yuku pinci, N: saltwater crocodile; preying mantis, stick insect

yuku pongkobo, N: grasshopper

yuku ponthe, N: stringybark (Eucalyptus tetradonta)

yuku pudhi, N: nest

yuku punga, N: nautilus

yuku pupi, N: matchwood

yuku putu, N: Eucalyptus sp: ghost gum (E. papuana) or bloodwood (E. terminalis)

yuku tha'u kuman, N: root

yuku thala, N: centipede

yuku thampi, N: lancewood (Acacia Rothii)

yuku thawa, N: native bee

yuku thaympa, N: boxwood

yuku thone, N: bark canoe

yuku thoyowo, N: hammerhead shark

yuku thuci, N: mother of pearl

yuku thumbudhu, N: paperbark tree (Melaleuca leucadendra)

yuku thuuyu, N: ti-tree

yuku uku, N: big bark container

yuku upun, N: eel

yuku wa'i, N: jellyfish

yuku waawi, N: earthworm

yuku thata, N: frog

yuku wagalnda, N: caterpillar

yuku wage, N: white gum

yuku wamara, N: willy willy, twister

yuku watha, N: green ant

yuku wati, N: bark

(yuku) weenga, N: boomerang

yuku wele, N: bailer shell

yuku wolo, N: blowfly

yuku wongbo, N: Christmas beetle, Rhinoceros beetle

yuku wooyodho, N: she oak (Casuarina)

yuku wotho, N: screw palm (Pandanus spiralis)

yuku woye, N: figtree (Ficus infectoria)

(yuku) woyo, N: throwing stick

(yuku (kantu)) woyodho, N: nulla nulla, fighting stick

yuku wutpa, N: sleeping platform

yuku wuuyuwuya, N: cockroach

yuku yeban, N: bivalve shell

yuku yengbe, N: ladyapple tree (Eugenia suborbicularis)

yuku yewo, N: whale

yumpi, Vtr: make, do

7.3   LIST OF GRAMMATICAL MORPHEMES

-dha, 2plIMP V Sfx 3.4.4

-dha, CAUSative V Sfx 3.4.10[3]

-dha, HAVing Adj Sfx 3.2.3[1]

-dhan, 3plPAST V Sfx 3.4.3

-dhani, CAUSative V Sfx 3.4.10

-dhu, MAY Clit 4.12[4]

-ku, EXCLamation Clit 4.13[5]

-la, Pro 3duNOM 3.3.2

-la, Pro 3sgNOM 3.3.2

-lan, Pro 3duDAT/ACC 3.3.2

-lanam, Pro 3duABL 3.3.2

-le, Pro 1duincNOM 3.3.2

-li, 1duincIMP V Sfx 3.4.4

-li, THEN Clit 4.12[9]

-lin, Pro 1duincDAT/ACC 3.3.2

-linam, Pro 1duincABL 3.3.2

-m, ABLative Clit 3.2.1[4]

-ma, EMPHatic Clit 4.13[1]

-ma, INTransitive V Sfx 3.4.12
assimilating Eng. loans 3.4.13
-(ma)-ku, IMPerative Pcl/Clit 4.13[4]
-mala, REFL Pro Sfx 3.3.1
-monh, NONFACTual Clit 4.12[7]
-mpa, Pro 1plincNOM 3.3.2
-mpara, Pro 1plincDAT/ACC 3.3.2
-mparam, Pro 1plincABL 3.3.2
-mu, 1plincIMP V Sfx 3.4.4
-n, 2sgPAST / UNMarKeD PRES V Sfx 3.4.3
-n, LOCative Clit 3.2.1[7]
-n, VOCative Clit 3.2.1[8]
-na, DATive Clit 3.2.1[3]
-na, Pro 1duexcNOM 3.3.2
-na, Pro 2sgACC 3.3.2
-nam, ABLative Clit 3.2.1[4]
-nan, Pro 1duexcDAT/ACC 3.3.2
-nanam, Pro 1duexcABL 3.3.2
-ng, 1sg V Sfx 3.4.3
-ng(a), LOCative Clit 3.2.1[7]
-ng(u), ERGative Clit 3.2.1[2]
-nga , CAUSative V Sfx 3.4.10[1]
-ngan, 2sgPRES V Sfx 3.4.3
-ngku, Pro 2sgDAT 3.3.2
-ngkurum, Pro 2sgABL 3.3.2
-ngu, Pro 3sgDAT 3.3.2
-ngurum, Pro 3sgABL 3.3.2
-nh, INFinitive V Sfx 3.4.8
-nha, CAUSative V Sfx 3.4.10[2]
-nha, Pro 3sgACC 3.3.2
-nha, UNMKD IRRealis V Sfx 3.4.3
-nhca, Pro 1plexcNOM 3.3.2
-nhcara, Pro 1plexcDAT/ACC 3.3.2
-nhcaram, Pro 1plexcABL 3.3.2
-nhin, 3plIRRealis V Sfx 3.4.3
-nhum, HISToric V Sfx 3.4.5
-nhun, 2sgIRRealis V Sfx 3.4.3
-ni, SUBORDinator Clit 4.7.1
-nta, Pro 2sgNOM 3.3.2
-nyi, Pro 1sgACC 3.3.2
-o, RECIProcal V Sfx 3.4.9
-pa, Pro 2duNOM 3.3.2

-(i)madha, VerBaLiSeR V Sfx for
-(pa)la, HITHER Clit 4.12[10]
-pan, Pro 2duDAT/ACC 3.3.2
-panam, Pro 2duABL 3.3.2
-(pu)yu, THITHER Clit 4.12[10]
-ra, COMitative Clit 3.2.1[5]
-ran, Pro 3plDAT/ACC 3.3.2
-ranam, Pro 3plABL 3.3.2
-tho, HORTative Clit 4.13[2]
-thu, Pro 1sgDAT 3.3.2
-thurum, Pro 1sgABL 3.3.2
-wi, INCHOative V Sfx 3.4.11
-wu, 3IMPerative/2duIMPerative V Sfx 3.4.4
-wu, DATive Clit 3.2.1[3]
-ya, CAUSative V Sfx 3.4.10[4]
-ya, Pro 2plNOM 3.3.2
-ya, You Know Clit 4.12[8]
-yara, Pro 2plDAT/ACC 3.3.2
-yaram, Pro 2plABL 3.3.2
-yi, PRIVative Clit 3.2.1[6]
-yin, 3plPRES V Sfx 3.4.3
-yinha, CAUSative V Sfx 3.4.10[5]
aara, Dem distABS 3.2.2
agawu, Dem distDAT 3.2.2
agu, Gen PLACE 5.2.6
alang, Dem distERG 3.2.2
aman, Dem distABL 3.2.2
angan, Dem distLOC 3.2.2
epa, AFFirmation Pcl 4.12[5]
iguwu, Dem 1proxDAT 3.2.2
iiru, Dem 1proxABS 3.2.2
ilung, Dem 1proxERG 3.2.2
imun, Dem 1proxABL 3.2.2
ingun, Dem 1proxLOC 3.2.2
ka'i(m), NEG Pcl, LIKE, 4.10
kana, PERFective Pcl 4.12[3]
kugu, Gen SPEECH 5.2.8
kuyu, Gen WOMAN 5.2.7
kuyu+waya, Gen OLD WOMAN 5.2.7
mayi, Gen VEGETABLE 5.2.3
minha, Gen ANIMAL, MEAT 5.2.1
nga'a, Gen SEAFOOD 5.2.2
ngale, Pro 1duincNOM 3.3.1

ngalina, Pro 1duincDAT/ACC 3.3.1
ngalinamu, Pro 1duincABL 3.3.1
ngampa, Pro 1plincNOM 3.3.1
ngampara, Pro 1plincDAT/ACC 3.3.1
ngamparamu, Pro 1plincABL 3.3.1
ngana, Pro 1duexcNOM 3.3.1
nganana, Pro 1duexcDAT/ACC 3.3.1
ngananamu, Pro 1duexcABL 3.3.1
nganhca, Pro 1plexcNOM 3.3.1
nganhcara, Pro 1plexcDAT/ACC 3.3.1
nganhcaramu, Pro 1plexcABL 3.3.1
nganyi, Pro 1sgACC 3.3.1
ngathu, Pro 1sgDAT 3.3.1
ngathurumu, Pro 1sgABL 3.3.1
ngaya, Pro 1sgNOM 3.3.1
ngingkurumu, Pro 2sgABL 3.3.1
nhaaru, Dem 2proxABS 3.2.2
nhaguwu, Dem 2proxDAT 3.2.2
nhalung, Dem 2proxERG 3.2.2
nhamun, Dem 2proxABL 3.2.2
nhangun, Dem 2proxLOC 3.2.2
nhila, Pro 3sgNOM 3.3.1
nhingku, Pro 2sgDAT 3.3.1

nhingu, Pro 3sgDAT 3.3.1
nhingurumu, Pro 3sgABL 3.3.1
nhinta, Pro 2sgNOM 3.3.1
nhipa, Pro 2duNOM 3.3.1
nhipana, Pro 2duDAT/ACC 3.3.1
nhipanamu, Pro 2duABL 3.3.1
nhiya, Pro 2plNOM 3.3.1
nhiyana, Pro 2plDAT/ACC 3.3.1
nhiyanamu, Pro 2plABL 3.3.1
nhunha, Pro 3sgACC 3.3.1
nina, Pro 2sgACC 3.3.1
pama, Gen MAN 5.2.7
pama+muwa, Gen OLD MAN 5.2.7
pukpe, Gen CHILD 5.2.7
pula, Pro 3duNOM 3.3.1
pulana, Pro 3duDAT/ACC 3.3.1
pulanamu, Pro 3duABL 3.3.1
thaarana, Pro 3plDAT/ACC 3.3.1
thaaranamu, Pro 3plABL 3.3.1
thana, Pro 3plNOM 3.3.1
waka, Gen GRASS 5.2.4
waya, LIKE Pcl/operator 4.12[6]
ya'a, NEG Pcl 4.10
ya'an / yaan, JUST Pcl 4.12[1]
yuku, Gen TREE, THING 5.2.5
yupa / -pa, FUTure Pcl/Clit 4.12[2]

AUTHOR'S NOTE

Nearly twenty years have passed since Steve Johnson and I undertook the fieldwork on which this grammar is based. The delay in getting this description into print is due to a number of factors, foremost being the difficult employment situation in which we both found ourselves. A year after we returned from the field, Steve left Monash University, where we were both on temporary contracts, and spent a number of years in Britain and Germany in non-academic purgatory before finding a post at the University of the West Indies, Mona. Subsequently, he moved to the School of Australian Linguistics and finally to the University of New England, where he founded the first linguistics programme. I had a less varied, though still uncertain career, and it was not until 1988 that permanent employment came my way. The draft on which this grammar is based was completed in late 1985, but geographical separation and preoccupation with other matters delayed the additional work needed to make a book-length grammar. Steve's untimely death in 1990 was a blow to Australian linguistics as well as a great personal loss to those who knew him. Unfortunately, for the foreseeable future my personal circumstances rule out undertaking the additional fieldwork required for a full grammar. It is therefore appropriate that our analysis should appear under the *Handbook's* rubric of 'sketch grammar', even though it is somewhat longer and more detailed than this name suggests.

The analysis presented here is essentially that of our 1985 manuscript, responsibility for which we shared equally. In preparing the manuscript for publication, I have made a few analytical changes that seemed warranted by a review of the data (notably to our treatment of diphthongs (2.1.2[2]), of reciprocals (4.5.1) and of certain directionals (5.4)). Chapter 1 has been enlarged to include relevant material from our 1986 article and 1987 manuscript on the sociolinguistics of the Nganhcara community; a third text has been included; and various other additions have been made where the *Handbook's* plan called for them or where they seemed useful. Finally, the organisation has been thoroughly reworked to fit the *Handbook*'s prescribed format.

Ian Smith
July 1997

ACKNOWLEDGEMENTS

Our greatest debt of gratitude is to the people of Edward River and Aurukun who welcomed us into their midst and especially to those who patiently helped us to study their language. Maymona Holroyd Mayi Monolinh was our principal Uwanh collaborator and the one with whom we worked most closely; she also provided information on Yi'anh, her mother's language. Paddy Yantumba worked with us extensively on Iyanh, Silya Peters Wura was our principal Muminh consultant until a family tragedy called her away; Nellie Yantumba Nga'antha 'api assisted with Ugbanh. Matthew Gordon Wanhcam furnished texts and lexicon in Uwanh. Stingaree Barney and George Lowdown provided chiefly lexical information on Mu'inh as did Toby Holroyd Nhunji and Doris Thupi Yomolo on Muminh. The administrative staff of Edward River and Aurukun were most helpful in making our fieldwork possible. We are particularly grateful for their help in finding suitable accommodation.

We thank the Australian Research Grants Commission, which provided funding for our 1979 field trip and York University, which awarded a grant for subsequent collaborative work and manuscript preparation. We are grateful to the Atlantic Provinces Linguistic Association and to Anthropological Linguistics for permission to reuse material from Smith and Johnson (1986) in chapter 1 and from Smith and Johnson (1985) in chapter 3. Our sometime colleague and good friend Barry Blake read earlier versions of the manuscript and gave us encouraging comments and helpful criticisms. Bob Dixon did the same for a later version of the manuscript. Amanda Lissarague worked as a research assistant for Steve Johnson before his death and passed on as much of his material as she could find. Janis Young has worked tirelessly at much of the tedious aspects of manuscript preparation. There are doubtless others whose names Steve would have added to this list; hopefully, they will excuse their omission.

References

Aboriginal and Torres Strait Islander Commission (1995), *Annual Report 1994–5* (Canberra: AGPS).

Aboriginal Communities of the Northern Territory and the Traditional Aboriginal Medicines Project Team (1993), *Traditional Aboriginal medicines in the Northern Territory of Australia* (Darwin: Conservation Commission of the Northern Territory).

Aboriginal Education Unit (1996), *Living languages* (video) (Adelaide: Department for Education and Children's Services).

Allen, M. (1985), *Concentrated language encounters of the Kriol kind* (Barunga, Northern Territory: Barunga School).

Alpher, B. (1993), 'Out-of-the-ordinary ways of using a language', in M. Walsh and C. Yallop (eds) (1993), 97–106.

Amery, R. (1993), 'Encoding new concepts in old languages: a case study of Kaurna, the language of the Adelaide Plains', *Australian Aboriginal Studies,* 1: 37–47.

Amery, R. (1994), 'Heritage and second language programs', in D. Hartman and J. Henderson (eds) (1994), 140–62.

Amery, R. (1995), 'Its ours to keep and call our own: Reclamation of the Nunga languages in the Adelaide region, South Australia', *International Journal of the Sociology of Language,* 113: 63–82.

Amery, R. (1996), 'Language reclamation', in C. Walton and M. Babia (eds) (1996), 145–79.

Anderson, S.R. (1984), 'Kwakwala syntax and the Government-Binding theory', in E.D. Cook and D.B. Gerdts (eds), *The syntax of Native American languages, syntax and semantics* 16 (Orlando: Academic Press), 21–75.

Angelo, D. (1996), 'Language revitalisation programs in the Katherine region', in C. Walton and M. Babia (eds) (1996), 97–131.

Armstrong, G. (1967), *Social change at Maningrida* (Dip. Anthrop. thesis, University of Sydney).

Armstrong, G. (1973), 'The Gunavidji people of northern Arnhem Land', *Journal of the Anthropological Society of South Australia* 11 (4): 6–14.

Ash, A. (1994), *Use 'em or lose 'em: The theory and practice of Aboriginal language maintenance* (BA Honours thesis, University of New England, Armidale).

Austin, P. (ed.) (1983), *Papers in Australian Linguistics 15: Australian Aboriginal lexicography* (Canberra: Pacific Linguistics).

Austin, P. (1991a), 'Australian lexicography', in F.J. Hausmann, O. Reichmann and H.E. Wiegand (eds), *Encyclopaedia of lexicography* (Berlin: Walter de Gruyter), 2638–41.

Austin, P. (1991b), 'Australian Aboriginal languages', in M. Clyne (ed.), *Linguistics in Australia: Trends in research* (Canberra: Academy of the Social Sciences in Australia), Chapter 4.

Australian Indigenous Languages Framework Project Team (1996a), *Australia's indigenous languages* (Adelaide: Wakefield Press).

Australian Indigenous Languages Framework Project Team (1996b), *Australian indigenous languages framework* (Adelaide: Senior Secondary Assessment Board of South Australia).

Australian Indigenous Languages Framework Project Team (1996c), *Australian indigenous languages in practice* (Adelaide: Senior Secondary Assessment Board of South Australia).

Australian Institute of Aboriginal and Torres Strait Islander Studies (1993), *Annual Report 1992–3* (Canberra: AIATSIS).

Baldauf, R.B., P. Mühlhäusler, J. Clayton and L. Hill (1996), *Backing Australian languages: Review of the Aboriginal and Torres Strait Islander Languages Initiatives Program* (Canberra: National Languages and Literacy Institute of Australia Limited).

Bavin, E. and T. Shopen (1985a), 'Children's acquisition of Warlpiri: comprehension of transitive sentences', *Journal of Child Language,* 12 (3): 597–610.

Bavin, E. and T. Shopen (1985b), 'Warlpiri and English: languages in contact', in M. Clyne (ed.), *Australia, meeting place of languages* (Canberra: Pacific Linguistics), 81–94.

Bell, J. (ed.) (1982), *Language planning for Australian Aboriginal languages* (Alice Springs: Institute for Aboriginal Development in association with the Aboriginal Languages Association).

Bell, S. (1995), 'Background and context of the NAATI Draft National Strategy' (paper presented at Proper True Talk: National Forum: Towards a National Strategy for Interpreting in Aboriginal and Torres Strait Islander Languages, Alice Springs (convened by Attorney General's Department and the National Accreditation Authority for Translators and Interpreters).

Berndt, R. (1955), '"Murngin" (Wulamba) social organization', *American Anthropologist* 57: 84–106.

Black, P. (1982), 'Why and how languages change', in J. Bell (ed.) (1982), 14–21.

Black, P. (1993), 'New uses for old languages', in M. Walsh and C. Yallop (eds) (1993), 207–23.

Blake, B. (1977), *Case marking in Australian languages* (Canberra: Australian Institute of Aboriginal Studies).

Blake, B. (1979), 'Australian case systems: some typological and historical considerations', in S.A. Wurm (ed.), *Australian Linguistics Studies* (Canberra: Pacific Linguistics), 323–94.

Blake, B. (1987), *Australian Aboriginal grammar* (London: Croom Helm).

Blake, B. (1991), *Australian Aboriginal languages: A general introduction*, second edition (St. Lucia: University of Queensland Press).

Bowden, M. (1994), 'The Arrernte language program at the Ntyarlke unit of the Catholic High School', in D. Hartman and J. Henderson (eds) (1994), 66–77.

Bradley, J. (1988), *Yanyuwa country: The Yanyuwa people of Borroloola tell the history of their land* (Richmond, Victoria: Greenhouse Publications).

Brennan, G. (1979), *The need for interpreting and translation services for Australian Aboriginals, with special reference to the Northern Territory* (Canberra: Department of Aboriginal Affairs).

Brown, P. and S. Levinson (1987), *Politeness: Some universals in language usage* (Cambridge: Cambridge University Press).

Brown, R and A. Gilman (1960), 'The pronouns of power and solidarity', in T. Sebeok (ed.), *Style in language* (Cambridge, Mass: MIT Press), 253–76.

Brumby, E. and E. Vaszolyi (eds) (1977), *Language problems and Aboriginal education* (Mount Lawley, W.A: Mount Lawley College of Advanced Education).

Burbidge, A., K. Johnson, P. Fuller and R. Southgate (1988), 'Aboriginal knowledge of the mammals of the central deserts of Australia', *Australian Wildlife Research,* 15: 9–39.

Buyuminy, D. and B. Sommer (1978), 'Milingimbi Aboriginal children's speech' (paper presented at Australian Linguistic Society annual meeting, Australian National University).

Capell, A. (1940), 'The classification of languages in north and north-west Australia', *Oceania* 10: 241–72 and 404–33.

Cappell, A. (1943), 'Languages of Arnhem Land, North Australia', *Oceania* 13 (1): 24–50 (continued from *Oceania* 12 (4): 364–92).

Capell, A. (1963), Linguistic survey of Australia (Canberra: Australian Institute of Aboriginal Studies).

Carroll, P. (1969) 'Matrix permutations applied to a Gunwinggu prefix' (ms).

Carrol, P. (1976), *Kunwinjku: a language of Western Arnhem Land* (Masters thesis, Australian National University).

Carroll, P. (1995), *An Aboriginal language interpreter service* (consultancy report prepared for the Office of Aboriginal Development and the Sub-committee on Public Safety and Social Development, Darwin).

Cataldi, L. (1990), 'Bilingual education and language maintenance at Lajamanu School', in C. Walton and W. Eggington (eds) (1990), 83–7.

Christie, M. (1994), 'Yirrkala Community Education Centre', in D. Hartman and J. Henderson (eds) (1994), 117–25.

Coleman, C. (1991), 'Progress report: The production of encyclopaedic "resource packages" at Maningrida CEC', *NT Bilingual Education Newsletter,* 91 (2): 46–54.

Coleman, C. and M. Strauss (1996), 'Different kinds of language programs', *NT Aboriginal Languages and Bilingual Education Newsletter,* 96 (1): 22–35.

Cook, L. and K. Buzzacott (1994), 'Yipirinya School', in D. Hartman and J. Henderson (eds) (1994), 78–91.

Craig, C. (1977), *The structure of Jacaltec* (Austin: University of Texas Press).

Craig, C. (1986), 'Jacaltec noun classifiers: a study in language and culture', in C. Craig (ed.), *Noun Classes and Categorization* (Amsterdam: John Benjamins), 263–93.

Crowe, G. (1994), 'Aboriginal languages in teacher training at Batchelor College', in D. Hartman and J. Henderson (eds) (1994), 341–54.

Crowley, T. (1978), *The Middle Clarence dialects of Bandjalang* (Canberra: Australian Institute of Aboriginal Studies).

Dench, A. and N. Evans (1988), 'Multiple case-marking in Australian languages', *Australian Journal of Linguistics*, 8: 1–47.

Dench, A. (1995), *Martuthunira: A language of the Pilbara Region of Western Australia* (Canberra: Pacific Linguistics).

Department for Education and Children's Services (1995), *Indigenous languages in South Australian schools*, first draft, December 1995 (Adelaide: Department for Education and Children's Services).

Department of Aboriginal Affairs (1979), *Aboriginal Newsletter* 35.

Department of Aboriginal Affairs (1980), *Aboriginal Newsletter* 72.

Department of Aboriginal Affairs (1982a), *Aboriginal Newsletter* 100, February.

Department of Aboriginal Affairs (1982b), *Aboriginal Newsletter* 113.

Department of Aboriginal Affairs (1986), *Aboriginal Newsletter, Central Australia,* 4 (1), May.

Department of Employment, Education and Training (1991a), *Australia's language. The Australian Language and Literacy Policy* (Canberra: Australian Government Publishing Service).

Department of Employment, Education and Training (1991b), *Australia's language. The Australian Language and Literacy Policy: Companion volume to the Policy Information Paper* (Canberra: Australian Government Publishing Service).

Devlin, B. (1990), 'Some issues relating to vernacular language maintenance: a Northern Territory view', in C. Walton and W. Eggington (eds) (1990), 53–74.

Dixon, R.M.W. (1971), 'A method of semantic description', in D.D. Steinberg. and J.A Jacobovits (eds), *Semantics: An interdisciplinary reader in philosophy, linguistics and psychology* (Cambridge: Cambridge University Press), 436–71.

Dixon, R.M.W. (ed.) (1976), *Grammatical categories in Australian languages* (Canberra: Australian Institute of Aboriginal Studies).

Dixon, R.M.W. (1980), *The languages of Australia* (Cambridge: Cambridge University Press).

Dixon, R.M.W. (1991), *Words of our country: Stories, place names and vocabulary in Yidiny, the Aboriginal language of the Cairns–Yarrabah region* (St Lucia: University of Queensland Press).

Dixon, R.M.W. and M. Duwell (eds) (1990), *The Honey-ant Men's Love Song and other Aboriginal song poems* (St. Lucia: University of Queensland Press).

Dixon, R.M.W. and G. Koch (1996), *Dyirrbal song poetry* (St. Lucia: Queensland University Press).

Dixon, R.M.W., W.S. Ramson and M. Thomas (1990), *Australian Aboriginal words in English: Their origin and meaning* (Melbourne: Oxford University Press).

Drysdale, I. and M. Durack (1974), *The end of dreaming* (Adelaide: Rigby).

Eades, D. (1984), 'Misunderstanding Aboriginal English: the role of socio-cultural context', in G. McKay and B. Sommer (eds) (1984), 24–33.

Eades, D. (1988), 'They don't speak an Aboriginal language, or do they?', in I. Keen (ed.), *Being Black: Aboriginal culture in settled Australia* (Canberra: Aboriginal Studies Press), 97–115.

Eather, B. (n.d.a.), 'Some aspects of the kinship system in Maningrida: "Skin" groups of subsections', unpublished paper in the course *Ndjébbana for Balánda* (Maningrida: Department of Education).

Eather, B. (n.d.b.), 'Verb parataxis and aspectual constructions in Nakkara', unpublished notes (Maningrida: Department of Education).

Eather, B. (1990), *A grammar of Nakkara (Central Arnhem Land coast)* (PhD thesis, Australian National University).

Eather, B. et al. (n.d.), *Ndjébbana for* Balánda (file of ms and typed material held in the Maningrida Ndjébbana Bilingual Education Centre).

Eckert, A. (1982), 'Analysis of written style: an imperative for readable translations', in G. McKay and B. Sommer (eds) (1982), 18–25.

Eckert, P. and J. Hudson (1991), *Wangka Wiṟu: A handbook for the Pitjantjatjara language learner* (Adelaide: University of South Australia).

Elkin, A., R. Berndt and C. Berndt (1951), 'Social organization of Arnhem Land I: western Arnhem Land', *Oceania* 21 (4): 253–301.

Elwell, V. (1977), Multilingualism and lingua francas among Australian Aborigines: a case study of Maningrida (BA Honours thesis, Australian National University).

Elwell, V. (1982a), 'Some social factors affecting multilingualism among Aboriginal Australians: a case study of Maningrida', *International Journal of the Sociology of Language* 36: 83–103.

Elwell, V. (1982b), 'Language planning and Aboriginal interpreters', in J. Bell (ed.) (1982), 83–92.

Fraser, J. (1977), 'A phonological analysis of Fitzroy Crossing children's pidgin', in J. Hudson (ed.), *Five papers in Australian phonologies,* Work Papers of SIL AAB A (Darwin: SIL), 145–204.

Gale, K. (1983), *Encouraging children to write: The Kriol experience at Barunga* (Barunga, NT: Bamyili Press).

Gale, K., D. McClay, M. Christie, and S. Harris (1981), 'Academic achievement in the Milingimbi bilingual education program', *TESOL Quarterly,* 15 (3): 297–314.

Gale, M.A. (1990), 'A review of bilingual education in Aboriginal Australia', *Australian Review of Applied Linguistics,* 13 (2): 40–80.

Gale, M.A. (1992), *Dhangum Djorra'wuy Dhäwu: The development of writing in Aboriginal languages in S.A. and the N.T. since colonisation* (MA thesis, Northern Territory University).

Gale, M.A. (1994a), 'Bilingual education programs in Aboriginal schools', in D. Hartman and J. Henderson (eds) (1994), 192–203.

Gale, M.A. (1994b), 'Dhangum Djorra'wuy Dhäwu: a brief history of writing in Aboriginal Australia', *The Aboriginal Child at School,* 22 (2): 33–42.

Gale, M.A. (1996), 'AnTEP comes of age', *The Australian Journal of Indigenous Education,* 24 (1): 17–25.

Gardner, P. (1991), *Northern Territory statistical summary 1991* (Darwin: Australian Bureau of Statistics, Northern Territory Office).

Garnduwa Amboorny Wirnan Aboriginal Corporation, Musicians Union of W.A. and Ausmusic (1992a), *All this spirit in the land: Traditional songs recorded live in the Kimberleys, Western Australia* (audio tape and lyrics booklet) (Fremantle, W.A: A Jovial Crew/Production Function Project).

Garnduwa Amboorny Wirnan Aboriginal Corporation, Musicians Union of W.A. and Ausmusic (1992b), *Singing up the country: Traditional and contemporary songs from the Kimberleys, Western Australia* (audio tape and lyrics booklet) (Fremantle, W.A: A Jovial Crew/Production Function Project).

Garnduwa Amboorny Wirnan Aboriginal Corporation, Musicians Union of W.A. and Ausmusic (1992c), *Walking along the edge: Contemporary music from the West Kimberley, Western Australia* (audio tape and lyrics booklet) (Fremantle, W.A: A Jovial Crew/Production Function Project).

Glasgow, D. and K. Glasgow (1967), 'The phonemes of Burera', *Papers in Australian Linguistics* 1 (Canberra: Pacific Linguistics), 1–14.

Glasgow, K. (1964a), 'Four principal contrasts in Burera personal pronouns', in R. Pittman and H. Kerr (eds), *Papers on the Languages of the Australian Aborigines, Occasional papers in Aboriginal Studies 3* (Canberra: Australian Institute of Aboriginal Studies), 109–17.

Glasgow, K. (1964b), 'Frame of reference for two Burera tenses', in R. Pittman and H. Kerr (eds), *Papers on the Languages of the Australian Aborigines, Occasional papers in Aboriginal Studies 3* (Canberra: Australian Institute of Aboriginal Studies), 118.

Glasgow, K. (1984), 'Burarra word classes', *Papers in Australian Linguistics* 16 (Canberra: Pacific Linguistics), 1–54.

Goddard, C. (1990), 'Emergent genres of reportage and advocacy in the Pitjantjatjara print media', *Australian Aboriginal Studies* 2: 27–47.

Goddard, C. (1994), 'The Pitjantjatjara story-writing context, 1988', in D. Hartman and J. Henderson (eds) (1994), 316–23.

Goddard, C. and N. Thieberger (1997), 'Lexicographic research on Australian Aboriginal languages 1968–1993', in D. Tryon and M. Walsh (eds), *Boundary Rider Essays in Honour of Geoffrey O'Grady.* (Canberra: Pacific Linguistics), 175-208.

Godfrey, M. (1979), 'Notes on paragraph division in Tiwi', in C. Kilham
    (ed.), *Four grammatical sketches from paragraph to discourse,* Work
    Papers of SIL-AAB A-3 (Darwin: SIL), 1–22.
Godfrey, M. (1985), 'Repetition in Tiwi at clause level', in S. Ray (ed.),
    Aboriginal and Islander grammars: Collected papers, Work Papers of
    SIL-AAB A-9 (Darwin: SIL), 1–38.
Graber, P. (1987), 'Kriol in the Barkly Tableland', *Australian Aboriginal
    Studies* 2: 14–19.
Green, R. (1989), 'Reconstructing verb inflections in the parent language of
    Ndjebbana, Nakkara, Gurrogoni and Burarra' (paper presented to
    Preconference Workshop on Comparative Non-Pama-Nyungan
    Linguistics, Australian Linguistic Society Conference, Monash
    University, Melbourne).
Green, R. (1995), *A grammar of Gurr-goni (North central Arnhem Land),*
    (PhD thesis, Australian National University).
Gumperz, J.J. and R. Wilson (1971), 'Convergence and creolization: a case
    from the Indo-Aryan/Dravidian border in India', in D. Hymes (ed.),
    Pidginization and Creolization of Languages (Cambridge: Cambridge
    University Press), 151–67.
Hale, K. (1976a), 'Wik reflections of Middle Paman phonology', in
    P. Sutton (ed.), *Languages of Cape York* (Canberra: Australian
    Institute of Aboriginal Studies), 50–60.
Hale, K. (1976b), 'The adjoined relative clause in Australia', in R.M.W.
    Dixon (ed.) (1976), 78–105.
Hanks, W. (1990), *Referential practice: Language and lived space among
    the Maya* (Chicago: University of Chicago Press).
Harkins, J. (1994), *Bridging two worlds: Aboriginal English and
    crosscultural understanding* (St. Lucia: Queensland University
    Press).
Harper, H. (1996), 'Having language and getting language back: traditional
    language use in Injinoo today', *Australian Aboriginal Studies,* 1:
    34–44.
Harris, J.K. (1969a), *Descriptive and comparative study of the
    Gunwingguan languages, Northern Territory* (PhD thesis, Australian
    National University).
Harris, J.K. (1969b), 'Preliminary grammar of Gunbalang', *Papers in
    Australian Linguistics* 4: 1–49.
Harris, J.K. (1970), 'Gunkurrng, a mother-in-law language', in S.A.
    Wurm and D.C. Laycock (eds), *Pacific Linguistics studies in honour
    of Arthur Capell* (Canberra: Pacific Linguistics), 783–9.
Harris, J.W. (1986), *Northern Territory pidgins and the origin of Kriol*
    (Canberra: Pacific Linguistics).
Harris, J.W. (1993), 'Losing and gaining a language: the story of Kriol in
    the Northern Territory', in M. Walsh and C. Yallop (eds) (1993),
    145–54.
Harris, J.W. and J. Sandefur (1994), 'The Creole language debate and the
    use of Creoles in Australian schools', *The Aboriginal Child at School,*
    22 (2): 7–21.
Harris, P. (1991), *Mathematics in a cultural context: Aboriginal perspectives
    on space, time and money.* (Geelong, Victoria: Deakin University).

Harris, S. (1995), 'A brief historical look at bilingual education, and where it might go in the future' (plenary paper delivered to participants at the workshop on language challenges and strategies in Aboriginal schools, organized by the Northern Territory Department of Education, Batchelor, April).

Harris, S., B. Graham and P. Buschenhofen (1984), 'Aboriginal bilingual education in the Northern Territory: priorities for the second decade' (paper presented at the Ninth Annual Congress of the Applied Linguistics Association of Australia, Alice Springs).

Harris, S. and P. Jones (1991), 'The changing face of Aboriginal bilingual education in the Northern Territory: a 1990 update', *The Aboriginal Child at School,* 19 (5): 29–53.

Hartman, D. and J. Henderson (eds) (1994), *Aboriginal languages in education* (Alice Springs: IAD Press).

Hartman, D., R. Riley and C. Brocklebank (1995), 'The Intelyape-lyape Akaltye project: Arrernte early childhood development', *Bilingual Network News: The Bilingual Schools Newsletter Operations South* 1 (Alice Springs: Northern Territory Education Department).

Haviland, J. (1979), 'How to talk to your brother-in-law in Guugu Yimidhirr', in T.A. Shopen (ed.), *Languages and their speakers* (Cambridge, Mass: Winthrop).

Heath, J. (1976), 'Substantival hierarchies: addendum to Silverstein', in R.M.W. Dixon (ed.) (1976), 172–90.

Heath, J. (1982), 'The Awabakal Aboriginal Co-operative', in J. Bell (ed.) (1982), 124–6.

Hercus, L. and P. Sutton (eds) (1983), *This is what happened: Historical narratives by Aborigines* (Canberra: Australian Institute of Aboriginal Studies).

Hiatt, L.R. (1965), *Kinship and Conflict: A study of an Aboriginal community in northern Arnhem Land* (Canberra: Australian National University).

Hoogenraad, R. (1993), *Report on the Language in Education Survey of the Barkly and Sandover regions* (unpublished report, Northern Territory Education Department, Alice Springs).

Hoogenraad, R. (1994), 'Grass-roots Aboriginal language and culture programs in schools in the Barkly and Sandover regions of the Northern Territory', in D. Hartman and J. Henderson (eds) (1994), 172–91.

Hopper, P. and S. Thompson (1980), 'Transitivity in grammar and discourse', *Language* 56: 251–99.

House of Representatives Standing Committee on Aboriginal and Torres Strait Islander Affairs (1992), *Language and culture — A matter of survival: Report of the Inquiry into Aboriginal and Torres Strait Islander Language Maintenance* (Canberra: Australian Government Publishing Service).

Howitt, A. (1904), *The native tribes of south-east Australia* (London: Macmillan and Co.).

Hudson, J. (1978), *The core of Walmatjari grammar* (Canberra: Australian Institute of Aboriginal Studies).

Hudson, J. (1981), *Grammatical and semantic aspects of Fitzroy Valley Kriol,* Work Papers of SIL-AAB A-8 (Darwin: SIL).

Hudson, J. (1994), 'Framework for the teaching of Aboriginal languages in primary schools', in D. Hartman and J. Henderson (eds) (1994), 163–171.

Hudson, J. and P. McConvell (1984), *Keeping language strong: Report of the Pilot Study for the Kimberley Language Resource Centre (long version)* (Halls Creek: Kimberley Language Resource Centre).

Institute for Aboriginal Development (1993), *Teaching our way: Development of Aboriginal curricula for Aboriginal schools* (VHS Video, 10 minutes) (Alice Springs: IAD Press).

Jernudd, B.H. (1974), 'Articulating Gunwinjgu laminals', *Papers in Australian Aboriginal Languages: Linguistic Communications* 14: 83–109.

Johnson, K. (1994), 'The Djabugay language at Kuranda State School', in D. Hartman and J. Henderson (eds) (1994), 40–44.

Johnson, S. (1974), *Investigations in the sound patterns of Kugu Uwanh and Wik Iyanh* (BA Honours thesis, University of Queensland).

Johnson, S. (1986), *Report on possible problems in Ndjebbana orthography,* ms (Batchelor, Northern Territory: School of Australian Linguistics).

Johnson, S. (1988), 'The status of classifiers in Kugu Nganhcara nominals', *Aboriginal Linguistics* 1: 198–203.

Johnson, S. (1991), 'Linguistic change in an unstratified Aboriginal society', in P. Baldi (ed.), *Patterns of change, change of patterns: Linguistic change and reconstruction methodology* (Berlin: Mouton de Gruyter), 203–17.

Johnson, S. and I. Smith (1986), 'The syntax of number in Kugu Nganhcara' (Paper read at the Australian Linguistic Society annual meeting, Brisbane).

Johnson, S. and I. Smith (1987), 'From Kugu to Wik: Mungkanization at Aurukun' (ms).

Kaldor, S. and Malcolm, I. (1991) 'Aboriginal English — an overview', in S. Romaine (ed.), *Language in Australia* (Cambridge: Cambridge University Press), 67–83.

Kilham, C. (1974), 'Compound words and close-knit phrases in Wik-Munkan', in C.E. Furby, L.A. Hercus and C. Kilham, *Papers in Australian Linguistics* 7 (Canberra: Pacific Linguistics), 45–73.

Kilham, C. (1977), *Thematic organization of Wik-Munkan discourse* (Canberra: Pacific Linguistics).

Kilham, C. (1996), *Translation time: An introductory course in translation* (Darwin: SIL-AAIB).

Kilham, C.A., M. Pamulkan, J. Pootchemunka and T. Wolmby (1986), *Dictionary and source book of the Wik-Mungkan language* (Darwin: Summer Institute of Linguistics, Australian Aborigines Branch).

Klavans, J.L. (1985), 'The independence of syntax and phonology in cliticization', *Language* 61: 95–120.

KLRC (1991), *Bunuba wordbook* (Halls Creek, W.A: Kimberley Language Resource Centre).

KLRC (forthcoming), *Thangani Bunuba: Stories from the Bunuba elders of the Fitzroy Valley* (Halls Creek, W.A: Kimberley Language Resource Centre).

Koch, G. (compiler and ed.) (1993), *Kaytetye country: An Aboriginal history of the Barrow Creek area* (Alice Springs: IAD Press).

Kolig, E. (1972), 'BI:N and Gadeya: an Australian Aboriginal model of the European society as a guide to social change', *Oceania* 43: 1–18.

Kolig, E. (1977), 'From tribesman to citizen?', in R.M. Berndt (ed.), *Aborigines and change* (Canberra: Australian Institute of Aboriginal Studies), 33–53.

Kolig, E. (1981), *The silent revolution: The effects of modernization on Australian Aboriginal religion* (Philadelphia: ISHI Publications).

Kyle-Little, S. (1957), *Whispering wind: Adventures in Arnhem Land* (London: Hutchinson).

Latz, P. (1995), *Bushfires & bushtucker: Aboriginal plant use in Central Australia* (Alice Springs: IAD Press).

Laughren, M. (1984), 'Warlpiri baby talk', *Australian Journal of Linguistics* 4.1: 73–88.

Lee, J. (1987), *Tiwi today: A study of language change in a contact situation* (Canberra: Pacific Linguistics).

Lee, P. (1993), *Bilingual education in remote Aboriginal schools: Developing first and second language proficiency* (a report to the Catholic Education Office of Western Australia) (Broome, W.A: Catholic Education Office Kimberley Region).

Leeding, V. (1979), 'Report on research of the children's speech at Hooker Creek (Lajamanu)' (unpublished report, Northern Territory Department of Education, Darwin).

Lo Bianco, J. (1987), *National Policy on Language.* (Canberra: Australian Government Publishing Service).

Lo Bianco, J. (1995), *Consolidating gains, recovering ground: Languages in South Australia* (Report of the Review of the Teaching of Languages in the South Australian Department for Education and Children's Services) (Belconnen, ACT: National Languages and Literacy Institute of Australia (NLLIA)).

Marett, M. (1987), 'Kriol and literacy', *Australian Aboriginal Studies* 2: 69–70.

Marmion, D. (1994), 'The Yamaji Language Centre', in D. Hartman and J. Henderson (eds) (1994), 370–80.

Marr, J., B. Oscar and B. Wirrunmarra (1990), *Bunuba stories* (recorded and transcribed by Alan Rumsey).

McConnel, U.H. (1930), 'The Wik-Munkan tribe of Cape York Peninsula', *Oceania*, 1: 97–104 and 181–205.

McConnel, U.H. (1939), 'Social organization of the tribes of Cape York Peninsula, north Queensland', *Oceania*, 10: 54–72.

McConnel, U.H. (1940), 'Social organization of the tribes of Cape York Peninsula, north Queensland. Marriage systems — Wikmunkan', *Oceania*, 10: 434–55.

McConvell, P. (1983), '"Only" and related notions in Guurinji' (ms).

McConvell, P. (1985), 'Domains and codeswitching among bilingual Aborigines', in M. Clyne (ed.), *Australia — Meeting Place of Languages* (Canberra: Pacific Linguistics), 60–76.

McConvell, P. (1991), 'Understanding language shift: a step towards language maintenance', in S. Romaine (ed.), *Language in Australia* (Cambridge: Cambridge University Press), 143–55.

McConvell, P. (1994), 'Two-way exchange and language maintenance in Aboriginal schools', in D. Hartman and J. Henderson (eds) (1994), 235–56.

McConvell, P. and G. McKay, (1994), 'Aboriginal and Torres Strait Islander language maintenance intervention activities' (paper presented to Workshop on Language Shift and Maintenance in the Asia-Pacific Region, Australian Linguistic Institute, La Trobe University, Melbourne).

McGregor, W. (1987), 'The structure of Gooniyandi narratives', *Australian Aboriginal Studies,* 2: 20–28.

McGregor, W. (1988a), 'A survey of the languages of the Kimberley region — report form the Kimberley Language Resource Centre', *Australian Aboriginal Studies,* 2: 90–102.

McGregor, W. (1988b), *Handbook of Kimberley languages, volume 1* (Halls Creek, W.A: Kimberley Language Resource Centre).

McGregor, W. (1988c), *Handbook of Kimberley languages, volume 1: General information* (Canberra: Pacific Linguistics).

McGregor, W. (1989), 'Greenberg on the first person inclusive dual: evidence from some Australian languages', *Studies in Language* 13: 437–51.

McGregor, W. (1990), *Functional grammar of Gooniyandi* (Amsterdam: Benjamins).

McGregor, W. (1994), 'Introduction', in N. Thieberger and W. McGregor (eds) (1994), xi–xxxv.

McGregor, W. (1996), 'The pronominal system of Gooniyandi and Bunuba', in McGregor, W. (ed.), *Studies in Kimberley language in honour of Howard Coate* (Munich: Lincom), 159–73.

McKay, G. (1975), *Rembarnga: A language of Central Arnhem Land* (PhD thesis, Australian National University).

McKay, G. (1978), 'Pronominal person and number categories in Rembarrnga and Djeebbana', *Oceanic Linguistics* 17 (1): 27–37.

McKay, G. (1979), 'Gender and the category *unit augmented*', *Oceanic Linguistics* 18 (2): 203–10.

McKay, G. (1980), *Ndjébbana (Kunibidji) verb conjugations (interim account),* ms (Maningrida, Northern Territory: Department of Education).

McKay, G. (1981a), *Glossary of miscellaneous Ndjébbana (Kunibidgi) words,* ms (Maningrida, N.T: Department of Education).

McKay, G. (1981b), *Glossary of Ndjébbana (Kunibidji) adverbials,* ms (Maningrida, N.T: Department of Education).

McKay, G. (1981c), *Glossary of Ndjébbana (Kunibidji) nominals,* ms (Maningrida, N.T: Department of Education).

McKay, G. (1981d), 'Gunibidji social, cultural and linguistic orientation', *Oceania* 51: 214–19.

McKay, G. (1982a), 'Attitudes of Kunibidji speakers to literacy', *International Journal of the Sociology of Language* 36: 105–14.

McKay, G. (1982b), *Glossary of Ndjébbana (Kunibidji) verbs*, ms (Maningrida, N.T: Department of Education).

McKay, G. (1982c), 'Social, cultural and linguistic aspects of orthography development in Kunibidji', *Applications of linguistics to Australian Aboriginal contexts, Applied Linguistics Association of Australia Occasional Papers* 5: 26–33.

McKay, G. (1984a), Ndjébbana (Kunibidji) grammar: Miscellaneous morphological and syntactic notes', *Papers in Australian Linguistics* 16 (Pacific Linguistics), 119–51.

McKay, G. (1984b), 'Stop alternations in Ndjébbana (Kunibidji)', *Papers in Australian Linguistics* 16 (Pacific Linguistics), 107–17.

McKay, G. (1988), 'Figure and ground in Rembarrnga complex sentences', in P. Austin (ed.), *Complex sentence constructions in Australian languages* (Amsterdam: Benjamins), 7–36.

McKay, G. (1990), 'The Addressee: Or is the second person singular?', *Studies in Language* 14.2: 429–32.

McKay, G. (1991), 'Linguistics in the education of speakers of Aboriginal languages: the first decade of the School of Australian Linguistics', in I. Malcolm (ed.) *Linguistics in the service of society: Essays to honour Susan Kaldor* (Perth: Institute of Applied Language Studies, Edith Cowan University), 6–21.

McKay, G. (1995), 'Body parts, possession marking and nominal classes in Ndjébbana', in H. Chappell and W. McGregor (eds), *The grammar of inalienability: A typological perspective on body part terms and the part-whole relation: Empirical approaches to language typology* 14 (Berlin: Mouton de Gruyter), 293–326.

McKay, G. (1996), *The land still speaks* (Commissioned Report No. 44) (Canberra: National Board of Employment, Education and Training).

McKay, G. and B. Sommer (eds) (1982), *Applications of linguistics to Australian Aboriginal contexts* (Melbourne: Applied Linguistics Association of Australia), Occasional Papers No. 5.

McKay, G. and B. Sommer (eds) (1984), *Further applications of linguistics to Australian Aboriginal contexts* (Melbourne: Applied Linguistics Association of Australia).

McKnight, C. (1976), *The voyage to Marege: Macassan trepangers in northern Australia* (Melbourne: Melbourne University Press).

Merlan, F. (1981), 'Land, language and social identity in Aboriginal Australia'. *Mankind* 13: 133–48.

Merlan, F. (1982), '"Egocentric" and "altercentric" usage of kin terms in Mangarayi', in J. Heath, F. Merlan and A. Rumsey (eds), *Languages of kinship in Aboriginal Australia.* (Sydney: Oceania Publications), 125–40.

Merlan, F. and J. Heath (1982), 'Dyadic kinship terms', in J. Heath, F. Merlan and A. Rumsey (eds), *Languages of kinship in Aboriginal Australia* (Sydney: Oceania Publications), 107–24.

Michaels, E. (1986), *The Aboriginal Invention of Television in Central Australia 1982-1986.* (Canberra: AIATSIS.)

Mithun, M. (1986), 'When zero isn't there', *Proceedings of the twelfth annual meeting of the Berkeley Linguistic Society* (Berkeley: California), 195–211.

Mithun, M. (1987), 'Is basic word order universal?', in Tomlin, R.S. (ed), *Coherence and grounding in discourse* (Amsterdam: John Benjamins), 281-299

Moizo, B. (1991), *We all one mob but different: Groups, grouping and identity in a Kimberley Aboriginal village* (PhD thesis, Australian National University, Canberra).

Morphy, F. (1983), 'Djapu, a Yolngu, dialect', in R.M.W. Dixon and B.J. Blake (eds), *Handbook of Australian languages, volume 3* (Canberra: Australian National University Press), 1–188.

Murtagh, E. (1979), *Creole and English bilingual education: Some research findings* (Darwin: SIL-AAB).

Nash, D. and J. Simpson (1989), 'The AIAS archive of machine-readable files of Australian languages: the national lexicography project', *Australian Aboriginal Studies* 1: 57–9.

Nekes, H. and E.A. Worms (1953), *Australian languages* (*Micro-Bibliotheca Anthropos*, 10) (Frieburg: Anthropos Institute).

Nicholls, C. (1994), 'Vernacular language programs and bilingual education programs in Aboriginal Australia: issues and ideologies', in D. Hartman and J. Henderson (eds) (1994), 214–34.

Northern Territory Department of Education (1986), *Handbook for bilingual education in the N.T* (Darwin: N.T. Department of Education).

Northern Territory Department of Education (1994), *Aboriginal Education News*, 5 (Darwin: N.T. Department of Education).

Northern Territory Department of Education (1995), *Aboriginal Education News. No. 6.* (Darwin.)

Northern Territory division of of the Australian Department of Education (1975), *Not to lose you my language* (motion picture) (Sydney: Film Australia).

O'Grady, G., C. Voegelin and F. Voegelin (1966), 'Languages of the world: Indo-Pacific fascicle six'. *Anthropological Linguistics* 8(2).

Perlmutter, D.M. (1971), *Deep and surface structure constraints in syntax* (New York: Holt, Rinehart and Winston).

Plank, F. (1988), *Relational typography* (Berlin: Mouton).

Plank, F. (ed.) (1995), *Double case: Agreement by suffixaufnahme* (Oxford: Oxford University Press).

Read, P. and J. Read (eds) (1991), *Long time, olden time: Aboriginal accounts of Northern Territory history* (book and cassette tapes) (Alice Springs: IAD Press).

Read, P. and J. Read (eds) (1993), *Long time, olden time: Aboriginal accounts of Northern Territory history* (CD-ROM) (Penrith, N.S.W: Firmware Publishing).

R.E.A.D. School Support Centre (1992), *Which language?* (video) (Brisbane: Queensland Department of Education).

Reynolds, R. (1988), *Cohesion in Arrernte discourse* (MA thesis, Monash University, Melbourne).

Reynolds, R. (1994), 'Ltyentye Apurte Community Education Centre, Ltyentye Apurte (Santa Teresa), NT', in D. Hartman and J. Henderson (eds) (1994), 105–16.

Rhydwen, M. (1992a), 'Kriol: what is it, who speaks it and what's it got to do with me?' (typescript 15p. Department of Linguistics, University of Sydney).

Rhydwen, M. (1992b), 'The extent of the use of Kriol, other creole varieties and varieties of Aboriginal English by schoolchildren in the Northern Territory and its implications for access to English literacy' (Project of National Significance (DEET) Report, typescript 118 p. University of Sydney).

Rhydwen, M. (1993), 'Kriol: the creation of a written language and a tool of colonisation', in M. Walsh and C. Yallop (eds) (1993), 155–68 .

Rhydwen, M. (1996), *Writing on the back of the Blacks: Voice, literacy and community in Kriol fieldwork* (St. Lucia: University of Queensland Press).

Riley-Mundine, L. and B. Roberts (1990), *Review of National Aboriginal Languages Program*, AACLAME Occasional Paper No. 5 (Canberra: AACLAME).

Roberts, S. (1996), 'Pronouns and the elsewhere principle', in McGregor, W. (ed.), *Studies in Kimberley language in honour of Howard Coate* (Munich: Lincom), 149–58.

Rockman, P. and L. Cataldi (1994), *Warlpiri dreamings and histories (Yimikirli)* (London: Harper Collins).

Rumsey, A. (n.d.), 'A brief tentative description of Bunaba'.

Rumsey, A. (1980a), 'Prolegomena to a theory of Australian grammatical case systems', *Papers in Australian linguistics 13: Contributions to Australian linguistics* (Pacific Linguistics), 1–29.

Rumsey, A. (1980b), Review of R.M.W. Dixon (ed.), 'Grammatical categories in Australian languages', *Language* 56: 669–73.

Rumsey, A. (1982a), 'Gun-gunma: An Australian Aboriginal avoidance language and its social functions', in J. Heath, F. Merlan and A. Rumsey (eds), *Languages of kinship in Aboriginal Australia* (Sydney: Oceania Publications), 160–81.

Rumsey, A. (1982b), *An Intra-sentence grammar of Ungarinjin, North-western Australia* (Canberra: Pacific Linguistics).

Rumsey, A. (1990), 'Wording, meaning, and linguistic Ideology', *American Anthropologist* 91: 346–61.

Rumsey, A. (1993), 'Language and territoriality in Aboriginal Australia', in M. Walsh and C. Yallop (eds) (1993), 191–206.

Rumsey, A. (1994), 'On the transitivity of 'say' clauses in Bunuba', *Australian Journal of Linguistics* 14: 137–53.

Rumsey, A. (1996), 'On some relationships among person, number and mode in Bunuba', in W. McGregor (ed.), *Studies in Kimberley language in honour of Howard Coate* (Munich: Lincom), 139–48.

Sandefur, J. (1985), *A Language coming of age: Kriol of North Australia* (MA thesis, University of Western Australia).

Sandefur, J. and J. Sandefur (1979), *Language survey, pidgin and creole in the Kimberleys, Western Australia* (Darwin: SIL-AAB).

Santangelo, A. and T. Vennemann (1976), 'Italian unstressed pronouns and universal syntax', in V. Lo Cascio (ed.), *On clitic pronominalization* (Italian Linguistics 2) (Lisse: Peter De Ridder), 37–43.

Sayers, B. (1976), *The sentence in Wik-Munkan: A description of propositional relationships* (Canberra: Research School of Pacific Studies, ANU).

Sayers, B.J. (1982), 'Aurukun children's speech: language history and implications for bilingual education', in G.R. McKay and B.A. Sommer (eds), *Application of linguistics to Australian Aboriginal contexts* (Applied Linguistics Association of Australia, Occasional Papers Number 5).

Schebeck, B. (n.d.), 'The glottal stop in north-east Arnhem Land' (unpublished letter, copy held in the Australian Insitute of Aboriginal and Torres Strait Islander Studies library, Canberra).

Schebeck, B. (1972), *Les systèmes phonologiques des langues Australiennes* (PhD thesis, Paris).

Scheffler, H.W. (1972), 'Afterword', in D.F. Thomson, *Kinship and behaviour in North Queensland: A preliminary account of kinship and social organization on Cape York Peninsula* (Canberra: Australian Institute of Aboriginal Studies), 37–52.

Schmidt, A. (1985), *Young people's Djirbal* (Cambridge: Cambridge University Press).

Schmidt, A. (1990), *The loss of Australia's Aboriginal language heritage* (Canberra: Aboriginal Studies Press).

Senior Secondary Assessment Board of South Australia (1996), *Australia's indigenous languages* (Adelaide: SSABSA).

Senior Secondary Assessment Board of South Australia (1996), *Australia's indigenous languages* (CD-ROM) (Adelaide: SSABSA).

Senior Secondary Assessment Board of South Australia (1996), *Australia's indigenous languages in practice* (Adelaide: SSABSA).

Senior Secondary Assessment Board of South Australia (1996), *Australian indigenous languages framework* (Adelaide: SSABSA).

Sharp, J. and L. Injie (1994), 'Training language workers in Western Australia', in D. Hartman and J. Henderson (eds) (1994), 324–40.

Sharp, R.L. (1939), 'Tribes and totemism in north-east Australia', *Oceania*, 9: 254–75 and 439–61.

Sharpe, M. (1993), 'Bundjalung: teaching a disappearing language', in M. Walsh and C. Yallop (eds) (1993), 73–84.

Sheppard, N. (1992), *Alitji in Dreamland: Alityinya ngura tjukurmankuntjala* (East Roseville, NSW: Simon and Schuster Australia).

Shnukal, A. (1988), *Broken: An Introduction to the Creole Language of theTorres Strait.* (Canberra: Pacific Linguistics.)

Silverstein, M. (1976), 'Hierarchy of features and ergativity', in R.M.W. Dixon (ed.) (1976), 112–71.

Simpson, J. (1993), 'Making dictionaries', in M. Walsh and C. Yallop (eds) (1993), 123–44.

Simpson, J. and D. Nash (1987), 'Australian bicentennial dictionary of Aboriginal languages', *Australian Aboriginal Studies* 2: 88–9.

Smith, A.M. (1989), 'A Wangkatja news item from Kalkurli', *Australian Aboriginal Studies* 1989 (2): 72–3.

Smith, I. (1978), *Wik: Aboriginal society, territory and language at Cape Keerweer, Cape York Peninsula, Australia* (PhD thesis, University of Queensland).

Smith, I. (1986), 'Language contact and the life or death of Kugu Muminh', in J.A. Fishman et al. (eds), *The Fegusonian impact 2: Sociolinguistics and the sociology of language* (The Hague: Mouton), 513–32.

Smith, I. (1991), 'Language in Aboriginal Australia: social dialects in a geographic idiom', in S. Romaine (ed.), *Language in Australia* (Cambridge: Cambridge University Press), 49–66.

Smith, I. and S. Johnson (1979), 'The cliticisation of case markers in Nganhcara' (paper read at the Australian Linguistic Society annual meeting, Canberra).

Smith, I. and S. Johnson (1985), 'The syntax of clitic cross-referencing pronouns in Kugu Nganhcara', *Anthropological Linguistics* 27: 102–11.

Smith, I. and S. Johnson (1986), 'Sociolinguistic patterns in an unstratified society: the patrilects of Kugu Nganhcara', *Journal of the Atlantic Provinces Linguistic Association* 8: 29–43.

Smith, I. and B. Rigsby (1979), 'Linguistic communities and social networks on Cape York Peninsula', in S.A. Wurm (ed.), *Australian Linguistic Studies* (Canberra: Pacific Linguistics), 713–32.

Stokes, B. (1982), *A Description of Nyigina: A language of the West Kimberley, Western Australia* (PhD thesis, Australian National University, Canberra).

Strelhow, T.G.H. (1971), *Songs of Central Australia* (Sydney: Angus and Robertson).

Swartz, S. (1988), *Constraints on zero anaphora and word order in Warlpiri narrative text*, Work Papers of SIL-AAB (Darwin: SIL-AAIB).

TAFE Queensland (1995), *Indigenous language workers' courses* (Cairns: Aboriginal & Torres Strait Islander Curriculum Consortium, Department of Employment Vocational Education, Training and Industrial Relations).

Teichelmann, C.G. and C.W. Schürmann (1840), *Outlines of a grammar, vocabulary and phraseology of the Aboriginal language of South Australia, spoken by the natives in and for some distance around Adelaide* (Facsimile edition, 1982) (Adelaide: Tjintu Books).

Thieberger, N. (1992), 'Dictionaries project', *Australian Aboriginal Studies* 1: 104–5.

Thieberger, N. (1993), 'Dictionaries project', *Australian Aboriginal Studies* 2: 120–23.

Thieberger, N. and W. McGregor (eds) (1994), *Macquarie Aboriginal words* (Sydney: The Macquarie Library Pty Ltd).

Tindale, J. (1994), 'Training for Aboriginal language teachers in Central Australia', in D. Hartman and J. Henderson (eds) (1994), 355–69.

Thies, K. (1987), *Aboriginal viewpoints on education: A survey in the East Kimberley region* (Research Series No. 5, National Centre for Research on Rural Education, The University of Western Australia, Perth).

Thomson, D.F. (1936), 'Fatherhood in the Wik Monkan tribe', *American Anthropologist,* 38: 374–93.

Tsunoda, T. (1981), *The Jaru language of Kimberley, Western Australia* (Canberra: Pacific Linguistics).

Tunbridge, D. (1988), *Flinders Ranges dreaming* (Canberra: Aboriginal Studies Press).

Vaarzon-Morel, P. (1995), *Warlpiri karnta karnta-kurlangu yimi: Warlpiri women's voices* (Alice Springs: IAD Press).

Varcoe, N. (1994), 'Nunga languages at Kaurna Plains School', in D. Hartman and J. Henderson (eds) (1994), 33–9.

Vászolyi, E. (1979), *Teach yourself Wangkatja, an introduction to the Western Desert language (Cundeelee District)* (Perth: Mount Lawley College).

Vászolyi, E. (1982), 'Teaching Aboriginal languages to Australians', in G. McKay and B. Sommer (eds) (1982), 1–4.

von Sturmer, D.E. (1980), *Rights in nurturing: The social relations of child-bearing and rearing amongst the Kugu Nganychara, Western Cape York Peninsula, Australia* (MA thesis, Australian National University).

von Sturmer, J.R. (1973), *Lurugu* (video) (Canberra: Australian Institute of Aboriginal Studies).

von Sturmer, J.R. (1978), *The Wik region: Economy, territoriality and totemism in Western Cape York Peninsula* (PhD thesis, University of Queensland).

Waddy, J. (1982), 'Folk biology and the Northern Territory science curriculum', in G. McKay and B. Sommer (eds) (1982), 80–97.

Walker, A. (1984), 'The Yolngu stop controversy: Wood's prosodic hypothesis revisited' (paper presented to the Australian Linguistic Society Conference, Alice Springs).

Walker, A. and R.D. Zorc (1981), Austronesian loanwords in Yolngu-Matha of northeast Arnhem Land, *Aboriginal History,* 5 (2): 109–34.

Walsh, M. (1993), 'Languages and their status in Aboriginal Australia', in M. Walsh and C. Yallop (eds) (1993), 1–13.

Walsh, M. and Yallop, C. (eds) (1993), *Language and culture in Aboriginal Australia* (Canberra: Aboriginal Studies Press).

Walton, C. and M. Babia (1996), *EAL551 Teaching Australian indigenous languages: Study guide* (Darwin: Northern Territory University, Faculty of Education).

Walton, C. and W. Eggington (eds) (1990), *Language: Maintenance, power and education in Australian Aboriginal contexts* (Darwin: NTU Press).

Warlpiri Media Association (1991–94), *Manyu-wana.* (Series of 10 VHS videos, Yuendumu, N.T.).

Warlukurlangu Artists (1987), *Kuruwarri: Yuendumu doors* (Canberra: Aboriginal Studies Press).

Waters, B.E. (1980), 'Djinang phonology', *Papers in Australian Linguistics* 14 (Pacific Linguistics), 1–71.

Waters, B.E. (1989), *Djinang and Djinba – A grammatical and historical perspective* (Canberra: Pacific Linguistics).

Watts, B.H., W.J. McGrath and J.L. Tandy (1973), *Recommendations for the implementation and development of a program of bilingual education in the Northern Territory* (Canberra: Department of Education).

Williams, D. (1981), *Learning an Aboriginal language* (Canberra: Curriculum Development Centre).

Willmot, E. (1984), *Out of the silent land: Report of the Task Force on Aboriginal and Islander Broadcasting and Communications* (Canberra: Australian Government Printing Service).

Wilson, G. (1996), *Indigenous languages in South Australia's preschools and schools* (in draft form) (Adelaide: Department for Education and Children's Services).

Wood, R. (1978), 'Some Yuulngu phonological patterns', *Papers in Australian Linguistics* 11 (Pacific Linguistic), 53–117.

Wordick, F.J.F. (1982), *The Yindjibarndi language* (Canberra: Pacific Linguistics).

Worms, A. (1949), 'An Australian migratory myth', *Primitive Man* 22: 33–8.

Wrigley, M. (1990), 'Community involvement in orthography development: devising an orthography for Bunaba', *Australian Aboriginal Studies* 1990(2): 87–9.

Wrigley, M. (1994), 'The Gogo School Language Program', in D. Hartman and J. Henderson (eds) (1994), 45–55.